The European Library.

THE LIFE OF MARTIN LUTHER.

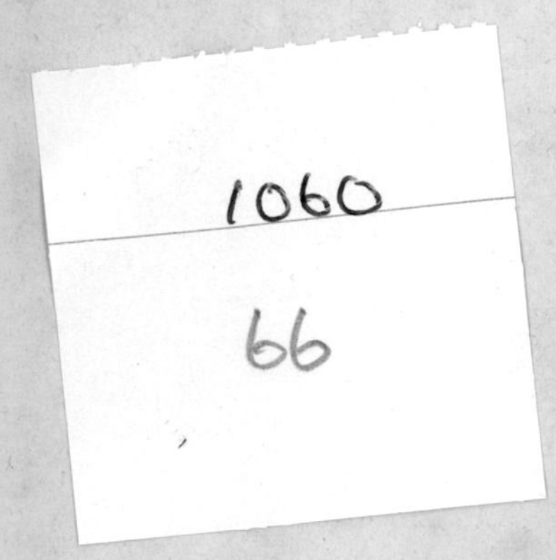
1060
66

From the Original Picture by
LUCAS CRANACH.

London, D. Bogue, 86, Fleet Street.

THE
LIFE OF LUTHER.

WRITTEN BY HIMSELF.

COLLECTED AND ARRANGED

BY M. MICHELET,

MEMBER OF THE INSTITUTE, AUTHOR OF "HISTORY OF FRANCE," ETC.

TRANSLATED BY WILLIAM HAZLITT, ESQ.

OF THE MIDDLE TEMPLE, BARRISTER-AT-LAW.

LONDON:
DAVID BOGUE, FLEET STREET.
MDCCCXLVI.

ADVERTISEMENT.

"These memoirs," writes a critic in Blackwood's Magazine, for Dec. 1835, "are composed altogether of letters and papers written by Luther himself, and give us a complete picture of the man as he was in life. Hitherto, the too common idea of the great reformer's character has been that it was a mere compound of violence and ruggedness. These traits have been made so prominent, that the finer lines of his portrait have been completely shaded from sight. If, in fact, we knew nothing of Dr. Johnson but his occasional bursts of savage and uncouth manners, we should not have a more erroneous impression of him than is generally entertained of Luther. Another reason of our misconception is, that we too often honour mere *daintiness* of mind with the names of delicacy, sensibility, humanity, virtue; whilst the rough exterior and the passionate expression, smack, to the taste of drawing-room, fashionable, *élite* society, whence opinions are usually circulated, only of brutality and ferocity. Perhaps, however, the finest, richest, and most generous species of character is that which presents to the *dainty* the most repulsive surface. Within the rough rind the feelings are preserved unsophisticated, robust, and healthy. The *noli me tangere* outside keeps off that insidious swarm of artificial sentimentalities which taint, and adulterate, and finally expel all natural and vigorous emotions from within us. The idea of a perfect man has always been figured forth in our minds by the emblem of the lion coming out of the lamb, and the lamb coming out of the lion. Of this description of character was Luther. Nothing could exceed his submissiveness and humility when a choice was left him whether to be humble or daring; but when conscience spoke, no other consideration was for a moment attended to, and he certainly did then shake the forest in his magnificent ire. But if we behold him one moment, to use his own quotation from Scripture, *pouring contempt upon princes*, and highly raging against the highest upon earth, we see him the next in his familiar correspondence a poor, humble, afflicted man, not puffed up with pride at the great things he had accomplished, but rather struck down by a sense of his own unworthiness. As to his violence, it was part of his mission to be violent, and those who lay it to his charge as blameworthy, seem to us not to accuse him, but to accuse Providence. Not to have been violent, would in him have been not to have been in earnest. And here it must be observed, that his violence was only verbal; it was merely the rousing *voice* to awaken Europe from the lethargy of ages. In his opinions and views he was the most moderate of all the reformers. In his coarseness, however, his low origin certainly speaks out, yet there is something sublime in the peasant (the miner's son) dragging popes and kings into his wrestling ring, and handling them with as much roughness and as little ceremony as he would a hobnailed clown from a country market-place. But let us follow him into private life. Here it is that we shall best learn to appreciate him. We will not dwell upon his constant contentment in poverty, and his contempt for riches, because this is the characteristic of almost all great men who are really worth more than gold can procure them; but his long unbroken friendship with Melancthon—a character so opposite to his own, and in some respects so superior, as he was the first to acknowledge himself—has always struck us as a proof that he possessed much sweetness and gentleness of disposition. Envy or jealousy never interrupted for a moment the fraternal affection that subsisted between these great men. Of those passions, indeed, Luther seems not to have been susceptible. Neither did personal ambition come near him. Though he had so many titles to it, he never claimed the supremacy over his contemporary reformers. Notwithstanding the great things he had performed, he gave himself no air of grandeur or importance. He seemed to consider himself as a common man among common men. He was doctor Martin Luther, and nothing more. There was a simplicity and commonness in his habits and conversation which contrasts wonderfully with the mighty revolution he brought about. This simplicity, we were going to say, shows his native greatness, but we correct ourselves, and add, that it exhibits that apostolic frame of mind which all the messengers of God, from Moses downwards, have displayed. Such men are moulded at once by the hand that sends them. The accidents of this world have no power (as they have upon others) to change or modify their moral conformation. There is a oneness, a wholeness, an uncompoundedness of character in these elect instruments; on their moral frame is chiselled by the divine finger one idea, and one only—and that external to their earthly condition. Hence was begotten the simplicity and homeliness of Luther's walk in life. Had he acted the great man, he would have proved that he was not the apostle. The frank, popular, coarse, and somewhat peasant-bearing which marked him, has made him the hero of the populace to this day in Germany. What is also remarkable in a man of his indubitable and profound piety is, that he had no sanctified airs, no austerity. On the contrary, he loved painting, music, singing, and decent conviviality. We wish, indeed, it were not considered necessary how-a-days to assume a peculiar solemnity, a peculiar formality of manners, as a badge of piety. Nothing makes so many hypocrites as this. The pious man should endeavour to avoid, as much as possible, the external manifestations of his piety, all that can be imitated without being realized. In this matter Luther was a perfect model. We feel thoroughly convinced, that all which he possessed was real, precisely because there was no show, no parade whatever of sanctity about him. In his family, and among his neighbours, he was jovial, affectionate, *debonnaire.* His piety was not put on him, but broke out of him. It flowed in a mingled stream with his everyday life and conversation. The gravel and the gold rolled together in the rich channel of his mind, and he made no effort to exhibit only the one and to conceal the other."

The volume thus warmly commended by so orthodox an authority, I have done my best to render complete. Having found that M. Michelet's work, more especially in reference to the earlier portion of Luther's career, was comparatively bare of detail, I looked around me for materials with which to supply the deficiency, and I found nearly all that I needed in M. Audin's *Histoire de Luther*, (fifth edition, Paris, 1845,) a production of a high order of merit in a literary point of view, but uncompromisingly Roman-catholic in its principle and purposes. From the narrative portions of this work, I have adopted such additions as I considered it desirable to make for the purpose of giving completeness to the present volume. I have, also, carefully compared M. Michelet's translations from Luther with those by M. Audin, and with the original documents which he supplies; in some cases, indeed, I have ventured to render M. Michelet's text itself fuller and more satisfactory from these sources; as, for instance, in the narrative of the proceedings of the diet at Worms, where I have filled up many an *hiatus maxime defendus* in M. Michelet's work. Luther's remarkable narrative of his Conference with the Devil, which finds no place in Michelet's volume, is given here. I have paid especial attention to the many extracts from the *Tischreden*, comparing them and M. Michelet's translation of them with the translations by Audin, by Captain Bell (the first English translator), and with the more modern English version. My peculiar anxiety on this point arose from the imputations which have been cast, by a controversialist, on the accuracy of M. Michelet's rendering of the *Table Talk*. I can only say, that I have found very little occasion to modify M. Michelet's version, and in no case have I found that version to depart, in any degree, from the spirit and purport of his original. Besides Audin's book, I have referred as much as I could to the other authorities who have treated of Luther, and I think I may fairly state as the result, that the present *Life of Luther* is the most complete that has yet appeared.

WILLIAM HAZLITT.

MIDDLE TEMPLE,
April, 1846.

PREFACE OF THE AUTHOR.

The present work is not an historical romance, founded on the life of Martin Luther; nor is it a history of the establishment of Lutheranism. It is simply a biography, composed of a series of translations. Excepting in that portion of it which has reference to his childhood, and which Luther himself has left undescribed, the translator has rarely found occasion to make his own appearance on the scene. He has, in fact, scarcely done anything beyond selecting, dating, and arranging the scattered texts before him; it is almost invariably Luther himself who speaks; almost invariably Luther related by Luther.

Who indeed, except in a case of absolute necessity, would be presumptuous enough to mix up his words with those of such a man. The only course for the translator was to remain silent, and leave Luther to tell his own tale; this is the course which, as closely as possible, has been acted upon in the following pages.

The present work, first published in 1835, was drawn up in the years 1828-9. The translator of the *Scienza Nuova*, vividly felt at that time the necessity of redescending from theory to practice, of studying the general in the particular, history in biography, humanity in individual man. For this purpose he needed one who had exhibited himself to the world as of the very highest power; an individual who was at once a real personage and an idea; a man perfect in thought and action; a man whose whole life was known in fullest detail, whose every word, whose every deed, had been marked and treasured up.

If Luther did not absolutely write his own Memoirs, he at all events prepared ample materials for the biographer.[1] His correspondence alone is scarcely less voluminous than that of Voltaire; and there is, moreover, scarcely one of his dogmatical or polemical works in which he has not unconsciously inserted some illustrative detail, some circumstance available to the biographer. Nor are the personal *memorabilia* supplied by Luther's own hand the only materials of this description which the compiler has at his disposal. There was not a word which fell from the great Reformer's lips which was not eagerly caught up by his disciples, transmitted forthwith to paper, and so to posterity; good, bad, and indifferent, everything was taken down; whatever Luther said, to whomsoever he said it, wheresoever it was said, at the fireside, in the garden, at table after supper, to his friends, to his wife, to his children, to himself, straightway the pen of his disciples did its work. As one inevitable consequence, a man so closely followed, so closely observed, must have constantly let fall something or other which he would afterwards wish to have recalled, and the Lutherans subsequently found occasion to regret that such things had been perpetuated; they would fain have blotted out this paradox, that passionate extravagance, but it was too late: *Quod scriptum est, scriptum est.*

It is, however, owing to this very circumstance that we are here enabled to lay before the world the genuine *Confessions of Luther;* confessions all the more true, that they were not deliberately drawn up by the confessor, but are collected for the most part from the words which fell from his lips from time to time, in open, honest, heedless intercourse with his friends and family. Those of Rousseau are, beyond question, far less honest; those of St. Augustine less complete, less various.

[1] We have followed for the German works of Luther, the edition of Wittemberg, 1539—1559, 12 vols. folio; for the Latin works, that of Wittemberg, 1545—1558, 7 vols. folio, and occasionally that of Jena, 1600—1612, 4 vols. folio; for the *Tischreden* (Table Talk), the edition of Frankfort, 1568, 1 vol. folio; for the *Briefe* (Letters), that of De Witte, Berlin, 1825, 5 vols. 8vo. Besides Luther's own works, we have availed ourselves of Ukert, Seckendorf, Marheinecke, and other authors who have written upon or in connexion with the subject.

As a biography, that of Luther's, had he written it throughout himself, would take its place between the two we have just mentioned. It presents in combination the two aspects which they exhibit separately. In the Confessions of St. Augustine, passion, nature, human individuality only appear in order to be immolated to Divine grace. They are a history of a crisis of the soul, of a new-birth, of a *Vita Nuova;* the *Saint* would have blushed to relate more than he has done of the life of the man, which he had quitted. With Rousseau the case is precisely the reverse; here grace is nothing, nature everything; nature dominant, triumphant, displaying herself with a daring freedom, which at times amounts to the distasteful—nay, to the disgusting. In Luther we see, not the equal balance of grace and of nature, but their fierce and painful struggle. Many other men have undergone the trials of the flesh, and the still higher and more perilous temptations of doubt; Pascal manifestly so: he stifled them in his own breast, and died in the contest. But Luther has concealed nothing, he kept nothing to himself, he fought the battle out openly, and he has thus enabled us to see and sound in him this deep and awful wound of our Nature. He, indeed, is perhaps the only man in whom we can fully study this terrible anatomy.

Hitherto, the only point of view in which Luther has been presented to the observation of mankind, is his duel with Rome. The present work exhibits his entire life, his spiritual fights, his doubts, his temptations, his consolations. The man here occupies as much of our attention as the party-leader, and even more. We show him, the violent and terrible Reformer of the north, not only in his eagle's nest at Wartburg, as braving the emperor and the empire at the diet of Worms, but also in his house at Wittemberg, seated at table amidst his grave-visaged friends and disciples, his children playing beside him, or walking with him in his garden, on the margin of the little pond in the grounds of that sombre monastery once sacred to celibacy, but now become the abode of the married Luther and of his family; we hear him meditating aloud, and finding in all that he looks upon, the flowers, the fruits, the birds flying over his head or singing in the trees, topics for grave and pious thoughts.

Whatever sympathy, however, may be felt with this

amiable and winning individuality of Luther, it must not be suffered to influence our judgment with reference to the doctrines which he, on all occasions, inculcates, or blind us to the consequences which are its necessary result. It must be borne in mind that this very man, who made so energetic, so immense a use of liberty, was he who revived the Augustine theory as to the annihilation of liberty. He sacrificed free-will to grace, man to God, morality to a sort of providential fatality.

In our own times, the friends of liberty have laid great stress upon the authority of the fatalist Luther; a circumstance, however, which, though strange at first sight, is susceptible of explanation. Luther fancied that he recognised himself in John Huss, in the Waldenses, the partisans of free-will. The solution of both the one circumstance and the other is, that these speculative doctrines, however opposed they may appear to each other, are upon common ground in their principle of action, the sovereignty of individual reason, resistance to the traditional principle, to authority.

It is not, therefore, inexact to say that Luther was, in point of fact, the restorer of liberty to the ages which followed his era. He denied it theoretically, indeed, but he established it in practice; if he did not absolutely create, he at least courageously signed his name to the great revolution which legalized in Europe the right of free examination. To him it is, in great measure, owing that we of the present day exercise in its plenitude that first great right of the human understanding, to which all the rest are annexed, without which all the rest are nought. We cannot think, speak, write, read, for a single moment, without gratefully recalling to mind this enormous benefit of intellectual enfranchisement. The very lines I here trace, to whom do I owe it that I am able to send them forth, if not to the liberator of modern thought?

This tribute paid to Luther, we the less hesitate to admit, that our own sympathies are not with him in the religious revolution he operated. This, however, is not the place for us to enumerate the causes which rendered the triumph of protestantism inevitable. We shall not, after the example of so many others, lay bare the sores of a church in whose bosom we were born, and which is still dear to us. We shall, in another place, explain the grounds on which we regard the Roman-catholic doctrine as, if not more logical, at least, more judicious, more fertile, more complete, than that of any of the sects which have risen up against it. Its feebleness, and its grandeur also, is, that it excludes nothing which belongs to man; that it has sought to satisfy, at one and the same time, all the contradictory principles of the human mind. This, alone, readily laid it open to the attacks of those who reduce man to this or that particular principle, and reject all the rest. The *universal*, in whatever sense the word may be taken, is feeble against the *special*. *Heresy* is a *choice*, a specialty—there is specialty of opinion, specialty of country. Wickliffe, John Huss, were ardent patriots; the Saxon Luther was the Arminius of modern Germany. Universal in time, in space, in doctrine, the church was, as against each of its opponents, deficient in a common medium. She had to struggle for the unity of the world against the particular forces of the world. As a body infinite in numbers, she was hampered by the baggage, as it were, of the lukewarm and the timid. As a government, she had to encounter all the worldly temptations. As the centre of religious traditions, she received, from all parts, a crowd of local beliefs, against which she had great difficulty in defending her unity, her perpetuity. She presented herself to the world such as the world and time had made her. She appeared before it in the party-coloured robe of history. Comprehending humanity at large, she shared also its miseries, its contradictions. The little heretic societies, made fervent by zeal and by their danger, standing apart, and purer by reason of their youth, disavowed the cosmopolitan church, and compared themselves with her, much to their own satisfaction. The pious and profound mystic of the Rhine and Low Countries, the simple, rustic Waldensians, pure as a flower amid Alpine snows, triumphed when they accused of adultery and prostitution her who had received all, adopted all. In the same way, each brooklet, doubtless, may say to the ocean: I come from my own mountain; I know no other waters than my own; whereas, thou receivest the impurities of the world. "Ay," is the answer, "but I am the ocean."[1]

[1] Upon the preceding passages the writer in *Blackwood*, already quoted, remarks:—"We would not desire a clearer statement of the

This is what it would be necessary to say and to develop. And there is no book which, more than the present, would seem to require such an introduction. To understand how it was that Luther was obliged to cause himself to undergo what he describes as *the most extreme misery;* to comprehend this great and unhappy man, who gives a new impulse to the human mind, who puts it in renewed motion at the very moment when he considers he is placing it at rest on the pillow of grace; to appreciate this futile attempt at union between God and man, it would be necessary to describe the more consistent efforts made, before and afterwards, by the mystics and rationalists—in other words, to sketch the history of the Christian religion.

I may be asked, why put this off, too! Why commence so many things, and always stop short less than half way? If the reader is anxious to know, I will readily tell him:

In the middle of my "Roman History," I met with Christianity in its origin; half through my "History of France," I encountered it again, aged and decrepit; here, I find it again.

general character of the Roman-catholic church than the above. But Monsieur Michelet has overlooked the real question, viz.—Whether this character corresponds with the character of Christianity? We feel quite sure that if his honest and conscientious mind would examine the matter, with the aid of the New Testament, he would find that Christianity itself is truly described as he has described heresy, viz.—It is a *choice*, a specialty. Indeed, a moment's reflection will show him that truth, compared with error, must always be a *choice*, a specialty, and that error has always the same kind of universality as he so much admires in catholicism. To carry on the same sort of parallel between *them* as he has established between protestantism and catholicism, Truth might say to Error, 'You are an adultress, a prostitute;' to which Error might reply, 'Triumph as you like, you are but a little miserable creature, inhabiting obscure corners; but I am universal, *I receive all, I adopt all;* you are but a river, I am the ocean.' In his zeal to do honour to catholicism, Monsieur Michelet has precisely pointed out its general all-pervading characteristic, which most thoroughly condemns it, by completely identifying its features with those of falsehood. Falsehood also excludes nothing, rejects nothing. It also would embrace humanity in the gross, by winding itself about every fibre of the heart, and satisfying every contradictory principle. Though not logical, it is judicious, fertile, and complete in taking every point, touching every point, meeting every case, and compounding with every difficulty. Like catholicism, too, its grandeur is, that it is all-accommodating, all-enveloping; and its feebleness likewise resembles that of its stupendous offspring—it is feeble against a *specialty*—against Truth."

In whatever direction I turn, it bars my way, and prevents my passing on.

To touch upon Christianity! Those alone hesitate not to do so, who know not what it is. . . . For myself, I recall to mind the nights wherein I watched the bedside of a sick mother; she suffered from remaining long in the same position, she wanted to change her place, to turn round, but my filial hands hesitated—how could I think of agonizing her still more, by moving her limbs, so full of acute pain?—

'Tis now many years that these ideas have been working within me. In the present period of outward storms, they constitute the exciting reveries of my solitude. At all events, these conversations that I hold with myself are soothing in their influence, and I am as yet in no hurry to sever myself from such long-cherished thoughts.

August, 1835.

LIFE OF LUTHER.

BOOK THE FIRST.

1483—1521.

CHAPTER THE FIRST.

1483—1517.

Birth and education of Luther—His ordination and temptations—His journey to Rome.

"I HAVE often conversed with Melancthon, and related to him my whole life, from point to point. I am the son of a peasant; my father, my grandfather, my great-grandfather were all mere peasants. My father went to Mansfeldt, and became a miner there. It was there I was born. That I was afterwards to become bachelor of arts, doctor of divinity, and what not, was assuredly not written in the stars, at least, not to ordinary readers. How I astonished everybody when I turned monk! and again, when I exchanged the brown cap for another. These things greatly vexed my father—nay, made him quite ill for a time. After that, I got pulling the pope about by the hair of his head; I married a runaway nun; I had children by her. Who saw these things in the stars? Who would have told any one beforehand they were to happen?"[1]

[1] Tischreden (Table Talk) (Frankfort, 1568), 240. Cochlæus, in his hostile life of the Reformer, gravely asserts that Luther was engendered by an incubus. An Italian Theatine, Cajetano Vicich, in his poem called *Thieudos,* says that Martin was born of Megæra, one of the furies, and sent express from hell into Germany. Many of his opponents designate him, as a matter of course, *son and disciple of the devil.*

"When he was a monk," Cochlæus adds, "he was suspected of having

Hans (John) Luther, or Lutter,[1] father of the Luther who became so celebrated, was of Mœrha or Moer, a village in Upper Saxony, near Eisenach. His mother (Gretha, or Margaret Lindemann) was the daughter of a tradesman of the same place, or rather, according to a preferable tradition, of Nieustadt, in Franconia. If we are to believe a modern writer, who, however, gives no authority for the statement, John Luther had the misfortune to kill, under the impulse of passion, another peasant, whom he found trespassing on a field of his with some cattle; and it was this which compelled him to retire, first to Eisleben, and afterwards to the valley of Mansfeldt. It is certain, at all events, that he did retire successively to these places. His wife, who accompanied him, lay in immediately upon their arrival at Eisleben.[2] The child was Martin Luther. The father, who was only a poor miner, found it a very difficult matter to maintain his family;

commerce with the devil. One day, when he was listening to the gospel, at the place where mention is made of a deaf and dumb devil, whom Christ compels to quit the body of a possessed person, Luther fell convulsively to the ground, exclaiming—*Non sum, non sum!* In one of his sermons, he tells the people himself, that he and the devil had known one another for a very long while; that they were in constant communication with each other; and that he, Luther, had eaten more than one grain of salt with Satan."—COCHLÆUS, *Life of Luther*.

Some Spaniards who were at the Diet of Augsburg (1530), seriously believed that Luther and his wife were destined to produce Anti-Christ.—LUTHER'S *Werke*, (1612,) i. 415.

Some of his opponents maintained, among other things, that he was a Bohemian—endeavouring to account for his heresy by identifying it with the opinions of Jerome of Prague and John Huss. Luther himself took notice of this, and charged the statement on a professor of Leipsic:—"A wretched quarrelsome fellow. Why, I was never in all my life nearer Bohemia than Dresden."

[1] Lotharius, Ludher, Lutter. The name Lutter, observes Mr. Roscoe, in his life of Leo X., afforded one of the reformer's adversaries a subject for the following lines, more remarkable for scurrility than for wit:—

"Germanis *Lutter*, scurra est, latro Bohemis;
Ergo quod est *Lutter*, scurra latroque simul."

But, on the other hand, quere, *Lut-herr*, chief of men?

[2] The house in which Luther was born was destroyed by fire in 1594. But it was afterwards rebuilt at the expense of the town, and is now used as a public school, to which there is a building attached as an establishment for the poor.

and it will be seen further on, that his children were fain at times to beg alms for their sustenance. Yet, despite his extreme poverty, instead of making them labour with him at his own occupation, he sent them to school.[1] He appears to have been a man of fine unsophisticated honesty and firm faith. When his pastor was affording him religious consolation in his last moments, he said : "Sir, that must be a poor creature who has not the soul to believe in God and his mercy." His wife survived him scarcely a year, dying in 1531.[2] They had at this time a small independence, which they doubtless owed to their son Martin. John Luther left a house, two forges, and about a thousand thalers in ready money.

The arms of Luther's father—for the German peasantry had arms, as well as their betters—were, simply, a hammer on a granite block. Martin was not ashamed of his parents : he has consecrated their names in his formula of marriage service:—*Hans, wilt thou take Gretha?*

"'Tis with me a pious duty," he says, in a letter to Melancthon, announcing John Luther's death, "to weep for him whom the Father of Mercy destined to give me birth—for him, by whose labour and sweat God nourished me, and made me what I am, such as that is. Oh, how I rejoice that he lived long enough to see the light of the truth! Blessed be God for ever, in all his counsels and decrees! Amen."

[1] "Luther, at six years old, could read and write with ease. His parents, though fond of their children, were very strict with them. Luther mentions that one day, for merely stealing a hazel-nut, his mother beat him till the blood flowed; and he says, that he had such fear of his father that he always hid in the chimney-corner when he had done anything to anger him."—AUDIN, *Histoire de Martin Luther*, 5th edit., 1845.

[2] "Margaret Lindemann, Luther's mother, was originally a servant at the baths—a virtuous, chaste, and God-fearing girl. She was considered the pride of Mœrha. John Luther, some time after he became a miner, managed to purchase out of his savings a plot of ground; and we find him, subsequently, filling a magisterial office, delegated to him by the friendship and esteem of his fellow-townsmen. It is not known how many children he had besides Martin. There were two who died of the plague which desolated Europe in the commencement of the 16th century; and one of his daughters married the scribe Ruhel de Mansfeldt, whose name occasionally occurs in Luther's correspondence. When Melancthon married, John Luther was invited to be present, and took his seat among the hellenists, doctors, savans, and literary men, there assembled."—AUDIN.

Martin Luther, or Ludher, or Lutter, or Lother[1]—for he signed his name all these ways—was born at Eisleben, on the 10th November, 1483, at eleven o'clock in the evening.[2] Sent at an early age to the free school of Eisenach (1489), he used to sing before people's houses to gain his daily bread, as was the wont, at that time and later, with many poor students in Germany. It is from himself that we learn this circumstance: "Let no one in my presence speak contemptuously of the poor fellows who go from door to door, singing and begging bread *propter Deum!* You know the psalm says—*Princes and kings have sung.* I myself was once a poor mendi-

[1] The papists, it has been observed, reckon Luther the beast of the Apocalypse, and have seriously endeavoured to discover in his name the famous mystical number—666. Lindanas and Astulphus have adopted the following calculation:—M, 30; A, 1; R, 80; T, 100; I, 9; N, 40; L, 20; A, 1; U, 200; T, 100; E, 15; R, 80=666. Floramond de Remond, too, calculates this number from the Greek word Λουθερανα, *Lutherana*, thus:—Λ, 30; Ο, 70; Υ, 400; Θ, 9; Ε, 5; Ρ, 100; Α, 1; Ν, 90; Α, 1=666: while another writer calculates 666, from the name *Martin Lutera.—De Mysteriis Numerorum*, p. 6[illegible]6. It is worthy of remark, that a similar calculation of this jargon is made by the same enthusiast in Hebrew. These fanciful conjectures are refuted by David Pareno, (*Comment. in Apoc.* xiii. 747,) who denies that the number 666 can be found by these numeral letters. "Nomen Lutheri verum, Græcè vel Hebræcè, quomodocumque scribas, numerum 666 non reddit. Est Græce, λουτερ, sicut 908; vel λουθηρ, 717; vel λουθερος, 847."

[2] No trifling disputes among the learned have there been on the date of Luther's birth, chiefly agitated by Roman-catholic writers, after he appeared, as they term him *the grand heresiarch*. In this they turned astrologers, falsifying the day and hour of his birth, that they might draw his character to their liking—believing, or pretending to believe, that no man could have effected such a singular revolution in the church, unless he had been under the influence of the devil. Some maintained that he was born on the 22nd October, 1483—specifying even the hour and the minute, as Floramond de Remond, and the famous Jerome Cardan declare; while a writer named Gauricus, a Romish prelate, says it was on the 22nd October, 1484, at ten minutes past one P.M.—thus differing from his contemporaries a whole year, though he found his astrological reveries to coincide completely with those of Remond and Cardan. It is amusing to see the inference which Gauricus, in common with the others, draws from this calculation. 'This is strange, and, indeed, terrible; five planets, Jupiter, Venus, Mars, Saturn, and Mercury, to which may be added the Sun and Moon, being in conjunction under Scorpio, in the ninth station of the heavens, which the Arabians allotted to religion, made this Luther a sacrilegious heretic, a most bitter and profane enemy to the Christian faith. From the horoscope being directed to the conjunction of Mars, he died without any sense of religion

cant, seeking my bread at people's houses, particularly at Eisenach, my own dear Eisenach!"

After awhile[1] he obtained a more regular subsistence, and an asylum in the house of dame Ursula Cotta, widow of Hans Schweikard, who took compassion on the poor wandering boy. By the assistance of this charitable woman, he was enabled to study four years at Eisenach.[2] In 1501, he was entered at the university of Erfurt, in Thuringia,[3] where his father, now in better circumstances, managed to support him. Luther, in one of his works, records the goodness of his benefactress, in words glowing with emotion; and he was through-

His soul, most impious, sailed to hell, there to be scourged for ever with the fiery whips of Alecto, Tisiphone, and Megæra.'

On the other hand, Tycho Brahe and Nicholas Prucker declare that Martin was born under fortunate auspices.

"I have often," says Melancthon, quoted by Audin, "asked Margaret at what hour of what day it was her son Martin came into the world; she recollected the hour and the day perfectly, but had forgotten the year. She stated that she was brought to bed on the 10th November, at eleven o'clock in the evening, at Eisleben, whither she had gone to buy provisions at the fair that was held every year in that place, and the child was baptized the next day, after the name of the saint whose festival they were celebrating at the time, St. Martin." Luther's brother, James, an honest worthy man, believed that the year of Martin's birth was 1483.

[1] "In the month of May, 1497, two scholars wended their way along the high road from Mansfeldt to Bernburg, knapsacks on their backs, sticks in their hands, and great tears rolling down their cheeks: they were, Martin Luther, aged fourteen, and his comrade, Hans Reinicke, about the same. Both had just quitted the paternal roof, and were proceeding on foot to Magdeburg, to avail themselves of the *currend schulen*, celebrated seminaries in the middle ages, which still subsist. Here each boy paid his board and education by means of alms collected from the richer townsmen, under whose windows they used to sing twice a-week, and of money they earned as choristers. Martin quitted this place in 1498, and directed his steps towards Eisenach."—AUDIN.

[2] "At Eisenach, Luther studied grammar, rhetoric, poetry, under a famous master, J. Trebonius, rector of the convent of the Bare-footed Carmelites. It was the custom of Trebonius to give his lessons with head uncovered, to honour, as he said, the Consuls, Chancellors, Doctors, and Masters who would one day proceed from his school. The young scholar's ready comprehension, his natural eloquence, his rare power of elocution, his skill in composition, both prose and poetical, soon made him the object of his master's especial favour."—AUDIN.

[3] "In the registers of the university we find, under the year 1501, the name of Luther, there written by the rector, Jodocus Truttvetter—*Martinus Ludher, ex Mansfield*. In 1502, the name appears, Martinus Luder,

out life grateful, in a more especial manner, to the whole sex for her sake

After having tried theology, he was induced, by the advice of his friends, to embrace the study of the law, which, at that period, was a stepping-stone to the most lucrative positions not only in state, but in church. He seems, however, never to have had any liking for this pursuit.[1] He infinitely pre-

Baccalaureus philosophiæ. Luther's instructors at Erfurt were Jodocus Truttvetter, whose death he afterwards accused himself of having hastened, by his rebellion against scholastic theology; Jerome Emser, who explained the poetics of Reuchlin; Gerard Hecker, an Augustine monk, who afterwards became a convert to protestantism, and introduced the Reformation into his convent; Bartholomew Usinger, surnamed Arnoldi, who vigorously opposed the new doctrine; John Grevenstein, who loudly protested against the execution of John Huss, and regarded the curate of Bethleem as a martyr; and John Bigand, who remained throughout life zealously attached to his pupil."—AUDIN.

[1] "It was in the conventual library of Erfurt that Luther passed his happiest hours. Thanks to Guttenberg, printing had been bestowed on the world; Mayence and Cologne had reproduced the Scriptures in every variety of form. The monastery of Erfurt had purchased at heavy cost several Latin Bibles. When first Luther opened one of these, his eye fell with inexpressible delight upon the history of Hannah and her son Samuel. 'Oh, God!' he murmured, 'could I have one of these books, I would ask no other worldly treasure!' A great revolution then took place in his soul. Human words clothed in poetry, however noble, seemed to him worthless in comparison with the Inspired Word. He at once conceived a distaste for the study of the law, to which his father had wished him to devote himself. He was now twenty, and deep study had worn him; he fell ill. An old priest came to confess him: the patient was pale, and gave way to a depression which aggravated his sufferings. 'Come, my son,' said the good priest to him, 'courage, courage; you will not die of this sickness. God has a great destiny in store for you; He will make a man of you, and you will live to console others in your turn; for God loveth those whom he chastens.'"—AUDIN.

"He was admitted into holy orders in 1507. Hitherto his mind had been regulated in the usual manner by the system of which he formed a part, and the religious opinions which universally prevailed. But the discovery of a Latin Bible turned his thoughts into a new channel. Previously to this, he informs us he never saw the Bible in any shape, and knew no more of it than those selections from the gospels and epistles which are inserted in the Romish missal. The monks, who rarely received their religious opinions from this source, profoundly ignorant of its contents, and equally careless or indifferent, beheld with amazement the ardent application of Luther in his study of the Scriptures, and of theology in general. The learning and eloquence of Luther, the correctness of his moral conduct, the devotion which he manifested in the church, and the zeal with which he pursued his

ferred the *belles lettres*[1] and music. Music, indeed, was his favourite art. He cultivated it assiduously all his life, and taught it to his children. He does not hesitate to say that music appeared to him the first of the arts after theology: "Music is the art of the prophets; it is the only other art, which like theology, can calm the agitations of the soul, and put the devil to flight." He played both the guitar and the flute. It is probable that he might have been equally successful in the other arts, had he essayed them. He was intimate with the great painter, Lucas Cranach. He had, moreover, it appears, a taste for mechanics, and could turn a lathe skilfully.

This inclination to music and literature, the assiduous cultivation of the poets, which he alternated with the study of logic and of law, presented no indication that he was at an early period to play so important a part in the history of religion. Various traditions, moreover, would give us to believe that, notwithstanding his application, he took his share in the amusements of the German student-life of the period: that gaiety in indigence, those boisterous manners and martial exterior with a gentle spirit, a peaceful disposition within, that ostentation of vice and real purity of life. Assuredly, they who saw Martin Luther travelling on foot from Eisenach to Mansfeldt, on the third day of the Feast of Easter, in the

studies, were soon generally known and appreciated at Wittemberg; and in 1508, when Frederick, elector of Saxony, founded the university of Wittemberg, Luther was appointed first to the professorship of philosophy, and afterwards to that of divinity, in both of which chairs he raised the fame of the infant establishment, and attracted pupils from every quarter of Europe.

[1] "At Erfurt," says Melancthon, in his Life of Luther, "Martin read most of the writings that remain to us of the ancient Latins, Cicero, Virgil, &c. At the age of twenty, he was honoured with the title of Master of Arts, and then, by the advice of his relations, he began to apply himself to jurisprudence. In the monastery he excited general admiration in the public exercises by the facility with which he extricated himself from the labyrinths of dialectics. He read assiduously the prophets and the apostles, then the books of St. Augustin, his *Explanation of the Psalms*, and his book on the *Spirit and the Letter*. He almost got by heart the treatises of Gabriel Biel and Pierre d'Andilly, bishop of Cambray; he studied with earnestness the writings of Occam, whose logic he preferred to that of Scotus and Thomas. He also read a great deal of the writings of Gerson, and above all, those of St. Augustin."

year 1503, his sword on one thigh, his dagger on the other, and wounding himself with his own weapons,[1] had no conception that the awkward student before them was so soon to overthrow the domination of the catholic church throughout one-half of Europe.

In 1505, an accident gave to the career of the youthful Martin an entirely new direction. He saw one of his friends killed at his side by a stroke of lightning. He sent forth a cry at the terrible spectacle : that cry was a vow to St. Anne that he would become a monk, if he were himself spared. The danger passed over, but he did not seek to elude an engagement wrung from him by terror. He solicited no dispensation from his vow. He regarded the blow with which he had seen himself so nearly threatened, as a menace, as an injunction from Heaven. He only delayed the accomplishment of his vow for a fortnight.

On the 17th July, 1505, after having passed a pleasant convivial evening with some musical friends, he entered the Augustine monastery at Erfurt, taking with him nothing but his Plautus and his Virgil.

Next day, he wrote a brief farewell to various persons, sent word to his father of the resolution he had carried into effect, and returned the ring and gown he had received from the university on being admitted to his mastership of arts ; and for a month would not allow any one to see him. He felt the hold which the world still had upon him ; he feared the possible effect upon him of his father's venerated features, filled with tears.[2] Nor was it until two years had expired,

[1] It was while on his way to visit his friends that this accident happened to him ; when just out of Erfurt, his knife or dagger fell from its sheath, and severed the crural vein. The Brother who was accompanying him took him on his shoulders, and carried him back to Erfurt, where the wound was cured.—AUDIN.

[2] "His monastic life was that of a thorough hermit. 'If,' says he, 'Augustin went straight to heaven from the walls of an abbey, I, too, ought to do so : all my brethren would give me this testimony. I fasted, I watched, I mortified, I practised all the cenobite severities, till I absolutely made myself ill. It is not our enemies who will believe this—the men who talk only of the pleasantness of the monastic life, and have never undergone any spiritual temptation.' Sometimes he alleviated the monotony of his days by singing a hymn. He was particularly fond of the Gregorian chant ; and his greatest delight was to take a part with some young chorister. His own voice was a fine counter-tenor. At other times, he

that John Luther gave way, and consented to be present at his son's ordination. A day was selected for the ceremony on which the miner could quit his avocation, and he then came to Erfurt with several friends, and ere he returned, gave to the son he was thus losing, the savings he had managed to put by: twenty florins.[1]

We are not to suppose that in undertaking these formidable engagements, the new priest was impelled by any peculiar degree of religious fervour. We have seen with how mundane an equipment he had furnished himself on entering the cloister; let us now hear his own statement as to what were the feelings he carried with him thither. "When I said my first mass at Erfurt, I was well nigh dead; for I had no faith. My only

would leave the monastery at daybreak, proceed into the country, and at the foot of some tree, preach the word of God to the shepherds. Then he would go to sleep, lulled by their simple minstrelsy. His novitiate was one of peculiar hardship and trial. His superiors, who had perceived the somewhat haughty tendency of his mind, tried his fitness for his adopted vocation in various ways. Luther, more frequently than any other person undergoing the novitiate, was set to sweep out the cells, to open and shut the church doors, to wind up the clock, and to go, a large bag at his back, to beg for his monastery. (*Primum ejus officium*, says Pfefferkorn, indeed, *in cœnobio fuit cloacæ expurgatio.*) Fra Martin murmured against these inflictions. The university of Wittemberg interfered, as did the worthy Staupitz, who put an end to these physical trials."—AUDIN.

Luther had great difficulty in supporting the obligations imposed on him by the monastic regulations. He relates how, at the commencement of the Reformation, he still endeavoured, but without success, to read his Hours regularly. 'If I had done nothing,' he says, 'but relieve men from this tyranny, they owe me a large debt of gratitude.' This constant repetition, at a fixed hour, of the same meditations—this materialization of prayer, which weighed so heavily on the impatient turn of mind of Luther, his contemporary, Ignatius Loyola, was endeavouring to exalt into still higher honour by his singular *Religious Exercises*.

[1] "After the ceremony, those present sat down to dinner. Hans sat by his son, who had hoped to receive from his father's lips expressions of joy and congratulation. 'My dear father,' at length said he, 'why are you so sad? Why should you regret my assuming the monk's robe? It is a becoming robe, is it not?' Hans rose, and addressing the company—'Is it not written in the Word, that a man should honour his father and his mother?' 'It is,' said they. Hans looked expressively at his son, who remained silent. The rest began to talk of indifferent matters. Suddenly Hans exclaimed—'Pray Heaven this be not a snare of the devil! But come, let us drink.' Luther trembled greatly when he ascended the altar; at the canon he was seized with such a fear, that he would have fled without completing the ceremony, had he not been detained."—PFIZER's *Luthers' Leben.*

notion about myself was that I was a very worthy person indeed. I did not regard myself as a sinner at all. The first mass was a striking thing, and produced a good deal of money. They brought in the *horas canonicas*, surrounded by large flambeaux. The *dear young lord*, as the peasants used to call their new pastor, had then to dance with his mother, if she were still alive, the spectators all weeping tears of joy; if she were dead, he put her, as the phrase ran, under the chalice, and saved her from purgatory."[1]

Luther having obtained what he had sought, having become priest, monk, all being accomplished and the door of the world closed upon him, became a prey, we will not say to regret, but to sadness, to perplexities, to temptations of the flesh, to the mischievous shafts and subtleties of the mind. We of the present day can hardly comprehend what this rude strife of the solitary soul can have been. We keep our passions more in order, or rather, we kill them at the birth. Amid our enervating distraction of business, of facile studies and enjoyments, our precocious satiety of the senses and of the mind, we cannot figure forth to ourselves the spiritual warfare which the spiritual man of the middle ages waged with himself, the dolorous mysteries of a life of abstinence and fanatic dreamings, the infinite hard fights that have been fought, noiselessly and unrecorded, in the monk's dark, narrow cell. An archbishop of Mayence used to say: "The human heart is like a millstone; if you put wheat under it, it grinds the wheat into flour; if you put no wheat, it still grinds on, but then, 'tis itself it wears away."[2]

"When I was a monk," says Luther,[3] "I frequently corresponded with Dr. Staupitz.[4] Once, I wrote to him: *Oh, my sins! my sins! my sins!* Whereto he replied, *You would fain be without sin; you have no right sin, such as murdering of parents, blaspheming, adultery, and the like. Thou hadst better keep a register of right and true sins, that so thou mayst not afflict thyself about small matters. Remember that Christ came hither for the pardon of our sins.*"[5]

[1] Tischreden, 281. [2] Ibid. 230. [3] Ibid. 102.

[4] Vicar-general of the monastery into which Luther had entered.

[5] "Luther did not attend to this counsel. Often was he seen at the foot of the altar, his hands clasped, his eyes, full of tears, raised towards Heaven, earnestly beseeching pardon for his sins. Often, on returning to

"I often confessed to Dr. Staupitz, and put to him, not trivial matters, but questions going to the very knot of the question. He answered me as all the other confessors have answered me: *I do not understand.* At last, he came to me one day, when I was at dinner, and said: 'How is it you are so sad, brother Martin?' 'Ah,' I replied, 'I am sad, indeed.' 'You know not,' said he, 'that such trials are good and necessary for you, but would not be so for any one else.' All he meant to imply was, that as I had some learning, I might, but for these trials, have become haughty and supercilious; but I have felt since that what he said was, as it were, a voice and an inspiration of the Holy Spirit."

Luther elsewhere relates, that these temptations had reduced him to such a state, that once for a whole fortnight, he neither ate, drank, nor slept.

"Ah, if St. Paul were alive now, how glad I should be to learn from himself what sort of temptation it was he underwent. It was not the thorn in the flesh; it was not the worthy Tecla, as the papists dream. Oh, no, it was not a sin that tore his conscience. It was something higher than despair resulting from the sense of sin; it was rather the temptation of which the Psalmist speaks: *My God! my God! why hast thou*

his cell for the night, he would kneel at the foot of his bed, and remain there in prayer until daybreak."—PFIZER.

"One morning, the door of his cell not being opened as usual, the brethren became alarmed; they knocked; there was no reply. The door was burst in, and poor Fra Martin was found stretched on the ground, in a state of ecstasy, scarcely breathing, well-nigh dead. A monk took his flute, and gently playing upon it one of the airs that Luther loved, brought him gradually back to himself."—SECKENDORF, *De Lutheranismo.*

"When I was young," says he, in his Table Talk, "it happened that I was taking part, in my priest's habit, in a procession on Corpus Christi day, at Eisleben. All at once, the sight of the holy sacrament, borne by Dr. Staupitz, so terrified me, that I perspired at every pore, and thought I should die with fear. When the procession was over, I confessed to Dr. Staupitz, and related what had happened to me. He replied:—*Thy thoughts are not according to Christ; Christ does not terrify, he consoles.* These words filled me with joy, and were a great relief to my mind."

"Doctor Martin Luther related, that when he was in the monastery at Erfurt, he once said to Dr. Staupitz—'Ah, dear doctor, our Lord God acts in an awful manner towards us! Who can serve him, if he thus strikes all around him?' To which he replied—'My son, learn to form a better judgment of God: if he were not to act thus, how could he overcome the headstrong and wilful. He must take care to the tall trees, lest they ascend to heaven.—*Tischreden,* 150.

forsaken me; as though the Psalmist would have said: *Thou art my enemy without cause;* and, with Job: *Yet I am innocent, nor is iniquity in me.* I am sure that the book of Job is a true history, of which a poem was afterwards made. Jerome and other fathers never experienced such trials. They underwent none but trivial temptations, those of the flesh, which indeed, have quite enough pains of their own accompanying them. Augustin and Ambrose, too, had trials, and trembled before the sword: but this is as nothing compared with the Angel of Satan, *who strikes with the fists.* If I live, I will write a book on temptations, for without a knowledge of that subject, no man can thoroughly understand the Holy Scriptures, or feel the due love and fear of the Lord."

". . . I was lying sick at the infirmary. The most cruel temptations tortured and wore out my frame, so that I could scarcely breathe. No man comforted me: all those to whom I represented my piteous condition, replied, *I know not.* Then, I said to myself: Am I then the only one amongst you who is to be thus sad in spirit? Oh, what spectres, what terrible figures did I see constantly before me! But, ten years ago, God sent me a consolation by his dear angels, enabling me to fight and write for Him."

A long time after this, only the year which preceded that of his death, he himself explains to us the nature of these so terrible temptations. "Even when I was at school, in studying the Epistles of St. Paul, I was seized with the most ardent desire to understand what the apostle meant in his epistle to the Romans. One single phrase stopped me: *Justitia Dei revelatur in illo.* I hated this expression, *Justitia Dei,* because, according to the custom of doctors, I had learned to understand by it that active justice, whereby God is just, and punishes the unjust and sinners. Now, I, who led the life of a harmless monk, and who yet felt painfully within me the uneasy conscience of a sinner, without being able to attain an idea as to the satisfaction I might offer up to God, I did not love, nay, to say the truth, I hated this just God, punisher of sin. I was indignant against Him, and gave silent utterance to murmuring, if not altogether to blasphemy. I said to myself: 'Is it not, then, enough that wretched sinners, already eternally damned for original sin, should be overwhelmed with so many calamities by the decrees of the decalogue, but God must further add misery to misery by his gospel, menacing us even there with his justice and his anger?' It was thus the trouble of my conscience carried me away, and I always came back to the same passage. At last I perceived that the *justice*[1] of God is that whereby, with the blessing of God, the just man lives, that is to say, *Faith;* and I then saw that the meaning of the passage was thus: *The gospel reveals the justice of God, a passive justice, whereby the merciful God justifies us by faith.* Thereupon, I felt as if born again, and it seemed to me as though heaven's gates stood full open before me, and that I was joyfully entering therein. At a later period, I read St. Augustin's book, *On the Spirit and the Letter*, and I found, contrary to my expectation, that he also understands by the justice of God, that wherewith God clothes us in justifying us. I was greatly rejoiced to find this, though the thing is put somewhat incompletely in the book, and though the father explains himself vaguely and imperfectly, on the doctrine of imputation."[2]

To confirm Luther in the doctrine of grace it only needed for him to visit the people from among whom grace had departed. We refer to Italy. We shall be dispensed from painting in detail that Italy of the Borgias. It certainly presented at this period something which has seldom, nay, which has at no other time, been exhibited in history: a systematic and scientific perversity; a magnificent ostentation of wickedness; in a word, the atheist priest proclaiming himself monarch of the universe. That was a feature peculiar to the period. Another feature, belonging to the country, and which is of all time, was that invincible paganism which has ever subsisted in Italy. There, do what you may, nature is pagan; and as is the nature of a country, so will its art be. It is a noble drama, the scenery, so to speak, by Raffaello, the sounding poetry by Ariosto. The grave solemnity, the elevation, the divinity of Italian art, the men of the North were far from appreciating. In what they there saw before them they recognised mere sensuality, mere temptations of the flesh, against which they deemed it their surest defence to close their eyes, to pass on quickly, and, as they passed, to mutter or shout, as it might be, a curse against the unclean thing.

[1] Rendered in our English version, *the righteousness.*

[2] Lutheri, *Op. Lat.* (Jenæ, 1612,) 1, *præf.*

On its more austere side, its politics and its jurisprudence, Italy was equally a stumbling-block for the northerns. The German nations have always instinctively rejected and anathematized the Roman law. Tacitus relates that on the defeat of Varus, the Germans eagerly took their revenge for the judicial forms to which he had essayed to subject them. One of these barbarians, as he nailed to a tree the head of a Roman legist, pierced his tongue, bitterly exclaiming, "Hiss now, hiss now, viper, if thou canst!" This hatred of the lawyers, perpetuated throughout the middle ages, was, as will be seen, given energetic expression to, on all occasions, by Luther, and naturally enough. The lawyer and the theologian are asunder as the two Poles; the one has faith in liberty, the other in grace; the one in man, the other in God. The first of these faiths has ever been that of Italy. The Southern reformer, Savonarola, who appeared somewhat before Luther, limited his views to a change in works, in manners; he contemplated no reformation in faith.

Behold Luther in Italy.[1] It is a moment of ineffable joy, of boundless hopes, in which we begin the descent of the Alps, to enter for the first time that glorious land. And for Luther, there was the further aspiration to confirm his wavering faith in the holy city, and throw aside all the growing burden of uneasy doubt at the tomb of the apostles. Old Rome, too, the Rome of classic ages, was a powerful attraction to him, as the seat and sanctuary of the learning he had cultivated with such ardour in his poor Wittemberg.

He was received at Milan in a marble convent, and from that he visited one convent after another, or, rather one palace after another, for such they were. In each he found good cheer, sumptuous entertainment. The simple-minded German was somewhat astonished at all this magnificence of humility, at all this regal splendour of penitence. He once ventured to suggest to the Italian monks that they would do well, at least to abstain from meat on Friday; the impertinence was near costing him his life; it was with the greatest difficulty he got out of the hands of the offended epicures.

[1] He was deputed thither by his monastery, in 1510, to adjust some differences before the pope, which had arisen between it and the pope's vicar general.

Undeceived and sorrowful, he proceeded on foot over the burning plains of Lombardy. He reached Pavia ill; he went on, and when he entered Bologna, he was sick well nigh unto death. The traveller's poor head had been too violently assailed by the sun of Italy, and even more than by this, by the strange things, the strange manners, the strange discourse he saw and heard around him on his way. He kept his bed for awhile in Bologna, the throne of the Roman law and of the legists, and looked upon himself for some time as a dead man. Ever and anon, he murmured to himself, to strengthen and confirm his mind, the words of the prophet and apostle: *The just shall live by faith.*

In one of his conversations, he gives us naïvely an idea of how terrible Italy was to the imaginations of the simple-hearted Germans: "The Italians only require you to look in a mirror to be able to kill you. They can deprive you of all your senses by secret poisons. In Italy, the air itself is pestilential; at night, they close hermetically every window, and stop up every chink and cranny."[1] Luther assures us that both himself and the Brother who accompanied him, were taken ill, solely in consequence of having slept with the casement open, but they ate two pomegranates, by which means it pleased God to save their lives.[2]

He went on his journey,[3] merely passing through Florence without stopping, and at length entered Rome, He proceeded to the convent of his order, near the *Porto del Popolo.*[4] "On arriving, I fell on my knees, raised my hands to Heaven, and exclaimed: 'Hail, holy Rome! made holy by the holy martyrs, and by the blood which has been spilt here.'" In his fervour, he adds, he hastened to view the sacred places, saw all, believed all. He soon perceived, however, that he was the only person who did believe; Christianity seemed totally forgotten in this capital of the Christian world. The

[1] Tischreden, 440.

[2] The occasion on which he cured himself and his companion by eating pomegranates, was when he had drunk some stagnant water on the way side.—Audin.

[3] His object in making all possible haste was to arrive at Rome by St. John's Eve; "for," says he, "you know the old Roman proverb: 'Happy the mother whose child shall celebrate mass in Rome on St. John's Eve.' Oh, how I desired to give my mother this happiness! but this was impossible, and it vexed me greatly to find it sò."

[4] Tischreden 441.

pope was no longer the scandalous Alexander VI., but the warlike and choleric Julius II. This father of the faithful breathed nothing but blood and ruin. We know that his great artist, Michel-Angelo, represented him overwhelming Bologna with his benediction. The pope had just at this time commanded the sculptor to prepare for him a funereal monument, as large as a church: of this projected monument, the *Moses*, with some other statues which have come down to us, were to have formed a part.

The sole thought that occupied the pope and Rome at this juncture, was the war against the French. Luther had manifestly slight chance of a favourable opportunity for discoursing of grace and the inefficacy of works, to this singular priest who besieged towns in person, and who only just before, had refused to enter Mirandola otherwise than by the breach he had made in its walls. His cardinals, apprentice-officers under him, were politicians, diplomatists, or, more generally, men of letters, upstart *savans*, who read nothing but Cicero, and who would have feared to hurt their Latinity by opening the Bible. When they spoke of the pope, it was of the *Pontifex Maximus;* a canonized saint was, in their language, a man *relatus inter Divos;* and if they at any time referred to grace, they phrased it thus: *Deorum immortalium beneficiis.*

If our poor German took refuge in the churches, he had not even the consolation of a good mass. The Roman priest despatched the divine sacrifice with such celerity, that before Luther had got through the gospel, the minister said to him, *Ite, missa est.*[1] "These Italian priests often say mass in such a manner that I detest them. I have heard them make a boast of their fearful temerity in free-thinking. Repeatedly, in consecrating the host, they would say, 'Bread thou art, and bread thou wilt remain! wine thou art, and wine thou wilt remain!'" The only thing to be done was to flee, veiling the head, and shaking off the dust from the feet: Luther quitted Rome at the end of a fortnight.

He carried back with him into Germany the condemnation of Italy, and of the Roman church. In the rapid and mournful journey he had made, the Saxon had seen sufficient to condemn, but not sufficient to comprehend. And, in truth,

[1] Tischreden, 441.

for a mind intent upon the moral point of view of Christianity, there needed a rare effort of philosophy, an historical enthusiasm, hardly to be expected in those days, to discover religion in that world of art, of jurisprudence, of politics, which constituted Italy.

"I would not," he says somewhere,[1] "I would not for a hundred thousand florins have missed seeing Rome, (and he repeats these words thrice.) I should have always felt an uneasy doubt whether I was not, after all, doing injustice to the pope. As it is, I am quite satisfied on the point."[2]

[1] Tischreden, 441.

[2] "On the recommendation of Dr. Staupitz, Luther, at about this time, was appointed professor of philosophy in the new university of Wittemberg. The prince's letter requiring him to come and occupy this chair was so urgent, that Luther had scarce time to bid adieu to his friends. His portmanteau was a light affair: it contained a coarse stuff robe, two Bibles, one Latin and one Greek, some ascetic books, and a small stock of linen. The books named, with a few volumes of Latin poetry, a Concordance, and some of Aristotle's treatises, comprehended the entire library of the monk of Wittemberg. The physics and ethics to which his attention was now directed, were by no means so much to his taste as theology, *that mistress of the world, that queen of the arts*, the study of which he so loved, and upon which he has passed so many a magnificent eulogium. Accordingly, to one of his friends, who had asked him how he liked his college life, he said: "Thank God, I am well; but I should be much better if I were not compelled to profess this philosophy." The philosophy was that of Aristotle, that devil's master, as Luther afterwards called him, who wanted to build upon man, instead of upon God. The senate of Wittemberg, on the recommendation of Dr. Staupitz, named Luther town preacher, the bishop sanctioning the appointment. This was a new mission for Martin, and he grew alarmed at his responsibility. He feared he should not be equal to the task, and he related to Dr. Staupitz the terrors that besieged him. The doctor encouraged him. "You want to kill me, doctor," exclaimed Luther. "I shall not be able to carry on the thing for three months." "Well, my son," said Staupitz, "even if you die, 'twill be in the service of the Lord; how noble a sacrifice!" Luther yielded. He preached by turns in his monastery, in the royal chapel, and in the collegiate church. He soon showed how mistaken he had been with respect to the extent of his powers; his success was of the most marked description. His voice was fine, sonorous, clear, striking; his gesticulation emphatic and dignified. He had told Staupitz that he would not imitate his predecessors, and he kept his word. For the first time, he presented the spectacle of a Christian orator ceasing to quote the old masters of the schools, and drawing, instead, his images from the inspired writers. Whenever he had leisure, he returned to his beloved theology; he especially loved to peruse the epistles of St. Paul and the sermons of Tauler. His dearest wishes were ere long in a way to be accomplished: he was admitted bachelor in theology, and could now, without giving up his professorship, read lectures on the sacred text. This daily exercise prepared

CHAPTER II.

1517—1521.

Luther attacks indulgences—He burns the pope's bull—Erasmus, Hutten, Franz von Sickingen—Luther appears before the Diet of Worms—He is carried off.

THE papacy was far from suspecting its danger. Ever since the thirteenth century, men had been disputing with it, had been railing against it, but apparently with no effect. The world, it imagined, had been quietly and permanently lulled to sleep by the dull and uniform clatter of the schools. It seemed as though scarcely anything new remained to be said about the matter. Everybody had talked and talked, till they had all fairly lost breath. Wickliff, John Huss, Jerome of Prague, persecuted, condemned, burned though they were, had nevertheless lived long enough to say all they had to say. The doctors of the most catholic university of Paris, the Pierres d'Andilly, the Clemenges, mild Gerson himself, had all, very respectfully, had a fling at the papacy; yet papacy

him for the great struggle he was about to sustain against the papacy. Never in any Saxon professional chair had there been heard so luminous an explanation of the Old and New Testaments, as that made by Luther. He conceived a passion for this kind of labour, passed whole nights in preparing for it. Sometimes eminent doctors came to listen to his course, and retired full of admiration. The venerable Pollich, known by the soubriquet of *Lux Mundi*, heard him, and, struck with wonder, exclaimed: "This father has profound insight, exceeding imagination: he will trouble the doctors before he has done, and excite no slight disturbance."—On the 16th Oct. 1512, St. Luke's day, Luther was admitted doctor of divinity, and on the 17th, he was invested with the insignia of the doctorate, by Andrew Bodenstein (Carlstadt.) Luther quitted the chair for a while to fulfil other occupations confided to him by Staupitz, who, compelled by his avocations to absent himself, charged his protegé to visit the convents in his province. This afforded Luther an opportunity of investigating the interior life of the cloister. According to him, "The Bible is a book which is rarely found in the hands of the monks, who know St. Thomas much better than St. Paul." His powers were very extensive; he could depose persons guilty of scandalous conduct. At Erfurt, he recognised as his superior, John Lange, who was afterwards one of the first to throw off the monastic robe and

endured nevertheless; it managed, with patient tenacity, to live on from hand to mouth, if nothing better, and so the fifteenth century passed away. The councils of Constance and Bâle made a great noise, indeed, but produced very little effect. The popes let them have their say, procured the revocation of the Pragmatic Sanction, quietly re-established their preponderance in Europe, and founded a powerful sovereignty in Italy.

Julius II. conquered for the church; Leo X. for his family. This youthful pope, a thorough man of the world, a man of pleasure, a man of letters, a man of business, in common with all the other Medici, had the passions of his age, as well as those of the former popes, and those of his own particular period. His aim was to make the Medici family monarchs. He himself played the part of the first king of Christendom. Independently of the costly diplomatic relations which he maintained with all the states of Europe, he kept up a scientific correspondence with the most distant regions. He opened communications even with the extreme north, and employed persons to collect the monuments of Scandinavian history. At Rome he was proceeding with St. Peter's, the construction of which had been bequeathed to him by Julius II.; the latter pontiff, in resolving on the work, had not calculated his resources; and indeed, when Michel-Angelo brought such

marry. The convent of Nieustadt was a prey to great disputes among its inmates; Luther re-established order, calling upon Michael Dressel, the prior, whose vacillation had occasioned most of the disorder, to resign his post. His letter to this monk is a mixture of firmness and gentleness; if he opens wounds, he has honey at hand to soften them. Humility and love are the two virtues he recommends to him: "Humility, above all," says he, "the mother of charity." He gives in a letter to Lange an amusing account of his occupation at this time:—"I had need have two secretaries to keep up my correspondence; pity my unhappy fortune. I am conventual *Concionator*, table preacher, director of studies; I am vicar, or in words, eleven priors in one, conservator of the ponds at Litzkau, pleader and assessor at Torgau, Paulinic reader and collector of psalms; add to all these, the assaults of the world, the flesh, and the devil." There was one assault, at this period, which he nobly withstood: the plague appeared at Wittemberg, and his conduct on the occasion stands out gloriously: his friends conjured him to imitate their example, and fly: "Fly," exclaimed the brother, "my God! no! for a monk, the world will not perish. I am at my post: obedience tells me to remain there till obedience shall make it a duty for me to withdraw Not that I have no fear of death, I am not the apostle Paul—but the Lord will deliver me from fear."—AUDIN.

or such a plan, who would have thought for an instant of haggling about the cost? It was he who said of the Pantheon: "I will raise that temple three hundred feet in the air." The impoverished Roman state was not in a position to carry out the magnificent projects of men with conceptions so vast, that the ancient empire, when sovereign of the world, could scarce have realized them.

Leo X. had commenced his pontificate with selling to Francis I. what did not belong to him, the rights of the church of France. At a later period, as a means of raising money, he created thirty-one cardinals at once;[1] but these were small matters. He had no Mexico to have recourse to. His mines were the old faith of the nations, their easy credulity. He had entrusted the working of this mine in Germany to the Dominicans, who had accordingly succeeded the Augustines in the sale of indulgences. The Dominican, Tetzel,[2] a shameless mountebank, went about from town to town, with great display, pomp, and expense, hawking the commodity in the churches, the public streets, in taverns and ale-houses. He paid over to his employers as little as possible, pocketing the balance, as the pope's legate subsequently proved against him. The faith of the buyers diminishing, it became necessary to exaggerate to the fullest extent the merit of the specific; the article had been so long in the market, and in such great supply, that the demand was falling off. The intrepid Tetzel stretched his rhetoric to the very uttermost bounds of amplification. Daringly piling one

[1] On the 13th June, 1517. The same day, a storm overthrew the angel that stood on the top of the Castel di San Angelo, struck an infant Jesus in a church, and knocked the keys out of the hands of a statue of St. Peter.—RUCHAT, i. 36.

[2] This Tetzel or Totzel, *italice* Tottila, was a man of notoriously immoral character. At a subsequent period his own party abandoned him. "The lies and frauds of this Tetzel," wrote Miltitz to Pfeffinger, "are perfectly well known to me; I have warmly reproached him for them, and proved them against him in the presence of many spectators. I have sent an account of all his conduct to the pope, and await his judgment. By a letter of an agent of the Fuggers, whose duty it was to keep an account of all the money received from the indulgences, I have convicted Tetzel of having taken every month eighty florins for himself, and ten for his servant, beyond the amount paid him for the two, and for the keep of three horses. This is without reckoning what he has otherwise embezzled or wasted. You see how the wretch served the holy Roman church and the archbishop of Mayence, my excellent lord."—SECKENDORF, i. 62.

lie upon another, he set forth, in reckless display, the long list of evils which this panacea could cure. He did not content himself with enumerating known sins; he set his foul imagination to work, and invented crimes, infamous atrocities, strange, unheard of, unthought of; and when he saw his auditors standing aghast at each horrible suggestion, he would calmly repeat the burden of his song: "Well, all this is expiated the moment your money chinks in the pope's chest."

Luther assures us that up to this time he had no very definite notion what indulgences were. But when he saw the prospectus of them proudly set forth with the name, arms, and authorization of the archbishop of Mayence, whom the pope had charged with the superintendence of their sale in Germany, he was seized with indignation.[1] A problem of mere speculation would never have placed him in antagonism with his ecclesiastical superiors. But this was a question of good sense, of common morality. A doctor of divinity, an influential professor in the university of Wittemberg, which the elector had just founded, provincial vicar of the Augustins, and entrusted by the vicar-general with the pastoral visitation of Misnia and Thuringia, he doubtless deemed himself responsible more than any other person for the Saxon faith so extensively confided to him. His conscience was struck: if he spoke, he ran great risks; if he remained silent, he believed he should incur damnation.

"It was in the year 1517, when the profligate monk Tetzel,[2] a worthy servant of the pope and the devil—for I am certain that the pope is the agent of the devil on earth—came among us selling indulgences, maintaining their efficacy, and impudently practising on the credulity of the people. When I beheld this unholy and detestable traffic taking place in open day, and thereby sanctioning the most villanous crimes, I could not, though I was then but a young doctor of divinity, refrain from protesting against it in the strongest manner,

[1] "When I undertook to write against the gross error of indulgences, Dr. Staupitz said: 'What, would you write against the pope? What are you about? They will not permit you to do this!' 'But suppose they must needs permit it?' replied I."—*Tischreden*, 384.

[2] The character of Tetzel was notoriously immoral. It is said that he had been convicted of adultery, and ordered to be thrown into the Inn, but received a pardon at the intercession of the elector Frederick of Saxony He died of a broken heart in 1519.

not only as directly contrary to the Scriptures, but as opposed to the canons of the church itself. Accordingly, in my place at Wittemberg—in which university, by the favour of God and the kindness of the illustrious elector of Saxony, I was honoured with the office of professor of divinity—I resolved to oppose the career of this odious monk, and to put the people on their guard against the revival of this infamous imposition on their credulity. When I put this resolution into practice, instead of being abused and condemned, as I have been, by these worthless tyrants and impostors, the pope and his mercenaries, I expected to be warmly encouraged and commended, for I did little more than make use of the pope's own language, as set forth in the decretals, against the rapacity and extortion of the collectors. I cautioned my hearers against the snares which were laid for them, showing them that this was a scheme altogether opposed to religion, and only intended as a source of emolument by these unprincipled men. It was on the festival of All-Hallows Eve that I first drew their attention to the gross errors touching indulgences; and about the same time I wrote two letters, one to the most reverend prelate Jerome, bishop of Brandenburg, within whose jurisdiction Tetzel and his associates were carrying on their scandalous traffic; the other to the most reverend prelate and prince, Albert, archbishop of Magdeburg, pointing out to them the consequences of this imposition, and praying them to silence Tetzel. My letter to the archbishop was in these terms:

"'To the most reverend father in Christ, my most illustrious lord, prince Albert, archbishop of Magdeburg and Mayence, marquis of Brandenburg, &c. Luther to his lord and pastor in Christ, in all submission and reverence.

JESUS.

"'The grace and mercy of God, and whatever can be and is. Pardon me, most reverend father in Christ, illustrious prince, that I have the temerity, I who am the lees of mankind, to raise my eyes to your sublimity, and address a letter to you. Jesus, my Lord and Saviour, is witness for me, that, long restrained by the consciousness of my own turpitude and weakness, I have long delayed commencing the work which I now undertake with open and upraised brow, impelled by the fidelity I owe to Jesus Christ; deign then, your grace, to cast a look upon the grain of sand who now approaches you, and to receive my prayer with paternal clemency.

"'Persons are now hawking about papal indulgences, under the name and august title of your lordship, for the construction of St. Peter's at Rome. I say nothing about the vapourings of the preachers, which I have not myself heard; but I complain bitterly of the fatal errors in which they are involving the common people, men of weak understanding, whom, foolish as they are, these men persuade that they will be sure of salvation if they only buy their letters of plenary indulgence. They believe that souls will fly out of purgatory, the moment that the money paid for their redemption is thrown into the preacher's bag, and that such virtue belongs to these indulgences, that there is no sin, howsoever great, even the violation, which is impossible, of the Mother of God, which the indulgences will not absolutely and at once efface.

"'Great God! And is it thus that men dare to teach unto death, those who are entrusted to your care, oh reverend father, and make more difficult the account which will be demanded from you in the great day! When I saw these things I could remain silent no longer. No; there is no episcopal power which can insure to man his salvation; even the infused grace of our Lord cannot wholly render him secure; our apostle commands us to wash out our salvation in fear and trembling: *The righteous scarcely shall be saved*, so narrow is the way which leads to life. Those who are saved are called in the Scripture, brands saved from the burning; everywhere the Lord reminds us of the difficulty of salvation. How, then, dare these men seek to render poor souls fatally confident of salvation, on the mere strength of purchased indulgences and futile promises? The chiefest work of bishops should be to take care that the people learn truly the gospel, and be full of Christian charity. Never did Christ preach indulgences, nor command them to be preached: what he preached and commanded to be preached, was the gospel. . . . I would implore you to silence these ill preachers, ere some one shall arise, and utterly confuting them and their preachings, cast discredit upon your sublimity, a thing to be avoided, but which I fear must needs occur, unless you take measures for silencing these men. . . . I intreat your grace to read and consider the propositions, wherein I have demonstrated the vanity of these indulgences, which the preachers thereof call all-powerful.'[1]

"To this letter I received no answer, and indeed I knew not at the time that the archbishop had bargained with the pope to receive one-half of the money raised from these indulgences, and to remit the other half to Rome. These, then, were my first steps in the matter, until the increased insolence and the lying representations of Tetzel, which seemed to be fully sanctioned by the silence of his superiors, as well as my determination to maintain the truth at all hazards, induced me to adopt more decisive measures than a mere personal remonstrance, in a series of cautions to those with whom I was more particularly connected, to beware of these arch impostors and blasphemers. So finding all my remonstrances disregarded, on the festival of All Saints, in November, 1517, I read, in the great church of Wittemberg, a series of propositions against these infamous indulgences, in which, while I set forth their utter inefficiency and worthlessness, I expressly declared in my protest, that I would submit on all occasions to the word of God and the decisions of the church. At the same time I was not so presumptuous as to imagine that my opinion would be preferred above all others, nor yet so blind as to set the fables and decrees of man above the written word of God. I took occasion to express these opinions rather as subjects of doubt than of positive assertion, but I held it to be my duty to print and circulate them throughout the country, for the benefit of all classes—for the learned, that they might detect inaccuracies—for the ignorant, that they might be put on their guard against the villanies and impositions of Tetzel, until the matter was properly determined."

These propositions were affixed to the outer pillars of the

[1] To this letter, dated All Saints' Eve, 1517, the propositions presently given were appended. The bishop of Brandenburg had sent him a letter in reply, by a Carthusian monk, in which he pointed out to him that in what he was doing, he was assailing the church, and advised him to remain silent for the sake of peace.

gate of the church of All Saints, at midday, on the 31st October, 1517. They open thus :

" From a desire to elicit the truth, the following theses will be maintained at Wittemberg, under the presidency of the reverend father Martin Luther, of the order of the Augustins, master of arts, master and lecturer in theology, who asks that such as are not able to dispute verbally with him, will do so in writing. In the name of our Lord Jesus Christ. Amen."

Let us quote from the ninety-five propositions which form the series, the following :

" When our Lord and Master Jesus Christ says, 'Repent,' he means that the whole life of his followers on earth shall be a constant and continual repentance.

" This word cannot be understood of the sacrament of penance (that is to say, of confession and satisfaction) as it is administered by the priest.

" Yet the Lord does not mean, in this, to speak only of internal repentance : internal repentance is null, if it does not produce externally all kinds of mortification of the flesh.

" Repentance and grief, that is to say, true penitence, last as long as a man is displeased with himself, that is to say, until he passes from this life into the life eternal.

" The pope cannot and will not remit any other penalty than that which he has imposed at his own good pleasure, or in conformity with the canons, that is, with the papal orders.

" The pope cannot remit any condemnation, but only declare and confirm the remission that God himself has made of it ; unless he do so in the cases that pertain to himself. If he does otherwise, the condemnation remains wholly the same.

" The laws of ecclesiastical penance should be imposed only on the living, and in no respect concern the dead.

" The commissioners of indulgences deceive themselves when they say, that by the pope's indulgence man is delivered from all punishment, and saved.

" The same power which the pope has over purgatory throughout the entire church, every bishop has in his own diocese, and every vicar in his own parish. Besides, who knows whether all the souls in purgatory desire to be redeemed ? They say St. Severinus' did not.

"They preach devices of human folly, who assert, that the moment the money sounds at the bottom of the strong box, the soul flies away out of purgatory.

"This is certain, to wit, that as soon as the money sounds, avarice and the love of gain spring up, increase, and multiply. But the succour and the prayers of the church depend only on the good pleasure of God.

"Those who think themselves sure of salvation with their indulgences will go to the devil with those who taught them so.

"They teach doctrines of Antichrist who assert, that to deliver a soul from purgatory, or to buy an indulgence, there is no need of contrition or repentance.

"Every Christian who feels a true repentance for his sins has a full remission of the penalty and of the transgression, without its being necessary that he should have recourse to indulgences.

"Every true Christian, living or dead, has part in all the good things of Christ or of the church, by the gift of God, and without letter of indulgence.

"Still we must not despise the pope's distribution and pardon, regarded as a declaration of God's pardon.

"True repentance and sorrow seek and love chastisement; but the pleasantness of indulgence detaches from chastisement, and makes one conceive a hatred against it.

"Christians must be taught, that the pope thinks not nor wishes that any one should in any wise compare the act of buying indulgences with any act of mercy.

"Christians must be taught, that he who gives to the poor or who lends to the needy does better than he who buys an indulgence.

"For the work of charity enlarges charity and makes the man more pious, whereas indulgences do not render him better, but only more confident in himself and more self-secure from punishment.

"Christians must be taught, that he who sees his neighbour in want, and who, in spite of that, buys an indulgence, does not buy the pope's indulgence, but lays upon him the wrath of God.

"Christians must be taught, that if they have nothing superfluous, it is their duty to reserve what is required for their houses to procure necessaries, and that they ought not to lavish it on indulgences.

"Christians must be taught, that to buy an indulgence is a free-will act, and not one by command.

"Christians must be taught, that the pope, having more need of a prayer offered with faith than of money, more desires the prayer than the money when he distributes indulgences.

"Christians must be taught, that the pope's indulgence is good, if one does not put one's trust in it, but that nothing can be more pernicious if it cause the loss of piety.

"Christians must be taught, that if the pope knew of the extortions of the indulgence-preachers, he would rather the metropolitan church of St. Peter were burnt and reduced to ashes than see it built with the skin, the flesh, and the bones of his sheep.

"The change of the canonical penalty into the purgatorial, is a tare, a tarnel of dissension; the bishops were manifestly asleep when this pernicious plant was sown.

"The pope must needs desire that if these pardons, things so trivial, are celebrated with a bell, a ceremony, a solemnity, the gospel, a thing so great, should be preached with a hundred bells, a hundred ceremonies, a hundred solemnities.

"The true treasure of the church is the sacro-sanct gospel of the glory and grace of God.

"Many have reason to hate this treasure of the gospel, for by it the first become the last.

"Many have reason to love the treasure of the indulgences, for by them the last become the first.

"The treasures of the gospel are the nets with which they fish for men of worth.

"The treasures of the indulgences are the nets with which they fish for men worth money.

"To say that the cross placed on the arms of the pope, is equivalent to the cross of Christ, is blasphemy.

"Why does not the pope in his very holy character, clear out purgatory at once, wherein so many souls are suffering? This would be bestowing his power far more worthily, than for him to deliver souls for money (money so gained brings calamity with it); and for what purpose, moreover? For a building!

"What is this strange compassion of God and of the pope, which, for so many crowns, changes the soul of an impious wretch, enemy of God and man, into a soul holy and agreeable to the Lord?

"Cannot the pope, whose treasures at this time exceed the most enormous accumulations elsewhere, cannot he with his own money, rather than with that of impoverished Christians, raise a single church, for the metropolitan cathedral?

"What does the pope remit, what does he give, to those who, by their complete contrition, have already purchased a right to plenary remission?

"Fie on the prophets, who say to Christ's people: *The cross! the cross!* and show us not the cross.

"Fie on the prophets who say to the people of Christ: *Peace! Peace!* and give us not peace.

"Christians must be taught to follow Christ, their Chief, through pain and punishments, and through hell itself; so that they may be assured that it is through tribulations heaven is entered, and not through security and peace, &c."

These propositions, negative and polemical, received their complement in the dogmatical theses[1] which Luther sent forth at about the same time:

"It is not in the course of nature for man to desire God to be God. He would rather himself be God, and that God were not God.

"It is false that the appetite is free to go as it will in the two senses: it is not free, but captive.

"There is not in nature, in the presence of God, anything but concupiscence.

"It is false that this concupiscence may be regulated by the virtue of hope. For hope is contrary to charity, which seeks and desires that only which is of God. Hope does not proceed from our merits, but from our passions, which efface our merits.

"The best, the infallible preparation and sole disposition for receiving grace, is the choice and predestination decreed by God from all eternity.

"On the part of man, nothing precedes grace, but the non-disposition to grace, or rather, rebellion.

[1] Opera Lat. ii. 56.

"It is false that invincible ignorance can be put forward as an excuse. The ignorance of God, of oneself, of good works, is the invincible nature of man."

"Some copies of my propositions," continues Luther, "having found their way to Frankfort-on-the-Oder, where Tetzel was then acting as inquisitor and selling indulgences under the archbishop-elector of Mayence, he, foaming with rage and alarm at the propositions I had set forth, published a set of counter-resolutions in reply, to the number of one hundred and six, in which he maintained the most insolent and blasphemous doctrines respecting the pretended power and infallibility of the pope; and in a second series of propositions, he assumed the office of general interpreter of the Scripture, and railed against heretics and heresiarchs, by which name he designated myself and my friends, and he concluded his insolence by burning my themes publicly in the city of Frankfort. When the news of this madman's proceedings reached Wittemberg, a number of persons collected together, and having procured Tetzel's productions, retaliated upon him by burning them in the great square, amid the cheers and derision of a large proportion of the inhabitants. I was not sorry that such a mass of absurdity and extravagance should meet with the fate it really merited; but, at the same time, I regretted the manner in which it was done, and solemnly affirm that I knew nothing of it at the time, and that it was done without the knowledge either of the elector or of the magistrates.

"I soon found that Tetzel was not the only opponent resolved to take the field against me, although I had maintained nothing in my propositions inconsistent with the avowed doctrines of these hirelings; and had, indeed, advanced my propositions more by way of doubt than in a positive manner. John Eck[1] made his appearance in a violent attack upon me: but as his observations were more in the nature of mere abuse than of conclusive argument, that person did a vast deal of harm to his own party, while he rendered me unintentional service. Another antagonist also entered the lists against me, in the person of Silvestro Prierio, a Dominican,[2] who with the

[1] Vice-chancellor of the university of Ingoldstadt.

[2] Master of the Apostolical chamber at Rome, and licencer of books.

pedantry peculiar to his office of censor in the metropolis of popery, chose to answer all my propositions in a way most convenient to himself, by declaring, in a manner altogether begging the question, that they were all heretical. In my reply, I exposed the absurdity of this method of proceeding, which, however, is the usual style of argument adopted by the Romish tyrants and their slaves. Prierio again attacked me; but when I found the man asserting that the authority of the pope was superior to the councils and canons of the church, and that even the sacred Scriptures depended for their interpretation on the mere dictum of that representative of Antichrist, I thought it unnecessary to reply further, than by simply declaring my conviction, that the said Prierio's book, being a compound of blasphemies and lies, must certainly have been the work of the devil; and that if the pope and cardinals sanctioned such writings, which I did not then believe, although I now know it well, Rome must be the seat of Antichrist, the centre of abomination, and the synagogue of Satan. Who is Antichrist, if the pope is not Antichrist? O Satan, Satan, how long wilt thou be suffered to abuse the patience of God by thy great wickedness? Unhappy, abandoned, blasphemous Rome! the wrath of God is upon thee, and thou richly deservest it, for thou art the habitation of all that is impure and disgusting! a very pantheon of impiety![1]

"In this way passed the year 1517, I maintaining the truth, and these apologists for impiety railing against me with their false accusations; for hitherto pope Leo had taken no notice of the matter, not wishing, as I was afterwards informed, to interfere at all, thinking that the zeal of both parties would soon subside. Meantime I began to consider what measures to adopt, for I knew that no reasonings of mine would have any weight with such obstinate and insolent disputants as Tetzel, Eck, and Prierio, bigoted slaves[2] of that system of

[1] "Habitatio draconum, lemurum, larvarum, et juxta nomen suum confusio sempiterna, idolis avaritiæ, perfidis, apostatis, cynædis, priapis, latronibus, simonibus, et infinitis aliis monstris ad os plena."

[2] While, however, Luther occasionally utters these strong expressions to denote the abhorrence in which he held the opinions of his adversaries, he was always respectful in his public controversies. Prierio he usually styles the *reverend in Christ*, and *reverend father*, while Prierio addresses Luther as *carissime Luther*.

iniquity and licentiousness which I myself had witnessed when at Rome."[1]

The publication of these theses and the sermon in German, which Luther delivered in support of them,[2] struck upon the whole of Germany like a huge thunderbolt. This sacrifice of liberty to grace, of man to God, of the finite to the infinite, was at once recognised by the German people as the true national religion, as the faith which Gottschalk proclaimed in the time of Charlemagne, from the very cradle of German Christianity, the faith of Tauler and of all the mystical preachers of the Low Countries. The people, accordingly, threw themselves with the most hungry avidity upon this religious pasture, from which they had been shut out ever since the fourteenth century. The propositions were printed in thousands, devoured, spread abroad, diffused in every direction. Luther himself was alarmed at his success. "I am sorry," said he, "to see them so extensively printed and distributed; this is not a good way wherein to set about the instruction of the people. I myself feel some doubts upon points. There are things I should more closely have investi-

[1] Another opponent took the field, in the person of James Hoogenstraaten, a German divine, of the Dominican order, who, however, subsequently wrote with equal virulence against Erasmus and others. This monk, in the true spirit of his order, told the pope, that, in his opinion, it would be best to convince Luther by chains, fire, and flames.

[2] "In the first five paragraphs, and again, more especially in the sixth, which is extremely mystical, he explains in a very clear manner the doctrine of St. Thomas: he then proves, from Scripture itself, against that doctrine, that the sincere repentance and conversion of the sinner can alone secure pardon for his sins:—'Even though the church should really declare that indulgences efface sins better than works of satisfaction, it were a thousand times fitter for a Christian not to buy them, but rather to do the work of repentance, and suffer the penalties; for indulgences are and can only be dispensations from good works and from salutary penalties. It were far better and surer to give what you can spare towards the construction of St. Peter's, than to buy the indulgences preached for that purpose But, first of all, if you have to spare, you should give it to your poor neighbour—that is better than to give it to raise up stone walls; and if there be no one in your neighbourhood who requires your assistance, then give it to the churches of your own town. If any then remain, give it to St. Peter, and not before. My desire, my prayer, and my advice is, that you buy not these indulgences. Leave it to bad, idle, sleepy churchmen to buy them; you can dispense with them. Whether men can be drawn from purgatory by the efficacy of indulgences, I cannot say; but I do not believe they can. Some doctors say they can; but they cannot prove it, and the

gated and ascertained, others which I should have altogether omitted, had I foreseen this result."

And he at this juncture seemed exceedingly disposed to throw up the whole matter, and to submit without further cavilling. "I will obey, implicitly," said he; "I had rather so than perform miracles, even though I had the gift of performing miracles."

Tetzel himself shook this pacific resolution by burning, as has been seen, Luther's propositions in public, whereupon the students of Wittemberg forthwith made reprisals upon Tetzel's own propositions. Though this circumstance was one, as Luther has informed us, which he regretted, he followed it up by sending forth his *Resolutions*, in support of his first propositions. "You will see," he wrote to a friend, "my *Resolutiones et responsiones*. Perhaps, in certain passages, you will find them more free than was absolutely necessary; and if they seem so to you, they will *à fortiori*, appear perfectly intolerable to the flatterers of Rome. They were published before I was aware, or I would have modified them in some respects."[1]

church says nothing about the matter; and, at all events, the surest way is to have recourse to prayer. What I teach is true, is founded on Scripture. Let the scholastic doctors keep to their scholastics; all of them put together are not enough to warrant a preaching up of indulgences. The indulgences, instead of preaching expiation, leave the Christian in the mire of sin. If we are not allowed to say anything against indulgences, there ought not to be so much said about their efficacy. They that preach up indulgences make fools of you; they are not looking after your salvation, but after your pennies. Let some charitably charge me with heresy, because I have told out truths that do harm to their shop, what care I for their brawling? Empty pates, that never opened the Bible, who know nothing of the doctrines of Christ, or even about themselves, and are ever groping in the dark. God give them understanding.'" These extracts seem less a sermon than notes on which for Luther to dilate. They are derived from the seventh volume of his works. [" One of the fathers came up to Luther after the sermon, pulled him by the sleeve, and said, shaking his head—'Doctor, you are going too far, you will do us much harm. The Dominicans are laughing in their sleeves at us.' 'Father,' replied Luther, 'if it comes not from God, it will fall: if it proceeds from his Holy Spirit, it will triumph.'"—AUDIN.]

[1] "If," observes Mr. Roscoe, "Tetzel and the rest did not discredit Luther's doctrines by their arguments, they exasperated his temper by their abuse to such a degree, that he was no longer satisfied with defending victoriously the ground which he had already assumed, but, carrying the war into the precincts of his adversaries, he began, with an unsparing hand, to lay waste all that seemed to oppose his progress."—ROSCOE, *Life of Leo X.*

The report of this controversy spread beyond the confines of Germany, and, in due course reached Rome. It is said that Leo X. believed, in the first instance, that the whole affair was merely a professional squabble between the rival Augustins and Dominicans, and that he observed respecting it: "Monkish jealousies; nothing more. Fra Luther is a man of fine genius."[1]

"While I was attacked and misrepresented, beloved reader, I knew well the malevolence of Tetzel, Eck, and the rest of them. Nor in this feeling was I mistaken, for I found that everywhere they were assiduously inculcating among the people that I was not only an obstinate heretic, but the enemy of all religion whatever. By disseminating these and other lies, unnecessary for me to mention, they hoped to excite the prejudices of the people against me, and while they carried on their detestable traffic of indulgences, retain the poor souls in the chains of that disgusting and odious despotism under which the pope and his satellites blind and overwhelm their unfor-

[1] Luther elsewhere gives a different account of the matter:—"When my first positions (he says in his Table Talk) concerning indulgences were brought before the pope, he said, 'A drunken Dutchman wrote them; when he hath slept out his sleep, and is sober again, he will then be of another mind.' In such sort he contemneth every man." Luther, however, gave the Italians, in the way of contemptuousness, as good as they brought. "If this Sylvester," he writes on the 1st September, 1518, "does not cease annoying me with his trash, I will put an end to the matter, and, giving the rein to my thought and my pen, show him that there are men in Germany who thoroughly comprehend his tricks, and those of his fellow Romans, and I don't care how soon I do this. For a long time past, the Romans, in their juggling, their quips, and their craft, have been amusing themselves at our expense, as though we were heavy blockheads."

"I am delighted that Philip (Melancthon) has himself experienced for himself the Italian character of mind. It is a philosophy that will not credit aught but on experience. As to myself, I can no longer place trust in any Italian, not even in the emperor's confessor. My dear Cardinal loved me so tenderly, that he would have poured out for me every drop of blood in—my veins. They are bad fellows. When you can get hold of a good Italian, he is very good; but a good Italian is as great a prodigy as a black swan." (21st July, 1530.)

"I want Sadoleto to believe that God is father of men, even out of Italy; but you cannot drive this into an Italian's head."

"The Italians," adds Hutten, "who charge us with incapacity to produce any writer of genius, are compelled to admire our Albert Durer, and do so with such fervour, that their painters, to sell their own works, are fain to put our Albert's name to them."

tunate and superstitious slaves. So to show the whole world the characters of these men, and how unscrupulous they are in publishing daring lies to serve their own purposes—a common practice in that mystery of iniquity called popedom, of which, I verily believe, the devil is the agent—I wrote to the pope Leo the following most submissive letter, for at that time my eyes were not fully open to the abominations of Rome.

"To the most holy father, Leo X., Martin Luther, of the Augustin order of monks at Wittemberg, wishes eternal salvation.

"I have heard, most holy father, that some most idle charges have been made against me to you, which bring me under your holiness' censure, as though I had contrived a plot to undermine the authority of the church, and the power of the supreme pontiff. I am called a heretic, an apostate, a traitor, and no end of odious names. My ears are shocked, my mind is lost in amazement, at these accusations. One testimony to my upright conduct is with me, however, the testimony of a good and quiet conscience. I do not mention these circumstances as if I had never heard of them before, for the men to whom I refer, who pretend to be most trustworthy and honest, have cast such names upon me in my own country; and, conscious of their falsehood, have imputed to me the most ignominious conduct, that they may justify their own villanies. But you, most holy father, are the best judge of the matter in dispute; you only, impartial and unprejudiced, are worthy to hear it from me.

"At the time that the jubilee of the apostolic indulgences was announced, certain persons, under the sanction of your authority, imagining they might say and do what they pleased, publicly taught the most blasphemous heresies, to the serious scandal and contempt of the church, as if the decretals contained nothing in them condemning the impositions of these extortioners. Not content with the unwarrantable language which they used in propagating their poison, they moreover published little pamphlets, and circulated them among the common people, in which—proving that I say nothing unjust of the insatiable and monstrous imposition of their conduct—they themselves maintained these same blasphemies and heretical doctrines, and so determinedly, that they bound themselves by oath to inculcate them fixedly on the people.

"If these men deny the facts I speak of, their pamphlets are in existence to prove their conduct to have been what I say. They carried on this traffic prosperously, and the poor people were thoroughly deceived by false hopes ; as the prophet says, *the very flesh was taken from their bones*, the impostors themselves living meantime in all luxury and gluttony.

"One argument they oftenest put forwards was the authority of your name, threatening summary punishment upon all who differed from them, and branding them as heretics. The language they used is indescribable, nor shall I say how fiercely they resented opposition, and even the merest doubt respecting them. If this mode of propagating error be sanctioned, schisms and seditions cannot fail to appear.

"Soon stories began to get abroad, in the shops and public places, concerning the avarice of these indulgence-hawkers, and prejudicial to the authority of the holy see ; this is well known throughout the country. I confess that I myself, for the sake of Christ, as I believed, burned with indignation at the preposterous proceedings of these men, though I did not for a while make up my mind what to do. I privately sent intimations to certain prelates of the church as to what was going on. Some treated me with utter silence, others wrote to me slightingly; the influence of your alleged authority prevailing with them. At last, finding humble remonstrance of no avail, I resolved to challenge these indulgence-sellers to prove their dogmas in disputation with me. I published a list of propositions, inviting only the doctors, if they were so disposed, to discuss with me, as may be seen in the preamble to my propositions.

"And this is partly why they rage so, being furious that I, only a master in theology, should claim to discuss in the public school, though after the custom of all universities and of the whole church, not only concerning indulgences, but also concerning the power of remission of sin, the divine authority of indulgences, and other important matters. Now though I resent their denying me the privilege conceded by your most holy licence, 'tis with reluctance I take up the controversy with them, and declare against their proceedings, wherein they mix up the dreams of Aristotle with theology, and set forth silly matters concerning the divine majesty above and beyond the power vested in them. Now what shall I do? I cannot recal that which I have done, and I perceive a determined hatred bursting forth against me. I am publicly discussed, according to the various views people take. By some I am called ignorant, stupid, unlearned, in this most refined and illustrious age, which even, as to learning and the arts, eclipses the age of Cicero. Others call me a paltry imitator. But I am compelled to answer geese in their own language.

"Therefore, that I may mitigate the anger of honest enemies, and satisfy the doubts of many, I forward to your holiness my humble propositions, and I do so, secure in your protection and authority, by which all may understand how entirely and implicitly I reverence and respect the ecclesiastical power and authority, and at the same time how falsely, how infamously, my opponents have maligned me. Were I what they call me, it is not probable the illustrious prince Frederick, duke of Saxony and elector of the empire, a prince devotedly attached to the catholic and apostolic truth, would tolerate such a pest in his own university, nor should I have the support of our own learned and virtuous body. I put forward these things in my favour, knowing they will carefully be suppressed by those who seek to embitter you against me.

"Wherefore, most holy father, I prostrate myself at the feet of your clemency, with all which I have and am. Bid me live, or slay me, call, recall, approve, disapprove, as it pleases you; I acknowledge in your voice the voice of Christ speaking and presiding in you. If I am worthy of death, I shall not refuse to die; for 'the earth is the Lord's, and the fulness thereof, who is blessed for evermore. Amen.' May he preserve you to all eternity! Trinity Sunday, 1518."

"Protest of the reverend father, Martin Luther, of the Augustin order at Wittemberg.

"Because this is a theological disputation, touching which some individuals inclined to peace may peradventure take offence, by reason of the recondite nature of the subject, I protest:

"First, that I have never held or taught anything but what

is contained in the sacred Scriptures, in the writings of the fathers of the church, and acknowledged by the Roman church in the canons and pontifical decretals. Yet, if any opinion of mine cannot be refuted or proved by these authorities, I shall hold it for the sake of discussion only, for the exercise of reason, and for the promotion of knowledge and inquiry, always having respect to the judgment of my superiors.

"Further, I venture to challenge, by the law of Christian liberty, what were the acknowledged opinions of St. Thomas, Buonaventure, and the other casuists and schoolmen, without any gloss or interpretation. I am resolved to refute or to admit, as circumstances may render necessary, according to the advice of St. Paul, 'Prove all things : hold fast that which is good.' I know the opinion of certain Thomists, that St. Thomas should be approved in all things from the church, but St. Thomas, at all events, is sufficiently acknowledged for an authority. I have shown enough in what I may be wrong, but I am no heretic, though my enemies roar and rage in their vociferations that I am so."

And Luther here inserts his ninety-five propositions for the pope's perusal, occupying seventy-two folio pages.

"Moreover," proceeds Luther, "I thought it necessary to write to several noble and reverend prelates, in justification of my conduct ; and to refute the calumnies of those scandalous monks who were deceiving the people and ensnaring their souls, and more especially to the illustrious prince and most reverend father, Albert, archbishop of Magdeburg, to whom I also sent my disputations.

"To my reverend father, Staupitz, I wrote thus :—

"'I remember, reverend father, among the many most delightful and pleasing conversations with which, by the grace of our Lord Jesus Christ, I was often peculiarly edified by you, to have occasionally heard you observe respecting the doctrine of penitence, as connected with indulgences, especially referring to those who are troubled in conscience, and those pretenders who torture them with innumerable and burdensome advices, on the manner of confession—and we hailed the sentiment as truly in accordance with divine authority—that that is true penitence which results exclusively from a sense of the love and justice of God, its origin rather than its end and accomplishment.

"'Your observation made as deep an impression on my mind, as though I had been pierced with the sharp arrow of the hunter, and I began to consult the Scriptures as to the real nature of penitence. The declaration rendered this occupation in many respects most pleasant and delightful to me, and I became satisfactorily convinced that whereas formerly there was no term in the Scriptures at which I felt more uneasiness than that of penitence, even when I would have attempted diligently to please God, and to exhibit a fixed and determined love to him, now there was none which yielded me greater pleasure and delight. Thus the commandments of God become enticing, not only as they are made known to us in his holy word, but as we see them exemplified in the obedient sufferings of our blessed Saviour. While thus meditating, certain individuals began to tune their pipes and to give us some strange music, and with much parade they sounded their new instruments respecting indulgences, which drew me into the field of controversy. In short, by neglecting or perverting the true doctrine of penitence, they had the presumption to enhance, not repentance, not even its most worthless part, which is called *satisfaction*, but the remission of that to me most worthless part, as it never had been previously held and estimated. And now they teach those impious, false, and heretical tenets with such boldness —I had almost said insolence—that he who presumes to express an opinion to the contrary, however diffidently, is forthwith branded as a heretic, as one who should be consigned to the flames of hell, to be eternally punished.

"'Unable to restrain the ravings of these men, I resolved in the gentlest possible manner to dissent from them, to call in question mildly their headstrong and impious assertions, trusting to the authority of all learned men and of the church, maintaining that it is better to render satisfaction (for sin, by repentance) than that the satisfaction should be remitted for money, namely, by the purchase of indulgences; nor has any doctor ever taught otherwise. I therefore disputed with and differed from them, and because I did so, I provoked their utmost resentment against me, (alas! that such things should be said of souls) my sole offence being in my interference with these zealots in their schemes for obtaining money from the people. And these men, so practised in their profitable knavery, when they could not refute me, pretended that I was injuring the authority of the pope.

"'This is the reason, reverend father, why I am now talked of malignantly in public, who have always been a lover of retirement, choosing rather to attend to the improvement and cultivation of the mind, than to make myself at all an object of public observation. But it behoves me to take these things patiently, and so far, I would rather be the topic of their slander than of their praise.

"'I request, therefore, that you will accept these my brief explanations, and transmit them as soon as possible to the holy father Leo X., because the representation of these malignant men may be injurious to me, and I have no other advocate in that quarter. I do not wish you, however, to be brought into trouble on my account; I desire to answer for myself, and to bear the whole responsibility. Our Saviour Christ knows whether what I have advanced be of myself, or agreeable to his will, without whose approbation the sanction of the pope is of little avail, nor that of any prince whom he guides and commands. But, nevertheless, I expect a decision to be pronounced at Rome.

"'To the threatenings with which I am assailed, I have little to say, except with Reuchlin, that he who is poor has nothing to fear, because he has nothing to lose. He who is deprived of fame and rewards, loses what I neither possess nor desire. One unworthy thing remains, my humble body, fatigued by cares and anxieties; so that whatsoever, with God's permission, they may do by force or stratagem, they can only deprive me of a few hours of life. 'Tis sufficient for me to know my blessed Lord and Saviour, to whom I shall sing praises as long as I live; if any one will not sing praises with me, that is not my concern; he may growl by himself if he pleases. May the Lord Jesus Christ preserve you, my beloved father, in his holy keeping for ever.

"'MARTIN LUTHER.'"

These two letters, of the 30th May, 1518,[1] are dated from Heidelberg, where the Augustins were then holding a pro-

[1] After despatching these letters, we find Luther this year sedulously engaged in delivering a course of lectures *on the Commandments*, in the church of Wittemberg; also four discourses :—*on the efficacy of Excommunication;*

vincial synod, and whither Luther had proceeded for the purpose of maintaining his doctrines against all comers. This famous university, close to the Rhine, and consequently on the most frequented high road in Germany, was certainly the most effective arena in which to champion the new doctrine.

Rome began to put itself in motion.[1] The master of the ceremonies to the sacred palace, the old Dominican, Sylvestro de Prierio, wrote in support of the doctrine of St. Thomas against the Augustin monk, and drew down upon himself a crushing reply, (towards the end of August, 1518.) Luther immediately received orders to appear at Rome within sixty days.[2] The emperor Maximilian had in vain called upon them not to precipitate matters, undertaking himself to do all the pope might order to be done with respect to Luther. But the zeal of Maximilian himself had begun to be somewhat distrusted at Rome. There had reached the holy city certain expressions of his which sounded disagreeably in the ears of the pope. "That which your monk is doing is not to be despised," the emperor had said to Pfeffinger, one of the elector of Saxony's councillors; "the game with the priests is beginning. Take care of him; it may happen that we shall have need of him." More than once he had bitterly complained of the priests and clergy: "This pope," said he, speaking of Leo X., "has acted towards me like a rogue. I

on the suitable preparation of the mind for receiving the Holy Sacrament, and on the manner in which Christ's Passion should be considered; on Threefold Justice; and *on Twofold Justice.* Also an exposition of the passage in *Ecclesiastes,* " There is not a just man on the earth, who doeth good and sinneth not;" with *an abridged Instruction for the Confession of Sins according to the Decalogue.* In none of these discourses does Martin make any allusion to himself or his position.

[1] The first step taken by the pope had been to write to Dr. Staupitz, exhorting him to use conciliatory means to reclaim Luther, and to soften the animosities which his controversy with Tetzel and his associates had excited. "The reverend father, Dr. Staupitz, my dear friend, and the chief of the Eremites, who was himself convinced of the truth, who loved the word of God, and loathed the impieties and blasphemies of Rome, as soon as he received his instructions from the pope, communicated them to me, and by letters and conversations urged me to reconciliation and forbearance. To do pope Leo justice, these instructions were written in a manner friendly towards me, breathing the spirit of paternal care and solicitude for the peace of the church. I listened to these instructions; I assured my reverend father of my willingness to obey in all things, save those of conscience and duty."

[2] The citation bears date 7 August, 1518.

can fairly say that I have never found in any pope I have met with sincerity or good faith; but, please God, I hope this will be the last of them."[1] These expressions were menacing. It was recollected, moreover, that Maximilian, by way of definitively settling the dispute between the empire and the holy see, had thought of making himself pope. Leo X. accordingly took good care not to leave to him the decision of this dispute, which every day assumed fresh importance.

Luther's main hope was in the protection of the elector. This prince, whether out of the interest he took in his new university,[2] or from a personal attachment to Luther, had always shown him peculiar favour.[3] He had proposed to take

[1] Seckendorf, De Lutheranismo, 44.

[2] The increasing celebrity of Luther attracted to Wittemberg an immense concourse of students. It was a complete hive, Luther himself tells us. An author, nearly contemporary, says :—" I have heard from our preceptors, that students from all nations came to Wittemberg to hear Luther and Melancthon. As soon as they got within sight of the town, they returned thanks to God with clasped hands ; for from Wittemberg, as heretofore from Jerusalem, proceeded the light of evangelical truth, to spread thence to the uttermost parts of the earth."—(*Sculletus, annalibus*, anno 1517.) The patronage accorded by the elector, however, was not the most liberal in the world. " I have asked you a dozen times," writes Luther to Spalatin, " to ascertain from the prince, whether it is his intention that this academy should crumble away and perish. I should much like to be satisfied on the point, so that I may not fruitlessly detain here those who are called upon from other quarters. The people at Nuremberg are warmly soliciting Melancthon to join them, the rumour is so prevalent that this school is given up. But we must not press the prince too closely."

After the death of the elector, Luther sent to Spalatin a plan for the better organization of the university. (20th May, 1525.)

[3] The elector himself wrote to Spalatin: " Our Martin's affair is proceeding favourably, Pfeffinger has good hopes for him." (Seckendorf, 53.) He sent word to Luther that he had got the legate to write to Rome to have the matter referred to particular judges, and in the meantime exhorted Luther to rest patient, and that, perhaps, the papal censure would not be sent at all. (Seckendorf, 44.)

The members of Luther's own order, the Augustins, who viewed the Dominicans as rivals, were not displeased at Luther's invectives against the latter, and in some degree coalesced with him in lessening the credit of the sellers of indulgences. This circumstance originated the common but false report, circulated by Roman-catholic and other writers, that Luther's conduct resulted from disappointment that his own order had not been selected for the traffic. Hume says, in his History of England, 'that the Augustin friars had been usually employed in Saxony to preach indulgences, and from this trust had derived both profit and consideration ; and Arcimbaldo, having given this employment to the Dominicans, Martin Luther, an

upon himself the expenses attending his protegé's obtaining his doctor's degree. In 1517, Luther thanks him, in a letter, for having sent him, at the beginning of winter, cloth to make him a gown. He felt pretty sure, too, that the elector by no means owed him any grudge for getting up an excitement of a nature to annoy the archbishop of Mayence and Magdeburg, a prince of the house of Brandeburg, and consequently an enemy to that of Saxony. Finally, the elector had announced that he recognised no other rule of faith than the words of Scripture themselves; and this afforded Luther a powerful argument for deeming himself secure in that quarter. Luther reminds the elector of this circumstance in the following passage of a letter, dated 27th March, 1519. "Doctor Staupitz, my true father in Christ, has related to me that conversing one

Augustin friar, professor in the university of Wittemberg, resented the affront thus put upon his order, and began to preach against the abuses that were committed in the sale of indulgences; and being provoked by opposition, proceeded even to deny indulgences themselves.' These assertions of Hume's are founded on a passage of Father Paul, in his History of the Council of Trent, which, as Mr. Maclaine, in his able translation of Mosheim, observes, has been abundantly refuted by Prierio, Pallavicini, and Gravesor, Luther's inveterate enemies. Father Paul affirms:—'It was a custom in Saxony, that whenever indulgences were sold there by order of the popes, the friars of the order of the Eremites were employed to publish them. The pardon-mongers, ministers of Arcimbaldo, would not go to them, because, being so accustomed to manage this merchandise, they might use some device to draw secret profits to themselves; so they went to the Dominicans. These, in publishing the indulgences, in order to amplify the value of them more than had been done before, spake many strange things, which gave cause of scandal; whereon Martin Luther, an Eremite, being stirred up, began to speak against the new pardoners; first, reprehending these excessive abuses only; afterwards, being provoked by them, he set himself to study the matter, being desirous to see the foundation and root of the doctrine of indulgences.'

Now, in the first place, the Augustin friars had *not* usually been employed to preach indulgences in Saxony; that privilege had been conferred alternately on the various mendicant orders, and sometimes on all of them collectively—namely, the Augustins, the Carmelites, the Dominicans, and the Franciscans; but from the year 1229, it had been principally entrusted to the Dominicans. In all the records which relate to indulgences, the name of an Augustin is rarely found, and not a single instance in which the pontiff grants the office to that order. From 1450 to 1517, when indulgences were sold with the most shameless impudence, no Augustin monk was employed, if we except a monk named Palzius, a truckler to Raymond Peraldi, the papal quæstor. *Secondly*, Arcimbaldo was never appointed to publish the indulgences, his district being Flanders

day with your electoral highness respecting these preachers who, instead of giving forth the pure word of God, preached to the people nothing but miserable quirks or human traditions, you said to him, that the Holy Scripture speaks with so imposing a majesty,[1] with such completeness of proof, that it has no need of all this adventitious aid of polemics, and that it places in one's mouth, involuntarily, these words: 'Never man spoke thus: this is the finger of God; this teaches not as the scribes and pharisees teach, but as the direct organ and mouthpiece of Almighty Power.' Staupitz approving these words, you went on: 'Give me your hand, and promise me, I entreat, that henceforth you will follow the new doctrine!'" The natural continuation of this passage is to be found in a manuscript life of the elector, by Spalatin. "With what pleasure would he listen to such sermons, and

and the Upper and Lower Rhine. *Thirdly*, Luther was not instigated by the superiors of his order to attack the Dominicans. The act was quite his own. It was of little consequence to him who promulgated the indulgences. *Fourthly*, the traffic in indulgences had become so notoriously infamous, that even many Franciscans and Dominicans, towards the end of the 15th century, opposed it publicly in their writings; and the very commission which first excited Luther's indignation, had actually been tendered by Leo to the Augustins, and by them refused. *Lastly*, Luther was never accused by the most hostile of contemporary writers on this subject. Guicciardini candidly admits, that Luther's opposition 'was, doubtless, honest, and, at all events, from the just occasion given for it, in some degree excusable. Not to mention, however, this historian, or Erasmus, Sleidan, and de Thou, who, although popish writers, may be charged with partiality to Luther, those whom the reformer assailed with more vehemence than prudence, Cajetano, Hoogenstraat, Prierio, Emser, and Tetzel himself, make no such allegation. 'Even,' observes Maclaine, 'the lying Cochlæus was silent on this head, though, after the death of the great reformer, he broached the calumny I am here refuting. Can it be imagined that motives to action which escaped the prying eyes of Luther's contemporaries, should have discovered themselves to us, who live at such a distance of time from the period of action—to M. Bossuet, to Mr. Hume, and other abettors of this ill-contrived and foolish story? Either there are no rules of moral evidence, or Mr. Hume's assertion is entirely groundless. and of no application

[1] Schenck had been commissioned to buy relics for the collegiate church of Wittemberg; but in 1520, the commission was revoked, and the purchased relics sent to Italy, to be sold for what they would fetch. "For here," writes Spalatin, "the common people despise them, in the firm and very legitimate persuasion, that all that is necessary is to learn well the Scriptures, to have faith and confidence in God, and to love one's neighbour."—SECKENDORF, 223.

read the word of God, especially the Evangelists, from whom he was always citing fine and consolatory sentences. But that which more especially was always on his lips was the expression of Christ in the gospel according to St. John: 'Without me, ye can do nothing.' He made use of this sentence as an argument against free will, even before Erasmus of Rotterdam had ventured to support, in several writings, this wretched freedom of the will in opposition to the word of God. He used often to say to me: 'How can we have free will? since Christ himself has said: Without me ye can do nothing, *Sine me nihil potestis facere.*'"[1]

Yet it would be an entire misconception to understand from the above passages that Staupitz and his disciple were merely the instruments of the elector. The Reformation of Luther was evidently a spontaneous principle of his own. The prince, as we shall have occasion to observe elsewhere, was rather alarmed at the daring of Luther. He embraced, he loved, he profited by the initiated Reformation: he would never himself have commenced it.

Luther had written on the 15th February, 1518, to his prudent friend Spalatin, the chaplain, secretary and confidant of the elector: "Here are bawlers who go about saying, to my infinite vexation, that all this is the work of our illustrious prince, that it is he who has urged me on to it, for the sake of spiting the archbishop of Magdeburg and Mayence. I wish you maturely to consider whether or no it is desirable to mention the matter to his highness. I am truly afflicted to see him suspected on my account. To be a cause of discord between such mighty lords, is an awful thing." He holds the same language to the elector himself, in his account of the conference at Augsburg. On the 21st March, writing to M. Lange, afterwards archbishop of Saltzburg, he says: "Our prince has taken Carlstadt and myself under his protection, and without any solicitation on our part. He will not permit them to drag me to Rome. This they know, and it is this vexes them so;" which would obviously lead us to suppose that Luther had already received from the elector definitive promises. Yet, on the 21st August, 1518, in a letter, still more confidential,

[1] Seckendorf, 79.

to Spalatin, he says: "I do not at all see at present how I can escape the censures with which I am threatened, if the prince does not come forward to my succour, though I would rather undergo the censure of the whole world, than have his highness blamed for my sake. This, therefore, is the course which it appears to our learned friends best for me to pursue, that I should demand of the prince a safe-conduct (salvum, ut vocant, conductum, per meum dominum). He will refuse it me, I am certain, and I shall then, say our friends, have a valid excuse for not appearing at Rome. I would ask you, then, to obtain from our illustrious prince, a rescript setting forth that he refuses me the safe-conduct, and makes me responsible, if I persist in setting out, for all the dangers I may incur. By so doing, you will render me an important service. But the thing must be done at once: time presses, the assigned day is near at hand."

Luther might have saved himself this letter. The prince, without having communicated with him on the point, had been taking measures for his security.[1] He had managed that

[1] The university of Wittemberg also addressed two letters on the subject, one to the pope, the other to Charles de Miltitz, a Saxon nobleman, who had previously been in military service, but was now papal councillor and apostolic chamberlain. The letter to the pope was couched in the following terms:

"The University of Wittemberg to the holy Roman pontiff, Leo X., testifying the integrity of Father Martin Luther, and excusing him for not proceeding to Rome:

"Most holy father, your most courteous and truly pastoral kindness will not, we humbly submit, accuse us of forwardness and presumption, when we make bold to approach your holiness by these our letters, seeing that piety and truth sanctioning our dutiful regard, will, we hope, secure to us your consideration, as it is munificently bestowed on every occasion.

"A certain brother, Martin Luther, master of arts, and professor of divinity, a faithful and worthy member of our body, has petitioned us, trusting to the success of our application, and requested our mediation with your holiness, to which we have affixed our testimonial of his life and doctrine, which are now called in question by questionable persons.

"By a commission, instituted under the authority of your holiness, to investigate certain disputes connected with indulgences, our brother is cited to appear personally at Rome. But, on account of the state of his health, and the dangers attending the journey, he is not able to undertake what he would otherwise be most anxious to do. On duly considering this his petition, we add our certification respecting him:

"We, the most obedient and devoted sons of your holiness, humbly and

Luther should be examined by a legate in Germany, in the free town of Augsburg; where he himself was at this time, and where he had doubtless come to an understanding with the magistrates to guarantee the safety of Luther during the dangerous conference. It was, we may be pretty sure, to this invisible Providence hovering over Luther, that we are to assign the almost painful anxiety evinced by these magistrates to preserve the reformer from the snares that might be laid for him by the Italians. As to him, he went straightforward on, strong in courage and in simple faith, quite uncertain to what extent the prince was disposed to act in his favour.

"I have said, and I repeat it, I would not in this business have our prince, who is throughout blameless, take the least step towards defending my propositions. If he can do it without compromising himself, let him guard me against actual violence; but if he cannot safely do this, I am ready to meet the utmost peril that may threaten me."[1]

earnestly implore you, most holy father, that our brother may be thought worthy of credit. Our opinion of him is, that he has never swerved from his true duty towards the holy Roman church, nor become infected with heretical opinions. He has merely exercised his right of debating freely, which his adversaries have also done; he has asserted nothing. We ourselves, holy father, would be held as a body determined to have no fellowship with any who oppose the genuine doctrines of the catholic church, resolved, in the midst of all things, by your favour and that of holy church, to be obedient to our Lord Jesus Christ, who, we pray, will move your holiness to listen favourably to our petition.

"Given at Wittemberg, September 25, 1518."

[1] "Luther departed from Wittemberg at daybreak, on foot, without a penny in his pocket, and dressed in a worn-out gown. Great and small, clergy and laymen, were waiting to take leave of him at the gates. When he appeared, they cried—'Luther for ever!'

"'Christ for ever, and his word!' replied Martin. Some of the crowd quitted the main body, and approached him. 'Courage, master,' said they, 'and God help you!'

"'Amen!' replied Luther.

"His friends accompanied him several miles on the way, and then separated from him with a warm embrace:

"'*In manus tuas Domine, commendo animum meam!*' said Luther.

"'Amen!' returned his disciples, in chorus.

"Luther went gaily on his way, though ever and anon terrible pains in his stomach wellnigh impelled him to turn back; but his heart was stronger than the malady. On his road, when he found no monastery to take up his abode in, he availed himself of private hospitality.

"At Weimar, he passed the night of the 28th in the house of the curate

The pope s legate, Thomas de Vio, cardinal of Caieta, was certainly a judge little open to suspicion. He had, indeed, himself written that it was permissible to interpret the Scripture, without following the torrent of the fathers, *contra torrentem patrum*, and this freedom had rendered him somewhat liable to an imputation of heresy; but, as the pope's man in this affair, he took it up entirely as a political matter, and assailed the doctrine of Luther only in the point of view, where it shook the political and fiscal domination of the court of Rome. He limited himself to the practical question of the *treasure of the indulgences*, without extending his interrogatories to the speculative principle of grace.

"In the year 1518, the 9th of October," says Luther, "when I was cited to Augsburg, I came and appeared: Frederick, prince-elector of Saxony, having appointed me a strong convoy and safe-conduct; and recommended me to the people of the city, who were very attentive, and warned me in no case to have conversation with the Italians, nor to repose any trust

Myconius, who soon after threw off the monk's gown, and married a young girl of Gotha. Luther preached next day in his church.

"Some days after, he embraced at Nuremberg his friend Winceslaus Linck, who made him a present of a handsome black gown, and accompanied him, together with an Augustin named Leonard, to Augsburg. For some way, all three travelled on foot; but, at a few miles from the city, Luther could scarcely walk; a vehicle was then hired by Linck, and all three proceeded by it the remainder of the journey. On the evening of his arrival in Augsburg, Luther wrote thus to his friend Philip Melancthon, then a professor in the university of Tubingen, afterwards his colleague and associate at Wittemberg:

"'There is nothing new or wonderful here at present known to me, except that I am the subject of conversation throughout the city, my name in every man's mouth. All are anxious to see him who is to be the victim of such a conflagration. You, meantime, will continue quietly and faithfully to discharge your duty, without alarm, instructing rightly, as you have ever done, the youth under your care. For you and for them I go onward, ready to be sacrificed, if such be the will of Heaven. I am not only ready to die, but, what were far worse to me, to be deprived of your dear society, rather than retract the truths I have maintained, or be the means of affording the stupid and bitter enemies of liberal studies and elegant learning an opportunity of achieving a triumph. Italy is prostrate in Egyptian darkness, and her people are ignorant of Christ and of those who love Christ. But we know some influential men who regard true religion. The wrath of God may be administered by our agency, as it is written—'I will make their princes as children, and the feeble shall reign over them.' Farewell, beloved Melancthon, and avert the wrath of God from us by your faithful prayers. Augsburg, October 12, 1518.'"—AUDIN.

or confidence in them, for I knew not, they said, what sort of wretches they were. I was three whole days in Augsburg without the emperor's safe-conduct. In the meantime, an Italian [Urban di Serra Longa] came to me, invited me to go to the cardinal, and earnestly persuaded me to recant. I should (said he) need to speak but only one word before the cardinal, *Revoco;* and then the cardinal would recommend me to the pope's favour, so that with honour I might return safely again to my master, the prince-elector. He quoted several examples, among others, that of the famous Joachim de Flores, who had submitted, and was consequently no heretic, though he had advanced heretical propositions. When he urged me no longer to delay waiting on the cardinal, I replied that certain excellent individuals to whom I had been recommended by the elector Frederick, had urged me first to procure the emperor's safe-conduct. Thereupon he replied, with much warmth: 'What! do you think the elector will take up arms on your account?' 'I should be unwilling,' said I, 'to be the occasion of such an extremity.' 'But if you had the pope and cardinals in your power,' returned he, 'what would you do with them?' 'I would show them all reverence and honour,' I replied. He paused, snapped his fingers after the Italian manner, and cried *Hem!* after which he departed, and I saw him no more.

"At the expiration of three days, the bishop of Trent came, who, in the emperor's name, showed and declared to the cardinal my safe-conduct. Then I went unto him in all humility, fell down first upon my knees, then prostrate upon the ground, where I remained at his feet, till after the cardinal had three times bad me rise; thereupon I stood up. This pleased him well, hoping I would consider, and better bethink myself.

"The next day, when I came before him again, and would absolutely revoke nothing at all, he said to me, 'What! thinkest thou the pope cares much for Germany? his little finger is more powerful than all Germany. Or dost thou think the princes will raise arms and armies to defend thee? Oh, no! where, then, wilt thou remain in safety?' I replied, 'Under heaven.'

"After this the pope lowered his tone, and wrote to our church, even to the prince-elector's chaplain, and to one of his counsellors, Pfeffinger, that they would surrender me into his hands, and procure that his commands might be put in execution. And the pope wrote also to the prince-elector himself as thus :

" 'Although, as touching thy person, thou art to me unknown, yet I have seen thy father (prince Ernest) at Rome, who was altogether an obedient son to the church ; he visited and frequented our religion with great devotion, and held the same in highest honour. I wish that thy illustrious serenity would tread in his footsteps,' &c.

" But the prince-elector well marked the pope's unaccustomed humility, and his evil conscience ; he was also acquainted with the power and operation of the holy Scriptures. Therefore he remained where he was, and merely returned thanks to the pope for his affection towards him.

" My books and resolutions in a short time went, or rather flew throughout Europe, therefore the prince-elector was confirmed and strengthened, insomuch that he utterly refused to execute the pope's commands, and subjected himself fully to the acknowledgment of the Scriptures.

" If the cardinal had handled me with more discretion at Augsburg, and had received me when I fell at his feet, things would never have come thus far; for at that time I saw very few of the pope's errors which now I see; had he been silent, so had I held my peace. It was at that time the style and custom of the Romish court, in dark and confused cases, for the pope to say: *We, by virtue of our papal power, do take these causes unto us, we annul them and destroy them ;* and the parties had nothing left for it but to weep.

" I am persuaded that the pope willingly would give three cardinals to have the matter where it was, before he began to meddle with me." [1]

Let us add some other details from a letter of Luther's to Spalatin, that is to say, to the elector, dated 14th October.

" On the day I was first admitted to an audience, I was received by the most reverend cardinal legate, not only with kindness but with marked deference and respect ; for he is a very different man from some of the more violent of his brethren. He had no inclination, he said, to debate with me.

[1] Tischreden, 377—380.

but he mildly and feelingly proposed to compromise the matter, by submitting to me three conditions sanctioned by the pope:—1. That I should alter my opinions, and retract my erroneous propositions; 2. That I should engage to abstain from propagating such doctrines in future; and, 3. That I should not circulate any opinions opposed to the authority of the church. I immediately desired to be informed in what respect I had erred, as I was not conscious of inculcating any error, for that the opinions I had set forth at Wittemberg had occasioned me no trouble or opposition there, and I was not aware I had changed any of my sentiments since I had arrived in Augsburg. This went on for four days, the prelate still refusing to have any controversy with me publicly or privately; all he did was to repeat, over and over and over again, 'Retract!—acknowledge thy error, whether thou believest it an error or not. The pope commands thee to do this.' At length, he was induced to consent that I might explain myself in writing, which I accordingly did, in presence of the seigneur de Feilitzch, the elector's representative. But when I had done, the legate refused to receive what I had written, and renewed his cry of *Retract! retract!* Next he hurled out some long harangue or other in the romance of St. Thomas, with which he fancied he would utterly crush me, and reduce me to silence. Ten times did I essay to speak, and ten times did he stop me short; raging and tyrannizing over me throughout the whole affair. At last he referred me to the Extravagant of pope Clement VI., entitled *Unigenitus*, and objected on the strength of it to my 58th proposition: 'That the merits of Christ were not the treasure of the *indulgences*.' He strenuously urged me to retract the proposition, and he paused for a little, in confidence of my submission, for he flattered himself, nay seemed almost certain, that I was ignorant of the Extravagant referred to, and he was the more confident about this, in that it is not inserted in all the collections.

"I then, in my turn, took to raising my voice somewhat. 'Come,' said I, 'if you can show me that your decretal of Clement VI. says expressly that the merits of Christ *are* the treasure of the indulgences, I retract.' Lord, what a laugh there was at this! The legate snatched the book, and ran over the pages in breathless haste, till he came to the place where it is written that 'Christ by his passion *acquired* the treasures,' &c. I stopped him at the word 'acquired.'

"By and bye, upon my asserting that the pope had no power except *salvâ Scriptura*, the cardinal laughed, and said: "Do you not know that the pope is above all councils? Has he not recently condemned and punished the council of Bâle?" "Yes," I replied; "but the university of Paris has appealed from his decision." The cardinal: "The university of Paris will be punished too." After a while, I spoke of Gerson. The cardinal said: "What are the Gersonists to me?" I asked him, who the Gersonists were? "Bah!" said he; "let's speak no more about them," and so he turned the conversation to something else.[1]

"After dinner, the legate sent for the reverend father Staupitz, and endeavoured to cajole him into bringing me to a retractation, adding, that I should have a difficulty in finding any one who had a more friendly feeling towards me than he had.[2]

[1] See Appendix I.

[2] Staupitz and Wenceslaus Linck accordingly had an interview with Luther, who thereupon wrote a letter to the legate, conceived in these terms:—"I present myself before you again, my father, but only in a letter. I have seen our vicar, John Staupitz, and my brother, maître Wenceslaus Linck: you could not have selected mediators more agreeable to me. I am moved at what I have heard. I have no longer any fear: the fear I experienced is changed into filial love and respect. You were at full liberty to make use of force: you have chosen rather to employ persuasion and charitable kindness.

"I fully admit that I have been violent, hostile, insolent, towards the pope. I should have treated so grave a matter with more reverence. I am penitent for my conduct; I solicit your pardon for it, in the eyes of all men, and I promise you, that henceforward I will speak and act in an entirely different manner. I will say nothing further about indulgences, provided you will impose the same silence on those who have brought me into this deplorable position.

"As to the retractation, reverend sir, which you and our vicar require of me with such pertinacity, my conscience will not permit me to give it; and there is nothing in the world, neither command nor counsel, nor the voice of friendship nor of mere prudence, which could induce me to act against my conscience. There remains but one voice to be heard, which has higher claims than any other—that of the bride, which is the same with the voice of the bridegroom.

"I, therefore, in all humility, supplicate you to bring this affair immediately under the eyes of our holy father, pope Leo X., so that the church may definitively pronounce what is to be believed, and what rejected."—AUDIN.

The legate transmitted Luther's answer to the pope by a special courier. He had previously sent word to Luther, that the affair might easily be arranged, if he would revoke what he had said about indulgences. "As to the point about the faith necessary for the holy sacrament, that may be left."

The disputants pursued courses diametrically opposed the one to the other: conciliation was impossible. The friends of Luther feared a snare for him on the part of the Italians: he accordingly quitted Augsburg, leaving behind him an *Appeal to the Pope better informed*,[1] and at the same time addressed a long narrative of the conference to the elector.[2] In it he entreats that prince not to deliver him up to the pope: "I call upon your illustrious highness to follow the dictates of honour and conscience, and not to send me to the pope. The legate certainly has not in his instructions any guarantee for my security at Rome. For them to demand of you to

[1] Luther left Augsburg altogether hastily. Staupitz gave him a horse, and provided him with a guide who knew the country well. A magistrate of Augsburg, Langemantel, led him in the night, through the by-streets, to a postern, and there took leave of him. Next morning, a monk, by order of the prior of the Carmelites, who himself forthwith absconded, affixed Luther's appeal to the gates of the convent. Its purport runs thus:—

'If Luther has controverted indulgences, it is because indulgences are not accordant with the divine word, or with its spirit. He would never have entertained the idea of controverting the catholic faith, or its discipline, or its symbols.

'2. He has invariably declared his readiness, his desire, to submit his theses to the judgment of the church and the sovereign pontiff.

'3. The judges assigned him were not impartial. Sylvestro Prierio, who has written dialogues against him, has never occupied himself with genuine theology; he is a mere Thomist.

'4. If he did not proceed to Rome, as enjoined, it was because at Rome, where once dwelt justice, murder now has taken up its abode: *justitia habitavit in eâ, nunc autem homicida.*

'Oppressed, then, struck at in his liberty, in his honour, and in his writings, which he once more submits to the judgment of his holiness:

'FROM THE POPE ILL INFORMED, HE APPEALS TO THE POPE BETTER INFORMED.'

'On the 18th, the cardinal received the following note from Luther, apprising him of his intended departure.

'Your reverence has seen my obedience, in this great journey I have undertaken, infirm as I am in body, poor, without the means of living. I cannot remain longer here, losing my time, and being a charge to the dear fathers Carmelite, who have lodged and entertained me. I go, therefore, confiding in God.'—AUDIN.

[2] While Luther was at Augsburg, he was often requested to preach in that city, but he invariably refused to do so, though courteously, fearing lest the legate might impute his preaching, under the circumstances, to bravado or personal impertinence. Luther said, on quitting Augsburg, that if he had four hundred heads, he would lose them all, rather than recant his article respecting faith. "There is no one in Germany," says Hutten, "who more utterly despises death than does Luther."

send me thither, is to ask you to spill Christian blood, to become a homicide. To Rome! why the pope himself does not live in security there! They have plenty of pens and ink in the Eternal City, plenty of scribes, scribes innumerable. They can easily put down in writing what my errors are. It will cost them less money to draw up an indictment against me absent, than to have me to Rome, and destroy me there by treachery.

"What affects me most especially is, that my lord the legate speaks ill of your electoral grace, as though it were upon you that I relied in undertaking all these things. There are even liars, who go about saying that it was your grace's exhortation that induced me to commence discussing the question of indulgences; whereas, in point of fact, even among my dearest friends, there was no one who knew beforehand of my intention, except the archbishop of Magdeburg, and the bishop of Mayence."

His fears were well grounded; the court of Rome was at the time making direct application to the elector of Saxony. It insisted upon having Luther at any rate. The legate had already complained bitterly to Frederic of the audacity of Luther, entreating him either to send him back to Augsburg, or to expel him from his dominions, if he did not desire to sully his glory and that of his ancestors, by protecting this miserable monk. "I heard yesterday, at Nuremberg, that Charles von Miltitz is on his way, armed (as I am assured from an eye-witness worthy of implicit credit) with no fewer than three briefs from the pope, to take me bodily and deliver me over to the pontiff. But I have appealed from him and his briefs to the future council." It was, indeed, necessary for him thus to repudiate the pope, for, as the legate had communicated to Frederic, Luther was already condemned at Rome.[1] He, however, put forth this new protest, with all the regular forms, declared he would submit readily to the judgment of the pope, well informed of the whole matter, but that the pope was fallible, as St. Peter himself had been fallible; and he therefore appealed to a general council, superior to the pope, with respect to all that the pope might

[1] The bull, issued by Leo as a preliminary proceeding to the absolute excommunication of Luther, was published on 9th November.

decree against him. Meantime, he feared some sudden violence; he might perhaps be carried off from Wittemberg. "They have misled you," he writes to Spalatin: "I have not bid farewell to the people of Wittemberg. All that I said to them was this: You every one know that I am a preacher, somewhat given to moving about from place to place. How many times have I quitted you abruptly, without saying farewell. Should the same thing happen again, and I should not return, you must assume that I have bid you adieu beforehand."

On the 2nd December he writes: "I am advised to request the prince to shut me up, as though I were a prisoner, in some castle, and then that he should write to the legate, that he holds me in sure custody, where I shall be compelled to answer all that the pope may put to me."

"There cannot be a moment's doubt that the prince and the university are for me. I have had related to me a conversation that passed on the subject at the court of the bishop of Brandenburg. Some one observed that Erasmus, Fabricius, and other learned personages supported Luther. 'The pope would not humble himself much for that,' replied the bishop, 'if it were not that the university of Wittemberg and the elector are also on his side.'" Still Luther passed the autumn of 1518 in constant alarm. He even thought of quitting Germany. "In order not to involve your highness in any danger, I will leave your territory; I will go whither the mercy of God shall lead me, confiding myself, in all things, to his divine will. I therefore now humbly offer my respects to your highness. Among whatsoever people I may retire I shall preserve an eternal recollection, an undying gratitude for all the good you have done me," (19 November.) Saxony, in truth, might well appear to Luther a somewhat insecure retreat. The pope was seeking to gain over the elector. Charles von Miltitz, a Saxon nobleman, canon of Mayence, named by Leo his agent in the matter, was commissioned to offer him the consecrated Golden Rose, a distinction which the court of Rome seldom accorded to other than kings, as a recompence for peculiar filial piety towards the church. This was putting the elector to a severe trial. It became necessary for him to make a definite explanation, one way or the other, and thus perhaps to involve himself in very considerable danger. The elector's hesitation on this occasion appears from a letter of Luther: "The prince at first altogether dissuaded me from publishing the proceedings of the conference of Augsburg; then he permitted me to publish them, and they are at this moment being printed. In his anxiety for me he would prefer I were anywhere else. He sent for me to Lichtenberg, where I had a long conversation with Spalatin on the subject: 'If the censures come,' I said, 'I will remain not a day longer.' He told me, however, not to be premature in setting out for France."

This was written on the 13th December. On the 20th, Luther was quite re-assured. The elector had replied to the pope, with truly diplomatic coolness, that he acknowledged himself an obedient son of holy mother church; that he entertained very great respect for his pontifical holiness, but that he wished the affair to be examined by judges not liable to suspicion. This was an infallible means of delaying the business, and, meantime, some circumstance or other might arise to lessen, or, at all events, put off the danger. The great point was to gain time: and the expectation was fulfilled. In January, 1519, the emperor died; and during the interregnum which followed, Frederic, by the express choice of Maximilian, acted as regent of the empire.

On the 3rd March, 1519, Luther, thus restored to confidence, wrote to the pope a letter, high in its spirit, though respectful in its form. It ran thus:

"Most holy father, necessity once more compels me, refuse of society and dust of the earth that I am, to address your exalted majesty; and I implore your holiness to listen to the bleatings of the poor lamb that now approaches you.

"Charles von Miltitz, private chancellor to your holiness, a just and worthy man, has, in your name, accused me to the illustrious prince Frederic of presumption, of irreverence towards the Roman church, and demanded, in your name, satisfaction; and I have been filled with grief at the misfortune of being suspected of disrespect towards the column of the church—I, who have never had any other wish than to assert and defend its honour.

"What am I to do, holy father? I have none to counsel me, on the one hand; on the other, I dare not expose myself to the effects of your resentment. Yet how avoid them? I know not. Retract, you say. Were the retractation demanded from me possible, it should be made. Thanks to my adversaries, to their fierce resistance, and to their rabid hostility, my writings have spread abroad far more widely than I had anticipated; my doctrines have penetrated too deeply into men's hearts for them now to be effaced. Germany is at this time flourishing in men of learning, of judgment, of genius: if I desire to do honour to the Roman church, it will be by revoking nothing. A retractation would only injure her in the estimation of the people, and expose her to ill representations.

" They whom I oppose, most holy father, are the men who have really injured and disgraced the holy Roman church; those adorers of filthy lucre, who have gone about, in your name, involving the very name of repentance in discredit and opprobrium, and seeking to throw the whole weight of their iniquities upon me, the man who struggled against their monstrosities.

" Ah, holy father, before God, before the whole creation, I affirm that I have never once had it in my thought to weaken or shake the authority of the holy see. I fully admit that the power of the Roman church is superior to all things under God; neither in heaven nor on earth is there aught above it, our Lord Jesus excepted. Let no credit be given by your holiness to any who seek to represent Luther to you in any other light.

" As to indulgences, I promise your holiness to occupy myself no further with them, to keep silence respecting them for the future, provided my adversaries, on their side, remain silent; to recommend the people, in my sermons, to love Rome, and not to impute to her the faults of others; not to give implicit faith to all the severe things I have abusively said of her, in the excitement of combating these mountebanks; so that, by God's help, these dissensions may, in brief time, be appeased; for my whole desire has been, that the Roman church, our common mother, should not be dishonoured by the base lies and jargon of these lucre-hunters, and that men should learn to prefer charity to indulgences."

Luther had formed his determination. Already, a month or two previously, he had written: " The pope has not chosen to allow me a just judge, and I will not admit the judgment of the pope. He then will be the text, and I the commentary." Elsewhere, he says to Spalatin (13th March), "I am at work on the Epistle of St. Paul to the Galatians. I have in contemplation a sermon on the Passion. Besides my ordinary lessons, I teach a number of children every evening, and explain to them the Lord's Prayer. In the intervals, I am looking through the decretals, with a view to my new discussion, and I find Christ so altered and crucified therein, that I have not made up my mind (let me whisper it in your ear) whether the pope is Antichrist himself, or only the apostle of Antichrist."

Whatever progress Luther might make in violence, the pope had thenceforward but very little chance of wresting from a powerful prince, to whom the majority of electors had delegated the empire, that prince's favourite theologian. Miltitz accordingly modified his tone. He declared that the pope would still be satisfied with a retractation. He visited Luther on apparently the most friendly and intimate terms. He essayed to flatter his vanity, by admitting that he had got all the world on his side, away from the pope.[1] He assured him, that on his way from Italy, he had not found more than two men out of five favourable to Rome. He wanted to persuade him to go and explain his views to the archbishop of Treves, but he did not profess that he was authorized to make this proposition either by the pope or by the archbishop. The good faith of the advice was matter of very great doubt indeed. Luther knew that he had been burned in effigy at Rome, (*papyraceus Martinus in Campo Floræ publicè combustus, execratus, devotus.*) His reply to Miltitz was cold and harsh, and he warned him that one of his messengers had excited such suspicions at Wittemberg, that the reformers there had been on the point of throwing him into the Elbe. "If, as you say, you are compelled, by my refusal, to come yourself, God give you a happy voyage. As to me, I have no time and no money to go wandering about in that manner. Farewell, worthy sir."

[1] Luther's works had already a very large circulation. John Frobin, a celebrated printer of Bâle, writes him word on the 14th Feb. 1519, that his books are read and approved of, even at Paris, nay, even in the Sorbonne; that he has no more than one copy left, of all those he had reprinted at Bâle, which were spread throughout Italy, Spain, and elsewhere, and everywhere admired by the learned. Seckendorf, 681.

On the arrival of Miltitz in Germany, Luther had said he would hold his peace, provided his opponents did the same; but they themselves released him from his engagement. Eck solemnly challenged him to come and dispute with him at Leipsig,[1] and he accordingly proceeded with Carlstadt to the place of meeting. But first, to enable him to appear in a decent garb at Leipsig, he was obliged to request a gown from the parsimonious elector, who, for the last two or three years, had omitted to supply him with clothes. The letter is curious:—"I beseech your electoral grace to have the kindness to purchase for me a white surplice and a black one. The white one I humbly ask for. As for the black one, your highness owes it to me, for you promised it me two or three years ago; and Pfeffinger has such difficulty in loosening his purse-strings, that I have been obliged to procure one for myself. I humbly beseech your highness, who thought that *the Psalmster* merited a black surplice, not to deem *Saint Paul* unworthy of a white one."

His journey to Leipsig is thus described by Seckendorf: "First came Carlstadt alone in a chariot; on the way one of his wheels broke, near St. Paul's church, and he was thrown out, which was considered a bad omen for him. Next came the chariot of Barnim, prince of Pomerania, who

[1] "Eck was at Augsburg, when Luther presented himself before cardinal Cajetano. He had just proposed a theological controversy upon the questions which were agitating the world, with Carlstadt, who had accepted the challenge. Luther arranged its matter and manner. Eck, in a programme which he distributed in large numbers, pompously announced the intelligence, and in doing so attacked with considerable bitterness some of Luther's theses.

"Luther, who asked nothing better than a disputation, sent forth another programme; his letter, forwarding it to Carlstadt, ran thus:—'All health to you: Our worthy Eccius, that illustrious master, has published a *schedula*, wherein he sets forth, in his usual inflated style, that he is going to have a controversy with you at Leipsic. You remember, that during my stay at Augsburg, I arranged the plan of a friendly discussion between you and Eccius, which you readily undertook. But now the fellow, totally forgetting all his engagements, after grossly insulting you, and all the while pretending to assail you, is, in reality, aiming at me his frog or fly blows, I don't know which to call them.

". . Now, my dear Andrew, I would not have you present yourself alone to this miserable disputant, for, in the first place, he attacks me as well, and, secondly, it were unjust that a man of your learning should condescend to the defence of what may be considered my fantastic imaginings.'"—AUDIN.

was at that time a student at Wittemberg, with the title of honorary rector. Beside him were Luther and Melancthon, and around and following the chariot was a large body of armed students."[1]

Eck gives this account of his interview with Luther:—"He came in great state to Leipsig with two hundred students of Wittemberg, four doctors, three licentiates, several masters, and a great number of his partisans; Dr. Lange, of Erfurt, Egranus, a preacher of Gorlitz, a citizen of Anneberg, some schismatics from Prague, and some Hussites, who glorify Martin as a stupendous apostle of truth, as equal even to their own John Hussinetz. The dispute was fixed for the 20th June; I granted that the Leipsigians should not be umpires, though many were well disposed towards me. Throughout the town the only talk was of my anticipated defeat. I, as an old doctor, was there to make head against all enemies. Meantime, the prince sent me a fine stag, and a fawn to Carlstadt. The citadel was prepared as our battle field. The place was guarded by seventy-six soldiers, to protect us, in case of need, from the insults of the people of Wittemberg and the Bohemian schismatics. When Luther entered, I saw clearly enough that he had no intention of disputing. He refused to recognise any judges whatever. I proposed to him successively as persons to be deputed, prince George, and the university of Leipsig, or any other university he might prefer in Germany; or, if Germany were too narrow a field, in France, Italy, or Spain. At last, certain doctors of Erfurt and Paris were chosen umpires." The authorities, however, were on the side of authority, and the faculties of Paris, Louvain, and Cologne, condemned Luther's propositions.

Luther was by this time so completely re-assured, that, not content with going to defend himself at Leipsig,[2] he assumed the offensive at Wittemberg. "He ventured," says his catholic biographer, Cochlæus, "with the sanction of the prince who protected him,[3] solemnly to cite the most able inquisitors, men who deemed themselves able to

[1] Seckendorf, i. 92. [2] See Appendix II.

[3] Luther could scarcely doubt the protection of the elector, when he found Spalatin, the confidant of this prince, translate into German, and publish his *Consolation to all Christians.*

swallow iron or split flints, to come and dispute with him;[1] offering them a safe conduct from the prince, who moreover undertook to provide them with board and lodging."

At this period, Luther, still undecided in his ideas of reform, sought to clear up his doubts by discussion: he requested, he demanded public conferences. On the 15th June, 1520, he wrote to the emperor Charles V., thus:

"Grace and peace in the name of our Lord Jesus Christ. That I should venture to write to your most serene majesty, dear emperor Charles, is a circumstance that will astonish all the world: 'tis, indeed, a strange thing that the king of kings, the master of the masters of the world, should be thus approached by a dwarf of base extraction.

"But astonishment will cease, when due attention is paid to the magnitude of the subject, that subject being gospel truth. If truth be worthy to approach the throne of celestial Majesty, it may well address itself to a prince of this world; nay, the princes of this world, the image of celestial Majesty, should take it as their model, and though dwelling on high terrestrially, look down without scorn upon things crawling beneath, raise the beggar, and take the poor man from his dunghill: a beggar and a poor man, I throw myself at the feet of your royal majesty.

"I have published various works, which have drawn down upon me much and powerful hostility. I had thought I should have remained free from these attacks—first, because it is altogether against my own inclination that I have been involved in the struggle; I having been absolutely compelled into the public arena, instead of staying quietly, as I had wished, in my little hole; and secondly, because, by the testimony of men of rare probity, that which I have sought to defend against the superstitious absurdities of tradition, is the truth of the gospel. It is now three years since I have been incessantly exposed to hatred, danger, opprobrium. In vain have I called for mercy, in vain have I offered to hold my peace, in vain have I offered conditions, in vain have I implored to be enlightened as to my errors: what my opponents desire is to stifle me and the gospel.

"After all I have done, it only remains for me, after the example of St. Athanasius, to invoke the aid of your impe-

[1] See Appendix III.

rial majesty—that is, if God permit you to come to the aid of His holy cause. Most serene majesty, dear king of the kings of the earth, behold me at your feet; deign to take me under your wings, or rather not me, but the truth, for whose protection alone you are entrusted with the sword. I ask you to defend me only until I shall clearly understand whether I am conqueror or conquered. I ask nothing at your hands, should it be really proved against me that I am guilty of impiety or heresy. "Your faithful servant."[1]

On the 4th Feb., he also wrote to the archbishop of Mayence and to the bishop of Magdeberg, letters full of submission and respect, supplicating these prelates not to credit the calumnies circulated against him, and affirming that his only aim was to enlighten his understanding, and clear up his doubts.[2]

Meantime, the principal adversary of Luther, Dr. Eck, had proceeded to Rome, to solicit the condemnation of the reformer, and Luther was judged and sentenced beforehand.[3] All that was left to him to do, was to judge his judge, and repudiate his authority in the face of the world, and this he accordingly did in his terrible book On the captivity of Babylon, wherein he maintained that the church was captive, that Jesus Christ, constantly profaned in the idolatry of the mass, set aside in the dogma of transubstantiation, was the pope's prisoner.

He explains in the preface, with daring freedom, the manner in which he found himself daily driven more and more to extremities by the conduct of his adversaries: "Whether I will or no, I become each day more learned and expert, driven about as I am, and kept in active exercise by so many antagonists at once. I wrote on the indulgences two years ago, but in a way that makes me repent I sent forth what I had written to the public. At that time I was still pro-

[1] Opera Latina, ii. 42. [2] Ib.

[3] The first special condemnation of Luther was issued at Rome, 15th June, 1520. It selects forty-one of Luther's propositions, and denounces them as heretical, scandalous, and damnable, and prohibits any one, under pain of excommunication, from in any way propagating or sanctioning them; and it further condemns all Luther's writings to the flames. It finally gives Luther and his followers one last opportunity of saving themselves from utter excommunication and damnation, by returning to the bosom of the church, and abandoning their errors, and allows them sixty days for this purpose.

digiously attached to the papal power, so that I dared not altogether reject the indulgences. I saw them, moreover, sanctioned by great numbers of intelligent persons—in fact, I was left to roll the great stone by myself. But since then, thanks to Sylvestro and the other brothers who so warmly defended them, I have found that they were nothing more than mere impostures invented by the flatterers of Rome, to ruin men's faith and their pockets. Would to God I could induce the booksellers, and all those who have my writings on the indulgences, to put them into the fire, and replace them by this single proposition:—*Indulgences are delusive trash, invented by the parasites of Rome.*

"After that, Eck, Emser, and their gang came to tackle me on the question of the pope's supremacy. I am bound to admit, in gratitude towards these learned personages, that the trouble they took in this matter was not without its effect, and that a considerable effect, on my advancement. Previously, I merely denied that popery was founded on right divine, admitting that it had human right on its side. But, after having heard and read the ultra-subtle subtleties on which these poor people found the rights of their idols, I have arrived at a sounder conclusion, and am convinced that the reign of the pope is that of Babylon, and of *Nimrod the mighty hunter.* And so I request all booksellers and readers (that nothing may be wanting to the success of my good friends) to burn, also, whatever I have written hitherto on this matter, and to stick to this simple proposition: *the pope is the mighty hunter, the hunter of Roman episcopacy.*[1]

At the same time, in order that it might be clearly understood that he was attacking popery rather than the pope, he wrote a long letter, both in German and in Latin,[2] to Leo X., wherein he repudiated any personal ill will to himself.

"Amid the monsters of this age, with whom I have been at war these three years, my thoughts and recollections turn towards you, most holy father: I protest—and my memory is a faithful one—I have never spoken of you but with honour and respect. Were it otherwise, I should be ready to retract

[1] Opera, ix. 63.

[2] The German translation, observes M. Audin, differs in many passages from the original Latin, and its general phraseology is far more energetic, more violent.

anything I had said against your person. Did I not call you the Daniel in the lion's den? Did I not defend your innocence against the man Sylvestro Rierio, who dared to impugn it? You cannot deny it, my dear Leo. The see in which you are seated surpasses in corruption the Babylon and Sodom of old, and it is against that impious Rome of yours I have set myself. I rose indignant when I saw men, under the authority of your name, shamelessly tricking Christ's people: it is against the Rome of those bad men that I have been fighting, and against which I will fight while a breath of faith remains in me. Not that I believe—for it were impossible—that my efforts will prevail against the crowd of flatterers who reign in your disordered Rome; but, charged to watch over my brethren here, I would not have them fall a prey to the Roman plague. Rome is a sink of corruption and iniquity; for it is clearer than light itself, that the Roman church, once of all churches the most chaste and pure, has become a cavern foul with robbers, the most obscene of brothels, the very throne of sin, of death, and hell! and that its wickedness could go no further, even were Antichrist reigning there in person.

"Ay, Leo, you are as a lamb amidst the wolves, as Daniel amidst the lions, as Ezekiel amid the scorpions. And to all these monsters what have you to set in contrast?—three or four cardinals of learning and faith. But what are these three or four in so vast a crowd of infidels and reprobates? You would be poisoned by them, were you to attempt to remedy such great evils, long before you had thought of a remedy. . . The days of Rome are numbered; the anger of God has been breathed forth upon her. She hates councils, she dreads reform, she will not hear of a check being placed upon her desperate impiety. It will be said of her, as was said of her mother: *We would have healed Babylon, but she is not healed; let us flee from her.* It was for your cardinals to have remedied all these mischiefs, but the disease now defies the physician, even were he at hand; the horses scorn the reins.

"Full of love for your person, I have often groaned in spirit to see you placed in the pontifical chair in an age like this of ours; you well merit that your destinies should have been cast in a happier time. The papal throne is not worthy of you; it should be occupied by Satan, who does, in truth, reign more potently than you in that Babylon. Is it not true I ask you, that under the vast canopy of heaven there exists nothing so corrupt, so wicked, so pestilential as Rome? Rome assuredly surpasses in impiety the Turk himself. Rome heretofore the gate of heaven, is now the jaws of hell, which the anger of God keeps wide open: scarcely shall we be able to save a few souls from the infernal gulf. Unhappy Leo, to be on this cursed throne! I tell you the truth, because I desire your welfare. If St. Bernard commiserated his pope Eugenius, how must we pity you, the corruption of whose throne is augmented by the lapse of three hundred years! Yes; you would thank me for your eternal salvation, were I to succeed in breaking the chains of that dungeon, of that hell in which you are kept a prisoner. . . .

"I do not come to you, holy father, with empty hands. I offer you a small treatise, published under the auspices of your name, as a pledge of my desire for peace, as an illustration of the mode in which I should have preferred to occupy my leisure hours, had your flatterers permitted me to follow my own inclinations; a present of small value, if you regard merely the form of the work, but highly precious—unless I deceive myself—if you consider the spirit of the book. I, a poor monk, have nothing better to offer you, and you need no gift but a spiritual gift.[1]

When the bull of condemnation[2] arrived in Germany, it found a whole nation in a state of ebullition. At Erfurt, the students took it from the booksellers' shops, tore it in pieces, and threw it into the water, saying, with more vehemence than point—"It is a bull; let us see if it can swim." Luther at once sent forth a pamphlet, *Against the execrable Bull of Antichrist.*[3] On the 10th December, 1520, he publicly burnt the Pope's anathema at the gates of the town, amid the exulting shouts of the people; and on the same day wrote to Spalatin, his ordinary medium of communication with the Elector: "This day, the tenth of December, in the year

[1] The treatise referred to, was his *De Libertate Christianâ*. With reference to the date of this letter, great controversy has taken place. In the edition of Jena, it bears the date 6th April, 1520. Seckendorf places it in October of the same year; that is to say, long after the publication of Leo's bull. We refer the reader to the Appendix, for what appears to us a satisfactory statement on the subject, by Mr. Roscoe.

[2] See Appendix IV. [3] See Appendix V.

1520, at nine o'clock in the morning, were burnt at Wittemberg, at the east gate, opposite the church of the Holy Cross, all the pope's books, the rescripts, the decretals of Clement VI., the extravagants, the new bull of Leo X., the *Somma Angelica*, the *Chrysopasus* of Eck, and some other productions of his, and of Emser's. This is something new, I wot." He adds, in the report he drew up on the subject: "if any one asks me why I act thus, I will answer him, that it is an old custom to burn bad books. The apostles burned books to the value of five thousand deniers."

According to the tradition, he said, on throwing the book of the decretals into the flames—"Thou hast afflicted the holy of the Lord: may eternal fire afflict thee, and consume thee."

All this was, indeed, as Luther said, something new. Hitherto most of the sects and heresies that had arisen from time to time, had formed themselves in secret, and were only too happy if their existence remained unknown; but here was a simple monk placing himself on an equality with the pope, and constituting himself the judge of the church's supreme head. The chain of old tradition was thus broken, its continuity destroyed, the seamless robe torn. Nor is it to be believed that Luther himself, with all his determination and violence of character, took this last decisive step without pain; for it was tearing from his heart at a blow the memory of a past which his youth had been taught to venerate. He believed, indeed, that he was retaining the Scripture; but then, after all, it was the Scripture interpreted otherwise than it had been for the last thousand years. His enemies have often said this; but none of them more eloquently than he himself: thus he writes, on the 29th November, to the Augustines of Wittemberg—"I feel more and more every day, how difficult it is to lay aside the scruples which one has had so long within one. Oh, how much pain it has cost me, though I had the Scripture on my side, to justify it to myself that I should dare to make a stand alone against the pope, and hold him forth as antichrist. What have the tribulations of my heart not been! How many times have I not asked myself with bitterness the same question which the papists put to me—*Art thou alone wise?* Can everybody else be so mistaken? Can so many ages have been mistaken? How will it be, if, after all, thou thyself it is who art wrong, and art thus involving in thy error so many souls, who will then be eternally damned? 'Twas so I fought with myself, till Jesus Christ, by his own infallible word, fortified my heart against these doubts, till it became as a coast of rocks, defying the waves which impotently dash against it."[1]

"Doubtless," he writes to Erasmus, in the beginning of his mournful book, *De Servo Arbitrio*, "doubtless you feel yourself somewhat embarrassed in presence of so long a succession of learned men—in presence of the sanction against you of so many centuries, wherein have flourished men, distinguished for their conversancy with sacred literature, wherein appeared such noble martyrs, glorified by numerous miracles; and all these backed by more recent theologians, by innumerable academies, councils, bishops, pontiffs. On that side, then, are ranged learning, genius, numbers, grandeur, rank, power, sanctity, miracles, and what not. On mine, Wickliffe and Lorenzo Valla (and also Augustin, whom you seem to have forgotten), and Luther, a poor creature, a man of yesterday, standing well-nigh alone with a few friends, unsupported by anything approaching the learning, or the genius, or the numbers, or the grandeur, or the sanctity of the other party, and as to miracles, they altogether could not cure a lame horse. *Et alia quæ tuplurim a fanda enumerare vales.* What are we, poor fellows? As the wolf said of Philomela—*Vox et præterea nihil.*

"I confess, my dear Erasmus, you have some reason to hesitate in presence of all these things. I myself, ten years ago, hesitated. I could hardly believe that this Troy, which for so many ages had victoriously resisted all the attacks made upon it, would one day fall. From the bottom of my soul, I call God to witness, that I should have continued in my fear, should have hesitated and hesitated up to the present day, and onward, had not my conscience, had not the force of truth compelled me to speak. I have not, as you well know, a heart of stone; and even though I had, beaten about as it has been, by such infinite fierce waves and storms, it would have yielded and broken when the whole power of authority burst upon my head, as a deluge about to overwhelm me."

[1] Luther's Briefe, ii. 107.

He says elsewhere: "I have learned from the Holy Scripture, that it is a thing terrible and full of danger, to raise one's voice in the church of God, to speak in the midst of those whom we shall have for judges, when, in the last day of judgment, we shall find ourselves in the presence of God, and of his angels—every creature there looking, listening, bending the ear to dwell on the Divine Word. Certes, when I think on it, I feel that I could heartily wish to bury all in silence, and pass a sponge over what I have written. To have to render an account to God of every heedless word—'tis hard, 'tis horrible!"[1]

On the 27th March, 1519, he writes—"I was alone, and thrown into this struggle without previously weighing the matter maturely. Under such circumstances, I at first gave up to the pope many essential articles. Who was I, a poor miserable monk, that I should make head against the majesty of the pope, before which the kings of the earth (nay, earth itself, hell, and heaven) trembled? What I suffered during the first and second year; into how deep a dejection I fell—no imaginary or affected dejection, but a regular prostration of mind, or rather, utter despair—cannot be conceived by those who, with easy confidence, have since rushed along the beaten road to attack the pope with such fierceness and presumption. Obtaining no light, to light me on my dark path, from the dead, mute masters (I speak of the books of the theologians and priests), I desired to seek the living counsel of the churches of God; so that, if there existed pious men, illumined by the Holy Spirit, they might take compassion upon me, and give me sound and assured advice, for my own good, and that of all Christendom. But it was impossible for me to recognise them: I looked only to the pope, the cardinals, bishops, theologians, canonists, monks, priests; it was from them I sought the spirit; for I had so thoroughly filled and stuffed myself with their doctrine, that I no longer knew whether I

[1] It is curious to compare these words of Luther with the so different passage in Rousseau's Confessions—

"Let the trumpet for the last judgment sound when it may, I will come, this book in my hand, to present myself before the Supreme Judge. I will say aloud, This is what I have done, what I have thought, what I was .... and then let any one present say, if he dare, *I was better than that man!*"

was awake or asleep. Had I then braved the pope, as I do now, I should have expected the earth to open and swallow me up on the spot, as it did Korah and Abiram. When I heard the name of the church sent forth, I trembled, and offered to yield. In 1518, I said to the cardinal of Gaeta at Augsburg, that I would thenceforward hold my peace, if only, as I humbly prayed, silence was also imposed upon my enemies, and their clamours put an end to. Far from granting me this concession, they threatened, if I did not instantly retract, to condemn all I had taught, without exception or condition whatever. I had already sent forth the catechism, by which, under the blessing of God, many men had grown better: I could not permit it to be condemned.

"I was thus compelled to the step, which at the time I regarded as the worst of evils. But I am not going now to relate my history; I only wish to confess the folly, weakness, and ignorance which once afflicted me, and, at the same time, to silence those presumptuous brawlers and scribblers, who assume merit to themselves in the struggle, without having ever borne the cross, or undergone the temptations of Satan."

Against the tradition of the middle ages, against the authority of the church, Luther sought a refuge in the Scripture, anterior to tradition, superior to the church itself. He translated the Psalms, he wrote his *Postilla* on the Evangelists and the Epistles. At no other period of his life did he make a nearer approach to mysticism than at the present time. He now relied as much upon St. John as upon St. Paul, and seemed ready to go through all the degrees of the doctrine of love, without being deterred by the deplorable consequences which resulted thence for the freedom and morality of man: "There are," says he, in his book on Christian Liberty, "two men in man; the inner man, the soul, and the outer man, the body; there is no relation between them. As works proceed from the outer man, they cannot affect the soul; let the body frequent profane places, let it eat, drink, let it omit to pray, let it omit to do all that the hypocrites do; the soul will suffer from none of these things. By faith, the soul is united to Christ, as the bride to her husband. Then all is common to them, the good alike with the bad. All of us who believe in Christ, are kings and pontiffs. The Christian, elevated by his faith above all things, becomes, by that spiritual power, lord of all things, so that nothing can hurt him, *imo omnia ei subjecta coguntur servire ad salutem.* If I have faith, all things, good and ill, turn into good for me. 'Tis this is the inestimable power and liberty of the Christian.[1]

"We must proceed, in our study of the Gospel of St. John, upon a totally different principle from that with which we regard the other Evangelists. The idea of this Evangelist is, that man can do nothing, is nothing, has nothing, of himself; that all he holds or is, proceeds from divine compassion and mercy. I repeat, and will repeat again and again: he who would elevate himself to a salutary idea, a salutary speculation respecting God, must make everything subordinate to the humanity of Christ. Let him constantly represent to himself Christ in his action and in his passion, until he find his heart softened. Let him not stop there, but penetrate and push further on with his thought; it is not of his will, but of that of God the Father, that Christ does this or that. It is then he will begin to feel the infinite sweetness of the will of the Father revealed in the humanity of Christ."

"If thou feel thy heart hesitate and doubt, it is high time for thee to go to the priest, and request absolution for thy sins. Thou oughtest to die a thousand deaths, rather than question the priest's judgment, for that is the judgment of God. If thou canst heartily believe in that judgment, thy heart may well be joyful and praise God, who, by the medium of man, has consoled thy conscience. If thou dost not think thyself worthy of pardon, it is because thou hast not done enough, because thou art not sufficiently imbued with faith, and dwellest too much on works. It is a thousand times more important to have firm faith in absolution, than to be worthy of it, or to do works to procure satisfaction. 'Tis faith renders thee worthy, and which constitutes true satisfaction. The man may, with faith, joyfully serve God, who, without that, from the disquietude of his heart, never doth any good work. 'Tis this which is called the light burden of our Lord Jesus Christ."[2]

This dangerous doctrine was cordially received by the

[1] Luther, opera ii. *De Libertate Christianâ.*
[2] Sermon preached at Leipzig, in 1519, On Justification.

people, and by the large majority of the learned. Erasmus, the most celebrated of them all, seems almost alone to have foreseen the inevitable consequences. Of a critical and doubting turn of mind, emulous of the able Italian, Lorenzo Valla, who in the fifteenth century wrote a book, *De Libero Arbitrio*, Erasmus himself wrote a treatise against Luther under the same title. In 1519, he received the advances of the monk of Wittemberg with great coolness. The latter, who felt how much at this time he needed the support of men of letters, had written complimentary letters (1518, 1519) to Reuchlin and Erasmus. The reply of the latter is cold and significant: "My attention is entirely directed to aiding as best I may the restoration of literature. In my opinion, greater progress towards good is effected by political moderation, than by violence. It was by his moderation Christ brought over the world to his law; it was by moderation Paul abolished the law of Moses. It is better to raise one's voice against those who abuse the authority of the priesthood, than against the priesthood itself; and so with regard to kings. Instead of throwing scorn upon the schools, it were advisable to bring them back to sounder studies. When we take in hand matters too deeply rooted in men's minds to be torn out by a single effort, we must proceed by discussion, by close, stringent argumentation, and not by mere assertion. We must ever be careful not to say or do anything with an air of arrogance or revolt; at least, such, in my opinion, is the method more consonant with the spirit of Christianity. What I here say, is not to teach you what you ought to do, but simply to confirm you in always doing that which you now do."[1]

This timid reserve was not suitable to such a man at such a period. The excitement was immense. The nobles and the people, the castles and the free towns, rivalled each other in zeal and enthusiasm for Luther. At Nuremberg, at Strasburg, even at Mayence, there was a constant struggle for his least pamphlets.[2] The sheet, yet wet, was brought from the press under some one's cloak, and passed from shop to shop. The pedantic bookmen of the

[1] Erasmi Epistolæ, iii. 445.

[2] The celebrated painter, Lucas Kranach, made designs for Luther's minor works.—(Seckendorf, 148.)

German trades' unions, the poetical tinmen, the literary shoemakers, devoured the good news. Worthy Hans Sachs raised himself above his wonted common-place; he left his shoe half made, and wrote his most high-flown verses, his best productions. He sang, in under tones, *The Nightingale of Wittemberg*, and the song was taken up, and resounded all over the land.

Nothing lent more powerful assistance to Luther than the zeal manifested by the printers and booksellers in favour of the new ideas. "The books in support of Luther," says a contemporary, "were printed by the typographers with minute care, often at their own expense, and vast numbers of copies were thrown off. There was a complete body of ex-monks, who, returned to the world, lived by vending the works of Luther throughout Germany. On the other hand, it was solely by dint of money that the Catholics could get their productions printed, and they were sent forth with such a host of faults, that they seemed the work of ignorant barbarians. If any printer, more or less conscientious than the rest, gave himself any trouble with any Catholic work, he was tormented to death by all his fellows, and by the people in the public streets, as a papist, and as a slave of the priests."[1]

Great as was the zeal of the towns, it was more especially to the nobles that Luther had appealed, and they responded to the call with an enthusiasm which he himself was at times compelled to moderate. In 1519, he wrote, in Latin, a Defence of the Articles condemned by the bull of Leo X., which he dedicated to the Count Fabien von Ferlitsch in these terms: "It having appeared to me desirable to write henceforward to you laymen, I determined, God willing, to commence under the favourable auspices of your name. Let this present work, therefore, recommend me, or rather, let it recommend the true Christian doctrine, to yourself and the other nobles." He had, at first, contemplated dedicating

[1] Cochlæus, 54. It was the same at Augsburg. The Confession of Augsburg was printed and diffused all over Germany, even before the Diet was concluded; the Refutation, by the catholics, which the emperor had ordered to be printed, was given to the printers, but did not appear. Luther reproached the catholics that they dared not publish it, and called it a night bird, a bat, an owl.

the translation of this treatise to Franz von Sickengen, and another work to the Counts of Mansfeldt, but he abstained from doing so, "least," as he says, "he should arouse the jealousy of many others, and more especially that of the Franconian nobles." In the same year he published a violent pamphlet, addressed *to the Christian nobles of Germany, on the amelioration of Christianity.* Four thousand copies of this production were sold off instantly.

"To his imperial majesty and the Christian nobility of the German nation, Martin Luther wishes grace and the strength of our Lord Jesus Christ.

"The Romanists have skilfully raised around them three walls, by means of which they have hitherto protected themselves against all reform, to the great detriment of Christianity and Christendom. First, they pretend that the spiritual power is above temporal power; next, that to the pope alone it appertains to interpret the Bible; third, that the pope alone has the right to convoke a council.

"God aid us and give us one of those trumpets, which heretofore overthrew the walls of Jericho, that we may level with the ground these walls of straw and paper, expose to full light the tricks and lies of the devil, and recover by penitence and amendment the grace of God. Let us begin with the first wall.

"*First wall.*—All Christians are of spiritual condition, and there is among them no difference, but that which results from the difference of their functions, according to the words of the apostle, (1 Cor. xii.) 'The body is one, and hath many members, but the body is not one member, but many.'

"We have all the same baptism, the same gospel, the same faith, and we are all equal in our capacity of Christians. It should be with the spiritual minister as it is with the civil magistrate, who, during the exercise of his functions, is above his fellow citizens, but on resigning his office, becomes as he was before, merely one among them. Indelible characters are a chimæra. The secular power being constituted by God, for the purpose of punishing the wicked and protecting the good, its ministration should extend over all Christians, without consideration of any person whatever, pope, bishop, monk, nun, or what not. If a priest is killed, the whole district is put under interdict. Why not just the same when a poor peasant has been murdered? Whence such a difference between Christians, whom Jesus Christ calls equals? The distinction arises simply and solely from laws and human inventions.

"*Second wall.* We are all priests. Does not the apostle (1 Cor. ii.) say, "He that is spiritual, judgeth all things, yet he himself is judged of no man?" We have all one mind in the faith, says the gospel elsewhere; why, then, should we not feel, as well as the popes, who are often infidels, what is conformable, what is contrary to the faith?

"*Third wall.* The first councils were not convoked by the popes. That of Nicæa itself was convoked by the Emperor Constantine. When a town is surprised by the enemy, the honour is to him who first of all cries *to arms*, whether he be burgomaster or not. Why should not the same be the case with reference to him, who, a watchful sentinel against our infernal enemies, should be the first to see them advance, and the first to assemble Christians against them? Must he needs be pope to do this? . . . Let the pope put an end to the preposterous luxury with which he is surrounded, and make an approach to the poverty of Jesus Christ. His court swallows up enormous sums. It has been calculated, that more than three hundred thousand florins are sent off every year from Germany to Rome. Twelve cardinals would be amply sufficient for all purposes, and the pope ought to maintain them. Why should the Germans permit themselves to be despoiled by cardinals, who monopolize all the rich preferments, and spend the revenues at Rome? The French do not suffer it. . . . Let us not give another farthing to the pope, as subsidies against the Turks; the whole thing is a snare, a miserable pretext for the purpose of draining us of more money. . . . Let us no longer recognise his right to investiture. Rome draws everything into her bag by the most impudent chicanery. There is one man in that city, a mere courtier, who alone possesses twenty-two benefices, seven priories, and forty-four prebends. Let the secular authority henceforward abstain from sending to Rome the *annates* it has been in the habit for the last hundred years of sending. Let it be sufficient, for the installation of bishops, that they be confirmed by the two nearest bishops, or by their archbishops, conformably with the enactment of the council of Nicæa. . . .

"My only object in writing this, is to afford matter for confirmatory reflection to those who are disposed to aid the German nation in becoming once more Christian, and once more free, after the deplorable government it has suffered at the hands of the Antichrist, the pope . . . Let there be fewer pilgrimages to Italy . . . Let the mendicant orders become extinct. They have degenerated, and no longer fulfil the intentions of their founders. . . Let us permit priests to marry. . . It will be well to suppress a great proportion of the saints' days, and make them coincident with Sundays. . . The celebrating the festivals of patron saints is prejudicial to society. Let fast days be put an end to. There are many things which may have been desirable under other circumstances and in other times, which are far worse than useless now. Let mendicity be extinguished, by each parish being bound to take charge of its own poor. It will be good to prohibit the foundation of private masses. The doctrine of the Bohemians should be inquired into more impartially and fully than has yet been done. And we might with good effect unite with them in resisting the court of Rome. Let the decretals be abolished. Let the houses for prostitution be suppressed.

"I have another song in my head upon Rome and the Romanists : if their ears itch for it, they shall have it, to the very last octave. Dost thou hear me, pope of Rome ? Thou art the greatest sinner of all : thy throne is not suspended from heaven, but fixed to the gate of hell. Who gave thee power to set thyself above thy God, and trample under feet His precepts and commandments?[1]

". . . Poor Germans that we are,—we have been deceived ! We were born to be masters, and we have been compelled to bow the head beneath the yoke of our tyrants, and to become slaves. Name, title, ensigns of royalty, we possess all these ; force, power, right, liberty, all these have gone over to the popes, who have robbed us of them. For them the grain, for us the straw. It is time we should cease to content ourselves with the mere image of empire ; it is time we resume the sceptre, and with the sceptre our body, and our soul, and our

[1] Luther's Werke, vi. 544.

treasure; it is time the glorious Teutonic people should cease to be the puppet of the Roman pontiff. Because the pope crowns the emperor, it does not follow that the pope is superior to the emperor. Samuel, who crowned Saul and David, was not above these kings, nor Nathan above Solomon, whom he consecrated. Let the emperor then be a veritable emperor, and no longer allow himself to be stripped of his sword or of his sceptre!"[1]

Luther's principal friends among the nobility were Silvester Von Schauenberg, Franz Von Sickengen, Taubenheim, and Ulrich Von Hutten. Schauenberg had confided the education of his young son to Melancthon, and offered to assist the elector of Saxony with troops, in the event of his becoming involved in any danger from his advocacy of the cause of the Reformation. Taubenheim and others sent money to Luther. "I have received," he says, "a hundred gold pieces, sent me by Taubenheim; Schart has given me fifty more; and I begin to fear least God should pay me here, instead of hereafter; but I have already protested, that I must not be thus gorged with money, or I should be fain to throw it all up again." The Margrave of Brandenburg had solicited to see him, as a great favour; Sickengen and Hutten promised him their active aid against all and any assailants. "Hutten," says he, "in September, 1520, sent me a letter, burning with indignation against the Roman pontiff; he wrote me that he was about to fall with pen and with sword upon sacerdotal tyranny; that he was furious at the pope's having tried to use the poniard and poison against him, and had written to the bishop of Mayence, that he would send him, bound hand and foot, to Rome. "You see," adds Luther, "what Hutten would have; but I would never consent to aid God's cause by aid of violence and murder, and so I wrote him word."[2]

[1] Opera Luth. vi. 544.

[2] It was also in this spirit of a desire that Germany should separate peaceably from the holy see, that he wrote, in 1520, to Charles V. and the German nobles. According, however, to Cochlæus, a very doubtful authority indeed, he had, at this time, preached actual war against Rome: "Let the emperor, the king, the princes, belt on their swords, and march forth to strike down this pest of the world. We must settle the matter by cold steel: there is no other remedy. There are lost, insane men who say, violence should be left to antichrist; but I say, if we have the gallows for thieves, axes for brigands, the faggot for heretics, why should we not

Meantime, the emperor had summoned Luther to appear at Worms, before the imperial diet;[1] and the two parties were now about to meet face to face.[2]

"Would to God!" said Hutten, "I could be present at the diet; I would make a stir! I would get up a tumult that should shake some of them!"[3] On the 20th April, he wrote to Luther:—"What atrocities have I not heard of? There is no *furia* comparable with the fury of these people. I see very clearly that we must come to swords, bows, armour, and cannon. Do thou, my father, fortify thy courage, and despise these wild beasts. I see each day the number of thy partizans augment; thou wilt be in no want of defenders. Many have come to me, saying—'Please God, he give not way: please God, he answer courageously, that he suffer himself to be overcome by no terrors!'"[4] At the same time, Hutten sent letters in every direction to the magistrates of different towns, exhorting them to form a league with the nobles of the Rhine; or, in other words, to arm against the ecclesiastical princes. He wrote to Pirkeimer, one of the principal magistrates of Nuremberg:—

"Arouse the courage of your people; I have great hope that you will find partizans in many towns that are animated by the love of liberty. Franz Von Sickengen is for us, full of zeal. The words of Luther have penetrated his very soul. I have Martin's minor works constantly read to him, as he sits at table. He has sworn not to desert the cause of liberty, and what he says, he will do. Set forth his example among

use worldly weapons against these children of perdition, these cardinals, these popes, the whole rout of the Roman Sodom, who corrupt the church of God. Why should we not wash our hands in their blood?" Cochlæus though he attributes these words to Luther, assigns no authority for them.

[1] The emperor's mandate was in the following terms:—"Honourable, dear, and devoted Luther,—Ourself and the states of the holy Roman empire, assembled at Worms, having resolved to demand an explanation from you on the subject of your doctrines and your books, we forward you a safe-conduct, to ensure your personal immunity from danger. We would have you immediately set forth on your journey hither, so that within twenty days of the receipt of our mandate, you may appear before us and the states. You have neither violence nor snares to fear. Relying upon our imperial word, we expect your obedience to our earnest wishes."—LUTHER'S *Werke*, ix. 106.

[2] The final bull of excommunication was fulminated against Luther on the 6th January, 1521.

[3] Hutten, op. iv. 292. [4] Ib. 295.

your citizens. There lives not a nobler soul in all Germany."[1]

Even in the diet at Worms, there were partizans of Luther. In one of the sittings, somebody openly produced a paper, setting forth that four hundred nobles had sworn to defend him, and after reading it, cried out, "*Buntschuh! Buntschuh!*"[2] —the rallying word of the insurgent peasantry. The catholics, indeed, were not altogether sure of the emperor. During the diet, Hutten writes: "Cæsar has, they say, made up his mind to side with the pope." In the town itself, among the populace, the Lutherans were numerous. Hermann Busch writes to Hutten, that a priest, coming out of the imperial palace with two Spanish soldiers, attempted, at the very gates of the palace, to take away eighty-four copies of the *Captivity of Babylon*, that a man was selling, but was soon compelled by the indignant people to take refuge in the interior of the palace. At the same time, to induce Hutten at once to take up arms, he describes to him the Spaniards insolently parading about the streets of Worms on their mules, and making the people give way before them.

"The audacity of the Romanists," he writes to Hutten, "grows greater and greater; for, as they say, you bark, but don't bite." [3]

Another man of letters, Helius Eobanus Hessus, also urged Hutten to take up arms for Luther. "Franz Von Sickengen will be there to back us, and you two together, I predict, will be the thunder and lightning that shall crush the monster of Rome." [4]

The hostile biographer of Luther, Cochlæus, relates in a satirical manner, the reformer's progress to the diet:—"A chariot was prepared for him in the form of a closed litter. Around him were many learned personages; the provost Jonas, Doctor Schurf, the theologian Amsdorff, &c. Wherever he passed, there was a great concourse of people. In the taverns was good cheer, joyous libations, and even music. Luther himself, to draw all eyes upon him, played the harp like another Orpheus—a shaved and capuchined Orpheus.

[1] Hutten, op. iv. 276.

[2] Buntschuh, *shoe of honour*. The shoe had already served as a distinctive sign in the twelfth century. *Sabatati* was a name of the Vaudois.

[3] Hutten, op. iv. 306. [4] Id. ib.

Although the safe-conduct of the emperor prohibited him from preaching on his route, he yet preached at Erfurth on Easter Sunday, and had his sermon printed."[1] This portrait of Luther by no means accords with the one given of him by a friendly contemporary, Mosellanus, some time before the diet:—

"Martin is of the middle height; cares and studies have made him so thin, that one may count all the bones in his body; yet he is in all the force and verdure of his age. His voice is clear and piercing. Powerful in his doctrine, wonderful for his knowledge of the Scriptures, every one of the verses of which, almost, he could recite one after another, he learned the Greek and Hebrew for the purpose of comparing and weighing the translations of the Word. He is never at a loss, and has at his disposition a world of thoughts and words. In his conversation he is agreeable and easy, and there is nothing hard or austere in his air. He even

[1] On the 2nd of April, Luther arrived at Leipsig, where the Cup of Honour was offered him, according to the old custom of that and many other places; on the 3rd, at Naumburg, where he dined at the table of the burgomaster Græssler, with the herald; on the 4th, at Weimar, where duke John of Saxony sent him the money necessary for the remainder of his journey.

John Crotus, rector, Helius Eobanus Hessus, professor of rhetoric, and Justus Jonas, accompanied by nearly forty horsemen, met the Doctor two miles from Erfurt. He was received at his old convent by the prior, John Lange, and by Bartholomew Arnoldi Usingen. It was the 6th April, the evening before Easter Sunday. It was nightfall; a small wooden cross, raised over the grave of a brother whom he had known, and who had died peacefully in the Lord, encountered his observation and agitated him. He pointed out the grave to Dr. Jonas: 'See, my father; he reposes there, while I——' and he turned his gaze towards heaven. Before retiring to rest, he went back to the grave, and sat meditating upon it for upwards of an hour. Amsdorff was obliged to come and remind him that the bell of the monastery had sounded the hour of retirement to rest. Before proceeding to his chamber, he saw the superior, and obtained permission from him to preach on the following day.

Next morning, the little church of Erfurt was crowded, long before the hour of service. Everybody was anxious to hear this monk who had been making such a noise for the last three years, who from his narrow cell was agitating whole empires. In the midst of the orator's discourse, a portion of the exterior walls gave way with a loud crash; terror seized upon the audience, who rose to fly tumultuously, and were breaking the windows, in order to escape what they regarded as imminent death. Luther remained firm and unmoved in his pulpit; he made a sign, which the crowd at once obeyed, and paused in their flight, to collect his words. 'My brethren,' said he, with a reassuring smile, 'see you not that this is merely the hand of the

permits himself to enjoy the pleasures of life. In society he is gay, jocund, and unembarrassed; and preserves a perfect serenity of countenance, despite the atrocious menaces of his adversaries. It is difficult to believe that this man could undertake such great things without Divine protection. The only reproach that almost everybody joins in making against him, is, that he is too caustic in his replies—hesitating at no bitterness of expression when he is angry."

We are indebted to Luther himself for a fine narrative of what took place at the diet—a narrative in all essential points conformable with that which has been given of it by his enemies:—

"The herald summoned me on the Tuesday in Holy Week, and brought me safe-conducts from the emperor, and from several princes. On the very next day, Wednesday, these safe conducts were, in effect, violated at Worms, where they condemned and burned my writings. Intelligence of this

lemon who desires to prevent you from hearing the word of God, which I nnounce to you. Remain where you are: Christ is with us and for us.' And at once, says the narrator, Daniel Gretzer, the whole throng turned ack, and came still nearer the pulpit to listen to the divine word.

At Eisenach, his dear Eisenach, where he paused for awhile, with tears n his eyes, beneath the window of the worthy Cotta, Luther was on the oint of arresting his journey, the pains in his stomach caused him such uffering. After awhile, however, they diminished in their intensity, and he ontinued on his way. At Frankfort on the Maine, which he reached April 4, he blessed two students whom Wilhem Nesse presented to him.

On the road, he received from a priest of Naumburg the portrait of Savonarola, with a letter exhorting him to persevere for the glory of God. Luther affectionately kissed the portrait. (He retained through life a great eneration for Savonarola, whom he regarded as a martyr whom God had rmed with the sword of the faith. See his *Werke*, Halle, xiv. 224, and the *Tischreden*, passim.) The procession advanced but slowly. It was from Frankfort that his friends at home received their first news of him, in a etter to Spalatin: 'We are proceeding on, my dear friend,' he says, 'notwithstanding the physical sufferings with which Satan has afflicted me, in rder to delay my progress; for you must know, all the way from Weimar o this place, I have undergone greater pain than I ever experienced before. But Christ lives, and I will go to Worms, to brave the gates of hell and the owers of the air.

The party stopped at Oppenheim to take some repose. Luther might asily have escaped, for Sturm, the herald, left him altogether at his own isposal. His companions advised him to flee:

'Flee!' exclaimed Luther, 'oh, no! I will go on; I will enter the town n the name of Jesus Christ.'

At Pfifflingheim, near Worms, Luther saw a peasant planting elms by he wayside. 'Give me one of them,' said he, 'and I will place it in the

reached me when I was at Worms. The condemnation, in fact, was already published in every town, so that the herald himself asked me whether I still intended to repair to Worms.

"Though, in truth, I was physically fearful and trembling, I replied to him—'I will repair thither, though I should find there as many devils as there are tiles on the house tops.' When I arrived at Oppenheim, near Worms, Master Bucer came to see me, and tried to dissuade me from entering the city. He told me that Glapion, the emperor's confessor had been to him, and had entreated him to warn me not to go to Worms; for that if I did, I should be burned. I should do well, he added, to stop in the neighbourhood, at Franz Von Sickengen's, who would be very glad to entertain me.

"The wretches did this for the purpose of preventing me from making my appearance within the time prescribed; they knew that if I delayed only three more days, my safe-conduct would have been no longer available, and then they

earth: God grant my doctrine may flourish as the branches of this tree will doubtless flourish.' The tree did flourish, and beneath its shade have been laid, from time to time, the bodies of enthusiastic Lutherans, whose dying breath had directed they should be buried near the Reformer's Elm.

The tree having been struck with lightning in 1811, was cut down by the remorseless owner.

On the 16th, Luther came in sight of Worms; and at once on beholding its old bell towers, he arose in his chariot, and began to sing the hymn of which, it is said, he had improvised the words and the music two days before, at Oppenheim, the *Marseillaise* of the Reformation, his—

"Ein feste Burg ist unser Gott."[1]

Leffler, the duke of Bavaria's jester, was in waiting for the Doctor at the gate of Worms, holding in one hand a cross, and in the other a lighted taper, which he had borrowed from the altar of a neighbouring church. On the approach of the monk, the jester gravely preceded him into the choir, walking backwards, exclaiming with sonorous voice: *Ecce advenit quem expectamus in tenebris.* The partizans of Luther smiled, saying to one another: 'Children and fools tell the truth.'

An eye-witness, Veit Von Warbeck, gives the following account, in a letter to the Elector John, of Luther's entrance into Worms:—

"'This day, 16th April, Luther arrived at Worms, accompanied by a brother of his order, John Pezenstein, d'Amsdorf, and a noble Dane Suaven. Before the car marched the imperial herald, in full dress, the eagle in his hand. Justus Jonas and his servant came next after the car A great number of men had preceded the monk, Bernard Von Herschfeldt John Scholte, Albert Von Lendenau, &c., &c., all on horseback. At ten, he made his entry into the city, and several thousands of the citizens, who ac-

[1] See Appendix, No. VI.

would have shut the gates in my face, and, without hearing what I had to say, have arbitrarily condemned me. I went on, then, in the purity of my heart, and on coming within sight of the city, at once sent forward word to Spalatin that I had arrived, and desired to know where I was to lodge. All were astonished at hearing of my near approach; for it had been generally imagined that, a victim to the trick sought to be practised on me, my terrors would have kept me away.

Two nobles, the seigneur Von Hirschfeldt and John Schott, came to me by order of the elector, and took me to the house in which they were staying. No prince came at the time to see me, but several counts and other nobles did, who gazed at me fixedly. These were they who had presented to his majesty the four hundred articles against ecclesiastical abuses, praying that they might be reformed, and intimating that they would take the remedy into their own hands if need were. They had all been freed by my gospel!"[1]

companied him to his lodgings, the next house to the Swan; where several town councillors alighted with him: Frederic Thunau, Philip d'Alitsch, and field-marshal Ulrich Von Pappenheim.'

Luther passed nearly the whole night at his window, sometimes meditating with earnestly upcast eyes, sometimes breathing the air of his hymn upon his flute.

He was summoned early the next morning to appear before the diet. On the departure of the herald, he fell on his knees and sent forth a prayer, of which Mathesius has preserved the following fragments:

"God, God, O my God! come thou to my aid, and protect my cause and thine against the wisdom of the world. Grant me this prayer, which thou alone canst grant. It is thy cause, O my God, and not mine; it is not for me, but for thee to defend me against the great ones of the earth. It is thy cause, the cause of justice and of eternity. God of all time, come to my aid, that aid which none among men can afford me. Flesh is flesh; man a poor weak, failing, faltering creature. O my God, hast thou not ears? Dost thou not hear me? Art thou dead? No, thou canst not die. Then, O my God, aid me in the name of thy well-beloved Son, Jesus Christ, my strength and my help, my citadel and my rampart. Where art thou, O my God, where art thou? Come, come! I am ready to give up my life as 'twere a lamb. It is the cause of justice—it is thy cause, and I will not separate myself from thee. The world cannot prevail, and were it given up to even a greater legion of devils, even though the work of thy hands were to give way and the earth open its abysses before me, I remain firm: my soul is thine, and is thine, and with thee to all eternity. Amen. O my God, aid me. Amen."—Audin.

[1] "Each of the electors of the empire, on setting out for Worms, took with him a copy of the Appeal which Luther had published and distributed

"The pope had written to the emperor desiring him not to observe the safe-conduct. The bishops urged his majesty to comply with the pope's request, but the prince and the states would not listen to it; for such conduct would have excited a great disturbance. All this brought me still more prominently into general notice,[1] and my enemies might well have been more afraid of me than I was of them. The landgrave of Hesse, still a young man at that time, desired to have a conference with me, came to my lodgings, and after a long interview said, on going away: 'Dear doctor, if you be in the right, as I think you are, God will aid you.'[2]

"On my arrival, I had written to Glapion, the emperor's confessor, entreating him to come and see me at his first leisure; but he refused, saying it would be useless for him to do so.

"I was then cited, and appeared before the whole council of the imperial diet in the town hall, where the emperor, the electors, and the princes, were assembled.[3] Dr. Eck,[4] official of the archbishop of Treves, opened the business by saying to me, first in Latin, and then in German:

"'Martin Luther, his sacred and invincible majesty, with the advice of the states of the empire, has summoned you hither, that you may reply to the two questions I am now

To the Emperor and to the German nobility. Accordingly, when the question was brought forward of the subsidies which the Emperor demanded on his going to Rome to be crowned by the pope, the states, for the first time, in granting him the troops he required, stipulated, that, while the nomination of the colonels should remain in his hands—the colonels, however, were to be, of necessity, Germans—the choice of the captains, who were also to be Germans, should belong to the respective squadrons. The national spirit, excited by the manifesto of Luther, thus speedily gave expression to its hatred of the foreign power which he had succeeded in rendering odious to it. And his Tyrtæan hymn as effectually roused the nobility: had the emperor but given the word, the whole body would have sounded to horse, and have marched over the Alps to combat Rome, to the chorus of Luther's war-song."—AUDIN.

[1] See Appendix VII.

[2] The landgrave came to consult Luther upon a curious point: whether a young woman might quit an elderly husband for a more juvenile spouse. Luther smiled at this proposition, and said, "Dear master, I never taught anything of the sort, nor may such things be."—LUTHER'S *Werke*, Halle, xv. 227.

[3] There were present at the diet, besides the emperor, six electors, an archduke, two landgraves, five margraves, twenty-seven dukes, and a great number of counts, archbishops, bishops, &c.; in all 206 persons.—LUTHER'S *Werke*, ix. 104.

[5] Not the theologian of Ingoldstadt, but the jurist Eck.—AUDIN.

about to put to you: do you acknowledge yourself the author of the writings published in your name, and which are here before me, and will you consent to retract certain of the doctrines which are therein inculcated?' 'I think the books are mine,' replied I. But immediately, Dr. Jerome Schurff added: 'Let the titles of the works be read.' When they had read the titles, I said: 'Yes, the books are mine.'

"Then he asked me: 'Will you retract the doctrines therein?' I replied: 'Gracious emperor,—as to the question whether I will retract the opinions I have given forth, a question of faith in which are directly interested my own eternal salvation, and the free enunciation of the Divine Word—that word which knows no master either on earth or in heaven, and which we are all bound to adore, be we as great as we may—it would be rash and dangerous for me to reply to such a question, until I had meditated thereupon in silence and retreat, least I incur the anger of our Lord and Saviour Jesus Christ, who has said, *He who shall deny me before men, I will deny him before my Father which is in heaven.* I therefore entreat your sacred majesty to grant me the time necessary to enable me to reply with full knowledge of the point at issue, and without fear of blaspheming the word of God, or endangering the salvation of my own soul.'[1] They gave me till the next day at the same hour.

"The following morning I was sent for by the bishops and others who were directed to confer with me, and endeavour to induce me to retract. I said to them: 'The Word of God is not my word: I therefore cannot abandon it. But in all things short of that, I am ready to be docile and obedient.' The margrave Joachim then interposed, and said: 'Sir doctor, as I understand it, your desire is to listen to counsel and to instruction on all points that do not trench upon the Word?' 'Yes,' I replied, 'that is my desire.'

"Then they told me that I ought to place myself entirely in the hands of his majesty, but I said, I could not consent to this. They asked me, whether they were not themselves

[1] "At these words there was manifested no slight surprise on the part of most of those present; on that of the persons who believed Luther inspired, more especially so. The Spaniards smiled, the nuncios whispered, the catholic theologians shook their heads. The emperor said on one side, "This man, at all events, wont make a heretic of me."—AUDIN.

Christians, and entitled to have a voice in deciding the questions between us, as well as I? Whereunto I answered, 'That I was ready to accept their opinions in all points which did not offend against the Word, but that from the Word I would not depart,' repeating, that as it was not my own I could not abandon it. They insisted that I ought to rely upon them, and have full confidence that they would decide rightly. 'I am not,' rejoined I, 'by any means disposed to place my trust in men who have already condemned me without a hearing, although under safe-conduct. But to show you my zeal and sincerity, I tell you what I will do; act with me as you please; I consent to renounce my safe-conduct, and to place it unreservedly in your hands.' At this my lord Frederic de Feilitsch observed, 'Truly this is saying quite enough, or indeed, too much.'

"By and by they said: 'Will you, at all events, abandon some of the articles?' I replied: 'In the name of God I will not defend for a moment any articles that are opposed to the Scripture.' Hereupon two bishops slipped out, and went and told the emperor I was retracting. At this a message came to me, asking whether I really consented to place myself in the hands of the emperor and of the diet? I answered: that I had consented to nothing of the sort, and should never consent to it. So I went on, resisting, alone, the attempts of them all, for Dr. Schurff and my other friends had become angry with me for my obstinacy, as they called it. Some of my disputants said to me, that if I would come over to them, they would in return, give up to me and abandon the articles which had been condemned at the council of Constance. To all which I simply replied: 'Here is my body, here my life: do with them as you will.'

"Then Cochlæus came up to me, and said: 'Martin, if thou wilt renounce the safe-conduct, I will dispute with thee.' I, in my simplicity and good faith, would have consented to this, but Dr. Jerome Schurff replied, with an ironical laugh: 'Ay, truly, that were a good idea—that were a fair bargain, i'faith; you must needs think the doctor a fool.' So I refused to give up the safe-conduct. Several worthy friends of mine, who were present, had already, at the bare mention of the proposition, advanced towards me, as if to protect me, exclaiming to Cochlæus: 'What, you would carry him off a prisoner, then! That shall not be.'

"Meantime, there came a doctor of the retinue of the margrave of Baden, who essayed to move me by fine flourishes: I ought, he said, to do a very great deal, to grant a very great deal, for the love of charity, that peace and union might continue, and no tumult arise. All, he urged, were called upon to obey his imperial majesty, as being the supreme authority; we ought all to avoid creating unseemly disturbances, and therefore, he concluded, I ought to retract. 'I will,' replied I, 'with all my heart, in the name of charity, do all things, and obey in all things, which are not opposed to the faith and honour of Christ.'

"Then the chancellor of Treves said to me: 'Martin, thou art disobedient to his imperial majesty; wherefore depart hence, under the safe-conduct which has been given thee.' I answered: 'It has been as it pleased the Lord it should be. And you,' I added, 'do all of you, on your part, consider well the position in which you are.' And so I departed, in singleness of heart, without remarking or comprehending their machinations.

"Soon afterwards they put in force their cruel edict—that ban, which gave all ill men an opportunity of taking vengeance with impunity on their personal enemies, under the pretext of their being Lutheran heretics; and yet, in the end, the tyrants found themselves under the necessity of recalling what they had done.

"And this is what happened to me at Worms, where I had no other aid than the Holy Spirit."

We find other curious details in a more extended narrative of the conference at Worms—written immediately afterwards, by Luther himself, in all probability, though he speaks in the third person:

"The day after, at four in the afternoon, the imperial chamberlain, and the herald who had accompanied him from Wittemberg, came to him at his inn, The Court of Germany, and conducted him to the town hall, along bye-ways, in order to avoid the crowds which had assembled in the leading streets. Notwithstanding this precaution, there were numbers collected at the gates of the town hall, and who essayed to enter with him, but the guards kept them back. Many persons had got upon the roofs of houses to see Dr. Martin. As he proceeded up the hall, several noblemen successively addressed to him words of encouragement. 'Be bold,' said they, 'and fear not those who can kill the body, but are powerless against the soul.' 'Monk,' said the famous captain George Freundesberg, putting his hand cheeringly on Martin's shoulder, 'take heed what thou doest; thou art adventuring on a more perilous path than any of us have ever trod. But if thou art in the right, God will not abandon thee.' Duke John of Weimar had previously supplied the doctor with the money for his journey.

" Luther made his answers in Latin and German.

" The official opened the proceedings: 'Martin Luther, yesterday you acknowledged the books published in your name. Do you retract those books, or not? This is the question we before addressed to you, and which you declined answering, under the pretext that it was a question of faith we were putting, and that you had need of time for reflection ere you replied, though a theologian like you must know very well that a Christian should always be ready to answer any questions touching his faith. Explain yourself now. Will you defend all your writings, or disavow some of them?'

" 'Most serene emperor,' replied Martin, 'illustrious princes, most clement lords, I am again before you, appearing at the hour appointed, and supplicating you to listen to me with benevolence and equity. If in my statement or my replies, I should omit to give you the titles of honour due to you, if I offend against the etiquette of courts, you will, I trust, pardon me, for I have never been accustomed to palaces; I am nothing but a poor monk, the inmate of a humble cell, who have, I assure you, never preached aught, never written aught, but in singleness of heart, and for the glory of my God, and the honour of the Gospel.

" 'Most serene emperor, and princes of the empire: to the two questions put to me yesterday, whether I acknowledged as mine the books published in my name, and whether I persevered in defending them, I answer now, as before, and as I will answer to the hour of my death—Yes, the books which have been published by me, or which have been published in my name, are mine; I acknowledge them, I avow them, and will always avow them, so long as they remain the same as I sent them forth, undistorted by malice, knavery, or mistaken prudence. I acknowledge, further, that whatever I have written, was first matured in my mind by earnest thought and meditation.

" 'Before replying to the second question, I entreat your majesty and the states of the empire to consider that my writings do not all treat of the same matter. Some of them are preceptive, destined for the edification of the faithful, for the advancement of piety, for the amelioration of manners; yet the bull, while admitting the innocence and advantage of such treatises, condemns these equally with the rest. If I were to disavow them, what practically should I be doing? Proscribing a mode of instruction which every Christian sanctions, and thus putting myself in opposition to the universal voice of the faithful.

" 'There is another class of writings in which I attack the papacy and the belief of the papists, as monstrosities, involving the ruin of sound doctrine and of men's souls. None can deny, who will listen to the cries and the evidences of the conscience within, that the pope's decretals have thrown utter disorder into Christianity, have surprised, imprisoned, tortured the faith of the faithful, have devoured as a prey this noble Germany, for that she has protested aloud against lying tales, contrary to the gospel and to the opinions of the fathers. If I were to retract these writings, I should lend additional strength and audacity to the Roman tyranny, I should open the floodgates to the torrent of impiety, making for it a breach by which it would rush in and overwhelm the Christian world. My recantation would only serve to extend and strengthen the reign of iniquity; more especially when it should be known that it was solely by order of your majesty, and your serene highnesses, that I had made such retractation.

" 'Finally, there is another class of works, which have been published under my name; I speak of those books of polemics, which I have written against some of my adversaries, advocates of the Roman tyranny. I have no hesitation in admitting that in these I have shown greater violence than befitted a man of my calling; I do not set up for a saint, I do not say that my conduct has been above reproach; my dispute is not about that conduct, but about the doctrine of Christ. But though I have been violent overmuch at times, I cannot consent to disavow these writings, because Rome would make use of the disavowal, to extend her kingdom and oppress men's souls.

" 'A man, and not God, I would not seek to shield my books under any other patronage than that with which Christ covered his doctrine. When interrogated before the high-priest, as to what he taught, and his cheek buffeted by a varlet: "If I have spoken evil," he said, "bear witness of the evil." If the Lord Jesus, who knew himself incapable of sin, did not reject the testimony which the vilest mouths might give respecting his Divine Word, ought not I, scum of the earth that I am, and capable only of sin, to solicit the examination of my doctrines?

" 'I therefore, in the name of the living God, entreat your sacred majesty, your illustrious highnesses, every human creature, to come and depose what they can against me, and, with the Prophets and the Gospel in their hands, to convict me, if they can, of error. I stand here, ready, if any one can prove me to have written falsely, to retract my errors, and to throw my books into the fire with my own hand.

" 'Be assured I have well weighed the dangers, the pains, the strife, and hatred that my doctrine will bring into the world; and I rejoice to see the word of God producing, as its first fruits, discord and dissension, for such is the lot and destiny of the Divine Word, as our Lord has set forth: *I came not to send peace, but a sword, to set the son against his father.*

" 'Forget not that God is admirable and terrible in all his counsels; and beware, least, if you condemn the Divine Word, that Word send forth upon you a deluge of ills, and the reign of our noble young emperor, upon whom, next to God, repose all our hopes, be speedily and sorely troubled.

" 'I might here, in examples drawn from Holy Writ, exhibit to you Pharaoh, king of Egypt, and the kings of Israel, ruined from seeking to reign at first by peace, and by what they termed wisdom. For God confounds the hypocrite in his hypocrisy, and overturns mountains ere they know of their fall: fear is the work of God.

" 'I seek not herein to offer advice to your high and mighty understandings; but I owed this testimony of a loving heart to my native Germany. I conclude with recommending myself to your sacred majesty and your highnesses, humbly entreating you not to suffer my enemies to indulge their hatred against me under your sanction. I have said what I had to say.'

"Then the emperor's orator hastily rose, and exclaimed that Luther had not directed himself to the question; that what the assembly had to do was not to listen to a discussion whether councils had decided right or wrong, but to ascertain from Luther whether he would retract; this was the question to which he had to reply: ay or no.

"Thereupon Luther resumed in these words:

"'Since then your imperial majesty and your highnesses demand a simple answer, I will give you one; brief and simple, but deprived of neither its teeth nor its horns. Unless I am convicted of error by the testimony of Scripture, or by manifest evidence (for I put no faith in the mere authority of the pope, or of councils, which have often been mistaken, and which have often contradicted one another, recognising, as I do, no other guide than the Bible, the Word of God), I cannot and will not retract, for we must never act contrary to our conscience.

"'Such is my profession of faith, and expect none other from me. I have done: God help me! Amen!'

"The states retired to deliberate; on their return, the official thus addressed Luther:

"'Martin, you have assumed a tone which becomes not a man of your condition; and you have not answered the questions put to you. Doubtless you have written some pieces which are in no way liable to censure; and had you retracted those works of yours, in which you inculcate your mischievous errors, his majesty, in his infinite goodness, would not have permitted any proceedings to be taken against those which contain only right doctrine. You have resuscitated dogmas which have been distinctly condemned by the council of Constance, and you demand to be convicted thereupon out of the Scriptures. But if every one were at liberty to bring back into discussion points which for ages have been settled by the church and by councils, nothing would be certain and fixed, doctrine or dogma, and there would be no belief which men must adhere to under pain of eternal damnation. You, for instance, who to-day reject the authority of the council of Constance, to-morrow may, in like manner, proscribe all councils together, and next the fathers, and the doctors; and there would remain no authority whatever, but that individual word which you call to witness, and which we also invoke. His majesty, therefore, once more demands a simple and precise answer, affirmative or negative; will you defend all your principles, as catholic principles, or are there any of them which you are prepared to retract?'

"Then Luther besought the emperor not to permit him to be thus called upon to belie his conscience, which was bound up with the sacred writings. They had required of him a categorical answer, and he had given one. He could only repeat what he had already declared: that unless they proved to him by irresistible arguments that he was in the wrong, he would not go back a single inch; that what the councils had laid down, was no article of faith; that councils had often erred, had often contradicted each other, and that their testimony, consequently, was not convincing; and that he could not disavow what was written in the inspired books.

"The official sharply observed, that Luther could not show the councils to have erred.

"Martin said he would undertake to do so at any time that might be assigned him.

"By this time, the evening drawing in, it grew dark, and the diet arose. When the man of God left the town hall to return to his lodging, he was followed and insulted by some Spaniards.[1]

"Next day, the emperor[2] sent for the electors and states to discuss with them the form of the imperial ban against Luther and his adherents. The safe-conduct, however, was retained in it.[3]

[1] "Martin had spoken more than two hours, repeating in Latin what he first said in German. The perspiration rolled down his face, his face was haggard, and he needed rest. On his return to his lodgings, he found on the table a small can full of Eimbeck beer, that had been sent him. He emptied it at one draught. On putting down the can, he asked: 'Who made me this present?' 'Duke Eric of Brunswick,' replied Amsdorf. 'Ah,' said Luther, 'as duke Eric has this day thought of me, so may God one day think of him.'"—AUDIN.

[2] Spalatin relates in his Annals (50), that after Luther's second appearance, the elector of Saxony, on his return from the town hall, sent for him and said: "Doctor Martin has spoken well before the diet, but somewhat too boldly."

[3] "The imperial rescript was in the following terms: 'Our ancestors, kings of Spain, archdukes of Austria, and dukes of Burgundy, protectors and

"Meantime, Luther was visited by a great number of princes, counts, barons, prelates, and other persons of distinction, lay and ecclesiastical. ['The doctor's little room,' writes Spalatin, 'could not contain all the visitors who presented themselves. I saw among them duke William of Brunswick, the landgrave, Philip of Hesse, count Wilhelm of Henneburg, the elector Frederick, and many others.']

"On the Wednesday following, (eight days after his first appearance before the diet,) he was requested by the archbishop of Treves to wait upon him. Luther accordingly presented himself before that prelate, attended by the imperial herald, and accompanied by the friends who had followed him from Saxony and Thuringia. In the apartment of the archbishop they found assembled Joachim of Brandenburg, the elector George, the bishops of Augsburg and Brandenburg, count George, grand-master of the Teutonic order; John Boeck of Strasburg, and Dr. Peutinger. Veh, (Vehus,) chancellor of Baden, opened the proceedings, in the name of those present, by declaring that they had not invited Luther there with any view to polemical discussion, but out of a pure feeling of charity and kindness towards him.

"Then Veh commenced a long harangue on the obedience due to the church and its decisions, to the councils and their decrees. He maintained that the church, like any other power, had its constitutions which might be modified according to the requirements of the particular nations to which they were applied, the diversity of manners, of climate, of

lefenders of the catholic faith, have preserved its inviolability with their swords and with their blood, and have ever taken care that the decrees of the church should meet with that obedience which they are entitled to. We shall not lose sight of these examples, we shall walk in the footsteps of our ancestors, and defend, with all our might, that faith which we have received as a heritage. And, therefore, a monk having dared to come forward and assail at once the dogmas of the church and the head of the Catholic communion, persisting obstinately in the errors into which he has fallen, and refusing to retract, we have deemed it essential to oppose ourselves to the further progress of these disorders, even though at the peril of our life, of our dignities, of the fortune of the empire, in order that Germany may not sully herself with the crime of perjury. We will not again hear Martin Luther, who has given ourself and the diet such manifest proofs of his inflexible obstinacy; and we order him to depart hence under the faith of the imperial safeguard we have given him, prohibiting him at the same time from preaching or exciting any commotion on his way."—AUDIN.

epochs; and that herein lay the apparent contradictions which Luther had denounced as existing in the internal system of the church. These contradictions, in fact, only proved more emphatically the religious care with which the church regulated its spiritual administration, and in no degree affected the integrity of the catholic dogma. That dogma was yesterday what it is to-day, and what it will continue to be till the end of time. He called Luther's attention to the disturbances to which his innovations were everywhere giving rise. 'See,' said he, 'your book, *De Libertate Christiana:* what does that teach men? To throw off every species of subjection—to erect disobedience into a maxim. We no longer live at a time when every child of the Christian family had but one heart and one soul; when the precept was one, like the society; when the rule was one, like the precept. It became necessary to modify all this, when time itself had modified society; but without the catholic dogma ever receiving the slightest prejudice. I am quite aware, Martin,' he added, 'that many of your writings breathe a sweet odour of piety; but we have judged the general spirit of your works, as we judge a tree, not by its flowers, but by its fruits. The advice given you by the states of the empire is given in a desire of peace, with all good feeling towards yourself. Those states were established by God to watch over the security of a people whose tranquillity your doctrines are calculated to disturb. To resist them is to resist God. Doubtless, it is better to obey God than to obey man; but do you think that we, any more than yourself, are deaf to his word, or have not meditated thereupon?'

"Luther, after having expressed his thanks for the peaceful and charitable expressions made use of towards him, proceeded to answer what Veh had said respecting the authority of councils. He maintained that the council of Constance had erred in condemning this proposition of John Huss: '*Tantum una est sancta, universalis ecclesia quæ est numerus prædestinatorum.*' 'No retractation!' he said, in conclusion, with an animated and firm voice: "you shall have my blood, my life, rather than a single word of retractation; for it is better to obey God than to obey man. It is no fault of mine that this matter creates confusion among you. I cannot prevent the word of Christ becoming a stumbling block to men. If the sheep of the good Shepherd were fed upon evangelical marrow, faith would live, and our spiritual masters would be honest and trustworthy. I know well that we must pay obedience to the civil magistrate, even though he be not a man after God's own heart; and I am quite ready to pay that obedience in all things that does not shut out the Word of God.

"Luther was then about to take his leave, but he was told to remain, and Veh pressingly urged upon him his previous arguments, and conjured him to submit his writings to the decision of the princes and states of the empire.

"Luther gently replied: 'I would fain have it understood, that I do not decline the judgment of the emperor and of the states; but the word of God, on which I rely, is to my eyes so clear, that I cannot retract what I have said, until a still more luminous authority is opposed to that Word. St. Paul has said—*If an angel from heaven preach any other gospel to you, let him be accursed;* and I say to you, do not offer violence to my conscience, which is chained up with the Scripture.'

"The meeting then broke up; but the archbishop of Treves retained Luther, and went with him into another apartment. Jerome Schurff and Nicholas followed. John Eck, and Cochlæus, dean of the church of the Holy Virgin at Francfort, were already in the room. Eck addressed Luther:—

"'Martin,' said he, 'there is no one of the heresies which have torn the bosom of the church, which has not derived its origin from the various interpretation of the Scripture. The Bible itself is the arsenal whence each innovator has drawn his deceptive arguments. It was with biblical texts that Pelagius and Arius maintained their doctrines. Arius, for instance, found the negation of the eternity of the Word—an eternity which you admit, in this verse of the New Testament —*Joseph knew not his wife till she had brought forth her first-born son;* and he said, in the same way that you say, that this passage enchained him. When the fathers of the council of Constance condemned this proposition of John Huss—*The church of Jesus Christ is only the community of the elect*, they condemned an error; for the church, like a good mother, embraces within her arms all who bear the name of Christian, all who are called to enjoy the celestial beatitude.' Luther replied, reproducing all the arguments he had before made use of. Cochlæus took him by both hands, and conjured him to restore peace to the church. Luther was inflexible, and so they separated.

"In the evening, the archbishop of Treves sent word to Luther that, by order of the emperor, his safe-conduct had been extended two days, and requested him to wait upon him the next day, to have another conference.

"Peutinger and the chancellor of Baden came to see Luther next morning, and renewed the conversation of the preceding evening, using every argument they could devise to induce him to submit his writings to the judgment of the emperor.

"'Yes,' said Luther, 'I am ready to do so, if you will come and controvert me, Bible in hand; otherwise, not. God has said by the mouth of the prophet-king: *Put not your trust in princes, for in them there is no salvation;* and, by the mouth of Jeremiah, *Cursed be he who putteth his trust in man.*' They urged him still more pressingly: 'I will submit everything to the judgment of man,' said he, 'except the Word of God.' They then left him, saying they would return in the evening, when they hoped to find him in a better frame of mind. They came; but it was all in vain.

"There was another interview with the archbishop. In this last conference, the prelate said: 'But, dear doctor, if you will not submit this matter to the diet, or to a council, by what means shall we avert the troubles which menace the church? What remedies can we apply?'

"Luther replied: 'Nothing better can be said in this case than was said, according to St. Paul, by Gamaliel: *If this work be of men, it will come to nought.* The emperor and the states may write to the pope thus: if the work of Luther is not an inspiration from on high, in three years it will be no more spoken of.'

"The archbishop persisted: 'Suppose,' said he, 'that we made from your books faithful extracts of articles we object to: would you submit them to a council?'

"'Provided they were none of those,' returned Luther, 'which the council of Constance has already condemned.'

"'But if they were——'

"'Then,' said Luther, 'I would not consent to submit them to a council, for I am certain that the decrees of that council condemned the truth: I would rather lose my head than abandon the divine word. In what concerns the word of God and the faith, every Christian is as good a judge for himself as the pope can be for him; for each man must live and die according to that faith. The word of God is the common heritage of the whole Christian world, each member of which is competent to explain it. The passage of St. Paul (1 Corinthians, xiv.): *If anything be revealed to another that sitteth by, let the first hold his peace*, proves clearly that the master must follow the disciple, if the latter understand the word of God better than he himself does.'

"And thus ended the conference.

"Soon after this, the official sent for Luther, and in the presence of the arch-chancellor, read to him the imperial sentence.

"'Luther,' he added, 'since you have not chosen to listen to the counsels of his majesty and of the states of the empire, and to confess your errors, it is now for the emperor to act. By his order, I give you twenty days, wherein to return to Wittemberg, secure under the imperial safe-conduct, provided that on your way you excite no disorders by preaching or otherwise.'

"As the official concluded, Sturm, the herald, inclined his staff, in token of respect.

"Luther bowed, and said: 'Be it as the Lord pleases; blessed be the name of the Lord.' He added the expression of his warm gratitude towards the emperor personally, and towards his ministers, and the states of the empire, for whom, he affirmed, with his hand on his heart, he was ready to sacrifice life, honour, reputation—all, except the word of God.

"Next day, 26th April, after a collation given him by his friends, the doctor resumed the route to Wittemberg.[1]

[1] "The Catholic himself," observes M. Audin, "if he will for a moment orget the sectary in the man, cannot but contemplate with admiration, in his grand historical scene of the diet of Worms, that black-robed monk, tanding face to face with, and bearding the throng of princes and nobles in heir steel panoply, their gauntleted hands grasping the massive handles of heir swords; and his heart will swell within him as he hears the clear, firm oice of the obscure brother Martin defying all the powers of the earth. hat youthful emperor, on whose head rests all the interests of Germany, nd whom a mere monk stops short at every turn of the conference; those rave priests, Amsdorf and Justus, pressing, full of love and enthusiasm, lose up to their master, and ready to defend him with their arms, if need e, as well as with their learned voices; that populace, in whose eyes the ugustin was all wonderful, as the latest novelty of the time; that old

"On his arrival at Freyburg, Luther wrote two letters one to the emperor, the other to the electors and states assembled at Worms. In the first, he expresses his regret a having found himself under the necessity of disobeying hi majesty: 'But,' says he, 'God and his word are above man. He laments, further, that he had not been able to obtain discussion of the evidences he had collected from Scripture adding that he was ready to present himself before any othe assembly that might be convened for the purpose, and t submit himself in all things without exception, provided th word of God received no detriment. The letter to the elec tors and states is written in the same spirit.[1]

To Spalatin (in a letter, dated 14th May) he says: 'Yo would hardly believe the civility with which I was receive by the abbot of Hirschfeldt.[2] He sent forward his chancello and his treasurer a full mile on the road to meet us, and h himself came to receive us at a short distance from his castl attended by a troop of cavaliers, who escorted us into th town. The senate received us at the great gate. The ab bot entertained us splendidly in his monastery, and assigne me his own bed to sleep in. On the fifth day, they absolutel forced me to preach in the morning, though I represented t them that they ran a risk of losing their privileges, shoul the imperialist party choose to treat this as a violation of m undertaking not to preach up my doctrines on the way. Bu then, I added, that I had never pledged myself to chain u the word of God; nor will I.

"'I preached also at Eisenach, in presence of the ministe who was in a great fright, and of a notary and his witnesse

Frundsburg, who addresses the pilgrim monk as though he were an arm warrior; that archbishop, his venerable head whitened in the service of Go conspicuous among the steel casques glittering in the sun's rays; that Vehu eloquent by mere force of logic; those warm, excitable southern faces, fu of restless energy, contrasting with the motionless features of the Germa spectators: all this forms a magnificent spectacle. At each word that fal from the monk's lips, the heart quails fearfully within one at the thought th the emperor is there, listening intently to all that is said, and that the mere gesture from him would suffice to crush the rebellious brother to the eartl All honour for his moderation be to that young crowned head, in whom h age would have served to excuse even a violent outbreak, and who had the on either hand, all around him, instruments ready at a word, at a nod, fulfil the dictates of his anger."

[1] Luther, Werke, ix. 107. [2] Crato Milius.

who formally protested against what I was doing, but excused themselves privately to me on the ground that, otherwise they dreaded the resentment of their tyrants. So, very likely, you will hear it said at Worms, that I have broken my faith; but I have not broken it. To chain up the word of God is a condition it is not in my power to enter into.

"Our friends met us on foot a little way out of Eisenach, and accompanied us into the town, in the evening. Our companions had set out in the morning with Jerome.

"As to myself, I was proceeding to rejoin my relations through the forest, and was on my way to Walterhausen, when near the fortress of Altenstein, I was taken prisoner. Amsdorf no doubt knew that it was arranged to seize me, but he is not aware to what place they carried me.

"My brother, who saw the horsemen coming up,[1] jumped out of the carriage, and, without saying a word, ran off through the wood, and, as I am told, reached Walterhausen in the evening. As for me, the horsemen took off my robe, and put me on a military garb, desiring me to let my hair and beard grow, and meanwhile put me on a false beard. You would scarcely recognise me; indeed, I hardly knew myself. However, here I am, living *in libertate Christianâ*, free from the chains of the tyrants."

When taken to the castle of Wartburg, Luther was not at all certain to whom it was he owed the pleasant and honourable captivity in which he found himself. He had sent away the imperial herald as soon as they had got a few leagues from Worms, and his enemies have thence concluded that he was aware of the contemplated proceedings; but it fully appears, from his own correspondence, that he was not. Meantime a cry of grief arose throughout Germany. It was believed that he had perished, and the pope and the emperor were accused of his death. In reality, it was the elector of Saxony, Luther's patron, who, alarmed at the imperial sentence fulminated against the reformer,[2] and at once incapable

[1] Their names were Hans Von Berletsch and Burcard Von Hund.—AUDIN.

[2] The edict, drawn up by Aleandro, and published by the emperor on the 25th May, is indeed, a severe one: it prohibits all persons, under penalty of high treason, from affording to Luther, after the 15th May, the day on which his safe-conduct expired, any aid or asylum whatever; and, on the contrary,

of openly supporting him against his enemies, or of allowing him to fall their victim, had conceived this mode of saving him from the effects of his own daring, and to gain time wherein to strengthen the party. To conceal Luther for awhile was a sure means of augmenting the public excitement in Germany, by arousing its fears for the champion of the reformed faith.

enjoins all persons to watch for and seize him, and place him in safe custody until justice shall have decided his destiny. It orders that all the Heresiarch's works, in Latin and in German, wheresoever found throughout Germany or the Low Countries, shall be burned; and it requires all the emperor's subjects to give aid and assistance to the apostolic commissioners entrusted with carrying into effect the decrees of the holy see. It menaces with severe penalties all booksellers and printers who shall publish or sell any of the monk's writings, or shall dare, in any manner, to circulate any publications calculated to bring into contempt the sovereign pontiff, the Roman church, prelates, princes, or the universities. It orders, that wheresoever any such publication, of whatever kind, image, engraving, or printed book, shall be found, it shall be forthwith torn or broken up, and burned, and its authors and publishers severely punished according to the laws. And in order that similar attacks upon religion, the holy see, the church, and dignitaries may not recur, the edict orders that, in future, no work treating of religious matters shall be published until it has been subjected to the examination of the ordinary, or of the faculty of theology of the nearest university."

'You have got to the end of the tragedy,' wrote the Spaniard, Alfonso Valderas, to his friend Piero d'Anghiera, at this juncture; 'the end, according to some—but, in my opinion, the beginning, for the Germans are exceedingly indignant against the Holy See.' The Spaniard was right; the very next day after the burning, according to the emperor's edict, of Luther's works in the public square at Worms, the booksellers of that city went about offering a number of other copies for sale from door to door, and had even the audacity to call with them at the Imperial residence.—AUDIN.

BOOK THE SECOND.

1521—1528.

CHAPTER THE FIRST.

1521—1524.

Luther's residence at the castle of Wartburg—He returns to Wittemberg without the elector's sanction—His writings against the king of England, and against princes in general.

WHILST in Worms the Roman party was furious at having allowed the audacious innovator to escape, he himself was securely looking down upon his enemies from the platform of the donjon of Wartburg. In that quiet retreat, he was at full leisure to resume his flute, to sing his German psalms, to translate his Bible, and to thunder forth against the pope and the devil.[1]

"The rumour has gone abroad," writes Luther, "that it was friends from Franconia who took me prisoner." And

[1] "At times the chatelain sent secretly for some of Luther's acquaintance, the nearest at hand, who repaired to Wartburg at night, and, rising early in the morning, assembled around the monk in one of the castle halls, and heard from his lips the words of his doctrine, returning to their homes at nightfall. Luther's table was well served, daily provided with game and with plenty of the glorious Rhine wine, the monk was always so fond of. The chatelain was courteous, attentive, respectful to his *prisoner*, who at one time felt a mistrust that he was living at the worthy man's expense: 'But after all,' he writes to Spalatin, 'I am satisfied it is the prince who is paymaster; I would not remain here another hour, if I really thought, upon reflection, that I was living at my guardian's cost. At the cost of the prince, with all my heart; for, if one must be a charge to somebody, it is well to be a charge upon princes; princes and thieves, you know, are pretty well synonymous terms. But I wish you to ascertain the precise state of the case, and let me know.'"

elsewhere: "They imagined, as I suspect, that Luther had been killed, or condemned to eternal silence, in order that the common weal might once more fall powerless beneath the weight of sophistical tyranny, the downfall of which its abettors so hated me for having commenced." He took care, however, to let his friends know that he was still alive. He writes to Spalatin (June, 1521): "I would not for the world have the letter I now send you fall by any negligence of your own, or of those about you, into the hands of our enemies. . . I wish you to get the portion of Gospel I send you herewith, copied by some careful person; it is essential that my hand should not be seen in the matter just at present."—"I had fully intended in this, my solitude, to dedicate to my host, a book on the Traditions of Men, for he has asked me to give him some information on that subject; but I have not done so, least I should thereby disclose the place of my retreat."—"It is with great difficulty I have obtained permission to send you this letter, so fearful are they of its becoming known where I am."

"The priests and the monks, who played their gambols while I was at liberty, have become so afraid since my captivity, that they themselves are beginning to modify the preposterous extravagances they were wont to send forth against me. They find they can no longer resist the pressure of the increasing crowd of questioners, and they know not in what direction to make their escape. See you not herein the arm of the Mighty One of Jacob, all that he is doing for us, while we hold our peace, while we stand aside, while we pray to him. Is not this a fulfilment of the sayings of Moses: *The Lord shall fight for you, and you shall hold your peace.* One of the fellows at Rome, has written to a Mayence hoopoe:[1] "Luther is quashed just as we wished; but the people are so excited about him, that I fear we shall run a chance of losing our lives, if we do not go in search of him, candle in hand, and bring him back."

Luther dates his letters: *from the region of the air; from the region of birds; or, from amidst the birds which sing sweetly on the branches of the tall trees, and praise God,*

[1] This description, applied to one of the dignitaries of the church, reminds one of Rabelais' marvellous birds, his *papegots*, his *evêgots*, &c.

night and day, with all their might; or, again, *from the mountain; from the Isle of Patmos.*

It was from this spot that, in a series of mournful but eloquent letters to various persons, he unfolded the sad thoughts that came over him in his solitude (*eremo meo*): "What art thou doing now, my Philip?" he writes, to Melancthon (12th May). "Prayest thou for me? As to myself, I sit gloomy all the day long, I place before my eyes the figure of the church, and I see these words of Psalm lxxxix.: *Wherefore hast thou made all men in vain.* Oh God! how horrible a form of the anger of God, is this abominable rule of the Antichrist of Rome! I hate the hardness of my heart, which does not dissolve in torrents of tears, weeping the children of my slaughtered people. There is not one among them who rises up, who puts himself in the front, for God's sake, who makes of himself a rampart for the house of Israel in this day of desolation and anger. O reign of the pope, refuse of ages! God have mercy upon us."

On the 24th May, he writes thus: "When I consider this horrible season of anger, I only ask to find in my eyes floods of tears to lament the desolation of men's souls, occasioned by this kingdom of sin and perdition. The monster has its seat in Rome, in the very midst of the church, and proclaims itself God; pontiffs adulate it, the sophists offer it incense, and there is nothing which the hypocrites refuse to do for it. Meanwhile, hell's heart is gladdened, and its immense jaws are opening wide; Satan's sport is in the perdition of souls. As to me, I sit still all day long, drinking and doing nothing. I read the Bible in Greek and in Hebrew. I shall write something in German one of these days, on the Liberty of Auricular Confession. I shall also continue the Psalter and the Commentaries, directly I receive from Wittemberg the books I need for that purpose; among other things, there is the *Magnificat*, which I have already begun." The mournful solitude in which he now found himself, brought with it a recurrence of Luther's early trials and temptations. Thus he writes to Melancthon (July 13): "Thy letter displeased me in a twofold point of view; first, because I see by it that thou bearest thy cross with impatience, that thou yieldest too much to the affections, that thou art, according to thy wont, too tender-hearted; secondly, because thou exaltest me far above my merits; thou art under sad error, in attributing to me such qualities and such virtues, as though I were a man who devoted myself to the cause of God. The high opinion thou hast of me confounds me, agonizes me, seeing myself, as I do see myself, insensible and hardened, a slave to sloth, rarely, alas, praying—unable even to send forth a groan for the church. Let me confess the horrible truth: my flesh, my flesh, my untamed flesh, burns with a devouring flame, with a flame which should only animate my spirit to good. Idleness, sluggishness, the lusts of the flesh come around me, assail me closely and fiercely. Is it because thou hast ceased to pray for me to God, that he has thus turned his face from me? It were well for thee to take my place, thou so much more richly endowed by God, so much more pleasing in his sight.

"Here have I been eight days without praying, without studying; whether from temptations of the flesh, or from some other vexations that are upon me, I know not. If things do not take a better turn with me, I will return publicly to Erfurt, and thou wilt see me there; for I must fain consult the physicians or the surgeons, whichever of them it be I need."

He was ill at this time, suffering cruel torments in the stomach. He has left us a description of his malady, but in terms so undisguised, and, sooth to say, coarse, that we may not translate them.[1] But his spiritual sufferings were even still more painful and more profound than those of his body.

"When, in 1521, on my quitting Worms, I was taken prisoner near Eisenach, and conducted to my Patmos, the castle of Wartburg, I dwelt far apart from the world in my chamber, and no one could come to me but two youths, sons of noblemen, who waited on me with my meals twice a day. Among other things, they had brought me a bag of nuts, which I had put in a chest in my sitting room. One evening, after I had retired to my chamber, which adjoined the sitting room, had put out the light, and got into bed, it seemed to me all at once that the nuts had put themselves in motion, and, jumping about in the sack, and knocking violently against each other, came to the side of my bed to make

[1] "Dominus percussit me in posteriora gravi dolore; tum dura sunt excrementa ut multa vi usque ad sudorem extrudere cogar: et quo diu tuis differo, magis durescunt; heri quarto die excrevi semel."

noises at me. However, this did not alarm me, and I went to sleep. By and by, I was wakened up, by a great noise on the stairs, which sounded as though somebody was tumbling down them a hundred barrels one after another. Yet I knew very well that the door at the bottom of the stairs was fastened with chains, and that the door itself was of iron; so that no one could enter. I rose immediately to see what it was, exclaiming: 'Is it thou?—Well, be it so!'[1] And I recommended myself to our Lord Jesus Christ, of whom it is written: *Thou hast put all things under his feet,*—Psalm viii.—and I returned to bed." — "The wife of John Berblibs came to Eisenach. She suspected where I was, and insisted upon seeing me; but the thing was impossible. To satisfy her, they removed me to another part of the castle, and allowed her to sleep in the apartment I had occupied. In the night, she heard such an uproar, that she thought there were a thousand devils in the place."[2]

On his arrival at Wartburg, Luther had found very few books there. He applied himself with ardour, as soon as he had obtained the requisite materials, to the study of Greek and Hebrew; he drew up an answer to the work of Latonus, so prolix, he calls it, and so ill written. He translated into German the Apology of Melancthon against the "blockhead theologians of Paris," adding a Commentary of his own. It was here, too, that he commenced his translation of the Bible.[3] In fact, though he speaks of himself as doing nothing, he displayed the most extraordinary activity in his Patmos, and from its height inundated Germany with his writings. "I have published," he writes, on 1st November, "a little volume against that of Catharinus on Antichrist; a treatise in German on Confession; a commentary in German on the 67th Psalm; another, also in German, on the Canticle of Mary; a third on the 37th Psalm, and a Consolation to the Church of Wittemberg. Moreover, I have in the press, a commentary in German, on the Epistles and Gospels for the year; I have just sent off a public reprimand to the bishop of Mayence, on the Idol of the Indulgences he has raised up again at Halle,[4]

[1] The antagonist here anticipated, was Satan.

[2] Tischreden, 208. [3] See Appendix VIII.

[4] The archbishop of Mayence, unconvinced by Luther's arguments, had continued the sale of indulgences in his diocese; and just before this time,

and I have finished a commentary on the gospel story of the Ten Lepers. All these writings are in German: I was born for the good of my dear Germans, and I will never cease to serve them. While I was at Wittemberg, I commenced a series of sermons to illustrate in a popular manner the Two Testaments; I had got in Genesis as far as the xxxii. chapter, and in the New Testament to John the Baptist. Here I stopped."

On the 9th September, he writes: "I am full of trembling, and my conscience troubles me, for that when at Worms, yielding to your advice and that of your friends, I allowed the spirit within me to give way, instead of showing another Elias to those idols. They should find things very different on my part, if I were once again to come in contact with them."

The affair of the archbishop of Mayence, which is referred to in the letter just quoted, deserves a more detailed mention. It is curious to observe the energy displayed by Luther in the matter, and how cavalierly he treats princes and potentates, the cardinal-archbishop, and the elector himself. Spalatin had delayed to print his pamphlet against the archbishop of Mayence. Luther wrote to him in the following terms:

"I sent you some time back, my books on the Mass, on Vows of Celibacy, on the Tyrant of Mayence. . . . Have they been intercepted, or has the messenger lost them. Did I think they had reached you, and that you kept them locked up, nothing would annoy me more. If you have them, at once lay aside your untimely caution; I will have them printed, I tell you, at Wittemberg or somewhere else. Oh, if I knew for certain that you were suppressing them, I should be perfectly furious; you would incur my severest displeasure. And to what end? You may burn the senseless paper I sent you, but you cannot extinguish the spirit that produced them.

"Don't tell me that the elector will not permit me to attack

a priest at Halle had ascended the pulpit by the prelate's direction, to urge the purchase of pardons by the public. On this occasion, however, the money raised was to be devoted, not to the erection of St. Peter's, but to the extermination of the hordes of Musselmen, who were menacing Hungary. —AUDIN.

the Mayence hang-dog, or that the public peace will be disturbed by what I write. Rather than not carry out what I see fit in the matter, I would annihilate the whole set of you, prince and all. What! shall I who fear not to resist the pope, the creator of the Mayence fellow, give way to the creature?

"A fine thing, truly! You would not have the public peace disturbed forsooth, but you would stand by and see the eternal peace of God compromised by all these sacrilegious abominations! No, Spalatin! No, prince! This is not well. Whether you will or not, I will resist with all my might, in behalf of the Lamb of God, against this devouring wolf, as I have struggled against the rest of them. I send you, therefore, another copy of my book against him, which was ready when your letter came, a letter which, you will see, has not induced me to alter a word of what I had written. I might, perhaps, have submitted it to the examination of Philip (Melancthon); who, if any one, is the person to suggest changes in it; but, as it is, take care not to transmit to him, till it is published, and seek not to dissuade me from giving it forth; my mind is made up, and I shall not hear a word you may say!"

This was written on the 11th. He had before this written to the archbishop twice, and addressed some days after this, another letter to him in these terms: "The first faithful exhortation which I addressed to your electoral grace, having only been met with ridicule and ingratitude, I wrote to you once again, offering to receive with respectful attention your nstructions and advice. What was your grace's reply to that second letter of mine? Harsh, rude, unworthy of a bishop, of a Christian.

"But though my two former letters have been thus treated, I will not suffer myself to be rebuffed; and, conformably with he Gospel, I now forward to your grace a third exhortation. You have just set up again at Halle the idol which kills soul and body, which robs poor simple Christians of their money here, and destroys them hereafter; and you have thus publicly declared, that whatever Tetzel did, he did it in concert with he archbishop of Mayence.

"But my God lives, be assured, and he is well able to fight gainst a cardinal of Mayence, even though he had four mperors at his side. It is His pleasure to break the cedars, and to abase proud, hardened Pharaohs. I entreat your grace not to tempt the anger of that great God!

"Or did you think Luther was dead? No! no! Luther is not dead; he lives, and, fortified by the protection of that God who has already humiliated the pope, is ready to begin with the archbishop of Mayence a game that nobody expected, perhaps. You are now warned; if your grace will not abandon these idolatrous practices, I shall take the matter actively in hand—I, a man of faith and of eternity; I will treat you as I have treated the pope, and will show the world what difference there is between a wolf and a bishop. Let your highness take heed in time, and act accordingly. If men contemn me, there will come one who will contemn contempt, according to the word of the prophet.

"I declare to you, that if within a fortnight from this time I have not received a precise and positive and satisfactory answer from you, I will publish my little book on the idol of Halle. So much the worse for you, if your people keep back my letter, and prevent its reaching you: it is the duty of a bishop to have honest and trustworthy people about him.

"Given in my desert, this Sunday after St. Catherine (15th November, 1521.) Your humble well-wisher,

"MARTIN LUTHER."

To this letter the cardinal wrote, with his own hand, thi humble reply:

"DEAR DOCTOR,—I have received your letter, dated th Sunday after St. Catherine, and have read it in all good wil and friendliness of feeling. But I am greatly astonished a its contents, seeing that, long since, a remedy has bee applied to the abuses against which it is directed.

"I will henceforth conduct myself, God aiding, as become a good prince, a good priest. I acknowledge fully that I hav great need of the assistance of God, poor, weak sinner that am, sinning each day of my life, and wandering aside fro the right path. Well do I know that without God's help can do nothing, vile dust of the earth that I am.

"This is my answer to your benevolent exhortation, for would fain show you how well disposed I am towards yo I am ever ready to submit to a paternal and Christian repr mand, and I pray to God that he will grant me His grace an

His strength, to enable me to live, in this as in other things, according to His will. Given at Halle, this St. Thomas's Day, (21st December, 1521.)

"ALBERTUS, *manu propria*."[1]

The archbishop's preacher and councillor, Fabricius Capito, in reply to another letter of Luther's, had blamed him for the harshness of his language, remarking that it is necessary to observe some degree of reserve in our intercourse with great people; to make allowances for them; sometimes even to shut our eyes to their defects. Luther, in his answer, says: "You ask me to be gentler in my language, to exercise a greater restraint on my tongue: I perfectly understand what you mean. But is there anything in common between the Christian and the hypocrite? The Christain faith is an open, a public, a sincere faith; it sees things as they really are, it proclaims them to be what they really are. My opinion is, that we ought to unmask all hypocrites and ill-doers, that we ought to spare none of them, to excuse none of them, to shut our eyes to none of their proceedings, so that truth may remain free and manifest, as on a broad, open field. *Cursed be he that doeth the Lord's work deceitfully*, says Jeremiah, (xlviii.) It is one thing, my dear Fabricius, to praise or extenuate vice, and another to set about its cure with kindness and gentleness. Before all things, it is essential to declare, aloud and unequivocally, what is just and what is unjust; afterwards, when our hearer is thoroughly imbued with that lesson, we should soothe him and assist him, despite of—nay, all the more for—any weaknesses whereunto he may fall back. *Brethren, comfort ye the feeble-minded*, says St. Paul. I trust that no one will ever have cause to charge me with any want of charity or patience towards the feeble-minded. If your cardinal had written his letter in true sincerity of heart, O God! with what joy, with what humility would I fall at his feet! how unworthy should I deem myself to kiss the dust before him!—for I myself, what am I but dust and filth? Let him truly accept the word of God, and we will all of us obey him as faithful and

[1] This *soft answer* did not *turn away the wrath* of Luther, who published his book immediately afterwards.

submissive servants. With respect to those who persecute and condemn the Word, the highest charity consists precisely in resisting their sacrilegious fury in every possible way.

"Do you imagine that Luther is a man who will consent to shut his eyes, provided he is tickled with a few cajoling speeches? My dear Fabricius, I really ought, in justice to myself, to address you in far harsher language; my *love* is ready to die for you; but touch my *faith*, and you touch the apple of my eye. Jest at, or honour the *love*, as you think fit; but the *faith*, the word, this you should adore, this you should look upon as the Holy of Holies. I pray you earnestly to do so. Ask anything of our *love*, but fear, dread our *faith*.

"I do not reply to the cardinal himself, not knowing how to write to him without either sanctioning or censuring his sincerity or his hypocrisy. Do you, therefore, communicate to him Luther's feelings on this matter. From my desert, St. Anthony's day. (17th Jan., 1522.)"[1]

Let us further quote the preface he placed at the head of his Commentary on the Gospel History of the Lepers, and which he especially sent to several of his friends.

"Poor lost brother that I am! here have I lighted up another great flame; here have I again let a great hole in the papists pockets. What will become of me by and by! Whence will the Romans collect together enough sulphur, pitch, and firewood, to burn the poisonous heretic? And as to their oratory, it will be necessary, at the very least, to take out the windows from all the churches, so as to give more space for the preachments of the holy priests on this Commentary—that is to say, to their bitter abuse, their furious vociferation against Luther. And what else should they preach to their poor benighted flocks? Every preacher must preach according to what he can, and to what he knows.

"'Kill! kill!' cry they—'kill that heresiarch who seek to overthrow the whole church—who seeks to rouse all Christendom against us!' I hope that, in due season, if I b worthy of such an end, I may attain it, and that in me thes men may fulfil the measure of their anger; but it is not ye time, my hour has not yet come; I have first to make thi

[1] Luther's Werke, ix. 129.

race of vipers still more furious against me, and thoroughly to earn the death they desire to inflict on me.[1]

From the depth of his retreat, when he himself could not come forward in the lists, he thus exhorts Melancthon:

"Even though I should perish, the gospel would lose nothing, for thou art far more important to it than I am now; thou art the Elisha on whom the spirit of Elias rests. Suffer not thyself to be cast down, but sing in the night the song of the Lord which I gave you; I will sing it also, having no other care than for the Word. Let him who is ignorant, be ignorant if he will; let him who perishes, perish; our care must be that they have no cause to complain of us that we failed in our duty to them." (26th May, 1521.)

He was at this time urged to resolve an important question he himself had raised, and the discussion of which did not turn upon theological controversies, the question of monastic vows; the monks in every direction were anxious to throw them aside, but Melancthon dared not take the settlement of the question upon himself. Even Luther, when it came to the point, approached the subject with considerable hesitation:

"You have not yet convinced me," he writes, "that we must regard under the same point of view the vow of priests and that of monks. I am strongly impressed with the feeling that the sacerdotal orders instituted by God is free; but it is a great question whether this principle applies to monks, who have chosen their condition, and offered themselves of their own full accord, to God. On the whole, however, I should be very much inclined to decide, that such of the inmates of these cut-throat places as have not yet attained the age of marriage, or who have not exceeded it, should be allowed to recal their vows without scruple; as to those who are past the proper age for conjugal life, and who have grown old in their present state, I am not prepared to form the same judgment respecting them.

"As to the priests, St. Paul gives, concerning them, a decision at length, saying that it was devils who forbade them to marry; and as the voice of St. Paul was the voice of divine Majesty, I have no doubt, but that we ought to follow it.

[1] Luther's Werke, 113.

Accordingly I would say that priests, even though at the time of their professing they bound themselves by this engagement of the devil, now that they know what sort of an engagement it is, are at full liberty without any hesitation to renounce and throw it off. (1 Aug.) As to myself, I have annulled unceremoniously vows made by me before I was twenty years of age, and I would annul them again; for every one must see, who chooses to open his eyes, that such vows as these were made without due deliberation, without adequate knowledge of the matter. But I admit of this dispensation only, with reference to those who have not as yet actually entered upon their office; to them who have administered the functions of their profession in the monasteries, I cannot say, I have as yet made up my mind to extend the same licence. Truly my brain is confused and obscured with this matter." (6 Aug. 1521.)

At times he became more confident on the subject, and spoke out plainly; "As to the vows of monks and priests," he writes to Gerbell, 19th May, 1521, "Philip and I have entered into a determination to prosecute a vigorous crusade against them, and not to rest till we have utterly destroyed and annihilated them. That miserable celibacy of young people of both sexes, constantly presents to my eyes such monstrosities of nature, that now nothing sounds more disagreeably in my ears than the words nun, monk, priest; and marriage appears to me a paradise, even though accompanied the depth of poverty." (1 Nov.)

In Luther's preface to his book, *De Votis Monasticis*, addressed, in an epistolary form, to his father (21 Nov. 1521), we find him saying: "It was not of my own deliberate will I became a monk. In the terror excited by a sudden apparition, threatened by death, and believing myself called upon by Heaven, I entered into my vow, without reflection, and as it were, on compulsion. When I mentioned this to you in an interview some time ago, you exclaimed, 'God grant it may not have been a delusion of the devil!' That observation of yours struck me deeply, as though it had been the word of God sent forth by your lips; but I shut my heart as closely as I could, against what you had thus said. So again, when I reproached you for the resentment you manifested at my turning monk, you made answer in words which

ected me at the time more than any other words ever did, which are constantly present in my recollection, which are graven on my heart: you said: 'And have you not also heard this: *My son, keep thy father's commandment?* But at that time, I was hardened by a supposed feeling of devotion, and I paid no attention to what you said, as coming only from a man; but, in the bottom of my heart, I have never been able to get over the effect of those words."

Elsewhere, too, he says: "I remember well, after I had taken the vows, my father in the flesh, who was at first very incensed against me, exclaimed, when he had moderated his resentment: '*Please God this may turn out to be no trick of Satan*,' words which struck into my heart with such deep roots, that I have ever since had them constantly before me. It seems to me still that God spoke by his mouth."

Acting upon the views he had expressed, he sent word to Wenceslaus Link to give the monks permission to quit their convents, without, however, any attempt to induce them to do so. "I am sure," he says, "you will do nothing yourself, nor suffer anything to be done, contrary to the gospel, even though the safety of all the monasteries in Christendom were at stake. I do not at all approve of the turbulent manner in which, as I understand, whole flocks of monks and nuns have quitted their convents; but though they have acted herein ill and unbecomingly, it would not be well or becoming in us to recal them, now the thing is done. After the example of Cyrus, in Herodotus, I would have you give full liberty to those who desire to leave their seclusion, but by no means compel any to leave it, nor, on the other hand, force any to stay who wish to go."

He had manifested the same toleration, when the people at Erfurt proceeded to acts of violence against the catholic priests. At Wittemberg, Carlstadt in a very short time fulfilled, and indeed exceeded, the instructions of his master.

"Good God!" exclaims the latter, in a letter of the 6th of August to Spalatin, "our people at Wittemberg seem as though they were all going to marry, even the very monks! As to me, they will not persuade me to take a wife. And do you, too, take care not to marry, so that you may not fall into the tribulation of the flesh."

This hesitation, this caution on the part of Luther, sufficiently manifest that he followed rather than preceded the movement which was at this time drawing men's minds out of the old track.

"Origen," he writes, to Spalatin (9th September), "gave instruction apart to the women; why should not Melancthon attempt something of the sort? He can do it, and ought, for the people are hungry and athirst.

"I should be very glad for Melancthon to preach in public, in the afternoons of holidays, to attract the people from guzzling and gambling; they would thus accustom themselves to the bringing back of liberty, and to the fashioning it on the model of the ancient church.

"For, as we have broken through man's corruptness, and shaken off their yoke, is Melancthon to be stopped, because his head is not anointed and shaved, and because he is married? He is veritably a priest, and fulfils the functions of a priest; that is, if a priest's office be the teaching of the Word. If such objections as those of the Romans be valid against Melancthon, then Christ himself was not a priest; since we find him teaching, now in the synagogues, now in a boat, now on the sea-shore, now on the mountain. In all places, at all times. he filled the character, and never, in one instance ceased to be himself.

"Melancthon must read to the people the gospel in German, as he read it to them in the first instance in Latin, and so qualify himself by degrees to be a German bishop, as he has already become a Latin bishop."

Meantime the emperor being fully occupied with his war against the arms of France, the elector grew more at ease respecting the safety of his *protégé*, and accordingly allowed him more liberty than he had previously enjoyed at Wartburg. "I have been out sporting two whole days," he writes on the 15th September. "I have long had a desire to appreciate for myself this princely pleasure, this γλυχυπιχρον; I caught two hares, and two poor little partridges. Tis a fine occupation for any one who has got nothing else to do. However, I did not entirely waste my time, for I theologized amid the nets and the dogs, and I found a mystery of grief and pain in the very heart of all the joyous tumult around me. Is not this hunting the very image of the devil going about seeking what poor beasts he may devour by the aid of his nets, his traps, and his trained dogs—that is to say, of his bishops and his theologians. There was an incident which made the mystery and the image still more manifest. I had saved alive a poor little hare I picked up, all trembling from its pursuers; after keeping it in my sleeve some time, I set it down, and the creature was running off to secure its liberty, when the dogs getting scent of it, ran up, and first broke its leg, and then pitilessly killed it. The dogs were the pope and Satan, destroying the souls which I seek to save, as I sought to save the poor little hare. I have had enough of such hunting as this; the hunting I shall keep to is that wherein I desire to pierce with sharp darts and javelins, wolves, bears, foxes, and the whole iniquitous troop of Roman beasts that afflict the world. Ah, vile courtiers of Rome, eaters of poor hares and partridges, and eaters of us, too, you will find in the other world that you yourselves have become beasts, whom Christ, the great hunter of all, will cage up. While you think you are hunters, 'tis you who are hunted!"

Towards the end of November 1521, the desire to see and encourage his disciples induced him to make a short excursion to Wittemberg; but he took care the elector should know nothing of the matter. "I conceal from him," he writes to Spalatin, "both my journey and my return; I need not tell you why; you understand my motive."

That motive was the alarming character which the Reformation was assuming in the hands of Carlstadt,[1] and the demagogue theologians, the image-breakers, the anabaptists and others, who were beginning to come forward.[2] "We

[1] See Appendix VI.

[2] In the commencement of 1522, Carlstadt, followed by Didymus (Gabriel Zwilling) and a number of persons of the lower class, whom he had fanaticised by his discourses, entered the church of All Saints at Wittemberg, during divine service, and commenced breaking and destroying the statues, the pictures, the images of saints, vociferating: 'Thou shalt not make unto thee any graven image, nor the likeness of anything that is in heaven above, or that is in the earth beneath, or that is in the waters under the earth.' At the enunciation of this text, which seemed to dazzle their understandings, the magistrates of Wittemberg remained passive, and Carlstadt extended his work of destruction to other churches . . . .
At Zurich, it was thought but fair to try the graven images before they were condemned, and a pamphlet was accordingly circulated, entitled, *Judgment of God upon Images*, wherein these mute emblems were of course sentenced, and the work of destruction was then actively carried into

have seen the prince of these prophets.[1] Claus Storch, who goes about in the dress, and having all the appearance of the troopers we call *lanzknechts;* there is another of them dressed in a long robe, and Dr. Gerard, of Cologne. This Storch appears to be pre-eminently characterized by a levity of mind which prevents him from being very fixed in his opinions. It is of such men Satan makes his market." (4th Sept. 1522.)

Luther for a while attached no great importance to the incipient movement: "I shall not quit my retreat; I shall not stir a day the sooner for these prophets, for they give me very little uneasiness."

In a letter dated 13th June, 1522, he thus directs Melancthon to test the real worth of these men: "If you would ascertain the title of the new prophets to inspiration, ask them if they have felt those spiritual agonies, those inward deaths, that inward hell, those divine new births whereof I have so often spoken to you. . . . . If you hear from them nothing but soft, peaceable, *devout* things, heed not a word they say, though they vow to you they have been carried away to the third heaven. You may then know that the sign of the Son of Man, the touchstone, the sole test of Christians, is wanting; that the rule for discerning the true condition of men's

effect. The magistrates having put an artisan named Hottinger in prison for heading the iconoclasts, Zwinglius mounted the pulpit and declaimed vehemently against graven images and likenesses, producing great excitement on the subject. And not only was the image in stone or marble, and the representation on canvas, condemned and executed by public fury, but even the illuminated missal and the painted windows of the churches were involved in the common ruin. All men with the slightest feeling for art in their souls, regarded this proceeding of Carlstadt's as a public outrage. Erasmus was the first to protest against such acts of fanaticism. Thus he writes on the subject, (book xxxi. ep. 59,) "He who takes painting from life, deprives existence of one of its most soothing and delightful charms; painting is often a better interpreter than words. It is erroneous to say that images are of no use. In the temples of the Jews there were images; cherubim, strange figures of men and animals. The symbols which adorn our Christian temples are not placed there for the adoration of the faithful; they are elegant decorations, or pious memorials. Do you suppose that the material representations on the walls of our sacred edifices, of the events in the life of Jesus Christ, do not direct the soul to the contemplation of his divine works? Once again, I say, the catholic does not put forward these images for the adoration of men; the homage paid them has reference solely to the saints whom they respectively represent."—AUDIN.

[1] See Appendix VII.

minds is against them. Would you bear in mind the places, the time and the manner of Divine interviews? Listen: *As a lion, so has he broken all my bones; Thou hast withdrawn the light of thy countenance from me; my soul is full of troubles; and my light draweth nigh.* The divine Majesty does not speak, as some pretend, immediately, directly, so that men may see it. No: *Thou canst not see my face and live.* This is the reason why God speaks by the mouth of men, because we cannot all endure his voice. Even the Virgin was troubled at the sight of the angel. Hear, too, the prayer of Daniel and of Jeremiah: *Correct me, but with judgment, not in thine anger.*"

On 17th June, he writes: "Take care that our prince does not stain his hands with the blood of these new prophets."

"It is by the aid of the Word alone we must combat; by the Word alone we must conquer; by the Word alone we must pull down that which our opponents have raised up by force and violence.

"I condemn only by the Word; let him who believes, believe and follow me; let him who believes not, believe not, and go his own way in peace. No one must be compelled to the faith or to the things of the faith against his will; he must be prevailed upon by faith alone. I also, condemn images, but I would have them assailed by the Word, and not by blows and fire; I would deal with them so that the people should no longer have the faith in them which they have heretofore had; to effect this great object, must be the work of the Word, and not of violence. Be assured, the images will fall of themselves, when tbe people, becoming enlightened, shall know that they are as nothing in the eyes of God; it is in this way I would efface from men's consciences, by the power of the Word alone, all these devices of the pope as to confession, communion, prayer and fasting."[1]

[1] "The voice of Luther thundered too far off to be heard with any effect at Wittemberg. Carlstadt, having thrown down the images, had proceeded to preach against image-worship; Staupitz showed him the reformer's letter, but Carlstadt only smiled, replying, 'It is written, *We ought to obey God rather than man.*' Staupitz warmly urged the pain which the profanation of these sacred places had given their common leader. The archdeacon replied, "It is nothing new for the world to be troubled by the word of God. Herod was agitated, with all his court, when he learned the birth of Christ;

To the inhabitants of Wittemberg he wrote (Dec. 1521): "You are directing your energies against the mass, images, and other unimportant matters, and in doing so, laying aside that faith and charity of which you have so much need. You have afflicted, by your outrageous conduct, many pious men —men perhaps, better than yourselves. You have forgotten what is due to the weak. If the strong run on at the utmost of their speed, regardless of their feebler brethren, who come more slowly after them, the latter, thus left helpless behind, must needs succumb.

"God granted you a great blessing, in giving you the Word pure and undefiled. Yet I see none the more charity in you. You extend no helping hand to those who have never heard the Word. You take no thought for our brothers and sisters of Leipsig, of Meissen, and infinite other places, whom we are bound to save in common with ourselves. You have rushed into your present proceedings, eyes shut, head down, like a bull, looking neither to the left nor to the right. Reckon no longer upon me; I cast you off, I abjure you. You began without me; finish how you may."[1]

Matters, however, assumed such an aspect at Wittemberg, that Luther could not permit himself to remain any longer in his donjon. He departed accordingly, without asking the elector's consent. One of the historians of the Reformation relates a curious incident of the journey:

"John Kessler, a young theologian of St. Gall, was proceeding with a friend to Wittemberg, to finish his studies

the whole world was moved and the sun's light obscured at the death of our Saviour. A token that my doctrine is true, is, that the multitude and the sages are offended with it.' 'But,' rejoined Staupitz, 'our father condemns images as you do; all he requires is that we should not proceed against them by violent means.' 'Hold your peace,' replied Carlstadt; 'you forget what Luther has said: *The word of the Lord is not a word of peace, but a sword.*' Staupitz then menaced him with the rigour of the secular power. Carlstadt smiled: 'My father,' said he, 'the same menace was addressed to brother Martin by the messenger of cardinal Cajetano; you recollect his reply: *I will go where God pleases, beneath his heaven.* My father, I make the same answer to you.' With these words, the interview terminated; Staupitz immediately communicated the particulars to Luther, who from that day forth vowed against his old master in theology a hatred which time neither extinguished nor weakened."—AUDIN.

[1] See Appendix VIII. [2] See Appendix IX. [3] See Appendix X.

there, when, one evening, in an inn, situated close to the gate of Jena, he met with Luther, dressed as a cavalier.[1] Neither of the young men was acquainted with the person of the reformer. The cavalier was seated at a table, reading a little book, which the young men afterwards ascertained to be the Psalter in Hebrew. He politely saluted them, and asked them to take their seat at his table. In the conversation which ensued, he asked them what was thought of Luther in Switzerland. Kessler replied that some there knew not how enough to honour him, and daily thanked God for having sent him on earth to vindicate and raise up the truth, while others, and more particularly the priests, denounced him as a heretic, who ought to be condignly punished. From some words which fell from the landlord of the inn, the young travellers at one time were disposed to think that the mysterious trooper who read Hebrew Psalters was Ulrich Von Hutten. By and by, in came two merchants. One of them soon after his arrival, pulled out of his pocket a pamphlet of Luther's, just published, and not yet bound, and asked the rest of the company whether they had seen it. In the course of the conversation which arose hereupon, the cavalier spoke of the indisposition to approach serious subjects manifested by the princes then assembled at the diet of Nuremberg. He also expressed a fervent hope, "that evangelical truth would bear fuller fruit in the persons of future teachers, not poisoned, like their predecessors, with papal errors." One of the merchants replied: "I am not learned in these matters; but, to my mind, Luther must be decidedly one of two things; either an angel from heaven, or a demon from hell; and at any rate, he is so remarkable a person that I have put by ten florins to go and confess to him." This passed at supper. Previously to the meal, Luther had arranged with the host to pay the bill for the whole party. When they separated for the night,

[1] He had allowed his beard to grow, and laid aside his pilgrim's staff for a riding whip. His monastic habiliments were exchanged for the steel cuirass, the long heavy sword, the plumed casque, the spurs and boots of the man-at-arms of the 16th century. It is in this warlike costume, amidst a crowd of valets and a cloud of dust, that the painter, Lucas Cranach, has represented him making his entry into Wittemberg. He had laid aside his name, too, for the moment; he was not the monk Martin Luther, but the cavalier George.—AUDIN.

Luther, giving a hand to each of the young Swiss (the merchants had gone out on their business), requested them, on their arrival at Wittemberg, to go and salute, on his part, their countryman, Doctor Jerome Schurff. On their asking him what name they should mention to the doctor: "Merely tell him," replied Martin, "that he who is to come, salutes him; he will not fail to comprehend these words." When the merchants, on their return to the inn, learned that it was Luther with whom they had supped, they were inconsolable at not having known this earlier, so that they might have paid him greater respect, and saved themselves the shame of having made many indifferent remarks. They got up early in the morning, to wait upon him before his departure, and offered a thousand apologies. Luther, however, only tacitly admitted that it was he.[1]

On his way to Wittemberg, he wrote to the elector, who had enjoined him not to quit Wartburg:

"I would have your grace know, that it is not from men, but from Heaven, through our Lord Jesus Christ, that I hold the gospel. I might long since, and I shall do it in future, have called and subscribed myself his servant and apostle. If I have several times asked to be examined, it was not that I doubted the goodness of my cause, but simply to prove my deference and humility. But, as I see that this excess of humility only humbles the gospel, and that the devil, if I yield him an inch of ground, will seek to occupy all, my conscience compels me now to act otherwise. It is surely enough that, to please your electoral grace, I have passed a year in retirement. The devil well knows it was not fear made me do this: he saw my heart when I entered Worms, and knows perfectly well, that, had the city been as full of devils as there are tiles on the house-tops, I would joyfully throw myself among them. Now duke George[2] is even less in my eye than a devil. As the father of infinite mercy has given me power, by his gospel, over all the devils and over death, and has given me the kingdom to come, your electoral grace must see clearly that it were an insult on my part

[1] Marheinecke, 1.

[2] Duke George had complained to the elector of the religious movement at Wittemberg, and, as a member of the Germanic diet, had invoked the rigours of the episcopal authority upon the agitators.—Audin.

towards my Master not to put my full trust in him, or to forget that I stand far above the anger of duke George. If God called me to Leipzig, as he does to Wittemberg, I would go there, though for nine whole days together it were to rain duke Georges, and every one of them were nine times more furious than this devil of a duke is. He takes my Christ for a straw, a reed; he shall find that neither Christ nor I will permit this any longer. I will not conceal from your electoral grace that I have more than once wept, and prayed that God would enlighten the duke; and I will do so once more, with earnestness, but this shall be the last time. I supplicate your electoral grace also yourself to pray, and to have prayers offered up, that, by our united solicitations, we may turn away, by God's mercy, the terrible judgment which each day more and more nearly menaces the duke. I write this to let you know that I am going to Wittemberg, under a protection far higher than that of princes and electors. I have no need of your help; 'tis you who need mine, which will be of greater use to you, than yours can be to me. Nay, if I thought you would persist in offering me your protection, I would not set out at all. This is a matter which requires neither sage councils, nor the edge of the sword; God alone, and without any paraphernalia of visible force, God alone is my master, and my protector. He among men, who has the fullest faith, is the best able to protect me; you are too feeble in the faith for me to regard you as a protector and saviour.

"You wish to know, doubtless, what you have to do on this occasion, persuaded as you are that hitherto you have not done enough. I will tell you, in all respect, that you have already done more than was desirable, and that now you have nothing to do at all. God will not permit you to share my griefs and my torments; he reserves them to himself and to his ministers. If your grace really have faith, you will find it bring you peace and security; but whether or not that be so, I believe, and I must leave your grace to undergo the penalties with which God afflicts the incredulous.

"In disobeying the directions of your grace, I relieve you, in the sight of God, from any responsibility should I be thrown into prison, or be deprived of life by the tyrants. Let, therefore, the emperor take his own course; do you obey him respectfully as becomes a prince of the empire; if he take my life, it will be his business to account for it, and no longer yours. You will not be angry with me, prince, for that I do not consent to involve you in my own misery and danger; Christ has not instructed me to show myself Christian at the expense of my neighbour. Wanting faith, I would not have you revolt against power. I hope that they will act so far consistently with common sense and decency, as not to call upon a person of your grace's exalted condition to be my gaoler; but should they be mad enough to require you to lay hands upon me, this is what I would have you do: obey them, without taking any heed to me, for I would not desire you to suffer on my account, in mind, body, or estate.

"God be with you, prince! some other time, if necessary, we will discourse at greater length. I dispatch this letter in haste, fearing least your electoral grace should be made uneasy at the news of my arrival; for it is my duty, as a good Christian to comfort all men, and to do ill to none. In you, I have to do with a very different man from duke George: I know that duke well, and he knows me not indifferently. If your grace believed, you would see the kingdom of God; as you do not believe, you have as yet seen nothing. Love and honour to God for ever. Amen. Given at Borna, by the side of my guide, this Ash-Wednesday, 1522. Your grace's humble servant.

MARTIN LUTHER."

On hearing of Luther's departure from Wartburg, the elector had dispatched Schurff to meet him, and persuade him to return, or at least to furnish him with an explanation of his conduct, which he might show to the emperor. In his answer to the elector, dated 7th March, Luther gives three reasons for his proceeding; first, that the church of Wittemberg had earnestly solicited his return; secondly, that disorder had crept in among his flock;[1] thirdly, that he wished to avert, as far as in him lay, the insurrection which he regarded as threatening the country:

"I have been called," he says, "and I will go; time

[1] The course of sermons which he delivered on his return, had the effect of at once restoring order. The prophets who had disturbed it quitted Wittemberg. (See Appendix XI.)

presses; let destiny be accomplished, in the name of Jesus Christ, master of life and of death. Satan, during my absence has penetrated into my fold, and committed ravages there which my presence alone can repair. A letter would answer no purpose; I must make use of my own eyes and my own mouth to see and to speak. My conscience will permit me to make no longer delay, and rather than act against that, I would incur the anger of your electoral grace, and of the whole world. The Wittembergers are my sheep, whom God has intrusted to my care; they are my children in the Lord. For them I am ready to suffer martyrdom. I go, therefore, to accomplish, by God's grace, that which Christ demands of them who own him. If my written word sufficed to drive away this great ill, do you think they would send for me thus urgently? I will die rather than delay any longer: die for the salvation of my neighbour as becomes me."

Writing to his friend, Hartmuth Von Kronberg, in March, shortly after his return to Wittemberg, he says: "Satan who always *presents himself among the sons of God*, according to Job, i. 6, has just done us all, and myself in particular, a cruel injury at Wittemberg. My worst enemies, near as they have often been to me, have never given me so hard a blow as that I have just received from my own people. I am fain to own that this ill smoke they have sent up, has pained me sharply, both in the eyes and in the heart. I can imagine Satan grinning, and saying to himself: 'Now I shall have depressed Luther's courage, and conquered his so unbending mind. This time, he will not get the better of me.'

"Perhaps God designs herein to punish me for having, at Worms, to please those about me, put a check upon myself, and spoken with too little vehemence in presence of the tyrants. The pagans, indeed, have since charged me with having manifested too much, rather than too little haughtiness on that occasion, but they know not what faith is.

"I yielded, as I have said, entirely to the entreaties of the good friends who were with me, and who were anxious I should not appear too harsh and exacting; but I have since often reflected with bitter regret upon the deference and humility I displayed.

"As for me, I know not Luther,[1] and will not know him, or hear of him. What I preach comes not from him, but from Christ Jesus. The devil may fly away with Luther, if he can; I care not, so that he leave Jesus Christ to reign in man's heart."[2]

Towards the middle of this year, Luther broke out with the greatest violence against princes and potentates. A number of secular and ecclesiastical dignitaries (Duke George among them) had prohibited the sale of the translation he was then publishing of the Bible, and offered to return the money paid by those who had already purchased the work. Luther unhesitatingly accepted the defiance thus cast at him: "We have triumphed over the papal tyranny which weighed down kings and princes; it will be still easier to demolish the kings and princes themselves.... I much fear that if they continue to heed what that blockhead duke George says, there will arise throughout Germany disturbances which will involve in ruin all the princes and magistrates, and drag down at the same time the whole body of the clergy. This is the aspect in which I view coming events. The people on all sides are in a state of excitement; they have opened their eyes, so long closed, and they will not, they cannot, suffer themselves to be oppressed any longer. It is the Lord himself who is bringing this about, and who shuts the eyes of the princes to the threatening symptoms which all else see; it is He who will accomplish the inevitable results, by means of the blindness and violence of these haughty men. I see before me Germany swimming in blood!

"Why will they not perceive that the sword of civil war is suspended over their heads? They are exerting all their efforts to destroy Luther, while Luther is doing his utmost to save them. It is not for Luther, but for them, that perdition approaches; and they, instead of seeking to avert, advance it. In what I am now saying, I verily believe the Spirit speaks by my lips. But if the decree of anger is passed in Heaven, and neither prayer nor prudence can avert its effects, we will obtain that our Josias shall fall asleep in peace, and that the world shall be left to itself in its Babylon. Though exposed every hour to death, in the very midst of

[1] See Appendix XII. [2] See Appendix XIII.

my enemies, without any human aid, I have ever entertained the most perfect contempt for these stupid menaces of prince George and his fellows. The Spirit, doubt it not, will thoroughly master duke George and his emulators in folly. I write this fasting, quite early in the morning, my heart filled with a pious confidence. My Christ lives and reigns, and I too shall live and reign" (19th March).

In the middle of the year appeared the book which Henry VIII. had got his chaplain, Edward Lee, to draw up in his name, and in which he put himself forward as the champion of the Roman church.[1]

"There is, indeed, in this book," observes Luther, (22nd July,) "a plentiful manifestation of royal ignorance; but its virulence and mendacity are the exclusive property of Lee." Luther's reply was not long in making its appearance; its violence surpassed anything that even his attacks on the pope might have led us to expect.[2] Never before had a private man addressed to a sovereign-prince words so contemptuous, so daring. "Two years ago," he says, "I published a little book called, *The Captivity of the Church at Babylon.* It horribly vexed and confounded the papists, who spared neither lies nor invective in replying to it. I readily forgive them both the one and the other, neither having hurt me. There were some who tried to swallow it down with a laugh; but the hook was too hard and too pointed for their throats. And now, quite recently, the lord Henry, not by the grace of God king of England, has written in Latin against my treatise. There are some who believe that this pamphlet of the king's did not emanate from the king's own pen; but whether Henry wrote it, or Hal, or the devil in hell, is nothing to the point. He who lies is a liar; and I fear him not, be he who he may. This is my own notion about the matter: that Henry gave out an ell or two of coarse cloth, and that, then, this pituitous Thomist, Lee, this follower of the Thomist herd, who, in his presumption, wrote against Erasmus, took scissors and needle and made a cape of it. If a king of England spits his impudent lies in my face, I have a right, in my turn, to throw them back down his very throat. If he blasphemes my sacred doctrines; if he casts his filth at the

[1] See Appendix XIV. [2] See Appendix XV.

throne of my monarch, my Christ, he need not be astonished at my defiling, in like manner, his royal diadem, and proclaiming him, king of England though he be, a liar and a rascal.

"He thought to himself, doubtless: 'Luther is so hunted about, he will have no opportunity of replying to me; his books are all burnt, so my calumnies will remain unconfuted; I am a king, and people will needs believe me. I need not fear to throw anything that comes first to hand in the poor monk's teeth, to publish what I like, to hunt down his character as I think fit.' Ah! ah! my worthy Henry! you've reckoned without your host in this matter: you have had your say, and I'll have mine; you shall hear truths that wont amuse you at all; I'll make you smart for your tricks. This excellent Henry accuses me of having written against the pope out of personal hatred and ill-will; of being snarlish, quarrelsome, back-biting, proud, and so conceited that I think myself the only man of sense in the world! I ask you, my worthy Hal, what has my being conceited, snappish, cross-grained—supposing I am so—to do with the question? Is the papacy free from blame because I am open to it? Is the king of England a wise man, because I take him to be a fool? Answer me that. The best of it is, that this worthy monarch, who has such a horror of lying and calumny, has assuredly collected together more lies and more slanders in this little book than can be charged upon me, by my worst enemies, in the whole extent of my writings. But, forsooth, in these quarrels, we must be respecters of persons; that is to say, a king, so he fawns upon the pope, may abuse a poor monk to the top of his bent. What most surprises me, is, not the ignorance of this Hal of England, not that he understands less about faith and works than a log of wood, but that the devil should trouble himself to make use of this man against me, when he knows perfectly well that I don't care a straw for either one or the other. King Henry justifies the proverb: *Kings and princes are fools.* Who sees not the hand of God in the blindness and imbecility of this man? I shall say very little more about him at present, for I have the Bible to translate, and other important matters to attend to; on some future occasion, God willing, when I shall be more at leisure, I will reply at greater length to this royal driveller of lies and poison. . . I imagine that he set about his book by way of penance, for his conscience is ever smiting him for having stolen the crown of England, making way for himself by murdering the last scion of the royal line, and corrupting the blood of the kings of England. He trembles in his skin, least the blood he has shed be demanded at his hands; and this it is makes him clutch hold of the pope to keep him on his throne, makes him pay court, now to the Emperor, now to the king of France. Tis precisely what might have been expected in a conscience-haunted tyrant. Hal and the pope have exactly the same legitimacy: the pope stole his tiara as the king did his crown; and therefore it is they are as thick together as two mules in harness."

Then turning upon the Thomists, Luther thus defies them: "Come on, pigs that you are! burn me if you dare! I am here to be seized upon. My ashes shall pursue you after my death, though you throw them to all the winds—into all the seas. Living, I shall be the enemy of popery, dead, I should be doubly its enemy. Pigs of Thomists, do what you can: Luther will be the bear in your path, the lion in your way; he will pursue you wheresover you go, he will present himself incessantly before you, will leave you not a moment's peace or truce, till he has broken your iron head and your brazen front—for your salvation or your damnation, as you shall then act.

"As to myself, to the words of the fathers, of men, of angels, of devils, I oppose, not old customs, nor the multitude of men, but the Word of Eternal Majesty, that gospel which my adversaries themselves are compelled to recognise. There I take my stand, there I take my seat, there I take my resting-place; there is my triumph, there my glory; from thence I defy popes, Thomists, Henricists, sophists, and the gates of hell. I heed very little the words of men, whatever their sanctity may have been; and as little do I heed tradition or custom, fallacious custom. The Word of God is superior to all else. If I have the Divine Majesty on my side, what care I, even though a thousand Augustins, a thousand Cyprians, a thousand churchfuls of Henrys rise up against me. God cannot err or deceive; Augustin and Cyprian, in common with the rest of the elect, may err and have erred.

"The mass once conquered, we shall, I think, have conquered papacy. The mass was the rock on which papacy rested, with its monasteries, its bishoprics, its colleges, its altars, its ministers, and its doctrines; its belly and its members. All these will crumble away with the abomination of their sacrilegious mass.

"In the cause of Christ, I have trampled under foot the idol of the Roman abomination which had put itself in the place of God, had established itself mistress of kings and of the whole earth. Who then is this Henry, this new Thomist, this disciple of the monster, that I should respect his blasphemies and his violence? He is defender of the Church, forsooth; yes, of his own church, that he exalts so preposterously, that prostitute clothed in purple and drunk with debauchery, that mother of fornications. As for me, my leader is Christ; and I will strike with the same blow this flagitious church and its defender; they are one and the same in this, and I will crush them together.

"I am sure that my doctrines proceed from heaven. I have made them triumph against him who, in his little finger, has more force and cunning than all the popes, all the kings, and all the doctors that ever were. My dogmas will stand, and the pope will fall, despite all the gates of hell, all the powers of the air, of the earth, of the sea. They have challenged me to war: well, they shall have war: they have contemptuously rejected the peace I offered them; they shall not have peace. God will see which of us will soonest cry *quarter*, the pope or I. Thrice already have I appeared before them. I went unhesitatingly to Worms, though I knew well enough that the emperor was urged by all about him to violate the public faith in my person. Luther, the fugitive, the trembler Luther, threw himself under the very teeth of Behemoth, while they, the terrible giants who were going to eat me up all at once, what have they done? How many of them in the three past years have presented themselves in Wittemberg? not one. And yet they would have come in full safety under the peculiar protection of the emperor. Ah, the cowards! and do they think to triumph now? Even during my retreat, they could not rise from out of their shameful ignominy: how should they do so now, when all the world thoroughly knows them for what they are, knows that the whole gang of them have not ventured to face Luther alone."[1]

He was still more violent in the German treatise he sent forth at about the same time on the secular power, and which opens thus:

"God has heated the brains of princes. They think they are fully entitled to follow out their own caprices; they put themselves under the wing of the emperor, and, according to their own account, in what they do, merely execute his orders like obedient subjects, as if they could in this way conceal their iniquity from men's eyes. Knaves that pass themselves off as Christian princes! And these are the hands to which Cæsar has confided the keys of Germany; madmen who would extirpate faith from our land, and establish blasphemy in its place, if we did not resist them by the mighty power of the Word. And resist them I will; I, who feared not to

[1] Henry complained of this letter to the elector, who in his reply, pro-:ested his love for the gospel, stated that it was against his order that Luther nad quitted Worms, and expressed his full reliance upon the result of a council to be held shortly, but said not one single word about the language which Luther had made use of toward the monarch.—AUDIN.

Luther's answer offended, as he himself tells us, many of his own partisans; and among these, king Christiern, after a while induced him to write to Henry, who, as the king said, was about to establish the Reformation in England. Luther's epistle to Henry, on this second occasion, is of a very different composition from the first. It is very humble in its terms, and apologizes for the writer's former violence on the ground that it had been excited by the language addressed towards himself, which, he had since been credibly informed, was not attributable to Henry, but to the shameless sophists about him, and more especially to *that enemy of God and man, Lee, archbishop of York*, and in conclusion he offers to recant all he has said wrongfully (*pallinodiam cantare*). The letter, which is dated, 1st Sept. 1525, produced no effect. Henry VIII. had been too deeply wounded in the monk's attack, to be willing to forgive the assailant, and Luther accordingly got nothing by his advances. 'These tyrants,' says he, a few months after, (Dec. 1525), 'with their woman's hearts, are poor, mean creatures; they are only worthy to be slaves of the people whom fortune enables them to domineer over. For myself, by Christ's grace, I am amply avenged upon them, in the thorough contempt I have for them, and Satan their god.'

The defence of Henry against Luther was undertaken in England by Fisher, bishop of Rochester, in a learned work published under the pseudonyme of William Ross, and by Thomas More, in a pamphlet which, intended to denounce more especially the coarse and ribald style in which the German reformer was wont to indulge, essayed to effect this object by sarcasm and raillery, by beating Luther at his own weapons, but he is not very successful in the attempt.—AUDIN.

take the pope by the horns, that great idol of Rome, am not likely to be intimidated by his scales and peelings. . . . Princes are of this world, and this world is the enemy of God, so that they live according to the world, and against the law of God. Be not astonished, therefore, at their furious violence against the gospel, for they cannot act counter to their own nature.

"The simple fact is, that God abandons these reprobates to their own perverted courses; he will put an end to them and to the great ones of the church; their reign is over, and they are about to descend into the tomb—the whole mob of scoundrels, princes, bishops, monks, covered with the contempt and hatred of mankind.

"Ever since the world was the world, a wise and prudent prince has been a *rara avis;* and an *avis* still more *rara*, has been a prince who was at the same time an honest man. What have we always found great men to be, at least almost always? Great fools, great knaves, the greatest knaves under the sun; lictors and hangmen in high places, whom God has made use of in punishing the other wicked ones of the earth : for God being a great and mighty king, it was necessary that the hangmen and lictors he employed should be noble, rich, illustrious persons, men in high and world honoured places, men feared by the world. It has pleased his divine will that we should address his hangmen and lictors as *most gracious lord, most exalted prince*, and so forth ; that we should prostrate ourselves at their feet; that we should be their dutiful, and obedient, and humble subjects. But beyond the hangman and lictor business, these men never carry their artifice so far as to pretend to be good shepherds of us their sheep. Oh, no; if we meet, in history or our experience, with a prudent, honest, Christian prince we cry *A miracle! a miracle!* and regard it as a precious token of divine favour; for generally it happens to us as to the Jews, whom God thus menaced, *I will give them a king in my anger*.

"Fine princes, these Christian princes of ours, who protect the faith, forsooth, and devour the faith! Take good heed how you trust such worthies. In their wonderful wisdom, they'll do great things for you. No doubt, on the one hand, they'll break their own necks, but then they'll plunge the nation into disaster and misery. But I'll do my best to open the eyes of the blind to these five words of the 107th Psalm: *he poureth contempt upon princes.* Ay, princes, the hand of God is suspensive over your heads. Contempt will be poured upon you; you will die, were your power greater than that of the Turk himself; and it will avail you nothing to puff and swell yourselves out, and to grind your teeth. Already your just reward is at hand; you are estimated at what you really are, rogues and rascals; you are weighed in a just balance, and found wanting; the people know you thoroughly, and the terrible chastisement, which God terms contempt, is hemming you round about, closer and closer, and will not be turned aside. The people, utterly wearied of you, will no longer endure your tyranny and your iniquity, nor will God. The world now is not the world as it used to be, wherein, at your good pleasure, you chased men, as though they were wild beasts."

Here, again, is an observation of Luther's, with reference to two severe orders which the emperor had issued respecting him. "I exhort all good Christians to pray with us in behalf of these blind princes, whom, doubtless, God sent us in his anger, and not to follow them against the Turks. The Turk is tenfold more able, ay, and more religious than our princes. How can these fools and ill-doers, who tempt and blaspheme God in so horrible a manner, ever think he will enable them to succeed against their enemy? Here is that poor, miserable creature, our emperor, a man not sure of his life for a single five minutes together, see how impudently he glorifies himself as the true and sovereign defender of the Christian faith.[1]

"The Holy Scripture says that faith is a rock against which shall not avail the gates of hell, death, the devil, or any other power; that it is a divine power; and that this divine power may be vindicated against all opposing powers by the merest child. Oh, God, how senseless, then, are the worldly princes and potentates, in acting as they do! There is the king of England, entitling himself, in his turn, *Defender of the Faith!* So, too, the Hungarians boast of being the protectors of God, and presumptuously sing in their Litany, "*That it may please*

[1] See Appendix XVI.

thee to hear us, thy defenders! By and by, we shall have some princes putting themselves forward as *defenders of Jesus Christ*, and others as *defenders of the Holy Ghost!* Should this be so, the Trinity, truly, will be fitly guarded!"

These daring freedoms alarmed the elector, and Luther had some difficulty in reassuring him. "I recollect, my dear Spalatin," he writes on the 12th Oct. 1523—"I recollect well what I wrote to the elector from Borna, and I would to God that, warned by the manifest signs then vouchsafed by God, you had strengthened and confirmed yourselves in faith. Does he not see that here have two years passed over since I left Wartburg, and yet I am safe and sound, uninjured by any of the attacks made upon me. As to the elector himself, not only is he, at the worst, safe in his own person, but for the last year he must have seen that the fury of the princes is appeased. Let him be certain that Christ will have no difficulty in defending his cause in my cause; that cause to which the elector, by an impulse from heaven, has engaged himself? If I knew how to extricate him from any difficulty or dilemma wherein he may find himself placed, without shame or detriment to the gospel, I would willingly do it, at the risk of my own life. For myself, I had fully calculated, that before a year of my return to the world had expired, I should be dragged to execution; and I had looked forward to this as an effectual means of relieving the elector. It has pleased God that this should not be; and now, incapable as we are of comprehending His designs, we shall be perfectly secure in saying: Thy will be done.[1] I have no doubt whatever, but that the prince will be entirely safe from any attacks, so long as he abstains from giving his public consent and approbation to our cause. He is under no necessity of sharing the odium which attaches to us amongst his class, though God knows, it were no real injury or peril for him to do so, but, on the contrary, a great help to his salvation."

That wherein consisted the real security of Luther at this period was the circumstance that a general disorder in the political world seemed close at hand. The populace in every direction were murmuring in a tone not to be mistaken. The gentry and the lower class of the nobility, still more dis-

[1] See Appendix XVII.

contented and impatient than the people, were taking the initiative in the social changes called for. The wealthy, overgrown ecclesiastical principalities lay spread out before the eyes of all, as a fair prey, in the pillage of which civil war might best be commenced. The catholics themselves called, though in a regular, legal way, for the reformation of those abuses in the church against which Luther had taken his stand. In March, 1523, the diet of Nuremberg[1] suspended the execution of the imperial edict against Luther, and drew up against the Roman clergy the list of grievances and accusations known as the *Centum gravamina.*[2] Already the most ardent of the Rhine nobles, Franz Von Sickingen, had commenced the struggle of the lesser lords against the princes, by attacking the palatine. "This," observes Luther, "is a very sad circumstance, and with other presages renders well nigh certain a general disorder in our political system. I have no doubt but that Germany is menaced with a very fearful civil war, if not altogether with destruction." (16th Jan. 1523.)

CHAPTER II.

Rise of the Lutheran church—Attempts at organization.

THE period succeeding the return of Luther to Wittemberg was the most active and laborious of his whole life.[3] He had to carry on the Reformation, to make further progress each day in the path he had opened, to remove the new obstacles which constantly presented themselves, and all the while to pause, from time to time, in the work of destruction, to rebuild, or patch up this thing or the other. His life no longer presented that uniformity which characterized it at Wartburg. Descended from his poetical solitude, plunged into the most pitiful realities, exposed, so to speak, as a prey to the whole world, it was to him that all the enemies of Rome addressed themselves. All flocked to him, besieging

[1] It had been opened in November, 1522. [2] Seckendorf, i. 251.

[3] In 1520, he published a hundred and thirty-three works; in 1522, a hundred and thirty; in 1523, a hundred and eighty-three, to almost all of which were prefixed a little woodcut, from Luther's own design.—AUDIN.

his door hourly—princes, doctors, and citizens. He had to give answers to Bohemians, Italians, Swiss, to men from every country in Europe. There were assembled in Wittemberg fugitives from all directions. Of these the most embarrassing, questionless, to Luther were the nuns, who, having escaped from their convents, and being rejected by their families, came to seek an asylum with Luther. Imagine this man of thirty-six, obliged to receive all these women and girls, and be towards them as a father! Poor monk! necessitous as his own condition was, he managed, though with great difficulty, to extract some assistance for them from the parsimonious elector, who, year after year, had allowed Luther himself to remain in a destitute condition. Since his triumph at Worms, to fall into all this wearing and constant anxiety was enough to calm any exaltation with which the reformer might have been previously inspired. The answers which he gave to crowds who came to consult him are impressed with a liberality of spirit, from which we shall hereafter sometimes find him deviating when, become the chief of an established church, he shall himself experience the necessity of checking the movement he had given to religious thought.

First, we find the pastor of Zwickau Hausmann calling upon Luther to fix the limits of gospel liberty; he replies: "We give entire liberty as to both the one kind and the other, but only to those who approach the matter becomingly, and in a spirit of due fear; as for the rest, let us leave it all as it is, according to the accustomed rites; let every one follow the dictates of his own judgment; let every one listen to his own conscience to satisfy the gospel." Next come (26th March, 1522) the Moravian brothers, the Waldenses of Moravia: "The sacrament itself," writes Luther to them, "is not in itself so necessary as to render superfluous, faith and charity. It is mere folly to squabble about such trifles as those which for the most part engage our attention, while we neglect things truly precious and salutary; wherever we find faith and charity, sin cannot be, whether the sin of adoring, or the sin of not adoring. On the other hand, where charity and faith are not, there is sin, sin universal, sin eternal. If these cavillers will not speak concomitantly, let them speak otherways, and cease all this disputation since we are agreed as to the broad ground-work. Faith, charity adores not: I speak of the adoration of the saints, because faith, because charity knows that we are not commanded to adore, and that we sin not in not adoring. Thus faith and charity pass in Christian liberty through the midst of these people, leaving to all of them to follow each his own interpretation of such matters. Faith and charity forbid men to dispute and arbitrarily to condemn one another, for faith and charity hate sects and schisms. I would resolve the question as to the adoration of God in the saints, by saying that it is a thing entirely free and indifferent." He expresses himself, it is to be observed, upon the latter subject with a singular degree of disdainfulness.

"The whole world so pesters one with questions, a thing I wonder at, about the worship of saints, that I find myself compelled, once for all, to publish my judgment on the matter. I would have the question then left peaceably alone ; for this simple reason, that it is in no way necessary to the solution of the great general question. (29th May, 1522.)

"As to the exposition of relics, I believe the whole collection of them have been already quite enough exhibited, and re-exhibited in every possible place. As to purgatory, I think it a very uncertain thing. It is probable, in my opinion, that, with very few exceptions indeed, the dead sleep in utter insensibility till the day of judgment. As to purgatory itself, I do not agree with the sophists in thinking it a determinate place. Who will venture to give an assured opinion on the subject ? On what authority can it be said that the souls of the dead may not sleep out the interval between earth and heaven, or hell, or purgatory, in the same way that the living pass in profound slumber the interval between their down-lying at night and their uprising in the morning. I believe that this pain of purgatory is that foretaste of hell whose torments Christ, Moses, Abraham, David, Jacob, Job, Hezekiah, and many others have so deeply suffered from. As, then, it is like unto hell, but yet temporary in its duration, whether it takes place in the body or out of the body, it is, in my view of it, purgatory." (13th January, 1522.)

In the hands of Luther, confession loses the character which had been given it by the church. It is no longer the formidable tribunal which opens or closes the gates of heaven. The priest, upon Luther's system, merely places his wisdom and his experience at the service of the penitent. Instead of a sacrament, which it was before, confession becomes, in the hands of the priest, merely a ministry of consolation and good counsel: "In confession, it is not necessary that people should relate all their sins: it is sufficient that they disclose what they think fit to disclose. We shall not stone them for any omissions of that sort. If they confess, from the bottom of their hearts, that they are poor sinners, we shall content ourselves with that.[1] If a murderer were to say before the tribunals, that I had absolved him, I should reply: I know not whether he is absolved or no; it is not I who confess and absolve, but Christ. A woman at Venice had killed and thrown into the water a young fellow who had slept with her. A monk gave her absolution, and then denounced her. The woman, by way of her defence, showed the monk's absolution. The senate hereupon ordered the monk to be burned alive, and the woman to be banished from the city. It was a wise decision; but if I were to give a billet, signed by my hand, to relieve an alarmed conscience, and a judge were to obtain possession of this billet, I might justly reclaim it, as I did on one occasion from duke George. For he who has got hold of other people's letters without a good title to them, and will not give them up, is nothing better than a thief."[2]

On the 11th October, 1533, he thus writes to the parish of Esslingen:—"It is true, I have said confession was a good thing. And in the same way, I do not forbid any person to fast, to keep festivals, to go pilgrimages, &c. All I say is, that I would have these things left open for each person to use his own discretion about them, and that it should not be considered a mortal sin to omit their performance. I would have man's conscience wholly free in all things that do not affect faith, and the love of one's neighbour.

"But as there are many consciences still held captive by the laws of the pope, you do well not to eat meat on fast days in the presence of these men, still feeble in their faith. This abstinence on your part becomes, indeed, a work of charity, in that its object is to respect the conscientious feelings of your neighbour. In themselves, these things have never

[1] Tischreden, 176. [2] Ib. 163.

been commanded by the Scripture; and as to the directions of the pope, they should go for nothing."

On the 16th October, 1523, he thus writes to Michel Vander Strassen, toll-collector at Borna, on the subject of a preacher at Oelnitz, who was carrying out Luther's principles to an extravagant degree: "You have seen my opinion on the matter, in my book, *On Confession and on the Mass.* I have there laid it down, that confession is good when it is free and unconstrained, and that the mass, without being either a sacrifice or a good work, is yet a testimony of religion, and a blessing of God. The error of your preacher is, that he flies too high, and is throwing away his old shoes, before he has got new ones. He should begin with thoroughly instructing the people upon faith and charity. A year hence, when the parish shall understand Jesus Christ, it will be time enough to touch upon the points which he now makes the subjects of his sermons. What good can result from all this precipitation with the, as yet, ignorant people? I myself preached for nearly three years, before I broached such questions, while these people think to settle the whole business in half an hour. Rely upon it, all this excessive haste is calculated to do us a great deal of harm. I beg you will get the principal at Oelnitz to enjoin the preacher to observe more moderation in future, and to begin with making his people thoroughly understand Jesus Christ; if he will not do this, let him leave off forthwith his absurd preachments and begone. Let him, above all, absolutely discontinue to prohibit confession, and to punish those who confess. He is evidently a petulant and intemperate person, who has seen the smoke rising, but knows not where the fire is."

As to the mass, ever since 1519, he had treated it as entirely an indifferent matter, with regard to its external forms. At that time he wrote to Spalatin, "You ask me for a form of celebrating mass. I entreat you to trouble me no more about these *minutiæ;* let the conscience be kept quite free on the subject. It is by no means a thing of such importance that, on its account, we should chain down the spirit of liberty with additional rules, regulations, and traditions; we have already quite enough of them, and to spare." "If it please God," he wrote, on November, 1524, "I will abolish the mass altogether; or at least try something else in its stead.

I can no longer endure the tricks and machinations of these three demi-canons against the unity of our church."

"I have at length," he says, on the 2nd December, 1524, "I have at length induced our canons to consent to the abrogation of these masses."

"These two words, mass and sacrament, are as far removed from one another as light and darkness—the devil and God. May God give to all Christians such a heart that they may henceforth hold in horror the very word mass, and when they hear it pronounced, may cross themselves as they would do at the mention of one of the devil's veriest abominations."

Towards the close of his life, in 1542, (10th November,) he writes to Spalatin: "With respect to the elevation of the host, do what you think fit; I would not have people chained down by arbitrary rules in indifferent matters; this is what I have always said, and what I always shall say to those who weary me about this question."

He was fully impressed, however, with the necessity for outward worship. Thus he writes on the 11th January, 1531: "Although ceremonies are not necessary to salvation, yet they produce an effect upon rude and uncultivated minds. I refer principally to the ceremonies of the mass, which you may retain, as we here, at Wittemberg, have done." . . .

"I condemn no ceremony," he writes on the 14th March, 1526, "which is not contrary to the gospel. We have preserved the baptistry and baptism, with this difference, that in the ceremony we make use of the vernacular tongue. I permit images in the temple, and the mass is celebrated with the accustomed rites and in the same costume as formerly; and here, again, the only difference is, that we sing some hymns in German, and that the words of consecration are in German. Indeed, I should not have abolished the Latin mass at all, or have substituted the vernacular, in celebrating it, had I not found myself compelled to do so."

"You are about to organize the church of Kœnisberg; I entreat you, in the name of Christ, to make as few changes as possible. You have in your neighbourhood several episcopal towns, and it is not desirable that the ceremonies of our new church should vary in any marked degree from the old ritual. If you have not already abolished the Latin mass, do not abolish it, but merely introduce into it a few German hymns. If it be abolished, at all events retain the old order and costumes." (16th July, 1528.)

The most important change to which Luther subjected the mass was the translating it into the vernacular tongue: "The mass shall be celebrated in German for the use of the laity, but the daily service may be in Latin, with the addition of some German hymns." (28th October, 1525.)

"I am glad to see that the mass is now celebrated in Germany in the German tongue; but for Carlstadt to insist upon this, as not merely desirable, but as essential, is carrying the thing too far. He is truly incorrigible; always new laws, always laying down this as a necessity, and that as a sin; but it is impossible for a mind constituted like his to proceed otherwise. I would gladly have the mass in German, and I am endeavouring to effect this object; but, at the same time, I would have it carried out in a truly German spirit, and assume a truly German air; merely to translate the Latin text, preserving the old tone and measure, might, in strictness, answer the purpose, but this is a compromise which in itself does not sound well to the ear, and does not satisfy my mind. I would have the whole thing, text and notes, accent and action, an emanation of our own tongue, suited to our own German voices; otherwise it will be mere apeing, grimace, and commonplace imitation.[1]

"I desire, rather than promise, to give you a mass in German, for I do not feel myself capable of a work which requires at once a high order of mind, and a great knowledge of music," (12th November, 1524.)

"I send you back the mass. I suppose I must allow it to stand as it is, though I don't at all approve of retaining Latin music for German words. I should much prefer the adoption of German music," (26th March, 1525.)

"I am of opinion that it would be well, after the example of the prophets and of the ancient fathers of the church, to compose psalms in German for the use of the people. With a view to this object, we are seeking poets in every direction, and, gifted as you are with such elegant and powerful eloquence, versed as you are in the German tongue, I

[1] Werke, 229.

would pray you to aid me in my labour, by translating some psalm on the plan which I myself, as you know, have adopted. I would have you exclude new words and fine phraseology. To be understood by the people, we must speak to them in the simplest and most ordinary language, though, at the same time, pure and correct; each expression should be perfectly clear, and as close to the text as possible," (1524.)

It was no easy thing to organize the new church. The ancient hierarchy was broken up, and the principle of the Reformation being the bringing back all things to the text of the gospel, it was necessary, in accordance with this design, to restore to the church the democratic form it wore in the first ages of Christianity. To this, Luther at first seemed disposed.

In his *De ministris Ecclesiæ instituendis*,[1] addressed to the Bohemians, he says:

" 'Tis a fine invention of the papists, truly, that the priest is invested with an indelible character, of which no fault he may commit can deprive him. The priest should be elected by the suffrages of the people, and afterwards confirmed by the bishop; that is to say, after the election, the first, the most venerable among the electors, should lay his hands upon the elected. Did Christ, the first priest of the New Testament, did he have need of the tonsure, and all these mummeries of episcopal ordination?—did his disciples, his apostles, need them? . . . . All Christians are priests; all may teach the word of God, may administer baptism, may consecrate the bread and wine, for has not Christ said: *do this in remembrance of me?* All we who are Christians have the power of the keys. Christ said to the apostles, who were the representatives about him of mankind at large: *Verily verily, I say unto you, whatsoever you shall bind on earth shall be bound in heaven. . . .*

" The names to be borne by the priests are respectively those of minister, deacon, bishop (overlooker), dispenser.[2] If the minister ceases to be faithful to his trust, he should be deposed; his brethren may excommunicate him, and put another minister in his place. The first office in the church

See Appendix XVIII. [2] Appendix XIX.

is that of preaching. Jesus Christ and Paul preached, but did not baptize.[1] (1523.)

He did not, as we have seen, desire that all the churches should be subjected to one unvarying rule. "It is not my opinion," (he writes, 12th Nov. 1524,) "that the whole of Germany should have our Wittemberg regulations enforced upon it." And again: "I am not at all clear that it will be judicious for our people to hold a council to establish a uniformity of ceremonies; however good the intention may be, these things have an ill effect, as has been proved in the case of all the councils of the church, from the very beginning. Even in the councils of the apostles, they discussed works and traditions more than faith; and in all the subsequent councils there has been no mention made of faith, but always *opinions* and *questions;* so that at last the very name of council has become as much a matter of distrust and odium as the name of free-will. Unless our church wishes to resemble the other in some of its worst features, why seek to impose obligations on our people in matters of form, by decrees of councils, which soon become fixed laws, and nets wherein to catch men's souls." (12th Nov. 1524.)

There was, however, he felt, a point beyond which the liberty he advocated as a general principle might be going too far, so as to involve the Reformation in a host of abuses: "I have read your ordination, my dear Hausmann," he writes on the 21st March, 1534, "but I think it would be well not to publish it. I have, for a long time past, regretted much that I have done; since every one of our leading men has taken it into his head to propose reforms of his own, the number and variety of ceremonies have increased to an infinite extent, so that ere long we shall exceed in dimensions even the great ocean of papal formulas."

In order to give something like uniformity to the ceremonies of the new church, the leaders instituted annual visitations, which were carried into effect throughout the whole of Saxony. The duty of the visitors was to make inquiries into the life and doctrines of the various pastors, to guide aright the faith of those who gave indications of wandering from the true faith, and to expel from the priesthood those

[1] Op. Lat. ii. 364.

whose moral conduct was liable to animadversion. These visitors were appointed by the elector, on the nomination of Luther, who, having now fixed his residence at Wittemberg, formed, with Jonas, Melancthon, and some other theologians, a sort of central committee for the direction of all the ecclesiastical affairs of the new church.[1] Here is one of their official communications:

"The parishioners of Winsheim have requested our illustrious prince to permit you to come and preside over their church; upon our advice he has rejected their application. He is ready, however, to allow you to return to your own district, if, on consideration, we shall deem you worthy of that ministry. (Nov. 1531.)

"Signed, LUTHER, JONAS, MELANCTHON."

Among Luther's letters, we find a great number of these missives, signed by him and other protestant chiefs.

In his letter to the council of Stettin, 12th Jan. 1523, he decides that the canons are compellable to share with the citizens the burden of public offices. He had, naturally, frequent applications made to him by persons desirous of a living in the reformed church. "Be not uneasy about getting a parish," he writes to some one on the 16th of Dec. 1530; "there is a great deficiency of faithful pastors; so that we are obliged to ordain and institute ministers in a peculiar way, without tonsure, without unction, without mitre or staff, without gloves or incense; in a word, sad to say, without bishops." (16th Dec. 1530.)

In 1531, we find the inhabitants of Riga and prince Albert of Prussia commissioning Luther to send them ministers of the new faith; and in April, 1539, Gustavus I., king of Sweden, applied to him for a preceptor to the young heir to his crown.[2]

Although Luther was invested with no rank or title, expressly placing him in authority over the other pastors of his church, we find him exercising a sort of supremacy and control: "Here," he writes in July, 1532, "here are fresh complaints against you and Frezhans, on account of your having excommunicated some barber; I do not wish to decide be-

[1] See Appendix XX. [2] Seckendorf, ii. 100.

tween him and you, but I should be glad of your informing me, what is the meaning of this excommunication."

"We cannot refuse the communion to any one," he writes in June 1533; "to attempt giving religious excommunication all the effect and power of political excommunication, would be merely to render ourselves ridiculous by essaying that which is opposed to the spirit of the age, and which is altogether beyond our strength. The civil magistrate and his functions should be kept quite apart from all these matters." Excommunication, however, was a weapon which he occasionally found it convenient to make use of. For instance, a tradesman of Wittemberg having bought a house for thirty florins, sought, after making some trifling repairs, to sell it again for four hundred. Luther's sense of fair dealing was shocked at the transaction: "If the man persists in this monstrous bargain," he says, "I will excommunicate him. Truly, excommunication must be had recourse to, in such extreme cases as this, if we can make no other remedy effectual."[1] Mention having been made of an idea of re-establishing consistories, the advocate, Christian Bruck, said to Luther—"the nobles and the merchant are afraid that, after having done with the peasantry, you will be coming about their ears." "Lawyer," replied Luther, "keep to your law, and to what concerns external order." In 1538, on hearing that an inhabitant of Wittemberg openly expressed his contempt for God, the Holy Word, and His servants, Luther sent two of his chaplains to menace him with his displeasure, if he did not amend his conduct. Some time after this, we find him interdicting the sacrament to a nobleman who had been guilty of usury.

One of the points which gave the greatest disquietude to the Reformer was the abolition of monastic vows. In 1522, he sent forth an exhortation on this subject to the four mendicant orders. The Augustines, in the month of March, the Carthusians in August, declared energetically in his favour.

To the lieutenants of his imperial majesty at Nuremberg, he writes, in August, 1523: "It is inconsistent with the nature of God to require vows which it is impossible for

[1] Tischreden, 176.

human nature to keep. . . Dear lords, we implore you to unbend in this matter. You know not what horrible and infamous cruelties the devil exercises in convents; render not yourselves accomplices in his wickedness, charge not your consciences with his guilt. If my bitterest enemies knew that which I learn every day from all the countries about us—ah, I am sure they would at once assist me in overthrowing the convents! You compel me to cry out louder than I otherwise would. Give way, I entreat you, ere these scandals burst forth more scandalously than they need to do.

"The general order of the Carthusians, as to the liberty to be given to the monks to leave their convents and throw aside the monastic habit, pleases me very much, and I shall publish it. The example of so considerable an order will greatly aid us, and give a most valuable sanction to our decisions." (20 Aug. 1522.) He was all the while, however, desirous that the change should be effected with the least possible confusion, and so as to involve his followers in the least possible discredit with the world at large. He writes thus to John Lange: "Your quitting your monastery was not, doubtless, without good reasons; but I should have preferred your doing it so as to have raised your conduct above all suspicion; I do not condemn the liberty to quit monasteries, but I am most anxious that our adversaries should have no loop-hole through which to make a calumnious suggestion against those who avail themselves of this liberty."

It was to little purpose that he recommended that all confusion and violence should be avoided; his influence over the progress of the Reformation daily escaped more and more from his grasp, as its sphere grew daily more and more extended. At Erfurt, in 1521, the houses of several priests had been violently entered, and he had bitterly complained of the outrage; in 1522, in the Low Countries, matters were carried still further: "You have heard, I suppose, what has occurred at Antwerp, how the women went in a body and took Henry Zutphen forcibly from his convent, where the superior kept him confined to his cell. The other brethren who had embraced our principles have since been imprisoned in various places: some of them, having denied Christ, have been restored to favour, but the rest who are true to us, are still in prison. The new doctrines, however, had made such way in the convent, that the Romanist authorities have directed the furniture to be sold off, and the church to be closed as well as the convent; in fact, it is to be pulled down very shortly. The Host has been transferred to the church of the Holy Virgin, with an emphasis of pomp, a marked display, as though it were being rescued from a place tainted with heresy, beyond redemption. Many of the citizens, men and women, have been tortured and otherwise punished. Henry himself was on his way to us, but on arriving at Bremen he was induced, at the solicitation of the people, and a consequent order of the council, to stop there and teach the word, to the great indignation of the bishop. The people in all directions are animated with an earnest desire for the propagation of the truth, and admirable zeal in that object; some persons here have established an agency which procures all the books published at Wittemberg, as soon as they appear. Henry himself was desirous of having his letter of licence direct from you personally, but he could not communicate with you in time enough for that, so we gave him the letter in your name, under the seal of our prior." (19 December, 1522.)

All the Augustines of Wittemberg having one after the other quitted the convent, the prior gave up the building itself into the hands of the elector; and Luther himself at length threw aside the monastic robe. On the 19th October, 1524, he appeared in public, in a gown similar to that which preachers still wear in Germany; it was the elector who had given him the cloth for it.

His example encouraged a still greater number of monks and nuns to quit their convents. The latter thus suddenly emerging from the quiet cloister, and feeling themselves utterly embarrassed in a world of which they knew nothing, hastened to seek advice and assistance from him whose glowing words had caused them to leave the solitude of the monastery.

"I yesterday," he writes, on the 8th April, 1523, "received here nine nuns who had emancipated themselves from their captivity in the monastery of Nimpschen; amongst them were Staupitza, and two other women of the family of Zeschau.

"I greatly commiserate these poor girls, and still more

those others who still remain in their convents, undergoing a slow death from that cursed and incestuous chastity. 'Tis a monstrous thing; that sex—so feeble, so dependent—is united with our sex by the voice of nature, by the voice of God himself; if it be separated from us, it perishes. Oh cruel, oh tyrannical parents! . . . You ask me what I shall do with these girls; in the first place, I shall intimate to their relations my desire that they may be permitted to return home; if this be refused, I will take care that they shall obtain an asylum elsewhere. Their names are:—Magdalen Staupitz, Elsa Von Kanitz, Ava Grossin, Ava Schonfeldt, and her sister Margaret Schonfeldt, Laneta Van Golis, Margaret Zeschau, and Catherine Bora. The way in which they escaped was perfectly astonishing . . . Pray beg some money for me of your rich courtiers to enable me to keep these poor girls for a week or a fortnight, until I can send them home, or to those friends who have promised to receive them in the event of their being rejected by their parents." (10th April, 1523.)

"They call me ravisher; if so, I am a blessed ravisher, like Christ, who was also a ravisher in this world, when by his death he wrested from the prince of the earth his arms and his riches, and led him away captive.

"Anne Craswytzinne, escaped from her bonds at Leusselitz; is come to live with us. She has married John Sheydewyndt, and desires me to salute you with all friendship in her own name and that of three other emancipated nuns, Barba Rockenberg, Catherine Taubenheim, and Margaret Hirstorf." (11 January, 1525.)[1]

"My dear Spalatin, I am astonished at your sending back the woman to me, since you are so well acquainted with my handwriting. The reason which you assign for the proceeding, that my letter was not signed, is no reason at all . . . . Entreat the elector to give us ten florins, and some dresses, new or old, or anything else he may please, for the support of these poor virgins in spite of themselves." (22nd April, 1523.)

Leonard Koope, a considerable citizen of Torgau, had taken an active part in enabling the nine nuns just men-

[1] See Appendix XXI.

tioned to escape from their convent. On the 10th April, 1522, he received a letter from Luther, warmly approving of what he had done, and exhorting him not to allow himself to be intimidated by the outcries of the Romanists: "You have done a good work; and would to God we could release, in the same way, the many thousand other souls, whom the pope still holds captive.... The word of God, however, thanks be to his name, is now come forth into the world, and not imprisoned in convents."

On the 18th June, 1523, he wrote a letter of consolation to three young ladies, whom duke Henry, son of duke George, had expelled from his court, for having read the works of Luther: "*Bless those who curse you; pray for those who despitefully use you.* Dear friends, you are unhappily but too amply revenged for the injustice which has been committed towards you. We must pity these furious creatures, these mad men, who, in their blind rage, see not that they are destroying their own souls in seeking to injure you."

"You are, doubtless, aware that the duchess of Montsberg has escaped, almost by a miracle, from the convent of Freyburg. She is now in my house, with two other girls, Margaret Volckmerin, daughter of a citizen of Leipsig, and Dorothea, daughter of a citizen of Freyburg." (20th October, 1528.)

"The unfortunate Elizabeth Von Reinsberg, who was expelled from the seminary of Altenberg, having now nothing to live upon, has addressed herself to me. The prince, in answer to her plaint, having referred her to the sequestration commissioners, she has asked me to solicit your mediation with them in her behalf." (March, 1533.)

"That young girl of Altenberg I told you of, whose old father and mother were dragged away prisoners from their house, has sent to me, soliciting advice and assistance. What I can do for her in the matter, God knows!" (14th July, 1533.)

Various expressions which Luther lets fall, give us reason to suppose that his humanity was frequently abused by the women who flocked round him at this period, some of whom, it would seem, were mere impostors. "What expenses have I not been put to in supporting, for a greater or less period, the women who have escaped from convents; and truly, many of them were no nuns at all, but mere strumpets of various grades, high and low." (24th August, 1535.) These mortifying deceptions had the effect, at an early period, of modifying Luther's views with reference to the suppression of convents.

In a letter addressed to the parish Leisnick, in 1523, he advises them to take no violent steps for putting down their convent, but rather to allow it gradually to grow into desuetude by receiving no more novices. "As no one," he continues, "should have compulsion put upon him in matters of faith, we ought not to expel or ill use those who wish to remain in the convents, whether by reason of their advanced age, their love of idleness and good living, or from conscientious motives. Let us leave them where they are if they so desire it, for the gospel teaches us to do good even to the unworthy; and we must always bear in mind, in these cases, that the persons in question entered the monastic state blinded by the common error, and that they have learned no business by which they may earn their livelihood....The property of the convents should be applied in the following manner: first, as I have said, to the support of those who remain in them; then we ought to give a certain sum to those who leave (even though they contributed nothing on their entrance), so that they may be enabled to enter upon some sort of business, for it is very likely that many of them, while they were in the convents, may have learnt some handicraft. As to those who brought money with them, it is just that the greater part, if not the whole of it, should be returned to them. What remains after these disbursements should be put into a common chest as a fund for the assistance of the poor, in the shape of loans or free gifts, according to circumstances. In this way, we shall, at least, fulfil the intention of the founders, who, though seduced by monkish trickstering to leave their property in general terms to the convents, designed that it should be consecrated to the true honour and worship of God. Now, there is no truer or finer worship of God than the Christian charity which cometh to the assistance of the poor, as Jesus Christ himself will attest in the last day, according to his word given to us in the 25th chapter of St. Matthew. If, however, among the heirs of the founders there should be found any who are in want, it will be just and most conformable with true charity to restore to them a portion of the property, and even the whole, if it be necessary, it not having been, or, at all events, it not having rightfully been the intention of their fathers to take away the bread from their children's mouths, and to give it to strangers. . . .You will, perhaps, object that I shall, in this way, make the hole too large, and that nothing will be left, or very little, for the common chest I spoke of; there will be no end, say you, of people coming and pretending that they are entitled to this, that, and the other. But, as I told you before, this must be a work of charity and equity. Let every one examine his own conscience, and ascertain how much he shall honestly require for his honest wants, and how much, as far as he is concerned, he can leave to the common chest; then let each parochial community consider the various estimates of its members, weigh all the circumstances fairly, act honestly upon them, and, depend upon it, everything will go on well. Even though the cupidity of a few individuals should find its advantage in this arrangement, still that would be far better than the pillaging and disorder we have witnessed in Bohemia.[1] I would not advise persons advanced in age to quit the cloister, because returning helpless to the world, they must necessarily become a charge to other people, and would scarcely meet, in these uncharitable days, with the care and attention to which their age is entitled.

"In the interior of the monastery they are a burden to no one, they are under no necessity of recurring to the more than doubtful kindness of strangers; and, moreover, they are in a position to do a great deal in aid of the spiritual salvation of their neighbours, which, were they in the world, it would be difficult—nay, I will say, impossible for them to do."

At the end of his letter, Luther encourages a particular monk to remain where he is: "I myself lived in a monastery some years; I should have lived there longer; I should be there now, had my brethren and the state of the monastery permitted it." (28th February, 1528.)

Some nuns had written to doctor Martin Luther from a place in the Low Countries, recommending themselves to his

[1] Werke, ix. 536.

prayers. They were pious, God-fearing virgins, who supported themselves with the labour of their hands, and lived together in peaceful union. The doctor conceived a warm esteem for them: "We should leave poor nuns like these," he says, "to live on after their own fashion. And the case is the same with the *Feldkloster*, which were founded by princes and other great nobles for the reception of persons of their own class. But as to the mendicant orders, that is quite another thing; it is of their monasteries I spake just now, as places whence we may derive many able men for the discharge of important public offices, both in church and in state."

At this period of the life of Luther (1520-1528), he was absolutely overwhelmed with business, and he was no longer sustained as heretofore by the heat of contest, and the excitement of danger: "I implore you," he writes to Spalatin, "to come to my relief; I am so crushed under the weight of other people's affairs, that it makes my life a burden to me;" and he subscribes himself *Martinus Lutherus, Aulicus extra aulam et invitus*. "I am head over ears in business—visitor, reader, preacher, author, auditor, actor, runner, debater, and what not."[1] (29th Oct. 1528.)

And truly the carrying out the reformation of parishes, the establishing a uniformity of ceremonies, the drawing up the great catechism, replies to the newly appointed pastors, letters to the elector, whose consent it was necessary to obtain for each petty innovation—all this involved a great deal of labour and a great deal of vexation. And, meantime, Luther's adversaries left him not a moment of repose. Erasmus published against him his formidable book, *De libero Arbitrio*, to which Luther did not reply until 1525. Even the Reformation itself seemed to turn round on the Reformer. His old friend Carlstadt[2] had run in the path whereon Luther only walked. It was principally, indeed, to check him in his too rapid and violent innovations, that Luther so hastily quitted the castle of Wartburg; it was no longer religious authority alone that was in question; the civil authority itself was now about to be made matter of debate. Behind Carlstadt was seen Munzer;[3] behind the sacramentarians and the iconoclasts, there appeared in the distance

[1] See Appendix XXII. [2] Ib. XXIII. [3] Ib. XXIV.

the revolt of the peasants ajacquerie—a servile war more comprehensive in its plans, more levelling in its objects, and not less bloody in its progress than the servile wars of antiquity.

CHAPTER III.

1523—1525.

Carlstadt—Munzer—War of the peasants.

"PRAY for me, and assist me to crush under foot the Satan who has risen up at Wittemberg against the gospel, in the name of the gospel. We have now to combat an angel, become, as he thinks, an angel of light. It will be difficult to make Carlstadt give way by means of persuasion; but if he will not yield of his own accord, Christ will compel him to do so. For we, who believe in the Master of life and of death, are ourselves masters of life and of death." (12 March, 1523.)

"I have determined to interdict him the pulpit which he has rashly ascended without any call thereto, where he is in despite of God and man." (19th March.)

"Carlstadt is angry with me because I have interdicted his preaching and withdrawn his licence. I have not condemned his doctrine, though I am exceedingly displeased at his occupying himself almost entirely with ceremonies and external things, and neglecting the true Christian doctrine, that is to say, faith and charity. . . . With his foolish manner of teaching, he is leading the people to imagine that they are Christians if they fulfil the most trifling requisites; so they don't go to confession, and do break images, according to him, they well nigh perform all that is necessary. . . . His ambition is to set up as a new doctor on his own account, and to establish his rules and system on the ruin of my authority." (30th March.)[1]

"This morning I took Carlstadt aside, and entreated him to publish nothing against me; if he did, I said, I should be compelled to butt at him in right earnest, which I wished

[1] See Appendix XXV.

to avoid. He swore, by all that is sacred, he would not assail me." (21st April.)

"We must communicate instruction to the weak gently and patiently. Would you, after you yourself had done sucking, desire to cut off the breasts whence you had derived nourishment, in order that none after you might resort to the same life-supporting fountain? If mothers were to cast away and abandon the children which, in their first infancy, are unable to eat the same food they eat when they grow up, what would become of you? Dear friend, if you have sucked enough, and grown up enough yourself, I pray you to let others suck and grow up in their turn."

Carlstadt had abandoned his duties as professor and archdeacon at Wittemberg, though without resigning the salary, and retired, unauthorized by the elector or the university, first to Orlamund and then to Jena; a circumstance which had greatly contributed to the displeasure now manifested against him on the part of the other leaders of the Reformation. The university having earnestly called upon him to return to his duties, he not only refused to obey the mandate, but accompanied the refusal by a highly insulting message.

"Carlstadt," writes Luther, on the 7th Jan., 1524, "has set up a printing press at Jena, but the elector and our academy have promised, conformably with the imperial edict, to permit no publication to be sent forth which has not previously undergone the examination of the commissioners. It is not to be endured, that Carlstadt and his people should be alone permitted to emancipate themselves from due submission to the authorities." .... "Carlstadt is as indefatigable as ever; his new presses at Jena have, I am told, already sent forth, or will very soon have done so, no fewer than eighteen works." (14th Jan., 1524.)

"Let us leave gloom and disquietude to Melancthon, as better suiting the turn of his mind. For ourselves, we will fight out the fight, without taking more heed to him than is absolutely necessary; our cause is the cause of God, and not of individuals; it is the business of God, and it will be the work of God, the victory of God. He could fight and conquer without us, if he so thought fit. If, therefore, he judges us worthy to be accepted as his champions in this holy war, we may well be proud, we may well be earnest and ever ready to manifest our devotion in his service. I exhort you, and the rest through you, that you give way to no fear of Satan; that you permit not your hearts to fail within you. If we are, indeed, fighting an unjust fight, we shall of necessity be crushed beneath the attacks of our enemies; if our cause be just, as I say it is, there is a just God, who will make that justice of our cause shine forth in the eyes of all men as clearly as the sun at noonday. Perish who shall perish; live who shall live, 'tis no business of ours." (22 Oct. 1524.)

"We shall again summon Carlstadt in the name of the university to return to his duty, requiring him to quit the place where he has no authority to preach, and to resume his post at Wittemberg, where his assigned mission is; if he fail to obey the summons, we shall report him to the elector." (14th March, 1524.)

At last, Luther considered it his duty to visit Jena himself.[1] Shortly after his arrival, Carlstadt, who regarded himself as aggrieved by a sermon which Luther had delivered, solicited an interview with the latter. It took place in Luther's apartments, in the presence of a great number of witnesses. After infinite recriminations to and fro,[2] Carlstadt said, "Well, well, doctor, preach as much against me as you like, I shall be at no loss what to do on my part." *Luther*: "If you have anything to say, say it boldly, or write it, and fear not to express your whole mind." *Carlstadt:* "Be assured I will not; I fear no one." *Luther:* "Ay, write against me if you will, and publicly." *Carlstadt:* "If that be what you desire, I will satisfy you, and perhaps more than enough; I have plenty of materials, I can tell you." *Luther:* "'Tis a bargain, and I will give you a florin as my pledge of battle." *Carlstadt:* "A florin!" *Luther:* "Ay, call me liar, if I do not." *Carlstadt:* "Well, I accept your challenge." Thereupon Luther took a gold florin out of his pocket, and presented it to Carlstadt: "There is the money," said he; "and now begin as soon as you like; strike boldly; you shall have as good as you bring, rely upon it." Carlstadt took the florin, which he handed round for the inspection of each person present: "Dear brethren," said

[1] See Appendix XXVI. [2] Ib. XXVII.

he, "you see I've got my earnest money; it cannot now be said that I have no warrant for writing against Doctor Martin. Be you all witness to this matter." He then put the florin in his purse, and shook hands with Luther, who drank a bumper to his health, which Carlstadt responded to, saying, after he had done so: "Dear doctor, I entreat you to put no obstacle in the way of my printing what I shall desire to print; and that when this matter is settled, you will not seek to prevent my embracing the new kind of life I contemplate—that of cultivating the earth with the labour of my own hands." *Luther:* "Fear nothing; I shall of course let your printers print what you like, since 'tis I myself gave the challenge; have not I this moment handed you a florin as my pledge of fair battle? Let the attack be as unflinching as you will; the more rigorous it is, the better I shall like it." They once more shook hands, and then separated.[1]

Finding, however, that the townspeople of Orlamund espoused, with somewhat too active an enthusiasm, the opinions of Carlstadt—they drove away their minister, because he would not adopt them—Luther found it advisable to obtain an order from the elector for the removal of the innovator from that place.[2] Previous to his departure, Carlstadt assembled, by the ringing of the church bells, the population of Orlamund; first, all the men, and then all the women, in the public square, and read to them a solemn farewell letter, which drew tears from the whole of the congregation. "Carlstadt has written a farewell address to the people of Orlamund, which he signs: *Andrew Bodenstein, expelled, without a previous hearing or condemnation, by Martin Luther.* You see that I, who no long while ago just escaped being a martyr myself, am now, in my turn, a maker of martyrs. Egranus, also, I hear is setting up for a martyr; a martyr, as he says, to the papists and the Lutherans; *the papists and the Lutherans!*—a fine story, truly! You cannot think what a general sensation has been created here by Carlstadt's dogma upon the sacrament; 'tis in everybody's mouth. —— has made his recantation, and implores us to forgive him; he, too, had been compelled to quit the country by us cruel persecutors, and all for no fault of his own.

[1] Werke, ix. 211. [2] See Appendix XXVIII.

However, as he is penitent, I have sent to solicit his reinstatement; whether I shall obtain it, I know not. Martin of Jena has also received orders to quit the place; he delivered a farewell sermon, in which with tears in his eyes he entreated for pardon, but the only answer we gave him was five florins, which he subsequently made an addition to, by sending people round the town to beg for him. I think these things will do a great deal of good to such of our preachers as have a tendency to ride the high horse; they will derive thence an excellent lesson, teaching them to conduct themselves with becoming modesty." (27th Oct. 1524.)

Carlstadt on quitting Orlamund proceeded first to Strasburg and thence to Bâle. The direction thus taken would seem the result of instinct, for as his footsteps bent towards Switzerland, so the inclination of his doctrines was towards those of the Swiss Reformers, Œcolampadius, Zwinglius, &c.

"I defer writing upon the eucharist until Carlstadt shall have vomited forth the poisonous exhalations he threatened us with, at the time I gave him the gold florin. Zwinglius, and Leo the Jew in Switzerland, hold the same opinions with Carlstadt; and thus the new plague of Egypt is diffused from country to country; but Christ reigns, though for the present he fights not." (12th Nov. 1524).

He felt it necessary, however, to take notice of the charge that he had unjustly and arbitrarily driven forth Carlstadt from Saxony. "As to the reproach put forward against me, by Carlstadt, that I have tyrannically expelled him from our country, I should not take the matter much to heart, were the charge well founded; but I believe I can very effectually clear myself from it. In the first place I can safely say, I have never mentioned him to the elector, for I have never said a word to the prince at all; have never heard him speak, have never even seen him, except once at Worms, on the occasion of my second appearance before the emperor. I have often, however, written to his highness, by the medium of Spalatin, and latterly with most urgent entreaties, that he should resist the man, or rather evil spirit, of Alstet.[1] But my letters have produced no effect, and I have with reason

[1] Alstet was the residence of Munzer, the leader in the revolt of the peasants, of which we shall make mention presently.

conceived great resentment against the elector. Carlstadt, I can assure him, need have no apprehensions of the prince taking any measures against him, and so may spare his abuse in that quarter. As to duke John Frederick, I admit that I have often spoken to him on these matters, and have made him acquainted with the perverse ambition and nefarious proceedings of Carlstadt.

"Whatever may have occasioned this man's departure from amongst us, I am thoroughly glad we have got rid of him, and I may wish he had not taken up his abode among you.

"Upon the strength of one of his writings, he had almost persuaded me, not to confound the spirit which animates him with the seditious and homicidal spirit of the man of Alstet; but when, by order of my prince, I proceeded to Orlamund, I soon found, on observing the worthy Carlstadian Christians there, what sort of seed it was he had sown. I had to thank God most heartily that I was not stoned ere I got away from the place, for there were men among them, who, by way of a parting benison, said to me; 'Go, in the name of a thousand devils; we hope you will break your neck before you reach the gates!' A fine set, truly! They have represented themselves in very different colours in the little book they have lately published, but I know them thoroughly now. Still I am by no means disposed for violent measures; if the ass had horns—that is to say, if I were prince of Saxony, Carlstadt should not be banished, unless very strong representations indeed were made to me to that effect. I would seek to conciliate him, and urge him not to disdain the goodwill of princes.[1]

"Such scandalous disorders as these do great harm to the gospel. A French spy told me distinctly, that his king had regular information of all these proceedings, that he had thence acquired the idea that we had ceased to respect religious or political order, or even the institution of marriage, and that, in fact, we were living in a state no degree superior to that of the beasts of the field.[2]

"It will not do to scout at, or make a jest of Mr. Everybody

[1] Letter to the people of Strasburg; Luther's Werke, ii. 58. (See Appendix XXIX.)
[2] Tischreden, 417.

(*Herr Omnes*); God himself constituted certain authorities to direct the world; for it is a great feature in his magnificent system, that there shall be order here below."

Carlstadt at length threw off all disguise. "I yesterday," says Luther, in a letter dated 14th December, 1524, "received a communication from one of my friends at Strasburg, in reference to this man; after passing through that city, it seems, he went on to Bâle, and has since vomited forth five books, which are to be followed by two others to the same tune. In every one of them, I am denounced as a double papist, as the ally of Antichrist, and what not." In a letter, however, dated 13th June, 1525, he says: "My friends write me from Bâle, that Carlstadt's people there have been put in prison, and that his books had a very narrow escape from being publicly burned. He is still there, it seems, but in concealment. Œcolampadius and Pellican are writing in support of his opinions."

"Carlstadt had made up his mind to go and fix himself at Schweindorf; but Count Henneberg expressly refused him permission to do so, and directed the town council not to receive him for a single hour. I wish the count would do the same in reference to Strauss." (10th April, 1525.)

Luther was quite delighted at Carlstadt's open declaration of war: "The devil held his peace," says he, "until I bribed him with a florin. Thank God, that money was well placed, at all events! I never laid out money with a more satisfactory result." He proceeded to write several able pamphlets *Against the Celestial Prophets*.[1] "People," says he, "seem going to sleep, as though the devil himself were laid at rest, whereas, all the while, he is going round and round about, watchful as ever for whom he may devour. But, please God, though others are negligent, while I live he shall not gain his ends: while I live I will fight against him, let what will come of it.[1] All the people, now-a-days, reject that which does not happen to please each man's reason. 'Twas the same with the Arians, the Pelagians; and so, under the papacy, 'twas a founding proposition that free-will might be instrumental to grace. The doctrine of faith and a good conscience, is far superior to that of good works; for even though the works

[1] Werke, ii. 10.

are wanting, if there be faith, there is still hope of succour. Spiritual means alone should be employed in the inducing true Christians to acknowledge their sins.... But as to the rude herd, Mr. Everybody, they must, if necessary, be bodily driven to his work, so that, whether he will or no, he shall demean himself piously, under the influence of the law and of the sword, just as we keep wild beasts in good order by chaining them up.

"The spirit of the new prophet flies very high indeed; 'tis an audacious spirit that would have eaten up the Holy Ghost, feathers and all. Bible! sneer these fellows: Bibel, Bubel, Babel! And not only do they reject the Bible thus contemptuously, but they say they would reject God too, if He were not to visit them as he did his prophets. Well! since the evil spirit is thus obstinate in these men, I will not yield him an inch more than I have given him heretofore. I will speak of images, first according to the law of Moses, and I say that Moses prohibits only images of God.... Let us content ourselves with entreating our rulers quietly and gradually to suppress images, and meanwhile remove them from our own hearts."

Further on, Luther expresses an ironical astonishment that these modern inconoclasts did not extend their pious zeal to the getting rid of their own money, or of any other precious object belonging to them which bore the stamp of any graven image. "To assist the weakness of these pious personages," says he, "and to free them from that which so contaminates their appalled souls, a few pickpockets would not be without their use, seeing that the *celestial voice*, as they call it, is not loud enough to induce them to throw aside these vanities themselves. Perhaps even a little violence might be beneficial."[1]

"When I was at Orlamund, discussing the question of images with the disciples of Carlstadt, after I had demonstrated from Holy Writ, that in all the passages of Moses which they cited, the idols of the pagans were alone referred to, one of these men, who doubtless thought himself the most able among them, came forward, and said to me: 'Listen, thou for I suppose I may "thou" thee if thou art a Christian.' ...

[1] Werke, ii. 13.

answered him: 'Call me what thou wilt.' I saw very well he would infinitely have preferred striking me a blow to speaking to me; at all events, he was so full of the spirit of Carlstadt, that the others could not induce him to hold his peace. 'If thou wilt not follow Moses,' continued he, 'thou shouldst at least submit to the gospel; but thou hast thrown the gospel under the table. It is we who will raise it thence; it shall not be suffered to remain where thou hast put it.' 'What does the gospel say?' I asked. 'Jesus says in the gospel,' replied he, 'I know not where it is, but my brethren are well acquainted with it, that the bride should take off her shift on the marriage night; in the same way we should take off and destroy all images, that we may become pure and free from the creature.'—*Hæc ille.*

"What could I do in the midst of such people as these, with their marvellous notions about breaking images being, according to the gospel, the same thing with the taking off the bride's shift on the marriage night? These words, and that phrase about the gospel being thrown under the table he certainly got from his worthy master; for, doubtless, Carlstadt had accused me of throwing down the gospel, in order that he might say he was come to raise it up. This ambitious pride of his is the cause of all his misfortunes, is that which has thrust him from the light into darkness.

"We are full of courage and cheerfulness, and we fight all the more successfully against these melancholy, timid, downcast souls, who fear the sound of a falling leaf though they fear not God; for such is the wont of the impious. Their passion, their monstrous aim is to domineer over God, his Word, and his works, and to turn them to their own purposes. They would not be so daring if God were not invisible and intangible. If he were a man, visible and present to the eye, he would make them fly before him with but a blade of straw for his weapon.

"He whom God truly inspires speaks freely and openly, without asking himself whether he stands alone, or whether others are standing by him. Jeremiah did this, and I may boast that I also did so.[1] Without any doubt, then, this

[1] "The spirit of these prophets has always very carefully got out of the way of danger, yet none the less it glorifies itself as magnanimous and

evasive and homicidal spirit which slips behind, and then excuses itself on the ground that at first it had not been strong enough in the faith; doubtless, I say, this spirit is the devil; the Spirit of God makes no such excuses. I know thee well, devil of mine....

"... If you ask Carlstadt's people how this sublime spirit is arrived at, they refer you, not to the gospel, but to their reveries, to their vacuum. 'Place thyself,' say they, 'in a state of void tedium as we do, and then thou wilt learn the same lesson; the celestial voice will be heard, and God will speak to thee in person.' If you urge the matter further, and ask what this void tedium of theirs is, they know as much about it as Doctor Carlstadt does about Greek and Hebrew... Do you not in all this recognise the devil, the enemy of divine order? Do you not see him opening a huge mouth, and crying: 'Spirit, spirit, spirit!' and all the while he is crying this, destroying all the bridges, roads, ladders, in a word, every possible way by which the spirit may penetrate into you—that is to say, the external order established by God in the holy baptism, in the signs and symbols, and in his own Word. They would have you learn to mount the clouds, to ride the wind, but they tell you neither how, nor when, nor where, nor what; all these things you must learn of yourself, as they do."

".... Martin Luther, an unworthy member of the church and evangelist at Wittemberg, to all the Christians at Strasburg, the beloved friends of God. I could endure, up to a certain point, Carlstadt's excesses in the matter of images. I myself, in my writings, have done more harm to images than he will ever do by all his furious violence; but that which I cannot endure is, the urging and exciting people on to these courses, as though they were essential to salvation and as though he who breaks not images cannot be a Christian. Now, without doubt, works do not constitute the

chivalrous spirit. As to me, I may say, without ostentation, that I appeared openly at Leipsig, ready to dispute in the presence of a hostile public. I presented myself at Augsburg, unprovided with a safe-conduct before my greatest enemies; at Worms, before Cæsar and all the states of the empire, although I knew very well that my safe-conduct had been infracted. Throughout my spirit has remained free as a flower of the field." (1524.)

Christian; these external things, such as images and the sabbath, are left free in the New Testament, in common with all the other ceremonies of the law. St. Paul says, 'We know that an idol is nothing in the world.' If, then, idols be nothing, why then chain up and torture the conscience of Christians in the matter at all? If idols are nothing, whether they fall or whether they stand, what matters it?"

He passes on to a higher subject, the question of the real presence—that superior question of the Christian symbolism, in comparison with which the matter of images is of inferior importance. It was principally on this point that Luther found himself opposed to the reformation in Switzerland, and that Carlstadt was more peculiarly allied with that reformation, though the extreme nature of his political opinions might have led us to a very different conclusion.

"I confess that if Carlstadt, or any one else, had, five years ago, shown me that in the holy sacrament there is nothing but bread and wine, he would have rendered me a great service. I had at that time powerful temptations assailing me; I turned and twisted about, I struggled fiercely with my own thoughts; I should have been most joyful to have extricated myself from the doubts and difficulties which environed me round about. I saw well enough that, if I could make up my mind on the point, I could inflict in this way a most terrible blow on papism. . . . There are two others who have written to me on the subject, far abler men than Dr. Carlstadt, and who do not, like him, torture words into the shape which may happen to suit their present caprice or their present purpose. But, upon this matter, I am, as it were, chained up in a prison I cannot quit; the text is too powerful; nothing I have ever yet heard has lessened its effect on my mind.

"Even now, could some one prove to me, by solid reasoning, that there is nothing in the holy sacrament but bread and wine, there would be no need to employ all this violence in gaining me over to that view of the question. I am, unhappily, but too much inclined to that interpretation every time that the old man Adam makes himself felt within me; but as to what doctor Carlstadt sends forth on the subject, it affects me not at all, or rather, it confirms me in the opposite opinion; so that if I had not already arrived at a conclusion, such idle trash as his, derived as it were from the air, at all events, not from Scripture, would suffice to convince me that his views were erroneous."[1]

He had already, in his pamphlet *Against the celestial prophets*, thus expressed himself: "Carlstadt says, that, consistently with reason, he cannot conceive how the body of Jesus Christ should reduce itself into so small a compass; but I say, that, if we consult our reason, we shall no longer see any mystery in the matter. . . ." In the next page, Luther makes use of this almost incredibly daring buffoonery. "You think, perhaps, that Christ, having drunk too much at supper, muddled his disciples with unnecessary words."

This violent controversy of Luther against Carlstadt was embittered by the symptoms, which daily became more menacing, of a political outbreak in Germany. The doctrines of the daring theologian entirely corresponded with the thoughts and wishes which had for a long time pas occupied the minds of the popular masses in Suabia, Thuringia, Alsace; in a word, all the western part of the empire. The populace, the peasantry, for ages slumbering in a dull, heavy sleep beneath the weight of feudal oppression, had heard learned men and princes speak of liberty, of enfranchisement, and they applied to themselves that which was not at all designed to extend to them.[3] The protest of the poor peasants of Suabia, its barbarian simplicity wi

[1] Werke, ii. 58. [2] See Appendix XXX.

[3] The peasantry, however, had risen on several occasions previous to the Reformation. There had been insurrections in 1491, in 1492, in Flanders—when the insurgents, to the number of forty thousand, had painted on the standard the representation of an enormous cheese; and again, in 150: The free towns had followed this example; Erfurt in 1509, Spires in 151: and Worms in 1513. The disturbances had recommenced in 1524; b this time the insurgents were nobles. Franz Von Sickengen, their chie thought the moment was come for laying hands upon the property of eccl siastical princes; he had the audacity to lay siege to Treves. He was, it said, directed in his movements by the celebrated reformers, Œcolampa dius and Bucer, and by Hutten, who was then in the service of the arch bishop of Mayence. The duke of Bavaria, the palatine, the landgrave of Hesse, came to relieve Treves, and having done so, resolved to attac Mayence, as a punishment for the presumed connivance of the archbisho with Sickengen. The latter perished; Hutten was proscribed, and thenc forth unprovided with an asylum; he continued, however, to write h violent, furious pamphlets until the day of his death, which happened n long after, in the midst of utter misery.

remain as a monument of courageous moderation. By degrees, the undying hatred of the poor for the rich aroused itself. Less blind, indeed, than in the *Jacquerie*, and already aiming at a systematic form—which, however, it did not attain until the time of the English *levellers*—it embarrassed itself with the germs of religious democracy, which everybody thought extinguished. Lollards, Beghards, a whole host of Apocalyptic visionaries put themselves in motion. The rallying word, at a later period of the insurrection, was, the necessity of a second baptism; but from the very commencement throughout, the aim was a fierce war against established order, against order of every description: a war against property, it was a robbery of the poor man; a war against science, it broke up all natural equality, it attempted God, who revealed everything to his saints, and books and pictures, according to it, were inventions of the devil.

The peasantry of the Black Forest were the first to rise,[1] and their example was immediately followed by the people of Heilbron, of Frankfort, Baden, and Spires; thence the conflagration extended itself to Alsace, where it assumed a character more terrible than in any other direction. We next see its progress in the Palatinate, in Hesse, in Bavaria. In Suabia, the principal chief of the insurgents was one of the petty nobles of the valley of the Necker, the celebrated Goetz Von Berlichingen, *Goetz with the Iron Hand*, who, by his own account, however, only became their general on compulsion.

"Complaints and amicable demands of the united body of peasantry, with their Christian prayers; the whole briefly set forth in twelve principal articles.

"To the Christian reader, peace and divine grace by Jesus Christ.

"There are, at this time, many Antichristians, who take the occasion of the union of the peasantry to blaspheme the gospel, saying: these are the fruits of the new gospel, under which nobody is to obey, but all are to rear up, and insolently rise against their superiors, assembling and collecting together in great crowds and with unseemly violence, in the inten-

[1] See Appendix XXXI.

tion of abrogating all civil and ecclesiastical authority, and perhaps of slaying the persons who administer such authority. To this false and impious statement, the following articles will furnish a sufficient reply.

"First, they repel the opprobrium with which it is sought to cover the word of God; and, next, they offer a Christian exculpation of the peasantry from the reproach of disobedience and revolt.

"The gospel is not a cause of insurrection or disorder; it is the word which announces to us our Christ, our promised Saviour; the word and the life which it teaches are not hatred and violence, but love, peace, and patience. Since, then, the articles of the peasants, as will be manifestly seen, have no other aim than to make clear the gospel, and to live in conformity with it, how can the Antichristians designate the gospel a cause of disorder and disobedience. If the Antichristians and the enemies of the gospel resist such demands as ours, it is not the gospel which is the cause of this, but the devil, the mortal enemy of the gospel; who, by means of incredulity, has awakened in his followers the hope of oppressing and of effacing the word of God, which is only peace, love, and union.

"It clearly results, hence, that the peasantry who in their articles demand such a gospel for their doctrine and for their life, cannot be justly called disobedient or rebellious. If God calls us, and urges us to live according to his Word, if he is willing to listen to us, who shall find fault with the will of God, who shall assail his judgments, or contend against that which it is his pleasure to do? He heard the voice of the children of Israel, when they cried unto him, and he delivered them from the hand of Pharaoh. And can he not now also save his people from their oppressors? Yes, he will save them, and that soon. Christian reader, read the following articles with attention, and judge between us.

"1. In the first place, it is the humble demand and prayer of us all, it is our unanimous will, that henceforth we may have the power and the right of electing and choosing a pastor for ourselves; that we may also have the power and the right of deposing him, if he should conduct himself in a manner not befitting his calling. This pastor, so elected by us, should be allowed to preach to us the holy gospel, clearly, and in all its purity, without any addition of human precept or command. For, in announcing to us none but the veritable faith, occasion is given to us to pray God, to solicit his grace, to form within us, and to confirm it, that veritable faith necessary to salvation. If the divine grace enters not within us, we remain mere flesh and blood, and are good for nothing. It is perfectly clear from the Scripture, that we cannot arrive at God otherwise than by the true faith, that we cannot attain heavenly bliss otherwise than by his mercy. We, therefore, necessarily require such a pastor and guide as is appointed in the Scripture.

"2. Since tithe is established as lawful by the Old Testament (which the New Testament has confirmed in all things), we are willing to pay our legal tithe of corn, in a fair and legal manner. . . . It is our wish, that, in future, certain men, to be selected for that purpose by the inhabitants of each parish, may receive and collect the tithe; that out of it they may supply the pastor elected by the parish with enough to support him and his family in comfort and decency, and that what remains shall be applied to the relief of the poor of the parish. If there should still remain a surplus, it should be reserved to meet the expenses of war, of convoys, and other similar charges, and so deliver the poor peasantry from the taxes with which they have been hitherto oppressed for such purposes. In cases where it may have happened that villages have, under a pressure of poverty, sold their tithe, those who have purchased it will have nothing to fear from us: we shall be willing to make arrangements with them suitable to the circumstances, so as to indemnify them as speedily and as fully as possible. But as to those who have acquired the tithe of a village, not by a fair purchase, but by the arbitrary appropriation of themselves or their ancestors, we owe them nothing, and we shall give them nothing. The tithe, in such cases, will be applied in the manner already described. As to the small tithe, and the tithe of cattle and sheep, we shall pay none such; for the Lord our God created these animals for the free use of man. We regard this tithe as the invention of man, and consequently illegal, and we shall, therefore, cease to pay it."

In their third article, the peasants declare that they will no longer be treated as the property of their seigneurs. "For," say they, "Jesus Christ by his precious blood redeemed all men without exception, the herdsman equally with the emperor." They claim to be free, but free according to the gospel—that is to say, without licentiousness, and with a full recognition of authority, seeing that the gospel taught them to be humble, and to obey their rulers in all fitting and Christian things.

"4. It is contrary to all justice and charity, that the poor should have no share in the enjoyment of the game—the birds of the air, the fish in the running waters; and still more so, when all the while they are compelled to submit in silence to the enormous damage done to their fields by these beasts of the forest and birds of the air. It was not so ordained by God, who, when he created man, gave him power over all animals without distinction." . . . They add that, conformably with the Scripture, they would respect the just claims of such seigneurs as could prove, by clear title, their purchased right to particular fisheries; but that for the rest of the nobles, their alleged rights must forthwith cease and determine, without any indemnity whatever.

"5. All woods and forests, anciently common property, and which have passed into the hands of individuals by any other process than legal sale by legal parties, must return to their original proprietors, the local community, each of the members of which shall be entitled freely to derive thence the wood he requires for his use, in a proportion to be determined by the chief men in the parish.

"6. In this article, the peasantry demand an alleviation of the feudal services imposed upon them, and which they state are becoming day after day more and more overwhelming. They claim to serve *after the manner of their forefathers*, and according to the Word of God, and no otherwise.

"7. Let not the seigneur require at the hand of the peasant more gratuitous services than are set forth in their mutual compact.

"8. Many lands are rated too high. Let the seigneurs accept in this matter the award of such irreproachable men as may be selected, and diminish the rent according to their equitable decision, so that the peasant may not labour in vain; every labourer is entitled to the wages of his labour.

"9. Justice at present is administered with partiality. There are constantly new pains and penalties being established. We desire that henceforth no person may be favoured more than another, and that we may keep to the old laws.

"10. We desire that the fields and grass lands which have been severed from the commons, in any other way than by equitable sale, may be restored to the community.

"11. The fines and other payments made to the lord upon the death of vassals, are revolting in themselves, and openly opposed to the will of God, for they are a direct spoliation of widows and children; we desire that they may be wholly and for ever abolished.

"12. If it should be found on examination that one or more of the preceding articles are opposed to the Holy Scriptures (which, however, we do not believe), we at once renounce them by anticipation. If, on the contrary, the Scriptures should, on further examination, warrant us in additional protests against oppressions exercised by man on his neighbour, we, in like manner, reserve our right to make those protests, and do make them by anticipation."[1]

In this great crisis it was impossible for Luther to remain silent.[2] The nobles charged him with being the prime author of the disturbances; the peasants recommended their cause under the sanction of his name, and invoked him as arbiter in their demands: he did not refuse the dangerous and responsible charge.[3] In his reply to their twelve articles he constitutes himself judge between the prince and the people; in no part of his life, perhaps, did he assume a position more elevated or more commanding.

The reply runs thus: "Exhortation to peace in answer to the twelve articles of the peasants of Suabia, and also against the spirit of murder and rapine manifested by the insurgent

[1] Werke, ii. 64. The articles were drawn up by Christopher Schappeler.

[2] He had already, in 1524, exhorted the elector and duke John to take vigorous measures against the revolted peasants. " . . . Jesus Christ and his apostles did not overthrow temples or break images, they gained men's minds by the word of God; and this done, the images and the temples fell of themselves. Let us imitate their example. Let it be our aim to detach our brethren and sisters from convents and from superstition. This accomplished, let the authorities do what they think fit with the deserted convents and the condemned images. What matters it to us how long these stone walls and these stone or wooden images remain, so that mind is free? . . . . All this violence may serve the purpose of ambitious men, whose sole aim is notoriety, but it is not suited for those whose object is the salvation of souls." (21st August, 1524.)

[3] See Appendix XXXII.

peasants in other districts. The peasantry now assembled in Suabia have drawn up, and, by means of the press, extensively diffused twelve articles, setting forth their complaints and grievances, as against authority.

" In this document, what I most approve of, is that in the twelfth article they declare themselves ready to accept whatever gospel instruction shall be better than their own views, with reference to their complaints.

" If, indeed, this be their real intention (and making this declaration, as they have done in the face of men, without fearing the light, it befits not me to draw any other conclusion), there is still good ground to hope for a satisfactory termination of all this agitation and disorder.

" I must confess that I who am of the number of those who make the Holy Scriptures their constant study, being addressed by name by the peasants (who refer their case to me in one of their printed manifestoes),—I must confess, I say, that I feel peculiarly encouraged by this declaration on their part, to make public my opinion also on the matter in question, conformably with the precepts of charity which ought to unite all men. By so doing, moreover, I shall relieve myself before God and man from any reproach of having contributed by my silence to the evil, in the event of the present agitation terminating in a disastrous manner.

" It is possible that they have only made the declaration I have referred to, with a view to the producing an effect upon the public mind in their favour; and doubtless there are among them men wicked enough to attempt such an imposition; for it is impossible that in so great a multitude all should be good Christians; the likelihood being that many among them seek to pervert the honest feelings and upright views of the rest, to the promotion of their own private and sinister designs. Well, if there be imposture in this declaration, I announce to the impostors that they shall not succeed; and I tell them that even were they to succeed it would be at the cost of their eternal damnation.

" The matter in which we are now engaged, is great and dangerous; it affects both the kingdom of God and the kingdoms of the world, so nearly, that if this revolt were to extend itself and become successful, both one and the other would perish, the word of God and secular government, and ere long nothing would be seen throughout Germany, but universal devastation and ruin. Under such grave circumstances, therefore, it is urgently necessary that we should give our opinion, upon all the points involved, freely and without respect to persons. At the same time, it is not less necessary that all should become attentive and obedient, that we should cease to close up our ears and our hearts, in the manner we have hitherto done, and which has given to the anger of God so full a movement, so terrible a swing. The many fearful signs which, in these latter times, have manifested themselves in the heavens and on the earth, unquestionably announce great calamities to Germany; changes hitherto unprecedented. We, to our own misfortune, trouble ourselves little about them, but God will none the less pursue the course of his chastisement, until he shall have at length softened our iron hearts.

"FIRST.—*To the princes and nobles:* It is quite clear that we have no one upon earth to thank for all this disorder and insurrection, but you yourselves, princes and lords, and you especially, blind bishops, insane priests and monks, who, even to this very day, hardened in your perversity, cease not to clamour against the holy gospel, although you know it is just, and right, and good, and that you cannot honestly say anything against it. At the same time, in your capacity as secular authorities, you manifest yourselves the executioners and spoilers of the poor, you sacrifice everything and everybody to your monstrous luxury, to your outrageous pride, and you have continued to do this until the people neither can nor will endure you any longer. With the sword already at your throat, your mad presumption induces you to imagine yourselves so firm in the saddle, that you cannot be thrown off. If you alter not, and that speedily, this impious security will break your necks for you. I have many and many a time exhorted you to beware, least the verse of the Psalmist, *He poureth contempt upon princes,* become applicable to you. Thus far all your efforts have tended to the accomplishment of those words in your persons; you seem determined that the club raised over you shall fall and crush you; let me implore you to take counsel ere it be not wholly too late.

"The signs of the anger of God which have appeared in the heavens and upon the earth, are addressed to you, hitherto in vain. It is you, it is your crimes that God is about to punish. If the peasants, who are now attacking you, are not the ministers of his will, others, coming after them, will be so. You may beat them, but you will be none the less vanquished; you may crush them to the earth, but God will raise up others in their place; it is his pleasure to strike you, and he will strike you.

You fill up the measure of your iniquities by imputing this calamity to the gospel and to my doctrine. Go on with your calumnies; you will, ere long, discover their injustice. You refuse to learn from me what is the gospel, what my doctrine; there are others at your door who will teach you what both the one and the other are, in a way very different from mine, if you mend not speedily the error of your ways. Have I not at all times earnestly, zealously, employed myself in recommending to the people obedience to authority, to your authority even, tyrannous as it has been—intolerable as it has been. Who has combated sedition more energetically than I have always done? It is for this that the prophets of murder hate me as bitterly as they do you. You persecuted my gospel by all the means in your power, yet all the while that gospel called upon the people to pray for you, and aided you in supporting your tottering authority.

"See you not, that if I desired revenge, I should only have to stand silently by, laughing in my sleeve, and look on at the peasants carrying out their work; I might even, by making common cause with them, gash still deeper your wounds. God ever preserve me, as now, from such thoughts. Dear lords, whether you be friends or enemies to me, despise not the loyal succour I offer you—poor man though I be; and despise not, I entreat you, this sedition. I do not say that you are not stronger than those who have risen up against you; it is not they whom I would wish you to fear, but the Lord God in his anger. If he wills to punish you (and you have but too well deserved punishment at his hands), he will punish you; and if there were not peasants enough to act as his instruments, he would change stones into peasants; he would give power to one of them to kill a hundred of you; he would cause that against a weak unarmed peasant, neither your strength, nor your sharp weapons, nor your glittering armour should prevail.

"Dear lords, in the name of God retire before the anger of God, which you see let loose against you.

"We fear and avoid a drunken man. Cease your exactions, cease your cruel despotism; treat the peasants as a man of sense treats people who are drunk or insane.

"Enter into no contact with them, you know not how it may terminate. Use gentle means with them, least the spark now lighted, extending itself gradually round, catching from point to point, produce, throughout Germany, a conflagration which nothing can extinguish. You will lose nothing by gentleness, and even though you were to lose some trifling matter, the blessings of peace would make it up to you a hundredfold. Resort to war, and you may be all of you swallowed up, body and goods. The peasantry have drawn up twelve articles, some of these containing demands so obviously equitable, that the mere circumstance of their requiring to be made, dishonours you before God and man, and realizes Psalm cvii., for *it pours out contempt upon princes.*

"I myself have many articles, and even still more important ones, perhaps, that I might present against you in reference to the government of Germany, such as I drew up in my book addressed to the German nobility. But my words passed unheeded by you as the wind, and you must now therefore undergo the immediate and pressing demands of private interests.

"As to the first article, you cannot refuse them the free election of their pastors; they desire that these pastors should preach the gospel to them: authority may not and cannot interpose any prohibition of this, seeing, indeed, that of right it should permit each man to teach and to believe that which to him seems good and fitting, whether it be gospel or whether it be false. All that authority is entitled to prohibit is, the preaching up of disorder and revolt.

"The articles having reference to the physical condition of the peasants, the fines, and payments upon death, the exaction of illegal services, &c., are equally just; for authority was not instituted for its own ends, nor to make use of the persons subjected to it for the accomplishment of its own caprices and ill passions, but for the interests and advantage of the people. Now the people have become fully impressed with this fact, and, being impressed with it, they will no longer submit to your crying extortions. Of what benefit were it to a peasant that his field should produce as many florins as it produces grains of corn, if his lord may despoil him of the produce, and lavish, like dirt, the money he has thus derived from his vassal, in fine clothes, fine castles, fine eating and drinking. What you must do, first and foremost, is to put a stop to all this vain luxury of yours, to close up the holes through which this money runs, so that you may leave some little matter in the peasant's pocket.

"SECOND PART.—*To the peasants.*—So far, dear friends, for the princes; now let me, in all kindness and charity, address myself to you. I have acknowledged that the princes and lords who prohibit the preaching of the gospel, and who load the people with intolerable burdens, have well merited that the Almighty should cast them from their seats, seeing that they have sinned against God and against man, and are without excuse.

"Nevertheless, though your complaints are just, and your demands reasonable, it behoves you to prosecute those demands with moderation, conscience, and justice. If you act with conscience, moderation, and justice, God will aid you; and even though subdued for the moment, you will triumph in the end; and those of you who may perish in the struggle, will be saved. But if you have justice and conscience against you, you will fail; and even though you were not to fail, even though you were to kill all the princes, your body and soul, would be none the less eternally damned.

"Believe me, this is no trifling or jesting matter; it is a matter in which your body and your soul are intimately concerned. What you have to consider, is not your own strength or the wrongs you have sustained from your adversaries, but whether the course you pursue is consistent with justice and conscience.

"Put no trust, I pray you, in the prophets of murder whom Satan has raised up amongst you, and who proceed directly from him, though they sacrilegiously invoke the name of the holy gospel. They will hate me, I know, for the counsel I give you, they will call me hypocrite, but this I heed not a whit. What I desire is, to save from the anger of God the good and honest among you; I care not for the rest, I heed them not, I fear them not; let them despise me, if they will, I know One who is stronger than all of them put together, and he tells me in the 3rd Psalm to do that which I am now doing. The tens of thousands, and the hundreds of thousands, intimidate not me....

"You invoke the name of God, and you say that you will act according to his Word; forget not, before all things, that God punishes him who takes his name in vain. Dear friends, keep the fear of his anger ever before you. What are you, and what is this world? do you forget that He is the all-powerful and terrible God, the God of the deluge, the God who destroyed Sodom in his wrath? Now, it is easy to see that by your present conduct you do not honour to his name. Has not God said: *They that take the sword shall perish with the sword?* and Saint Paul: *Render, therefore, honour to whom honour is due.* How can you, after reading these precepts, still pretend that you are acting according to the gospel? Beware, beware, least a terrible judgment fall upon you!

"But say you, authority is wicked, cruel, intolerable; it will not allow us the gospel, it overwhelms us with burdens beyond all reason or endurance; it ruins us, soul and body. To this I reply, that the wickedness and injustice of authority are no warrant for revolt, seeing that it befits not all men indiscriminately to take upon themselves the punishment of wickedness. Besides which, the natural law says that no man shall be the judge in his own cause, nor revenge his own quarrel. The divine law teaches us the same lesson: *Vengeance is mine, saith the Lord, I will repay.* Your enterprise, therefore, is not only wrong according to Bible and gospel law, but it is opposed also to natural law and to equity; and you cannot properly persevere in it, unless you prove that you are called to it by a new commandment of God, especially directed to you, and confirmed by miracles.

"You see the mote in the eye of authority, but you see not the beam in your own. Authority is unjust, in that it interdicts the Gospel, and oppresses you with burdens; but you are still more in the wrong even than authority, you who, not content with interdicting the Word of God, trample it under foot, and arrogate to yourselves the power reserved to God alone. Which (I refer the decision of the question to yourselves) which is the greatest robber: he who takes a part, or he who takes the whole? Now authority, it is not to be denied, unjustly deprives you of your property, but you seek to deprive authority, not only of property, but also of body and of life. You say, indeed, that you will leave it something; but who will believe you? You aim to take from it power; he who takes all, does not hesitate, at will, to take also the part; when the wolf eats the sheep, he eats the ears also.

"Do you not perceive, my friends, that if your doctrine were tenable, there would remain upon the earth neither authority, nor order, nor any species of justice. Every man would act entirely as his own judge, his own vindicator, and nought would be seen but murder, rapine, and desolation.

"What would you do, if, of your own body, each member insisted upon his independence of the rest, administered his own justice, revenged his own quarrel? Would you permit this? Would you not say that it was for the leaders, for the superiors to judge of the matter?

"This is the law upon which even the Pagans, Turks, and Jews must act, who desire to maintain peace and order among them. So far, then, from being Christians, you would act worse than Heathens and Turks! What will Jesus Christ say, on seeing his name thus profaned?

"Dear friends, as I have said, Satan has sent among you certain prophets of murder, who aim at rule in this world, and think to achieve it by your means, without heeding for a moment the spiritual and temporal dangers into which they are hurling you.

"Let us pass on to the question of gospel law, a law which does not bind the heathen, as does the law of which we have just spoken. Jesus Christ, from whom you derive your title of Christians, says, in the gospel of St. Matthew, chap. V., *Resist not evil; but whosoever shall smite thee on thy right cheek, turn to him the other also.* Hear you that, assembled Christians? Now, I ask you, does your conduct answer to this precept? If you cannot suffer as our Lord calls upon you to suffer, at once lay aside his name, of which you are not worthy, or he himself will come in anger and tear it from you. *Love your enemies*, says Jesus Christ, *bless them that curse you, do good to them that hate you, and pray for them which despitefully use you, and persecute you.* Suffer the cross! Suffer the cross! That is the law taught you by Christ—the Law of laws! Yet, how do you obey that law? Oh, my friends, if you do these things, how can you fulfil the precept which commands you to love your enemies, and to do good unto them. . . Oh! would to God that the most of us, if nothing else, were at least good and pious pagans, who observed faithfully the natural law!

"In order to show you to what an extent your prophets have led you astray, I have only to recal to you one or two examples which manifest what the law of the gospel is. Consider Jesus Christ and St. Peter in the garden of Gethsemane: you recollect that St. Peter thought he was doing a good action in defending his Lord and master against those who came to betray him and to deliver him over to the hands of the executioners. And yet, you know, Jesus Christ reprimanded him, as though he were a murderer, for having resisted with the sword, saying: *They who take the sword, shall perish with the sword.*

"Another example: when Jesus Christ himself was bound to the cross, what did he? Did he not pray for his persecutors? did he not say, *Father, forgive them, for they know not what they do.* You know that Jesus Christ, after he had gone through his mortal sufferings, was glorified; you know that his kingdom has prevailed and triumphed. In the same way God would aid you, if you would submit lowlily and patiently to the long suffering he requires of you in this world.

"To take an example in the very times wherein we live: How, I ask you, has it happened that neither the emperor nor the pope has been able to effect anything against me? that the more strenuous the efforts they have made to arrest the progress of the gospel, and to destroy it, the more has the gospel gained ground and force. I have never drawn the sword; I have never taken a step towards revolt; I have always preached, always inculcated obedience to authority, even to the authority which was bitterly persecuting me; I always relied wholly upon God; I placed everything in his hands. It is for this reason, that, in despite of the pope and of the other tyrants, he has not only preserved my life, which is in itself a miracle, but he has also more and more advanced and spread my gospel; it is you yourselves, who, while you think you are serving the gospel, are in reality impeding it; you are giving it a terrible blow, you are destroying its effect in the minds of men, you are crushing it by your perverse and insane enterprise.

"I say all this unto you, my dear friends, that you may see to what an extent you are profaning the name of Christ and of his holy law; however just your demands may be, it befits not a Christian to draw the sword, or to employ violence; you should rather suffer yourselves to be defrauded, according to the law which has been given unto you (1 Corinthians, vi.), At all events, if you persist in carrying out the dictates of a perverse will, desecrate not the name of Christ, nor impiously make use of it as a pretext and cloak for your unrighteous conduct. I will not permit you to do so; I will not excuse it; I will wrest that name from you by any effort of which I am capable, sacrificing, if necessary, the last drop of blood in my veins. . .

"Not that I desire to justify authority; the wrongs it has committed are infinite, immense—I readily admit it; but what I desire is, that if, unhappily (which God forbid), if, unhappily, I say, you should come to blows, what I desire is, that neither the one nor the other of you presume to call yourselves Christians. It will be a war of pagans, and nothing else; for Christians fight not with swords or arquebuses, but with the cross and with patience, after the example of their general, Jesus Christ, who handled not the sword, but unresistingly suffered himself to be bound to the cross. Their triumph consists not in domination and power, but in submission and humility. The arms of our chivalry are of no corporeal efficacy; their force is in the Almighty.

"Entitle yourselves, therefore: men who follow nature, and will not endure evil; that is the name which befits you. If you do not assume it, but persist in retaining and incessantly pronouncing the name of Christian, I can regard you in no other light than that of enemies, equally with the pope and with the emperor, to myself and to the gospel. I would have you know, that, in this case, it is my determination to throw myself, in all confidingness, at the feet of God, and to implore him to enlighten your minds, and to save your souls, by taking part against you in this matter, so as to cause your enterprise to fail.

"I will risk my head herein, as I have already done in my resistance to the emperor and to the pope; for I see very

clearly that the devil, not having been able to get the better
of me by their means, aims at exterminating and devouring
me by means of the prophets of murder, who are among you.
Well, let him devour me: he will find me not very easy to
digest.

"But, dear friends, I entreat you humbly, and in a spirit
of sincere friendship, as one who wishes you well here and
hereafter, to pause before you proceed further in this matter,
to reflect most earnestly upon your real interests, and as the
fruit of your reflection, to relieve me from the painful duty
of fighting by prayer against you; for, though I am myself
but a poor sinner, yet I know that, in this case, reason is so
clearly on my side, that God would infallibly listen to my
solicitations. He himself has taught us in the Lord's Prayer
to say: *Hallowed be thy name on earth as it is in heaven.* It
is impossible that in your hearts you should feel confidence
in God, for the gospel and your own consciences alike condemn you—alike tell you that you are acting as heathens, as
enemies of the gospel. If you were Christians, you would
not resort to the sword, or to violence of any kind; but you
would humbly pray, *Thy will be done*; and, *Deliver us from
evil.* You yourselves set up to be your own God, your own
Saviour; the true God, the true Saviour, then, have abandoned
you.

"The demands you have drawn up, are not in themselves
contrary to natural law and to equity, but they are rendered
so by the violence with which you seek to force them from
the hands of authority; so, too, he who prepared them is not
a pious and sincere man; he has cited a great number of
chapters of the gospel, without giving the verses themselves,
which he has done for the purpose of seducing you, and involving you in danger by specious appearances, without
enabling you from the text itself to confute him.

"For I will tell you that when we come to read the chapters he has indicated, so far from their telling in favour of
your enterprise, they are, on the contrary, against you; for
they inculcate that all men should live and act as becomes
Christians. He who has thus essayed to attack the gospel
by your means, is assuredly a prophet of sedition and of
murder; but God will resist him, and preserve you from him.

"In the first place, you glorify yourselves in your preface, for that you only ask to live according to the gospel. But do you not yourselves admit that you are in revolt? How then, I ask you, can you have the audacity to cloak such conduct under the holy name of the gospel?

"You cite the example of the children of Israel. You say that God heard the cries which they sent up unto him, and delivered them from the hands of their enemies. Why ther do you not follow the example which you so complacently quote? Invoke God as they did, and wait in humble patience until he sends you also a Moses, who shall prove his missior by miracles. The children of Israel did not rise in insurrection against Pharaoh; they sought not to help themselves, a you seek to do. The example, therefore, which you quote, i directly against you, condemning your case, instead of establishing it.

"Nor is it true that your articles do, as you announce i your preface, teach the gospel; nor is it true that they ar conformable with it. Is there any one of the twelv founded upon evangelical doctrine? On the contrary, is no the sole object of them all the temporal emancipation o your persons and your property? Have they not all reference to temporal things? You covet power, and the good of the earth; you are unwilling to endure any wrong The gospel, on the contrary, has no heed to these things and constitutes the external life of Christians of suffering, o enduring injustice, of submitting to be defrauded, of bearin the cross, of patience, of contempt of life and of all th things of this world.

"It is absolutely essential, then, that you should eithe abandon your enterprise, and consent to endure the wrong that men may do unto you, if you desire still to bear th name of Christians; or else, if you persist in your resolution that you should throw aside that name, and assume som other. Choose one or the other of these alternatives: ther is no medium.

"You say that your tyrants prevent the gospel from comin unto you. I tell you that there is no power, either on eart or in heaven, which can do that. A public doctrine make its progress free and unconstrained beneath the wide vault c heaven. It is limited to no place, any more than the brigh star, which, traversing the air, announced to the wise men the east the birth of Christ. . . . If the gospel is interdicted in the town or village in which you happen to be, follow it to the town or village where it is preached. . . . Jesus Christ has said (Matthew x. 23), *When they persecute you in this city, flee ye into another.* He does not say, if they persecute you in one town, remain there, gather yourselves together against the lords in the name of the gospel, and make yourselves masters of the place.

"What! shall persons calling themselves Christians, dare to become, in the name of the gospel, thieves and robbers? Shall such men presume to entitle themselves followers of the gospel?

"Answer to Article 1.—If authority will not support a pastor who is agreeable to the feelings of a particular parish, the parish should support him at its own expense. If authority will not permit this pastor to preach, the faithful should follow him elsewhere.

"Answer to Article 2.—You seek to dispose of a tithe which does not belong to you; this would be a spoliation and robbery. If you wish to do good, let it be with your own money, and not with that of other people. God himself has told us that he despises an offering which is the product of theft.

"Answer to Article 3.—You wish to apply to the flesh the Christian liberty taught by the gospel, but I would ask you did not Abraham and the other patriarchs, as well as the prophets, keep bondmen? St. Paul himself tells us that the empire of this world cannot subsist without an inequality of persons.

"Answer to the eight last Articles.—As to your propositions respecting game, wood, feudal services, assessment of payments, &c., I refer these matters to the lawyers; I am not called upon to decide respecting them; but I repeat to you that the Christian is a martyr, and that he has no care for all these things; cease, then, to speak of the Christian law, and say rather that it is the human law, the natural law that you assert, for the Christian law commands you to suffer as to all these things, and to make your complaint to God alone.

"Dear friends, this is the monition and reply I have to give you, in answer to the demand you put to me. God grant that you may be faithful to your promise, to be guided in all your proceedings by the gospel! Do not cry out unreflectingly and hastily: Luther is a flatterer of princes, he speaks against the gospel; read calmly what I have written, and see whether it is not all based on the Word of God.

"Exhortation to both parties:—Since, then, my friends, neither the one nor the other of you are defending a Christian thing, but are both acting equally against God, abandon, I beseech you, all notion of violence. If you do not, you will cover Germany with horrible carnage, with disorder that will have no end. For as you are equally committing injustice, you will mutually ruin each other, and God will punish your wickedness by your own hands.

"You, lords, have against you Scripture and history; both teach you that tyranny has always been punished. You yourselves are tyrants and hangmen; you prohibit the gospel, and you can, if you persevere, have no hope of escaping the fate which has hitherto ever befallen men like you. Behold the empires of the Assyrians, of the Persians, of the Greeks, of the Romans,—all these have perished by the sword, because they rose by the sword. God has ever shown, in regard to all such dominations, that it is he who is the supreme judge and ruler of the earth, and that he will suffer no injustice to remain unpunished.

"You, peasants, have also against you Scripture and history. Never has revolt been truly successful or prosperous in its results, for God has ever provided for the strict fulfilment of his Word: *He that takes up the sword, shall perish by the sword.* Even though you were to triumph over the nobles, you, the conquerors of the nobles, would speedily tear one another to pieces like wild beasts. The spirit not ruling over you, but only the flesh and the blood, God would not delay to send among you an evil spirit, a destroying spirit, as he did to Sichem and its king.

"I am filled with anguish and pity when I reflect upon two inevitable calamities that are about to befal both parties: would to God I could avert them, by the sacrifice of my own life! In the first place, seeing that you both fight in an unrighteous cause, it is perfectly certain that all of you who shall perish in the struggle will be eternally lost, body and soul, for you will die in your sins, without repentance, without the succour of divine grace. The other calamity I foresee, with tearful eyes and bursting heart, is, that Germany will become a prey to devastation; for once such a carnage as is now threatened shall begin, it can hardly terminate until all parties are involved in the destruction. It is very easy to begin the battle, but it will not be in our power to put a stop to it, when once begun. Madmen! What have the old men, the women, and children, whom you will drag down with you into destruction—what have they done to you, that you should fill the country with blood and rapine, that you should make so many widows and orphans?

"Oh, this is a glorious, a joyful sight for the enemy of man! Satan must shout aloud with self-gratulation when he sees God thus terribly angry with us, thus menacing to overwhelm us with his wrath. Take heed, take heed, dear friends! you are all involved in the danger. I cannot think that, upon reflection, you will persist in damning yourselves eternally, and leaving behind you, in this world, a bleeding and burning country.

"My earnest counsel is, that you choose from among the nobles a certain number of counts and barons, and from among the commonalty an equal number of representatives, and that you leave it to these to arrange matters upon an amicable footing. You, lords, if you listen to me, will lay aside that insulting haughtiness which you have hitherto exhibited, but which you must, sooner or later, renounce, whether you choose or no; you will mitigate your tyranny, so that the poor man may at last enjoy a little ease and comfort. You, peasants, if you listen to me, will, on your part, make some concessions, will relinquish such of your articles as shall be considered to go too far. In this way, the matter, though not arranged according to the strict letter of the Gospel, will at least be accommodated consistently with human law.

"If you will not follow this my counsel (I pray God you may), I cannot prevent you from proceeding to open hostilities, but at least I shall be guiltless of the destruction of your goods, your lives, your souls. The burden of your sins will rest wholly upon yourselves. It will be, as I have said not a fight of Christians against Christians, but of tyrants and oppressors against robbers and profaners of the name of the gospel. They who perish in this struggle, will assuredly be eternally damned. For me, I shall now content myself with praying, together with my people, that God will prevent you from carrying out your unchristian purposes. I cannot but confess, however, that the terrible signs which have manifested themselves of late, in heaven and on the earth, have grievously afflicted my soul, and filled it with fear that the anger of the Lord has been too awfully aroused against us, and that he has said, as he said of others, in Jeremiah: *Though Moses and Samuel stood before me, yet my mind could not be toward this people.* God grant, however, that fearing his anger, you may repent and amend yourselves, so as at least to put off the evil day. These are the counsels which, as a brother and a Christian, I offer you in all sincerity, as my conscience testifies for me; God in his mercy permit that they bear good fruit. Amen!"[1]

The biographical character of this work, and the limits within which we are necessitated to confine ourselves, will not permit us to enter into the history of the German *Jacquerie* which now broke out. A few particulars respecting it will be found in the Appendix; here we shall content ourselves with giving the sanguinary proclamation of Dr. Thomas Munzer, chief of the insurgent peasants of Thuringia; it presents a singular contrast with the tone of gentleness and moderation which breathes throughout the Twelve Articles we have just cited. It runs thus:

"The true fear of God before all things. Dear brothers, how long will you sleep? Will you always continue in this disobedience to the will of God, because, blind-souled that you are, you think yourselves abandoned of him? How many times have I not already repeated to you my words of warning and of instruction? How many more times shall I have to repeat them? God will not, cannot reveal himself to you any more, disobedient as you are. Brothers, you must throw off this lukewarmness, you must stand forward firm and bold, or the sacrifice and the sufferings will all have been in vain; and you yourselves will begin to suffer then, again and worse than ever; this I predict to you. We must either suffer in the cause of God, or become the martyrs of the devil.

[1] Werke, ii. 66.

" Stand fast, then, resist, throw off this fatal fear and lethargy, cease to flatter the dreamers who have gone astray from the right path, and the impious reprobates who have never sought it. Arise, and fight the fight of the Lord! Make your brethren respect the testimony of God, or you will all miserably perish. Germany, France, Italy, have arisen in their strength; the Master, at length, wills to play his own game; the hour of the wicked is come.

" At Fulda, in Holy-week, four churches were sacked; the peasants of Klegen in Hegau, and those of the Black Forest, have risen, to the number of three thousand, and their number increases every day. All my apprehension is, least these heedless men should listen to some delusive compact, to the disastrous consequences of which they are blind. You are as yet but three thousand, it is true, but confiding in God, and vindicating his honour and glory, a hundred thousand enemies ought not to inspire you with a moment's fear.

" On—on—on! now is the time! the wicked tremble when they hear of you. Be pitiless, though Esau should give you fine words (Genesis, xxxiii.); heed not the groans of the impious ones; they will implore you with tender supplications, they will weep like children, but be not affected with their tears or their groans; God forbad Moses to show mercy (Deut. vii.), and he has revealed to us the same prohibition. Rouse up the towns and villages; above all, rouse up the miners of the mountains!

" On! on! on! on while the fire is burning—on while the hot sword is yet reeking with the slaughter! Give the fire no time to go out, the sword no time to cool. Kill all the haughty ones; while one of them remains alive, you will not be freed from the fear of man. While they reign over you, it is fruitless to speak of God.

" On! on! on! on while there is yet daylight. God marches on at your head; follow him firmly. The whole of this history is written and explained in St. Matthew, chapter xxiv. Fear not: God is with us, as it is written there, chapter ii., verse 2. God tells you to fear nothing. Be not intimidated by numbers. It is not your battle, but the battle of the Lord; it is he who fights, not you. Be bold, and you will receive the help of the Most High. Amen. Given at Mulhausen, 1525.—Thomas Munzer, servant of God against the wicked."

In a letter to the elector Frederic, and to duke John, Luther institutes a comparison between himself and Munzer: ". . . . I am but a poor man; I commenced my undertaking in fear and trembling; St. Paul did the same, as he himself confesses, Corinthians i., 3—6; yet he could truly boast of having heard a celestial voice. I hear no such voices, and I am not supported by the Spirit. With what humble reserve did I attack the pope in the first instance! How terrible were the struggles I had with myself! What earnest prayers did I offer up to God for aid and enlightenment! My very first writing proves all this. Yet with this poor spirit of mine, I did that which the terrible world-cracker yonder,[1] who, from his lofty position, scarce looks down upon us poor insects, I did that which he is afraid to do; I disputed at Leipsig, in the midst of a population altogether hostile to me; I appeared at Augsburg before my greatest enemy; I appeared at Worms, before the emperor and all the states of the empire, though I knew that my safeguard had been violated, and that snares and treachery awaited me.

"Poor and weak as I then was, my heart told me that I ought to repair to Worms, even though there were as many devils in it as there were tiles on the house-tops . . . . It was necessary, I felt, to dispute incessantly, against one, two, three, against as many as presented themselves, and in whatever method they might impose upon me. Weak and poor of mind, I was left to myself, like the flower of the field; I could select neither the adversary, nor the time, nor the place, nor the manner of the attack, nor its matter; I had to hold myself in readiness to answer all men that might assail me, or my doctrines and the true Word.

"But this wonderful spirit who has exalted himself as far above all of us as the sun is above the earth, who scarcely deigns to look down upon us poor worms and insects, he, forsooth, before he speaks, requires that the assembly he is to address shall be all favourable to his views, trusty adherents from whom no opposition, no doubt, is to be apprehended; resolutely refusing to hold any conference apart, with two or three disputants, who are not disposed to agree implicitly in

[1] Munzer, who had refused to engage in any controversy, or in any assembly, which was not favourable to his views.

his opinions . . . . We have no strength but that which Jesus Christ gives us; if we are left to ourselves, the sound of a falling leaf will make us tremble; but if He sustains us, our spirit is strong in his power and glory . . . . I am constrained at times to say more of myself, and more boastingly than I would wish, but St. Paul was also constrained to do so (Corinthians, ii. 11—16); I should be very willing to abstain from it, but I cannot, until these spirits of mischief and lying are effectually dispersed."[1]

Immediately after the defeat of the insurgent peasants, Melancthon published a brief history of Munzer. It is needless, perhaps, to add, that this narrative is altogether unfavourable to its subject. The author informs us that Munzer, having fled from the battle-field, so fatal to him, of Frankenhausen, concealed himself in a bed in a neighbouring cottage, and bound up his head, as though he were suffering from some malady, but a horseman of the opposite party, who came to the cottage, detected him by a paper in his portmanteau.

"While they were handcuffing him, he cried out several times, whereupon duke George, who had come up on hearing news of his arrest, said to him, 'Thou sufferest, Thomas; but the poor people suffered more who, led astray by thy persuasions, appeared in arms this day against authority, and have met their death at our hands.' 'They desired no other,' replied Thomas, with a loud laugh of a peculiar kind, which gave those present the idea that he was possessed of a devil."

On his trial, Munzer stated that the reformation of religion had long occupied his thoughts, and that he had availed himself of the insurrection of the peasants of Suabia as a favourable occasion for carrying his views on the subject into effect.

"On the approach of his last moments, he exhibited the most miserable pusillanimity; he was, indeed, so utterly stunned and overwhelmed with fear, that he could not even repeat the Belief. Duke Henry of Brunswick accordingly said it to him, and he followed the duke, paragraph by paragraph. He publicly admitted that he had been in the wrong,

[1] Werke, ii. 406.

but at the same time he exhorted the princes to be kinder and gentler towards the people, and to study the book of Kings; adding, that if they followed this advice, they need fear no repetition of the recent disorders. His head having been cut off, it was stuck at the end of a pike, and left exposed to public view for some time, as a warning to others."

A little while before his execution, he wrote to the inhabitants of Mulhausen, recommending his wife and children to their care, and entreating that none would visit his offences upon his family. In the same letter, he said: "Before I quit this world, I feel it my duty earnestly to exhort you all never again to have recourse to violence or revolt; strictly to avoid any further effusion of blood."

But whatever may have been the atrocities with which Munzer and the peasantry disgraced their struggle, one cannot but feel surprised at the harsh manner in which Luther speaks of them after their defeat. He could not at all get over the fact that their conduct had compromised the name of the Reformation .... "Miserable spirits of confusion! where are now the words with which you excited and aroused the poor misguided folk? When you told them they were the people of God; that God was fighting for them; that any one of them was able to cope with a hundred of the enemy; that with one sweep of a hat they could kill five adversaries; that the stones shot from the arquebuses against them, would turn against and destroy those who had discharged them? Where now is Munzer, with that great sleeve of his, in which he was to catch any weapon that should be hurled against his people? What God is that who for the last twelve months, has been prophesying by the mouth of Munzer?

"I think that all the peasants should perish, rather than the princes and magistrates, because the peasants have taken up the sword without divine authority.... No mercy, no toleration, is due to the peasants; on them should fall the wrath of God and of man." (30th May, 1525.) "The peasants are under the ban of God and of the emperor, and may be treated as mad dogs." In a letter of the 21st June, he enumerates the horrible massacres which had been committed by the nobles, without giving the least indication of sympathy with the fate of the victims.[1]

[1] See Appendix XXXIII.

He displayed more magnanimity with reference to his personal enemy Carlstadt, who was at this juncture exposed to very great danger, finding it very difficult, when called upon, to justify his conduct in having taught doctrines analogous to those of Munzer. He returned to Wittemberg, and humbled himself to Luther. The latter interposed in his favour, and obtained from the elector for Carlstadt the permission he had solicited, to establish himself as an agricultural labourer at Kemberg.

"I feel great commiseration for the poor man, and your grace need not be reminded that you should be kind and merciful towards the unfortunate, especially when they are not guilty in a moral point of view." (12th Sept. 1525.)

On the 22nd November, 1525, he writes again in these terms:—"Dr. Carlstadt has urgently entreated me to intercede with your electoral grace, that he may be allowed to inhabit the town of Kemberg; for he finds that the residence in a mere village is rendered disagreeable to him, and even dangerous, by the ill-will of the peasantry. Now, as he has kept himself quiet so far, and as, moreover, the provost of Kemberg can watch his proceedings for the future, I humbly beseech your electoral grace to comply with his request. I admit that your grace has already done a great deal for him, and that you have even involved yourself in calumny and suspicion on his account, but God will amply repay you for all these things. As to the salvation of Carlstadt's soul, that is his affair, and I trust he will see to it; in the meantime, he has immediate need of being put in a way to gain his livelihood; and I think we should do this for him."

".... To all dear Christians whom this writing shall reach, Dr. Martin Luther wishes the grace and peace of God the Father and of his Son Jesus Christ. Dr. Andrew Carlstadt has just sent me a manuscript, wherein he exculpates himself from the charge of having been one of the chiefs in the late rebellion, and he earnestly prays that I would cause this manuscript to be printed, in order to preserve the honour of his name, and perhaps even his life, which he finds in peril at the present moment, owing to the precipitancy with which they are proceeding against accused persons. It is, in point of fact, generally rumoured that authority is about to prosecute many poor people, and in such a spirit of blind anger that it is possible many innocent persons will suffer with the guilty, being allowed no time wherein to defend themselves from the charges brought against them; and I am inclined to believe the rumour, convinced as I am that the cowardly tyrants who of late trembled at the falling of a leaf, are now so insolently puffed up with their success, that they will go on glutting their cruelty until the appointed day when God shall throw them down in their turn.

"Now, though doctor Carlstadt is my greatest enemy in questions of doctrine, and though there is no chance or hope of our coming to a reconciliation on these points; the confidence which has inspired him to have recourse to me in his hours of peril, rather than to his pseudo-friends, who heretofore animated him against me, that confidence, I say, shall not be deceived, and I will render him this service, and any other that may be in my power."[1]

Luther then proceeds to express his opinion that, by the grace of God, all may yet turn out well with regard to Carlstadt, and that he will ultimately renounce his errors touching the sacrament. At the same time, he protests against the possible conclusions of those who may judge, from the course he takes in this matter, that he yields in the slightest degree any one of his points of doctrine. As to those who may accuse him of an excess of credulity, he replies by anticipation: "It befits neither myself nor any man to judge of the hearts of others. Charity is not suspicious; *Charity*, says St. Paul, *is long-suffering, and kind, and envieth not.*

"This, then, is my view of the case: as doctor Carlstadt offers to submit himself to a fair trial, and to undergo merited punishment if he can be shown to have taken part in the rebellion, I am bound to credit his word and his book, though, I confess, I had before felt disposed to believe him, in common with many others, animated with a spirit of sedition. But, under the altered aspect of his case, it is my duty to obtain for him the inquiry he solicits."

Further on, Luther charges the greater share of responsibility for the calamities which had lately befallen Germany,

[1] Werke, ii. 59.

upon the violence with which the princes and bishops had resisted the introduction of religious freedom. "Hence, among the people, has arisen that fury which, naturally enough will not abate until their tyrants are thrown down into the mud; that state of things cannot go on for ever, wherein the master's only idea is to inspire those under him with fear, instead of seeking to engage their affections also.

"Let our priestlings and our lordlings still keep their ears fast shut against all warnings; let them go on, let them have their swing for awhile; let them continue for awhile to throw upon the gospel the blame of the evil which they have brought upon themselves; let them mock the Word; ere long Another will come, who will say: 'I will have no prince nor bishop remain on the earth.' These men will very speedily find that which they have been so long seeking; the matter is in train. God grant they may repent in time, ere the thunderbolt strikes them! Amen."

". . . . I entreat the nobles, and the bishops, and all concerned, to allow Carlstadt to defend himself, since he assures us so solemnly he can exculpate himself from his alleged share in the rebellion, least God should become still more angry with us for our injustice, and the anger of the people be furiously, and with greater reason, aroused against authority. He who has promised to hear the cry of the oppressed, has never lied to us; and as he has the will to punish wrong-doers, so he has the power. May he grant us his grace! Amen." (1525.)[1]

"Germany is lost, I fear; she must, indeed, needs perish, since her princes will employ only the sword. Ah! they think they can thus pull out, hair by hair, the beard of the Great God. He will smite them, he will smite them!" (1526.)

"The minds of these tyrants are full of impotent malice, of cowardly malignity, of thoughts utterly opposed to honesty and honour. It is they, and not the people, who deserve to be slaves. Thank God, as far as I am concerned, I am sufficiently revenged for all they have done me, or can do me, in the thorough contempt I have for them and for Satan, their God." (Dec. 1525.)

[1] See Appendix XXXIV.

CHAPTER IV.

1524—1527.

Attacks of the rationalists upon Luther—Zwinglius, Bucer, &c.—Erasmus.

DURING the terrible tragedy of the peasants' war, the theological war upon Luther continued almost without intermission. The reformers of Switzerland and of the Rhine—Zwinglius, Bucer, Œcolampadius,—fully participated in the theological principles of Carlstadt, differing from him only in their submission to the civil authority. In all other respects, not one of them was prepared to remain within the limits which Luther had assigned to the Reformation. Cold, unbending logicians, they, bit by bit, sternly demolished what he had sought to preserve of the old poetry of Christianity. Less daring than they, but infinitely more dangerous, the king of the men of letters of that period, the phlegmatic but infinitely spiritual Erasmus, dealt doctor Martin, from time to time, some terrible blows.

It was long the great object with Zwinglius and Bucer,[1] men of great political capacity, to preserve, at all events, the apparent unity of protestantism. Bucer, *the great architect of subtleties*, as Bossuet calls him, concealed his opinions for a considerable period from Luther, and even executed the translation of his German works. "There is no one," says doctor Martin, "who has turned my writings into Latin with greater ability and exactitude than Bucer. He has mixed up with them none of his absurdities about the sacrament. I could not show my heart and thought better in words than he has done."[2]

A closer examination, however, showed him the infidelity

[1] The learned men of the 16th century were wont to translate their vernacular names into Greek. Thus Kuhhorn (Cow-horn) became Bucer; Hauschein (domestic light), Œcolampadius; Didier (*desiderium*, desire,) Erasmus; Schwartz-Erde (black-earth), Melancthon, &c. Luther and Zwinglius, the two popular reformers, alone retained their family appellations.

[2] Tischreden, 425.

of the translation. On 13th Sept. 1527, he writes to a printer to warn him that Bucer, in turning his works into Latin, had so altered certain passages as to make him say just the reverse of what he had said; and he earnestly requests his correspondent, in the event of his reprinting the volume in which these alterations by Bucer occurred, to intimate the fact to the public in a preface. In 1527, Luther attacked Zwinglius and Œcolampadius in a book, wherein he designated them new Wickliffites, and denounced their opinions as dangerous and sacrilegious.[1]

In 1528, we find him saying, with reference to Bucer: "I know too well the wickedness of Bucer to be at all astonished at his turning against myself what I have written for the sacrament.[2] Christ guard thee, poor Luther, surrounded as thou art with these wild beasts, these vipers, these lionesses, these panthers, far more in danger than was Daniel in the lion's den."

"Zwinglius I regard as having drawn down upon himself the just hatred of all good men, by his daring and criminal manner of treating the word of God." (27th Oct. 1527.)

"What a fellow is this Zwinglius! Ignorant as a block of grammar, and logic, and every other science." (28th Nov. 1527.)

In a second book he published against them in 1528, he says: "I reject and condemn, as unmixed error, all doctrine that proceeds upon the principle of free will." This was his grand quarrel with Erasmus. It had commenced in the year 1525, when Erasmus published his book, *De Libero Arbitrio.* Up to that period, the two men had been on terms of friendship. Erasmus had several times taken up the defence of Luther; and the latter, in return, had consented to respect Erasmus' neutrality on other points. The following letter will show that, in 1524, Luther still felt it necessary to observe some circumspection with reference to the powerful writer of Rotterdam.

"I have remained silent long enough, dear Erasmus; I have waited month after month, in the expectation that you, as being the greater man of the two, would be the first to renew our correspondence; as you have not done so, charity commands me to set you the example. I do not reproach you with

[1] See Appendix XXXV.

having kept apart from us, knowing that your wish was not to complicate or embarrass the cause you were maintaining against our enemies the papists. My only vexation is, that in the books you have published, you have, in several places, in order to conciliate their favour or mitigate their fury, dealt us sundry sharp side blows and cuts, which we had no reason to expect at your hands. We have seen, clearly enough, that the Lord has not seen fit to bestow on you, as yet, the energy and the direction of mind necessary to enable you to attack these monsters roundly and boldly; and we are not men to require from you efforts beyond your present strength. We have respected in you the will of God, who has meted out to you, in this respect, but limited gifts. On the other hand there is no one can deny that it is you who have mainly contributed to the flourishing rise of letters we have witnessed and which gives so powerful an assistance to the right understanding of Scripture; the powers which God has granted to you in this respect, are great, admirable, magnificent, and heartily do we thank him for bestowing them upon you Impressed with these feelings, I have never desired to see you step beyond the limits assigned you by Providence, and come over to our camp; you would render us great services there, doubtless, with your rare intellect and your fine eloquence; but since your heart falls short of the requisite degree of confidence, it is better you should serve us in your own way. My great fear has been least you should be induced by the seductions of our enemies, to write against our dogmas in which case I should have been compelled, though most unwillingly, to oppose you, face to face. As it is, I have had great difficulty in persuading some of our people to lay aside books they had written for the purpose of drawing you into the arena. I was deeply pained, influenced as I have throughout been by these views, when I saw Hutten's *Expostulatio* published, and still more so when I read your *Sponge for Hutten.* If you will reflect upon this production, you must admit that, however easy it may be to write lectures recommending moderation, and to charge Luther with intemperance of language and manner, it is difficult, nay impossible, to practise these lessons of yours, unless one is singularly favoured by Providence. Believe it or not, as you will, but Christ is my witness, I pity you from the bottom of my soul, when I see you exciting by your conduct so formidable a body of enemies, whose indignation and hatred cannot be matters of indifference to a mind constituted as yours is, so susceptible of human weakness. Yet, at the same time, I am not at all prepared to say that the anger entertained against you by our people, is not the result of a perfectly legitimate zeal, deeming, as they do, that your attacks upon them have been wholly unwarrantable and unprovoked.... For myself, I am, I admit, irritable, and often led away, under the impulse of indignation, to write with greater bitterness than I myself approve of upon reflection, but I have never yielded to such intemperance, except in the case of persons whom I deemed perversely obstinate. Gentleness and kindness towards all others, however wicked and foolish they might be, it has always been my care to observe; and my own conscience and the experience of many persons, fully bear me out in the assertion. In the same way, despite all your side blows at us, I have restrained my pen, and have promised I will restrain it, until you openly declared yourself against us, which I hope may not happen. For though we differ wholly on many subjects, though I am deeply pained to observe the manner in which you express your opinions, your doubts and disapprobation, on some of the most material points of religion, I cannot, and will not, charge you with what I deem perverse stubbornness.[1] But what am I to do? On both sides, the feeling is one of a very bitter character. For my own part, if I could be admitted to mediate, I would have our people cease from attacking you, and allow your old age to go to rest peacefully in the Lord. They would do so, I am persuaded, if they would once take into proper consideration your advanced years, and the greatness of the cause they are fighting for, and which you should not be blamed for not appreciating, seeing that its comprehension is above your grasp. They should bear in mind that things with us have attained such a position, that our cause would be but very slightly endangered, even though Erasmus were to concentrate against it the entire amount of his intellectual strength.....Yet it is quite intelligible that our people should feel sore at your attacks upon them, knowing, as we all do, what an influence the bare name of Erasmus exercises over mankind, how great his authority is as against any adver-

[1] See Appendix XXXVI.

sary; to have one bite from Erasmus, is worse than being assailed at once by the whole world of papists put together. I admit this, dear Erasmus, as a proof of the candour I desire to observe towards you, and because I would have God inspire you with a moral mind worthy of your exalted intellectual fame. If He should not send you, heart and soul, amongst us, at least let me entreat of you, that you remain a silent spectator of our tragedy. Do not join your forces with those of our adversaries; publish no books against me, and I will publish none against you. As to those who complain that they are attacked in the name of Luther, remember that they are men like you and me, to whom we must grant indulgence and pardon; and that, as St. Paul says, we should *bear one another's burdens.* The mutual biting and snarling I have deprecated is quite bad enough; but let us, at all events, refrain from absolutely devouring each other." (April, 1524.)

To Borner, our reformer writes thus: "Erasmus knows less about predestination than even the Sophists of the school did. He is in no degree formidable as to this matter, any more than he is on the other questions of Christian doctrine. I shall take care, however, not to assail or exasperate master Erasmus; and even though he should assail me once, nay twice, I would not answer him; for it would be very imprudent just now to bring him down upon us, with all the immense power of his eloquence. . . . Still, should the necessity arise, I shall take my stand in all firmness and confidence, face to face, even with the most eloquent Erasmus. I know myself to be a mere child in comparison with him; but, strong in the goodness of my cause, I care not for his credit, his name, his reputation. I have no ill-will to Mosellanus for attaching himself to Erasmus rather than to myself. Tell him from me he is at full liberty to be Erasmian all over." (28th May, 1522.)

It is evident that this state of things could not endure for any permanence; and, at length, the publication of the *De Libero Arbitrio* served as a regular declaration of war between the parties.[1] On its appearance, Luther at once admitted that the real question was now at last placed at issue.[2] "What I admire, what I praise in you, is that you alone

[1] See Appendix XXXVII. [2] Ib.

have gone to the root of the matter, to that which is the question of questions—free will. You alone do not weary me with quarrels foreign to the point, about the pope, and purgatory, and indulgences, and other insipid affairs; you alone have laid hold of the knot of the thing—you have seized it by the throat. Thanks, Erasmus.

"It is irreligious, say you, superfluous, a mere effect of idle curiosity, to seek to know whether God is endowed with prescience; whether our will is active in that which relates to eternal salvation, or merely passively suffers the action of grace; whether, as to what we do of evil or good, we do it, or suffer it. . . . Great God! if such an inquiry as this be irreligious, be superfluous, be trifling, what inquiry on earth is there that can be characterized as religious, grave, or useful? Erasmus, Erasmus, you can hardly allege ignorance as the excuse for the mischievous fallacy you here advance. In a man of your age and experience, who has lived so long amongst a Christian people, who has so long considered and weighed the Holy Scriptures, such conduct is without excuse, and leaves you exposed to the just animadversion of all good men. 'Tis monstrous that you, a theologian—you, a Christian doctor, not content with your habitual scepticism, should thus come forward and publicly decide that things are altogether superfluous, without which there is no longer God, or Christ, or gospel, or faith, or any one of the elements, I will not say of Christianity, but of Judaism!"[1]

It was to little purpose Luther put forth all his strength, all his eloquence; he could not burst the chains which circled him round about. "Why," asks the cool, subtle Erasmus, "why does not God remove the vice of our will, since our will is not in our power; or why does he make us responsible, if the vice of the will is inherent in man. The vase says to the potter: why did you create me for eternal flames? If man is not free, what is the meaning of *precept*, *action*, *recompence*, of the whole circle of such expressions? What is the meaning of, *Turn ye from your sins?*" . . . .

Luther had great difficulty in answering Erasmus: "God," says he, "speaks thus to us, solely for the purpose of convincing us that we are powerless, unless we implore His aid.

[1] See Appendix XXXIX.

Satan says: 'Thou mayest act.' Moses says: *Act;* in order, by practical proof, to convince us, against Satan, that we cannot act." An absurd, and, so to speak, cruel reply, as it appears to us, amounting to a proposition that people are to be bound, and that then a task-master is to say to them, *Walk!* in order practically to prove to them they cannot walk, and beat them, moreover, each time they helplessly fall. Retreating from before the consequences, which Erasmus draws or suggests, from his premises, Luther rejects all systems of interpretation of the Scriptures, though, at the same time, he himself is fain to have recourse to them, in order to escape from his adversary's conclusions. For instance, he explains, in the following manner, the *I will harden the heart of Pharaoh:* God does evil in us, that is to say, by us, not from any fault of his, but as the result of our own vices; for we are all sinners by nature, while God is incapable himself of doing aught but good. In virtue of his omnipotence, he draws us with him in his action; but, omnipotent as he is, all good as he is, he cannot help an evil instrument producing evil."

It must have been a subject of great exhilaration to Erasmus to see the triumphant opponent of popery painfully writhing under the blows which he inflicted upon him, and seizing, for the purpose of resistance, a weapon so dangerous to him who wielded it. The more Luther struggled, the greater his apparent advantage, the more did his victory involve him in perilous quagmires.[1] He plunged so deeply into immorality and fatalism, as to be compelled to admit that it was necessary for Judas to betray Christ. Luther, accordingly, retained a most bitter recollection of this dispute. He himself laboured under no delusion as to the real nature of what some called his triumph; he quite felt that the solution of the terrible problem was not furnished in his *De Servo Arbitrio;* and, until the latest day of his life, we find the name of him who had thus forced him on to the most immoral consequences of the doctrine of grace, mixed prominently up, in his writings and discourses, with his fiercest denunciations against the blasphemers of Christ.

He was more especially exasperated at the apparent mode-

[1] See Appendix XL.

ration of Erasmus, who, not daring to assail the edifice of Christianity at its base, seemed desirous of overturning it gradually, stone by stone. This manœuvring, this ambiguous method of proceeding did not at all suit Luther's straightforward energy.[1] "Erasmus," says he, "that amphibolous being, sitting calmly and unmoved on the throne of amphibology, cheats and deludes us by his double-meaning, covert phraseology, and claps his hands when he sees us involved in his insidious figures of speech, as a spider rejoices over a captured fly. Then, seeing the occasion arrived for the display of his rhetoric, he comes thundering down upon us, tearing us, flagellating us, crucifying us, throwing all hell at our heads, because we have, as he says, apprehended in a calumnious, infamous, and diabolical manner, words which, though he says not, he all the while meant we should understand in the sense wherein we have understood them. See him in another direction, crawling on like a viper to ensnare simple souls, after the manner of the serpent of old, which whispered in the ear of Mother Eve, and made her doubt the precepts of God." The quarrel, in point of fact, caused Luther, whatever he may say to the contrary, so much annoyance and embarrassment, that at last he refused to continue the discussion, and even forbade his people to take the matter up for him. "If I fight against mud, whether I get the better of it or no, I am all the same covered with mud, and so the best way is to let mud pass on."[2]

"I would not," he writes to his son John, "I would not for ten thousand florins ready money, take upon myself the peril in which Jerome, and still more Erasmus, will be, when they find themselves in the presence of Christ.

"If ever I get well and strong again, I will fully and publicly assert my God against Erasmus. I will not sell my dear Jesus. I am daily approaching the grave—nearer and nearer—and I am, therefore, anxious to lose no time in once more, and emphatically asserting my God in the face of all, against this bad man. Hitherto I have hesitated; I said to myself, if you kill him, what will happen? I killed

[1] See Appendix XLI.

[2] Hoc scio per certo, quod si cum stercore certo,
Vinco vel vincor, semper ego maculor.

Munzer, and his death at times weighs upon me, but I killed him because he sought to kill my Christ."[1]

One Trinity Sunday, again, Dr. Martin said: "I entreat all you present, with whom the honour of Christ and the gospel is felt to be a serious matter—I pray you all to vow enmity to Erasmus."

On another occasion he said to Dr. Jonas and Dr. Pomeranus, with peculiar and manifestly heartfelt emphasis: "I recommend it to you as my last will, to be terrible and unflinching towards that serpent.—If I myself am restored to health, by God's help I will write against him and kill him. We have suffered him to insult us, and to take us by the throat; but now that he seeks to do so to Christ, we will array ourselves determinedly against him. It is true that to crush Erasmus is like crushing a bug, but he has mocked and insulted my Christ, and he shall be punished."

"If I live, I will, God aiding, purge the church of this vile creature. It is he who sowed and cultivated Crotus, Egranus, Witzeln, Œcolampadius, Campanus, and other visionaries and epicureans. He shall be expelled the church, I tell him."

On seeing a portrait of Erasmus, one day, Luther burst out—"That fellow, as his face manifestly proves, is full of trick and underhand malice—a very fox—a knave who has mocked God and religion. He makes use, indeed, of fine-sounding words: 'The dear Lord Christ, the Word of Salvation, the Holy Sacraments,' and so on, but as to the truth, he cares not a straw for it. When he preaches, it rings false, like a cracked pitcher. He once attacked Popery, and now he is trying to pull its head out of the mud."

CHAPTER V.

1526—1529.

Luther's marriage[2]—Poverty—Depression—Illness—Belief in the approaching end of the world.

THE strongest mind could not be expected to resist so many shocks, and Luther's had been visibly giving way ever since the crisis in the year 1525.

[1] Tischreden, 299. [2] See Appendix XLII.

The part in which he had so long and so prominently appeared before the world, had been changed, and in a manner most painful to his own feelings. The opposition instituted by Erasmus was a clear manifestation of the estrangement from Luther of the men of letters, who had so powerfully aided his cause in the outset. This, in itself, had a very depressing effect; and the book, *De Libero Arbitrio*, was allowed to remain without any earnest answer. Again, the great innovator, the leader of the people against Rome, had since found himself left behind by the people, cursed by the people, in the war of the peasants. We need not, therefore, feel any surprise at the dejection of mind into which he fell at this period. As the intellectual man grew weaker, the empire of the flesh became stronger ; and, yielding to its impulse, Luther married. The next two or three years are a sort of eclipse of the sun of Luther ; whenever, during their course, we catch sight of him, we find him generally engaged in the material cares of life,[1] which, as may have been expected, did not serve to fill up the void in a mind like his. Accordingly, he, at last, gave way : a grand physical crisis marked the close of this period of atony.[2] He was aroused from his lethargy by the double danger of Germany—menaced from without by the arms of Soliman (1529), and within, as to its liberty and faith, by Charles V., at the diet of Augsburg, (1530.)

" Since from the very nature of woman as created by God, she necessarily requires the support and society of man, we need inquire no further : God is on our side : let us then honour marriage, as a thing honourable and divine.[3]

" This mode of life was ordained by the Almighty from the very beginning of the world; he has been pleased to continue it from that time to the present, and he will glorify it to the last. Where were the kingdoms and empires of this earth, when Adam, when the patriarchs, their sons, and their daughters married and were given in marriage? From what other state of life does empire itself descend, from generation to generation? The wickedness of man has caused it to be necessary for the magistrate to take the institution of marriage under his control to a great extent; and has occa-

[1] See Appendix XLIII. [2] Ib. XLIV. [3] Ib. XLIV.

sioned itself to become, as it were, an empire of war, but, in its early purity and simplicity, marriage was the empire of peace." (17th Jan., 1525.)

"You tell me, in your last letter, my dear Spalatin, that you are desirous of resigning your office and of retiring from the court. My advice is, that you remain there; unless, indeed, your intention, in retiring, is to marry. . . . For myself, I am in the hands of God, as a creature whose heart he may change and change again, whom he may kill or vivify at any hour, at any moment. Yet, in the state wherein my heart always has been, and still is, I shall not take a wife; not, God knows, that I have no consciousness of the flesh, not that I am a stock or a stone, but because my mind is not turned towards marriage at a period when every day I am in expectation of encountering torture and death as a heretic." (30th November, 1524.)

"Be not surprised that I do not marry, I who am *sic famosus amator.* And yet, perhaps, it is matter of wonder that one who has so constantly written in favour of marriage, and who has been so much in the society of women, should not himself, ere this, have been woman enough to marry. If you would regulate yourself by my example, here it is: I have had with me at one and the same time no fewer than three women, whom I loved and whom I should have liked to marry, but I have let two of them pass on and wed other husbands. The third is still with me, and I am holding on to her with my left hand; but, if I take not care, she too will escape me." (16th April, 1525.)

To Amsdorf he writes thus, on the 21st June, 1525: "I am a married man.[1] Hoping yet to live some time, I can no longer refuse to my father the desire he has so long expressed of leaving behind him a posterity through me. Moreover, I am anxious to be myself an example of what I have taught; and the more so, that many around me fail to practise that which is clearly commanded in the gospel. It is the will of God I follow in this matter; I do not feel towards my wife any burning passion, any lawless love, but simply affection."

The person whom Luther married was a young woman of noble family,[2] an escaped nun, twenty-four years old, and

[1] See Appendix XLVI. [2] Ib. XLVII.

remarkably handsome. Her name was Catherine de Bora. It seems that she had previously been attached to Jerome Baumgærtner, a young doctor and senator of Nuremberg; for we find Luther writing to the latter on the 12th October, 1524: "If you are anxious to have your Ketha, come here at once, or she will become the property of another, who has already got her with him in his house. However, she has not as yet conquered her love for you; and, after all, I should be perhaps better pleased that you, having a prior title, should be united to her."

On the 12th August, 1526, a year after his marriage, he writes thus to Stiefel: "Catherine, my dear rib, salutes you. She is quite well, thank God; gentle, obedient, and kind in all things, far beyond my hopes. I would not exchange my poverty with her, for all the riches of Crœsus without her."

His poverty, indeed, at this period was extreme; and anxious to provide for his wife, and the family he saw reason to anticipate, he determined to have recourse to some occupation for a livelihood: "If the world will not support us for the sake of the Word, let us learn to support ourselves by the labour of our hands." As a matter of choice, doubtless, had the matter been open to him, he would have selected one of the arts he so loved—that of Albert Durer and of his friend Lucas Cranach, or music, which he was wont to call the first science after theology; but, unprovided with a master to teach him either of these, he became a turner. "Since amongst us barbarians there is no man of art to instruct us in better things, I and my servant, Wolfgang have set ourselves to turning." In one of his letters, we find him directing Wenceslaus Link to purchase the necessary instruments for him at Nuremberg. He also applied himself to gardening and building. "I have laid out a garden," he writes to Spalatin, (December, 1525,) "and I have constructed a fountain, and have succeeded excellently well in both undertakings."

In April, 1527, writing to an abbot at Nuremberg, who had made him a present of a clock, he says: "I must put myself to school with some mechanician, so that I may understand the wonderful details of the clock you have sent me, for I never saw anything like it before." And, a month after, he writes: "I have received the turning tools, and the dial, and the cylinder, and the wooden clock. You omitted to mention how much more I have to pay you. For the present, I have got tools enough, unless, indeed, you have any instruments newly discovered that will turn of themselves, while that idle knave of mine is snoring or gaping about him. I have made considerable progress in clock-making, and I am very much delighted at it, for these drunken Saxons need to be constantly reminded of what the real time is; not that they themselves care much about it, for so long as their glasses are kept filled, they trouble themselves very little as to whether clocks or clockmakers, or the time itself, go right." (19th May, 1527.) "My melons," he writes, on the 5th July, "as well as my gourds and pumpkins are getting up famously; so you see the seeds you sent me were not thrown away."

Melons, gourds, and pumpkins, however, are but a miserable resource, and Luther soon found himself in a situation as singular as it was afflicting. Here was the man who had defied and fought popes and sovereign-princes, compelled to depend for his daily subsistence upon the precarious and scanty aid of the elector. The new church, in throwing off the thrall of popery, had placed itself in subjection to the civil authority, and the civil authority had left it, from its very birth, to starve.

In 1523, Luther wrote to Spalatin, proposing to resign the revenue of his convent into the hands of the elector: "Since we no longer read, nor sing, nor say mass, nor do anything our founder contemplated that we should do, we have no business to live upon his money, and we ought, therefore, to hand over the property to whomsoever may show a better title to it. (November.)

"Staupitz has not sent us our money yet, and meantime we are becoming more and more involved in debt.[1] I don't know what to do; whether to send once more to the elector, or to let things take their course, from bad to worse, until absolute misery and starvation compel me, for aught I know, to quit Wittemberg, and make it up with the pope and the emperor." (November, 1523.) "Here we are expected to pay everybody, and yet nobody pays us. Things are come

[1] See Appendix XLVIII.

to a fine pass, truly!" (1 February, 1524.) "I am becoming day by day more and more overwhelmed with debt; I shall be compelled to solicit alms, by and by." (24th April, 1524.) "This sort of thing cannot possibly continue. These delays on the part of the prince necessarily give rise to great suspicions in our minds. As to myself, I should long since have quitted the convent, to live elsewhere by the labour of my hands (though here, God knows, I labour hard enough,) had I not feared thereby to compromise the gospel and my prince." (December, 1524.)

"You ask me for eight florins: where on earth am I to get eight florins? As you know, I am compelled to live with the strictest economy, and yet my want of means, perhaps my want of care, has necessitated me to contract, during the past year, debts amounting to more than a hundred florins, which I must, somehow or other, and at some time or other, repay to various persons. I have been obliged to pawn three goblets, presents from different people, for fifty florins, and absolutely to sell one for twelve." (He writes elsewhere, with reference to this debt: "The Lord, who punished me so long for this imprudence of mine, has at length relieved me from its effects.") "Neither Lucas nor Christian will any longer accept me as security, for they have found that by doing so, they either lose all the money, or that my poor purse is drained of its last penny." (2nd February, 1527.)[1]

"Tell Nicholas Endrissus to send to me for some copies of my works. I have retained certain claims upon my publishers in this respect, as is just, seeing that, poor as I am, I get no money from them for my labour,[2] nor any other return, except that of, now and then, a copy or two of my productions.[3] This is not too much to expect, I should say, considering that other writers, even mere translators, receive a ducat a sheet for their manuscript." (5th July, 1527.)

"What has occurred, my dear Spalatin, that you should write to me in so menacing and imperious a tone? Has not Jonas already undergone enough of your contumely, and that of your prince, that you are still so inveterate against the excel-

[1] Luther's income never exceeded two hundred Misnian florins.

[2] See Appendix XLIX.

[3] The bookseller had offered him an annual stipend of four hundred florins for whatever he might write, be it less or more, but he did not think it right to take the money.

lent man. I know the prince's character well, I know with what slights he is in the habit of treating men. . . . Is it, I ask you, honouring the gospel, to refuse to its ministers a small subsistence? I tell you, it is at once gross injustice and treacherous meanness to order him privately to depart, and yet in public to wear an air as though you had given him no such order. Think you that your tricks will pass unobserved by Christ? . . . I don't imagine that we have been the occasion of any pecuniary loss to your prince; on the contrary, I am pretty certain that he has already realized a very handsome balance of the goods of this world by our means, and that he is likely to realize still more. I have no fear but God will provide us with food, if you refuse it us; but for your own sakes, dear Spalatin, I beseech you to treat us poor exiles in Christ with greater consideration and kindness. At all events, I request you to explain yourself distinctly and definitely, in order that we may know what we are about; whether we are to go or stay, and that we may be no longer made fools of by people, who, while they order us to go forth, are afraid of our naming, in our own justification, those who compelled us to take that step." (27th November, 1524.)

"We have received, dear Gerard Lampadarius, the letter and the cloth you have so benevolently bestowed upon us. . . We burn the lamp you gave us, every night; and both Catherine and myself frequently lament that we have been able to make you no little present in return, at once to mark our gratitude, and that you might have something about you which should retain us in your memory. I am ashamed of myself, that I have hitherto omitted to make you even a present of some printed paper, for that is in my power; but I will not delay to send you a parcel of my books. I would have forwarded you herewith a German Isaiah I have just published, but there has been such an overflowing demand for the work, that I have absolutely not got a copy left." (14th October, 1528.)

To Martin Gorlitz, who had sent him a barrel of beer, he writes: "Thy Cerealian gift from Torgau has been done noble justice to. I assure thee, that it has dispensed happiness in appreciating quarters. My co-visitors seemed as though they would never have done drinking and praising it, praising it and drinking it. They exalted its qualities above those of all the barrels of beer they had ever been at the broaching of. And here have I, lout that I am, omitted till this present moment, to thank thee and thy Emilia for the bounteous gift! But the fact is, I am a poor οιχοδεσποτης (housekeeper), so heedless of domestic affairs, so forgetful, that, until the other day, I had not recalled to mind that thy pleasant donation was in my cellar at all; and then it was my servant who brought it to my recollection. Salute, in my name, all our brethren, and, more especially, salute in my name, thy Emilia and her son, the graceful hind and the young fawn. May the Lord bless thee, and multiply thee a thousand-fold, in the Spirit as in the flesh!" (15th January, 1529.)

On the 29th March, 1529, Luther sends word to Amsdorf, that he is about to receive into his house the wife of a mutual friend, who is near her confinement: "If my Catherine should be brought to bed at the same time, so much the worse for thy pocket; so come, having first girded on, not a sword, but a bag with silver and gold therein, for I will not let thee off without a handsome present on the occasion."

To Jonas he writes: "I had read ten lines of your letter when it was announced to me that my Ketha had given me a daughter. *Gloria et laus Patri in Cœlis.* My little John has recovered. Augustin's wife is getting better, and so is Margaret Mochinn, whose escape from death seems an absolute miracle. On the other hand, we have lost five pigs, which is very disagreeable; however, I hope the plague will accept them as our full contribution: *Ego sum, qui sum hactenus, scilicet ut Apostolus, quasi mortuus, et ecce vivo.*"

The plague had broken out in Wittemberg, just as Luther's wife was on the eve of her confinement, and his little son very ill with his teeth. Two women who were on a visit in the house, Hannah and Margaret Mochinn, were attacked with the pestilence, so that he might truly say, as he did in a letter to Amsdorf, (1st Nov., 1527,) "My house has become a regular hospital."

"The wife of George, our chaplain, died a few days ago of the plague. Everybody seemed afraid to have any intercourse with the poor fellow, so we took him and his children into our house." (4th Nov., 1527.) "Thy little favourite, John, does not salute thee, for he is too ill to speak, but, through me, he solicits your prayers. For the last twelve days he has not eaten a morsel. 'Tis wonderful to see how the poor child keeps up his spirits; he would manifestly be as gay and joyous as ever, were it not for the excess of his physical weakness. Margaret Mochinn's imposthume was opened yesterday, and she is getting quite round again already; I have put her into our winter bedroom; we ourselves are in the great front room, Jenny in the chamber with the stove, and Augustin's wife in her own room; we are beginning to hope that the plague will soon disappear. Farewell; salute thy daughter and her mother in our name, and remember us all in thy prayers." (10th Nov., 1527.)

"My poor son was all but dead, but he has now recovered; he had eaten nothing for twelve days. It has pleased the Lord to increase my family with a daughter. We are all well, except myself, who, though sound in body and apart from the world, still suffer within from the assaults of Satan and all his angels. I am writing, for the second and last time, against the sacramentarians and their futilities." (31st Dec., 1527.)

"My little daughter, Elizabeth, is dead; 'tis wonderful how sick at heart her loss has made me; I feel a mere woman, so great is the agitation that has since pervaded me. I could never have dreamed that a man's soul could be filled with such tenderness even towards his child." (5th August, 1528.)

"I am now, unhappily, in a condition to explain to you truly what it is to be a parent, *præsertem sexûs, qui ultra filiorum casum etiam habet misericordiam valde moventem.*" (5th June, 1530.)

Towards the close of the year 1527, Luther was himself several times attacked with illness both of body and of mind.[1] On the 27th October, he thus closes a letter to Melancthon: "I have not yet read Erasmus' new work, and indeed, how should I read it—I, a poor sick servant of Christ, who can hardly keep life within him. This is no time for me to read, or write, or do anything at all. Yet it is hard: it would really seem as though God had resolved to overwhelm me with all the waves of his displeasure at once. Men who ought to have compassion upon me, are selecting the very moment of my bodily and mental prostration, to come and give

[1] Werke, ix. 238.

me a final thrust. God mend them and enlighten them! Amen."

Two intimate friends of Luther, doctor John Bugenhagen and doctor Jonas, have left us the following account of an alarming swoon into which Luther fell towards the end of this year: "On the Saturday of the visitation, in the afternoon, doctor Luther complained of great pains in the head, and of a violent buzzing in the ear. He felt convinced he was going to die. Early next morning, he sent for doctor Bugenhagen to receive his confession. He spoke to him with terror of the temptations which he had been undergoing of late, entreated his support and his prayers for him with God, and concluded by saying: 'Because I sometimes wear a gay and joyous aspect, many people fancy that my path is one of roses; God knows how different is the fact. God knows what is in my heart. I have often determined within myself that, for the public advantage, I would assume a more austere, a holier (so to speak) exterior, but God has not enabled me to carry this resolution into effect.'

"In the afternoon of the same day, he fell quite senseless on the floor, became cold, and gave no sign of life. When, by the zealous attentions lavished upon him, he was restored to himself, he began praying with great fervour: 'Thou knowest, O God,' said he, 'that I would willingly have poured forth my blood for thee, but thou didst ordain that it should not be so. Thy will be done! Doubtless, I was not worthy to become such a sacrifice. Death would be welcome; but, O my God, if thou so willest, I am ready to live on to spread abroad thy Holy Word, and console and strengthen those who are faint-hearted. If, on the other hand, my hour is come, Thy will be done; blessed be thy name! Thou art the master of life and of death.'

"'O my Lord Jesus Christ! I thank thee for that thou didst me the grace to let me know thy holy name. Thou knowest that I believe in thee, and in God the Father, and in the Holy Ghost; thou art my divine Mediator and Saviour. Thou knowest, O my Lord, that Satan has laid many snares for me, to kill my body by means of his tyrants, and my soul by his fiery darts, by his infernal temptations. Hitherto thou hast miraculously protected me against all his fury. Protect me still, O my faithful Lord, if such be thy will.

"Then he turned to us, and said: 'The world loves lying, and there will be many, who, when I am gone, will say that I retracted on my death bed. I therefore earnestly desire you now to hear, and having heard, to retain in your memories my profession of faith: I declare, in my conscience, that I have taught the true word of God, as the Lord taught it me. I declare that what I have preached as to faith, charity, the cross, the holy sacrament, and other articles of the Christian doctrines, is all just, good, and salutary.'

"'Many charge me with having been too violent, too harsh. I admit that I have sometimes been violent and harsh towards my enemies. But I will, on the other hand, affirm that I have never sought to injure any one, and still less have I ever sought to cause the perdition of any man's soul. I had proposed to myself to write upon baptism, and against Zwinglius, but, as it appears, God has decided otherwise.'

"Afterwards he spoke of the sects which he said would rise up to pervert the word of God, and assail the flock which the Lord had redeemed with his blood. He wept as he spoke of these things. 'Hitherto,' he added, 'God has permitted me to struggle at your side against these spirits of disorder, and I would willingly continue the good fight; but I fear me that alone you will not be able to bear up against them, they are so many and so furious. Yet have I confidence in Jesus Christ, for he is stronger than Satan with all his arms; he is master of Satan.'

"By and by, when the circulation was more fully restored by means of constant friction and the application of hot pillows, he said to his wife, 'Where is my little darling, my dear little John.' The child, when brought to him, smiled upon its father, who, with tears in his eyes, sobbed forth: 'My poor, dear little boy, I commend thee heartily to our Lord God, thou and thy good mother, my beloved Catherine. I leave you nothing, but God will provide for you, He who is the father of widows and orphans. Preserve them, O God; teach them, as thou hast preserved and taught me.' He then said a few words to his wife about some silver goblets, adding, 'Thou knowest, they are all we possess.'

"He then fell asleep, and the slumber proving long and deep, restored to him so much strength that the next day he found himself much better. 'I shall never,' he observed to

Dr. Jonas, 'I shall never forget the day I spent yesterday. The Lord leads man to the brink of hell, and then withdraws him from its rude jaws. The tempest which yesterday morning broke upon my soul, was infinitely more terrible than that which in the evening assailed my body. God kills and revives us. He is the master of life and of death.'"

"'For nearly three months,' he writes on the 8th Oct. 1527, 'I have been languishing not so much in body as in mind, so that I have scarce been able in that whole time to pen as many lines. These are the persecutions of Satan.

"'I want to answer the Sacramentarians, but if my soul does not acquire greater strength, I shall not be capable of doing that or anything else.' (1 Nov. 1527) 'I have not yet read Erasmus' recent books, nor the late productions of the Sacramentarians, with the exception of a few pages of Zwinglius. It is well done in them to take advantage of my debility to crush me under foot. I alone bear the burden of God's anger, because I have sinned towards him; the pope and the emperor, the princes and bishops, the whole people hate me and assail me; and, as if this were not enough, my own brethren now come to persecute me! My sins, death, the devil and his angels incessantly assail me. And who will guard me, who console me, if Jesus Christ also abandons me; He for whom I have incurred all this hatred! But he will not abandon the miserable sinner in his extremity; not even myself, for I think I shall be the last of all men. Oh, please God! please God, that Erasmus and the Sacramentarians may some day, if only for a quarter of an hour, undergo the agonies which my poor heart endures. (10 Nov. 1527.)

"'Satan makes me suffer terrible temptations, but the prayers of the saints do not abandon me, though the wounds of my heart are hard to cure. My consolation is that there are many others who have to fight the same internal fights. Doubtless, I have committed sins more than enough to warrant the torments I undergo; but my life and my strength is, the consciousness that I have taught, to the salvation of many, the true and pure Word of God; it is this which so infuriates Satan, who gnashes his teeth at the thought that he has not been able to drown and destroy me and the Word . . . . I have not suffered bodily the cruelties which the tyrants of this world have inflicted upon those who have been burned and slaughtered for the sake of Christ; but Satan has made me writhe all the more with the martyrdom of the soul.' (21 Aug. 1527.)

"When I try to work, my head becomes filled with all sorts of whizzing, buzzing, thundering noises, and if I did not leave off on the instant, I should faint away. For the last three days, I have not been able even to look at a letter. My head has lessened down to a very short chapter, soon it will be only a paragraph, then only a syllable, then nothing at all. . . . The day your letter came from Nuremberg, I had another visit from the devil. I was alone, Vitus and Cyriacus having gone out, and this time the evil one got the better of me, drove me out of my bed, and compelled me to seek the face of man." (12th May, 1530.)

"I am well in health, but sick at heart from the persecutions of Satan, so that I can neither read nor write. The last day, I feel convinced, is near at hand. Farewell. omit not to pray frequently for poor Luther." (28th Feb., 1529.) "One may extinguish the temptations of the flesh; but, oh! how difficult it is to struggle against the temptations of blasphemy and despair! We do not comprehend sin, and we are equally ignorant of the true remedy." After a week of constant suffering, we find him writing, on the 2nd August, 1527: "Having well-nigh lost my Christ, I was beaten about fearfully on the waves and tempests of despair and blasphemy."

Amidst all this internal disorder, Luther, so far from being supported and consoled by his friends, found them either simply luke-warm and hesitatingly sceptical, or else actually quitting him, and rushing onward in the path of mysticism which he himself, some years before, had thrown open. The first of these who openly declared his independence and new views, was Agricola, the leader of the Antimonians (*enemies of the law.*) We shall see further on, how painful to Luther, in his last moments, was the controversy thus necessitated with so dear a friend.

"Some one has told me a story about you, my dear Agricola," he writes on the 11th September, 1528, "and persists so determinedly in the truth of what he relates, that I promised him I would write to you, and satisfy myself on the subject. This story is, that you were propounding that one may have faith without works, and that you were defending this innovation against all comers, with great pomp of Greek words, and much rhetorical artifice. . . . I warn you to mistrust the snares of Satan. . . . I was never more astounded at anything than I was at the secession of Œcolampadius and Regius; and what have I not now to fear for these men, once my intimate associates? In even a still greater degree do I tremble for you: not for the world would I see you severed from us."

"Why should I fret and fume against the papists?[1] All they have done against me has been in fair, open war: we are declared enemies, and act as such. They who hurt me most are my own dear children. My brothers, *fraterculi mei, aurei amiculi mei*—they who, if Luther had not written, would know nothing of Christ, or of the gospel, and would not have shaken off the papal yoke; for even if they had had the power to do so, the courage would have been wanting. I thought I had gone through, had exhausted all the adversities the evil one could inflict; but it was not so. My Absalom, the child of my heart, had not deserted his father, had not poured out ignominy upon David; my Judas, the terror of the disciples of Christ, the traitor who delivered up his master, had not sold me: he has done so now.[2]

"There is now going on against us a clandestine but very dangerous persecution. Our ministry is contemned; we ourselves are hated, oppressed, left to starve.[3] Such is at present the lot of God's word; when it is offered to those who have need of it, they will not receive it. . . . Christ would not have been crucified had he left Jerusalem. But the prophet would not consent to die out of Jerusalem, though, as it is well known, a prophet is not honoured in his own country. 'Tis the same with us. . . . It will soon come to pass that the nobles of this duchy will have cleared it completely of ministers of the Word—driven away by hunger, to say nothing of other outrages." (18th October, 1531.)

"There is nothing known for certain about the preternatural appearances which have made so much noise in Bohemia.[4] Many people repudiate them altogether. As to the gulf, however, which opened here under my own eyes,

[1] See Appendix L. [2] Cochlæus, 146. [3] See Appendix LI. [4] Ib. LII.

on the Sunday after Epiphany, at eight o'clock in the evening, there is no doubt about that; and the same thing was witnessed in various places between this and the sea. Moreover, Dr. Hess writes me word, that, in December last, the whole heavens were seen on fire above the church of Breslau; and another day, there were witnessed in the same place two circles of fire, one within the other, and in the centre of them, a blazing pillar. These signs announce, it is my firm opinion, the approach of the Last Day. The empire is falling, kings are falling, princes are falling, the whole world totters, and, like a great house about to tumble down, manifests its coming destruction by wide gaps and crevices on its surface. This will infallibly happen, and ere long, unless the Turk, as Ezekiel prophesied of Gog and Magog, have fire sent against him by God, and be destroyed in his pride of conquest, together with his ally the pope."[1] (7th March, 1529.)

"Grace and peace in our Lord Jesus Christ. The world approaches its end, and it often comes into my thoughts that perhaps the day of judgment will arrive before I have finished my translation of the Bible. All the temporal events we find predicted therein have been accomplished. The Roman empire tends nearly to its ruin; the Turk has attained the summit of his power; the papal splendour is fast becoming eclipsed; the world cracks in every direction, as though about to fall in pieces. The empire, it may be said, has received a new impulse from our Cæsar, Charles; but this is, perhaps, its last effort, the flame of the candle burning up more brightly than ever for the moment preceding its extinction." . . .

"The Turk is about to thunder down upon us: he, unless I am much mistaken, will be found to be the reformer sent us by God in his anger." (15th March.)

"There is now in my house a man just arrived from Venice, who assures me that the son of the doge is, at the present moment, at the court of the grand Turk; so that we may fairly look forward to having the pope, the Venetians, and the French, ere long, impudently, and in the face of day, turning Turks, and fighting for their new master against us. The same man tells me that there were in the army of the

[1] Werke, ix. 542.

French, at Pavia, eight hundred Turks, three hundred of whom returned safe and sound home to their own country, when they got tired of fighting. From your not having referred to these monstrosities, I conclude you have not heard of them; but I can assure you they have been related to me, both *vivâ voce* and in writing, upon authority and with circumstantial details which do not permit me for a moment to entertain a doubt about them. The hour of midnight approaches, when the cry will be heard, *Behold, the bridegroom cometh, go ye out to meet him.*" (6th May, 1529.)

BOOK THE THIRD.

1529—1546.

CHAPTER THE FIRST.

1529—1532.

The Turks—Perils of Germany—Augsburg—Schmalcaldus—Dangers of protestantism.

LUTHER was raised from the state of depression into which he had sunk, and recalled into active life, by the perils which menaced the Reformation and Germany. When the scourge of God, whom he had awaited with resignation,[1] as the sign of the Day of Judgment, burst over the German states, when the Turks were seen pitching their tents before Vienna, Luther altered his mind, summoned his countrymen to arms, and wrote a book against the Turks, which he dedicated to the landgrave of Hesse. On the 9th of October, 1528, he addressed to this prince an exposition of the motives by which he had been actuated in composing this book.

"I cannot hold my peace. Unhappily there are amongst us, preachers who induce the people to believe that there is no need to trouble themselves about this war with the Turks. There are, on the other hand, fanatics who give out that under all circumstances it is forbidden to Christians to have recourse to temporal weapons. Others, again, who look upon the German people as upon a nation of incorrigible brutes, go to the extreme of hoping that they may become subject to the Turks. These absurdities, these atrocious calumnies, are all imputed to Luther and the Gos-

[1] See Appendix LIII.

pel, as three years ago was the revolt of the peasants; and as, in general every evil that occurs throughout the world. It is therefore now most urgent that I should write publicly upon this subject, as well to confound the calumniators, as to enlighten the consciences of the innocent in respect to that course which it behoves them to take against the Turks."

Again: "We heard yesterday that the Turkish host has, by a great miracle of God, left Vienna, and gone towards Hungary. For after having made twenty successive assaults, without effect, the enemy opened a breach in three places by springing a mine: but nothing could induce the Turkish troops to renew the attack—God had struck them with a panic; they preferred being decapitated by their chiefs to the attempt at a last assault. It is believed by some that they retreated from an apprehension of our bombards and of our future army; others think differently. The Almighty has evidently combated for us this year. The Turk has lost twenty-six thousand men, and of our troops there have perished, during their sorties, no more than three thousand soldiers. I have desired to communicate these tidings to you, in order that we may return thanks to the Most High, and that we may render our prayers in unison to Him—for the Turk, become our neighbour, will not allow us to enjoy peace for ever." (27th October, 1529.)

Germany was saved, but the protestantism of its people was all the more in imminent peril. The irritation of the opposing parties had been already carried to the utmost degree by an event which was anterior in point of date to the invasion of Solyman. If the Roman-catholic biographer of Luther is to be credited, the same Cochlæus whose work we have already cited, the chancellor of duke George, Otto Pack, formed, on paper, a league of the Catholic princes against the elector of Saxony and the landgrave of Hesse: he affixed to some letters respecting this supposititious league, the seal of the duke George, and then despatched these forged documents to the landgrave, who, deeming himself menaced, raised an army, and formed a strict alliance with the elector.[1]

The catholics, on their part, and the duke George[2] above all, strenuously denied that they had ever entertained a

[1] See Appendix LIV. Cochlæus, 171. [2] See Appendix LV.

thought of menacing the religious independence of the Lutheran princes. They threw upon the chancellor all the responsibility of the plot, he having probably only divulged the secret designs of his master. "Doctor Pack,[1] voluntary prisoner of the landgrave, is, according to my view, at present under the accusation of having formed this alliance of princes. He expresses his expectation of being able to bring himself out of the matter honourably. God send that the snare may entrap the imbecile rustic who is its inventor—that is to say, our great adversary! You know of whom I speak, (the duke George of Saxony.)" (14th July, 1528.) Shortly after, he writes again: "This league of impious princes, which, nevertheless, they deny to exist, you observe what trouble it has already excited. For myself, I regard the cold excuses of the duke George as an avowal. The Most High will confound this enraged madman, this Moab, whose pride towers far above his power to sustain it! We will pray without ceasing against these homicides; they have had enough indulgence. If they engage in any further plots, we will forthwith invoke the aid of God, and call the princes to our succour, in order that they may perish without mercy."[2]

Notwithstanding that the whole of the catholic princes had declared these letters to be forged, the bishops of Mayence, Bamburg, &c., were mulcted in the sum of one hundred thousand crowns of gold, as an indemnity for the expenses of the armaments that the Lutheran princes had prepared. These latter desired nothing more ardently than that hostilities should commence. They reckoned up their forces, and relied confidently upon them. The grand master of the Teutonic order[3] had already secularized the states of Prussia. The dukes of Mecklenburg and of Brunswick, encouraged by this important occurrence, had called into their dominions Lutheran preachers. (1525.) The Reformation was predominant throughout the North of Germany. In Switzerland, and upon the Rhine, the Zwinglians every day increasing in number, sought to bring themselves into communication with Luther; and, on the other hand, the

[1] See Appendix LVI. [2] Ukert, 216. [3] See Appendix LVII.

Turks, masters of Buda and Hungary, continually menaced Austria, and at the same time held the emperor in check. In the absence of this latter potentate, the duke George of Saxony, and the powerful bishops of the north, became the chief adversaries of the Reformation. A polemical dispute of more than ordinary rancour had raged between the prince (George of Saxony) and Luther for some considerable time. The duke thus addresses the reformer: "What! you fear that we have to do with hypocrites? These lines will let you see how that matter stands. If we dissimulate with you in these presents, you may henceforward say what you will of us and ours. If we do not dissimulate with you, as is the fact, look you for your hypocrites amongst those who style you prophet, the apostle of Germany, a Daniel, the evangelist! You imagine, forsooth, that you are an envoy of the Almighty to us, as were the prophets of old, to whom God gave the power, and confided the mission of converting the princes of the earth and the powerful. Moses was sent to Pharaoh, Samuel to Saul, Nathan to David, Isaiah to Hezekiah, St. John the Baptist to Herod; we know these facts. But amongst all these prophets we do not discover an apostate; they were all of them men faithful and constant to one doctrine; sincere and pious persons, devoid alike of pride and avarice, and observers of chastity. Neither do we hold in very great esteem your prayers, or the prayers of your associates. We know full well that God detests the assembly of your apostates. By our instrumentality, God has punished Munzer for his perversity; the same power may well do the same by Luther; nor shall we decline, in this instance, the task of becoming His unworthy instruments.

"Say rather, Luther, that thou wilt return to us. Do not suffer thyself to be betrayed by the same spirit which seduced the apostate Sergius. The church of Christ does not close its doors against the repentant sinner. If it be pride that has undone thee, cast thy thoughts upon that proud Manichean, St. Augustine, thy master, whose rules thou hast sworn to obey. Return as he did—return to thy faith and to thy vows; become, like him, a shining light of Christianity. These are the counsels which we bestow upon thee at the coming of the new year. If thou conform to them thou wilt be eternally recompensed by God, and we will do all in our power to procure thy pardon from the emperor."[1] (28th December, 1525.)

The following is found in the memorial of Luther against the duke George,[2] who had intercepted one of his letters, (1529.) "As for the very handsome manner in which the duke George speaks of me as a wretch, a scoundrel, a perjured, dishonoured man, I can only return him my thanks for his appellations. They are the rubies, the emeralds, the diamonds, wherewith the princes of the earth are in duty bound to decorate me, in consideration of the honour and power which their temporal authority derives from the restoration of the gospel.

"Would not any one gather that the duke George knows no superior? He, a miserable lordling, says of himself: 'I am sole master and prince, I am above all the princes of Germany, above the empire, above its laws and customs! I alone am to be feared. I alone am to be obeyed. My supreme will ought alone to constitute the law, in despite of any who may think and speak differently!' Friends, where will the pride of this Moab stop?[3] It now only remains for him to scale the heavens, to pry into and to punish the letters and thoughts of those who are sheltered even in the very sanctuary of God himself! Behold this petty prince!—and amidst all this he expects to be glorified, respected, adored, forsooth!"[4]

In 1529, the year in which the treaty of Cambrai and the siege of Vienna by Solyman occurred, the emperor convoked a diet at Spires (15th March.)[5] It was there decreed that the states of the empire should continue to obey the edict promulgated against Luther in 1524, and that every kind of innovation should still be interdicted, until a general council was convoked. It was at this moment that the party of the Reformation burst forth with vigour into light. The elector of Saxony, the margrave of Brandenburgh, the landgrave of Hesse, the dukes of Lunenburgh, the prince of Anhalt, and, together with them, the deputies of fourteen imperial towns, framed in concert a solemn protestation against the decree of

[1] Werke, ix. 231. [2] See Appendix LVIII. [3] Ib. LIX.
[4] Ib. LX. [5] Ib. LXI.

the diet, and declared it to be alike unjust and impious. They thence assumed and retained the name of *protestants*.

The landgrave of Hesse felt the stringent necessity of uniting together all the dissenting sects, and of forming out of them a party formidable to the catholics of Germany. He made an attempt to reconcile Luther with the sacramentarians.[1] Luther at once foresaw and predicted the utter uselessness of this attempt.

"The landgrave of Hesse," says he, "has convoked a meeting of our party at Marburg, on the day of Saint Michael, in order to try to effect a reconciliation between ourselves and the sacramentarians. I expected no good results from this step. The difficulties are too great, and I see only snares. My fear is that, as in the days of Arius, they will carry off the victory. Assemblies such as these have always proved more hurtful than beneficial. This young man of Hesse is of a troublous disposition, and full of ideas which ferment in his mind. The Almighty has preserved us during the last two years from two tremendous explosions which would have kindled a flame throughout Germany." (2nd August, 1529.)

Again Luther writes thus on the 12th of October, in the same year: "The landgrave has afforded us a most magnificent and liberal hospitality. There were at his court Œcolampadius, Zwinglius, Bucer, &c. All joined in suing me for peace with the most extraordinary humility. The conference lasted two days: I responded to the arguments of Œcolampadius and Zwinglius, by citing this passage: '*This is my body*;' and I refuted all their objections. In effect, they are ignorant and insufficient men, utterly incapable of sustaining an argument."

Another of his letters contains the following pithy exposure of the results of the Marburg meeting: "I congratulate myself, my dear Amsdorf, in witnessing your gratulations respecting our synod at Marburg: the thing looks very insignificant, but it is, in reality, of the deepest moment. The prayers of the pious have had the effect of enabling us to witness our adversaries' humiliation, confusion, and defeat."

And, again: "The whole of Zwinglius's argument may

[1] See Appendix LXII.

be shortly reduced to the following summary:—That the body of our Lord cannot exist without occupying space, and without dimensions. Œcolampadius maintained that the fathers styled the bread a symbol, and consequently, that it was not the real body of Christ. They supplicated us to bestow upon them the title of 'brothers.' Zwinglius even implored the landgrave with tears to grant this. 'There is no place on earth,' said he, 'where I so much covet to pass my days as at Wittemburg.' We did not, however, accord to them this appellation of brothers; all we granted was, that which charity enjoins us to bestow even upon our enemies. They, however, behaved in all respects with an incredible degree of humility and amiability. Their object, however, as is now apparent, was to bring about a feigned concord with us, in order to render us their partisans, and the patrons of their errors. Oh, thou wily Satan!—but Jesus who delivered us out of this snare is more able than thou! I am now no longer surprised at their impudent falsities; I perceive that they can act in no other manner, and I exult in their downfall." (1st June, 1530.)

This theological strife in Germany filled up the interstices of that great European war which Charles V. waged with Francis I. and the Turks. But during the most violent crises of the latter, the former struggle was but rarely relaxed or abated. It is a solemn and imposing spectacle that Germany offers, absorbed by a religious sentiment, and forgetting, in that entrancement, the imminent dangers in which her formidable enemies threatened to envelope her. Whilst the Turks were bursting through all the ancient barriers which once protected her, and whilst Solyman was even pouring his Tartar hordes into the country beyond Vienna, Germany was engaged in a dispute respecting transubstantiation and free-will. The most renowned of her warriors were seated in dietic assemblies interrogating the learned. Such was the intrepid phlegm of this great people; such their confidence in the force and members of the nation. The war of the Turks and that with France, the capture of Rome, and the defence of Vienna, occupied Charles V. and Ferdinand to that degree that the protestants secured toleration until the next council. But, in the year 1530, Charles V. seeing France prostrate, Italy quelled, and Solyman driven within his own boundaries, determined upon undertaking the decision of the great question of the Reformation. The two conflicting parties were summoned, and met at Augsburg. The sectaries of Luther, known by the general name of protestants, were desirous to be distinguished from the other enemies of Rome, the excesses committed by whom would have thrown odium upon their cause; to be distinguished from the Zwinglian republicans of Switzerland, odious to the princes and to the nobles; above all, they desired not to be confounded with the anabaptists, proscribed by all as the enemies of society and of social order. Luther, over whom there was still suspended the sentence pronounced against him at Worms, whereby he was declared a heretic, could not appear at Augsburg; his place was supplied by the learned and pacific Melancthon, a man timid and gentle as Erasmus, whose friend he continued to be, despite of Luther.

The elector, however, conveyed the great reformer[1] as near to the place of convocation as regard to his friend's personal safety rendered advisable. He had him stationed in the strong fortress of Coburg.[2] From this place, Luther was enabled to maintain with ease and expedition a constant intercourse with the protestant ministers. On the 22nd of April he thus writes to Melancthon—"I have at length arrived at my Sinai, dear Philip; but of this Sinai I will make a Sion: I will raise thereon three tabernacles, one to the Psalmist, another to the prophets, and, lastly, one to Æsop, (whose fables he was then translating.) There is nothing here to prevent my solitude from being complete. I reside in a vast abode which overlooks the castle: I have the keys of all its apartments. There are scarcely thirty persons within the fortress, of whom twelve are watchers by night, and two others sentinels, who are constantly posted on the castle heights."

To Spalatin he writes thus, on the 9th of the following month: "You are about to go to Augsburg without having examined the auspices, and not knowing as yet when they will permit you to commence. As for me, I am in the thick of another diet, in the presence of magnanimous sovereigns, kings, dukes, grandees, and nobles of another sort, who confer

[1] See Appendix LXIII. [2] Ib. LXIV.

together upon state affairs in all gravity of demeanour, and who fill the air with unceasing voice, promulgating their decrees and their preachings. They do not seat themselves shut up in those royal caverns, which you term palaces, but they hold their councils in the light of the sun, having the heavens for a canopy, and for a carpet, the rich and varied colours of the trees on which they are congregated in liberty—the only limits to their domains being the boundaries of the earth. The stupid display of silk and gold inspires them with horror. They are all alike, in colour as in countenance—black. Nor is their note different one from the other; the only dissonance being the agreeable contrast formed by the voices of the young mixing with the deeper tones of their parents. In no instance have I ever heard them speak of an emperor; they disdain with sovereign contempt the quadruped which is so indispensable to our cavaliers; they have a far better means of mocking the fury of cannon. In so far as I have been able to comprehend their decrees, thanks to my interpreter, they have determined upon waging an incessant war during the present year against barley, corn, and grain of all sorts—in short, against all that is most enticing and agreeable amongst the fruits and products of the earth. It is much to be feared that they may become conquerors wherever they direct their efforts; for they are a race of combatants, wily and adroit—equally successful in their attempts to plunder by force or by surprise. As for me I am an idle spectator, assisting willingly, and with much satisfaction at their consultations. The hope that I have of the victories which their courage will give them over the barley and grain, and all other of their enemies, has rendered me the faithful and sincere friend of these *patres patriæ*, of these saviours of the republic. And if by the most ardent wishes I can serve them, I shall entreat heaven that they be freed from the odious name of rooks, &c. This is a mere pleasantry; but it is a serious one, and necessary to me, in order to repulse the thoughts which overwhelm me, if, indeed they can thus be overcome."

In a subsequent letter, he pursues the same train of ideas "The noble seigneurs who constitute our councils of state,

[1] See Appendix LXV.

run, or rather sail through the air. In the morning, at an early hour, they go out to battle, armed with their invincible beaks, and, whilst they are engaged in pillaging, destroying, and devouring all that comes in their way, I am delivered, for the time being, from their everlasting songs of victory. In the evening, they return in triumph; fatigue speedily closes their eyes, but their slumbers are light and refreshing as those of a conqueror. Some days since, I penetrated into their palace, in order to behold the pomp of their empire. The unhappy wretches were in a state of considerable alarm. They imagined I had come to destroy the results of their industry. There was a clamour, a fear, and a consternation which was visible in their countenances. When I perceived that I alone occasioned such trepidation to all those Hectors and Achilles, I clapped my hands, and threw my hat into the air, thinking myself amply revenged on them by being enabled thus to mock their alarms. All this must not, however, be looked upon as mere trifling. There is an allegory couched under what I write—a presage of that which is about to happen. Thus, in like manner, will be shortly seen trembling and crouching under the Word of God, those harpies who are at this moment at Augsburg crying aloud, and Romanizing." (19th June.)

Melancthon, transformed at Augsburg into the chief of a party, having to do battle every day with legates, princes, and the emperor, found that the active duties imposed upon him accorded very ill with his natural disposition. He communicated his troubles on several occasions to Luther, who, by way of consolation, rebuked him harshly.[1]

"You talk to me of your labours, your dangers, your tears, and I!—is mine a bed of roses? Do not I bear part and parcel of your burthens? Oh, would to God my cause was one which admitted of tears!" (29th June, 1530.)

On the following day the great adversary of catholicism again addresses his colleague:—"God reward, according to his deserts, the tyrant of Saltzburg, who occasions you so much evil! He deserved a different sort of answer from you at your hands, such in fact as I should perhaps have made him; an answer like unto none that he has ever yet had. It will, I fear, be im-

[1] See Appendix LXVI.

perative that they hear repeated to them the words of Julius Cæsar—‘It was they who willed it.’

“But all that I can write here is utterly thrown away, seeing you are determined, according to your philosophy, to govern all things by the mere force of reason: that is to say, to make unreason dominate over reason. Proceed, however! Destroy yourself in this vain effort, and that without being able to perceive that neither your hand nor your mind can control the crisis, nor that it will have none of your aid.”—(30th June, 1530.)

In another letter Luther observes: “God has placed this cause in a certain position which neither your rhetoric nor your philosophy have been able to fathom—that position is the light of faith. There all things are inaccessible to human sight—whoever desires to render them visible, tangible, and comprehensible, only gets for his pains, trouble and tears, as you have done. God has declared to us that he dwells in the clouds, and is seated amidst the darkness. Had Moses sought to escape from the army of Pharaoh, Israel in all probability would have remained to this day in Egypt. If we are destitute of faith, why not seek consolation in the faith of others, for some there necessarily are who believe, even though we ourselves are devoid of belief? What, then! shall it be said that Christ has abandoned us, before the consummation of the appointed days? If He be not with us, where, let me ask you—where is He in this world? If we are not the church, or a branch of the church, where is the church? Is the church Ferdinand? Is it the duke of Bavaria?—the pope?—the Turks, or their likes? If God’s promise rests not with us, with whom is it? You do not comprehend the state of affairs. Satan has confounded you and rendered you feeble. That Christ may restore you and heal you, is my sincere and constant prayer!” (29th June.)

“My health,” says Luther, in his next letter, “is failing. But I despise this angel of hell who troubles me in the flesh. If I can neither study nor write, I can at least give way to my thoughts, and thus fight with the devil; and afterwards give myself time to sleep, to lie indolent, to play, and sing. As for you, dear Philip, do not wear yourself out in over anxiety about this cause, which is not in your hand, but in that of the Almighty, from whom none can wrest it." (31st July.)

Melancthon believed in the possibility of effecting a reconciliation between the two parties. Luther, at a very early period of the schism, saw that they were utterly irreconcilable. In the commencement of the Reformation, he had frequently had recourse to conferences and to public disputations. It was then of moment to him to resort to every effort, to try, by all the means in his power, to preserve the bond of Christianity, before he abandoned all hope of so doing. But towards the close of his life, dating from the period of the Diet of Augsburg, he openly discouraged and disclaimed these wordy contests, in which the vanquished would never avow his defeat. On the 26th August, 1530, he writes: "I am utterly opposed to any effort being made to reconcile the two doctrines; for it is an impossibility, unless, indeed, the pope will consent to abjure papacy. Let it suffice us that we have established our belief upon the basis of reason, and that we have asked for peace. Why hope to convert them to the truth?" And on the same day, (26th August,) he tells Spalatin: "I understand you have undertaken a notable mission—that of reconciling Luther and the pope. But the pope will not be reconciled, and Luther refuses. Be mindful how you sacrifice both time and trouble. If you succeed, in order that your example may not be lost, I promise you to reconcile Jesus Christ and Belial."

Luther had previously, in a letter dated July 21st, thus apprised Melancthon of his views in this particular respect: "You will see," says he, "whether or no I was a true prophet when I unceasingly repeated that there was no possibility of bringing the two doctrines into accordance with each other, and that it ought to suffice us if we succeeded in obtaining public peace."

These prophecies were, however, unheeded: the conferences took place, and the protestants were required to furnish their profession of faith. This was drawn up by Melancthon, who consulted Luther upon all the more important articles. In relation to this undertaking, Luther says to his coadjutor, in a letter without date: "I have received your apology, and I am utterly astonished at your inquiry, as to what we ought to concede to the papists. As to the position of the prince, and as to what ought to be permitted to him under contingent circumstances of danger, that is another question. With regard to myself, your apology contains, on my behalf, far greater concessions than were at all needful or proper; and if they are rejected by our opponents, I do not see that I can proceed further, unless, indeed, their reasonings and their writings shall hereafter appear to me much more forcible and convincing than I have hitherto found them. I work night and day in this matter, meditating, interpreting, discussing mentally, and diligently searching the Scriptures. Each successive day augments my conviction, and confirms me in my doctrine."

"Our adversaries," again he writes, on the 20th of Sept. "will not give way a hair's breadth, whilst on our side we are not only called upon to admit their canon of Scripture, the sacrifice of the mass, communion in its restricted form, the old jurisdiction, but likkwise it is to be incumbent on us to avow openly that their doctrines, their persecutions, all that they have done, all that they have imagined even, has been just and legitimate, and that we have been wrong in accusing them; that is to say, they will us to be condemned, and themselves to be justified by the force of our own testimony. Thus we are not simply called upon to retract, but ourselves to pronounce a triple malediction upon our own acts."

"I do not like your having called to your support in this cause my opinions—neither will I consent to appear as your chief. Not even when the most favourable construction is put upon this appellation, will I accept of such a title. If the cause is not your own, much less shall it be said to be mine, and that I have imposed its defence upon you. I will undertake its vindication myself, readily, provided that task be left to my efforts alone."

Two days antecedently to this date, he had written to Melancthon: "If I should hear that things are going amiss on your side, it will be with difficulty that I shall prevent myself from facing in person this formidable array of Satan's fangs;" and he follows this up some days after by saying (on the 21st July, 1530), "I would willingly have become th victim sacrificed by this last council, as John Huss was at Constance,[1] that of the last days of the papal fortunes."

The protestant confession of faith[2] was delivered to the Diet and "read aloud, by order of Cæsar, before the whole empire—that is to say, before all the princes and powers of the empire. It is a joyful circumstance for me to have lived until this hour, and thus to have witnessed Christ preached by his confessors before an assembly such as that, and in so noble a profession of faith." (6th July.) This confession was signed by five electors, thirty ecclesiastical princes, twenty-three secular princes, twenty-two abbots, thirty-two counts and barons, and thirty-nine free and imperial cities. In the letter quoted above, Luther enumerates the chief of these celebrated subscribers to the Augsburg Confession—"The prince elector of Saxony, the margrave George of Brandenburg, John Frederick, the younger, landgrave of Hesse, Ernest and Francis, dukes of Lunenburg, prince Wolfsang, of Anhalt, the towns of Nuremberg and Reutlingen. Numbers of the bishops incline towards peace without troubling themselves respecting the sophisms of Eck and Faber. The archbishop of Mayence is strongly disposed to peace;[3] so likewise is duke Henry of Brunswick, who familiarly invited Melancthon to dine with him, assuring him that he could not rebut the articles touching the two species (of communion), the marriage of priests, and the inutility of constituting any differences between the various kinds of food. It is admitted by all our adherents that no one displayed a more conciliating disposition during the various conferences, than did the emperor himself. He received our prince not only with kindness, but with respect." (6th July.)

The bishop of Augsburg, the confessor of Charles V., was favourably disposed towards the Lutherans. The Spaniard declared to Melancthon, that he was astonished to see them contesting in Germany the doctrine of Luther respecting the faith, for that he himself had ever entertained an opinion identical with Luther's, upon the point in question. (Spalatin's narrative.[4])

[1] See Appendix LXVII. [2] Ib. LXVIII. [3] Ib. LXIX.
[4] Werke, ix. 414.

Whatever may have been said by Luther of the favourable tendencies of Charles V., the latter put an end to the discussions by summarily calling upon the Reformers to renounce their errors, on penalty of being placed under the ban of the empire, if they refused. He, at one moment, even seemed disposed to have recourse to violent measures, and caused the gates of Augsburg to be closed for a short time. In a letter dated July 15, speaking of duke George, Luther observes: "If the emperor desires to send forth an edict, let him do so.[1] He issued one after the diet of Worms. To the emperor we will listen in his imperial capacity, but to no others. What care we for the clown George?"

In another letter he says: "Our cause is far more easily defended against violence and menace, than against the diabolical snares which I have eternally dreaded up to this hour. Let them restore to us Leonard Keiser,[2] and the hosts whom they have unjustly put to death. Let them restore the numberless souls whom they have lost by their impious doctrines. Let them give back the wealth which they have acquired by means of their false indulgences, and their frauds of every description. Let them render to God the glory they have tarnished by so many blasphemies. Let them re-establish, as well in respect to persons as to manners, that ecclesiastical purity which they have so shamefully sullied. What more shall I demand of them? When they have fulfilled these conditions, we shall be in a position to speak *de possessorio*." (13th July.) Later in the same year, we learn from one of his letters, that "the emperor is about to issue an ordinance, simply to the effect that all things are to be re-established in their former condition—that the reign of the pope is to recommence; which I fear," says Luther, "will excite such troubles as will infallibly ruin the priests and the clerical orders. The most powerful amongst the cities, Nuremberg, Ulm, Augsburg, Frankfort, Strasburg, and twelve others, openly reject the imperial decree, and make common cause with our princes. You have already heard of the inundations at Rome, and of those in Flanders and Brabant. These are signs proceeding from the Almighty, but the impious cannot comprehend their import. You are

[1] See Appendix LXX. [2] Ib. LXXI.

likewise informed of the monk's visions at Spires. Brentius writes me word, that at Baden there has been seen in the air a numerous army, and upon its flank a soldier brandishing a lance with a triumphant air, as he passed over the neighbouring mountain, and across the Rhine." (5th Dec.)

The diet had scarcely been broken up, when the protestant princes reassembled at Schmalkald, where they entered into a defensive league, by which they constituted themselves one united body. (31st December.) They protested against the elevation of Ferdinand to the rank of king of the Romans; preparations for battle were made;[1] their contingents were fixed; and they forwarded addresses to the kings respectively of France, England, and Denmark. Luther was accused of having urged the protestant princes to assume this hostile attitude.[2]

He thus meets the charge—"I did not, as has been asserted, urge or advise the resistance manifested to the emperor.[3] The advice which I as a theologian tendered, was this[4]—If the jurists can show that the course proposed is permitted by the law, I also permit them to follow the course of their law. If by the emperor's laws it is established that, under such circumstances as these, it is lawful to resist him, let him be amenable to that law which he himself has made. A prince is a political personage only. If he acts in his capacity as prince, he does not act in that of a Christian, for the Christian is neither prince, nor man, nor woman; nor any particular individual upon earth. If, therefore, it is lawful for the prince, in his capacity of prince, to offer resistance to Cæsar, let him do so according to his judgment and his conscience. As for the Christian, nothing is to him lawful or permissible; he is dead to the world." (15th Jan. 1531.)

In the same year, Luther wrote a pamphlet against a little book that had been published anonymously at Dresden, in which an accusation was made against the protestants, that they were secretly arming themselves, with the intention of suddenly falling on the catholics, these being, in the meantime, engrossed entirely by the wish to re-establish peace and harmony. "It is," says he, in this memorial, "most carefully

[1] See Appendix LXXII. [2] Ib. LXXIII. [3] Ib. LXXIV. [4] Ib. LXXV.

concealed whence this book has proceeded. Nobody is to know. Well, I am content to remain, likewise, in ignorance upon the subject. I will consent to have my nostrils closed up with rheum, that I may not smell the unlucky pedant. Nevertheless, I shall call into action all my own adroitness, and endeavour to strike a blow at the lion's skin, satisfied that if I hit the ass who is concealed beneath it, no fault will be imputable either to me or to him, but solely to the covering in which he has enveloped himself.

"Be it true, or be it not, that the Lutherans are making preparations and are assembling together, what is that to me? I have not enjoined or counselled them so to do. I neither know what they do nor what they do not; but since the papists announce, by means of this book, that they believe in the reality of these armaments, I welcome their report with pleasure, and I rejoice in their delusions and their alarms. I would even assist in augmenting these illusive fears if I only knew how, were it but to make them die of fright. If Cain kills Abel; if Annas and Caiaphas persecute Jesus, is it not just that they be punished? Let, then, our foes be in a state of agony; let them tremble at the sound of a falling leaf; let them see on every side the phantoms of insurrection and death; nothing can be more equitable.

"Is it not, ye impostors, true, that when our partisans presented their confession of faith at Augsburg, a papist exclaimed, 'Those fathers have presented a book written with ink. For my part, I would answer it with blood?'

"Is it not likewise true that the elector of Brandenburg and the duke George of Saxony promised the emperor to supply five thousand horse against the Lutherans?

"Is it not true that a vast number of priests and nobles wagered amongst themselves that before the day of Saint Michael it would be all up with the Lutherans?

"Is it not true that the elector of Brandenburg declared publicly that the emperor and the whole empire would devote themselves, body and goods, in order to attain this end?

"Do you believe that your edict is unknown to the world? Do you think people are ignorant of the fact that by this edict every sword in the empire is unsheathed and sharpened, that every arquebuse is charged, that every lance is ready to rush down upon the elector of Saxony and his party, to spread fire and blood, and to fill the world with desolation and weeping? Look at your edict! Look at your own murderous designs inscribed with your own seals and emblazoned arms, and will you pretend to call that peace, or dare to accuse the Lutherans of a desire to disturb the good understanding that exists? Oh, matchless impudence! Oh, boundless hypocrisy! But I understand your projects. You desire our people not to make any preparations for the war with which their enemies have so long menaced them, but that they quietly suffer their throats to be cut, like so many sheep in the slaughter-house, without either complaining or standing on their defence. Much obliged to you, good folks. I, a preacher of the Word, might indeed submit to such a proceeding—I know this well—and perhaps others to whom a like grace has been given might also quietly endure their fate. But I cannot guarantee to tyrants that all will follow my example. If I publicly offered this advice to our people, our tyrants would doubtless avail themselves of it, but I am by no means disposed to relieve them from the apprehensions they entertain of our resistance. Do they seek to win their spurs by massacring our congregations? Let them gain their honours as it behoves gallant soldiers, by braving real dangers. Cut-throats by profession, let them at least look to be met as such.

"The accusations made against me of being too violent[1] I care nothing about. I place my whole glory and honour henceforward in having it said of me that I rage and storm against the papists. Ten years have now elapsed since I have humiliated myself before them and constantly given them mild words. What advantages have I gained by these supplications? To make the evil still worse. These clowns are only thereby rendered more haughty. Well, then, since they are incorrigible—since there no longer exists a shadow of hope that their infernal determinations may be shaken by goodness and mild demeanour, I break with them;[2] and I now henceforward shall pursue them with my imprecations ceaselessly, leaving neither them nor myself repose until I have sunk into the tomb. Never again shall they have a good

[1] See Appendix LXXVI. [2] Ib. LXXVII.

word from me. I am determined to see them crushed and buried under the weight of my thunders and lightnings.

"I can no longer pray without intermingling maledictions with my orisons: if I exclaim, 'Hallowed be thy name,' I am, as it were, constrained to add, 'cursed be the name of papists and of those who blaspheme against thee.' If I say, 'Thy kingdom come,' I must put in, 'cursed be the papacy and all the other kingdoms which are opposed to thine.' If I pray, 'Thy will be done,' I rejoin, 'cursed be the papists and may their designs be overthrown who oppose thy commands.' Nevertheless, I entertain, within my heart, towards the whole world a kind and affectionate disposition, and even my greatest enemies know this.

"Oftentimes, during the night, when I cannot sleep, I endeavour to seek, when lying on my bed, in what manner to bring the papists to repentance, before the judgment which impends over them arrives. But it seems as if this is not to be. They repulse every idea of being to blame, and cry out loudly for our blood. The bishop of Saltsburg said to our Philip (Melancthon) at the diet of Augsburg, 'Why have such everlasting disputes? We are quite aware that you are in the right.' And another time he said, 'You won't give way; we will not give way either; one of us must, therefore, exterminate the other. You are the weak, we the strong; we shall soon see who will have the upper hand.' Never should I have believed that such words as these could have been uttered by any one."[1]

CHAPTER II.

1534—1536.

The Anabaptists[2] of Munster.

WHILST the two great leagues of princes were in presence of, and appearing to defy each other, a third arose between the two, to the common consternation of both. This time also, it is the people, as in the war of the peasants, but it is an organized people, masters, too, of a rich city. The *jacquerie*

[1] Werke, ix. 459.
[2] See Appendix LXXVIII.

of the north, better and more systematically organized than that of the south, offers the *beau ideal* of the German demagogues of the sixteenth century—a scriptural royalty. The mystical handicraftsmanship of Germany enthrones a tailor.

The tailor's enterprise was a bold one, but not altogether absurd. The anabaptism at this period was in great strength. It burst forth in full vigour only in Munster, but it had spread throughout Westphalia, Brabant, Gueldreland, Holland, Friesland, and the whole coast of the Baltic as far as Livonia.

The anabaptists put into form the curses which the conquered peasants had cast upon Luther. They detested, in his person, the friend of nobles, the upholder of civil authority, the *remora* of the Reformation. "Four prophets, two true and two false ones; the true are David and John of Leyden; the false Luther and the pope: but Luther is worse than the pope."

In what manner the gospel saw the light at Munster, and the mode in which it was quelled after the destruction of the Anabaptists. A true history, worthy of being read and retained in the recollection (for the germ of the anabaptists is still alive in Munster): by Henry Dorpius of that city.[1] We shall content ourselves with a short extract from this prolix recital.

The Reformation commenced at Munster in 1532; its originator there was Rothmann, a Lutheran or Zwinglian preacher. So great was its success that the bishop acceding to the intercession of the landgrave of Hesse, accorded to the evangelical ministers six of the churches under his control. At a later period, a journeyman tailor, John of Leyden, made known in that city the doctrines of the anabaptists, and promulgated them in several families. He was aided in his ministry by a preacher named Herman Stapraeda of Moersa, an anabaptist like himself. Their secret assemblies speedily became so numerous that catholics and reformers were alike alarmed, and drove the anabaptists from the city. But the latter soon returned, bolder than before; they intimidated the council, and compelled the authorities to appoint a day on which the question of infant baptism should be pub-

[1] Werke, ii. 391, 199.

licly discussed in the Town Hall. In this discussion, the pastor Rothmann went over to the party of the anabaptists, and became one of their leaders. One day, another of their preachers ran through the streets, crying aloud, "Repent! Repent!! Amend your ways; be baptized, or God will punish you." Whether it was from fear, or that they were stimulated by religious zeal, true it is that many people who heard these exclamations hastened to be baptized. The anabaptists then repaired to the market place, which they filled with their numbers, crying out, "Down with the pagans who will not be baptized." They seized the artillery and ammunition, obtained possession of the Town Hall, and maltreated all the catholics and protestants whom they encountered. These, in their turn, formed themselves into bodies, and attacked the anabaptists vigorously. After several indecisive combats, the two parties discovered the expediency of coming to an understanding, and mutually agreed to suffer each other to practise that form of worship which was conformable to their creed. But the anabaptists did not adhere to this treaty; they wrote secretly to the men of their own sect in the neighbouring towns, calling upon them to repair to Munster. "Leave all that you have," they wrote, "wives, children, wealth, quit everything and hasten hither. All that you have sacrificed shall be rendered to you tenfold." When the wealthier classes of Munster perceived the city to be filled with these strangers, they quitted it in the best manner they were able, leaving behind them of their own party none but those of the lowest classes. This was during Lent 1534.

The anabaptists, emboldened by these flights, and by the reinforcements which had joined them, deposed the town council, and elected another, composed of men of their own party.

A few days after this, they pillaged the churches and convents, and perambulated the city in tumultuous bodies, armed with halberds, arquebuses, and clubs, crying out, like maniacs: "Repent, repent!" and then—"Out with ye, impious wretches—out of the city, or you will be crushed!" In this manner they drove out, regardless of compassion, all who were not of their sect. Neither the aged nor the sick, nor women with child were exempted from this banishment. A considerable number of the wretched fugitives fell into the hands of the bishop, who was preparing to besiege the city. Regardless of the circumstance that they were not anabaptists, he imprisoned them, and many were put to death in the cruelest manner.

The anabaptists being masters of the city, their supreme prophet, John Matthiesen, commanded his disciples to cast all their possessions and wealth into one common treasury, without making any reservation, upon pain of death. The populace feared, and obeyed the ordinance. The property of the fugitives was also seized, and appropriated in a similar manner. The prophet next determined that no books should be retained by his sectarians except the Bible and the New Testament. Every other work which could be found was thrown into a fire kindled in the court yard of the cathedral. "Such is the will of the Father of Heaven," said the prophet, and twenty thousand florins worth of books were thus consumed.

A farrier having spoken disparagingly of the prophets, the whole community was called together into the market-place, where John Matthiesen put him to death by a musket shot. A short time after this event, the prophet ran wildly out of the city gate, with a halberd in his hand, exclaiming, that God the Father had commanded him to repulse his enemies! He had scarcely got outside the walls when he was slain.

John of Leyden succeeded him as supreme prophet, marrying, at the same time, his widow. He revived the courage of the anabaptists, which had been greatly depressed by the death of his predecessor. At the feast of Pentecost, the bishop gave orders for the assault, but the assailants were driven back with great loss. John of Leyden selected twelve of the faithful (amongst whom were three nobles), and nominated them the elders of Israel. He likewise announced that God had revealed to him some new doctrines respecting marriage; he held a disputation on the subject with the preachers, who ultimately adopted his views, and promulgated from the pulpit the doctrine of a plurality of wives. A considerable number of the inhabitants declared their sentiments against this innovation, and even imprisoned the ministers who recommended it, together with one of the prophets; but they were compelled very speedily to release them, and forty-nine of the dissidents perished.

On the feast of St. John, in the year 1534, a new prophet, formerly a goldsmith at Warendorff, called the people together, and communicated to the assembled multitude a revelation that had been made to him, according to which John of Leyden was ordained to reign over the whole earth, and to occupy the throne of David until the time that God the Father should appear and assume the government. The twelve elders were deposed, and John of Leyden proclaimed king.

The greater the number of wives that each of the anabaptists took to himself, the more did a libertine spirit obtain sway amongst them. They committed the most horrible excesses upon the persons of young females of ten, twelve, and fourteen years of age. These barbarous brutalities, together with the miseries inflicted by the besiegers outside the walls, irritated a portion of the populace. Many of them suspected John of Leyden of being an impostor, and thought how best to deliver him over to the hands of the bishop. The king (John of Leyden) redoubled his vigilance, and nominated twelve dukes to preserve order in the city, (Epiphany Sunday, 1535.) He promised to these twelve chiefs that they should reign in the place of all the princes of the earth, and distributed amongst them, in anticipation of this promise, the titles of electors, and princes. The "noble landgrave of Hesse" alone was an exception to the proscription of existing dignitaries. "That prince," said they, "will, we, hope, become our brother." The king named Easter Day as the period of deliverance for the city.

One of his queens having observed casually to a companion that she did not think it was conformable to the will of God that the poor people should be suffered to perish from misery and hunger, the king conducted her, together with his other wives, to the market-place, commanded her to kneel down, whilst they also were prostrate around her, and cut off her head. The companion queens sang aloud, "Glory to God in the Highest," and the people danced around them. Nevertheless, nothing but bread and salt remained in the city for the food of the besieged. Towards the end of the siege the famine pressed so severely, that the flesh of the dead was regularly distributed in rations, the only care exercised being that of not using the bodies of those who had died of contagious maladies. At the feast of St. John, 1535, the bishop was apprised, by a deserter, of the spot at which an assault might be successfully attempted. The city was taken the same day, and after an obstinate struggle, the anabaptists were put to the sword. The king, together with his vicar and lieutenant, were brought into the camp bound between two horses, a doubled chain round their necks, and their heads and feet bare. The bishop sternly questioned John respecting the horrible disasters which he had occasioned. The king replied, "Francis Waldeck," (the bishop was thus named,) "had I been able to control events, every man should have perished by famine ere I would have surrendered the city to thee."

We find various other interesting details respecting these events in a piece inserted in the second volume of the German writings of Luther (Witt's edition) under the title of *Tidings of the Anabaptists of Munster*, from which the following are extracted: "Eight days after the assailants were driven back by the anabaptists, the king began his reign by surrounding himself with a court upon the same footing as that of a secular prince. He instituted masters of the ceremonies, marshals of the palace, ushers, chief cooks, harbingers, chancellors, orators, servants of the table, cupbearers, &c.

"One of his wives was elevated to the rank of queen, and she likewise had a court establishment. This personage was a beautiful woman of a noble family of Holland; she had been previously married to another prophet, who was slain before the walls of Munster, and by whom she was at the time pregnant.

"The king appropriated to himself thirty-one horses, with housings of cloth of gold. He likewise caused garments to be prepared for him ornamented with gold and silver; these habits were made out of the parish church robes. His squire was clad like himself, in most superb garments also made from church ornamental robes, and he wore besides, golden rings, and it was the same with the queen, her virgins, and women attendants.

"When the king, in his state, traversed the city on horseback, he was attended by pages; one of them carried, at his right hand, his crown and the Holy Bible; on his left, another page bore a drawn sword. One of the pages was the son of the bishop of Munster. He was a prisoner, and he served the king in his private apartments.

"The king had a triple crown, over which was a chain of gold; precious stones also adorned it, forming an effigy of the world transfixed by a sword of gold and one of silver. In the centre of the pommel of these swords was a small cross, on which was inscribed, "A king of righteousness over the world." The queen wore ornaments similar to these.

"Clad in the apparel thus described, the king visited thrice a week the market-place, where he seated himself upon an elevated platform raised expressly for the purpose. The king's lieutenant, Knipperdolling stood on a step immediately below the throne, and the counsellors were ranged in order below him. Those demanding audience of the king came forward, bowed twice, and at the third inclination prostrated themselves on the earth, after which they were at liberty to state their demands.

"One Tuesday, they celebrated the Lord's supper in the Court of the Dome; they were all seated at table, to the number of four thousand two hundred persons. Three dishes were served—namely, boiled fresh beef, ham, and roasted meat. The king, his wives, and all their household, waited upon the guests.

"After the repast, the king and queen took a wheaten cake, broke it, and handed it round, saying, "Take, eat, and proclaim the death of our Lord." In like manner they served wine, saying, "Take, drink, all of you, and proclaim the death of our Lord." The guests also broke cakes in the same manner, handing pieces one to the other, pronouncing these words: "Brother, [or sister,] take, eat. In like manner as Jesus Christ offered himself for me, so do I devote myself to you; and as the grains of wheat in this cake are united together, and the grapes were pressed and mingled together to make this wine, so are we also united." They exhorted each other at the same time to utter no frivolous words, neither to say anything contrary to the law of the Lord. Afterwards they returned thanks to Almighty God, first, by offering up prayer, and then by singing psalms, particularly that commencing, "Glory to God in the highest!" The king and his wives, together with their servitors, then seated themselves at the board, as well as those who had remained on guard during the first repast. When all was finished, the king demanded of the whole assembly if they were disposed to do and to suffer the will of the Father. All replied, Yes. The prophet John Warendorff then rose up, and said: God had ordered him to send out some persons from amongst them, for the purpose of proclaiming to the world the miracles which they had witnessed. The prophet added, that, according to the will of God, those whom he should appoint would have to repair to four imperial cities, and to preach there. To each of the persons chosen there was given a golden fenin of the value of nine florins, together with some ordinary money, for the expenses of their journey, and they left the city that same night.

"On the eve of St. Gall, these missionaries made their appearance, each in the city to which he had been deputed, crying aloud, "Repent, and be converted, for the mercy of God is about to terminate! The axe is at the root of the tree. Let this city seek to be reconciled, or its inhabitants will perish!" When these fanatics were brought before the town councils of the four cities, they spread their mantles on the ground, and cast upon them the above-mentioned pieces of gold, exclaiming, "We are sent by the Father to you with tidings of peace. If you accept them, cast all your possessions into a common stock; if you reject them, we here protest, with these golden pieces, against you in the presence of God, and they shall be our witnesses that you have refused the peace which he sent to you. The time spoken of by the prophets has come, when God will no longer permit aught but righteousness to reign over the earth. And when the king (John of Leyden) shall have caused righteousness to be established throughout the world, then will Jesus Christ resign his power into the hands of God the Father."

"The missionaries were severally cast into prison, and questioned by the authorities respecting their belief, their lives, &c. (Here, in the original, follows the interrogatory.) They stated that there had been four prophets, two true ones and two false; that the true prophets were David and John of Leyden; the false, Luther and the pope; but that "Luther was even worse than the pope." They likewise held that all other sects of anabaptists save theirs were damned, wheresoever they might be found.

"In Munster," said these persons, "every man has five, six, or seven wives, according to his will and pleasure;[1] but he is compelled to cohabit with only one of them until such time as she proves with child—he may then do as he pleases with the rest. All the maidens who have reached their twelfth year are compelled to marry."

"The anabaptists of Munster destroyed the churches and other edifices appropriated to divine worship. They awaited in that city the arrival of the inhabitants of Groningen and others of the Dutch provinces. Those reinforcements arrived, the king would march with his united forces and subjugate the whole earth.

"They held, also, that it was impossible to comprehend the Scriptures without the aid of the prophets as interpreters or expounders. When in discussion their mission was asserted not to be justified or grounded upon any text in scripture : they replied that the Father had not empowered them to give any explanation. Others replied: The prophet has said it by command of God.

"There was not one of these missionaries who would retract his words, or who would accept of pardon on that condition. They continually sang hymns, praising God, and returning thanks in that they had been deemed worthy of suffering for the glory of his name."

The anabaptists summoned by the landgrave of Hesse to give some account of their proceedings in having elected a king, replied to him (January, 1535):

"That the period of restitution spoken of in the Holy Scriptures had arrived:—that the gospel had opened for them the prison of Babylon, and that now was the time when they must requite the Babylonians for their doings. That the careful perusal of the prophets, the apocalypse, &c., would speedily show the landgrave whether their choice of a king was their own act, or done by the command of God," &c.

There then follows the convention agreed to in the year

[1] One of the deponents states that the king had five wives; but, according to the account of others, the number ultimately reached seventeen.

1533, between the bishop of Munster and that city by the intermediation of the councillors of the landgrave. The anabaptists despatched to this prince a copy of their book, '*De Restitutione*.' He read it with sentiments of indignation, and commanded his theologians to reply to it, and in particular to set forth in opposition to the anabaptist dogmas, nine articles, which he himself suggested. In these articles the landgrave accused the anabaptists, amongst other things, firstly, of having made righteousness consist not in faith only, but in faith and good works combined; secondly, of having unjustly accused Luther of never having taught the doctrine of good works; thirdly, of having defended the doctrine of free will.

In their book, *De Restitutione*, the anabaptists divided the history of past ages into three principal epochs. The primæval world," said they, "which existed up to the time of Noah, was submerged in the deluge; the second world, that which now exists, and in which we ourselves have our being, will be dissolved and purified by fire; the third epoch of the terrestrial globe, will witness a new heaven and a new earth, wherein righteousness will have her sway. These things were shadowed out by the Almighty in his holy arc, wherein were the vestibule, the sanctuary, and the Holy of Holies. The advent of the third world will be preceded by the restitution of all things unjustly acquired, and by an universal chastisement. The wicked will be put to death, the reign of righteousness prepared, the enemies of Christ cast down, and all things restituted. This epoch is about to commence."

From a narrative of the period, intituled, *Interview or discussion which Antony Corvinus and John Kymeus had at Beverger with John of Leyden, the king of Munster*—the following passages are extracted:—

"When the king entered the apartments where we were, accompanied by the escort which had guarded him from his prison, we saluted him in a cordial manner, and invited him to take a seat by the fire. We then inquired of him respecting his health, and whether he suffered from his confinement. He said that he suffered from cold, and was very much depressed, but that it was his duty to bear his affliction with patience, since God had ordained he should be thus treated. Little by little, always under the most friendly guise, for in no other way could anything be got out of him, we succeeded in inducing him to speak of his kingdom and his doctrine, which he did in the following words :—

"First point of the Interrogatory.—*The ministers.*—'Dear John, we have heard the most extraordinary and horrible stories respecting your government. If these accounts are true, and unhappily there is too much reason to believe them, we cannot conceive in what manner you are able to justify such an undertaking as yours by Holy Writ.'

"*The king:* 'That which we have done and taught, we have done and taught by good right, and we are able to justify our enterprise, our actions, and doctrine before God, from whom they proceed.'

"*The ministers* suggested to him, that in the Scriptures the kingdom spoken of was the spiritual reign of Jesus Christ. 'My kingdom,' said our Saviour himself, 'is not of this world.'

"*The king:* 'I perfectly understand that which you allege respecting the spiritual reign of Christ, and I in no manner attack the passages of Scripture which you have cited. But you ought to be able to distinguish the spiritual kingdom of Jesus Christ, which refers only to the period of suffering, and of which, after all, neither Luther nor yourselves have any true idea, from the other kingdom—that which, after the resurrection, shall be established for the space of one thousand years on the earth. The texts which speak of the spiritual reign of Jesus Christ, have reference only to the period of suffering, whereas those which are to be found in the prophets and the apocalypse, respecting the temporal kingdom, are to be interpreted solely as indicating the period of glory and power which Jesus Christ is to possess in this world, together with his flock. Our kingdom of Munster was an image of this temporal reign of Christ. You know that God makes known his will upon earth by symbols and figures. We entertained a belief that our kingdom would endure until the coming of the Lord; but now we perceive that, in this respect, our understanding has failed us, and that our prophets themselves have been devoid of comprehension. God has opened our eyes, and revealed the truth to us in our prison.

'I am aware that you usually apply to the spiritual reign of Christ, those passages which you have cited, and other similar ones, which nevertheless, refer, without doubt, to the temporal kingdom. But what becomes of your spiritual interpretations, and of what use are they if none of them are ever to be realized on earth? God created the world chiefly that he might gratify himself by beholding man, in whom are reflected his might and dignity.'

"*The ministers:* 'And how will you justify yourself when God shall ask you at the day of judgment, "Who made thee king? Who commanded thee to fill the earth with such frightful errors, to the disparagement of my Word?"'

"*The king:* 'I shall reply: "The prophets of Munster commanded me to do so, in obedience to thy divine will, in testimony of which they pledged to me body and soul."'

"*The ministers* asked him respecting the divine revelations which were said to have been made to him on the subject of his elevation to the throne.

"*The king:* 'I have had no revelations upon this subject. It simply occurred to me that Munster ought to have a king, and that I ought to be that king. These ideas troubled and shook me exceedingly. I prayed to God that he would take my inaptitude into consideration, and abstain from imposing so heavy a burthen upon me. In the event of my not being spared this trial, I implored the Almighty to cause me to be appointed by the voices of prophets worthy of belief, and in the possession of his Word. I held secretly to that determination, and said not a word to any human being. But, fifteen days after this, a prophet arose in the midst of the community, and cried aloud, that God had signified to him his will that John of Leyden should be king. The same prophet announced these tidings to the council, which immediately conformed to his words, resigned the power confided to it, and proclaimed to the whole community that I was king. The council delivered to me the sword of justice, and thus I became king.'

"SECOND ARTICLE.—*The king:* 'We in no respect opposed the existing authorities, save only because they forbade to us our rite of baptism, and the Word of God. We resisted violence. You assert that, in so doing, we have acted unrighteously; but does not Saint Peter declare, that we must obey God rather than men? You would not censure our actions, did you but know how those things came to pass.'

"*The ministers:* 'Mitigate and justify your deeds as you may, you will not the less be everlastingly looked upon as rebels, guilty of the crime of treason. It is the duty of Christians to suffer, and not resist the evil doer. Even supposing, what was not the case, that the whole council was ranged on your side, you ought rather to have endured the utmost extremity of their violence rather than originate a schism and sedition; raising up a tyranny such as yours was contrary to the command of God, and in defiance of the majesty of the emperor, of the royal dignity, and of that of the electors and princes of the empire.'

"*The king:* 'That which we have done we fully comprehend. God be our judge!'

"*The ministers:* 'We likewise well know the foundation upon which our words rest. God be our judge also!'

"FIFTH ARTICLE.—*The king:* 'We were besieged and destroyed for the divine commands. It is in that cause that we have endured the extremities of famine, and every evil; that we have lost our kinsmen and friends, and that we have been overwhelmed by these lamentable calamities. Those of our friends who still live will permit themselves to be slain without resistance or complaint, like the lamb that is sacrificed.'

"FIFTH ARTICLE.—The king averred that he was for a long time of the same opinion as Zwinglius; but that he reverted to his former belief in the doctrine of transubstantiation. Only he did not admit to his interrogators that the eucharist was efficacious when administered to a person without faith.

"SIXTH ARTICLE.—*The ministers:* 'What do you make of Jesus Christ if you deny that he was invested with body and blood by his mother Mary? Do you mean to say he was a phantom, a spectre? It will be necessary for our Urbanus Regius to publish another book in order that you may learn to comprehend your mother tongue;[1] otherwise your ass-headed companions will eternally resist all instruction.'

[1] This observation refers to the interpretation given to the word born—*geboren*.

"*The king:* 'If you but felt the infinite consolation contained in the knowledge that Jesus Christ, God and Son of the living God, was made man and shed his blood, not the blood of Mary, to redeem our transgressions, (he who is pure and exempt from every fault,) you would not speak as you do, nor would you find our opinions so wrong.'"

"SEVENTH ARTICLE.—(On polygamy.)—The king cited the example of the patriarchs in this respect to the ministers. These entrenched themselves within the limits of modern times, and urged the general practice and usages of those times, declaring marriage to be *res politica*—a political institution. The king observed that it was better to have a plurality of wives than a multitude of prostitutes; and he put an end to the conversation, as in the former instance, by ejaculating—'God be our Judge!'

Although the ministers themselves drew up this report, the effect produced by reading the account of their discussions is not favourable to them. It is impossible to abstain from a sentiment of admiration at the firmness, the good sense, and the modest simplicity of the king of Munster, contrasted so strongly as his qualities are with the obdurate pedantry of his interrogators, who thus introduce their publication to its readers—

"Corvinus and Kymeus to the Christian Reader:

"We have here rendered an account of our different conversations with the king, nearly word for word, not omitting any one of his arguments. We have merely clothed them in our own language in terms more suitable than those employed by him. About eight days after our original interviews, he sent to us, requesting that we would again come and discuss matters with him. We went, and for two days more renewed our conversations. He was more docile than on the former occasion, and we attributed the change to a desire on his part to save his life. He declared, of his own accord, that if he were pardoned, he would, in conjunction with Melchior Hoffmann, and his queens, exhort the anabaptists of Holland, Brabant, England, and Friesland, in which countries they are exceedingly numerous, to hold their peace henceforward, and to obey, even to baptising their children, until such time as the authorities came to some understanding with them in matters of religion."

Then follows the new confession of faith of John of Leyden, wherein he modifies some points contained in his first formula. In exhorting the anabaptists to obedience, he meant that he merely instructed them to put on an external semblance of obedience. He gave up no single point of doctrine, and insisted upon perfect freedom of conscience. With respect to the Eucharist, he declared all his brethren to be of the opinion of Zwinglius upon this point, and that he had himself entertained the same views, but that whilst he was in prison God had made known to him his error. This confession of faith was signed in the Dutch language—"I, John of Leyden, signed with my own hand."

On the 19th January, 1536, John of Leyden, together with Knipperdolling and Krechting, his vicar and lieutenant, were brought forth from their cells. On the following day, the bishop sent his chaplain to confer separately with each of the prisoners, respecting his belief and the deeds of which he had been guilty. The king evinced repentance, and retracted his pretensions; but the two others persisted in their belief, and maintained that they were guiltless in every respect. On the 22nd, in the morning, the gates of Munster on every side were closed; no one was allowed to enter or to depart from the city. About eight A. M., the king, his body bared to the waist, was conducted to a scaffold erected in the market-place. Two hundred foot and three hundred horse-soldiers surrounded the cortège. The concourse of people was immense. He was fastened to a stake, and two executioners alternately tore his flesh from his bones with red hot pincers. At length, one of them plunged a knife into his breast, and thus finished the execution, which was an hour in duration.[1]

The first three wrenches with the red-hot pincers failed to extort a sound from the king. But afterwards he ceaselessly screamed out, and cried, his eyes turned upwards to Heaven: "Oh! Father have pity on me!" He prayed ardently to God to forgive him the sins he had committed. When he found himself sinking, he exclaimed—"Oh, Father! into thy hands I commit my spirit!" saying which, he expired.

The corpse was thrown upon a sledge and dragged to

[1] See Appendix LXXIX.

the space in front of the tower of St. Lambert: three iron frames were ready prepared there, on to one of which the dead man was strongly chained, and then the surrounding peasants, who were looking on, ran it up by means of a rope, to the top of the Tower, where it was finally suspended to a hook fastened in the masonry. The torments inflicted on Knipperdolling and Krechting were similar to those endured by their king. They persevered, whilst they had breath, in maintaining their opinions. "During the execution," says the narrator, "they invoked the name of the Father only, not mentioning Christ, as is the custom of their sect. Neither of them made use of any remarkable phrases—perhaps their silence was attributable to the torments they had endured whilst in prison—for they had more the semblance of dead than of living beings, when brought out for execution. Their bodies were made fast in the iron frames already mentioned, and swung by the peasants up to the tower of Saint Lambert, where they were suspended, one on each side of their king, about a man's stature below the height at which he hung. The city gates were then reopened, and there entered a vast multitude of persons who were too late to witness the execution." [1]

In the preface to the *Tidings respecting the Affairs of Munster*, Luther writes thus of these matters:—"What can I, and what ought I to write against, or respecting, these poor wretches at Munster. Is it not too plainly apparent that the devil reigns there in person, or rather, that there is a whole band of devils?

"Let us, nevertheless, acknowledge herein the grace and the infinite mercy of God. Although Germany has by her blasphemies, and by shedding the blood of so many innocents, well deserved to be governed with a rod of iron, the Father of mercy has not suffered the devil to play his own game, but has warned us betimes by means of this Satanic stupidity which is going on at Munster. The power of God has compelled the Spirit, whose wiliness is infinite, to suffer himself to be entrapped by the most clumsy, ill-imagined contrivances, in order that we may have time for repentance, whereby to escape from the far better devised schemes which the one had reserved for our overthrow.

[1] See Appendix LXXX

"In fact, the spirit which seeks to devour the whole world ought not to have commenced by taking women to himself, and by stretching out his hand to grasp crowns and royal sceptres, or by cutting people's throats. This is somewhat too gross a proceeding; every one sees plainly that this is the work of a spirit which only desires to effect its own elevation, and to oppress others. In order to be able to carry on a scheme of deceit successfully, you ought to put on a black or grey gown, and adopt a mortified and pitiful air, bending down your head, rejecting gifts of money, abstaining from flesh meat, avoiding women as though they were poisonous, denouncing all temporal power as damnable, renouncing the sword, and under these semblances and self-denials you may incline humbly before the crown, the sword, and the keys, in order the better to be in a condition to snatch or to seize them furtively. This is the way to succeed; this method of proceeding would deceive even the wisest, and those entirely given to spiritual things. That is really a fine sort of devil; a devil with an exterior more taking than all the feathers of peacock or pheasant could furnish. But to grasp in so impudent a manner a crown; to take not one, but as many women as his caprice and pleasure prompt him to desire!—this must be a sucking devil's, or a scholar devil's act—a devil at his A, B, C. Or, perhaps, it is Satan, the learned and wily Satan, bound hand and foot by the instrumentality of God, with chains so powerful that he has been unable to act more cleverly. It is in order to threaten us all, and to exhort us to fear his chastisements, before he lets loose upon us a far more adroit and diabolical adversary, who will attack us not with the alphabet of sin, but with the veritable text, the difficult text. If the enemy can, as a sucking devil, act as we perceive him to have done, what have we not to apprehend from him when he presents himself as a reasonable spirit of hell, wise, learned, a legist, and a theologian?

"When God is in anger, and deprives us of his word, no species of deceit practised by the devil is too palpable or gross. The first beginnings of Mahomet were thus of the grossest and most absurd nature; no impediment being offered by God to his so doing, that impostor created a kingdom of infamy and damnable deception, as is known to all the world. Had God not aided us in our struggles with Munzer, he would have created a Turkish empire like that of Mahomet. To have done: no spark is so minute but that when blown upon by the devil, under the permission of the Almighty, there will not issue forth a flame that may envelop the entire world, and which no person will ever be able to extinguish. The most potent weapon against the devil is the sword of the spirit, the Word of God. The devil is a spirit who jeers at cuirasses and at horsemen.

"But our nobles, our bishops, and princes, will not permit the gospel to be preached, nor that, by the Divine Word, the souls of men be snatched from perdition. They think, forsooth, that it is sufficient to cut throats. In this way, they save the bodies of men from the devil, and leave him possession of their souls. They will have the same success as the Jews, who thought they were exterminating Christ when they were crucifying him.

"The Munster fanatics, amongst other blasphemies, speak of the birth of Christ as if he was not of the seed of Mary, (such is their language,) and yet that he was, notwithstanding, of the seed of David. They do not, however, explain clearly their meaning. The devil keeps hot water in their mouths, and wont let them do anything but mutter 'mum, mum,' they probably wishing, all the while, to say something worse. The fact probably is, as far as I can understand their meaning, that, according to them, the flesh or the seed of Mary could not redeem our sins. Well, good devil, what next? Go on muttering, mumbling, and sputtering, as long as you please—the one little word 'born' knocks all that on the head. In every tongue throughout the whole earth, the word born means the child of flesh and blood which issues from the womb of the woman, and it means nothing else. The Scripture everywhere declares Jesus Christ to have been born of his mother Mary—that he was her firstborn. Thus Isaiah, Gabriel, and others: 'Thou shalt conceive a child in thy womb.' To conceive, worthy sirs, is not to be a mere pipe or conduit through which water flows, (according to the blasphemies of the Manicheans,) but it means that the child conceived partakes of the flesh and blood of his mother; that he is nourished within her; that he grows within her, and that he is at length brought by her into the world.

"The other proposition of these people—that under which they condemn the baptism of infants, and pronounce that rite to be a pagan ceremony—is equally absurd as the first. They look upon all that is possessed or bestowed by impious persons as evil. Why do they not hold this opinion with respect to silver and gold and other goods which they wrested from those same impious persons of Munster? It would have behoved them, in that case, to have made new gold and new silver.

"Their wicked kingdom is so evidently a kingdom of palpable imposture, and of revolt, that it is unnecessary for me to say anything respecting it: I have already said too much. I stop."[1]

CHAPTER III.

1536—1545.

Last years of Luther's life—Polygamy of the Landgrave of Hesse, &c.

ALTHOUGH the catholics and protestants united for a moment in order to crush the anabaptists,[2] their mutual hatred was in no degree abated; constant rumours of an approaching general council were no proofs that either of the two parties desired one to be called. In fact, the pope mistrusted such a proceeding, whilst the protestants were forward in denouncing it. "They write me word from the diet," says Luther, in a letter of the 9th July, 1545, "that the emperor has been urging our people to consent to a council, and that he has been much enraged by their refusal. I cannot comprehend such absurdities. The pope absolutely refuses to heretics like ourselves any standing in a council, whilst the emperor wills that we at once consent to its appointment, and obey its decrees. It is, perhaps, God who has caused them to become foolish; but I think I can fathom their absurd combination. As, up to the present time, they have not been able, under the titles of pope, church, emperor, diets, to render their unjust cause formidable, they now think to clothe themselves

[1] See Appendix LXXXI. [2] Ib. LXXXII.

with the name of a council, in order to be able to obtain an excuse for accusing us of being so utterly lost and without hope, that we will listen neither to pope, church, emperor, the edicts of the empire, nor even of the council itself, which we have so repeatedly called.

"Herein may be discovered the wonderful cleverness displayed by knowing Satan against poor half-witted God, who doubtless will have great difficulty in escaping from a snare so aptly contrived. No; it is our Lord who will mock the designs of those who lay toils for him. If we are now to consent to the appointment of a council entertaining such intentions towards us, why, let me ask, did we not submit ourselves, twenty-five years ago, to the supreme head of all councils, the pope, and to his bulls?"

The council thus proposed, might, had it been assembled, have reunited the bonds of the catholic hierarchy, but it could in no shape whatever have re-established those of the church. Arms alone could determine that question.[1] The protestants had already driven the Austrians out of Wittemberg. They despoiled, likewise, Henry of Brunswick, who was carrying into effect, for his own behoof, the decrees of the imperial chamber. They encouraged the archbishop of Cologne to imitate the example of Albert of Brandenburg, in secularizing his archbishopric, by which means they would have obtained a majority in the electoral council. There were not wanting, however, in the interval, several conciliatory attempts. Conferences were opened at Worms and Ratisbon[2] (1540—1541), which were equally futile with those that had preceded them. Luther never attended any of them; and, indeed, he paid little heed to disputes which every day assumed more decidedly a political, rather than a religious, character.

"I have received no tidings from Worms," says he in one of his letters, "save what is told me by Melancthon, who tells me there is such a swarm of learned persons from France, Italy, Spain, and Germany, as, as he says, never before were exhibited by any pontifical synod." (27th November, 1540.)

Shortly after this, Luther again writes: "I have heard from Worms, where our people are conducting matters with strength and wisdom, whilst our adversaries, like foolish and

[1] See Appendix LXXXIII. [2] Ib. LXXXIV.

unskilful people, resort only to barren craft and lies. One would almost think the devil himself could be seen at sunrise, running to and fro, seeking, without avail, some gloomy abode wherein he might shelter himself, and thus escape the flood of light which pursues him." (9th January, 1541.)

After another conference of the theologians of both parties, the opinion of Luther upon ten articles of faith, which had been mutually agreed on, was sought by them. Respecting this he writes, "Our prince learning that they were coming directly to me, without having recourse to him first, went at once to Pontanus, and these two drew up the reply in their own way."[1]

Had such an interference as this been ventured upon a few years before by the prince, Luther's indignation would have known no bounds. But here he speaks of it without any angry feeling; he was already beginning to flag, owing to the lassitude and disgust that had seized upon him. He clearly saw, that in labouring to restore the gospel to its primitive purity, he was only furnishing the princes of his time with the means of gratifying their earthly ambition; and that every day they sought to make a market of his Christ.

"Our excellent prince," says he, on the 4th April, 1541, "has sent for my perusal the conditions which he is about to propose, in order to bring about a peace with the emperor and our adversaries. I perceive that they all look upon this matter as if it were a comedy which they are acting amongst themselves,[2] whereas it is a solemn tragedy enacted between God and Satan, wherein Satan triumphs and God is humbled. But the catastrophe has yet to come, when the All Powerful, the author of the drama, will assign to us the victory. I am utterly indignant to see matters of such vast moment thus trifled with."[3]

We have seen at an early stage of the business, the lamentable dependence in which the Reformation was placed, in reference to the princes who protected the movement. Luther lived long enough to experience the consequences in which he had felt this would terminate. These princes were men; they must, therefore, be served, not only as princes, but as men, in their caprices, in the wants and desires of their frail

[1] See Appendix LXXXV. [2] Ib. LXXXVI. [3] Ib. LXXXVII.

humanity. Hence originated the expediency of making concessions which, without being contrary to the principles of the Reformation, seem very little to the honour of the Reformers.

The most warlike amongst the protestant chiefs, the impetuous and choleric landgrave of Hesse, caused it to be represented to Luther, that the state of his health required him to cohabit with more than one wife. The instructions given to Bucerus for negotiating this matter with the theologians of Wittemberg offer a curious mixture of sensuality, of religious apprehensions, and of daring frankness.[1]

"Ever since my marriage," so say the recorded instructions of the prince to his minister, "I have lived constantly in a state of adultery and fornication, and, as I will not forego this course of life, I am interdicted from taking the holy communion; for St. Paul expressly says, 'The adulterer shall not see the kingdom of heaven.'" The landgrave then proceeds to enumerate the reasons which have compelled him to follow his actual course of life. "My consort," says he, "is neither handsome nor of a pleasant disposition; she smells ill, drinks, and my chamberlains are well aware how she conducts herself when intoxicated." . . . "I am of a warm complexion, as my physicians can testify; I am obliged frequently to repair to the imperial diet. *Ubi lauté vivitur et corpus curatur; quomodo me ibi gerere queam absque uxore, eum non semper magnum gynæceum mecum ducere possim?* How would you have me punish fornication and other offences when I myself am guilty, and am liable to be told, 'Commence with yourself?' If we take arms in the cause of the gospel, I shall do so with a troubled conscience, in fear and trembling; for I cannot conceal from myself, that if I am slain I shall go to the devil direct. I have read with great attention the Old and the New Testaments, and I can discover no other resource save that of taking another wife; for I neither can nor will change my course of life; I call God to witness my words. Why am I not to be permitted that which was lawful to Abraham, to Jacob, David, Lamech, and Solomon?"

This question of polygamy had already been agitated

[1] Werke, i. 328.

during the early years of protestantism; the practice was everywhere recognised in the Scriptures to which the Reformation professed to bring back the world. The reformers, likewise, held marriage to be a political institution (*res politica*), and as such subject to the laws of the sovereign. At first Luther recoiled from the topic; the thing was repulsive to him; but he dared not condemn that which the Old Testament sanctioned; besides, the doctrine illustrated and invoked by the landgrave was precisely that which Luther had adopted in principle from the very commencement of his Reformation, although he did not recommend it to be carried into practice. He had already written thus on the point, in 1524 : " The husband must be certified in his own conscience, and by the word of God, that polygamy is permitted to him. As for me, I avow that I cannot set myself in opposition to men marrying several wives, or assert that such a course is repugnant to the holy Scripture. Nevertheless, I do not wish to see this practice introduced amongst Christians, to whose religion it is more conformable that they should abstain even from what is lawful, in order that they may avoid scandal, and preserve that *honesty* which St. Paul is so solicitous to maintain on all occasions. It is totally unworthy of a Christian to be running, on all occasions, after what appears to be his own personal advantage, even to the extreme limits of the liberty that is allowed him, and in the meantime to neglect the commonest and most necessary acts of charity. For these reasons, I determined not to open this question in my late sermon." On a subsequent occasion, Luther revives the subject: " Polygamy, which was permitted amongst the Jews and Gentiles, cannot, according to our faith, exist in a community of Christians, unless under circumstances of imperious necessity; as, for example, if one were compelled to separate from a leprous wife, &c. You will, therefore, enjoin these earthly men, that, if they would become Christians, they must subdue the flesh, and not give the reins to their desires. If they will continue to be Gentiles, let them; but theirs be the risk and danger." (21st March, 1527.)

One day Luther asked doctor Basil, whether, according to law, a husband whose wife was afflicted with an incurable malady, and was thus rendered, so to speak, more dead than alive, was authorized to take a concubine. The doctor having stated his opinion that, in certain cases, such a permission might probably be granted, Luther observed: "That is a very dangerous admission; for, if the practice be permissible in cases of bodily disease, it may happen that fresh reasons will every day be discovered for dissolving marriages." (1539.)

The application of the landgrave of Hesse occasioned extreme embarrassment to Luther. The whole of the theologians at Wittemberg assembled on the occasion, to frame a reply, in which they determined upon effecting a compromise with the prince. They acceded to his request for permission to take a second wife, but upon condition that she should not be publicly recognised. "Your highness," they state in their answer, "will, of your own accord, readily suggest to yourself the difference which exists between laying down a law to be universally promulgated, and one to serve a private and urgent exigency. We cannot publicly introduce or give our sanction, as by a law, to a permission for marrying a plurality of wives. We implore your highness to reflect upon the danger in which that man would be placed who should be convicted of having introduced into Germany a law such as this, whereby divisions would be instantly created amongst families, and a series of eternal law-suits arise. Your highness is of a frail constitution; you sleep little, and it is requisite to adopt very great precautions in your case. The great Scanderbeg frequently exhorted his soldiers to observe chastity, telling them that nothing was so detrimental to their pursuit as the pleasures of love. May it please your highness to examine seriously the various considerations involved in this matter; the scandal, the labours, the cares, the grief, and weakness, which, as has been shown to you, are involved in it. If, however, your highness is utterly determined upon marrying a second wife, we are of opinion that it ought to be done secretly. Signed and sealed at Wittemberg, after the feast of Saint Nicholas, in the year 1539. —Martin Luther, Philip Melancthon, Martin Bucer, Antony Corvin, Adam John Lening, Justin Wintfert, Dyonisius Melanther."[1]

[1] See Appendix LXXXVII.

It was truly a cruel proceeding to compel Luther, who, both as a theologian, and as the father of a family, maintained the sanctity of marriage, to declare that, according to the Old Testament, it was lawful for a man to take two wives and thus to introduce under one domestic roof, the hatreds jealousies, and angry passions of two females. He felt the burthen of his cross most painfully: "As for this *Mace-donian* business," he writes, soon after the completion o the transaction, "afflict not yourself too much respecting it matters are now come to a pass that renders utterly futile either joy or sadness? Why should we kill ourselves? Why suffer grief to destroy in us the thought of Him who ha vanquished death, and all the evils of this life? He wh has conquered the devil, and judged the prince of the world has he not likewise judged and overcome this scandal? I their eyes, our virtues are vices, when we do not worshi Satan together with them. Let Satan triumph, then; w will give way neither to grief nor sadness; but we will re joice in Christ, who has the power to avert the efforts o all our enemies." (18th June, 1540.)

It appears that, at one period, Luther entertained a hope tha the emperor would, by his intervention, save the protestant from the scandal of such a proceeding as that of the land grave; for in one of his letters, he says, "If Cæsar and th Empire willed, as they will be compelled to will, they migh speedily end by an edict this scandal, in order that it ma never become to future ages either an example or a law."

From this period, the letters of Luther, as well as those Melancthon, are filled with expressions of sadness and disgust.[1] Some one requested the former to give hi letters to the court of Dresden. Luther replied that he ha lost all his credit and influence in that quarter. In th correspondence anterior to this epoch, there occur occasion bitter expressions in regard to this court, "*Mundana ill caula.*"

"I will assist at your marriage, my dear Lauterbac; bu it will be in spirit and by prayer. As for being personall present, I am not alone hindered by the multiplicity of affair but also by the danger of offending these Mamelukes, and th

[1] See Appendix LXXXIX.

queen of this kingdom, (the duchess Catherine of Saxony?) for who is not now ruffled by the folly of Luther?"

"You ask me to send you, dear Jonas, consolation from time to time. But it is I who, more than any one, require your letters, in order that some animation may be infused into me, who, like Lot, have so much to suffer from this infamous and diabolical ingratitude—from this horrible disregard of the Word of the Lord. It has been reserved for me to witness the possession by Satan of the hearts of those who believe, that for themselves alone were reserved the high places in the kingdom of Christ."

The protestants had already began to relax in the severity of their demeanour and practice. They reopened the houses where debaucheries were wont to be carried on. "Better," observed Luther, "would it have been that the devil had never been banished, than that he should return in sevenfold strength." (13 September, 1540.)

"The pope, the emperor, the Frenchman, Ferdinand, have dispatched to the Turk an embassy charged with magnificent gifts, to demand peace. The finest feature of the proceeding is, however, that, in order to avoid giving offence to Turkish eyes, the whole *cortège* is to be habited in Turk's costume, quitting their own garments, and putting on the long robes of that nation. I do most ardently hope that these are the blessed signs of the immediate end of all things." (17 July, 1545.)

To Jonas he had thus written some time before:—"I must whisper in your ear a suspicion I have formed, that we Lutherans are about to be dispatched alone, and by ourselves, to fight the Turk. The king of Bohemia, Ferdinand, has levied throughout his states the war tribute, and, at the same time, has forbidden a single soldier to quit the kingdom. The emperor does nothing. What if it were their design to exterminate us by the Turk's agency?" (29th December, 1542.)

And in the early part of the same year, he communicates thus his fears: "Nothing new has transpired here, unless it be that the margrave of Brandenburg has got for himself a bad name throughout Germany in regard to the war in Hungary. Nor is that of Ferdinand a whit better. I discover so many circumstances, all bearing the same aspect and having the same tendency, as to be unable to divest myself of the belief that these are so many indications of a horrible and baneful treason." (20th January, 1542.)

"What," he again writes, "what will be the result of this horrible treason of the kings and princes?" (16th December, 1543.) And in a prior year thus—"God avenge our cause against these incendiaries." (He frequently vents his exclamations respecting the fires which were constantly happening at Wittemberg.) "Satan has discovered a new method of slaying us. They poison our wine;[1] put chalk into the milk. At Jena twelve persons were poisoned in their wine. Perhaps, however, they died of an excess of drinking. Nevertheless, there have been detected, I am assured, at Magdeburg and Northuse, several vendors of poisoned milk." (April, 1541.)

In another of his letters he gives a story of a poisoned eucharist. And from Amsdorf he thus speaks concerning the plague which was raging at Magdeburg: "The intelligence you send respecting the apprehensions of the plague which prevail with you, quite corresponds with the experience which former events of a like nature afforded me. I am astonished, I own, to observe that the more widely the word of life, through Jesus Christ, is spread, the greater becomes the fear of death amongst the people. Thus, whilst in former years, under the pope's domination, a false and illusory hope of eternal life diminished in men's estimation the fear of death, it seems as if, when the well-founded and certain expectation of the life to come is placed before them, it brought with it a sense of the weakness of our nature, in so far as the victory over death is in question. Or is it that God tempts us by means of these weaknesses of our nature, and thereby permits Satan to acquire more strength and boldness? So long as we held by the papal faith, we were like drunken men, stupid or asleep, mistaking death for life; that is to say, utterly ignorant of death and of the wrath of God. Now that the light has manifested itself, and that the wrath of God is better understood by us, human nature has extricated itself from the trammels of folly and of indolence. Hence it results that some have greater

[1] See Appendix XC.

apprehensions than they formerly entertained. I adjoin and apply to this reflection that passage of the seventy-first Psalm—'Cast me not off in the time of old age, forsake me not when my strength faileth;' for I believe that this supreme hour is of the latter days of Christ, and the hour of depression; that is to say, the last great assault of the devil, as in like manner David in his last days, when enfeebled by age, would have been slain by the giant, had not Abisai come to his aid. I have learnt during the last year to exclaim with Saint Paul: *Quasi mortui et ecce vivemus;* and also, *Per gloriam vestram quotidie morior*. When this apostle says to the Corinthians, *In mortibus frequenter*, he neither indulged in speculations, nor in meditation upon death; his idea was that of death itself, and he wrote as if he had no longer expectation or a hope of life." (20th Nov. 1538.)

"I ardently hope," says Luther, a few months before, "that amidst these internal dissensions on the earth, Jesus Christ will hasten the day of his coming, and that he will crumble the whole universe into dust." (12th Feb. 1538.)

BOOK THE FOURTH.

1530—1546.

CHAPTER THE FIRST.

Luther's table-talk—Wife—Children—Family ties—Nature.

Let us pause in this sad recital of the events of the last years of Luther's public life; let us retire, with himself, into his private life; let us seat ourselves at his own table,[1] surrounded by his wife, his children, and his intimate friends; and let us listen to the solemn and memorable sayings of the pious, the tender father of the family.

"He who insults preachers of the Word and women,[2] will never meet with much success. It is from women proceed children—a continuity which keeps up families and the commonwealth. Whosoever contemns them, contemns alike God and man.[3]

"The Saxon law, which assigns as the widow's portion, a chair and a distaff, is too severe. It ought to be interpreted largely, as implying by the first gift the right of remaining in the dwelling of her husband; and by the second, her subsistence, her maintenance. A man pays his servant more liberally; nay, he gives more than this to a beggar![4]

"There is no doubt that women who die in childbed, in the faith, are *ipso facto* saved; inasmuch as they die in the very fulfilment of that function for which God has especially created them.[5]

[1] See Appendix XCI. [2] Ib. XCII. [3] Tischreden, 241.
[4] Ib. 315. [5] Ib. 116.

There is a custom in the Low Countries for every young and newly ordained priest to choose a little girl, who is regarded as his betrothed; this is done in order to honour the holy state of marriage.[1]

Some one said to Luther: "If a preacher is bound to endure imprisonment and persecution on behalf of his love for the word of God, is he not far more imperiously called upon to endure the privation of celibacy?" The pastor replied: "It is far easier to endure a prison than to burn with hot passion—I myself have experienced this difficulty. The more I mortified my body, the greater the efforts I made to conquer my desires, the more fiercely they impelled me. Even supposing that a man had the gift of chastity bestowed upon him by nature, he ought nevertheless to marry in pure defiance of the pope! Had I been struck with death unexpectedly, I would have manifested the sense of honour which I entertain for the marriage state, by causing a pious young virgin to be brought to my bedside, whom I would have taken for my wife, and to whom I would have given two silver goblets as a wedding gift and token."[2]

In a letter to one of his friends, who requested his advice respecting marrying, Luther says: "If you burn, take a wife. You doubtless would have her to be handsome, pious, and rich: you may find such a wife, dear friend, in a picture—a wife with rosy cheeks and white legs. This sort of wives is of the most pious kind too; but what is the use of them in the kitchen or the bed-chamber? To rise betimes, and to marry young, are what no man ever repents of doing.[3]

"It is no more possible to do without a wife, than it is to dispense with eating and drinking. Conceived, nourished, borne by women, our very being is, in a great measure, their being; and it is utterly impossible for us to dissever ourselves altogether from them.

"If I ever felt disposed to make love to a woman, it was thirteen years ago, when I would have taken to myself Ave Schonfeldin, who is now the wife of doctor Basil, the Prussian physician. I was not then enamoured of my Catherine; I suspected her of pride and haughtiness; but it pleased God thus to order matters: he willed that I should take compassion

[1] Tischreden, 312. [2] Ib. [3] Ib. 315.

upon her, and the affair turned out well. May God be praised for it!

"The utmost blessing that God can confer on man is, the possession of a good and pious wife, with whom he may live in peace and tranquillity; to whom he can confide his whole possessions, even his life and welfare, and who bears him children. Catherine, thou hast a pious man who loves thee for a husband—thou art a very empress! Thanks be unto God!"[1]

Some one was excusing in Luther's presence a man who was in the habit of associating with loose women; the doctor observed: "He ought to know that he shows an utter contempt for the female sex in what he does. It is an abuse of woman, who was not created for such purposes. It is a high degree of happiness when a young woman inspires a constant passion: the devil seldom permits such a thing to happen. When I was at school, my hostess at Eisenach had a good saying: 'There is nothing on earth,' said the worthy woman, 'so sweet and consoling as the love of woman.'"

On Saint Martin's-day, the anniversary of Luther's birth, maître Ambrose Brend came and asked his niece in marriage. . . . . . . He surprised them one day discoursing together apart, in undertones: he burst into a laugh, and exclaimed: "I don't wonder at a bridegroom having so much to say to his betrothed. Can persons so circumstanced ever be fatigued with each other's company. So far, however, from placing any constraint upon them, I hold them privileged above law and custom." In granting to the doctor the hand of his niece, he made use of these words: "Sir, and dear friend, I here give unto you this young maiden, such as God in his goodness bestowed her upon me: I confide her to you. May God bless you, and render your union holy and happy!"[2]

Doctor Martin Luther was present at the marriage of the daughter of John Luffte. After supper, he conducted the bride to her bed, where he observed to the husband, that, according to the common practice, he ought to be the master in his own house—so long as his wife was not there. As a token of this, he took one of the bridegroom's shoes, and flung it upon the tester of the bed, by way of giving him dominion and chief rule.

[1] Tischreden, 313. [2] Ib. 316.

"Do as I myself did, dear comrade," said Luther, on another occasion, "when I was desirous of taking my dear Catherine to wife. I offered up my prayers to our Lord; I prayed earnestly. Do thou pray earnestly also. Thou hast not yet done so."[1]

On one occasion, in 1541, Luther was in an unusually gay and joyous mood when seated at table. "Do not be scandalized," said he to his associates, "to see me thus cheerful. I have received to-day various evil tidings, and I have just finished reading a letter of extreme violence against myself. Our affairs must be in a good train, since the devil rages so violently." He was wont to laugh at the futile chatter of his wife, and used to ask her whether, before she began her admirable sermon, she had said the Lord's prayer; "for if so," he would say, "God would assuredly have prevented thee from preaching."

"If," said he, on another occasion, "I were to marry again, I would carve an obedient wife for myself out of a block of marble; for, unless I did so, I should despair of finding one."

"The first year of married life brings with it strange ideas. If one is seated at table, the thought suggests itself—'Last year you were alone; now, you are two. A-bed, when one wakes up, another face is on the pillow.'

"In the first year of our marriage, my Catherine was wont to seat herself beside me, whilst I was studying; and once, not knowing what else to say, she asked me—'Sir doctor! in Prussia, is not the maître d'hotel the brother of the margrave?'[2]

"There ought to be no interval between the betrothal and the wedding. Oftentimes the friends of both parties interpose obstacles, as happened to me, in the case of maître Philip, and in regard to the marriage of Eisleben (Agricola). All my best friends cried out—'Not her! Some other!'"[3]

Lucas Cranach the elder drew the portrait of Luther's wife. When the picture was finished, and hung on the wall, the doctor saw it, and exclaimed—"I will have a man's portrait also taken, and the two shall be sent to the council at Mantua for the holy fathers to determine whether they would not, after all, prefer the marriage state to the celibacy of the ecclesiastics."

[1] Tischreden, 320. [2] Ib. 313. [3] Ib. 314.

"The certain sign of God's enmity to the papacy is, that he has refused to its ministers the blessings of paternity.

"When Eve was brought unto Adam, he became filled with the Holy Spirit, and gave her the most sanctified, the most glorious of all appellations. He called her Eva; that is to say, the mother of all. He did not style her wife; but simply mother—mother of all living creatures. In this consists the glory, and the most precious ornament of woman. She is *fons omnium viventium*, the source of all human life. This is a brief phrase; but neither Demosthenes nor Cicero could have paralleled it. It is the Holy Ghost himself who spoke thus through the medium of our first parent; and as he has conveyed herein so noble an eulogium on the marriage state, it is for us to conceal the frailty of woman. Nor did Jesus Christ, the son of God, contemn the marriage state. He himself was born of a woman, which is of itself the highest eulogy that could be pronounced on marriage."

"The image of marriage,"[1] continues Luther, "is discoverable in all living creatures; and not only in all animated creation, but also in trees and stones. Every one knows that trees, such, for instance, as the apple and the pear tree, stand mutually in sexual relations, and require mutual intercourse in order to be fruitful, only prospering when they are planted in contiguity one to the other.[2] The same observation applies equally to stones, more particularly the precious stones, coral, emeralds, and others. The heavens are likewise the husband of the earth: vivifying it by the rays of the sun, and thus rendering it capable of bringing forth all sorts of plants and fruit."[3]

The doctor's little children were one day standing at the table, looking intently at some peaches that had been served; Luther observed of them—"Whoso would behold the image of a soul which enjoys the fulness of hope, may find it in these infants. Ah, if we could but await with such joyful expectation for the life to come."[4]

They brought to Luther, one day, his little daughter Mag-

[1] See Appendix XCIII.

[2] Luther is wrong here. The apple and the pear have blossoms, which fructify themselves; it is the date tree and the family of palms, &c. that require external aid in order to produce fruit.

[3] Tischreden, 312. [4] Ib. 342.

dalen, in order that she might sing to him the hymn beginning, "The pope invokes the emperor and kings; they, &c.' The child, however, refused to obey, although her mother insisted on her compliance. The doctor interposed, saying—"Nothing good comes of violence. Without grace, the works of the law are nought."[1]

"Serve the Lord in fear, and rejoice in trembling," observed Luther. "There is no contradiction involved," continued he, "in this text, at least for me. My little boy, John, does exactly thus in respect to myself. But I cannot thus act towards God. If I am seated at table, and am writing or doing anything, John sings me a little song: if he sings too loud, and I tell him of it, he still sings on, but with some fear, and to himself, as it were. God wills that we also should be constantly gay, but that our gaiety be tempered with fear and reserve."[2]

On New Year's Day, one of Luther's children sobbed and cried to such a degree that no person was able to quiet it; the doctor and his wife were both saddened and discomposed for a full hour in consequence. He observed of the occurrence: "Such are some of the inconveniences of the marriage state; such its responsibilities. This probably is the reason why none of the Fathers has written anything worthy of note respecting this matter. Jerome has spoken of marriage in an obscene, and, I may say, in an antichristian manner. The reverse, however, holds good of Saint Augustine."[3]

Having one day been playing with his little Magdalen, his wife placed in his arms the youngest of his children; he observed, "I would willingly have died at the age of this child; I would willingly have renounced for that, all the honour I have gained, and all I am still to acquire in the world." The infant having thrown down a cup of wine over his wife's clothes: "Oh! how much more has our Saviour to suffer on our behalf than a mother on that of her child."[4]

Another time, he said to it—"Thou art the innocent little fool of our Lord, not under the law, but under grace. Thou art without fear or disquietude; all that thou dost is well done."[5]

"Children, after all, are the happiest. We older fools

[1] Tischreden, 124. [2] Ib. 10. [3] Ib. 314. [4] Ib. 47. [5] Ib. 49

constantly torment ourselves, and bring affliction on us by our eternal disputes about the Word! Is it true?—is it possible?—how is it possible? are our incessant inquiries. Whereas children, in the simplicity and the purity of their faith, possess a certainty, and doubt of nothing in which their salvation is concerned. In order to be saved, we ought to imitate their example, and hold fast to the Word of God alone. But the devil, in order to hinder us from so doing, is constantly throwing some obstacle in our path. This it is why it is better to die without questioning or doubting, and to pass quickly away from earth." [1]

On another occasion, when his little son, Martin, was taking the breast, the doctor said: "This babe and all who belong to me are hated by the pope, hated by duke George, hated by their partisans, hated by all the devils. Yet the dear child is disquieted by none of these foes; neither is he discomposed by the dread of the evil which these powerful princes and nobles wish to do him. He enjoys his meal cheerfully, and looks round, laughing aloud, leaving those who will to grumble and growl.[2]

The pastor of Zwickau, maître Leinhart Beier, and Spalatin, were one day at Luther's house, whilst he was caressing his little Martin, and fondling him, the baby, meanwhile, holding his doll and prattling to it. Luther said: "Such were our thoughts when in Paradise, simple and free: innocent, devoid of malice and hypocrisy; we should have been really and truly as this child is, when he speaks of God so assuredly." [3]

"What," said Luther on another occasion, "what must have been the feelings of Abraham, when he assented to sacrifice his only son, and to slay him? He would never have spoken of it to Sara; it would have cost him too dear. Truly, had God imposed such a command upon me, I should have contested the point with him." The doctor's wife took part in the conversation, and said, "I cannot believe that God would require any one to kill his child."

"How ardently my heart yearned after my family," said Luther one day, "at the time when I was sick almost unto death, at Smalkald! I believed that I should never again behold wife or children:[4] how heavily this separation weighed

[1] Tischreden, 134. [2] Ib. 45. [3] Ib. [4] Ib. 47.

upon me! No one is so thoroughly weaned from the flesh, as not to feel these impulses of nature. 'Tis a wonderful thing, the bond of association that unites man to woman.[1]

It was really touching to witness the manner in which the most common occurrences would arouse in Luther reflections of piety on the goodness of God, on the state of man before the fall, on the life to come, and other serious topics. Thus, a beautiful bough loaded with cherries, brought and put on the table by doctor Jonas, a few fishes from the little pond in his garden, that his wife placed joyfully on the board, the mere sight of a rose, or any other equally simple incident would rouse these pious sentiments in him. On the 9th of April, 1539, the doctor was walking in his garden, attentively looking at the trees and flowers, then in all the brilliancy of spring verdure; he exclaimed with admiration, "Glory to God, who, from the dead creation, thus raises up life again in the spring-time. Behold these branches, how strong, how beautiful they are! Already they teem, and are big with the fruit which they will bring forth. They offer a beautiful image of the resurrection of all men. The winter season represents death; the summer-tide, the resurrection. Then all things live again, all is verdant.

"Philip Melancthon and myself are overwhelmed with business and embarrassments. I, who am aged, and have gained my title of *Emeritus*, should prefer now to enjoy the pleasures of an old man in the garden, contemplating the wonders of God's creation in the trees, the flowers, herbs, birds, &c. I should have enjoyed these pleasures and this absence of care, had not my sins merited my privation of them, by causing me to be condemned to watch over these affairs, at once so pressing and often so fruitless." (8th April, 1538.)

On the 18th April, 1539, in the evening, a very violent storm occurred, followed by beneficent showers, which restored verdure to the trees and the earth. Doctor Martin, turning his eyes towards heaven, said: "How lovely is this weather! Thou hast granted to us, O Lord, this bounty, to us who are so ungrateful to thee, so full of wickedness and avarice. But thou art a God of goodness! This is no work of the

[1] Tischreden, 417. [2] Ib. 363.

devil! No; it is a bounteous thunder which shakes the earth and rouses it, cleaving it, that its fruits may come forth and spread a perfume like to that which is diffused by the prayer of a pious Christian." [1]

Another day, on his way to Leipsig, seeing the surrounding plains covered with the most luxuriant crops of wheat, he fell to praying with the utmost fervour, exclaiming: "O God of all goodness, thou hast bestowed upon us a year of plenty. But not because of our piety, O Lord, but in order to glorify thy holy name. Cause us, O Lord, to amend our lives, and to increase in faith, and in the belief of thy holy word. All in and around thee are miracles. Thy voice causes to spring out of the earth, and out of the sand of the desert, these beautiful plants, these green blades, which so rejoice the eye. O Father, give unto all thy children their daily bread."

"Let us support the difficulties which surround the functions exercised by us, with equality of soul, awaiting the help of Christ. Regard, in the violets and heartsease which you trample under foot whilst walking in your garden, an emblem of our condition. When we address the people, we offer to their view the broad robe of purple, the colour of sadness; but in the centre is the golden flower, which represents the faith which fades not."[2]

One evening, doctor Luther, seeing a little bird perching on a tree, and taking up its rest for the night, observed: "That little bird has chosen its shelter, and is about to go to sleep in tranquillity: it has no disquietude, neither does it consider where it shall rest to-morrow night, but it sits in peace on that slender branch, leaving it to God to provide for it."[3]

Towards night there came on another occasion two birds, who were busy in building their nest in the doctor's garden. They were often scared, whilst committing their petty thefts, by the passers to and fro. He observed of them: "Ah, poor little birds, fly not away; I wish you well with all my heart, if you would only believe me. Thus we ourselves refuse to trust in God, who so far from willing our condemnation, has given for us his own Son!"[4]

[1] Tischreden, 423. [2] Briefe, v. [3] Tischreden, 43.
[4] Ib. 24. See Appendix XCIV.

CHAPTER II.

The Bible—The fathers—The schoolmen—The pope—The councils.

DOCTOR MARTIN LUTHER had written with a piece of chalk upon the wall behind his stove the following words (Luke xvi. 10): "He that is faithful in that which is least is faithful also in much. And he that is unjust in the least is unjust also in much." "The child Jesus," said he, pointing to his effigy on the wall, "still sleeps in the arms of Mary, his mother. He will awake one day and call us to account for that which we have done."[1]

Luther one day was being shaved and having his hair cut in the presence of doctor Jonas; he said to the latter: "Original sin is in us like the beard—we are shaved to-day and look clean, and have a smooth chin; to-morrow our beard has grown again, nor does it cease growing whilst we remain on earth. In like manner original sin cannot be extirpated from us; it springs up in us as long as we exist. Nevertheless, we are bound to resist it to our utmost strength, and to cut it down unceasingly.

"Human nature is so corrupt, that it does not even desire celestial things. It is like a new-born infant, who, although you may offer it all the wealth and pleasures of the earth, is heedless of everything save its mother's breast. So, also, when the gospel offers us the eternal life which Jesus Christ promised mankind, we remain deaf to the divine words, we are benumbed by the flesh, and occupied only with frivolous and perishable ideas. Human nature has not any understanding, not even a sentiment, respecting that mortal malady by which it is overwhelmed.

"In divine matters the Father constitutes the *grammar;* for he supplies the words, and is the source whence flow all the good, pure, and beautiful expressions that can be made use of. The Son is the *logic;* he bestows the disposition, the

[1] Tischreden, 32.

method of arranging things in proper order, so that they follow and result one from the other. The Holy Ghost is the *rhetoric;* it is its province to expound, to enforce, and to display the topic; to give it life and force, so that it seizes upon men's hearts, and makes an impression on them.[1]

"The Trinity is discoverable throughout all creation. In the sun there co-exist body, brilliancy, and heat: in rivers, body, current, and strength; the same is true of the arts and sciences. In astronomy there are motion, light, and influence: in music, the three notes, *re, mi, fa;* and so on. The schoolmen have neglected these important signs for frivolities."

"The decalogue[2] is the *Doctrina doctrinarum;* the symbol is the *Historia historiarum;* the Father is the *Oratio orationum;* the sacraments are the *Ceremoniæ ceremoniarum.*"[3]

Luther was asked one day, whether, during the domination of the pope, those who had not been cognisant of the doctrine of the gospel which was taught in the present time (1539) could be saved. The doctor replied, "I know nothing of the matter; at least, unless I may think that baptism had the saving effect. I have seen many monks, to whom in their dying moments the crucifix was presented, as was the practice in those days. They might have been saved by their faith in the merits and sufferings of Jesus Christ."[4]

"Cicero far excelled Aristotle in philosophy and teaching. The *Officia* are better than the *Ethica.* And although Cicero lived in great care, and had upon him great burthens, labour, and pains in the government, yet he was far above Aristotle, who had money, wealth, and easy days.

"Cicero handled the best and finest questions in philosophy; as, Whether there be a God? what God is? whether he deals with human affairs? that there must be an everlasting mind, &c. Aristotle was a good logician, who handled the method and orderly way in teaching; but he taught not the business, the case, nor the kernel, so exquisitely as Cicero did. Whoso intends to learn upright philosophy, let him read Cicero.

"Cicero was a very wise man, he wrote more than all the philosophers, and read all the Grecian books through. I marvel that he was able to read and write so much amid so many

[1] Tischreden, 69. [2] See Appendix XCV. [3] Ib. 112. [4] Ib. 362.

great dealings and businesses. No man rightly understands Cicero's Epistles except he has been exercised in government twenty years. Cicero, a wise and diligent man, suffered and performed much; I hope God will be merciful unto him and to such as he was; howsoever, it is not our duty to speak certainly touching that point, but to remain by the word revealed unto us; namely, 'Whoso believeth and is baptized, the same shall be saved.' Yet, nevertheless, God is able to dispense and to hold a difference among the nations and heathen, but our duty is not to know nor to search after time and measure. For there will be a new heaven and a new earth,[1] much more extensive than now they be: God can give to every one according to his pleasure."

Luther was asked whether he who had been injured was bound to go to the extent of asking his injurer's pardon. He replied: "No: Jesus Christ himself has not left us such an example, nor has he anywhere commanded it to be done. It is sufficient if we pardon offences in our hearts,—publicly when occasion calls upon us to do so,—and that we pray for those who have injured or offended us. I myself went on one occasion to two persons who had injured me, Eisleben (Agricola) and doctor Jerome Schurf, but it fell out by chance that neither of them was at home, so I came back, and made no other endeavour to see them. I now return thanks to God that I was not permitted to do as I then wished."[2]

The doctor one day sighed heavily whilst meditating on the perturbators and the sectarians who despised the Word of God. "Ah!" said he, "were I but a great poet, I would write a magnificent poem on the utility and the efficacy of the divine word. Without that word what should we be?—For several years I read the whole Bible twice in every twelvemonth. It is a great and powerful tree, each word of which is a mighty branch: each of these branches have I shaken, so desirous was I to learn what fruit they every one of them bore, and what they could give me. Each time I succeeded in obtaining a couple of either pears or apples."[3]

"In former times, under the papacy, pilgrimages were undertaken[4] to visit the saints. People went to Rome, to Jerusalem, to Saint Iago of Compostella, to expiate their sins.

[1] Tischreden, 425. [2] Ib. 106. [3] Ib. 311. [4] See Appendix XCVI.

Now-a-days, we perform our Christian pilgrimages by means of faith. When we read diligently the Prophets,[1] the Psalms, and the Gospels, we arrive, not through the holy city, but through our hearts and thoughts, even unto God. This is journeying to the real land of promise, the paradise of eternal life."[2]

"Of what account are the saints in comparison with Christ?[3] They are no more than sparkling drops of the night dew upon the head of the bridegroom, scattered amongst his hair?"[4]

Luther did not love to hear any one insist on the miracles. He looked upon these as a very secondary class of proofs. "The convincing testimony," said he, "is to be found in the Word of God. Our adversaries read the translation of the Bible much more frequently than we do. I believe that duke George has read it more carefully than any one of the nobles who are with us. He (duke George) observed to some one, "If that monk only finishes his translation of the Bible, he may take his departure as soon as he likes." Luther said that he was compelled by Melancthon to translate the New Testament.

"Let our enemies indulge their transports of rage; God has not set up a stone wall to confine the waves of the ocean, nor has he controlled them by a mountain of steel. He thought it enough to place a shore, a boundary of sand.[5]

"I read very much in my Bible whilst I was a monk, during my youth; but this availed me nothing: I simply looked upon Christ as another Moses. We have now, however, found the dear Saviour again; let us return thanks, and hold fast by him, suffering on his behalf all that it behoves us to endure.

"What is the cause of the universal teaching and observance of the Ten Commandments? It is that the natural moral law is nowhere so well set forth and written down as by Moses. I wish they would borrow some more of his regulations in respect to temporal matters, such as the law of divorce, the jubilee, the year of enfranchisement, the tithes, &c. &c.: the world would be much better governed.

[1] See Appendix XCVII. [2] Tischreden, 311.
[3] See Appendix XCVIII. [4] Cochlæus, Leben Luther's, 226.
[5] Tischreden, 447.

The Romans compiled the laws of their twelve tables much in this way, from the institutions of Greece. As for the Sabbath or Sunday, there is no necessity for its observance; and if we do so, the reason ought to be, not because Moses commanded it, but because nature likewise teaches us to give ourselves, from time to time, a day's rest, in order that man and beast may recruit their strength, and that we may go and hear the Word of God preached.[1]

"Since there has been begun in this age a general replacing of things in their former state, as though it were the day of universal restoration, it occurred to my mind to try whether the laws of Moses could not be revived, and thus trace back all our laws and customs to their original source. I took, in the first instance, especial care to treat upon all subjects with the utmost possible simplicity, and not to suffer myself to be drawn into mystical explanations, as they are termed. I can conceive no other reason why God chose to form the Jewish people by these ceremonials, than because he saw the tendency of that race towards external things; and to the end that these ceremonies should not be empty phantoms and mere semblances, the Almighty gave them, by means of his Word, weight and substance, thus rendering them matters of grave and serious import. I have annexed to each chapter short allegories, not that I hold these in much esteem, but in order to hinder others from being seized with the mania for allegorizing. Thus you may see in Jerome, Origen, and other ancient writers, an unhappy and sterile practice of imagining allegories which refer everything to morality and good works, whereas everything should be referred to the Word of God and faith." (April, 1525.)

"The Lord's Prayer is that which I prefer. I constantly repeat it, mingling with it sentences from the Psalms,[2] praying that the false teachers may be confounded and covered with shame. The Lord's Prayer has no equal amongst prayers; I like it better than any of the Psalms.[3]

[1] Werke, 11. 16. [2] See Appendix XCIX.

[3] Tischreden, 153. ["At sitting down to and rising from our tables, at our rising and going to bed, and in every particular act, wherever prayer is wont to be introduced, I would have Christians always make use of the Lord's Prayer; if not that prayer alone, yet at least that prayer always. . . . The people should have it continually in their mouths; for it is most

"I candidly avow my ignorance as to whether I rightly understand the Psalms in their legitimate sense. I do not, however, doubt the verisimilitude of my version of them. Amongst those who have rendered them, one has been in error in one part, and another has mistaken the meaning in another part. I discover meanings that were overlooked by St. Augustine: others who come after me, will, I am aware, perceive much that has escaped me. Who will venture to affirm that any one has thoroughly understood a single psalm? Our life is a beginning and a progress, not a consummation. He is best who approaches nearest to the spirit. There are degrees in life and in action; why should there not be the same in mind. The apostle declares that we are transferred from one light to a greater one."

Respecting the New Testament, Luther remarked: "The gospel of St. John is the true and pure gospel—the chief of the gospels, inasmuch as it contains the greatest portion of our Saviour's sayings. Thus, also, the epistles of Saint Paul and of Saint Peter are higher in authority than the gospels of Saint Matthew, Saint Mark, and Saint Luke. In a word, Saint John's gospel, and his first epistle, the epistles of Saint Paul, more especially those to the Romans, the Galatians, and the Ephesians, together with the first epistle of Saint Peter, constitute that portion of the New Testament which most clearly show Christ, and which contain and teach all that it is useful and necessary to know, even were you never to see any other books.[1]

He did not consider the epistle to the Hebrews, nor that of Saint James, to be of apostolic origin. He thus delivered his sentiments respecting that of Saint Jude: "It is quite undeniable that this epistle is either an extract from, or a copy of the second epistle general of Saint Peter. The expressions are nearly identical in both. Jude speaks therein of the apostles as having been their disciple, and as writing after their decease. He quotes texts, and mentions circumstances which are nowhere else to be found in the Scriptures."

certain that all necessary petitions are comprehended in it, and that it is infinitely proper for all occasions. 'Tis the only prayer I use in all places and circumstances, and what I still repeat without changing."—Montaigne's Essays, by Hazlitt, book i. chap. 56, p. 147.]

[1] Ukert, 18.

Luther's opinion respecting the Apocalypse is remarkable: "Let each man judge of this book according to the light that is in him, and by his own particular perceptions. I do not desire to impose my opinion respecting it upon any one. I say, simply, that which I think of it myself. I look upon the revelations of St. John to be neither apostolic nor prophetic." On another occasion he said—"Many of the fathers of the church rejected this book; consequently, every man is at liberty to treat it according to the dictates of his own mind. For my part, one single reason has determined me in the judgment I have come to respecting it, which is, that Christ is neither adored in it, nor is he therein taught such as we know him."

Of the Fathers of the church,[1] Luther said: "Jerome may be consulted for the purposes of historical study. As to faith, and good true religion and doctrine, there is not a word about them in his writings. I have already proscribed Origen. Chrysostom possesses no authority in my estimation. Basil is but a monk, for whom I would not give the value of a hair. The apology of Philip Melancthon is worth all the writings of all the doctors of the church put together, not excepting those of Saint Augustine. Hilary and Theophylactus are good, as also is Ambrosius. The last is admirable, when he treats upon the most essential article, that of the forgiveness of sins.

"Bernard is superior to all the doctors in his sermons; but when he disputes, he becomes quite another man; he then allows too much to the law, and to free will.

"Bonaventure is the best of the school of theologians. Amongst the fathers, Saint Augustine holds unquestionably the first place, Ambrose the second, Bernard the third. Tertullian is a thorough Carlstad. Cyril contains the happiest sentences. Cyprian the martyr is a feeble theologian. Theophylactus is the best interpreter of Saint Paul."[2]

In order to demonstrate that mere antiquity does not add to authority, Luther said: "We observe how bitterly Saint Paul complains of the Corinthians and the Galatians. Amongst the apostles themselves, Christ found a traitor in Judas.

"The books written by the fathers respecting the Bible,

[1] See Appendix C. [2] Tischreden, 383.

contain in themselves nothing conclusive. They leave the reader suspended between heaven and earth. Read St. Chrysostom, the best rhetorician and orator of them all."

He remarked—"The fathers said nothing decisive, during their lives, respecting justification by grace; but at their death they believed in it. This was the more prudent course for them to follow, in order neither to encourage mysticism, nor discourage good works. These worthy fathers lived better than they wrote."

Luther eulogized very highly the history of Saint Epiphanius, and the poetry of Prudentius: "Augustine and Hilary have written with the greatest clearness and truth of them all; the other fathers must be perused with judgment (*cum judicio*).

"Ambrosius was mixed up in the affairs of the world, much in the same way as we are. We are obliged to devote more time to the matters relating to marriage brought before the Consistory, than to the Word of God.[1]

"Bonaventure was styled the seraphic doctor; Thomas, (Aquinas) the angelic; Scot, the subtle; Martin Luther will be denominated the arch heretic."

Saint Augustine was represented in a book that Luther saw, habited in a monk's garment. The doctor, on looking at the picture, observed: "The painter wronged the holy father, for he led an ordinary life, just like that of the rest of his countrymen. He had silver spoons and cups; he did not live apart like a monk.

"Macarius, Antony, Benedict, have all wronged, in a remarkable degree, the church of which they were members, by their monkery, and I consider that they will be placed in heaven many degrees below the man who has been a good citizen, the father of a family, of pious life and fearing God.

"Saint Augustine pleases me more than all the others. He has taught a pure doctrine, and has declared, with true Christian humility, his works to be subject to the Holy Scriptures. He is likewise well disposed to the marriage state. He speaks in favourable terms of the bishops who had been the pastors of the church up to this time, but the period in which he lived, and the disputes with the Pelagians

[1] Tischreden, 383.

soured his disposition, and did him great harm. Had he lived to witness the scandals of the papacy, he would doubtless not have suffered such things to be. Saint Augustine is the first of all the fathers of the church who treats of original sin."[1]

Having delivered his opinions respecting Saint Augustine, Luther added: "But since I became, by the grace of God, capable of understanding St. Paul, I have been unable to esteem any of these doctors; they have shrunk into insignificance in my estimation.

"There is not one of the fathers to whom I am so hostile as to St. Jerome. He writes only respecting fasts, sorts of food, virginity, &c. Doctor Staupitz was wont to say, 'I would like to know how Jerome can, by any possibility, be saved?'

"The nominals are in the upper schools a sect to which I once belonged myself. They controvert the views of the Thomists, the Scotists, and the Albertists. They call themselves Ockhamists. This is the newest, and now it is the most powerful of all the sects, more particularly at Paris."[2]

Luther entertained a high opinion of Peter Lombard's *Master of Sentences*. But in general, he thought that the schoolmen[3] assigned too small an influence to grace, and too much influence to free will.

"Gerson alone, amongst all the doctors, has mentioned spiritual temptations. Every one of the others, Gregory Nazianzene, Augustine, Scot, Thomas, Richard Ockham, describe bodily temptations only. Gerson is the sole writer who has treated of discouragement. The church, in proportion as she becomes more ancient, must necessarily experience spiritual temptations. We have now reached that epoch in the progression of our church.

"William of Paris experienced, in some degree, these spiritual temptations. But as to the schoolmen, they never acquired a knowledge of the catechism. Gerson alone, whom I have already mentioned, offers reassurance to, and restores the conscience of sinners. He has been the means of salvation to many poor souls in despair, by lessening and extenuating the rigour of the law, whilst, at the same time, he

[1] Tischreden, 98. [2] Ib. 384. [3] See Appendix CI.

uniformly upheld it. But Christ does not merely pierce the barrel, he staves it completely, and he says, 'Confide neither in the law, nor rest thy hopes upon it; but upon me, and in me, Christ. If thou are not good, I am.'

"Doctor Staupitz was speaking one day before us of Andrew Zacharias, who, as has been asserted, got the better of John Huss in argument. He narrated, that doctor Proles of Gotha, seeing a portrait of this Zacharias in a convent, represented with a rose in his bonnet, observed, 'God preserve me from wearing a rose like that; for he conquered John Huss unfairly, and by means of a falsified copy of the Bible.' There is in the thirty-fourth chapter of Ezekiel, this verse: 'It is I, saith the Lord, who will visit and punish my shepherds,'[1] to which there were surreptitiously added, 'but not my people.' The members of the council showed John Huss this text falsified in his own Bible, as in the others referred to, and came to the following conclusion: 'You see by this that you are not called upon to punish the pope; for God himself takes that charge upon him,' and thus the poor man was condemned and burnt.[2]

"John Agricola was one day reading a certain publication written by John Huss, full of spirit, but also of resignation as well as fervour, in which he set forth how in his person he suffered martyrdom from the stone, and at the same time saw himself rejected by the emperor Sigismund. Doctor Luther expressed his admiration at his spirit and courage, exclaiming, 'Great injustice is done to John Huss and myself in styling us heretics!'

"Huss died, not as an anabaptist, but as a Christian. He offers an example of Christian frailty, but at the same time there was roused in his soul a power as from God which sustained him. The struggle between the flesh and the spirit, with Christ and with Huss, is beautiful to behold. Constance is now a poor wretched city. I believe that God has thus punished it. John Huss was burnt, and I believe that I shall, if it pleases God, be also slain. Huss weeded from out of Christ's vineyard a few thorns, in attacking only the scandalous doings of the papists; whereas I, doctor Martin Luther,

[1] There is no such exact text in our Vulgate translation, though the sense is borne out.—Ed.

[2] Tischreden, 385.

found myself upon a well-tilled and already black mould—I attacked the doctrine of the pope, and I overthrew it.[1]

"John Huss was the seed which was to be buried in the earth and die, in order to revive and grow with force." [2]

Luther improvised one day, whilst sitting at table, the following verse:

"Pestis eram vivens, sed moriens ero mors tua, papa."

(In life I was your plague; dead, I shall be your death, pope.)

"Antichrist is at once typified in the Pope and the Turk. The pope is the soul; the Turk the flesh.[3]

"My poverty and the infirmity of my condition, not to speak of the righteousness of my cause, have occasioned the downfall of the pope. 'If,' said the pontiff, 'I have successfully defended my doctrine against so many kings and emperors, how is it possible for me to fear a mere monk?' Had he but considered me in the beginning a sufficiently dangerous foe, he might have stifled my voice at the very outset.

"I admit that I have frequently been guilty of too much violence; but never in respect to the papacy. There ought to be set aside for the special service of the popish battle, a tongue, every word of which is a thunder-bolt.[4]

"The papists are confounded and vanquished by the mere force of scriptural testimony. God be praised, I am alive to all their errors, under every aspect, from the *Alpha* to the *Omega*. Notwithstanding, however, that they themselves now admit the Scriptures to be opposed to them, such is the splendour and majesty of the pope, that it dazzles me sometimes; and it is in fear and trembling that I attack him.[5]

"The pope says to himself: 'What! shall I quail before a monk, who seeks to despoil me of my crown—my majesty? He would indeed be a fool who yielded in such a struggle.' I would give my two hands to believe as firmly in Jesus Christ, as the pope believes that Jesus Christ is nought.[6]

"Others have attacked the manners of the popes, as did Erasmus and John Huss; but I levelled the two pillars upon which popery rested—namely, vows and private masses."[7]

Of councils.—"Councils have no vocation in regard to lay-

[1] Tischreden, 386. [2] Ib. 127. [3] Ib. 241. [4] Ib. 249. [5] Ib. 255. [6] Ib. 259. [7] Ib. 192.

ing down articles of faith. Their proper occupation is that of regulating discipline in the church."

Doctor Martin Luther raised his eyes one day to heaven, and sighing, exclaimed: "Ah! would we had a general council, free to act, and of a truly Christian spirit! God knows well how to bring this about: the matter is in his hands: He knows and has charge of the most secret counsels.

"When Peter Paul Vergerius, the pope's legate, came to Wittemberg, in the year 1533, and I went up to the castle where he was, he cited us, and gave a summons to us to proceed to the council. 'I will go,' said I, adding, 'you papists are taking a great deal of pains very uselessly. If you resort to a council you wont open the questions respecting the sacraments, justification by faith, or good works; but you merely resort to child's play and idle words, such as fixing the length of robes, or the breadth of a priest's belt, or the extent of his tonsure, &c.' The legate turned away from me, and observed to his companion: 'This man goes to the point at once, &c.' Some one asked when the pope would convoke a council. Luther replied: 'It seems to me that we shall have none before the day of judgment. Then our Lord God will himself hold a general council.'"

Luther's recommendation was, not to refuse to attend at a council, but to require that it should be perfectly free. "If this is refused to us," said he, "we cannot have a better excuse."[1]

Of church property.[2]—Luther desired all church property, rents, &c., to be applied to the maintenance of schools, and of poor divines. He deplored the spoliation of the churches, and predicted that the spoils of those establishments would become very soon a subject of dispute amongst the princes.

"The pope," said he, "lavishes the property of the church on the catholic princes, in order that they may be his friends and allies.

"It was not so much our princes of the Augsburg confession of faith who pillaged the church, as Ferdinand, the emperor, and the archbishop of Mayence. Ferdinand compelled all the monasteries to pay a ransom. The Bavarians are the greatest church robbers of all. In that kingdom there

[1] Tischreden, 376. [2] See Appendix CII.

are very rich abbeys; whereas my gracious sovereign, and the landgrave (of Hesse) have in their dominions only some very poor monasteries of the mendicant orders. It was proposed at the diet to place all the monasteries under the control of the Emperor, who would have established in them a sort of military government. I advised as follows: 'You must first collect all the monasteries into one spot; for what prince would suffer in his territory the troops of the emperor?' This argument was thoroughly enforced by the archbishop of Mayence."

In the reply which Luther gave to a letter from the king of Denmark, asking advice of him, the doctor disapproved of the article whereby all the church property was vested in the crown, and observed: "See how differently our prince John Frederick acts: he applies the property of the church solely to the support of the pastors and the professors of religion."[1]

"There is good sense in the proverb which says, 'The more priests the less profit.' Burchard Hund, councillor to the elector John of Saxony, used to say: 'We nobles have united to our own properties the cloistral properties, whilst these latter, in their turn, have swallowed up our properties, so that there exists neither one nor the other.'" Luther adds to this, the fable of the fox who avenged the loss of her cubs by burning the tree, and the eaglets nestled in its branches.[2]

A former preceptor of Ferdinand, king of the Romans, whose name was Severus, narrated to Luther the fable of the dog who guarded the tray of meat; but who, finding himself overpowered by other dogs, seized upon a portion of the spoil, and devoured it. "That is precisely what the emperor is now doing," said Luther, "in regard to the church properties (of Utrecht and Liege.)"

Of cardinals and bishops.[3]—"In Italy, France, England, and Spain, the bishops are commonly called to his council by the king: they are poor, and that is the reason. But in Germany, where they are rich, powerful, and where, moreover, they are held in great consideration, the bishops govern for their own behoof, and in their own persons.[4]

[1] Tischreden, 380. [2] Ib. 60. [3] See Appendix CIII.
[4] Tischreden, 275.

"I would take every precaution to maintain the canonries, and smaller bishoprics; so that, by means of the revenues arising from these sources, we may establish preachers and pastors in the great cities. The larger bishoprics must be secularized."

On the day of Ascension, doctor Martin Luther dined with the elector of Saxony, and it was resolved that the bishops should preserve their authority and jurisdiction, provided they consented to abjure the pope. "Our people," said Luther, "will examine and ordain them by the imposition of hands. It was by this means that I myself became a bishop."

During the disputes at Heidelberg, it was asked whence the monks originated. The reply was, "God having ordained the priesthood, the devil wished, as usual, to imitate what he had done; but he shaved too much of the hair off his men.[1]

"Monkery can never be re-established, so long as the doctrine of justification is maintained in its purity.

"In former days, the monks had obtained such a degree of respect and consideration, that the pope dreaded them more than he did kings or bishops, for they had the common people entirely under their thumbs. The monks were the pope's best bird-catchers. 'Tis to small purpose the king of England refuses to recognise the pope as the supreme head of the Christian church. He does nothing but torment the body while strengthening the soul of the papacy." (Henry VIII. had not, at this period, suppressed the monasteries.[2])

CHAPTER III.

Of schools and universities, and the liberal arts.

"Schools must yield preachers and ministers; but what comes to cathedrals and vicarages, the same is lazy stuff in popedom, and does no good. Preachers and ministers must edify and preserve the church. Schools and ministers are better than the councils; therefore, in my little book, *De Con-*

[1] Tischreden, 271. See Appendix CIV. [2] Tischreden, 272.

ciliis, I have preferred them before and above the councils, which will sorely vex the papists.

"The youth have now good and convenient times to study, for every art is taught orderly and uprightly, insomuch as they may soon and easily comprehend them, except they be blockheads. Neither are the boys now so strictly and harshly treated as in former times, when they were called *martyrs of the schools;* especially, they were plagued with the *Lupus*, with *Casualibus*, and with *Temporalis*, which were altogether unprofitable, very irksome and unpleasing, wherewith they consumed time, and spoiled many a fine and expert brain.

"I hope, that if the world is to last awhile longer, the universities of Erfurt and Wittemberg will raise their heads, and regain strength, provided always they adopt a wholesome theology, which it seems they are already disposed to do. But some people must go to sleep first. I am astonished that a university should ever have been established in this town of Wittemberg. Erfurt is far better situated for such an establishment. There ought to be a city on that spot, even were the present one to be burnt, which God forbid! The university of Erfurt was formerly so renowned, that all others were, in comparison with it, considered only as so many petty academies. This pre-eminence and majesty have altogether abated now, and Erfurt exhibits now a mere shadow of a university.

"In those times of which I speak, the masters of the university were greatly promoted and honoured: they were attended by torch-bearers. For my part, I know of no worldly enjoyments which are comparable to such distinctions as they received. When the degree of doctor was conferred, a great festival always took place. They went in procession, on horseback, round the city: the university people dressed themselves with extreme care, and wore their robes. But none of this exists now: I only wish they would revive these good old customs.

"It will be an evil day for Germany when her schools are permitted to decay, or if they should ever be neglected or despised. Woe be to the archbishop of Mayence and of Erfurt, who, by a single word, could revive the universities of these two cities, and who, nevertheless, suffers them to remain desolate and deserted. One corner alone of Germany,[1]

[1] See Appendix CV.

that wherein we now are, still flourishes—God be praised!—through the purity of the doctrine taught there, and because, also, the liberal arts are cultivated amongst us. The papists have shut the stable-door, now that the steed is stolen. The fault lies with the bishop of Mayence, who has been the scourge of the universities, as of the whole of Germany. But he is justly punished: he has on his face a spot of a deathly hue, like dirt mingled with blood.

"It is at Paris, in France, that the most celebrated and most excellent university is to be found: there are upwards of twenty thousand students in it. The theologians have assigned to them, for their own private use, in the most agreeable part of the city, a street which is closed at both ends by gates, called the *Sorbonne.* Perhaps this word is derived from the Service tree, (*Sorbus,*) which is found on the shores of the Dead Sea, and whose fruits present a fair outside—within, only bitter dust. Such is the university of Paris: a great crowd of professors, students, &c., are collected there, but she is the parent of many errors. When they hold disputations, they gabble and scream, like drunken peasants, in French and in Latin. The masters are obliged to knock on the ground with their feet to obtain peace. No degree of doctor in theology is conferred at the Sorbonne—at least, not until the student has passed ten years amidst their sophisms and futile dialectics. The candidate has to sit the entire day, from six in the morning to six in the evening, maintaining a disputation with whosoever presents himself for that purpose.

"At Bourges, in France, when they confer the degree of doctor in theology, which ceremony takes place in the metropolitan church, a net is given to the newly made doctor, apparently to enable him to make a prey of men.

"We have amongst us—praised be God!—universities wherein the Word of the Lord is accepted. There are, likewise, many fine private schools, where the best disposition is observable, such, for instance, as Zwickau, Torgau, Wittemberg, Gotha, Eisenach, Deventer, &c."

Extract from Luther's Treatise on Education.—"Domestic tuition is quite insufficient. The magistrature ought to superintend the instruction of children. The establishment of schools is one of the most important duties which they have to perform; nor ought the functions of a teacher to be confided to any but the most learned men." Respecting the importance of the study of languages, Luther says—"The devil greatly dreads this sort of learning, and uses every means to extinguish it. The first gift Christ bestowed on the apostles was that of tongues." Luther complained that in the monasteries of Germany the monks not only were ignorant of the Latin language, but scarcely knew their mother tongue. "As for me," said the doctor, "if I should ever have children, and my means permit, I will have them well instructed and made proficients in languages and history; and also, they shall learn music and the mathematics." He then breaks into an eulogy on poets and historians.

"Children ought to be sent for at least an hour or two every day to school. They may employ the remainder of their time in learning household affairs, and acquiring some trade." "There ought, likewise, to be schools for girls." "Public libraries are necessary establishments; the basis being theological works in the Greek, Latin, and German languages; next in importance, lexicons, grammars, &c., for the purpose of teaching languages; after that, the poets, the orators, Greek and Latin, pagan and Christian. The authors who treat on the liberal arts and mechanics are not to be excluded, nor the writings of the jurists; the professors of medicine, annalists, chroniclers, historians, all of them in their own language, and these ought to constitute the principal contents of such a library, &c."

Of Languages.—"The wisdom of the Grecians, in comparison of the wisdom of the Jews, is altogether bestial, for without God no true understanding nor wisdom can be. The wisdom of the Grecians consists in an external, virtuous, and civil conversation; but the end of the wisdom of the Jews (such as are upright and godly) is to fear God and to trust in him. The wisdom of the world is the wisdom of the Grecians: hence Daniel names the kingdoms of the world (according to their kind) *ignorant beasts.* The Grecians have good and pleasing words, but not sentences; their language is soft, and of a courteous kind, but not rich. The Hebrew tongue, above other languages, is very plain, but withal it is majestic and glorious: it contains much in few and simple words, and therein surpasses all other languages. The Hebrew tongue is the best and richest in words; it is a pure language, which neither begs nor borrows of others. She has her own proper colour. Greek, Latin, and the German tongue beg of others; they have many *composita*, or compounded words; the Hebrew tongue, after the Babylonian captivity, fell away in such sort, that never since it could again be brought to perfection; for the most part they speak the Chaldean language, but corrupted, mingled, and impure, as the Walloons speak Latin. Languages of themselves make not a divine, they are only helps to him; for when one intends to speak of a thing, he ought to know and understand the business before. For my part, I use the common German tongue, to the end both high and low country people may understand me; I speak according to the Saxonian chancery, which is imitated in the courts of all German princes, insomuch that it is the general German language. Maximilian the emperor, and Frederick prince elector of Saxony, drew the German tongue into the *Roman empire*. I learned more Hebrew when, in reading, I compared one place and sentence with another, than when I directed the same upon and towards the grammar. If I were young, I would contrive a way and means for the perfect learning of the Hebrew tongue, which is both glorious and profitable, and without which the Holy Scriptures cannot rightly be understood; for although the New Testament be written in Greek, yet it is full of the Hebrew kind of speaking, from whence it is truly said, 'The Hebrews drink out of the fountain, the Grecians out of the springs that flow from the fountain; the Latins out of the ponds.' I am no Hebraist, according to the grammar rules, for I permit not myself to be tied, but go freely through. Although one have the gift of languages and understand them, he cannot so soon bring one into another to translate them. To translate, is a special gift and grace of God. The Seventy Grecian interpreters that translated the Hebrew Bible into Greek, were inexperienced and unpractised in the Hebrew language; their translations are very poor, for they contemned the letters, the words and manner of speaking, insomuch that the translation and interpretation of Jerome is to be preferred before them. I am persuaded that if Moses and the prophets should now rise again, they would not understand their own words and language, as now the same are screwed about.

Lyra, above all others, was the best Hebraist, and a diligent translator of the Old and New Testaments."

Of the Tongue.—"The tongue of man is a wonderful work and creation of God, which is able to show the words significantly, distinct and apprehensively. Every country has its particular kind of language and speaking; the Grecians pronounce the letter R only in the throat, with an H; insomuch as it was a very difficult and hard matter for Demosthenes, the most eloquent speaker in the Greek tongue, to pronounce this R without rattling in the throat, yet at last practice overcame nature, so that he was able to pronounce it plainly. For the superfluity of the moistness of the brain hinders the tongue, as we see in the drunken. Thus God gave to his creature, man, a working tool."

Of Grammar.—"Grammar is one thing, the Hebrew tongue is another, quite distinct. The Hebrew language, in so far as its grammar is concerned, has in a great measure been lost by the Jews; it fell together with Judaism, and with the comprehension of that dispensation, as is told us by Isaiah, (xxix.) No concessions, therefore, ought to be made to their rabbis in their interpretations respecting sacred things. They torture and do violence to the etymologies and meanings, because they determine the thing by the word, making it subservient to the word, whereas the thing itself ought to predominate.

"Similar to these, are the disputes between the Ciceronians and the other Latinists. I, for my part, am neither of the Latin, nor of the grammarian, nor still less of the Ciceronian school. Nevertheless, I approve of those who give the preference to the school of Cicero. So, also, in respect to sacred literature; I should greatly prefer being able merely to follow the real meaning of Moses, of David, or of Isaiah, in their writings, were that possible, than to be a Cumic Hebraist, or a follower of any other of the rabbinical schools." (1537).

"I regret very much not to be able to devote any time to the study of the poets and the rhetoricians; I once bought a Homer, in order to make myself a Grecian." (29th March, 1523.)

"Were I to write a treatise on dialectics, I would confine myself strictly to the German language, rejecting all such words as *propositio*, *syllogismus*, *enthymema*, *exemplum*, &c.

Those who have introduced new terms have also brought in with them new principles, as did Scot with his *reality* and his *hiccity* (his here-ness) and as also did the Anabaptists and the preachers of disturbances, with their jargon. Let people, therefore, be cautious in respect to those who make it their study to use new and uncommon words."

Luther once referred to the fable of the "Lion's Court," and said: "After the Bible, I know of no better books than the Fables of Æsop, and the writings of Cato." Thus also he pronounced Donatus to be, in his estimation, the best of the grammarians. "It was not one man," he said, "who wrote Æsop's fables; many great minds have contributed to the stock, at every successive epoch of the world."[1]

Of the learned—"Before many years shall have elapsed such want will be of learned people, that they would willingly dig them nine ells deep out of the ground if they could but get them; but all will be in vain: we too sorely provoke God to anger.

"Wisdom, understanding, learning, and the pen, these do govern the world. If God were angry, and took out of the world all the learned, then all people would become merely like wild and savage beasts."

To a friend he writes: "Do not trouble yourself with anxiety as to whether Germany may not retrograde in civilization, if the literature which our doctrine has called forth should subside. Such a result would be inevitable." (29th March, 1523.)

CHAPTER IV.

Drama—Music—Astrology—Printing—Banks, &c.

Of theatrical representations.—Luther, on the case being submitted to him, said he had no fault to find with a particular schoolmaster for having allowed his boys to play one of Terence's comedies. After enumerating the various aspects in which he regarded theatrical representations as useful, he observed: "If we keep away from theatres because the pieces

[1] See Appendix CVI.

acted often turn upon love, we must, on the same principle, refuse to read the Bible."

"Our dear Joachim has asked my judgment respecting the religious shows, which several of your ministers object to. Briefly, my opinion is this: it has been commanded unto all men to spread and propagate the word of God by every possible means, not merely by speech, but by writings, paintings, sculptures, psalms, songs, musical instruments; according to the Psalmist: *Praise him with the trumpet, praise him with the timbrel, praise him upon the loud and sounding cymbals.* Moses says: *Ye shall lay up these my words in your heart and in your souls, and bind them for a sign upon your hand, that they may be and serve as frontlets between your eyes; and thou shalt write them upon the door-posts of thine house, and upon thy gates.* Here Moses desires that the Word should *move* before the eyes; and how, I would ask, can this be more effectively and manifestly done, than by representations of this kind, grave and decent, of course, and not mere coarse buffoonery, such as they used to be under popery. These spectacles, properly conducted, strike the imagination of the people through their eyes, and move them often far more than public preaching. I know for certain, that in Lower Germany, where the public teaching of the gospel has been interdicted, sacred dramas, founded upon the law and the gospel, have converted great numbers." (5th April, 1543.)

Of music.[1]—"Music is one of the most magnificent and delightful presents that God has given us. Satan is the inveterate enemy of music, for he knows that by its aid we drive away temptations and evil thoughts: he cannot make head against music.

"Some of the nobles and courtiers grudge the three thousand florins a-year that my gracious master so judiciously lays out upon music, while they readily aid him to expend, in things worse than useless, ten times the amount.

"Duke George, the landgrave of Hesse, and the elector of Saxony, John Frederic, used to have each an establishment of musicians, vocal and instrumental. Now, it is the duke of Bavaria, the emperor Ferdinand, and the emperor Charles."

On the 17th December, 1538, Luther, among other

[1] See Appendix CVII.

friends assembled at his house, had some fine singers and players. After hearing them for awhile, he exclaimed, with enthusiasm: "If our Lord grants us such noble gifts as these in the present life, which is only a life of miserable trials, what will it not be in the life eternal! This is but a specimen.

"Singing is the best exercise there is: we have nothing else at all comparable with it. . . . I am very glad that God has denied to these obstinate rebels of peasants a gift so valuable, so full of consolation; they do not care for music, and they reject the word of God."

He said one day to a harper he had called in: "My friend, play me an air, as David did. Truly, I think if the Psalmist were to come among us now, he would wonder not a little to see how many are skilled in his art.

"How is it that we have such a number of fine things in secular minstrelsy, while all our spiritual music is poor and cold? [And here he sung, by way of illustration, first one or two German songs, and then one or two of the hymns in ordinary use.] . . . . As for them who despise music, the dreamers and mystics, I despise them. . . . I shall ask the prince, out of all this money we have got, to establish a good band." (April, 1541.)

On the 4th of October, 1530, we find him asking Ludwig Sienfel, one of the musicians to the court of Bavaria, to set to music for him the *In pace in id ipsum.* "The love of music," he adds, "has enabled me to surmount the fear of being repulsed, when you see at the foot of this request a name which is doubtless odious to you. The same love for, the same faith in music also inspires me with the hope that my correspondence will not involve you in any trouble or annoyance. The Turk himself could not make the receipt of a letter upon such a subject matter of reproach against you. . . . Except theology, there is no art which can be placed in comparison with music."

Of painting.[1]—Luther, introducing to his friend Amsdorf a painter, named Sebastian, says: "I do not know whether you have need of him, according to your own notions; but I confess I should like to see your house more decorated, more elegant in its details, if only to please the flesh, which needs

[1] See Appendix CVIII.

gratifications of an innocent and tranquil nature, to keep its attention from being diverted to others not of an innocent or tranquil nature." (6th Feb. 1542.)

Luther's pamphlets against the pope were almost always provided with some symbolical engraving or wood-cut. "As to the three Furies," he says in explanation of one of these satirical illustrations, "I had no other idea in my head, when I applied them to the pope, than to express the atrocity of the papal abomination by the most energetic, the most denunciatory figures known to the Latin tongue; for the Latins, as you are aware, had no notion whatever about Satan or the devil, any more than the Greeks and many other nations had." (8th May, 1545.)

It was Lucas Cranach who executed these figures. Luther observes about him: "Maître Lucas is not over refined in his ideas. He might, I think, spare the female sex, out of respect for our mothers and for the work of God. He might easily design other forms far more worthy of the pope—that is to say, more diabolical." (3rd June, 1545.)

"If I live, I will do my best to get Lucas to substitute a decent illustration for this obscene affair." (15th June.)

Luther entertained the highest admiration for Albert Durer. When he heard of his death he wrote: "It is, doubtless, very sad to have lost him, but, on the other hand, we should rejoice that it has pleased God, by so happy an end, to remove him from this world of trouble and misery, which, I am convinced, will ere long be torn in pieces by even still greater troubles than those which have hitherto afflicted it. The Lord was not willing that a man, worthy of the happiest times, should see misery, and he has therefore sent him to sleep in peace with his fathers." (April, 1528.)

On astronomy and astrology.—"It may be very true that astrologers can predict to the wicked their future destiny, and announce to them the death that awaits them; for the devil knows the thoughts of the wicked, and has them in his power."

Mention was made in his presence of a new astronomer,[1]

[1] Copernicus, no doubt, who completed, in 1530, his book, *De Orbium Cœlestium Revolutionibus*, which was printed in 1545, at Nuremberg, with a dedication to Pope Paul III. His disciple Rheticus, however, had previously (in 1540) made the new system public in a letter.

who sought to prove, that it was the earth which turned round, and not the firmament, the sun, and the moon; and who said, that the inhabitants of the world generally were in the same position with the person who, being in a chariot or in a ship, imagines he sees the coast, or the trees of the road-side, flying away behind him. "Ah," observed Luther, "this is quite the way of the world now-a-days; whosoever has any pretensions to superior cleverness, tries to make them out by setting aside as futile all that other people do and know. This silly fellow, for instance, wants to upset the old established astronomy; but, according to the Scripture, Joshua commanded the sun to stand still, and not the earth."

"The astrologers are wrong in attributing to the stars the evil influences which really result from the comets.

"Maître Philippe is very earnest about this matter, but he has not been able to get me over to his views. He pretends that the art itself is real, but that there is no person who understands it thoroughly."

Some one was showing Luther a horoscope that had been drawn out: "'Tis a pretty theory," said he, "and at first glance agreeable enough to reason. How regularly they proceed from one line to another! 'Tis with astrology as with the art of the sophists; *de decem prædieamentis realiter distinctis;* all is artificial and false, but throughout the vain and delusive structure there is an admirable unity of plan and of purpose; one century after another, one sect after another—Thomists, Albertists, Scotists, all have stuck to the same text, the same rules, on this subject.

"The science which has matter for its object, is uncertain; for matter is without form, and destitute of qualities and properties. Now astrology has matter for its object, &c.

"They predicted there would be a deluge in 1524, and the event did not happen till 1525, and then only in the shape of the inundation of the insurgent peasants. The burgomaster Hendorf was so sure of the matter, that he had a barrel of beer taken up to the top of his house, so that he might not be wholly unrefreshed during the deluge that was to be."

Maître Philippe said, that the emperor Charles would live to be eighty-four. Luther replied: "The world itself will not live so long. Ezekiel tells us to the contrary. And, again, if we drive forth the Turk, the prophecy of Daniel will be accomplished, and then you may rely upon it, the Day of Judgment is at hand."

A great red star which had appeared in the heavens in 1516, and gradually formed itself into a cross, re-appeared some years after: "But then," remarks Luther, "the cross seemed broken, for the gospel was obscured and endangered by sects and insurgents. After all, I can make out nothing at all certain in these signs; I believe they are for the most part delusions of the devil. We have seen no end of them in the course of the last fifteen years."

Of printing.—"Printing is the latest and greatest gift, by which God enables us to advance the things of the gospel. It is the last bright flame, manifesting itself just previous to the extinction of the world. Thanks be to God it came before the last day came! *Sancti patres dormientes desiderarunt videre hunc diem revelati Evangelii.*"

Some one having shown him a letter from a member of the Fugger family, in which were certain strange characters that nobody could make out, he said: "'Tis a device of clever, far-sighted men, but at the same time an indication that our age is very corrupt and evil. We read that Julius Cæsar made use of similar letters. It is said that the emperor, distrusting his secretaries, dictated to two of them, upon all matters of very great importance, rescripts the one totally contradictory of the other, and left it uncertain to which of the two he would affix his seal."

Of bankers. — "The cardinal bishop of Brixen dying suddenly at Rome, there was found nothing upon him but a scrap of paper written upon, fastened inside his sleeve. Pope Julius II. hearing of this, at once conceived it must be a bill of exchange, and taking charge of it, sent for the agent at Rome of the Fuggers, and asked him whether he knew the handwriting. 'Yes,' replied the agent, 'it is an acknowledgment for three hundred thousand florins that Fugger and Company owe the cardinal.' The pope asked whether he could pay him all that money. 'At any time your holiness pleases,' replied the man, very coolly. Whereupon the pope sent for all the cardinals of France and Rome, and asked them whether their sovereigns could command, in any given hour, three hundred thousand golden florins? 'No,' said they, 'certainly not.' 'Well then,' rejoined the pope, 'here is a citizen of Augsburg that can.'[1]

"Fugger being called upon one day by the council of Augsburg to furnish them with an estimate of his property, replied, that he did not know what he was worth, for that his money and goods were spread all over the world; in Turkey, in Greece, at Alexandria, in France, in Portugal, in Poland, &c.; 'but,' added he, 'if you merely want to know the value of what I have got here in Augsburg, I can ascertain that.'"

CHAPTER V.

On preaching—Luther's style—His admission of the violence of his character.

"Oh how I trembled when I was ascending the pulpit for the first time. I would fain have excused myself; but they made me preach. It was the regulation, that the junior brethren should preach to the rest.[2] . . . .

"Here, under this very pear-tree, I have, over and over again, argued with Dr. Staupitz, as to whether it was my vocation to preach. He said it was. I had fifteen reasons against it, and fifteen more when they were done. 'Doctor,' I used to say, 'you want to kill me. I shall not live three months, if you compel me to go on.' 'Our Lord,' the doctor would reply, 'our Lord requires the aid of able men: he needs your services, and must have them.'

"I feel very little anxiety, indeed, about the diffusion of my printed works. On the contrary, I have Saturn's hunger within me, and would fain devour them all, so that they should be no more seen. There is not one of them with which I am satisfied, except, perhaps, the *De Servo Arbitrio* and the *Catechism*. (9th July, 1537.)

"I don't at all like Philip to be present when I preach or lecture; but I make the best I can of it. I put the cross

[1] See Appendix CIX. [2] Tischreden, 181.

before me, and say to myself: 'Philip, Jonas, Pomer, and the rest of them, have nothing to do with the question in hand;' and I try to persuade myself, that I am as competent to fill the pulpit as they."[1]

Dr. Jonas said to him one day:[2] "Doctor, I cannot at all follow you in your sermons." Luther replied: "I cannot follow myself; for oftener than not, it is myself, or some particular matter connected with myself, that I take as the subject of my discourse, according to time, circumstances, or audience. If I had my time to go over again, I would make my sermons much shorter, for I am conscious they have been too wordy.

"I would have the people made thoroughly conversant with my catechism. I take that as the basis of most of my sermons. I discourse as plainly as possible; for I desire that the commonest people, that children, that servants should understand what I say. It is not for the learned we go up into the pulpit; they have their books."[3]

Dr. Erasmus Alberus, previous to his departure for Brandenburg, questioned Dr. Luther as to how he ought to preach before the elector. "Your sermons," replied Martin, "should be addressed, not to princes and nobles, but to the rude, uncultivated commonalty. If, in my discourses I were to be thinking about Melancthon, and the other doctors, I should do no good at all: but I preach in plain language to the plain, unlearned people, and that pleases all parties. If I know the Greek, Hebrew, and Latin languages, I reserve them for our learned meetings, where they are of use; for at these we deal in such subtleties and such profundities, that God himself, I wot, must sometimes marvel at us.[4]

"Albert Durer, the famous painter of Nuremberg, used to say, that he took no pleasure in works of art which were overladen with colouring, for that he much preferred those which were plain and simple in their execution; and so I say about sermons.

"Oh, how happy should I have been, when in the monastery at Erfurt, could I have heard once, only once, a sermon, however brief, upon the gospel, or upon the least of the psalms![5]

[1] Tischreden, 197. [2] Ib. 113. [3] Ib. 116. [4] Ib. 184.
[5] Luther's Werke, ix. 245.

"There is nothing more agreeable and more useful to the common class of auditors, than to preach to them the law and plain examples. Disquisitions upon grace, and upon the article of justification, however good in themselves, sound cold and uninteresting to such ears."

Among the other qualities which Luther requires in a preacher is this, that he should be handsome and well formed, so as to please the eyes of the women.[1]

In his treatise *On Monastic Vows*, Luther asks pardon of his reader for saying many things which it is not customary to say: "Though I understand not why we should not be at liberty to repeat that which the Holy Spirit, for the edification and instruction of men, dictated to Moses.[2] But we, forsooth, would have our ears purer than the mouth of the Holy One."

To J. Brentius he writes: "I do not flatter you, and I do not deceive you, any more than I deceive myself, when I tell you that I prefer your writings to my own. It is not Brentius that I here praise, but the Holy Spirit, which in you manifests itself gentler, more tranquil; your words flow in a purer, more limpid stream. I, whose style is impracticable, harsh, rough, pour forth a deluge, a chaos of words: my manner is turbulent, impetuous, fierce, as that of a gladiator contending with a thousand monsters, who assail him in uninterrupted succession. If I might compare small things with great, I should say, that I had given me somewhat of the quadruple spirit of Elias the prophet, who was rapid as the wind, whose word burnt like a lamp, who overthrew mountains, and burst asunder rocks. You, on the contrary, breathe forth the gentle murmur of the light refreshing breeze. One thing, however, consoles me—namely, that the Divine Father of the human race has need, for the instruction of that immense family, of both the one servant and the other—of the rugged, for the conquering of the rugged, the harsh, for the conquering of the harsh. To clear the air, and to render the earth more fertile, it is not enough that the rain should water and penetrate its surface; there needs, also, the thunder and the lightning." (20th August, 1530.)

"I am very far from thinking myself faultless, but I may,

[1] Tischreden, 183. [2] Seckendorf, i. 202.

at least, boast with St. Paul, that I cannot be accused of hypocrisy, and that I have always spoken the truth; perhaps, indeed, somewhat too harshly. I would rather offend man by the acerbity of my language in diffusing the truth, than offend God by keeping the truth captive within my breast. If the grandees are displeased at my method of proceeding, they are quite at liberty to leave me to myself; I and my doctrines can do without them. I have done them no wrong, no injustice. The sins I commit, it is for God to pardon." (5th Feb. 1522).

To Spalatin he writes, in Feb. 1520: "I cannot deny that I am often more violent than is absolutely necessary, but the fault is mainly in those, who, knowing the irritability of the dog, persist in teasing him. You yourself know how difficult it is to moderate one's energy, to keep one's pen in check, on a subject in which one is wholly interested. And this is why I have always hated to appear in public; but it is of no use; the more I hate doing it, the more I am forced to do it."

Dr. Luther used often to say, "I have three vicious dogs, Ingratitude, Pride, and Envy; he whom these bite, is well bitten.[1]

"When I am dead, the papists will find out how temperate an adversary I have been to them. Other preachers will not show them the same forbearance, the same moderation. As it is, compare me with Munzer, with Carlstadt, Zwinglius, and the anabaptists.

"When I get angry, I forget, for the time, my physical maladies, and my understanding seems sharpened; all temptations, all uneasy sensations of weariness disperse: I never write or speak better than when I am in a passion."[2]

He writes thus to Michael Marx:—"You cannot think how delighted I am, at seeing day after day, my adversaries rising higher and higher in their fury against me. I never feel prouder, more full of lofty daring, than when I hear, from time to time, of their denunciations upon me. Doctors, bishops, princes, what care I for the whole mob of them. *The heathen rage, and the people imagine a vain thing. The kings of the earth set themselves, and the rulers take counsel together, against the Lord and against his anointed; but he*

[1] Tischreden, 105. [2] Ib. 356.

that sitteth in the heavens shall laugh; the Lord shall have them in derision.

"I hold all these Satans in such scorn, that were I not kept here, I would go straight to Rome, in despite of the devil and all these princes.

"I must have patience with the pope, with my disciples, with my servants, with Catherine de Bora, with everybody; my life is a long lesson of patience."

BOOK THE FIFTH.

CHAPTER I.

Death of Luther's father, and of his daughter.

"THERE is no union, no society, more beautiful to look upon, more gentle and felicitous in itself, than a well assorted marriage. It is perfectly delightful to see a wedded pair living together in peace and mutual love. But, on the other hand, nothing is harder to bear, nothing more truly afflicting, than the severance of this bond; and, next to this affliction, is that of losing one's children. The latter misery I, alas, have had to endure![1]

"I write to you under the depression of heavy sadness, for I have just received intelligence of the death of my father, that good old man whom I so loved. And though, by my means, he passed hence easily and happily into the bosom of Christ, and now, escaped from the monsters of this world, reposes in eternal peace, yet my heart is sad and agitated to think that he is gone from me, he who gave me birth and nourished my early years." In a letter, written on the same day, to Melancthon, he says: "I succeed to his name and place; it is I now who am Old Luther. Presently, it will be my turn, my privilege to follow him through the jaws of death, to that kingdom which Christ has promised to all those of us who for his sake undergo misery and opprobrium upon earth . . . . Oh, how I rejoice that the old man lived long enough to see and accept the true light of truth. Blessed be God in all his works, in all his designs." (5th June, 1530.)

"News having come from Freyberg that Maître Hausmann

[1] Tischreden, 331.

was dead, we concealed the matter as long as we could from doctor Luther, telling him at first that Hausmann was simply unwell, and then that he was confined to his bed. When we, at last, informed him that his old friend had gone peacefully to sleep in the Lord, the doctor fell to weeping aloud. "These are perilous times," he said, "the Lord is sweeping out his barn and his threshing-floor. All I pray is, that he will not let my poor wife and children survive me, for I know not what is to become of them." All the remainder of that day he sat motionless on his chair, weeping and lamenting. There were with him, doctor Jonas, maître Philip (Melancthon), maître Joachim Camerarius, and Gaspard Von Keckeritz, and he sat in the midst of them, overwhelmed with his grief." (1538).[1]

When he lost his daughter Magdalen, who died in 1542, aged fourteen, he said to his wife, who was bitterly weeping: "Dear Catherine, console thyself; think where our daughter is gone, for sure she has passed happily into peace. The flesh bleeds, doubtless, for such is its nature; but the spirit lives, and goes to the place of its wishes. Children do not dispute; what we tell them, they believe. With them all is simplicity and truth. They die without pain or grief, without struggling, without temptations assailing them, without bodily suffering, just as though they were merely going to sleep."

"When his daughter was very ill, he said: 'I love her well; yet, O my God! if it be thy will to take her hence, I will resign her, without regret, into thy hands.' As she lay in bed, he said to her: 'My dear little daughter, my darling Magdalen, thou wouldst, doubtless, willingly remain here with thy poor father, but thou wouldst also go hence willingly to thy other father, if he call thee to him?' She replied: 'Yes, my dear father, as God shall please.' 'Dear girl,' returned Luther, ''tis not with thee that the spirit alone is willing. He then walked up and down the room for some time, saying to himself, but half aloud: 'Ah, I have loved her dearly! . . . If her flesh be so strong, what must her spirit be?'

"He further said, among other things, 'God has not, for a thousand years, bestowed so many great gifts upon any

[1] Tischreden, 274.

bishop as he has upon me. One should duly appreciate and pride oneself upon such gifts; but—I am mad with myself for it—I do not enough rejoice at them in my heart: I do not sufficiently return thanks for them. I sing, indeed, from time to time, a little song of praise to the Lord, but 'tis very inadequate.' . . . 'Well, whether we live or die, we are the Lord's; so, courage, doctor!'

"In the night which preceded the death of Magdalen, the doctor's wife had a dream: she thought she saw two beautiful, elegantly-dressed youths come to her, and ask her daughter in marriage. When Philip Melancthon visited her, next morning, she told him her dream, whereupon, he said to those who were present: 'The youths were a vision of the holy angels, who are about to carry away our dear virgin to the true nuptials of the heavenly kingdom.' Magdalen died in the afternoon.

"When she was in her last agony, her father fell on his knees at the bedside, and, weeping bitterly, prayed the Lord to save her life. Shortly afterwards she died, going to sleep gently in her father's arms. Her mother was at the other end of the same room, utterly overwhelmed with affliction. The doctor repeated, from time to time, 'God's will be done! —my daughter has still a father in heaven.' Maître Philip said: 'The love of parents for their children is an image of the Divinity imprinted on the heart of man. God no less loves the human race than parents their children.' When they put her into the coffin, her father said: 'Poor, dear little Magdalen, there thou art; peace be with thee!' Then, as he looked upon her, he said: 'Dear child, thou wilt rise again; thou wilt shine like a star—ay, like the sun. . . . I am joyful in spirit, but, oh! how sad in the flesh! 'Tis marvellous I should know she is certainly at rest, that she is well, and yet that I should be so sad.'

"When the people came to remove the body, and, as usual, expressed their sympathy with his affliction, he replied: 'Friends, be not grieved; I have sent a saint to heaven. Oh, would that we might have such a death! Could such a death be mine, I would joyfully die this moment!' When, at the funeral service, they sang, *Lord, remember not the sins of my youth!* he added, to those who were standing near him, 'Nor those of the present time; for truly we are avaricious, usurers, wicked in every way, and the scandalous outrage of the mass still exists.'

"On their return home, he said, among other things, 'Children are a source of great anxiety, and especially the poor girls. One does not so much fear for boys, they can manage to make a living, so that they are able to work at all; but girls can scarce do anything but beg. A boy can go to the schools, and acquire learning, by which he may live; a girl has no such opportunity, and the chances are, that she turns to evil courses. 'Tis therefore all the more resignedly that I give my poor girl to the Lord.'"[1]

On the same subject, he writes thus to Jonas: "You will have heard of the new birth into the kingdom of Christ of my daughter Magdalen. Though my wife and I ought, in reality, to have no other feeling than one of profound gratitude for her happy escape from the power of the flesh, the world, the Turk, and the devil, yet the force *της στοργης* (of natural affection) is so great, that we cannot support our loss without constant weeping and bitter sorrow—a thorough death of the heart, so to speak. We have ever before us her features, her words, her gestures, her every action in life and on her death-bed—my darling, my all dutiful, all obedient daughter! Even the death of Christ (and what are all other deaths in comparison with that?) cannot tear her from my thoughts, as it ought to do. . . . She was, as you well know, all gentleness, amiability, and tenderness." (23rd Sept. 1542.)

CHAPTER II.

Of equity and law—Difference between the theologian and the lawyer.

"THEORETICALLY, it is better to govern oneself by natural reason than by the written law, for reason is the soul and queen of the law. But where are we to find people in whom this discretion can be safely placed? Not above three or four occur in a whole century. Our gracious lord the elector Frederic, was such a man, and there was his councillor, Fabien Von Feilitsch, a layman, who, without having studied

[1] Tischreden, 300.

the matter at all specially, could give better answers about the *apices et medullam juris,* than the whole gang of lawyers could out of their books. There is maître Philip Melancthon, too, who teaches the liberal arts, so as to derive less light from them to himself than he himself gives to them. I also may say, that I carry my art to my books, and derive it not from them. Any one who fancies he could imitate the four men I have here named, had better lay aside his project, and content himself with listening. Such prodigies as these are very rare indeed. The written law is for the people, the commonalty. Natural law, and superior, independent judgment, for the men of whom I have spoken.[1]

"There is an undying struggle between the lawyers and the theologians; it is the same antagonism as between the law and grace.

"The law is a fine, beautiful guide, so long as she keeps to the nuptial couch. If she ascends another bed, and attempts to control theology, she becomes no better than a prostitute. Law must doff her cap in the presence of theology."[2]

To Melancthon he writes: "I retain entirely the same opinion as heretofore respecting the law of the Sword; I fully agree with you, that the gospel nowhere counsels or teaches such law, and that it ought not to be, seeing that the gospel is the law of freedom and liberty, which have nothing to do with the sword or the law of the sword; yet is not this law therein abolished."

"Before my time, no lawyer had comprehended what was the law, with reference to God. What they know upon the subject now they have from me. It is not set forth in the gospel that we are to venerate lawyers. When our Lord shall judge, he will require none of their aid. As to the world here below, I am willing to leave it to them; but in the things of God they must be subordinate to us. If one or the other must perish—perish law, and reign Christ!

"*The princes of the people have assembled together,* says David; but, according to the gospel, *God hath chosen the foolish things of the world to confound the wise, and the weak things of the world to confound the things which are mighty; not many wise men after the flesh, not many mighty, not many*

[1] Tischreden, 347. [2] Ib. 273.

noble, are called. Hear this, O kings of the earth, instruct yourselves thereby, O judges of the earth.

"If the lawyers persist in not praying for the pardon of their sins, and in not accepting the gospel, I will confound them, so that they shall not know how to relieve themselves from their perplexity. I know nothing about law, but I am the lord of law in all things that have reference to the conscience.

"We have to thank the lawyers for filling the world with such an infinitude of subterfuges, evasions, shifts, shirkings, and chicanery, that matters have become worse than they were in the Tower of Babel: there no man could understand his neighbour if he would; with us, thanks to the lessons of the knave lawyers, no man will understand his neighbour though he can. O sycophants, O sophists, pests of the human race! I address you, full of indignation; but I am by no means clear that I should speak to you in other terms were I ever so cool." (6th Feb. 1546.)[1]

The day before the authorities were going to make a doctor of law, Luther said: "There will be another viper hissing against the theologians."

"Lawyers are enemies to Christ. 'Tis a just saying, *A good lawyer a bad Christian:* for he applauds the righteousness of works, as if we were justified thereby, and saved before God. If a lawyer chance to turn Christian, then he is looked on as a monster among the lawyers: he must beg his bread, for by the other lawyers he is held rebellious. Ye lawyers take heed that ye tread not us divines under your feet; if ye do, then be assured that we will sting your heels. If I intended to study but two years in the laws, I would be better learned therein than Dr. Jerome Schurf; for I would discourse touching causes, as in truth they are and ought to be understood, of themselves uprightly, justly; but he contests only about words; he goes not upon the ground to speak of the plain truth, but he rests upon a *Quos,* which he may screw every way: they talk much, and make many words, but without understanding. Dr. Schurf may justly be called Dr. *Quos.* The doctrine of the lawyers is nothing but merely a *Nisi*—that is, unless this or that; *Nisi*

[1] Tischreden, 402.

must be in every case: but divinity goes not about with *Nisi*, but it is certain, and has a constant and sure ground which neither fails nor deceives. Lawyers have need of the help and assistance of divines, but we have no need at all of their voice and part-taking.

"The authority of the theologians consists in this, that they may put into the shade the universals, and all things that relate to the universals. They may exalt or debase. If the gospel makes itself heard on any point, therein must Moses and the emperor give way.

"The law of the Persians, and the law of the Greeks, have fallen into desuetude, are abolished. The Roman or Imperial law only hangs by a thread.[1] For if an empire or a kingdom falls, its laws and ordinances fall with it.

"Many people think that the theology which is revealed at the present time is nothing. If such be the case now, what will it not be when we are dead? On the other hand, many among us are full of the belief and they will bring it forth into life ere long, that law is nothing."

"I leave the shoemaker, the tailor, and the lawyer in their proper places. But let them beware how they intrude upon my province."

Again, in a sermon *against the lawyers*, he says: "Observe the conduct of our insolent lawyers here at Wittemberg. . . . They read not our books (which they call *catonical*, instead of *canonical*), heed not our Lord, and go not to our churches. Well, then, since they do not acknowledge Dr. Pomer as bishop of Wittemberg, nor myself as preacher to that church, I, on my part, no longer reckon them amongst my flock."

"'You are going against the imperial law,' cry these fellows. I care not a straw for any law that does wrong to the poor."[2]

He then tells a story of an advocate promising an attorney that if he will give him ten florins in hand, he will undertake to prolong a lawsuit they have in hand for full ten years: "Excellent, worthy people," he adds, "comparable only with Reynard the Fox, in the poem. My friends, you will agree with me that I have full warrant in being without pity or mercy for these knave lawyers. They prate about the Canon

[1] See Appendix CX. [2] Tischreden, 403.

law, the filthy decretals of the pope, and what not, that we have had such infinite trouble in kicking out from amongst us. Do they think we will suffer these vile things to come back. . . . I warn you, lawyers, to beware how you irritate the old dog;[1] arouse him, and you will not easily get him to his kennel again.

"The lawyers complain loudly of the manner in which I speak of them. I cannot help it; to save their miserable souls, I must thoroughly chastise them. There may be some honest, pious men among them; if so, I except them from my censures."[2]

CHAPTER III.

Faith—The law.

To Gerbellius.—"Amidst the wickedness that surrounds us on every side, be true to thyself, dear friend. For thy support and encouragement, I restore to thee the bride (faith) whom lately thou sendst me; I restore her to thee a virgin without stain. But what there is about her so admirable, so novel, so unprecedented, is, that while she desires and attracts around her an infinite number of competitors, she remains all the more chaste the more lovers she has. . . . Our rival, Philip Melancthon, salutes thee. Adieu; be happy with the bride of thy youth." (23rd Jan. 1523.)

To Melancthon.—"Sin, sin mightily, but have all the more confidence in Christ; rejoice more vehemently in Christ, who is the conqueror of sin, of death, and of the world. While we are in this world, we can do no other than sin, we must sin. This life is not the abode of righteousness; no, we merely await here, as St. Peter says, *new heavens and a new earth, wherein dwelleth righteousness.*

"Pray earnestly, for thou art a great sinner.

"I am now full of the doctrine of the remission of sins. I grant nothing to the law, nor to all the devils. He who can believe in his heart this doctrine, is saved.

"In the same way that it is impossible to meet anywhere in nature with the *mathematical, indivisible point,* it is im-

[1] See Appendix CXI. [2] Tischreden, 407. See Appendix CXII.

possible to find anywhere righteousness such as the strict law requires. No man can entirely satisfy the law, and the jurists themselves, notwithstanding all their art, are often obliged to have recourse to the remission of sins; for even they, cunning knaves, do not always attain the end they seek, and when they have given a false judgment, and the devil pricks their consciences, neither Baldus nor Bartolus, nor any other of their doctors, can do them any good; and then they are fain to shield themselves beneath the επιεικεια, the remission of sins doctrine. They do their best, according to their own account, to arrive at a right judgment, and after that, if they fail, all they can say is, *If I have judged ill, O God, pardon me!* Theology alone has mastered the mathematical point; theology alone does not go groping about, for she has the very word of God. She says, *There is but one righteousness, Jesus Christ; he who lives in him is righteous.*[1]

"The law, doubtless, is necessary, but not to salvation, for no one can fulfil it; but the remission of sins consummates and accomplishes it.

"The law is a regular labyrinth, which cannot fail to embarrass men's consciences; and the righteousness of the law is a minotaur—that is to say, a pure fiction, which carries us not to heaven, but to hell.[2]

Addition of Luther's to a letter written by Melancthon, on grace and the law.—"To get myself entirely out of sight of the law and of works, I do not even remain content with viewing in Jesus Christ, my master, my doctor, my giver, but I would have himself to be my doctrine and my gift, so that in him I possess all things. He tells us, *I am the way, the truth, and the life;* not, "I show you, or give you, the way, the truth, and the life, as if he merely wrought in me, and were nevertheless himself not in me."[3]

"There is but one single point in all theology—genuine faith and confidence in Jesus Christ. This article comprehends all the rest." "Our faith is an unutterable sigh." And elsewhere, "We are our own gaolers." (That is to say, we shut ourselves up in our works, instead of throwing ourselves confidingly into the arms of faith.)[4]

"The devil would have us cultivate only an active righte-

[1] Tischreden, 102. [2] Ib. 128. [3] Ib. 133. [4] Ib. 147.

ousness, a righteousness that we can ourselves put in motion within us, whereas we have, in reality, only a *passive* and extrinsic righteousness, which he wishes to deprive us of. If we were limited to the *active* only, we should be lost, for it is defective in all men."[1]

An English divine, Antony Barns, put it to Luther, whether Christians, when justified by the faith, were not entitled to reward for good works they might do afterwards, a question which had been much agitated in England. The answer was this: "1. We are still sinners, even after justification; 2. God promises to reward those who do well; and works, though they do not entitle us to heaven, still greatly adorn the faith by which alone we are justified. God only crowns the gifts which he himself has bestowed upon us."[2]

Fidelis animæ vox ad Christum:—Ego sum tuum peccatum, tu mea justitia; triumpho igitur securus," &c.

"Effectually to resist despair, it is not enough to have vain words on the tongue, nor a vain and feeble opinion; we must raise up our heads fearlessly, be firm of heart, and trust wholly in Christ against sin, death, hell, the law, and a bad conscience."

"When the law reproaches thee with thy faults, thy con science says to thee: Yes, God gave the law, and commanded it to be observed under penalty of eternal damnation; therefore thou must inevitably be damned. But thou wilt reply to thy conscience: I know very well that God gave the law, but he also by his Son gave us the Gospel, which tells us, *Whosoever liveth and believeth in me shall never die.* This gospel is greater than the law, for the law is terrestrial, and was delivered to us by a man; whereas the gospel is celestial, and was brought us by the Son of God.—No matter, returns Conscience, you have sinned, and transgressed the command of God; therefore you shall be damned.—*Answer:* I know very well that I have sinned, but the gospel has released me from my sins, because I believe in Christ; and this gospel is raised as far above the law as heaven is above the earth. The body must remain on the earth, and bear the burden of the law; but the conscience must quit it, and go up, with Isaac, to the mountain, and attach itself to the gospel, which

[1] Tischreden, 142. See Appendix CXIII. [2] Tischreden, 144.

promises eternal life to all who believe in Jesus Christ.—No matter, persists Conscience, you shall go to hell, you have not observed the law.—*Answer:* Yes, so I should, were heaven not to come to my help; but it has come to my help, it has opened its gates to me; the Lord has said: *Whosoever liveth and believeth in me shall never die.*[1]

"God said to Moses: *My back parts thou shalt see, but not my face.* The back parts are the law; the face, the gospel.

"The law does not endure grace, and in its turn grace does not endure the law. The law was given only for the haughty, the arrogant, the nobles, the peasantry, the hypocrites, and those who have set their hearts and take their pleasure in the multitude of laws; but grace was promised to poor suffering spirits; to the humble, the meek, and the afflicted; it is they whom the mission of Jesus concerns. To grace belong maître Nicholas Hausmann, Cordatus, Philip (Melancthon), and myself.[2]

"St. Paul is the only author who has written in a complete and satisfactory manner upon the law; it is death to reason to judge the law, the spirit alone is its proper judge." (15th August, 1530.)

"Good and true theology consists in practice, use, and exercise. Its basis and foundation is Christ, whose passion, death, and resurrection are made manifestly intelligible to us by faith. With reference to these things, there has started up, in our days, a *speculative theology*, which proceeds upon reason. This same *speculative theology* has for its author the devil in hell. Zwinglius and the sacramentarians *speculate* that the body of Christ is in the bread, but only in the spiritual sense. That was Origen's theology. David's theology was quite different: he acknowledged his sins, and said: *Have mercy upon me, Lord! Lord, have mercy upon me!*

"I have lately seen two signs in the heavens: I was looking out of my window in the middle of the night, and I saw the stars, the whole majestic vault of God, supporting itself, without my being able to perceive the columns upon which the Master rested it: yet it fell not. There are men now-a-days who insist upon finding out these invisible columns—

[1] Tischreden, 124. [2] Ib.

nay, who insist upon touching them with their own hands; and because they cannot achieve this, tremble, and lament, and beat their breasts, and fear the firmament is about to rush down upon them. The heavens will not stir any the more for their groping.

"In the morning, I saw huge, heavily-laden clouds floating over my head, like an ocean. I saw no pillars supporting the enormous masses; yet they fell not, but, saluting me gloomily, passed on; and as they passed on, I perceived beneath the curve which had sustained them, a delicious rainbow. It was very slender, very delicate, and some might have trembled least the heavy clouds should destroy it, yet its slight aerial line was strong enough to bear all that weight, and protect us from danger. We have among us too many who fear the clouds, and distrust the rainbow; they would fain ascertain, by some experiment of their own, what the exact force of the rainbow is; and as they cannot do this, they are all alarmed least the clouds should break, and overwhelm them in their fierce waves. The clouds are heavy, say they, your rainbow is very slight. But time will show its strength." (August, 1530.)[1]

CHAPTER IV.

Innovators—Mystics, &c.

"THAT same *Why*, has done us a great deal of harm. It was the cause of Adam's destruction.

"I fear two things; epicurism and enthusiasm, two schisms that have still to come.

"Take away the Decalogue, and there is no longer such a thing as heresy. The Holy Scriptures is the common book of all heretics.

Luther described the seditious and presumptuous spirits about him, as "precocious saints, who, long before they have attained maturity, are eaten into by a worm, and drop off the tree with the first breath of wind. The dreamers are like

[1] Tischreden, 125. See Appendix CXIV.

butterflies; first, a grub stuck against some wall, in a house of its own, then warmed by the sun into an ephemeral butterfly, which dies upon a tree in a few days, leaving a long row of eggs behind it, destined for a similar existence."

Doctor Martin Luther said, with reference to the false brothers and heretics who separated from him, that the only way was to let them alone, and not to trouble his head about them; if they would not listen to him, so much the worse for them; in the end they would be seen, with the worthies whom they resembled, all burning in hell together.[1]

"When I began to write against indulgences," says he, "I was for three years entirely alone, not a single soul holding out the hand of fellowship and co-operation to me. But now they all want to share in the triumph.

"I have quite trouble and anxiety enough with my open enemies; 'tis hard that my own brethren should help to throw stones at me. What is to be done I know not. These misguided friends of mine are most of them young men, new in the cause, and who have as yet done little or nothing to promote it. I am old, and well nigh worn out with my past labours and suffering. Osiander may very well give himself airs; he has a fine time of it; four hundred florins a year for just two sermons a week.[2]

"In 1521, a man from Zwichau called upon me, of the name of Marcus. He was agreeable enough in his manners, and very courteous, but frivolous and shallow-pated. As I found he went on talking about things entirely foreign to the Scriptures, I interrupted him by saying that I acknowledged only the Word of God, and that if he sought to set up anything else, he must in the first place prove his mission by miracles. 'Miracles!' said he, 'you shall have miracles in seven years. God himself could not deprive me of my faith,' he added; 'I can tell at once whether a person is one of the elect or not.' He then went on with a long rigmarole about *talent that must not be hidden*, and *unravelling*, and *tedium*, and *expecting*, and what not. I asked him what all this meant, and who understood him when he talked in this manner. He replied that he only preached to believing and skilled disciples. 'How know you that they are skilled?'

[1] Tischreden, 292. [2] Ib. 193.

asked I. 'I have only to look at them,' he replied; 'I can see their *talent* at a glance.' 'Well, my friend,' I rejoined, 'what *talent* do you see in me, for instance?' 'You are as yet only in the first degree of mobility,' he said, 'but there will come a time when you will be in the first degree of immobility, like myself.' Thereupon I cited to him several texts of Scripture, and so we parted. Some time after, he wrote me a letter very friendly in its tone, and full of exhortations; I returned for an answer simply this: *Good-bye to thee, dear Marcus.*

"On a later occasion, I was visited by a turner, who also described himself as a prophet. He met me just at the door as I was going out, and accosting me in a confident tone, said: 'Mr. Doctor, I bring you a message from my father.' 'Who is your father?' I asked. 'Jesus Christ,' he replied. 'He is our common father,' said I; 'what did he order you to announce to me?' 'I was to announce to you, on the part of my father, that God is angry with the whole world.' 'Who told you this?' 'Yesterday, as I was going out of the Koswick gate, I saw in the air a little cloud of fire, a sufficient proof that God is angry.'[1] He then told me of another sign: 'In a deep sleep,' said he, 'I saw a party of drunkards sitting round a table, crying one to another, Drink! drink! Above them was extended, menacingly, the hand of God. All at once, one of them threw a cup of beer at me, and I awoke.' 'Listen to me, my friend,' said I, calmly; 'you must not make a jest in this manner of the name and commands of God;' and I proceeded to reprimand him severely. When he saw how I took the affair up, he went away in a rage, muttering to himself: 'And yet there are some people who do not see what a fool this Luther is!'

"Another time, I had to do in the same way with a man from the Low Countries. He came and wanted to dispute with me about all sorts of things, *down to fire inclusively*, as he said. When I saw what a poor ignorant creature it was, I said to him: 'Hadn't we better dispute over a can or two of beer.' This quite irritated him, and he went away. The devil is a haughty spirit; and can't bear to be treated with contempt in any way."[2]

[1] See Appendix CXV. [2] Tischreden, 282.

Maître Stiefel came to Wittemberg, and, in a private interview with Dr. Luther, gave him, set forth in twenty articles, his opinion respecting the day of judgment. He considered that it would be on St. Luke's day. He was told to remain silent on the subject, and by no means to give forth his opinions publicly. He was very nettled at this. "Dear Doctor," said he, "I am astonished that you should forbid my preaching this matter, that you yourself should not believe what I tell you. I feel certain that I ought not to remain silent thereupon, though I should speak unwillingly, after what you have said." Luther replied: "Dear sir, you managed very well to remain silent upon the subject for ten years, under the reign of popery; you may well keep quiet respecting it for the little time that remains." "But this morning, early," urged Stiefel, "as I was on my way, I saw a very fine rainbow, and I at once thought of the coming of Christ." "There will be no rainbow in the case," returned Luther; "in one instant, one enormous thunderbolt will destroy every living creature, as one tremendous blast from the trump will awaken us all at the same moment; for it is no gentle breathing on a pipe that can make itself heard by those who are asleep in the tomb." (1533.)[1]

"Michael Stiefel thinks he is the seventh angel announcing the last day, and accordingly, he is giving away his books and his goods, as having no further occasion for them."[2]

"Bileas is certainly damned, though he has had great revelations, as great as those of Daniel, for he, too, takes in the four empires. He is a terrible example for the haughty ones. O brethren, let us humble ourselves, and be lowly!"[3]

"Doctor Jeckel is a worthy of the same class with Eisleben (Agricola.) He wanted to pay his court to my niece, but I at once said to him: 'That shall not be, if you were to live for a thousand years.' To the girl I said: 'If you marry that fellow, never appear before me again. I will neither see you, nor hear a word from you.'"[4]

When duke Henry of Saxony came to Wittemberg, Luther spoke to him twice in reprobation of Jeckel, and earnestly exhorted the prince to do his best towards remedying the evils

[1] Tischreden, 367.
[2] See Appendix CXVI.
[3] Tischreden, 367.
[4] Ib. 287.

the church was labouring under. Jeckel had preached this doctrine: "Do just what you like: provided you only believe, you will be saved." "He should have said," observed Luther, "when you have been born again, and are become a new man, then do what shall suggest itself to your regenerate mind. These fools do not understand what faith really is."

A minister at Torgau came to complain to Doctor Luther of the insolence and hypocrisy of Doctor Jeckel, who by his artifice was worming himself most undeservedly into the favour of the nobility in his district, into that of the council, into that of the prince himself. The doctor, on hearing the minister's statement, shuddered, sighed; then, after a moment's silence, began praying. The same day, he ordered that Eisleben (Agricola) should be forthwith called upon to make a public retractation, and, that if he failed to do so, he should be publicly confuted and disgraced.

"Dr. Luther having reproached Jeckel, for that he, having so little experience, and being so imperfectly acquainted with logic and rhetoric, should venture to set up opinions against his masters and preceptors, Jeckel replied: 'I must fear God more than I fear my masters; I have a God equally with yourself.' After supper, Luther was picking his teeth, as were the guests from Freyburg; Jeckel sat by in a very sullen mood. 'If I had made the court as pious as you have the world,' said Luther, 'I should have worked to fine purpose.' Jeckel made no reply to this, but sat sullen as before, his eyes fixed on the ground. At last, Luther rose to go away; hereupon Jeckel made a further attempt to explain his views, and discuss the matter with Luther, but the doctor now would not speak to him, and departed."[1]

Of the antinomians, and particularly of Eisleben.—"Ah, how painful it is to lose a friend that one has tenderly loved! That man used to be constantly at my table—he was my cherished companion; we used to laugh and joke together, and, now he has turned against me! . . . . This is intolerable. What! utterly to reject the law, without which there can be no church, no government! This is not piercing the barrel, but regularly staving it. . . . . There is no help for it; we must fight for it. What! while I live, shall he be al-

[1] Tischreden, 290.

lowed to puff himself up with pride, presumption, and vanity, seeking to rule and govern with his cold reasonings? . . No! . . . . It is nothing to the purpose that he attempts to excuse himself by saying, that he spoke only of Dr. Creuziger and of Maître Roerer. The Catechism, the Explanation of the Decalogues, and the Confession of Augsburg, are mine, not Creuziger's, or Roerer's. He seeks to teach repentance by the love of righteousness; so that he only preaches the revelation of the Divine wrath to pious and righteous men. He does not address himself to the unrighteous. Yet St. Paul said: *The law is not made for a righteous man.* In a word, while, taking away the law, he takes away also the gospel; he takes from our belief the firm support of conscience, in order to subject it to the caprices of the flesh.[1]

"Who would have thought of that mischievous sect the antinomians, the assaulters of the law? I have outlived and endured three cruel tempests, Munzer, the sacramentarians, and the anabaptists. Now they are stilled and gone, others come on, insomuch that there will be no end of writing. I desire to live no longer; for there is no more hope of peace.[2] Ancient Bernard said well, we should preach of four particulars, of virtues and vices, of rewards and threatenings. Doctor Eisleben flatters himself that his *Oportet* will do the deed: for he says: 'This and that must be done away; we will have none of it.' But he must swallow down that *must* again.

"On the 19th of April, 1539, Luther charged doctor Ambrose Bernd, that he, as master, should admonish the university professors, to take heed of factions, and not to induce schisms or separations. He gave charge also that Dr. Eisleben should not be chosen dean, 'to the end his pride, his presumption, and disobedience, may not be confirmed and strengthened; for he is a very shameless and proud enemy of the church, of schools, and of us all; we should, in so doing, harbour in our bosoms a serpent, which we ought not to feed, and nourish with milk, but with earth; unless he truly repent, he shall be rejected. Thus much would I have you signify to your facultists, and tell them, if they refuse to hearken unto you herein, I will publicly preach against them.'"

[1] Tischreden, 287. [2] Ib. 288.

On the last day of November, 1538, Luther was spending the evening pleasantly and jovially with his brother, his cousins, his sister, and some friends from Mansfeldt. Mention was introduced of Dr. Grickel, and the company entreated Luther to forgive him. The doctor, however, replied: "I regarded that man as one of my best and most trusty friends, but he deceived me. I shall write against him sharply; let him take heed to himself; there is no repentance in him.

"I had such full confidence in that man (Eisleben), that when I went to Smalkald in 1537, I left my church, my wife, my children, my house, all I had, all I held most dear, in his charge.

"On the last day of January, 1539, doctor Luther read out in the evening the propositions which Eisleben was going to maintain against him; he had put into them something or other, wholly inapplicable, about Saul and Jonathan, (*I did but taste a little honey, and lo, I must die!*) 'Jonathan,' observed Luther, 'of course, is Maître Eisleben, tasting the honey and preaching the gospel; I am Saul. . . . Ah, Eisleben, canst thou really be such a ——. But let me restrain myself.'

"If the law is thus transferred from the church to the council, to the civil authority, the latter will say in its turn: 'We too are faithful Christians; the law does not concern us;' and by and by, the hangman will say the same thing; and things will come to a fine pass. There will first be nothing talked of but grace and gentleness and loving-kindness, forsooth, and in the twinkling of an eye all this will become the very frenzy of capricious will, and abominable wickedness of all souls. That was how Munzer proceeded.[1]

In 1540, Luther gave an entertainment, at which were present the principal members of the university. Towards the close of the repast, when every one was in high spirits, a glass with circles marked upon it in colours was brought in. Luther filled it with wine, which he drank off to the health of his guests. The latter, each in his turn, reciprocated the toast out of the same glass. When it came round to Eisleben, Luther, on filling for him the glass, said: "Maître, the wine in this glass which is above the first circle, repre-

[1] Tischreden, 291.

sents the ten commandments; that down to the second circle, the *Belief;* that down to the third, the *Lord's Prayer;* the *Catechism* is at the bottom:" and with these words he drank off the whole contents of the glass, looking fixedly all the while at his guest, and then filling it once more, handed it to Eisleben. The latter drank only down to the first circle, and replaced the glass on the table, looking quite appalled. Luther, still with his eyes fixed on his guest, said to the rest of the company: "I knew very well that Maître Eisleben would only drink the Ten Commandments, leaving the *Belief*, the *Lord's Prayer*, and the *Catechism* untouched."[1]

Maître Jobst dining with Luther one day, showed him certain propositions he had drawn up, to the effect that the law ought not to be preached, since it is not the law which justifies us. Luther grew quite angry at this: "What!" he exclaimed, "shall our own people, while we ourselves are yet alive, propound such things as these? Ah! how highly ought we to honour Maître Philip (Melancthon), who inculcates with such perspicuity and truth the use and utility of the law. That which Count Mansfeldt prophesied to me in a letter is becoming fulfilled: *behind this new doctrine there will be seen another Munzer.* He who destroys the doctrine of the law, destroys at the same time political and social order. If you eject the law from the church, there will no longer be any sin recognised as such in the world; for the gospel only defines and punishes sin by reference to the law. (1541.)[2]

"If, heretofore, I in my discourses, spoke and wrote so harshly against the law, it was because the Christian church was overwhelmed with superstitions, under which Christ was altogether hidden and buried; and I am anxious to rescue pious and God-fearing souls from the tyranny of the conscience; but as to the law in itself, I never rejected it."

[1] Tischreden, 129. [2] Ib. 125.

CHAPTER V.

Temptations—Regrets and doubts experienced by his friends, by his wife, by Luther himself.

"MAÎTRE Philip Melancthon one day related the following apologue at Luther's table: 'A certain man had caught a little bird; the little bird begged and prayed to be set free, and at last it said to the man: "Dear friend, if you will release me, I will discover to you a fine pearl, worth thousands of florins." "You seek to deceive me," said the man. "Oh, no," replied the bird; "you may fully rely upon my word; come with me, and I will show it you." The man released the bird which flew off to a neighbouring tree, where it perched, and thence said to the man: "*Have small faith in other people; keep what you have got, pine not after that which is gone.*" It was a fine pearl the bird left him.'[1]

"Philip asked me one day to select a motto for him from the Bible, such a one as he should not grow weary of, but it is impossible to give a man anything of which he will not grow weary, sooner or later.[2]

"If Philip had not been so chastened with temptations, he would have some very singular ideas and opinions."

Luther's paradise is a very rude one. He conceived that into the new heaven and the new earth, the more useful animals would be admitted. "I often think about eternal life, and the joys to be experienced in it; but I cannot comprehend how we are to spend our time there; for there is to be no changes, no work, no eating, no drinking, no occupation of any sort; however, doubtless there will be an infinitude of objects to contemplate." Hereupon, Philip Melancthon very well said: "Maître, let us see God, and that will be all-sufficient."[3]

"The peasantry are not worthy of the multitude of products which the earth furnishes. I am more thankful to

[1] Tischreden, 145. [2] Ib. 29. [3] Ib. 195.

God for a single tree, than all the peasantry put together are for all their lands put together." "Ah, *domine doctor*," interfered Melancthon, "you must make an exception, at all events in favour of such men as Adam, Noah, Abraham, Isaac."[1]

"Doctor Jonas said one night at supper: 'Ah, how magnificently St. Paul discourses about his death; yet I cannot believe all he says.' 'In truth, it seems to me, also,' returned Luther, 'that even St. Paul himself could not feel upon this matter so forcibly as he writes. I myself, unhappily, cannot, with respect to this article, believe as stoutly as I preach, speak, and write—as stoutly as other people think I believe. Indeed, it perhaps were not well that we should implicitly do all that God commands us; for then, what would become of his Godhead: his own words would be falsified.'[2]

"A horribly impious book against the Holy Trinity having been printed in 1532, Luther said: 'These chimærists do not believe that other people have had their temptations on this subject. But how could I think of putting a thought that may come into my head, in opposition to the word of God and to the Holy Ghost. Any such opposition of mine would not stand the test of examination for a moment.'[3]

The doctor's wife said to him one day. "Doctor, how is it, that under popery we prayed so frequently and so fervently, and that now our prayers are cold and unfrequent?"

The doctor replied: "Popery is the devil's worship, and the devil incessantly urges on his servants to practise that worship."

"Dr. Luther, on one occasion, had been exhorting his wife to read and hear with earnest attention the Word of God, more especially the Psalms. She replied, that she already listened sufficiently, and that she read portions of the Scripture every day, so that she was able to repeat, God willing, a great number of passages from it. The doctor sighed: 'Thus,' said he, 'commences in mankind weariness of the word of God. 'Tis a sign of ill promise. One of these days, some new books will be started in competition, and the Holy Scripture will be slighted, despised, jerked into a corner, thrown, as they say, under the table.'"

[1] Tischreden, 305. [2] Ib. 137. [3] Ib. 70.

Luther asked his wife whether she, too, thought herself holy. She was amazed at this, and replied: "How can I think myself holy—I, who am a great sinner?" "Here," returned he, "is the terrible effect of the papal doctrine, which has wounded all hearts, and filled all minds with its pernicious dogmas, so that none are capable of seeing anything beyond the personal and external piety and sanctity of works, operated by man, of and by himself."

"The Lord's prayer and faith are my security against the devil. My little Magdalen and my little John, too, pray for me, as do many other Christians.[1] . . . . I love my Catherine, I love her more than I do myself; for I would die rather than any harm should happen to her or to her children. I love my Lord Jesus Christ, who, out of pure mercy, poured forth his blood for me; but my faith ought to be far greater and more vivid than it is. Oh, my God, judge not thy servant."[2]

"That which contributes in no slight degree to affect and try men's hearts, is, that God seems to them capricious and changeable. He gave to Adam promises and ceremonies, and these ended in the rainbow and the ark of Noah. He gave to Abraham circumcision, to Moses miraculous signs, to his chosen people, the law; but to Christ, and to us, through Christ, he gave the gospel, which is considered as annulling all that went before. And now the Turks are seeking to efface this divine word, crying, as they pass on—*Your new law has lasted sometime now, but it will be changed by and by.*" (Luther leaves off thus, without any further observation.)

CHAPTER VI.

The devil — Temptations.

"Once, in our monastery at Wittemberg, I distinctly heard the devil making a noise. I was beginning to read the Psalms, after having celebrated matins, when, interrupting my studies, the devil came into my cell, and thrice made a

[1] Tischreden, 135. [2] Ib. 140.

noise behind the stove, just as though he were dragging some wooden measure along the floor. As I found he was going to begin again, I gathered together my books, and got into bed. . . . Another time, in the night, I heard him above my cell, walking in the cloister; but, as I knew it was the devil, I paid no attention to him, and went to sleep.

"A girl, a friend of the old steward at Wittemberg, being ill in bed, there presented itself before her a vision, a beautiful and noble form, resembling Christ. She believed it to be our Lord, and rising from her bed, prostrated herself at its feet and began to pray. Those about her immediately sent for Dr. Luther, who, when he saw the figure, at once perceived it was a mere delusion and trick of the devil, and exhorted the girl not to allow herself to be any more deceived in this manner. He then spat in the face of the vision, which then changed itself into a great serpent, which glided up to the girl and bit her ear so sharply that the blood ran. The devil-serpent then vanished. Dr. Luther saw all this with his own eyes, in company with many other persons."[1]

A minister in the environs of Torgau complained to Luther that the devil made a most extraordinary noise and uproar every night in his house, throwing things down, and breaking the furniture and kitchen utensils, the pieces of which he said the devil threw at his head, laughing all the while very lustily. The poor man added, that he had been persecuted in this manner for a year past, and that matters had at last become so bad that his wife and children would no longer remain in the house. Luther replied: "Dear brother, be strong in the Lord, and give not way to this murderer-devil. If you have not yourself invited and brought this guest into your house by your sins, you may well say to him, firmly: 'I, by divine authority, am the master of this family, by celestial calling pastor of this church; but thou, devil, hast slipped in here like a robber and a murderer. Wherefore remainest thou not in thy own place? Who invited thee here. Go hence!"[2]

Of a possessed woman.—"Since the devil in this woman is a jovial spirit, and makes mock of us at his ease, we must

[1] The Editor of the *Tischreden*, whence this story is taken, does not pretend that he had it from Luther himself.

[2] Tischreden, 208.

first pray in all earnestness and grave seriousness in behalf of this poor girl, who suffers thus for our sins; and we must then despise this devil, and laugh at him in our turn, and not have recourse to exorcisms and that sort of thing, which the arrogant devil will only sneer at. Let us persevere in prayer on the one hand, and in despising the evil spirit, on the other; and in the end, by the grace of Jesus Christ, he will retire, for he cannot endure scorn. I would our princes would reform their vices, whereby the evil spirit manifests that he has possession of them too. As this affair appears to me of sufficient importance to be published to the world, I would have you forthwith make yourself acquainted with all the circumstances of the case. Among other things, in order to obviate any possibility of fraud, fully assure yourself that the pieces of gold which this girl swallowed are real pieces of gold, genuine gold coins; for I have all along been so beset with every sort of imposition, with such tricks, lies, machinations, and knaveries, that I feel disposed to disbelieve everything that I myself have not ocular or auricular proof of." (5th August, 1536.)

"The minister you speak of, need not be affected in conscience on account of having given burial to the woman who had killed herself, if, indeed, she did kill herself. I have known many cases of this kind, and I have had reason to think, in most of them, that the parties were killed, directly and immediately killed, by the devil, in the same way that a traveller is killed by a brigand. For when it is evident that the suicide has not taken place naturally, when all you find is a rope, a girdle, or as is the case of which you speak, a veil hanging without any knot whatever, wherein you could suspend a fly, in these cases, according to my view of the matter, the only solution of the affair is, that the devil has been deceiving the parties, and making them believe that they were doing something else, and so has killed them. Yet, still the civil magistrate is quite right in punishing this offence without exception, least the devil should make more and more way in this respect. The world merits such warnings, now that it has taken to epicurising, and setting down the devil as nothing." (1st Dec. 1544.)

"Satan once tried to kill our prior, by throwing down a piece of the wall upon him, but God miraculously saved him." (4th July, 1524.)

"Idiots, the lame, the blind, the dumb, are men in whom devils have established themselves; and all the physicians who heal these infirmities, as though they proceeded from natural causes, are ignorant blockheads, who know nothing about the power of the demon." (14th July, 1528.)

"In many countries there are particular places to which devils more especially resort. In Prussia there is an infinite number of evil spirits. In Switzerland, on a high mountain, not far from Lucerne, there is a lake they call Pilate's Pond, which the devil has fixed upon as one of the chief residences of his evil spirits, and they are there in awful numbers. In my part of the country, at Poltersberg, there is a lake similarly cursed. If you throw a stone into it, a dreadful storm immediately arises, and the whole neighbouring district quakes to its centre. 'Tis the devils kept prisoners there, who occasion this!"[1]

"At Sussen, the devil carried off, last Good Friday, three grooms who had impiously devoted themselves to him." (1538.)

One day, when there was a great storm abroad, Luther said: "'Tis the devil who does this; the winds are nothing else but good or bad spirits. Hark! how the devil is puffing and blowing!"[2]

"Two noblemen in the time of Maximilian had sworn to kill each other. The devil having, accordingly, killed one of them in his bed with the other's sword, the survivor was taken into the great square of the town in the middle of the day, and the executioner having dug up and thrown away as much of the surface of the ground as was covered by his shadow, the man himself was banished the country. This is what is termed *mors civilis*. I had this from Dr. Bruck, chancellor of Saxony."

Luther next gives us two stories of persons who had been warned beforehand that they would be carried off by the devil, and who, though they had received the holy sacrament, and were guarded around by their friends, kneeling in prayer, and holding consecrated tapers, were, nevertheless, carried off on the day and hour indicated. "He crucified even our Saviour himself; but, provided he carry not our souls off, no matter."[3]

[1] Tischreden, 212. [2] Ib. 219. [3] Ib. 214.

"The devil takes some people about in their sleep, and makes them do various things just as though they were awake. The papists, superstitious animals as they are, say, in reference to such persons, that they were never christened, or, that if they were, it was by a drunken priest."[1]

"In the Low Countries, and in Saxony, there is a monstrous dog which scents out people that are going to die, and prowls about them till they are gone."[2]

"Some monks were taking a possessed man to their convent. The devil, who was in him, said in smooth tones to the monks, '*Popule meus, quid tibi feci?*' "[3]

Some one related at Luther's table, that as a cavalcade of gentlemen were riding along, two of them said to one another, spurring their horses, *Devil take the hindmost!* and that the one who was beaten in the race, was immediately carried off through the air by the devil. Luther observed on the occasion: "We need not invite the devil to our table; he is too ready to come without being asked. The air all about us is filled with demons; even we, who watch and pray daily, have but too much to do with him."[4]

"An old minister, kneeling at prayer one day, heard behind him the devil, who was endeavouring to hinder him from his devotions, by grunting like a whole herd of pigs. The old minister, not permitting himself to yield to fear, turned round, and exclaimed: '*Maître* devil, you have only got what you deserved; you were a glorious angel, and now you are only a filthy pig;' whereupon the grunting ceased, and the devil fled away, for he cannot endure to be treated with contempt. Ah, faith is a wonderful thing! it makes the weak strong; it enables one to prostrate the devil as though he were an infant."

"The devil fears the word of God. He can't bite it; it breaks his teeth."

"A young rascal, a mad, reckless vagabond, was drinking one day with some companions in a pot-house. His money being all spent, he cried out that if anybody would treat him to a can of good wine, he would sell him his soul for it. Shortly after, there came into the room a man who began drinking with the scapegrace I speak of, and by and by asked

[1] Tischreden, 213. [2] Ib. 221. [3] Ib. 222. [4] Ib. 205.

him whether he was really willing to sell his soul. The fellow daringly answered that he was. Whereupon the new comer provided him with as much drink as he liked for the rest of the day. Towards evening, when the young man was quite drunk, the stranger said to the rest of the company: 'Gentlemen, how say you; when one has bought a horse, don't the saddle and bridle go with it?' The people sitting round were alarmed at these words, and for a while made no answer. However, the stranger pressing for a reply, they said: 'Yes, the saddle and bridle go with it;' whereupon the devil, for it was he, clutched hold of the miserable young man he had bought, and flew off with him through the ceiling, since which time nothing has been heard of the impious creature."

On another occasion, Luther related the story of a soldier who had deposited some money with his landlord, in Brandenburg. The landlord, when the soldier asked him for his money, denied that he had received any from him. Hereupon, the poor fellow furiously assailed the knavish landlord, who, to get rid of him, handed him over to the town-guard, on the charge of disturbing the peace. The soldier being in prison awaiting his trial, the devil came to him and said: "To-morrow thou wilt be condemned and executed, but if thou wilt sell me thy soul, I will deliver thee." The soldier resolutely refused. "Well," said the devil, "at all events, thou mayest do this: To-morrow, when thou art before the judges, I will be near thee, in a blue hat with a white feather. Do thou then ask the judges to let me plead thy cause, and I will get thee out of thy difficulty." Next day, the soldier acted upon the devil's advice, and when the landlord persisted in his denial of having received the money, the advocate with the blue cap said to him: "Friend, how canst thou perjure thyself thus? Thou knowest well enough that the money is in thy bed, under the bolster. The sheriffs, if they send there, will find it at once." When the landlord heard this, he vociferated, with a great oath: "If I received the money, may the devil fly away with me on the spot!" The sheriff's men, however, who had gone to search the bed, soon came back with the money, which they found just where Blue-cap said it was. Then the latter rubbed his hands and chuckled, and said: "I knew I should have one of the two, the soldier or the publican;" and with that he twisted the knave landlord's neck, and flew off with him into the air. Luther, on finishing this story, added, that he was not at all pleased with people making such use of the devil's name; "For," said he, "the scoundrel is never very far off; you need not call very loud for him to hear."[1]

"There were at Erfurt, two students, one of whom had fallen so desperately in love with a girl, that he seemed on the point of going mad. The other, who, unknown to his companion, was a sorcerer, said to him one day: 'If thou wilt promise not to kiss her, or to take her in thy arms, I will manage for her to come and see thee.'—'Agreed,' returned the young man; and the girl was brought accordingly. But on sight of her, the lover could not restrain his passion, and he caught her in his arms and kissed her, whereupon, she fell down, and died on the spot. When the two men saw her lying dead, they were in a great fright, and the sorcerer said: 'I must employ my last resource.' That last resource was the devil, who, upon being summoned, restored the girl to apparent life, and carried her secretly back to her parents, where she continued for a while to do the work she had been accustomed to do about the house, but was deadly pale, and spoke not a word. At the end of three days, the parents, amazed at her appearance and conduct, went in search of certain divines, and asked them what it would be best to do. Immediately guessing how the matter stood, the divines came to the girl, and sharply adjuring the devil within her, the latter withdrew, and the girl then fell stiff on the floor, a putrid corpse."[2]

"Doctor Luke Gauric, the sorcerer you sent for from Italy, has often admitted to me that his master in the black art used constantly to have conferences with the devil."[3]

"The devil can so completely assume the human form, when he wants to deceive us, that we may very well lie with what seems to us a woman, of real flesh and blood, and yet all the while 'tis only the devil in the shape of a woman: Satan, according to St. Paul, has great power over the children of unrighteousness. 'Tis the same with women, who may think it is a man in bed with them, yet 'tis only the devil; and when it is considered that the result of this connexion is

[1] Tischreden, 205. [2] Ib. 215. [3] Ib. 216.

oftentimes an imp of darkness, half mortal, half devil, such cases are peculiarly horrible and appalling. How often have not the demons called *Nix*, drawn women and girls into the water, and there had commerce with them, with like fearful consequences. The devil, too, sometimes steals human children; it is not unfrequent for him to carry away infants within the first six weeks after their birth, and to substitute in their place imps, called in Latin *supposititii*, and by the Saxons *kilkropff*.

"Eight years ago, I myself saw and touched at Dessau, a child of this sort, which had no human parents, but had proceeded from the devil. He was twelve years old, and, in outward form, exactly resembled ordinary children. He did nothing but eat, consuming as much every day as four hearty labourers or threshers could. In most external respects he was, as I have mentioned, just like other children; but if any one touched him, he yelled out like a mad creature, and with a peculiar sort of scream. Whenever anything went wrong in the house, if there was any misfortune or accident, he danced about and shouted for joy; when, on the other hand; matters proceeded smoothly, he was always weeping. I said to the princes of Anhalt, with whom I was at the time, If I had the ordering of things here, I would have that child thrown into the Moldau, at the risk of being held its murderer. But the elector of Saxony and the princes were not of my opinion in the matter. I then told them, at all events, to have prayers offered up in the churches to God, that he would be pleased to remove the demon. Prayers to that effect were accordingly said every day for a year, and at the end of that time the child died."

When the doctor had done relating his story, some one asked him how he could have made up his mind to throw the child into the river? "Why," he replied, "children like that are, in my opinion, a mere mass of flesh and bone, without any soul. The devil is quite capable of producing such things; just in the same way that he annihilates the faculties of men, when he possesses them corporally, so as to deprive them of reason, and render them mentally blind and deaf for a period, just in the same way, I say, he inhabits these masses of flesh, which seem to us children, and is himself their soul, the only soul they have."

"The devil must needs be very powerful, to hold the intellectual part of us so closely captive. Origen, as it seems to me, did not sufficiently comprehend or appreciate this power, or he would never have suggested the possibility of the devil's obtaining pardon in the day of judgment. How horrible a sin was his to revolt, wilfully and determinedly, against his God, his Creator!

"In Saxony, not far from Halberstadt, there was a man who had one of these kilkropffs in his house. This demon child could exhaust at one meal the whole of his supposed mother's milk, and that of five other women, and would devour, besides, whatever was presented to it. The man was advised to take the child a pilgrimage to Holchelstadt, to the shrine of the Virgin there, and dedicating it to the Virgin, leave it to be nursed in the immediate vicinity. The man adopting this advice, was on his way to the shrine, carrying the child in a basket, when, on passing a bridge, another devil, from the water below, cried out, *Kilkropff! kilkropff!* The child in the basket, who until that moment, had never said a single word, replied: 'Oh, oh, oh!' The devil in the river continued, 'Where art thou going?' The one in the basket replied: 'Oh, oh! I'm going to our blessed mother's at Holchelstadt, to be nursed!' The countryman, all aghast at this dialogue, threw basket and child into the river, and immediately the two devils rose from the water, and flew off through the air, crying, 'Oh, oh, oh!' and turning one over another, in sportive mockery of the countryman!"[1]

One day, as Luther was coming out of the chapel of the castle in which he had been preaching, a lansknecht came up to him, and complained to him of the manner in which the devil constantly assailed him with temptations and threats of carrying him off through the air. While he was stating his case, Doctor Pomer, who was passing by, came up and assisted Luther in giving comfort and hope to the poor man. "Do not despair," said they; "despite all these temptations of the evil one, we clearly perceive that you are not one to fall into his clutches. Our Lord Jesus Christ also was tempted by him, but he triumphed over him by aid of the Word of God; do you defend yourself in like manner by the Word of God, and by prayer." Luther added: "If the devil should again assail you, and threaten to carry you off, address him thus, in

[1] Tischreden, 216.

a firm tone: 'I belong to Jesus Christ, my Lord and Saviour, in whom I believe, and with whom hereafter I shall be eternally; and he has assured me that no power can tear away Christians from his protecting hand.' My friend, keep your thoughts fixed upon your God, who is in heaven, rather than upon the devil, and cease to alarm yourself about the devices of Satan. I know perfectly well that he would gladly carry you off, but I know also, that without your own consent, he cannot do so. He is like the robber, who desires to lay hands upon the rich man's money-box, and would do so, but that it is well guarded. Do you keep guard over yourself, and God will not permit the spirit of darkness to hurt a hair of your head. Listen devoutly to the divine word, pray constantly, and with fervour, keep yourself in full occupation, be not too often alone, and you will find that God will deliver you from Satan, and will preserve you amongst his flock."

A young farrier had been giving out in the neighbourhood that he was haunted wherever he went by a spectre. Luther sent for the young man, and questioned him on the matter in the presence of several learned persons. The farrier stated, that the spectre which pursued him charged him with impiety, in having received the communion in both kinds, and had thereupon threatened him: If thou returnest to thy master's house, I will twist thy neck; and this, he said, was the reason why, as was the case, he had not gone to his master's for several days past. The doctor, after having narrowly questioned him, said, very seriously: "Be careful, my friend, not to lie in such matters as these. Fear God, and listen attentively to his Word. Doing this, thou mayest return in all security to thy master's house, and proceed honestly with thy allotted work. Should Satan return, say to him: 'I will not obey thee; I will obey God, who has called me to this condition of life; I will remain here at my work, and even though an angel should come, I will not be led from it."

"As Dr. Luther advanced in years, he experienced comparatively few temptations on the part of men; but the devil, as he himself tells us, kept constantly at his side, even in the cloister, tormenting and tempting him. There were one or two devils, in particular, who kept watch upon him. And when they could not make their way to his heart, they used to seize hold of his head, and torment him in that quarter.[1]

[1] Tischreden, 222.

". . . . Oh, that has very often happened to me. Sometimes, when, I have had a knife in my hand, terrible thoughts have come upon me. At other times, the devil has prevented me from praying, when I have sought to do so, and has driven me out of my chamber in search of human faces. I and some others of us have to do with the great devils, devils who are complete doctors in theology; the Turks and papists have arrayed around them mere imps, not theologians, but only lawyers.[1]

"I know, thanks be to God therefore, I know that my cause is a good and divine cause; otherwise, if Christ were not indeed in heaven, and Lord of the world, my case were very bad indeed. Yet, I own, the devil often presses me so closely in debate, that I am all in a sweat. His anger against me is eternal and unceasing; I know that perfectly well. He lies with me, nearer even than my Catherine, and gives me more pain than she gives me pleasure. . . . Sometimes he thinks to get me quite in a corner: 'The law,' he says 'is also the Word of God; why be always putting it in opposition to the gospel in this manner?' Ay, I reply, it may be so; but it is as far beneath the gospel, as earth is beneath heaven."[2]

"The devil, it is true, is not exactly a doctor who has taken his degrees,[3] but he is very learned, very expert for all that. He has not been carrying on his business during thousands of years for nothing. . . . If he has sometimes quitted the bodies of possessed persons at the exorcisms of the papist priests and monks, leaving behind him some sign, a broken pane of window, a bit of wall knocked open, or something of that sort, he did not go away entirely, you may rely upon it, but merely made people believe he had quitted the body, in order more effectually to take possession of their minds, and confirm them in their superstitions."[4]

In January, 1532, Luther fell seriously ill, as the physician imagined from an apoplectic attack. Melancthon and Roerer, who were sitting by his bed-side, having alluded to the joy which any intelligence of his death would doubtless occasion throughout the Roman catholic world, he said in a confident

[1] Tischreden, 220. [2] Ib. 224. [3] See Appendix CXVII.
[4] Tischreden, 202.

tone: "I feel quite certain that I shall not die yet for some time, for I am satisfied that it is not God's will to confirm that abominable popery by my death. He will not, so soon after the departure of Zwinglius and of Œcolampadius, give the papists a new subject of triumph. Satan, indeed, is bent upon killing me, and for that purpose never quits me for an instant, that so he may lose no opportunity for effecting his object, but when I die, not his, but the Lord's will is accomplished.[1]

"My malady, which consists of a series of headaches, vertigoes, and so on, is decidedly not natural; nothing I take remedies it in the slightest degree, though I implicitly obey my physician's directions."[2]

"In 1536, he was summoned to Torgau to unite in marriage duke Philip of Pomerania, and the elector's sister. In the midst of the ceremony, the nuptial ring escaped from his hold, and fell to the ground. He was seized with a temporary alarm, but, soon recovering himself, exclaimed: "Hark ye, devil, this is no affair of thine! 'tis all lost time for thee," and he proceeded with the service.[3]

"One day, as doctor Luther was talking after dinner with some friends, his wife suddenly rose, and ere she had reached the door, fainted. When she came to herself, the doctor asked her what had passed through her mind during the swoon. She said that she had experieneed certain peculiar trials, which she regarded as undoubted signs of approaching death, striking her to the heart more effectually than a bullet or an arrow. 'To him who undergoes such temptations,' replied the doctor, soothingly, 'I would give this sound advice—that he forthwith turn his thoughts to something gay and diverting; that he drink a good cup of wine, and engage in some amusing pastime, or rather, perhaps, compel his attention to some serious occupation. The best remedy of all, however, and without which all the rest are as nought, is to believe firmly in Jesus Christ.'[4]

"When the devil finds me idle, and not thinking upon the Word of God, he insinuates into my mind doubts and apprehensions that I have not taught aright; that I have over-

[1] Ukert, i. 320. [2] Tischreden, 210. [3] Ukert, i. 322.
[4] Tischreden, 184.

turned and destroyed authority without just cause, that my doctrine has occasioned all this confusion and disorder unrighteously. But as soon as I get hold of the word of God again, I am strong as ever, and say to the devil: 'What is the opinion of the world, great as that world is, to God? has not He set his Son over that world as its Lord and King? If the world attempts to unthrone its Lord, God will overturn the world and reduce it to ashes; for he has himself said: This is my son, reverence his words. *Be wise now, therefore, O ye kings! be instructed, ye judges of the earth!*[1]

"The devil, above all things, is anxious to tear from our hearts the article of the remission of sins. *What*, says he, *how dare you preach that which no man has taught for so many centuries! Suppose this were to anger God?*

"When I wake up in the night, the devil immediately comes to me and disputes with me, and gives me strange thoughts, until, at last 'I grow enraged beyond all endurance, and give him ill words. 'Bah, beast,' I say; 'the Lord is not so irritated against us as thou sayest.'[2]

"Early this morning when I awoke, the fiend came and began disputing with me. 'Thou art a great sinner,' said he. I replied, 'Canst thou not tell me something new, Satan? I knew that thou now sayest long since. I have sins enough upon me, without the addition of any of thy invention.' He went on: 'What hast thou done with the monasteries?' 'What is that to thee,' I replied; 'thou seest that thy sacrilegious worship subsists still, though we have got rid of the monasteries.'[3]

One evening, at supper, the conversation fell upon Dr. Faustus. Luther said, very gravely, "The devil has never employed the agency of sorcerers against me; if he could have done so, doubtless he would have set about it long ago. He has often had very hard hold of me, but he has always been obliged to let go at last. I know the devil thoroughly well; he has over and over again pressed me so close that I scarcely knew whether I was alive or dead. Sometimes he has thrown me into such despair, that I even knew not whether there was a God, and had great doubts

[1] Tischreden, 185. [2] Ib. 218. [3] Ib. 222.

about our dear Lord Christ. But the Word of God has speedily restored me."[1]

"The devil is always placing before my eyes the law, sin, and death, and makes use of this Trinity to torment me."[2]

"The devil has sworn our death; but he will stick his teeth into a hollow nut."[3]

"The temptation of the flesh is a small matter; 'tis a malady the first woman you come to may cure very speedily. Eustochia would have been a complete cure for St. Jerome; but God defend us from the great temptations which touch upon eternity; when we are beaten about among these, we know not whether God is the devil or the devil God. These temptations are not so easily dispersed."[4]

"When I am troubled with thoughts which concern only worldly or domestic affairs, then I take a Psalm, or some sentences out of St. Paul, and lay me down to rest and sleep thereupon; but the cogitations which come of the devil, are more chargeable to me, and require a good sturdy effort of the mind to get rid of them. Oftentimes, merriment and buffoonery serve the turn."[5]

"That same barley has much to endure from man. First, it is thrown into the earth to rot; then, when the new germ has come forth, and has assumed the form of a full, ripe ear, it is cut, and beaten in the barn, and dried, and then cooked up into beer, to be consumed by drunkards. Flax, too, is a great martyr in its way. When it is ripe, it is torn up, and soaked, and then dried, and then beaten, and then peeled, and dressed, and woven, and made into shifts, and cassocks, and what not. When it is worn out in these shapes, it is torn up and converted into menial dusters, or bandages for wounds, or has plasters put upon it, or it is made into wicks for candles, or it is sold to the paper maker, and pounded and pulled all to pieces, and then made up into paper. The paper is printed upon, and written upon, and made into playing-cards, and then torn up again, and applied to all sorts of base uses. These plants, then, in common with many other creatures, which are very useful to us, suffer much at our hands; and the good and pious among Christians have, in the same way,

[1] Tischreden, 12. [2] Ib. 220. [3] Ib. 362. [4] Ib. 318. [5] Ib. 226.

endless sufferings to endure in this world at the hands of the wicked."[1]

"When the devil comes to me in the night, I say to him, 'Devil, I must now sleep; for it is the command and ordinance of God that we labour by day, and sleep by night.' If he goes on with the old story, accusing me of sin, I say to him, to vex him: '*Holy Spirit Satan, pray for me!*—Go,' I say to him, '*physician, cure thyself.*'"[2]

"If you are preaching to one who is under temptation, you must kill Moses and stone the law. When he comes to himself, and has forgotten the temptation, the law may be preached to him. *Let him who has been afflicted be afflicted no more.*

"The best way of getting rid of the devil, if you cannot do it with the words of the Holy Scripture, is to rail at and mock him. He cannot bear scorn."[3]

"Some persons afflicted with temptations may be relieved by having a good supper given them, but this remedy will not do for everybody, and is especially inapplicable to young people. As to myself, an old man, I find that a cup of wine has often the effect of driving away evil thoughts, by sending me comfortably to sleep for the night.[4]

"An efficient medicine against temptations is to turn your thoughts to some pleasant subject, to tell or hear jests and merry stories out of Marcolphus, or Eulespiegel, or some facetious book of that kind. Music, too, is very good; for the devil is a saturnine spirit, and music is hateful to him, and drives him far away from it."[5]

The important extract we will now lay before our readers may be regarded as, to a certain extent, a narrative of the obstinate war which Satan waged against Luther throughout his life.

"*Written by Dr. Martin Luther, some time previous to his death.*—Whoever will read with attention the history of the church, the works of the holy fathers, and, more especially, the Bible, will clearly see that ever since the origin of the church, things have followed exactly the same course. Each time that the Word has made itself heard, and that

[1] Tischreden, 216. [2] See Appendix CXVIII. [3] Tischcreden, 227.
[4] Ib. 231. [5] Ib. 238.

God has assembled together in his service a small flock, the devil has at once caught sight of the divine light forcing its way through the darkness, and has forthwith set himself to work, puffing, blowing, storming from every direction, with all his might, in order to extinguish it. It has been to no purpose that one or two holes have been stopped up, he has soon found out another through which to blow his rage. Thus it has gone on from one century to another, and thus it will go on until the day of judgment.

"I hold that I myself (not to speak of the ancients) have undergone more than twenty tempests, twenty fearful assaults of the devil. First, there were the papists. All the world, I believe, knows how many hurricanes, in the shape of bulls, books, diets, and what not, the devil dashed against me by the agency of the papists; the lamentable manner in which I have been torn to pieces, devoured, demolished by them. It is true that I puffed away at them a little, but that was to slight purpose, for they stormed and raged more than ever, vomiting forth fire and flames. And so it has gone on to this very day, without intermission.

"I had, at one time, ceased for a moment to fear these tempests of the devil, when all at once he burst out upon me through another hole, in the shape of Munzer and his revolt, whereby the light was all but dashed out. Christ had scarcely stopped this hole, when, behold, the devil was at me again in the person of Carlstadt, breaking in my windows, and roaring and tornadoing to such a furious extent that I thought he was going to carry off the light, wax, wick, and all. But God stepped forward to the succour of his poor light, and would not allow it to be extinguished. Then came the sacramentarians and the anabaptists, who dashed open doors and windows in their determination to put out the light, and did, indeed, place it in very great danger; but, thank God, their evil intentions also were frustrated!

"Others, again, have stormed at once against the old masters, the pope, and Luther, anathematizing all these together by a strange combination; Servetus and Campanus were among the men of whom I now speak. . . . As to those who have not publicly assailed me in printed books, but who have discharged their poisoned arrows against me in the form of manuscript pamphlets, I will not put them down in the present account. It is sufficient for me to show that I have learned by my own experience (for I had not credited history upon the point) that the church, for the love of its dear Word, of its blessed light, cannot have rest, but must be constantly prepared for new storms raised against it by the devil, as it has been from the beginning, is now, and ever shall be.

"And even were I myself to live another hundred years, were I to succeed in appeasing the tempests which now assail us, and those which will assail us, yet this would not, I see clearly, give rest to those who come after me. So long as the devil lives and reigns, there will be no peace for the world. I therefore pray Almighty God to grant me one little hour of a state of grace; I ask not to live longer.

"As for you who shall come after us, be it your care to pray to God, fervently and constantly, to observe his word assiduously, and to take good care of the poor candle of God, for the devil never sleeps, never stands still at his work, and will not die before the last judgment. You and I, and those who succeed us from generation to generation, will die, but he will remain as he is, fighting as furiously as ever against the gospel. . . .

"I see him there, not very far off, puffing out his cheeks till they are all red, blowing, and blowing, and blowing against the light; furious, mad; but our Lord Jesus Christ, who, in the outset, gave him one good blow on his inflated cheek, still combats him vigorously, and will combat him until the end of things. This our Lord himself has assured us of, and he is incapable of falsehood. *I will be with you alway, even unto the end of the world;* and again, *The gates of hell shall not prevail against my church;* and, in St. John, *And I give my sheep, eternal life, and they shall never perish neither shall any pluck them out of my hand;* and in St. Matthew, x., *The very hairs of your head are all numbered—fear not them which kill the body, but are not able to kill the soul.*

"Yet, it is commanded us, that we ourselves watch and guard the light to the utmost extent of our power. It is said: *Watch; the devil is a roaring lion, walking about, and seeking whom he may devour.* Such he was when St. Peter so described him, and such he will continue to be unto the end of the world." . . . .

(Luther, after subsequently enlarging upon the aid of God, without which all our own efforts are futile, proceeds:) "Thou and I were nothing, were silent a thousand years ago, and yet the church was saved; it was saved, without our assistance, by him of whom it has been said, *The same yesterday and for ever.* And, just in the same way, it is not we who, in the present day, preserve the church; for it is not within our capability to reach the devil, who is in the pope, and in seditious and wicked men; it would perish beneath our very eyes, and ourselves with it, were there none others than ourselves to protect it. We must place our faith in him, who *will be for ever the same as to-day*. . . .

"'Tis a lamentable thing to witness the haughty pride, the arrogant audacity which we exhibit, despite the terrible and scandalous examples afforded us by those who, in their conceit, have imagined that the church was built upon them. To speak of our own times: what was the end of Munzer, he who monstrously thought that the church could not endure, unless he were at hand to support and govern it? And, quite recently, have not the anabaptists been a fearful warning, reminding us that a devil, still more cunning than they, is ever hovering about us; that our finest thoughts may be the most dangerous; and that it is essential for us, as Isaiah points out, to look well into our hands, whenever we pick up anything, to see whether it is God, or an idol—whether it is gold, or mere clay.

"But, unhappily, all these warnings are thrown away upon us; we live on in full security; for, of course, the devil keeps a good distance from *us; we* have nothing of that flesh, which even St. Paul was afflicted with, and of which he could not rid himself, notwithstanding all his efforts (Romans vii.). *We*, we are great heroes, invincibles, men who need be under no apprehensions at all respecting the flesh and thought; *we* are pure spirits; *we* hold in captivity the flesh and the devil, chained together; and whatever comes into *our* heads, is infallibly an inspiration of the Holy Ghost. The result of all which impertinence and wickedness is, that both horse and rider break their necks.

"The papists, I know, will here turn upon me, and say: 'Ah, ha! this is good: here art thou thyself complaining of disorder and sedition! What caused both the one and the other? Was it not thou and thy doctrine?' A mere trick by which they seek to overthrow Luther and his word; but I care not for them. Let them calumniate me—let them lie on as much as they like; they must, perforce, hold their peace by and by. This fine argument of theirs, or whatever they may call it, is not worth a rush; if it were, all the prophets would, on the same principle, have been really the heretics, and seditious perturbators which they were all of them considered by their own nation; as which they were persecuted, and as which, most of them were put to death.

"Jesus Christ our Saviour himself had to submit to hear it said by the Jews, and, in particular, by the pontiff, the pharisees, the scribes, by all those highest in power, that he had a devil in him, that he drove out devils only by means of other devils; that he was a Samaritan, a companion of publicans and sinners. He was even at the last condemned to die on the cross, as a blasphemer and seditious perturbator. Hear what St. Stephen said to the Jews who were about to stone him: *Which of the prophets have not your fathers persecuted? And they have slain them which showed before the coming of the Just One, of whom you have been now the betrayers and murderers.*

"The apostles and disciples were not more fortunate than their Master; they all fulfilled the predictions he had made respecting them. . . .

"If this, then, be the case, and the gospel shows that it is, why should we be astonished that we who, in these awful times, preach Jesus Christ, and put ourselves forward, as his servants, are, after his example, persecuted and condemned as heretics, as perturbators? For what are we in comparison with those sublime geniuses who were immediately enlightened by the Holy Ghost, adorned by God with such admirable gifts, and endowed with such strong and impregnable faith?

"Let us not, then, be ashamed of the calumnies and the insults with which we are assailed by our enemies: let us not fear all they may do unto us; but let us regard it as our greatest glory, as our greatest happiness, to receive at the hands of the world the same wages which, from the beginning, it has almost invariably meted out to the saints, in recompence for their faithful services. Let us rejoice in God that we poor despised sinners have been judged worthy by the master of all things to undergo this ignominy, for Christ's sake. . . .

"The papists, in their grand arguments, are like a man who should contend, that if God had not created good devils, there would have been no devils, seeing that these were once good angels. On the same principle, Adam reproached God for having given him a wife, seeing that if God had not created Eve, he would not have sinned; whence it would appear that God himself was the only sinner in the case, and that Adam and his children were all pure, pious, holy personages.

"Say they: there have arisen out of the doctrine of Luther, many spirits full of disorder and revolt; consequently, that doctrine is an emanation of the devil. But, as St. John says, *They went out of us, but they were not of us.* Judas was one of the disciples of Christ; consequently, according to their argument, Jesus Christ was a devil. Heretics have never proceeded from among the pagans; they have all come out of the bosom of the holy Christian church; consequently, according to the papist argument, holy church is the work of the devil.

"It was the same with the Bible under the pope; it was publicly said that the Bible was the book of heretics, and it was charged with giving its sanction to the most condemnable opinions. Even to the present hour, the papists cry: *The church, the church, against and above the Bible!* Emser, that sage man, could not at all make up his mind that it was advisable for the Bible to be translated into German; possibly he was not quite satisfied that it was well for it to have been written in Hebrew, Greek, or Latin, or written at all; for truly the Bible and the church differ on a good many points.

"If, then, the Bible, the book and the word of the Holy Spirit, has such things to endure at their hands, we, surely, may be contented to submit to their imputing to us all the heresies and seditions that burst forth from time to time. The spider sucks poison from the sweet and gentle rose whence the bee derives only honey: is it the fault of the flower that in the foul spider its honey becomes poison?

"*Give a dog an ill name and hang it*, says the proverb: *The sheep that the wolf wanted to devour, had disturbed the water*, the wolf said, though the poor thing stood lower down the stream than where it was disturbed. Æsop tells us this story. Just so, the very men who have notoriously filled the church with error and bloodshed, with lies and murder, say that it is we who have disturbed the water above us; that we, who have all along done our best to resist sedition, and to disperse practical errors, are the perturbators and the heretics! Well, wolf, do thy worst: eat, eat away, my worthy friend; a bone will stick in thy throat, rely upon it. . . . It is impossible for these wretches to do otherwise than as they do; 'tis their nature, the nature of their world and of that world's god. When you find them calling the Master of the house Beelzebub, can you expect they will treat his servants well? When you find them calling the Bible the *book of heretics*, is it to be supposed that our works will receive honour? The living God is the Judge of us all: he will one day settle all this business; he will one day let it be clearly seen whether or no 'tis an heretical book, and not to be believed, this sacred Scripture, which so many times has testified of him.

"May Jesus Christ, our beloved Saviour, the guardian of our souls which he has redeemed with his most precious blood, may he preserve the little flock faithful to his word, so that it may increase in grace, in light, in faith! May he deign to sustain it against the temptations of Satan and of the world, and take pity on its deep groans, and the expectation full of painful suspense, with which it looks forward to the glorious coming of Him its Saviour, when the fiery and deadly bites of the serpents shall at length cease, and for the children of God shall commence the revealing of liberty and beatitude, which they hope for, and await in patience. Amen! amen!"[1]

CHAPTER VII.

Illness—Yearnings after death and judgment—Death of Luther, 1546.

"THIS tooth-ache and ear-ache I am always suffering from, are worse than the plague. When I was at Coburg, in 1530, I was tormented with a noise and buzzing in my ears, just as though there was some wind tearing through my head. The devil had something to do with it.[2]

[1] Werke, ii. 1. [2] Tischreden, 1.

"We should live high and drink wine, when we are not well." He followed this agreeable regimen when he was ill at Schmalkald, in 1537.

A man was complaining to him, one day, of the itch; said Luther: "I should be very glad to change with you, and to give you ten florins into the bargain. You don't know what a horrible thing this vertigo of mine is. Here, all to day, I have not been able to read a letter through, nor even two or three lines of the Psalms consecutively. I have not got beyond more than three or four words, when, buzz, buzz! the noise begins again, and often I am very near falling off my chair with the pain. But the itch, that's nothing; nay, it is rather a beneficial complaint."[1]

One day, when he had been preaching at Schmalkald, he had, after dinner, a severe attack of the stone,[2] whereupon he knelt down and prayed fervently: "O my God, my Lord Jesus! thou knowest with what zeal I have preached thy word; *if it be for the glory of thy name*, come to my succour; if not, close my eyes. I will die the enemy of thy enemies, I will die full of hatred of that villain pope, who has essayed to exalt himself above thee, O Christ." And he composed forthwith four Latin verses on the subject.

"My head is so weak, so unsteady, that I can neither read nor write, especially when fasting." (9th Feb. 1543.)

"I am feeble, and weary of life; I would fain bid adieu to the world, which is now given over to the evil one. God grant me a favourable hour for my departure, and a prosperous journey. Amen." (14th March.)

To Amsdorff he says, on the 18th August, in the same year: "I write this to thee after supper, for when fasting, I cannot, without great danger, even look at a book or at paper. I don't understand this wretched malady at all; whether it is one of Satan's blows at me, or the effect of nature's decay."

"I take it that my malady is made up, first of the ordinary weakness of advanced age; secondly, of the results of my long labours, and habitual tension of thought; thirdly, above all, of the blows of Satan; if this be so, there is no medicine in the world will cure me." (7 Nov. 1543.)

To Spalatin he writes (30th Jan. 1544): "I confess to

[1] Tischreden, 362. [2] See Appendix CXIX.

thee, that in my whole life, throughout our whole struggle, I have never spent a more unpleasant year than the last has been to me. I have had a most terrible business with the lawyers, on the subject of secret marriages; I have found in those whom I regarded as devoted friends to the church, most bitter enemies. This is enough to plague me, is it not?

"I am indolent, weary, indifferent, in other words, old and useless. I have finished my journey, and nought remains but for the Lord to reunite me to my fathers, and give the worms and rottenness their due. I am weary of life, if this can be called life. Pray for me, that the hour of my departure may be pleasing to God and salutary for myself. I think no more about the emperor and the empire, except to recommend the one and the other to God in my prayers. The world seems to me to have reached its last hour, to be grown old like unto a garment, as the Psalmist expresses it; 'tis time it were changed." (5th Dec. 1544.)

"If I had known in the beginning that men were so hostile to the word of God, I should certainly have held my peace, and kept myself quiet. I imagined that they sinned merely through ignorance."[1]

On one occasion he said, "Nobles, citizens, peasants, everybody, anybody, knows the gospel better than Dr. Luther, or even St. Paul himself. They all despise the pastors of God, or rather, the God and master of pastors."[2]

"Our nobles want to govern, but they don't know how to set about it; the pope does. The least papist of them all is more capable of governing than ten of our court nobles put together. They may rely upon that."

Some one told Luther that in the diocese of Wurtzburg there were six hundred rich livings vacant. "There will no good come of that," replied he; "and it will be the same with us, if we persist in despising the word of God and his servants. . . . If I wanted to become rich, all I need do were to abstain from preaching. . . . The ecclesiastical visitors asked the peasantry in several places, why they did not support their pastors? Oh, returned they, we've enough to do to keep our shepherds and pigherds, and we can't do without them. They thought they could very well dispense with their soul-herds."[3]

[1] Tischreden, 6. [2] Ib. 5. [3] Ib.

Luther, during six months that he did not preach in the church, used to read the services and deliver sermons on the Sabbath in his own house. "I do this," said he to Dr. Jonas, "to acquit my own conscience by fulfilling my duty as father of this family; but as to any other result, I see very clearly that the Word of God will be no more heeded here than it is in the church.

"It is you, Dr. Jonas, who will succeed me in my pulpit; I hope you will acquit yourself of the duty conscientiously."[1]

He one day came out of the church in disgust, at seeing some people talking. (1545.)[2]

On the 16th Feb., 1546, Luther observed: "The best thing Aristotle ever wrote was the fifth book of the Ethics, where he pays a fine and well-merited homage to moderation, wherein I entirely concur." (This tribute in favour of moderation is very remarkable, given, as it was, in the last year of Luther's life.)

The count of Mansfeldt's chancellor, dining with Luther at Eisleben, on his way from the diet of Frankfort, mentioned that the pope and the emperor were proceeding sharply against Hermann, bishop of Cologne, and were even thinking of expelling him from his electorate. Luther said: "They wont be able to do anything; they find that God and the holy gospel will not aid them against us, so they are resolved to see whether world wisdom, violence, cunning, will stand them in stead; but they will fail, for our Lord is with us. Do they think that God will suffer himself and his Son to be always regarded as nobodies? Even were they to kill me, they must, to do themselves any good, utterly destroy and extinguish all I have taught. I have the advantage over them. My Lord has said, *I will raise you up at the last day*; and when the last day comes, he will say, *Dr. Martin, Dr. Jonas, Maître Michael Cœlius, come to me*; for he will call you by your names, as he has promised in 1 John: *I will call my own sheep by name.* Be not afraid, then.[3]

"God has now and then a fine game at cards, all of them court cards—kings, princes, and so on. He deals them out, and plays them against one another—the pope against Luther, for instance; and, by and by, as children do when they've

[1] Tischreden, 195. [2] Ib. [3] Ib. 19.

been fighting at beggar-my-neighbour for a long time without result, gets tired, and throws the cards under the table.[1]

"The world is like a drunken peasant: put him on his horse on one side, and he tumbles over on the other. Take him in what way you may, you cannot help him; he wont let you. The world is bent upon going to the devil."[2]

Luther used often to say, that if he died in his bed, it would be a great disgrace to the pope: "You, all of you, pope, devil, kings, princes, and lords—you are all of you enemies to Luther, and yet you can't do him any harm. It was not so with John Huss. I am persuaded that, for the last hundred years, there has not existed a man whom the world at large hated more than it hates me. I, in my turn, am hostile to the world; there is nothing, *in tota vitâ*, which gives me any pleasure: I am utterly weary of life. I pray the Lord will come forthwith, and carry me hence. Let him come, above all, with his Last Judgment: I will stretch out my neck, the thunder will burst forth, and I shall be at rest." He subsequently consoles himself for the ingratitude of the world by calling to mind the example of Moses, Samuel, St. Paul, and Christ.[3]

One of his guests observed, that if the world were to subsist another fifty years, a great many things would happen which they could not then foresee. "Pray God it may not exist so long," cried Luther; "matters would be even worse than they have been. There would rise up infinite sects and schisms, which are at present hidden within men's hearts, not yet mature. No; may the Lord come at once! let him cut the whole matter short with the Day of Judgment, for there is no amendment to be expected."[4]

"You will see that before long such wickedness will prevail, life will become so terrible to bear, that in every quarter the cry will be raised: God! come with thy Last Judgment." And having a necklace of white agates in his hand at the time, he added: "O God, grant that it may come without delay. I would readily eat up this necklace to-day for the Judgment to come to-morrow."[5]

The conversation one day having turned upon eclipses, and the little influence they in reality exercised over the death of

[1] Tischreden, 32. [2] Ib. 448. [3] Ib. 449. [4] Ib. 295. [5] Ib. 15.

kings and princes, the doctor said: "No; eclipses no longer have any influence over such matters, and the reason I take to be that the Lord is shortly about to bring matters to a real crisis, to settle everything with the Judgment. I was meditating upon this the other afternoon, as I went to sleep, and I said to myself, soon I shall *go to rest in the Lord.* The Judgment must needs be at hand, for what help is there for the world? The papal church will not reform itself; that is out of the question; and the Turks and the Jews are as little inclined to amendment. Our empire makes no progress towards improvement: here have we been for the last thirty years assembling diets from time to time, yet nothing is done. When I am meditating, I often ask myself, what prayer I ought to offer up for the Diet. The bishop of Mayence is naught, the pope is worse than naught. I see no other prayer that is fitting but only this: *Thy kingdom come.*" [1]

"Poor creatures that we are! We gain our bread even in sin. Up to seven years old, we do nothing but eat, drink, play, and sleep. Thence, up to twenty-one, we go to our studies, perhaps, three or four hours a-day, and the rest of our time follow out our own caprices, running about, drinking, and what not. After that, we begin to work, and go on working till we are fifty, and then we become children once more. All along, we sleep out one-half of our lives. Ah, shame upon us! we do not give to God even a tenth of the time; and yet we imagine that with our good works, forsooth, we merit Heaven! What have I myself done? chattered two hours, been at my meals three, sat quite idle four. Ah! *enter not into judgment with thy servant, O Lord!*" [2]

In a letter to Melancthon, dated 18th April, 1541, after relating his sufferings, he says: "Please Christ to remove my soul into the peace of the Lord. By the grace of God, I am ready and desirous to go. I have lived out and finished the course assigned me by God. O, may my soul, wearied with so long a journey on earth, now ascend to Heaven!"

"I have no time to write to thee at any length, my dear Probst, for though I am overwhelmed with age and weariness: *old, cold, and half blind,*[3] as the saying is, yet I am not per-

[1] Tischreden, 304. [2] Ib. 48.

[3] Luther had been for some time afflicted with a disease in one of his eyes.

mitted as yet to take my repose, besieged as I am by circumstances which compel me to write on, on, on. I know more than thou dost about the destiny of our world: that destiny is destruction; it is inevitably so—seeing how triumphantly the devil walks about, and how mankind grow daily worse and worse. There is one consolation, that the Day of Judgment is quite close at hand. The word of God has become a wearisome thing to man, a thing viewed with disgust. The very circumstance that no new false prophets have arisen up amongst us of late, is in itself an unfavourable symptom; there is no occasion, no place for new heresies, where the universal sentiment is an epicurean contempt for the word of God altogether. Germany has been: and it will never be again what it has been. The nobles are solely intent upon grasping what they can from other people; the towns are only thinking of themselves (and so far, are very much in the right of it); the effect of all this is that the nation is divided against itself, which ought to be firmly united for the purpose of making head against that army of devils let loose, the Turks. We trouble ourselves very little as to whether God is for us or against us; for we imagine we are to conquer, by our own strength, against Turks, and devils, against God himself. The self-confidence of this poor dying Germany amounts to sheer insanity. Yet we can do nothing for her. Lamentations are vain, tears are vain, exhortations are vain. Nothing remains but to pray: *thy will be done.*" (26th March, 1542.) [1]

"All around me I observe an unconquerable cupidity prevalent; this is another of the signs which convince me that the last day is at hand; it seems as though the world in its old age, its last paroxysm, was growing delirious, as sometimes happens to dying people." (8th March, 1544.)

"I consider that we are the last trumpet which is to prepare and precede the coming of Christ. However weak we ourselves are, however low the note we sound in the ear of the world, yet the sound we give forth in the ears of heaven's angels is loud and telling, and they, aiding our weakness here, will take it up, prolong, and give it out in full blast. Amen." (6th August, 1545.)

One seems to read traces of all these sad thoughts in the portrait of Luther when dead, which Zimmer, of Heidelberg, has in his collection. There is in the portrait, moreover, the unquestionable expression of long-continued and strenuous effort for some cherished object.

During the last two or three years of his life, his enemies from time to time spread abroad a rumour that he was dead, colouring the rumour, moreover, with circumstances of a most extraordinary and tragical description. To put an end to this annoyance, Luther, in 1545, printed in German and Italian, a pamphlet entitled: *Lies of the Italians, touching the alleged death of Martin Luther.*

"I said long ago to Dr. Pomer, that he who after my death shall slight the authority of this school and this church, must be regarded in no other light than as a perverse-minded man and a heretic. For it was in this school that God purified his word, and made a new revelation of it. Twenty-five years ago, who could do anything at all in the way of freedom and faith? Twenty-one years ago, how many were there standing at my side? None."

"I reckon up the progress of things from time to time, and I find that we are getting very near to the close of the forty years, at the expiration of which, according to my calculations, all this will have a final end. St. Paul preached only forty years, and 'twas the same with Jeremiah and St. Augustine. In all these cases, on the termination of the forty years respectively during which the word of God had been preached, the word ceased to be heard, and great calamities immediately ensued."[1]

The electress dowager, one day when Luther was dining with her, said to him: "Doctor, I wish you may live forty years to come." "Madam," replied he, "rather than live forty years more, I would give up my chance of Paradise. I have ceased consulting the physicians. They tell me I am to live another year—so, meantime, I shall get on as well as I may, and make myself as comfortable, eating and drinking whatever I fancy.[2]

"I would to God our adversaries would kill me by some violence, for my death at their hands would be far more useful to the church than my life."[3]

On the 16th of February, 1546, during his last visit to Eisleben, the conversation having turned upon sickness and death, Luther said: "If I get back to Wittemberg, I will take to good eating and drinking, so that the worms may have a fine fat doctor to devour."

[1] Tischcreden, 416. [2] Ib. 361. [3] Ib. 147.

Two days after this, on the 18th of February, 1546, Martin Luther died at Eisleben.[1]

. . . . We may here insert an impromptu of Luther's on the frailty of life:

> "Dat vitrum vitro Jonæ (vitrum ipse) Lutherus,
> Se similem ut fragili noscat uterque vitro."[2]

We retain this couplet in its original language, for it would lose whatever merit it possesses by translation.

The following notes upon various subjects were written by Luther at Eisleben, two days before his death: "No man can thoroughly understand Virgil's *Bucolics* who has not been five years engaged in the raising of cattle and sheep. No person can appreciate Virgil's *Georgics* who has not been five years engaged in the cultivation of the earth. No person can comprehend Cicero's Letters, who has not for twenty years been mixed up with state affairs.

"Let no person imagine that he has a thorough appreciation of the Holy Scriptures who has not for a hundred years governed the churches with the prophets Elias and Elijah, with John the Baptist, Christ, and the Apostles.

"*Hanc tu ne divinam Æneida tentas, sed vestigia pronus adora.*[3]

'We are wretched beggars, one of another, from beginning to end. *Hoc est verum*, 16th Februarii, Anno 1546."

. . . . *Prediction of the reverend father, doctor Martin Luther, written in his own hand, and found after his death*

[1] Tischreden, 362. [2] Ib. 358.

[3] We find Luther on one occasion, however, essaying, not, indeed, an emulation of the Æneid, but a parody upon some lines in it. "Notwithstanding the gravity of his cause," observes Mr. Roscoe, in his *Life of Leo X.*, "Luther was sometimes sarcastically jocular, and a parody of his on the first lines of the Æneid, while it shows that he was not unacquainted with profane writers, contains an additional proof of his endeavours to mark his enemies as the enemies of all improvement." The verse in question, a Satire upon Cochlæus, run thus:—

> Arma viramque cano, Mogani qui nuper ab oris,
> Liucoream, fato stolidus, Saxonaque venit
> Littora; multum ille et furiis vexatus ab æstro,
> Vi scelerum, memorem Rasorum cladis ob iram;
> Multaquoque et Satana passus, quo perderet urbem,
> Inferretque malum studiis, genus unde malorum
> Errorumque Patres, atque Alti gloria Papæ.

in his library, by those whom the most illustrious John Frederic I., elector of Saxony, had ordered to examine the doctor's books and papers.

"The time has come when, on the authority of ancient prediction, there will present themselves, after the revelation of antichrist, men who will live without God, each according to his own desires and his own illusions. Not long since the pope was a god, above God; now everybody is disposed to dispense with any god at all, and the papists more especially; though, unhappily, our own people, for the most part, now that they are emancipated from the laws of the pope, desire to be so also from the law of God, to follow only their own changeable policy, and to follow even this only as it may suit their caprices. We imagine that the persons to whom the before cited prediction applies, are still far off, whereas it applies to ourselves, to the present generation. There are amongst those who desire rule in this world, men who have begun to expel from the church the decalogue and the law. One of these is Maître Eisleben, (Agricola) . . . . . . I am very apprehensive of the papists; they are flattering up the pope, ostensibly out of hatred to us, but in reality to achieve power for themselves, until eventually they will become formidable to the miserable pope himself. . . . . . I feel greatly consoled when I see the flatterers of the pope laying snares for him infinitely more dangerous than any that I, his declared enemy, ever set for him. . . . . 'Tis the same with our people, who give me greater trouble and uneasiness, and threaten me with greater dangers than all popery put together; for as to popery it can never again do us any harm. . . . How true it is, that if an empire is to be destroyed, it can only be so by turning its own weapons against itself. Look at Rome:

> "Mole ruit suâ . . . . . .
> . . . Corpus magnum populumque potentem
> In sua victrici conversum viscera dextrâ."[1]

Towards the close of his life, Luther had conceived a distaste for Wittemberg as a place of residence. In July, 1545, he wrote to his wife from Leipzig, where he was staying at the time: "Grace and peace to thee, dear Catherine. Our John will tell thee how we got here. Ernst von Schonfeldt

[1] Opera Latina (1612.)

received us very well at Lobnitz, and our friend Scherle received us even still better here. I have a great desire so to arrange matters as not to return to Wittemberg. My heart is cooled towards that town, and I no longer like to reside there. I would, therefore, have you sell the smaller house, with the court and garden, (the large house I shall return to our gracious master, who made me a present of it), and we will then establish ourselves at Zeilsdorf. With my salary, we may put our farm into good order, for I suppose my lord will not refuse to continue it in my hands, at least for this next year, which I firmly believe will be the last of my life. Wittemberg has become a perfect Sodom, and I will never return thither. The day after to-morrow I am going to Merseburg, on the earnest invitation of count George. I would much rather spend my remnant of life travelling about in this way, or even begging my bread, than have my poor last days afflicted with beholding the wickedness of Wittemberg, and the reflection constantly recurring that all my pains, all my labour, have been utterly thrown away upon that reprobate place. You may make Philip and Pomer acquainted with my intention, and ask them to give the town one more blessing in my name. I myself will never again see it."

Luther was so fixed in this resolution, that it required the most urgent entreaties on the part of his friends, of the whole body of the academy, of the elector himself, to induce him to renounce it. He did, however, yield, and returned to Wittemberg on the 18th of August.

It was destined that Luther's should be a life of labour and excitement to its very close; well nigh his last days were occupied in the difficult and delicate task of bringing about a reconciliation between the counts of Mansfeldt, of whom, by birth he was the vassal. "A week, more or less," he writes to count Albert, who had asked him to come to Eisleben, as arbiter, "a week, more or less, will not stop me from coming, though truly I am very much occupied with other affairs. But I feel that I shall lie down on my death-bed with joy, when I have seen my dear lords reconciled and once more friends." (6th December, 1545.)

On his arrival he wrote thus to his wife: "To the very

[1] See Appendix CXX.

learned and deeply profound dame Catherine Luther, my most gracious spouse.—Dear Catherine, we are terribly annoyed here in one way and another, and would willingly return home, but I think we shall have to remain a full week longer. You may tell Maître Philip from me, that he would do well to revise his notes on the Gospel; for he does not seem, in writing them, to have rightly understood why our Lord, in the parable, calls riches thorns. This is the school in which we really learn these things. The Scripture throughout menaces thorns with the eternal fire; this at once alarms me, and gives me patience with life, for I must exercise my utmost powers in settling this matter, by God's aid." . . . (6th February, 1546.)

"To the gracious dame Catherine Luther, my dear spouse, who is tormenting herself quite unnecessarily. Grace and peace in our Lord Jesus Christ.—Dear Catherine, thou shouldst read St. John, and what the catechism says respecting the confidence we ought to have in God. Thou afflictest thyself just as though God were not all-powerful, and able to raise up new doctor Martins by dozens, if the old doctor Martin were to be drowned in the Saale, or perish in any other way. There is One who takes care of me in his own manner, better than thou and all the angels could ever do: He sits by the side of the almighty Father. Tranquillize thyself, then. Amen. . . . I had intended this very day to depart *in my anger*, but the affliction in which I see my native place involved, still detains me. Would you believe it? I am become a lawyer! I doubt, however, whether I shall do much good in that line; they had much better let me exercise my own profession. It were a great blessing for these people, if I could succeed in humbling their arrogant pride. They speak and act as though they were gods, but I fear they will rather become devils, if they continue in their present course. They should bear in mind that it was by pride the angels fell. Hand this letter to Philip; I have no time to write separately to him." (7th February, 1546.)

"To my sweet wife, Catherine Luther Von Bora. Grace and peace in the Lord. Dear Catherine,—we hope to be with you again this week, if it please God. The Almighty has manifested the power of his grace in this affair. The lords have come to an agreement upon all the points in dispute, except two or three; and, among other great ends achieved, counts Gebhard and Albert are reconciled. I am to dine with them to-day, and will endeavour, before we separate, to make them once more brothers. They have written against each other with great bitterness, and, during the conferences, have not as yet interchanged a single word. . . . Our young nobles are all gaiety now; they drive the ladies out in sledges, and make the horses' bells jingle to a pretty tune. God has fulfilled our prayers.

"I send thee some trout that countess Albert has given me. This lady is full of joy at seeing peace re-established in her family. There is a rumour current here, that the emperor is advancing towards Westphalia, and that the French are enlisting lanzknecht, as well as the landgrave, &c., &c. Let them go on with their news,—true or false, it matters little which: we await in patience God's declaration of his will. I commend thee to his protection. Martin Luther. 14th February, 1546."

Luther had arrived at Eisleben on 28th January, and, although very ill, he took part in the conferences which ensued, up to 17th February. He also preached four times, and revised the ecclesiastical regulations for the territory of Mansfeldt. On the 17th he was so ill that the counts entreated him not to quit his house. At supper, on the same day, he spoke a great deal about his approaching death; and some one having asked him whether we should recognise one another in the next world, he said he thought we should. On retiring to his chamber, accompanied by maître Cælius and his two sons, he went to the window, and remained there for a considerable time, engaged in silent prayer. Aurifaber then entered the chamber, to whom he said: "I feel very weak, and my pains are worse than ever." They gave him a soothing draught, and endeavoured to increase the circulation by friction. He then addressed a few words to count Albert, who had joined him, and laid down on the bed, saying, "If I could manage to sleep for a half hour, I think it would do me good." He did fall asleep, and remained in gentle slumber for an hour and a half. On awaking about eleven, he said to those present, "What! are you still there? will you not go, dear friends, and rest yourselves?" On their replying that they would remain with him, he began to pray, saying with fervour: *In manus tuas commendo spiritum meum; redemisti me, Domine, Deus veritatis.*"[1] He then said to those present, "Pray, all of you, dear friends, for the gospel of our Lord; pray that its reign may extend, for the Council of Trent and the pope menace it round about." He then fell asleep again for about an hour. When he awoke, Dr. Jonas asked him how he felt. "O my God!" he replied, "I feel very ill. My dear Jonas, I think I shall remain here at Eisleben, here, where I was born." He took a turn or two in the room, and then lay down again, and had a number of clothes and cushions placed upon him to produce perspiration. Two physicians, with the count and his wife, entered the chamber. Luther said to them, feebly: "Friends, I am dying; I shall remain with you here at Eisleben." Doctor Jonas expressing a hope that perspiration would, perhaps, supervene, and relieve him: "No, dear Jonas," he replied, "I feel no wholesome perspiration, but a cold, dry sweat; I get worse and worse every instant." He then began praying again: "O my father, thou, the God of our Lord Jesus Christ, thou, the source of all consolation, I thank thee for having revealed unto me thy well beloved Son, in whom I believe, whom I have preached, and acknowledged, and made known; whom I have loved and celebrated, and whom the pope and the impious persecute. I commend my soul to thee, O my Lord Jesus Christ! I am about to quit this terrestrial body, I am about to be removed from this life, but I know that I shall abide eternally with thee." He then thrice repeated: *In manus tuas commendo spiritum meum; redemisti me, Domine, Deus veritatis!* All at once his eyes closed, and he fell back in a swoon. Count Albert, and his wife, and the physicians, made every effort to restore him to life, but for some time, altogether in vain. When he was somewhat revived, Dr. Jonas said to him: "Reverend father, do you die firm in the faith you have taught?" He opened his eyes, which were half closed, looked fixedly at Jonas, and replied, firmly and distinctly: "YES." He then fell asleep; soon after, those nearest him saw him grow paler and paler; he became cold, his breathing was more and more faint: at length, he sent forth one deep sigh, and the great Reformer was dead.[2]

[1] "Into thy hands I commend my spirit: thou hast redeemed me, O Lord God of truth."

[2] See Appendix CXXI.

His body was conveyed, in a leaden coffin, to Wittemberg, where it was interred on the 22nd February with the greatest honours.[1] He sleeps in the castle church, at the foot of the pulpit.[2]

The following is Luther's will, dated 6th January, 1542:—

"I, the undersigned Martin Luther, doctor of divinity, do hereby give and grant unto my dear and faithful wife, Catherine, as dower to be enjoyed by her during her life, at her own will and pleasure, the farm of Zeilsdorf, with all the improvements and additions I have made thereto; the house called *Brun*, which I purchased under the name of Wolff; and all my silver goblets, and other valuables, such as rings, chains, gold and silver medals, &c., to the amount of about a thousand florins.

"I make this disposition of my means, in the first place, because my Catherine has always been a gentle, pious, and faithful wife to me, has loved me tenderly, and has, by the blessing of God, given me, and brought up for me, five children, still, I thank God, living, beside others who are now dead. Secondly, that out of the said means she may discharge my debts, amounting to about four hundred and fifty florins, in the event of my not paying them myself before my death. In the third place, and more especially, because I would not have her dependent on her children, but rather that her children should be dependent on her—honouring her, and submissive to her, according to God's command; and that they should not act as I have seen some children act, whom the devil has excited to disobey the ordinance of God in this respect, more particularly in cases when their mother has become a widow, and they themselves have married. I consider, moreover, that the mother will be the best guardian of these means in behalf of her children, and I feel that she will not abuse this confidence I place in her, to the detriment of those who are her own flesh and blood, whom she has borne in her bosom.

"Whatever may happen to her after my death, (for I cannot foresee the designs of God,) I have, I say, full confidence that she will ever conduct herself as a good mother towards

[1] See Appendix CXXII.

[2] Ukert, i. 327. Derived from the personal narrative of Luther's death, drawn up by Jonas and Cælius.

her children, and will conscientiously share with them whatever she possesses.

"And here I beg all my friends to testify the truth, and to defend my dear Catherine, should it happen as is very possible, that ill tongues should charge her with retaining for her own private use, separate from the children, any money they may say I left concealed. I hereby certify that we have no ready money, no treasure of coin of any description. Nor will it appear surprising to any who shall consider that I have had no income beyond my salary, and a few presents now and then, and that, yet, with this limited revenue, we have built a good deal, and maintained a large establishment. I consider it, indeed, a special favour of God, and I thank him daily, therefore, that we have been able to manage as we have done, and that our debts are not greater than they are. . . .

"I pray my gracious lord, duke John Frederick, elector, to confirm and maintain the present deed, even though it should not be exactly in the form required by the law.[1]

"Signed, MARTIN LUTHER.

"*Witnesses*, MELANCTHON, CRUCIGER, BUGENHAGEN."

[1] See Appendix CXXIII.

APPENDIX.

I. (p. 51.)—The materials for the narrative now under the reader's observation are derived from Luther's letters and other works, Melancthon's Life of Luther, Seckendorf, &c.

II. (p. 59.)—The reader who is desirous of studying the controversy at Leipzig, is referred, besides Luther's own works, to Riederer, *Nachricht zur Kirchengeschichte*, *Menzel*, *Neuere Geschichte der Deutschen*, (vol. i.); Hagenbach, *Vorlesungen*, (vol. i.); Huber, *Vita Mart. Lutheri;* Gretschel, *Leipzig, und seine umgebungen*, &c. &c.

III. (p. 60.)—He was exceedingly violent in his language against his adversaries in the writings he sent forth at this time. Eck is a miserable upstart, puffed up with wind, a *glorianus*, a *gloriensis*, a *gloriosus;* the Lipsians, *asses with doctors' caps* on their heads; Alfeld, who had asserted the supremacy of the pope in a book, "Super Apostolica Sede," is a *bull in head, face, and mouth.*—Audin.

IV.—The Ciceronians of the pontifical court, the Sadoletis, &c., had called all their learning, all their literature into requisition in drawing up the bull of Leo X. Their fine invocation to all the saints to stand forward against Luther, at once calls to mind the famous peroration of Cicero's speech, *De signis*, in which he adjures all the gods to come and testify against Verres, who has outraged their altars. Unfortunately, the pope's secretaries, more intent upon the rhetorical forms of antiquity than upon the history of the church, did not perceive that they were evoking against Luther precisely the apostle on whom he relied as against them. *Ex surge, tuquoque, quæsumus, Paulle, qui Ecclesiam tuâ doctrina illustrasti. Surgit novus Porphyrius......*(Luther *opera lat.* ii. 52.)

Leo X. while condemning in this bull Luther's books, once more offered him a safe conduct to Rome, and promised to pay his expenses.

The universities of Louvain and Cologne approved of the pope's bull, and accordingly drew upon themselves Luther's attacks. He charged them with unjustly condemning Ockham, Pico de la Mirandula, Lorenzo Valla, John Reuchlin. "To weaken the authority of these universities," says Cochlæus, "he was constantly assailing them, even in the books he read, writing in the margin of any of them, when he came across a barbarism or an ill-turned sentence: *lavanialiter* (a Louvain phrase)—*colonialiter* (a Cologne phrase.)

V. (p. 64.)—The next day he preached against the bull, pursuant to notice. The church was crowded. "I burned yesterday," said he, "the Satanic works of the popes. It would have been better had it been the pope himself we had burned, I mean the pontifical see. If you do not break off with Rome, woe to your souls! Let every Christian well reflect that in holding communion with the papists he renounces his eternal salvation. Abomination on the modern Babylon!—While I have a breath in my body, I will cry, abomination!" —AUDIN.

VI. (p. 80.) The following is the original of this noble hymn. The translation appended is derived from *Fraser's Magazine*:

"Ein' feste Burg ist unser Gott,
Ein' gute Wehr und Waffen.
Er hilft uns frei aus aller noht,
Die uns jetzt hat betroffen.
Der alt böse Feind
Mit Ernst er's jetzt meint;
Gross' Macht und viel List
Sein' grausam Rüstung ist'.
Auf Erd' ist nicht seins' Gleichen.

"Mit unser Macht ist nichts gethan,
Wir sind gar bald velohren;
Es streit für uns der rechte Mann,
Den Gott selbst hat erkoren.
Fragst du, wer er ist?
Er heisst Jesus Christ,
Der Herr Zebaoth;
Und ist kein andrer Gott,
Das Feld muss er behalten.

"Und wenn die Welt voll Teufel wär,
Und wollt uns gar verschlingen,
So fürchten wir uns nicht so sehr,
Es soll uns doch gelingen;
Der Fürst dieser welt,
Wie sau'r er sich stellt,
Thut er uns doch nichts;
Das Macht, er ist gericht't.
Ein Wörtlein kann ihn fällen.

"Das Wort sie sollen lassen stehn,
Und kein Dank darzu haben;
Er ist beì uns wohl auf dem Plan
Mit seinem Geist und Gaben.
Nehm'n sie uns den Leib,
Gut, Ehr, Kind und Weib,
Lass fahren dahin,
Sie haben kein Gewinn;
Das Reich muss uns doch bleiben.

TRANSLATION.

"A safe stronghold our God is still,
A trusty shield and weapon;
He'll help us clear from all the ill
That hath us now o'ertaken.
The ancient prince of hell
Hath risen with purpose fell,
Strong mail of craft and power
He weareth in this hour—
On earth is not his fellow.

"With force of arms we nothing can,
Full soon were we down-ridden;
But for us fights the proper Man,
Whom God himself hath bidden.
Ask ye, Who is this same?
Christ Jesus is his name,
The Lord Zeboath's Son,
He and no other one,
Shall conquer in the battle.

"And were this world all devils o'er,
And watching to devour us,
We lay it not to heart so sore,
We know they can't o'erpower us.
And let the prince of ill
Look grim as e'er he will,
He harms us not a whit,
For why? His doom is writ—
A word shall quickly slay him.

"God's word, for all their craft and force,
One moment will not linger,
But, spite of hell, shall have its course,
'Tis written by his finger.
And though they take our life,
Goods, houses, children, wife,
Yet is their profit small,
These things shall vanish all,
The city of God remaineth."

VII. (p. 82.)—The various sources consulted in the preparation of the following narrative of the proceedings, before the Diet of Worms, are, Luther's own works, the account given by Gaspard Ulemberg, Cochlæus, Melancthon's Life of Luther, Roscoe's Life and Pontificate of Leo X. &c. &c.

VIII. (p. 103.)—Several German versions of the Bible had already been published at Nuremberg, in 1477, 1483, 1490; and at Augsburg, in 1518; but they were not adapted for popular reading. "They were not permitted to be read," says Seckendorf, "and were in themselves wholly unsatisfactory, as well with reference to style as to the manner in which they were printed."

Before the end of the 15th century, Germany possessed at least twelve editions of the Bible, in the vernacular tongue, while in Italy there were only two, and in France only one. ["Giacomo de Voragine," says M. Audin, "bishop of Genoa, and author of the Golden Legend, translated the Bible into Italian towards the close of the 13th century. Another version was made at Venice about 1421, by a Camaldolese monk, Nicoli Malermi, or Malerbi; there were nine editions of this translation printed in the 15th century, and twenty in the following century. There was another version by Fra Guido; and in 1530, Brucioli published another translation. In France, Jean Lefevre published a translation of the Bible, at Etaples, in 1523."]

The adversaries of the Reformation themselves contributed to augment the number of Bibles in the vulgar tongue. Jerome Emser, for instance, published a translation of the Scriptures in opposition to that by Luther. Luther's own version was not completed until 1534.

The Institute of Canstein, in Halle, alone printed, in the space of a hundred years, two million Bibles, a million New Testaments, and as many Psalters. (Ukert, ii. 339.)

"I was twenty years old," says Luther himself, "before I had ever seen the Bible. I had no notion that there existed any other gospels or epistles than those in the service. At last, I came across a Bible in the library at Erfurt, and used often to read it to Dr. Staupitz, with still increasing wonder." (Tischreden, 255.)

"Under popery, people knew nothing about the Bible. Carlstadt did not begin to read it till after he had got his doctor's degree, about eight years since." (Tischreden, 6.)

"At the Diet of Augsburg, the bishop of Mayence one day took up the Bible. One of his people coming up to him, said: 'Gracious lord, what is your electoral grace doing with this book? 'I don't know what book it is,' replied he, 'all I know is that what I have been reading in it is clear against us.' Dr. Usinger, an Augustine monk, who was my preceptor at the convent of Erfurt, used to say to me when he saw me reading the Bible with such ardour: "Ah, brother Martin, why trouble yourself with the Bible? Rather read the ancient doctors who have collected together for you all its marrow and honey. The Bible itself is the cause of all our troubles." (Tisch. 7.)

Selneccer, a contemporary with Luther, relates that the monks seeing Martin very busily engaged with the Holy Scriptures, grumbled at him, saying that it was not in occupying himself that way, but in begging and collecting bread, meat, fish, eggs, and money, that he must be useful to their community."

"Formerly, the times were not favourable for study; the heathen Aristotle was held in such honour, that any one who should have ventured to say a word against him would have been condemned at Cologne as a heretic. Not that they understood Aristotle, as how should they, seeing that the sophists had thrown such a veil of mystification over him. I remember a monk, preaching on the subject of the Passion, puddled about for more than two hours in this question: *Whether is, quality in reality distinct from substance?* and by way of illustration he said: '*My head may pass through this hole, but the bigness of my head cannot pass through it.*'" (Tisch. 15.)

"The monks despised such among them as had any pretensions to learning. The brotherhood in my convent used to snarl at me for studying: '*What should you be different from us for?*' asked they. *Sic mihi, sic tibi: saccum per naccum* (with sack round the neck, go begging as we do). They made no sort of distinction among people." (Tisch. 272.)

"Formerly even the most learned of our doctors could not, I will not say compose merely, but even read, a Latin speech. They mixed up with their Latin, such as it was, all sorts of words, not German or anything else." (Tisch. 15.)

This ignorance on the part of the clergy was general throughout Europe. In 1530, a French monk said from the pulpit: 'They have found out a new language, called Greek; we must carefully guard ourselves against it. That language will be the mother of all sorts of heresies. I see in the hands of a great number of persons a book written in this language, called *the New Testament;* it is a book full of brambles with vipers in them. As to the Hebrew, whoever learns that becomes a Jew at once." (Sismondi, H. des Francais, xvi. 364.)

VI.* (page 113.)—On the 3rd of December, 1521, during the celebration of divine service in the parish church at Wittemberg, a number of young men rose up at a given signal, and, while some of them drawing their knives, cut up the mass-books, the rest violently ejected the priest from the church. Some of these young men were arrested, but the senate was obliged to dismiss them again, on the demand of a great crowd who surrounded the senate house.... Carlstadt was foremost among the revolters against authority. On Christmas day, he utterly threw aside the accustomed forms, and shortly afterwards putting in practice the theory of his pupil Martin, married a woman of equivocal character, and drew up a mass to be celebrated on the occasion of future marriages of persons situated like himself. The disorder extended itself to various parts of Germany.—AUDIN.

VII. ([b]p. 114.)—The three men who assumed a more prominent position among these prophets were Mark Stubner, a man of considerable literary ability; Nicholas or Claus Storch, of Zwichau, a tailor; and Munzer, formerly pastor of Alstet or Alstaedt, in Thuringia.—AUDIN.

VIII. ([b] p. 116.)—No longer subject to the influence of the searching eyes now hidden by the walls of Wartburg, the flock at Wittemberg, or at least some of the more daring disciples, determined to sound the mystery of the Lutheran idea. This was to be expected; they treated Luther as he had treated authority, they returned him doubt for doubt, abrogation for abrogation, and sought to separate from him in virtue of the very principle which he had himself asserted.—AUDIN.

IX. (p. 116.)—"What," asks Arnold, "what had Luther to reproach Carlstadt with? He had married a wife, indeed, but Luther had inculcated marriage. He had taken violent measures against the mass; but how many times had not Luther denounced the mass as an invention of the devil! He had overthrown images, but more than once, even from Wartburg itself, Luther had thundered against them."—AUDIN.

X. (p. 116.)—"Luther," it is M. Audin who speaks: "Luther was now undergoing the penalty for his revolt against authority; around him, he saw nothing but deception, doubt, scepticism; the glove he had cast down against authority was now thrown at him by his own people, and he was compelled to accept the challenge. It must have been a solemn sight to have looked upon him as he sat at his window in the castle at Wartburg, his mental eye fixed upon the tempest at Wittemberg, which even his powerful voice could not reach, and murmuring painfully forth his songs of grief and despondency at seeing himself abandoned by his disciples, by his old master. 'Rods, rods!' he cries, 'for the mutinous school-boys, who, defying their master, are tearing up their books.' The scholars reply coolly: 'It is written in St. Matthew, *neither be ye called masters*.'—'Direct Carlstadt to spare the images. Carlstadt replies: '*Thou shalt not make unto thyself any graven image*.'—'Baptize that infant,' he enjoins Didymus; but Didymus answers: '*He that believes and is baptized, the same shall enter into the kingdom of heaven*. Very true, but this infant does not believe!'—'Read, poor wretch, read what the church tells thee;' and Carlstadt, and Didymus, and Storch answer in chorus: 'Pope! know you not there is no authority but that of the Bible, no light but that of the Holy Ghost; 'tis to these we adhere.' 'You shall not see the face of the Lord!' exclaims Luther, and the prophets laugh him in the face."

XI. (p. 120.) By an order of the elector, Munzer and his adherents were directed to quit the electorate forthwith. Munzer made his hostile adieu to Luther like a regular Parthian, turning round and hurling at him a tract in which he made Martin out to be *Satan*. Carlstadt, on taking his departure, exclaimed: 'Condemned by my own people, without having been heard.'—Audin.

XII. (p. 122.)—*Charitable exhortation of doctor Martin Luther to all Christians, that they preserve themselves from the spirit of disorder and revolt.* (1524.)

"... In the first place, I pray you to lay aside my name, and no longer to call yourselves Lutherans, but Christians. Who is Luther or what? My doctrine comes not from myself. I have not been crucified for the world. St. Paul desired the people (1 Cor. iii.) not to call themselves Paulians, or Peterians, but Christians. How then would it become me, poor scum of the earth, to give my name to the children of Christ? Cease, dear friends, to assume these party names; let us lay them all aside, and call ourselves Christians, after him from whom our doctrine proceeds.

"It is just and right, indeed, that the papists should have a party name, because they do not content themselves with the doctrine and name of Jesus Christ, but desire, moreover, to be papists. Well, let them belong to the pope, who is their master. I neither am nor desire to be the master of one. I and mine simply wish to maintain the one and common doctrine — our one and common master." (Werke, ii. 4.)

XIII. (p. 122.)—The reader, if he desires to investigate the movement of ideas in Germany in 1522, may consult, among other books: Ulrichi de Hutten, Equitis Germ. Ad Carolum Imp. adversus intentatam sibi à Romanistis vim et injuriam. Conquestio ejusdem ad Albertum Brandenburgensem, et Fredericum, Saxonum Ducem. De Interdata esu carnum. Epistola Apologetica Erasmi, Rot. Pasquilus, sive Dialogus de Statu Romano.

XIV. (p. 123.)—*Assertio Septem Sacramentorum adversus Martinum Luterum.* The first edition of the book appeared in London, *In Ædibus Pynsonianis*, 1521. It was reprinted at Antwerp, in 1522. (In Ædibus Michaelis Hillenii.)

XV. (p. 123.)—At the same time that he so fiercely maltreated Henry VIII. and the princes, he passed all bounds in his attacks upon the holy see. His reply to the brief of pope Adrian VI. concludes thus: "I am sorry to be obliged to write so much good German upon this miserable kitchen-Latin of theirs. But God wills to confound antichrist in all things, leaving him nothing whatever—

art, learning, or language; he may really be said to be a mere drivelling idiot, quite in his second childhood. It is a shame to address us Germans in such wretched Latin, to present to people in their ordinary senses so bald and absurd an interpretation of the Scriptures." (1523.)

We take the following from Luther's preface to his observations upon two bulls, wherein Clement II. announced the celebration of the jubilee for 1525.

". . . . The pope says in his bull, that he will open *the golden gate*. We have for many a long year opened all our gates in Germany, but the Italian swindlers don't bring us back a farthing of the money they have robbed us of by their *indulgences* and *dispensations*, and other inventions of the devil. Worthy pope Clement, all your smooth words wont serve your turn here. We buy no more of your indulgences, rely upon that. Dear *golden gate*, beloved *bulls*, return whence you came; get the Italians to pay you. We, who know your true value, wont have you at any price. We here feel, thanks be to God therefore, that all they who hear and believe in the Holy Gospel, hold jubilee every hour of the year. . . . Dear pope, what think you we want with your bulls? Spare your lead and your parchment; they are quite thrown away upon us." (Werke, ix. 204.)

" I should like to make the pope and his cardinals into a bundle, and throw them all together, into that little ditch of a Tuscan sea of theirs. 'Tis a bath would do them good, I'll answer for it, and so will Jesus."

" My little Paul, my little pope, my little donkey, take care how you go; it's very slippery. If you don't mind, you'll fall and break a leg or so, and then the folks will say: What the devil's this—why the poor popelet has hurt himself!"

Explanation of the Monk-calf, and of two horrible Popish Monsters found in the Tiber, at Rome, in 1496. *Published at Friburg, in Misnia*, 1523, by *P. Melancthon and Martin Luther.*—" At all times, God has manifested, as with his finger, his anger and his mercy, and by miraculous signs announced to men the overthrow, the ruin, or the splendour of empires, as we see in Daniel, viii.

" During the pestilential domination of popery, he multiplied these signs of anger, and, but recently, has, in that horrible figure of the pope-ass, found in the Tiber, given so exact a representation of the papacy, that no human hand could have traced a closer resemblance.

" And first, there is the ass's head, which so well indicates the pope. The church is a spiritual body, which can rightly have no visible head or other member, but only Christ himself as Mediator, Lord, and Master. The Holy Scriptures illustrate by the ass, an irregular and carnal life, Exodus, xiii. And just as the brain of an ass differs from the intellect of man, so is the papal doctrine remote from the doctrine of Christ. Thus, ass's head, according to the Scripture, ass's head, according to the interpretation of natural law, and the light of reason, as is shown by the imperial priests, who say, a mere canonist, a mere ass.

" *The right hand resembling the foot of an elephant*, signifies the spiritual power of the pope, wherewith he bruises and breaks trembling consciences, in like manner as the elephant seizes, tears, and crushes its victims. For is popery anything else than a murderous immolation of consciences, by means of confession, vows, celibacy, masses, feigned penitence, indulgence-trickstering, the superstitious worship of saints; as Daniel says: *He shall kill the saints.*

" *The left hand of a man*, means the political power which the pope has arrogated, despite Christ's prohibition (Luke, xxii.); but which antichrist has seized upon, by help of the devil, in order to make himself master of kings and princes.

" *The right foot ending in a bull's hoof*, means the spiritual members of popery. The *bajuli* who aid and assist in the oppression of men's souls; the catholic doctors, preachers, confessors, the mob of monks and nuns, and above all, the scholastic theologians, that race of vipers, who insinuate and filter into the people the prescripts and ordinances of popery, and chain down consciences captive beneath the foot of the elephant; the very basis and foundation of papism, which without them would never have been able to subsist as long as it has. For what does the scholastic theology comprehend but insane, wild, foolish, execrable, Satanic, maddening dreams, monks' reveries, of no use but to trouble, fascinate, set to sleep, and destroy men's souls?

" *The left foot that of a griffin*, indicates the ministers of the pope's temporal power—namely, the canonists. When the griffin has got a victim in its claw, it keeps good hold of it; in the same way, these satellites of the pope, when, by means of their long canonical hooks, they have clawed hold of our property, take care not to let it go again.

" *The breast of a woman* means the papal *corps*—that is to say, the cardinals, bishops, priests, monks, the saints, and martyrs of the Roman calendar, the whole race of roaring lions and Epicurean pigs, who go about seeking what they may devour, eating and swilling, and shamelessly indulging in all sorts of filthy obscenity.

" *Fishes' scales on the arms, feet, and neck*, indicate the temporal princes and lords who obey this domination, united and folding over popery as the scales upon fish, though they know well enough the monstrous sins of popery, its horrible tyranny.

The head of an old man partly attached to the left thigh, implies the old age, the decline and fall of the papal kingdom. And, thank God, the base farce is well nigh over!

"*The eyes full of adultery*, and *the heart full of avarice*: these sons of malediction have abandoned the right path to follow Balaam; they will realize the reward of their iniquity."

XVI. (p. 129.)—"It is not surprising that our princes should merely see what they can get out of the new gospel as present profits. They are the mighty hunters of old revived. The light come upon us, enables us to see the world as it really is: the kingdom of Satan." (1524.)

XVII. (p. 130.)—Already depression and discouragement begin occasionally to manifest themselves in Luther's writings. This same year, 1523, in August, we find him writing thus to the imperial lieutenants, at the diet of Nuremberg: "It appears to me, also, that by the terms of the imperial mandate, issued in March last, I ought to be relieved from the ban and excommunication formerly directed against me, until the sitting of the next council; otherwise I do not understand what can be the meaning of the postponement, of which special mention is made in the said mandate; for I, on my part, consent to observe the conditions on which that postponement is granted.... However, it matters very little. My life is of small importance to myself or to any one else. The world has had enough of me, and I of it. But at least, dear lords, take pity on the poor people; it is in their name I entreat you to listen to me."... He proceeds to request that they would execute with leniency the imperial edict relative to the punishment of clergymen who should marry or quit their respective orders.

XVIII. (p. 138.)—As soon as Luther felt the necessity of introducing somewhat of order and regularity into the new church, when he found himself called upon every day to act as judge in matrimonial causes, to decide upon questions affecting the relationship of the church with the laity, he began to study the canon law. "In this marriage matter," he writes, on the 30th March, 1529, "which I mentioned to you had been brought before me, I decided according to the pope's own decretals. I have begun to read the regulations of the papists on these and similar subjects, and I find that they do not themselves observe them." .... "I would give my left hand to have the papists compelled to carry out their canon law; they would then be fiercer against it than against Luther."... "The decretals resemble a monster; the head that of a young girl, the body that of a devouring lion, the tail that of a serpent. They are all lies and deception from beginning to end—just like popery altogether." (Tischreden, p. 277.)

XIX. (p. 138.)—*Instructions to the Minister at Wittemberg.*—Dismiss all unworthy priests. Abrogate all venal masses and vigils. In the morning, instead of a mass *Te Deum*, a reading, and brief exhortation. In the afternoon, reading and commentary; after supper, compline. Let only one mass be celebrated, and that merely on Sundays and festivals." (Briefe, 19th August, 1523.)

In 1520, he published a catechism. Ten years later, however, he sent forth another, in which he only retained baptism and communion. Confession was omitted, the penitent being called upon instead to have frequent recourse to the experience of their minister, in the way of advice.

In order to relieve ministers from dependence on the civil authority, he was in favour of retaining tithes. "It seems to me," he writes on the 15th of June, 1524, "that tithes are the fairest thing in the world. Would to God that, all other taxes being abolished, there only remained tenths, or even ninths or eighths! Why, the Egyptians gave only a fifth, and yet their priests managed to live very well. We, forsooth, can't live upon tenths; but then we are heavily laden with charges."—"All ministers and preachers who conduct themselves discreditably, should be at once deposed and imprisoned. The elector has resolved to build a prison for such offenders.". . . . The doctor afterwards spoke of John Sturm, whom he had often visited when confined in the castle of Wittemberg, and who persisted in his belief, that Christ died only by way of example. He was, in consequence of his obstinacy, removed to the castle of Schwnitz, where he died." (Tischreden, 196.) Luther said that the anabaptists ought not to be punished with death, unless they coupled sedition with their religious errors. (Ib. 298.)

XX. (p. 140.)—The commission which the elector, on the recommendation of Luther, appointed in 1528, for the inspection of schools, consisted of doctor Jerome Schurff, the seigneur John Von Plaunitz, Asma Von Haubitz, and Melancthon.

In the instructions which the commission subsequently addressed to the various ministers of the electorate, with the sanction of Luther, we observe the following passage: "There are some who say that we ought not to defend the faith by the sword, but that we ought patiently to suffer all things, even as Jesus Christ and his apostles suffered all things. To this the reply is, that although persons not in rule should, as individuals, submit to suffer, and have no right to defend themselves against oppression, yet, on the other hand, authority is charged with the protection of its subjects against all violence and injustice, whether this violence and injustice have a religious source, or otherwise." (Werke, ix. 263.)

In 1527, the prince forwarded to Luther the reports of the commissioners, respecting the state of the churches, desiring to know from him whether they should be printed. (19th August, 1527.) "The prince replied to the university, that he wished the visitation of the parishes to be completed as soon as possible, in order that all these matters may be examined, and the churches constituted, that there may be the means of inflicting excommunication where necessary." (10th January, 1527.)

XXI. (p. 144.)—"In his treatise, *De Vitanda hominum doctrinâ*, he says of the bishops and dignitaries of the church: 'Let these frontless and lascivious men, who have ever in their mouths, and no where else: *Christianity! Christianity!* let them fully understand that it was with reference to them I wrote, touching the necessity of not abstaining from meat, of discontinuing confession, and doing away with images; as for them, I regard them as the impure ones who made foul the camp of Israel. My purpose in writing these things was to set free the captive consciences of the unhappy monks and nuns who yearned to lay aside their vows, but knew not whether they could do so without sin." (Seckendorf, 1, 56.)

To Spalatin he writes, 2nd January, 1523: "If you do not already know it, I can tell you that all the priests here pass the most scandalous lives; hardened in heart, despisers of God and man, they spend well nigh every night with abandoned women. . . . I have declared distinctly, that if we ourselves tolerate them in their impiety, the civil magistrate is bound to take notice of their conduct, and if they will not amend it, if the power of the flesh is so strong in them, they must marry. . . . You were saying, the other day, that you feared the elector could not be accused of openly favouring married priests."

To Wolfgang Reissenbach, preceptor at Lichtenberg, (27th March, 1525) . . . "My dear friend, let us not aim at flying too high, and let us not pretend to do better than did Abraham, David, Isaiah, St. Peter, St. Paul, and all the other patriarchs, prophets, and apostles, and many holy martyrs and bishops, who have all acknowledged without any shame, that they were men created by God, and that, faithful to his word, they did not remain alone. He who is ashamed of marriage. is ashamed to be man. We cannot make ourselves other than God willed we should be. Children of Adam ourselves, it is our duty to leave children behind us. Madness! we see every day of our lives how difficult it is to remain chaste, even in the married state; and yet we prohibit marriage. We try God beyond all measure, by these insane vows, and prepare the way for ourselves to Satan."

XXII. (p. 148.)—To Frederic of Nuremberg he writes: "You will do me the justice to believe, that my having so long delayed to congratulate you on your marriage is solely referable to my extensive occupation. What with my weak health, with so many books to publish, so many letters to send and to answer, so many matters to discuss and arrange, so many duties to fulfil towards my friends in one way and another, I can assure you I feel perfectly overwhelmed. I write this at supper, and in great haste. You will pardon my brevity; partly, on account of the supper; partly, on account of my wanting to join in the conversation going on around me; but not, I promise you, owing to my having drunk too much."

Amidst this multiplicity of affairs, he continued to keep up a tolerably regular correspondence with king Christian II. He says to Spalatin, (27th March, 1526): "I have had nobody to send them by, or I would before this have transmitted to you the last letters I have received from king Christian, the very unhappiest of men, I verily believe, and who seems to live only for Christ's sake." To Melancthon, he writes: "There is nothing new, except a letter from king Christian, addressed to us both, and in which he has sent us a silver goblet each. He entreats us not to credit those who describe him as a deserter from the gospel." (Nov. 1540.)

He had still to watch, with unremitting vigilance, over the interests of the reformers throughout Germany. For instance, the protestant parish of Miltenburg, in Franconia, was oppressed by the officer of the elector of Mayence, who cut off all correspondence between the parishioners and that city, whereupon Luther addressed a letter of consolation to his oppressed flock, which he had printed, in order that he might secure its reaching them, and at the same time sent word of the case to the elector, and asked him whether or no his officers were acting under his authority in the matter? (14th February, 1524.)

XXIII. (page 148.)—Carlstadt was canon and archdeacon of the collegiate church of All Saints; he was dean of it, when Luther took his doctor's degree, in 1512. (Seckendorf, i. 72.)

XXIV. (p. 148.)—*Letter of Dr. Martin Luther to the Christians of Antwerp*......"So long as the reign of the pope endured, we used to think that the noisy, disorderly spirits which used to be heard sometimes in the night, were the souls of men, which, in expiation of their sins, had to return to earth at certain times, and wander about. This error of ours has, we thank God, been cleared away by means of the Gospel, and we now know that they are not the spirits of men, but malignant and malicious devils, deceiving men by fallacious answers. It is they who have filled the world with such idolatries.

"The devil, seeing that this sort of confusion no longer serves his purpose, has devised another plan; he infuses into his limbs—I mean hereby the wicked ones of the earth—an insane excitement, by which he seeks to make way for all kinds of chimerical vanities and extravagant doctrines. One of his agents, thus acted upon, will have no more baptizing; a second denies the efficacy of the Eucharist; a third favours another world intervening between the present world and the day of judgment; others teach that Jesus Christ is not God; some say one thing, some another, until at last we shall have as many sects and faiths as there are men and women.

"I must give you an example in point, for I have to do with a great number of these worthies, every one of whom sets up to be wiser than Luther, every one of whom seeks to gain his spurs against

Luther. And, so far, would they were what they pretend to be, and that I were nothing. However, to proceed with the example I spoke of. This man assured me, amongst other things, that he had been sent to me by the God who created heaven and earth, about whom he proceeded to deliver sundry very fine things, but the clown was apparent in all he said.

"At last, he ordered me to read to him the books of Moses. I asked him for some sign confirming the alleged order. 'It is,' says he, 'written in the Gospel of St. John.' This clenched the matter, and having now had more than enough of him, I told him to go away, and come, if he liked, some other day, but that, at that moment, I had not time to read the books of Moses to him."

......"I have to listen to the absurdities of no end of these poor people, during the year. The devil comes nearer me in them than under any other form. Hitherto the world was full of these noisy spirits, without bodies, which gave themselves out to be the souls of departed men, but now they have put on bodies, and represent themselves as living angels.

"'During the pope's reign,' say they, 'no one ever heard of these disorders, this confusion.' No: for then the devil kept at home, quite secure in the exertions of the pope; but now that a stronger than he has come forward, who prevails against him and drives him off, the devil storms, and rages, and struggles.

"Dear friends, there has come among you one of these spirits of disorder, which have assumed the human form. He seeks to lead you astray by the inventions of his wicked pride; do you beware of him.

"*First*, he says that every man has the Holy Ghost within him; for that, *secondly*, the Holy Ghost is nothing else but our reason and our understanding; *thirdly*, he affirms that every man has faith; *fourthly*, that there is no such place as hell, or, at all events, that the flesh alone will be damned; *fifthly*, that every soul will enjoy eternal life; *sixthly*, that natural instinct of itself teaches us to do unto our neighbour that which we desire he should do unto us. This, say they, is faith; *seventhly*, that the law is not violated by concupiscence, provided the mind does not consent; *eighthly*, that he who has not the Holy Ghost, is also without sin, for he is without reason.

"All these are audacious and monstrous propositions, vain products of a diseased imagination. There is only one among them, the seventh, which is worthy of any answer whatever......

"It is sufficient for us to know that God desires we should not sin. As to seeking in what manner he may permit or will us to sin, that is a point which we should not even touch upon. A servant must not attempt to fathom the secrets of his master, but content himself with simply obeying his orders; how much less ought the poor creature man seek to scrutinize and sound the depths of the majesty and mystery of his God!

"We have enough to do, in this life of ours, to know the law of God, and learn his son Jesus Christ. (1525, Werke, ii. 61.)

XXV. (p. 149.)—Carlstadt had joined the insurgents in Franconia, but quitted them at the first cannon shot, and returned to his pamphleteering. To cover paper was his vocation, to throw ink at Luther or his disciples, his pastime and delight. He wrote night and day, and himself printed the lucubrations of his diseased brain. He had just now published two dissertations against the doctrines of the school of Wittemberg; the one 'on sin,' the other 'on Christian resignation.'—AUDIN.

XXVI. (p. 151.)—Carlstadt, in one of these disputes, cited Luther to the Last Judgment.—"When we were at the inn, discussing these matters, after he had undertaken to defend his doctrine to the very bottom, all at once he turned round upon me, and, cracking his fingers, exclaimed, 'I scorn you.' Now, if he scorn me, whom amongst us does he estimate more highly? It is not worth while to dispute with such a man. I have always thought that he regarded me as one of the most learned men in Wittemberg, yet here he says in my very teeth, *I scorn you.* How, after this, can one have faith in the sincerity of his statement, that he desires to be instructed?"—"Carlstadt used to dress himself at Orlamund with ostentatious simplicity. He would not allow people to call him *doctor*, he was only *brother Andrew*, *cousin Andrew*, forsooth! He placed himself, too, formally, under the jurisdiction of the magistrate of the little town, in order to be, said he, 'entirely on a footing with the other townsfolk.'" (Werke ii. 18.)

XXVII. (p. 151.)—*Carlstadt:* "Will you dispute with me at Erfurt; a friendly discussion after supper? or at Wittemberg, if you like. I do not fear the light of day; all I require is a guarantee for my personal safety."—*Luther:* "What should you fear? You'll be perfectly safe at Wittemberg."—*Carlstadt:* "I'm not clear about that. In a public dispute, we must get to high words; and I know, to my cost, that you have managed to make the people attached to you."—*Luther:* "No one shall hurt you, doctor, I give you my word."—*Carlstadt:* "Well, then, I will dispute with you in public, and will manifest the truth of God or my own disgrace."—*Luther:* "Manifest your own absurdity, doctor."—*Carlstadt:* "If I come to shame, at least it will be in the attempt to glorify the Lord."—*Luther:* "The shame shall come upon you, and heavily too. I like your menaces, i' faith. Who fears you, I wonder!"—*Carlstadt:* "And I, then: whom should I fear? My doctrine is pure; it comes from the Lord."—*Luther:* "If it comes from the Lord, how is it you could not infuse into your hearers the spirit which led you to break images at Wittemberg?"—*Carlstadt:* "That was a work which not I alone undertook; it was entered upon by authority of a resolution of the senate, and with the aid of your own disciples, who fled at the moment of danger."—*Luther:* "That's a lie, I protest."—*Carlstadt:* "And I protest it is not.... Call you it fair or right to strike me when I am disarmed, naked, bound hand and foot?"—*Luther:* "I strike you?"—*Carlstadt:* "Ay; and what call you your preaching, writing, printing against me, while all the time you prevent me from meeting you in any of these ways? If you had allowed me the exercise of my tongue and my pen, you would have found what spirit it is lives in me."—*Luther:* "You preach! Who gave you authority to preach?"—*Carlstadt:* "If you refer to human vocation, I am an archdeacon, and as such entitled to preach and teach; if of divine vocation, I also have my mission.... I defy you to show an instance wherein I have been wanting in charity to you, while all your conduct towards me has been characterized by violence and harshness.... Why did you not bring one of your friends with you, if you did not choose to come alone?" —*Luther:* Why, so I did; I brought Pomer and Philip with me into your stove of a place."—*Carlstadt:* "That is false!" &c. &c.

XXVIII. (p. 152.)—"Carlstadt is stated, by several eye-witnesses, to have had in his service a chaplain who performed the part of a spirit, in the feigned apparitions and supernatural revelations, by means of which his master imposed upon the people." (Luther's *Briefe*, [1826,] ii. 625.)

"Carlstadt was very daring; he even ventured to hold a public disputation at Rome, in the principal college. When he came back to Germany, he was quite magnificent in his habits and attire. His taking to the peasant-life afterwards was merely the result of baffled spite and jealousy."

"Carlstadt condemned university degrees. I remember him saying one day: 'I feel that I have done wrong in raising those two men to the doctor's degree, merely for the two florins they paid. I swear I will never make another!' He said this in the castle chapel at Wittemberg, and I rebuked him soundly for such an observation." (Tischreden, p. 416.)

"In the discussion at Leipzig, Carlstadt insisted upon speaking before me. He left it to me to combat the propositions of Eck, respecting the supremacy of the pope, and John Huss. He is a very poor disputant; he is as obstinate as a pig."

XXIX. (p. 154.)—On hearing of the death of Carlstadt, Luther observed (16th Feb. 1542): "I should like to know whether Carlstadt died repentant. A friend of mine, who wrote to me from Basle announcing his decease, mentions a curious circumstance: he assures me, that there is a spectre constantly wandering about Carlstadt's grave, and in the house where he lived, where he occasions great confusion, throwing stones and gravel about. However, the Athenian law forbad men to speak ill of the dead, and 'twas a good law: I will say nothing further about this matter." . . . "Carlstadt, they say, was killed by the devil. The story goes, that as he was preaching there appeared in his sight, and that of many of the congregation, a tall man, who, entering the church, seated himself not far from the altar; shortly afterwards he went out and proceeded to Carlstadt's house, where he took up his little son, who was there by himself, and seemed for a moment as though he were going to dash him to the earth; but eventually he left him, without doing him any harm, ordering him to tell his father that he would return in three days to carry him, the father, away; and so it happened: Carlstadt died on the third day from that time. It is added, that when the sermon was over, Carlstadt asked the person next to whom the stranger had seated himself, who he was; but the party answered that he had seen no one next to him. I imagine that this circumstance, whatever it was, inspired Carlstadt with a horrible degree of fear, and that it was this same fear of death which killed him. He always entertained a miserable dread of dying." (7th April, 1542.)

XXX. (160.)—" It was indeed a heavy oppression. At the death of the master of the family, the lord inherited his best pair of oxen; on that of the mistress, her best suit of clothes. This was the right of *Todfall*. Every peasant who changed masters, was obliged to pay a fine to the one he was leaving, the *Lehnschelling*: the finest bundle of wheat, the finest bunch of grapes, the finest fruits of his garden, the finest honey from his bees, all belonged to the lord. On Shrove Tuesday, he was bound to present him with a pig; on St. Martin's Day, with a couple of geese; at Michaelmas, with a pair of fowls. The temporal or spiritual lord treated his peasants like veritable slaves; body and mind they were wholly subject to him; if he changed his religion, the vassal was compelled to go over with him to the new faith. With these were coupled the exactions of the priesthood, often as cruel and oppressive as those of the temporal lord."—AUDIN.

XXXI. (p. 161.)—An important circumstance in the peasants' war was, that it broke out while the imperial troops were in Italy. Had it been otherwise, the insurrections would have been repressed far more speedily. The peasantry of count Sigismond Von Lupffen, in Helgovia, rose (1524) in consequence of the burdens which weighed upon them, as they declared to Wilhelm Von Furstenberg, who was sent to quell them; their insurrection had nothing to do with the question of Lutheranism. The first to imitate their example were the peasants of Kempten, who put forward as their reason the severities exercised over them by their seigneur, the abbot; they forced their way into all the towns and castles belonging to him, and broke all the images and church ornaments. The abbot being captured by them, was taken to Kempten, where he was compelled to sell all his seigneural rights for the sum of 32,000 gold crowns. This body of insurgents was soon joined by others, so that when they were all assembled near Ulm, they numbered fourteen thousand men; among their adherents were the peasantry of Leipheim and Guntzberg, and those of the environs of Augsburg. The two former towns, besieged by the League of Suabia, surrendered; the first was given up to be plundered by the infantry engaged; the second became the assigned spoil of the cavalry. The conquered peasants rose again, and this time plundered not only the monasteries, but the castles also of the nobles. Count Montford interposed in behalf of these wretched men, with the deputies of Ravensberg and Uberlingen; but a great many of them were nevertheless crucified, beheaded, and otherwise put to death.

This first insurrection was scarcely suppressed, when Munzer excited the peasants of Thuringia to revolt.

The pious, the erudite, the pacific Melancthon gave his testimony that the demands of the peasants were altogether consistent with the word of God, and with justice, and he exhorted the princes to clemency. Luther anathematized both the one and the other, peasants and princes.

The peasants of Thuringia, of the Palatinate, of the dioceses of Mayence, Halberstadt, and of Odenwald, assembled in the Black Forest, under the leadership of Metzler, of Ballenberg. They got possession of Mergentheim, and compelled several counts, barons, and knights to unite with them. The subjects of the counts of Hohenlohe, who were already in arms, soon joined them, whereupon, the counts of Hohenlohe having previously received from the peasant letters of safe-conduct, sealed with the head of the count palatine on a piece of money, a conference took place, and the counts promised to observe the *Twelve Articles* for a hundred and one years. At this concession, the peasants discharged, simultaneously, two thousand muskets, as a *feu de joie*. Several noblemen joined the peasants voluntarily, and others were compelled to do so. The town of Landau acceded to the League. At about the same time, the peasantry of the environs of Heilbronn rose, and, after some excursions by themselves, joined the main body. Several towns, one after another, acknowledged them, and opened their gates to them.

The treaty made by the peasants with the representative of the elector of Mayence was signed on their behalf by Goetz Von Berlichingen and George Metzler of Ballenberg. The peasants sent eight of their chiefs in different directions, to receive the oath of all the inhabitants of the diocese of Mayence. The clergy of that diocese had to pay them fifteen thousand gold florins within a fortnight. The peasants of the Rhingau, oppressed by the abbot of Erbach, rose about the same time, but the representative of the elector of Mayence having complied with their demands, the tumult as far as regarded them was appeased.

Those propositions were in substance as follow: "The ministers of religion shall be elected by their flocks. They shall have for their support one-thirtieth of the corn and wine, to be collected by the parishioners among themselves; if there be any surplus after paying the minister, it shall be reserved for the assistance of the poor, and towards the general expenses of the parish. All persons to be taxed fairly and impartially, without favour or exemption, unless authentic deeds are produced establishing a legitimate claim to such favour or exemption.

"No duty on the sale of wine by the grower; the retailer to pay all such charges. No excommunication for secular offences. Bondage to be abolished. The Jews to be expelled, by reason of their disgraceful usury; no man's goods to be seized for exorbitant interest; the capital lent and the fair per centage thereon to be alone recognised. The trade in wood for building purposes to be free as heretofore, without let or impediment thereto on the part of the people of Mayence. No person to be admitted into any monastery for the future, and all monks and nuns to be allowed to quit their convents if they desire it. The lord not to interfere in any way, directly or indirectly, in trials affecting his tenants. The magistrate of each place to watch over and take charge of widows, orphans, and wards. Pastures and rivers to be free to all, as well as the chase, respect being in all cases paid to the privileges of the magistrate and of the prince. The judge to be subjected to the same charges as the other citizens, noble or not noble. The secular causes not to be decided by the canon law, but by the local customs. No person to set up a claim to peculiar forest rights or property. If the district of the Rhingau hereafter frame any further articles, the same to be adopted by the people of Erbach." (Gnodalius, *apud* Schardt, *Rerum Germanicarum Script.* ii. 142-3.)

The insurrection having made considerable progress in Alsace, Duke Antony of Lorraine, an ardent defender of the church, assembled a body of troops, composed principally of the wreck of the battle of Pavia, and attacked the peasants on the 18th of May, 1525, near Luffenstein. He defeated them, burned the town of Luffenstein with all its inhabitants, took Saverne, into which a large body of peasants had retired, and a few days after, beat a third body of insurgents near Schurweiler. The number of peasants who perished in these three combats is carried by some historians as high as thirty thousand. Three hundred prisoners were decapitated. (Calmet, *Hist. de Lorraine*, i. 495; Hottinger, Hist. of Switzerland, ii. 28; Sleidan 115.)

General George Von Freunsdberg, who had distinguished himself at the battle of Pavia, and whom the archduke Ferdinand had recalled into Germany that he might put an end to the war, did not imitate the other catholic leaders in their cruelty. The peasants had taken up a position near Kempten. Convinced as he was that he should overwhelm them by the superiority of his forces, he desired to avoid the effusion of blood. He restrained the impatience of his colleague, George Von Waldburg, and privately sent a recommendation to the peasants to disperse in the woods and mountains. They took his advice, and thereby saved themselves. (Wachsmuth, 137.)

A Franconian song composed after the peasants' war, had for its refrain:

"Heed to thee, peasant, my horse will o'erthrow thee"—

a counter-cry to the refrain of the war song composed by the Dithmarsians, after they had defeated the Black Guard—

"Heed to thee, horseman, the peasant's upon thee."

The insurgent peasants had in general adopted, as a distinctive mark, a white cross. Some corps of them had banners on which was figured the wheel of Fortune, (not the wheel of a plough as an agricultural symbol.) Some had seals, on which were engraved a ploughshare, with a flail, a rake, or a fork, and a wooden shoe placed cross-wise. (Gropt, Chronicle of Wartburg, i. 97; Wachsmuth, 36.)

There appeared in 1525 a violent anonymous address, *To the body of assembled peasants*. This pamphlet, published in Southern Germany, bore on the title-page a wheel of Fortune, and under it the following inscription, in German verse:

"The time is come for the wheel to turn,
God knows, beforehand, which party will be at top.

Peasants,	Romanists,
Good Christians,	Sophists."

Then, a little lower down:

"What made us sweat so furiously?
The avarice of the seigneurs."

And at the bottom:

"Turn, turn, turn;
Whether you will or no, you must turn."

(Shobel, Memoirs on the Literature of the 16th century, ii. 44; Wachsmuth, 55.)

The peasants had boasted that their general council would last a hundred and one years. After the capture of Weinsberg, they resolved to give no quarter whatever to any prince, count, baron, noble, knight, priest, or monk—"in a word, to none of the men who live in idleness." They accordingly massacred all the nobles who fell into their hands, in order, they said, to avenge the death of their brethren in Suabia. Among these nobles killed by the peasants was the husband of a natural daughter of the emperor Maximilian; the lady herself they conveyed to Heilbronn, in a dung-cart. They destroyed a great number of convents; in Franconia alone, two hundred and ninety-three monasteries were pillaged and burned.

When they despoiled a castle or a monastery, they never failed to go in the first instance to the cellar, and clear off all the wine; they then divided among themselves, the church ornaments, and sacerdotal dresses.—Haarer (*Petrus Crinitus*) *apud* Freher, iii. 242. At the monastery of Erbach, in the Rhingau, there was an immense tun, capable of containing eighty-four hogsheads of wine. It was full when the peasants took possession of the monastery; when they went away, not above a third of the quantity remained. (Cochlæus, 108.)

They compelled the lords to send their own peasants to join them. "The common council," they used to send word, "has decided that you must assemble your people, and, having properly armed them, send them to join us. If you fail herein, your life and property, be assured, are in great jeopardy." (Haarer, *ut sup.*)

The women took part in the peasants' war. Those from Heilbronn formed a body of themselves, who marched under a banner of their own. (Jæger, Hist. of Heilbronn, ii. 34.)

"As the peasants were conveying count Lœwenstein prisoner through Weinsberg, a passer by respectfully saluted the captive nobleman. An old peasant, who observed this, came up and struck the man with his halberd, saying: 'Why bowest thou to him? thou art as good as he.' (Jæger, *ut sup.*)

The peasants of the diocese of Wurzburg, who were commanded by an able man, named James Kohl, required that all the castles should be demolished, and that no noble should be allowed to keep a war-horse. They denied that the nobles should have any privileges whatever, beyond that enjoyed by the community at large. (Stumpf, Hist. of Franconia, ii. 44; Wachsmuth, 58.)

"When Munzer was at Zwickau, he called upon a handsome girl there, and told her that he was sent towards her by a divine voice which had directed him to sleep with her; and without she consented to his doing so, he could not preach the word of God. The girl confessed this, and her compliance, on her death-bed." (Tischreden, 292.)

"Munzer laid down degrees in the state of the Christian: 1st, *the clearance state*, in which he disengages himself from the coarser sins, gluttony, drunkenness, lasciviousness; 2, *the state of study*, when one seriously thinks upon a future life, and strenuously labours at further amendment; 3, *contemplation*—that is to say, meditations upon sin and grace; 4, *tedium*—that is to say, the state wherein fear of the Law makes us hate ourselves, and inspires regret for having sinned; 5, *suspensionem gratiæ*, profound depression, profound incredulity, despair, such as that of Judas, or, on the other hand, entire abandonment of oneself to faith in God, placing everything wholly at his disposal, and letting things take their course under his guidance."

". . . He once wrote to me and Melancthon: "I like your attacking the pope, but as to your state of prostitution, that you call marriages, I don't approve of it at all." He taught that a man may not lie with his wife, unless he has been previously assured by a divine revelation that he will engender a holy child; without this, he would be committing adultery." (Tischreden, 292.)

Munzer was very deeply versed in sacred literature. He had received his doctrine, he said, by divine revelations, and he communicated no portion of them to the people; he simply ordered them what to do, telling them that his orders came direct from God. He had been expelled from Prague, and several other towns. Taking up his residence at Alstaedt, he declaimed against the pope, and, more dangerous still, against Luther himself. "The Scripture," said he, "promises that God will grant what is asked of him; he cannot, therefore, refuse a sign to him who seeks true knowledge of him. This inquiry is agreeable to God; and there can be no doubt he will declare his will by some certain signs." He added, that God would communicate to him his word, as he had to Abraham; and that if God did not do so, he would hurl darts against him, (or himself, *tela in se ipsum conjecturum.*) He said that God manifested his will by dreams. (Gnodalius, *ut sup.*)

While Munzer was haranguing the peasants previous to the battle of Frankenhausen, a rainbow appeared over their heads. As some of the insurgents had a rainbow for an emblem on their banner, they thought the appearance a sure prognostic of victory. (Melancthon's Life of Munzer.)

XXXII. (p. 165.)—*Sincere exhortation of Dr. Martin Luther to all Christians, to guard themselves against the spirit of rebellion.* (1524.) The labouring man, tried beyond all endurance, overwhelmed with intolerable burdens, will not, and cannot, any longer submit to that sort of thing, and he has, doubtless, good reasons for striking with the flail and the club, as John Pitchfork threatens to do . . . . I am delighted so far to see the tyrants trembling; as to myself, let who will menace, let who will fear, &c.

" . . . . It is the secular authority and the nobles who ought to put their hand to the work (of the Reformation); that which is done by the regular powers, cannot be looked upon as sedition. . . ."

After pointing out that what was needed was a spiritual, and not a temporal insurrection, he proceeds: "Spread yourselves, and aid others to spread the gospel; teach, write, preach, that all human establishments are vain; dissuade every one you severally know from becoming papist priest, or monk, or nun; persuade all who are now in the convents to quit them; cease to give money for bulls, and candles, and bells, and pictures, and churches; tell those who ask you for money for these and such like purposes, that the Christian life consists in faith and charity. Do these things for two years, and what will become of pope, bishops, cardinals, priests, monks, nuns, bells, church towers, masses, vigils, cassocks, copes, tonsures, rules, statutes, and the whole of the papal nuisance. It will have disappeared like smoke."

After having recommended gentleness and patience towards the feeble-minded, whom those he addressed should desire to enlighten, Luther continues: "If a brother had a cord tied tight round his neck, and, on hastening to his assistance, you pulled the cord with violence, or too precipitately made use of your knife to sever it, would not the result of this haste and violence be to strangle your brother outright, in the one case, or to wound him, in the other; and so to do him more harm than the enemy who had bound him? No; if you would succour your brother, you must assail that from which he suffers; the cord which confines him must be handled with precaution until you have disengaged his neck from it. 'Tis on the same principle you must proceed in the case before you. Spare not the hardened rogues and tyrants you find opposed to you. Give them the stoutest blows you can, since they will not listen to reason; but as for the men of simple minds, whom they have chained down in the bonds of their false doctrine, you must observe quite a different treatment towards them. You must disengage them by degrees. You must give them a reason and a cause for everything you do, and thus fit them for freedom as you are emancipating them. You cannot be too severe towards the wolves, too gentle towards the poor weak sheep."

XXXIII. (184.)—To John Ruhel, his brother-in-law, he expresses himself thus (23rd May, 1525): "'Tis a lamentable thing to see the peasants thus severely dealt with, but what was to be done? God willed that a sound terror should be diffused amongst the people, or Satan, ere long, would have done worse than even the princes are doing. We must prefer the lesser evil to the greater."

". . . . What especially induces me to write so violently against the peasants is, that I am indignant at seeing them compelling the timid to join their ranks, whether they desire to do so or no, and that they thus involve innocent men in the impending chastisement of God." (30th May, 1525.)

XXXIV. (p. 187.)—Carlstadt, after having obtained permission to establish himself at Kemberg, could not remain quiet, as he had promised to do. He had secretly printed and circulated various anonymous attacks upon Luther, and, at the same time, forwarded to the chancellor Bruck complaints, under various heads, of the conduct which he alleged his former pupil, and subsequent adversary, had pursued towards him. Luther, on hearing of this proceeding, wrote to the chancellor, and gave him an account of all that had passed between him and Carlstadt, and set forth in detail his opinion of that personage. (24th September, 1528.) ". . . . In fact, I hardly know what to say about some of his lamentations; for the least annoyance, the slightest misfortune that befalls him, is immediately set down to my account. . . . . From a feeling of compassion, I consented that he should come to my house, and explain the views on which he founded his scruples, and I endeavoured to satisfy his mind on the various points. He thanked me warmly for what I had said, yet since, I have perceived from one of his letters to Schwenkfeldt, he makes a mock of my kindly reception of him. This circumstance has turned my heart entirely away from him.

". . . . If he is not more narrowly watched, so as to be prevented from having these anonymous pamphlets published (for we know quite well that they are his), who will believe that it is without the consent of our gracious prince, and without our knowledge, that Carlstadt is residing within my lord's territory? On the other hand, were he to quit the electorate, he would, in all probability, excite disorder elsewhere, and people would not fail to make my lord responsible for it, seeing that he might have prevented it, by keeping this dangerous man in check at Kemberg. I confess, that the recollection of Munzer makes me most apprehensive on all these occasions. My opinion is, that he should be compelled to maintain the silence he swore to observe, and that he should not be allowed to quit the country—at all events, not until some new decision on the subject. It will be only necessary to talk to him severely about it; for he is a weak man, and readily yields to those who address him in a firm and decided tone. As for myself, I am well punished for having enabled him to return amongst us—for having so imprudently invited Satan to my table, as it were."

As evidence of the kindly feeling which had been exhibited on the part of Luther towards Carlstadt, we may add the following:—

"Yesterday we baptized Carlstadt's youngest son—a sort of rebaptism of baptism in this case. Who, last year, would have anticipated that the man who was then anathematizing and scorning baptism, would this year call upon his old adversary to stand godfather to one of his children. (February, 1526.) But his return to the dogma was not sincere. "He is living with us," says Luther, speaking of Carlstadt, on 28th November, 1527, "and we had hoped to bring him back into the right path, but the miserable creature becomes more and more hardened in his error every day, though he is afraid to say as much openly." Some months after, 28th July, 1528, we find in a letter of Luther's: "That viper, Carlstadt, whom I have been cherishing in my bosom, is moving about there, but, as yet, afraid to leave his resting-place. Would to God the fanatics had him among them, and I were rid of him!"

"Carlstadt has been absent for several weeks past, and it is thought he has gone back to his old nest, and his late companions. Let him go, since he is not to be persuaded to remain amongst us by reason and kindness." (27th October, 1528.) Carlstadt, in fact, no longer able to submit to the somewhat imperious protection of Luther, had fled into the Low Countries. "Carlstadt has taken up his quarters in Friesland. I hear he is quite triumphant, exhilarant. He has sent for his wife: his letter is a mere tissue of self-gratulation." (6th May, 1529.)

Sometime after, we find Luther using his influence with the elector's chancellor, Christian Bauer, to obtain a safe-conduct for Carlstadt: "Carlstadt's wife has been earnestly entreating me to solicit from our gracious lord a safe-conduct for her husband, who wishes to return amongst us. Though I can hardly expect a compliance with this application, I could not refuse her my support." (18th July, 1529.)

Luther entitled one of his writings against Carlstadt: "Touching the noble and gracious dame, called the skilled intelligence of Dr. Carlstadt, her observations on the Eucharist." (Werke, ii. 46.)

XXXV. (p. 189.)—On the 25th May, 1524, Luther writes thus to Capito (Kepstein): "There are persons who persist in affirming that I condemn your method of proceeding and that of Bucer...... These vain rumours have, doubtless, their origin in the letter I addressed to you, which has been so often reprinted, and which has just now been translated into German. I am really almost deterred from writing any letters at all, when I see them thus laid hold of, against my will, for the press. There are many things which pass, and which ought to pass, between friends, which one does not desire to see spread abroad among the public." On the 14th Oct. 1534, he writes to Bucer: "You will respectfully salute in my name J. Sturm and J. Calvin, whose books I have read with singular gratification."

"Œcolampadius and Zwinglius said: 'We remain at peace with Luther because he was the first by whose agency God restored the Gospel in our days; but after his death, we will enunciate and confirm our opinions.' They did not think I should last longer than they."

Luther said: "We ought to content ourselves with simply despising that miserable Campanus. He is not worth writing against. Melancthon observed, that, for his part, he thought the fellow ought to be hanged, and so he had told his master the elector.

"Campanus thinks he knows more Greek than Luther or Pomer. The Christian is, according to him, a man perfect and infallible; he makes out man to be a log of wood, as the stoics did. If we feel no struggles, no combats within ourselves, I would not give a farthing for all the preachings and sacraments that ever were, are, or shall be." (Tischreden, 283.)

"Zwinglius has the audacity to say: 'In three years we shall have with us all France, Spain, and England'...—introduces his books under my name from Switzerland into France, so that several towns have become infested with them......I have greater hopes from the people of Strasburg."

"Œcolampadius at first was a very worthy fellow, but he afterwards became soured and bitter. Zwinglius, too, who used to be a very lively, good-natured man, has become melancholy and saturnine." (Tischreden, 283.)

"When I heard Zwinglius at the conference of Marburg, I esteemed him to be an excellent man, and so with Œcolampadius... I have been very much vexed at your publishing Zwinglius' book, *To the most Christian King*, with commendations of the book from yourself; you must have known perfectly well that it contained many things which are highly displeasing, not only to myself, but to all pious people. Not that I begrudge Zwinglius the honours rendered him—his death was a source of great pain to me—but because no consideration whatever should induce any one to do that which militates against the purity of our doctrine." (14th May, 1538.)

"Maître Bucer used to think himself mightily learned, but he was quite out of his reckoning in this respect. He actually put forth in one of his books that all nations have in truth only one religion, by reason of which they are saved. This may be called mere raving." (Tischreden, 184.)

"Some one brought to Dr. Luther a large book written by a Frenchman named William Postellus, on *The Unity in the World*. He gave himself infinite pains therein to prove the articles of faith by arguments founded on nature and reason, his object being to convert the Turks and Jews, and to bring all mankind to one and the same faith. The doctor observed: ''Tis too much for one bite; we have already several similar works on natural theology. Our friend bears out the proverb: *The French have light brains and light heels*. By and by, we shall have visionaries who will undertake to give all the various sorts of idolatry an appearance of faith, and so excuse idolatry itself." (Tischreden, 68.)

Bucer made several attempts to become reconciled with Luther. "As far as I am personally concerned," writes the latter, in 1532, "I can very well make practical allowance for you, and admit your statement that you cannot return all at once; but I have hereabout (as you witnessed yourself at Schmalkald) a great number of men whom I cannot keep altogether in check. We cannot, by any means, permit you to assert that you have not been in error, or that we did not perfectly understand each other. Your best plan will be, either to avow frankly that you have been wrong, or, saying nothing more on the point, content yourself for the future with teaching the true doctrine. There are men amongst us who will not submit to any evasions on your part, Amsdorf, for instance, Osiander, and others."

After the revolt of the anabaptists, in 1535, there were other attempts made to unite the reformed churches of Switzerland, Alsace, and Saxony, under one and the same confession. Luther, on the 9th July, 1537, writes thus to Capito, a friend of Bucer, and minister at Strasburg: "My Catherine thanks you for the gold ring you sent her, and none the less so from the circumstance that she has unfortunately lost it. I never saw her more vexed than she was when she found out that it had been stolen, or that she herself had lost it from carelessness, which I do not believe, although she is constantly accusing herself of having done so. I had persuaded her that this gift was sent to her as a happy pledge of the future concord of your church with ours. The poor woman is all affliction at her misfortune."

XXXVI. (p. 191.)—"I have something about me which will enable me to defend my cause, even though all the world should rave against me—that, namely, which Erasmus calls my pertinacity of assertion." (1st Oct. 1523.)

XXXVII. (p. 192.)—"Though you say less, you, in point of fact, grant more to free will than all the rest do: you do not define free will, yet you give everything to it. I would much rather accept what is said on this point by the sophists and their master, Peter Lombard, with whom free will is merely the faculty of discerning and choosing good, if one is sustained by grace—evil, if grace fails us. Peter Lombard thinks with Augustine, that free will, if it be left without a guide, cannot but lead man to his ruin; that of itself it has no power, except for sin. Augustine, accordingly, in his second book against Julian, calls it *slave will*, rather than *free will*." (De Servo Arbitrio, 447.)

XXXVIII. (p. 192.)—No one will believe the utter disgust I feel for this treatise on *Free Will*, though I have, as yet, only read a few pages of it. . . . 'Tis a great annoyance to have to reply to so learned a book, by so learned an author." (1st Nov. 1524.)

However, he could not allow the work to pass unanswered. "I have killed," says he, somewhere—"I have killed, by my silence, Eck, Emser, Cochlæus." But in the case of Erasmus, it was impossible for Luther to remain silent. The immense reputation of that adversary rendered a refutation of his work, or an attempt at refutation, essential. Luther accordingly set himself to the work. He writes, on 28th Sept. 1525—"I am up to the ears in Erasmus and free will, and I will take care to leave him not a leg to stand upon."

XXXIX. (p. 193.)—"If God have prescience; if Satan be the prince of the world; if original sin ruined us; if the Jews, seeking righteousness, fell into unrighteousness; if Christ redeemed us with his blood, there is no free will for either man or angel. If there were, Christ were superfluous, or, rather, it must be admitted that he only redeemed the vilest part of man." (De Servo Arbitrio, 525.)

XL. (p. 194.)—Under the impulse of the spirit of contradiction and paradox, Luther went the length of laying down the following propositions: " Grace is gratuitously given to the most unworthy, the least deserving; we cannot obtain it by study, by works, by our own efforts, small or great; it is not even accorded to the most ardent zeal of the best, the most virtuous of men, the most earnest seeker after righteousness." (Ib. 520.)

XLI. (p. 195.)—" What you mention to me about Erasmus, and his ravings against me, I was already acquainted with, and his past letters gave me full reason to anticipate such conduct on his part. . . . He is a hare-brained, volatile man, who makes a jest of all religions, after the manner of his favourite Lucian, and who never writes anything serious, except out of spite and malice, and when he thinks he cannot assail the object of his malignity so effectually in any other way." (28th May, 1529.)

" Erasmus' conduct is quite worthy of himself, in thus persecuting the Lutheran name, though the Lutherans are his sole security. Why does he not go among his Dutchmen, his Frenchmen, his Italians, his English? . . . His object in all this flattering, is to provide himself with quarters, but he wont get any, and will fall to the ground between the two stools. If the Lutherans hated him as his own people hate him, it would be at the peril of his life he stopped at Basle. But Christ will judge this atheist, this Lucian, this Epicurus." (7th March, 1529.) This diatribe probably refers to the following publication: *Contra quosdam qui se falsò jactant Evangelos Epistola Desid. Erasmi, Rot. Jam recens edita et Scholiis Illustrata. Ad Vulturum Niocomum.* (*Frib.* 1529. 8vo.)

" You regret, my dear Erasmus, you bitterly complain in your writings, of the tumult which has of late prevailed, and you sigh for the good old times of peace and concord which have passed away. You may as well cease your complaints, your efforts to find a remedy for the supposed evil. This tumult arose by the will of God; by His will it still continues, and it will not terminate until the adversaries of the word of God have become as the mud beneath our feet." (De Servo arbit. 465.)

XLII. (p. 196.)—In advocating the marriage of priests, Luther's only idea was to put an end to the monstrous contradictions which their conduct daily gave to their vow of chastity; it did not occur to him at the time, that a married priest may prefer his family in the flesh to that which God has entrusted to his care. He himself could not always divest himself of this feeling of the family-man; there escape from him at times words which form a sad contrast with the charity and devotion professed, and to a great extent practised, by the Roman-catholic priests. " It is sufficient," he says, in one of his instructions to pastors, " it is sufficient for the people to receive the sacrament three or four times a year, and that publicly;

to give way to a practice of administering the sacrament at all times to individuals, would involve too weighty a charge upon ministers, more especially in times of plague. Besides, we must not make the church and her sacraments a mere slave, at the beck and call of everybody, of those, particularly, who contemn her, and yet require that the church shall be at all times ready to do whatever they need, though they themselves never do anything for her." (26th Nov. 1539.) He himself, however, did not act upon this principle; when occasion presented itself, he manifested the most heroic disinterestedness and charity.

"My house has become a regular hospital," he writes, on the 4th Nov. 1527. "Everybody else being frightened out of their wits by the plague, and refusing to receive him, I have taken in the poor minister, whose wife is just dead of the pestilence, and all his family."

"Dr. Luther, speaking of the death of Dr. Sebald and his wife, whom he had visited and touched in their malady, observed: 'They died rather of anxiety and vexation than of the plague.' He took their poor orphans into his house, and when some people told him this was no better than a tempting of Providence, replied: 'Ah! I have had masters who have taught me what tempting God really is; the present is nothing of the sort.'

"The plague was in two houses which a deacon had visited in the course of his duties. The people wanted to send this deacon away; but Luther would not permit it, having confidence in God, and being persuaded that the best method was to suppress the feeling of fear as much as possible." (Dec. 1538; Tischreden, 356.)

XLIII. (p. 197.)—"Poor as I am," he writes to Spalatin, "I would have returned you the beautiful golden orange you sent me, had I not been afraid of offending you."

"Salute your wife for me in my name; salute her for me when you are saluting her on your own account, and blessing God for having bestowed upon man such a treasure as woman. Praise and glory be to his name." (6th Dec. 1525.) "My little John is strong and lively; he is voracious, bibacious, loquacious." (May, 1527.) "Salute in my name old Melchior, for whom I desire a submissive wife, that will drag him by the hair of his head round the market-place seven times a day, and stun him with conjugal objurgations half the night; this would serve the fellow exactly right." (10th Feb. 1525.)

"We drink excellent wine out of the prince's own cellar, and should soon be perfect evangelists, if the gospel would only fatten us in the same way." (8th March, 1523.)

In a letter to J. Agricola, whose wife was on the eve of her confinement, he says: "Thou wilt give a piece of gold on my part to the new-comer, and another piece of gold to its mother, so that she may drink wine and have plenty of milk. If I could be present, I would be godfather. From the region of the birds, 1521."

The letters of Luther at this period generally terminate with one or other of these phrases "My rib Kitty, my lord Kitty, my empress Kitty, salutes you."

"Kitty, my lord and master, was at her new kingdom of Zeilsdorf (a small farm now possessed by Luther) when your letter arrived."

On the 15th May, he writes to Spalatin: "My Eve requests your prayers that God may preserve her two children, and grant her more."

Cochlæus designates Luther's wife, *dignum ollæ operculum*, (page 73.)

Luther thus, on 5th May, 1529, solicits Nicholas Amsdorf to act as godfather to his daughter Magdalen: "Excellent sir, the Father of all grace has given to me and to my good Catherine, a dear little girl. Under these circumstances, which fill us with joy, we entreat you to fulfil a Christian office, and to be the spiritual father of our poor little pagan, introducing her into the holy community of Christians by the divine sacrament of baptism. God be with you."

Luther had three sons, John, Martin, and Paul; and three daughters, Elizabeth, Magdalen, and Margaret. The first two girls died young, the one aged eight months, the other thirteen years. On the gravestone of Elizabeth was inscribed: *Hic dormit Elisabetha, filiola Lutheri.*

The male lineage of Luther became extinct in 1759. (Ukert, i. 92.)

In the church of Kierctzsch, a Saxon village, there is a portrait of Luther's wife, with this inscription: *Catarina Lutheri geborhne von Bohrau.* (1540.) This portrait once belonged to Luther. (Ib. 364.)

XLIV. (p. 197.)—He became, in his turn, indignant against preachers who exhibited an excess of vehemence. "If N——," he writes to Hausmann, "cannot manage to be more temperate, I will request the prince to dismiss him his dominions.

"I have already requested you," he says in a letter to the preacher in question, "to preach the word of God more quietly, abstaining from personalities, and from whatever is calculated to excite the people without beneficial result. . . . On the other hand, I understand you speak too coldly with reference to the sacrament, and that you do not communicate often enough." (10th Feb., 1528.)

"There has arrived here a preacher from Kœnigsberg, who wants to introduce all sorts of new regulations about bells and candles, and so on. . . . It is not desirable to preach too often; I hear that at Kœnigsberg, there are no fewer than three sermons delivered every Sunday. What is the need of so many? two would be quite enough, and two or perhaps three in the course of the week. When one preaches every day, one gets into the pulpit without having properly meditated upon the subject to be treated, and one says whatever comes first into the head; if nothing good occurs, one is driven to the indifferent, the flat. I pray God to moderate the tongues and spirit of our preachers. This one of Kœnigsberg is too vehement by half; he is always full of sombre ideas, and dismal, bitter declamation about the merest trifles." (16th July, 1528.)

"If I wanted to become rich, I need only give up preaching, and turn merry-andrew at fairs; I should have infinitely more people paying money to see me then, than I have auditors for nothing now." (Tischreden, 186.)

XLV. (p. 197.) We find him, so early as 25th May, 1524, writing thus to Bucer and Capito: "I like your encouraging these marriages between priests, and monks, and nuns; I entirely approve of this appeal of wedlock against the bishop of Satan. I fully sanction the choice you have made of ministers for the various parishes already regulated. In a word, your whole proceedings have given me unmixed satisfaction. Go on and prosper. . . . We have made quite concessions enough to the feeble-minded. Since they persist in hardening themselves more and more, we must act and speak, without reference to them. I am myself thinking of laying aside the monk's frock, which I have hitherto retained out of consideration for the weaker souls, and in mockery of the pope."

XLVI. (p. 198.) "The affair of the peasants has restored courage to the Papists, and greatly injured the cause of the gospel: it is incumbent upon us, on our part, to take decided steps, to raise our heads still higher. It is with this object, to testify to the gospel not only by my words, but by my actions, that I have just married a nun; at which my enemies have been triumphing, and crying, Io! Io. I was determined to show them, that though old and feeble, I was not going to beat a retreat before them. Ay, and I will do other things, yet, I hope, which shall disturb their rest, and strengthen the words I have enunciated." (16th August, 1525.)

Dr. Eck published a collection, entitled: *Epithalamia festiva in Lutherum Hessum (Urbanum Regium) et id genus Nuptiatorum.* Amongst these we find a hymn of nineteen strophes, headed: *Hymnus Paranymphorum*, and beginning with these words—'Io! Io! Io! Io! *gaudeamus cum jubilo*, &c. An *Additio dythrambica ad Epithalamium Mart. Lutheri*, in the same metre; an *Epithalamium Martini Lutheri*, in hexameters, commencing, *Dic mihi, musa, novum*, &c. Husemberg wrote a satire, entitled: *Ludus ludentem Luderem ludens.*

Luther answered these assaults upon himself, his wife, and his friends, in different pieces, which were subsequently collected under the title of, *The Fable of the Lion and the Ass.*

Luther had not been married more than a fortnight, when his enemies spread the report that his wife was already brought to bed of a son. Erasmus eagerly caught up the calumny, and hastened to communicate it to all his correspondents; but he subsequently found himself necessitated to contradict it. (Ukert, i. 189.)

Luther's own statement of his family in the Tischreden is as follows: "I married on the 14th June, 1525; on the 6th June, 1526, was born my eldest son John; in 1527, my second child, my daughter Elizabeth; in 1529, Magdalen; in November, 1531. Martin; 28th January, 1534, Paul; and, lastly, in 1536, Margaret."

XLVII. (p. 198.) She was of the family of Haubitz, and was born on 29th January, 1499. Her parents were of limited means, and, at twenty-two years of age, (4th April, 1521,) she entered the convent of Nemptsch, near Grimma, on the Muldau. Judging from the portrait of her by Lucas Cranach, it could hardly have been the external charms of the escaped nun which attracted Luther. Her face is large and bony, with round, unmeaning eyes, and wide, open nostrils. After the death of Luther, she was involved in the deepest distress, owing to the total neglect of her on the part of the protestant princes. Even king Christian gave her assistance on only one occasion. After wandering about, and begging her bread for some years, she died in 1552, at Torgau, and was buried in the parish church there. The *Petites Affiches* of Altona, for the 15th November, 1837, contains the following announcement, headed, "The Orphans of Luther:"

"These are the children of Joseph Charles Luther, born at Erfurt, 11th November, 1792, and who died in Bohemia, having previously returned to the bosom of the Roman-catholic church.

"M. Reinthaler, director of the institution of St. Martin, established at Erfurt in honour of Luther, received the poor orphans into his house.

"On the 6th May, 1830, the eldest, Antony, born in 1821, arrived at the ancient convent of the Augustines. Instructed in the principles of the Reformation, he received the communion in that faith at Easter. He was placed as apprentice with a cabinet-maker. Two of his sisters, Mary and Ann, are at service; the youngest, Theresa, is still at school."

M. Reinthaler made an appeal to the protestants in favour of the descendants of Luther, but with scarcely any effect. Frankfort-on-the-Main and Leipzig sent fifty thalers, and that was all....AUDIN.

XLVIII. (p. 200.) Notwithstanding the limited extent of his means, however, his generosity was very great. He would give away to the poor, in default of anything else, the presents which his children had received from their baptismal sponsors. A poor student asking him one day for relief, he desired his wife to give him some money; on her replying that there was none in the house, Luther took a silver cup that had been made a present to him, and handing it to the applicant, told him to sell it at the goldsmith's, and keep so much of the money. (Ukert, ii. 7.)

"I would willingly have given him money to carry him on his journey, but I was utterly overwhelmed, at the time, by the multitude of poor people, who, from far and near, come here as to an open house." (April, 1539.)

"I entreat thee, dear Jonas, for heaven's sake, to get for me, from the treasurer, the money his grace promised to G. Scharf. 'Tis really monstrous one should have such difficulty in realizing the sum. If necessary, give him a receipt in my name." (11th May, 1540.)

"Luther, walking one day with Dr. Jonas and some other friends, bestowed alms on some poor people who were passing by. Dr. Jonas followed his example, saying, with a smile, as he did so—*How do we know that God will render this unto us?* Luther gravely replied, *You forget that it was God gave it you.*" (Tischreden, 144.)

"Dr. Pomer, one day, brought Luther a hundred florins that a nobleman had sent for him; but he said he would not take them. He gave one half to Philip, and offered the other fifty to Pomer, who would not accept them." (Ib. 59.)

"I never asked my lord for a single farthing for myself." (Ib. 53.)

XLIX. (p. 201.)—"Legitimate commerce is blessed by God, as for instance, when one makes only five per cent.; but usurious gains are accursed. There is that publisher of mine, ——, realizing monstrous profits upon the books I give him to print—as much, I'll warrant, as a hundred per cent. How different from my other publisher, John Grunenberger. He said to me, one day, most honestly, 'Sir doctor, I should make too much at that rate: I must print more copies, and sell them for less.' He was a God-fearing man, and the Lord blessed all his undertakings." (Tischreden, 62.)

"Thou knowest, my dear Amsdorf, that, work as I may, I cannot supply all the presses that are craving their food at my hands. Why, here, in this one town, we have got nearly six hundred printers, of one sort and another." (11th April, 1526.)

L. (p. 209.)—Yet it would appear that they were endeavouring to get rid of him by poison. He himself tells us, in two letters, (Jan. and Feb. 1525,) of Polish Jews who had been sent to Wittemberg to poison him, and mentions the sum they were to receive for the work—two thousand ducats. As they refused, when arrested, to name their employers, they were about to be put to the torture; but Luther would not permit this, and even exerted himself to procure their liberation. He had no doubt, he says, as to who it was that sent them.

"They have promised gold to whomsoever shall kill me. 'Tis thus it fights now, thus it reigns and triumphs, this holy apostolic see, the regulator of faith, the mother of churches." (Cochlæus, 25.)

An Italian of Sienna came to Wittemberg, and stopped with Dr. Luther several weeks, taking all his meals with him, and constantly talking with him, probably to see how matters were going on. (Tischreden, 416.)

There were attempts of another kind made against him.

"Matthew Lang, bishop of Salzburg, fished for me in a similar manner, and, but for the especial assistance of our Lord, I should have been entrapped. In 1525, he sent one of his doctors to my house with twenty gold florins, which the man slipped privately into Catherine's hand; but as soon as I found the matter out, I returned him the money. 'Tis with money this bishop has got hold of the lawyers, who, accordingly, all think him very fine, he laughing slily at them all the while. Once, he sent one of our pastors a piece of damask, to induce him to disavow our gospel; and having succeeded in his object, by the gift and his flatteries, he said about everywhere: 'What dreadful knaves these Lutherans are! They'd do anything for money." (Tischreden, 274.)

Melancthon, who never broke off his private relations with the literary men of the papal court, was for some time suspected of having listened to offers from them.

One day, when a letter was brought to Sturm from Sadoleti, in which the Italian warmly eulogized Melancthon, Luther observed: "If Philip chose to make matters up with them, he might very easily become a cardinal, and keep his wife and children all the same.

"Sadoletus, who has been fifteen years in the pope's service, is a man of great wit and learning. He has written to Melancthon in the most friendly terms possible, after the Italian fashion, hoping, no doubt, to get him over to their side, by the bait of a cardinalship; for the good gentleman, Mr. Pope, is sadly perplexed; he knows not how to set about us. The same Sadoletus, though a clever man, knows nothing about the Scriptures, as he has manifestly shown in his commentary on the 51st Psalm. None of the papists, in fact, are conversant with the Scriptures; spiritually, they are not competent to govern one single parish church; they sit stiffly and uncompromisingly in their own particular government, and cry, 'The decrees of the fathers must not be questioned.' That's their song. They are fully of opinion that though the Pope should seek to lead the whole world openly into hell, no human creature is entitled to question him for the same, or to object in the slightest degree." (Tischreden.)

LI. (p. 209.)—On the occasion of two Augustine monks having been burned at Brussels, Luther thus writes: *To the Christians of*

Holland, Brabant, and Flanders.—"Oh, how miserably have these men perished. But, then, what glory will they not receive at the hands of our Saviour. To be persecuted and slain by the world is as nothing in the eyes of those who know that *precious in the sight of the Lord is the death of his saints*, as the Psalm says. What is this world in comparison with God?......What joy, what utter delight must the angels have felt when these two souls appeared before them. God be blessed and praised to all eternity, for having thus permitted us to see and hear true saints, true martyrs, in place of the false saints and martyrs that are constantly held up to our adoration! Our brothers of Germany have not, as yet, been deemed worthy to consummate so glorious a sacrifice, though many of us have had to undergo persecution. Therefore, dear friends, be ye glad and joyful in Christ, and join with us in returning him thanks for the signs and miracles he has been pleased to commence operating amongst us. He has refreshed our courage by these new examples of a death worthy of him. It is high time, indeed, that the kingdom of God should be established, not by words only, but by deeds and in reality." (July, 1523.)

"The noble dame Ursula Von Staufen, is sustaining a noble combat on this earth: she is full of the spirit, and word, and knowledge of Christ. She has inundated the academy of Ingolstadt with able writings, denouncing its conduct in having compelled a young man, named Arsacius, to make a disgraceful recantation. Her husband, who is one of our tyrants, and who has been dismissed from an office he held in consequence of her noble conduct, is in doubt what to do in the matter. She, amidst all the perils which surround her, maintains a firm courage, though, as she writes me word, fear sometimes comes very near her heart. She is a precious instrument of Christ; I commend her to you, hoping that Christ by this *weak vessel* will confound and bring to ruin the mighty ones, and those who glorify themselves upon their wisdom." (1524.)

To Spalatin he writes: "I send you some letters I have received from our dear Argula, that you may see how much labour and suffering that pious creature endures for the sake of Christ." (11th Nov. 1528.)

The translation of the Bible by Luther produced a general tendency to disputation on the subject of the Scriptures, thus thrown open to the examination of all classes. Even women came forward and challenged the theologians, declaring that they now saw all the doctors were ignorant persons. There were some women who actually claimed a right to preach from the pulpit; for, said they, Luther has declared that by baptism all mankind are rendered priests, bishops, popes. (Cochlæus, 51.)

One day, when at Luther's table, the conversation had turned upon the illiberality manifested by the Lutheran leaders towards the pastors of their church, Luther said: "The world does not deserve to have anything done for it by men of heart and conscience; the sort of people the world likes are bawling, brawling, impudent beggars, such as Friar Matthew. This worthy brother, by dint of pertinacious solicitation, had wrung from the elector a promise that he should have a fur mantle. Finding that the prince's treasurer did not furnish the garment, the preacher next Sunday, in the midst of his sermon before the elector, cried out aloud: 'Where's my fur mantle?' Thereupon the prince renewed the order to his treasurer, who, however, still neglected to execute it; next Sunday, out came another: 'Where's my fur mantle? I haven't got my fur mantle,' and so he went on, Sunday after Sunday, until he obtained what he desired." (Tischreden, 189.)

Luther himself complained of the miserable condition in which the protestant ministers found themselves. "They absolutely wont pay us," says he; "here we see noblemen who squandered away thousands of florins upon designing knaves who plundered them, refusing to give a hundred to a worthy pastor." (1st March, 1531.)

"We are establishing here (at Wittemberg) a consistory for the trial of matrimonial cases, to compel the peasants to observe some discipline, and to pay the pastors their dues. We need a consistory as to the latter point for some of our nobles and magistrates." (12th Jan., 1541.)

LII. (p. 209.)—"Joachim writes me word that there has been born at Bamberg, a child with the head of a lion; it died soon after its birth. There have also been crosses seen in the air over the towns, but the catholic clergy have stifled the rumour of these things." (22nd Jan., 1525.)

"The princes are dying off in great numbers this year; this is perhaps what the many signs we have had announced." (6th Sept., 1525.)

LIII. (p. 212.)—In the first instance, Luther had been disposed to regard the Turks as absolutely an aid sent him by heaven. "They are," says he, in 1526, "the ministers of divine wrath against our wicked ones." With the same feeling, he had urged the protestants not to take up arms against the Ottomans in favour of the papists; "for," said he, "the papists are not a jot better than the Turks." In the preface, he wrote for a book published by Dr. Jonas, he says that the Turks equal the papists, or indeed excel them, in points which the latter regard as essential to salvation—such as alms, fastings, maceration, pilgrimages, the monastic life, ceremonies, and other outward works, and it was for this reason the papists said nothing about the worship of the Mahometans. He takes this opportunity of exalting alike above these Mahometan and Romanist "practices," the pure religion of the heart and spirit inculcated by the gospel.

Elsewhere, he draws a parallel between the pope and the Turks which concludes thus: "If we must fight against the Turks, we must also fight against the pope." All this was when the danger was comparatively far off; when he saw the Turks nearly and seriously menacing the independence of Germany, he over and over again urged the necessity of keeping up a permanent army on the frontiers of Turkey, and daily called upon all who bore the name of Christians to implore God for the success of the emperor's arms against the infidels. He exhorts the elector, in a letter, dated 29th May, 1538, to take part in the war then preparing against the Turks, and to forget the intestine quarrels of Germany, in the one immediate object of expelling the common enemy.

"A man worthy of credit, who had been ambassador to the Turkish court, told Luther one day, that the sultan had asked him what sort of man Luther was, and of what age, and being informed that he was about forty-eight, replied: 'I would he were not so old; tell him that he has a gracious lord in me.' 'God preserve me from such a gracious lord,' cried Luther, crossing himself.'" (Tischreden, 432.)

LIV. (p. 213.)—Luther, in a letter to the chancellor Bruck, in speaking of the preparations for war set on foot by the landgrave, says: "Such an aggression on the part of our people would be a disgrace to our gospel. A revolt such as this, not of peasants, but of princes, would bring down upon Germany the most terrible evils. There is nothing would give Satan greater delight." (May, 1528.) He wrote several letters to the same purport to the elector. Yet at times he was tempted to let the landgrave have his way. After reading a letter from Melancthon, who was at the conference, he said: "What Philip writes here is good stuff, has a good body, is full of authority and meaning. He says much in a very few words. I conclude from his statement that we must needs have war. . . . 'Tis that cowardly knave of Mayence has done all the mischief. They must give us an answer speedily, or take the consequences. If I were the landgrave, as a matter of personal feeling, I would fall upon them, and either perish myself or exterminate them, since they would not give me peace when my cause was so just." (Tischreden, 151.)

LV. (p. 213.)—This prince from a very early period had manifested decided hostility to the Reformation. So long back as 22nd Dec., 1525, we find Luther writing to the duke, and earnestly entreating him to renounce his persecution of the new doctrine: "I throw myself at your feet to implore you to cease your impious proceedings against us. Not that I fear anything you may do to me, for I have nothing to lose but this miserable body of flesh, which, in any case, is soon about to return to its mother earth. If I sought my own advantage, I should in every possible way encourage persecution, seeing that hitherto it has served me beyond all expectation. And so again, if it were any satisfaction to me to render your grace unhappy, I should urge you with my utmost persuasion to continue in your present violent courses; but it is my duty, as it is my desire, to consult your grace's salvation, by supplicating you on my knees to cease your criminal assaults upon God and his word."

LVI. (p. 214.)—"My dear Amsdorf,—here is Otto Pack, a poor exile whom I recommend to your pity; he will be safer at Magdeburg than with me, for here I should be in constant apprehension of duke George's compelling me to surrender him." (29th July, 1529.)

LVII. (p. 214.)—"At my first interview with prince Albert, when he asked my opinion about certain matters affecting the rules of his order, I advised him to set at nought those absurd and unmeaning rules, to marry, and to give Prussia a political form, converting it into either a principality or a duchy. Philip fully concurred in my views, and gave the prince exactly the same counsel. I am sure the plan might be easily accomplished, if the people and nobles of Prussia would unite in petitioning the prince to that effect; this would at once encourage him, and supply him with powerful and satisfactory reasons for doing that which I am sure he himself desires to do. Do you, therefore, with Speratus, Amandus, and our other ministers, bring the people to the desired point; urge them, excite them, so that, instead of adhering to this abominable hermaphrodite principality, which is neither lay nor ecclesiastical, they may desire and demand a regular and proper principality. I should like to induce the Bishop of —— to take the same step; and I feel satisfied he would assent to our views, if his people would only urge the change upon him." (4th July, 1524.)

The bishop in question had been openly preaching the Reformation for six months past, "So that," writes Luther, in April, 1525, at the height of the peasants'war—"so that while the gospel is progressing at full sail and with uninterrupted course in Prussia, whither it was not called, in high and low Germany, where it came and entered of itself, it is blasphemed and despised."

LVIII. (p. 216.)—"Pray with me to the God of mercy, that He will either convert duke George to his gospel, or, if the prince be not worthy of this, that He take him from the world." (27th March, 1526.)

LIX. (p. 216.)—On 31st December, 1528, Luther writes thus to the elector, on the subject of his controversy with duke George: "I entreat your electoral grace to leave me and my case entirely to the judges, should duke George require it, for it is my duty to hazard my head rather than prejudice your grace in any way. Jesus Christ, I hope, will give me strength enough alone to resist Satan."

LX. (p. 216.)—Duke George was, after all, not an ill-natured persecutor. Having expelled eighty Lutherans from Leipzig, he gave them permission to retain their houses there, in the possession of their wives and children, and even to come on a visit to the latter thrice a year at the fair times. At another time, Luther having exhorted the protestants of Leipzig to resist the orders of their duke, the prince contented himself with requesting the elector of Saxony to prohibit Luther from communicating with his subjects. (Cochlæus, 230.)

LXI. (p. 216.)—Some time after this diet, Luther drew up the following propositions: "First, it is desirable that our party, excluding the Zwinglians, should speak for itself alone.

"In the second place, we should write to the emperor, representing in their very strongest light the benefits which the elector of Saxony has conferred on church and state; as thus:

"1. That he has caused to be taught Christ and his faith in all their purity, in such a manner as they have not been taught for the last thousand years; that he has abolished a crowd of abuses and monstrosities which had operated most injuriously to both church and state, such as the traffic in masses, the abuse of indulgences, excesses in excommunication, and many other things which the states themselves have acknowledged to be intolerable, and of which they required the abolition at Worms.

"2. That he resisted the seditious perturbators who were breaking images and desecrating the churches.

"3. That the imperial dignity has been honoured, glorified, vindicated, by him, more than it has been several centuries past.

"4. That it was we who did most, and underwent most, in suppressing the partisans of Munzer, and thus preserving the public peace and his majesty's crown.

"That it was we, and none else, who suppressed the sacramentarians, by whom, but for us, the papists would have been utterly annihilated, body and goods.

"That it was we, in like manner, who repressed the anabaptists.

"That it has been owing to us that the seed sown by wicked men in divers places, for the purpose of injuring the Holy Trinity, the faith of Christ, &c., has been prevented from attaining its growth. I mean hereby Erasmus, Egranus, and their coadjutors in wickedness." (May, 1529.)

LXII. (p. 217.)—Luther had made several attempts to restrain his party from going any further lengths. On the 22nd May, 1529, he wrote to the elector to dissuade him from entering into any league against the emperor, and to exhort him rather to refer all things to divine protection. In a letter to Agricola, dated 30th June, 1530, he expresses his approbation of the prudent conduct of the elector with reference to the emperor.

"Our prince did excellently well in recognising a lord in a foreign town, and not setting up a claim to be master there, as he might, had he been less prudent, have done. Christ says, *When they persecute you in one city, flee to another;* and elsewhere, *Quit this house.* In my opinion, our prince, as a member which cannot safely separate itself from the body, should not break with Cæsar. And he himself happily seems of this opinion; by observing silence, he has, so to speak, fled to another city, he has quitted the house."

To the landgrave of Hesse, in reference to his attempts to reconcile him with the sacramentarians, Luther writes: "Grace and peace in Jesus Christ. Most serene lord, I have received the letter wherein your highness seeks to induce me to proceed to Marburg, for the purpose of conferring with Œcolampadius and his friends on the subject of our differences of opinion on the holy sacrament. I cannot conceal from your highness, that I have very slight hopes of peace and union resulting from such a conference. Nevertheless, your highness is entitled to our thanks for the anxiety you manifest in this matter; and I, for my part, am quite ready to proceed to the place indicated, though I regard it as a wholly useless step. I would not leave to our adversaries the glory of having it to say that they were more desirous of peace and concord than we are. But I would humbly entreat you, gracious lord and prince, ere we meet together, to inform yourself whether they are disposed to make some concessions to us, for if they are not, I fear that our conference will do more harm than good, and that the result will consequently be just the reverse of that which your highness so sincerely and so laudably contemplates. It can serve no purpose of good for the two parties to meet and discuss, if each meets the other fully predetermined to yield not a jot of the points in dispute." (23rd June, 1529.)

In a paper drawn up on the same subject, and which is generally ascribed to Luther, the writer expresses a wish that "some grave and learned papists" should be present at the conference, as witnesses.

To his wife he writes (4th October, 1529): "Grace and peace in Jesus Christ. Dear Catherine, you must know that our amicable conference at Marburg is over, and that we have agreed upon no one point whatever, our adversaries persisting as strenuously as before in seeing merely bread in the Eucharist, and in admitting merely a spiritual presence of Jesus Christ. The landgrave is to address us once more, to make one more effort to unite us, or, at all events, to bring us to recognise each other as brothers, as members of the same body. He labours most indefatigably in this cause, but to little purpose. We are willing to hold them in all peace and charity, but we cannot accord them the name of brothers. To-morrow, or next day, I imagine we shall set out for Voigtland, whither the elector has summoned us.

"Tell Pomer that the utmost arguments of Zwinglius amounted to this: *that the body cannot exist without space, and that, consequently, the body of Christ is not in the bread;* while all that Œcolampadius could achieve was this: *that the holy sacrament is merely a symbol of Christ's body.* God has thoroughly blinded them; they could not answer us at all. The messenger who brings this is pressed for time, so I will conclude. Pray for us. We are all well, and live exactly the same as the princes. Embrace Maudlin for me, and little John. Your devoted servant, Martin Luther."

In another letter to the landgrave of Hesse, on the same subject, (dated 20th May, 1530,) Luther says: "I have undergone such perils and dangers for my doctrine, that assuredly I do not desire to have laboured in vain. It is from no feeling of vanity in myself, or hatred towards others, that I persevere in my resistance to these men; God is my witness, I should long since have adopted their views, had they shown me their views were right and true; but the reasons they have hitherto assigned are too feeble to influence me."

LXIII. (p. 219.)—He set out from Torgau on the 3rd of April, and arrived at Augsburg on the 2nd May. His suite was composed of a hundred and sixty horsemen. The divines he had with him were Luther, Melancthon, Jonas, Agricola, Spalatin, and Osiander. Luther, being under excommunication, and under the ban of the empire, remained at Coburg. (Ukert, i. 232.)

LXIV. (p. 219.)—"I am on the confines of Saxony, half-way between Wittemberg and Augsburg. The last town would not have been safe for me." (June, 1530.)

LXV. (p. 220.)—"My residence is now in the clouds, in the empire of the birds. Not to mention the infinity of other birds, whose songs, and chatterings, and confused cries would deafen the voice of the tempest, there is near me a wood, completely peopled, every branch of every tree in it, with rooks and crows. From morning till night—nay, sometimes from night till morning—there is a clamour so incessant, so indefatigable, as to make me fully convinced that in no other one spot in the world are there so many birds assembled together as there are here. They are not quiet for one single instant; old and young, parents and children, are eternally cawing away to the praise and honour of crows. Perhaps, by their so harmonious voices, they charitably intend to bring sleep gently to my eyelids. Pray God, I may find such to be the case to-night. 'Tis a noble race of birds, and, as thou knowest, very useful to the world! As I look at them, I seem to have before me the whole army of sophists and Cochlæists assembled together from all parts of the world, for the purpose of giving me a better idea of their wisdom and their pleasant language, and to let me see at my leisure what they are, and what they can do for the world of spirit and for the world of flesh. We have not as yet heard the nightingale, though the cuckoo, who announces and accompanies the more agreeable notes of Philomela, has for some time past been glorifying himself in the woods around me.—From the residence of the crows, this 22nd April, 1530."

LXVI. (p. 221,) — At times, however, he sent him words of consolation. " You have assisted Christ, offered peace, obeyed Cæsar, submitted to insults, undergone vilification. You have not returned evil for evil; in a word, you have worthily laboured in the holy work of the Lord, as befits saints to do; rejoice, therefore, in His holy name. You have long enough been afflicted and cast down by the world. Look up, raise your head firmly; the hour of redemption approaches. I will canonize you as one of Christ's most faithful servants; there needs no more than this for your glory." (15th September, 1530.)

LXVII. (p. 225.)—" Please God, we may be thought worthy to be burned or slaughtered by him (the pope). If, however, we do not merit to give testimony by our blood, let us at least implore God to grant us this grace, to testify by our life and words that Jesus Christ alone is our Lord, and that we adore him, *in secula seculorum*. Amen." (Op. Lat. ii. 270.)

LXVIII. (p. 225.)—" At the diet of Augsburg, duke William of Bavaria, who was strongly opposed to the evangelical doctrine, asked Dr. Eck: " Cannot we overthrow these opinions by the Holy Scripture?" " No," said Eck;" only by the fathers." Whereupon the bishop of Mayence observed: " Truly, our divines are making a pretty defence for us. The Lutherans show us their opinions in the Scripture, chapter and verse; we are fain to go elsewhere." The same bishop remarked: " The Lutherans have one article which we cannot gainsay, even though we could all the rest; and that is, their article about marriage." (Tischreden, p. 99.)

LXIX. (p. 225.)—Luther, in a letter addressed to the bishop, exhorting him to peace, says: " I cannot take away from before my weeping eyes poor Germany; so unhappy, so abandoned, so despised, sold to so many traitors at once. My dear country! I would give my life to see her happy!" (6th July, 1530.)

LXX. (p. 226.)—Luther was quite conscious of his real position, his real strength. " If I were to be killed by the papists, my death would serve as a secure protection for those who shall come after me, and the wild beasts, my enemies, would be more cruelly punished than they will be at my hands, or than I should perhaps wish them to be. For there is One who will some day cry, *Where is thy brother Abel?* And He will brand the murderers on the forehead, and send them forth as fugitives and wanderers over the face of the earth. Our race is now under the protection of the Most High, who has said: *I will show mercy unto thousands of them that love me, and keep my commandments.* I believe His word." (30th June, 1530.)

"If I were to be killed in some papist commotion, I should carry away with me in my suite plenty of papist bishops, and priests, and monks; so that the people would say: 'Truly Dr. Martin Luther is escorted to the tomb by a fine procession; he is, certes, a very grand doctor indeed, to be accompanied in his funeral by so many bishops, and priests and monks—all, to do him the more honour, stretched on their backs as dead as he;' for in that way we should make our last journey together." (Cochlæus, 211: extract from a book of Luther's, entitled, *Advice to the Germans.* 1532.)

"The catholics," it was said to him, "charge you with several wilfully false interpretations in your translation of the Scriptures." "They've got too long ears by half," replied he; "with their *hihau! hihau!* their heads are not sound enough to judge of a translation even from the Latin. Tell them that Dr. Martin Luther abides by his translation; regarding a papist and an ass as one and the same thing:

"Sic volo, sic jubeo, sit proratione voluntas."

(The only authority for this is Cochlæus.)

LXXI. (p. 226.) "He deserves not only the title of king, but even that of Cæsar, since he has conquered him whose power had no equal on the earth. He who thus offered his body a sacrifice for God's sake, is not merely a priest, he is a sovereign pontiff, a genuine pope. Justly is he called *Leon-hard*, that is to say, *Lion's-strength*, for he is a strong and intrepid lion." (22nd October, 1524.)

To Hausmann: "I suppose you have heard of Gaspard Tauber, the new martyr of Vienna, who has been beheaded and burned in that city for the sake of God's word. The same glorious fate has befallen a bookseller of Buda, in Hungary, whom they burned in the midst of his books." (12th November, 1524.)

There were, in point of fact, a good many partisans of the new doctrine in Vienna: "When, after the diet of Augsburg, cardinal Campeggio entered that city with king Ferdinand, the reformists dressed up a great wooden doll in the costume of a cardinal, tied round its neck an imitation of the pope's indulgence bull, with seal and all, and some indulgences, and setting the doll astride a dog, with a pig's bladder full of peas, fastened to its tail, sent it running down the street in front of the imperial and papal cavalcade." (Tischreden, 215.)

If we are to believe Cochlæus, Luther afterwards, in his turn, became a persecutor. According to this very doubtful authority, a Lutheran having, in 1532, gone back to the old faith, Luther had him brought to Wittemberg, imprisoned, and a prosecution commenced against him. As nothing warranting the interference of justice could be made out, the man was set at liberty; but he was ever afterwards bitterly persecuted by the protestants. (Cochlæus, 218.)

LXXII. (p. 227.) Both sides, however, were so apprehensive of the result of a struggle, that, contrary to all expectation, peace was maintained. "I admire, with profound devotion, this miracle of God, by which all threatening appearances have been dispersed, like a cloud of smoke. Everybody fully anticipated that in the spring Germany would be involved in a sanguinary war." (June, 1531.)

The fear of a new insurrection of the peasantry greatly contributed to preserve the peaceful attitude of the princes: "The peasants," writes Luther, on the 19th July, 1530, "are beginning to re-assemble. Sixty of them attempted the other night to take the castle of Hohenstein by surprise. You see that, notwithstanding the presence of the emperor, we must take precautions against another revolt. What a state of things, if the papists were to commence hostilities at such a juncture!"

LXXIII. (p. 227.) So far from anything of the sort, he had, as we have already observed, in 1539, urgently dissuaded the elector from entering into any league that might be formed against the emperor. "An alliance of such a kind could not possibly meet with our sanction. Should its result be, as it must be, some public calamity, perhaps even open war, we should feel ourselves responsible; and we prefer dying a hundred deaths to having to reproach ourselves with a single drop of blood shed for the gospel. It is not with such arms we fight. It is our part to suffer. It is not for us to avenge ourselves upon our oppressors; but to leave everything in the hands of God. I therefore humbly entreat your electoral grace not to allow any present danger to involve you in hostile measures. We will offer up our prayers to God; but our hands shall remain pure from blood and crime. Were it even to happen, (which I do not anticipate,) that the emperor should demand me or my friends to be delivered up to him, we will, under the protection of God, appear before him, rather than compromise your electoral grace in any degree, as I have repeatedly told your august brother, the late elector Frederick." (18th November, 1529.)

LXXIV. (p. 227.) In the Tischreden, (p. 397,) Luther speaks out more explicitly: "It is not for religion they will fight. The emperor has seized upon the bishops of Utrecht and Liege, and he has offered the duke of Brunswick to let him quietly take possession of Hildesheim. He absolutely hungers and thirsts after ecclesiastical territories;

he devours them. Our princes do not like this; for they want to have a share in the meal. He wont let them, if he can help it, and so they'll go to fisticuffs; but not about religion." (1530.)

"I have often been asked by my gracious lord what I should do if a highway robber were to attack me? I should resist, I have replied, for the sake of the prince whose servant and subject I am; and, so far, I consider I might kill the robber, and receive the sacrament afterwards, with a safe conscience. But if it is in the assertion of God, and in my capacity as preacher, that I am attacked, then my duty is to submit, recommending myself to the protection of God, to his vengeance, if I fall, upon my oppressor. I use the knife, therefore, only on the highway, and against the highway robber. The anabaptists are desperate rogues, but they abstain from carrying arms, and lay claim to great patience and long-suffering."

"As I was speaking in favour of peace, the landgrave of Hesse interrupted me: 'Sir doctor, your counsel is good, perhaps; but what if we follow it not?" (1536.)

To the question as to the right of resistance, Luther replied, "that according to public law, natural law, and reason, resistance to unjust authority was quite permissible. There is no difficulty on the point, till you bring it within the jurisdiction of theology.

"The question would not have been difficult to solve in the time of the apostles, for then all the authorities were pagans. But now that all the princes are Christians, or pretend to be so, it is far more difficult to decide, for a prince and a Christian are near relations. Whether a Christian may defend himself against authority, is matter for grave reflection. After all, it is from the pope I tear the sword, and not from the emperor."

He gives us the following summary of the arguments which he should have addressed to the Germans, had he decided upon exhorting them to resistance:

"1. The emperor has neither the right nor the power to order this; beyond a doubt, if he orders it, he ought not to be obeyed. 2. It is not I who excite disorder, I oppose it, and do my best to prevent it; it is they are the authors of it who order that which is contrary to God's Word. 3. Do not make so light of the matter. If you give the fool drink, take heed he spit not in your face. He is thirsty enough, for that matter, and asks nothing better than to drink his fill. Well, you will fight: bow your heads to receive the blessing: Good luck to you!—a joyful victory to you! I, Dr. Martin Luther, your apostle, have spoken to you—have warned you, as it was my duty to do."

He says, further on—"You slight my doctrine. You would catch Luther in his words, as the Pharisees sought to do with Christ. But, if I chose (which I do not), I could give you a gloss which should thoroughly perplex you. I would say, this resistance is not against the emperor, but against God. On the other hand, that a political person, a citizen, a subject, is not a Christian person; that it in no way entered into Christ's purpose to destroy the laws, the policy, and government of the world: *Render unto Cæsar the things which are Cæsar's, and unto God the things which are God's.* Only obey not in that which is counter to God and to his Word.

"I condemn revolt, at the peril of my body, of my life, of my honour, of my worldly goods. I would have you forbear. If you proceed, I will hold my peace, and perish with you. You will go to hell, in the name of all the devils, and I to heaven, in the name of Jesus Christ. They desire to abuse our doctrine, but they shall see that at least it is not erroneous in itself.

". . . . To kill a tyrant is not permitted to any man not invested with public functions, for the fifth commandment says, *Thou shalt do no murder*. But if I surprise a man with my wife or daughter, though he be not a tyrant, I have a full right to kill him, like any murderer or highway robber." (Tischreden, 397.)

"The worthy and truly noble seigneur, Gaspard von Kokritz, has requested me, my dear John, to give you my opinion whether, in the event of the emperor's making war upon our princes, on the subject of the gospel, it would be lawful for our people to resist, and defend themselves. I delivered my views upon this subject in the time of the late duke John. It is now somewhat late in the day to ask my opinion, since the princes have determined among themselves that it is lawful and right to resist and defend themselves, and since they will not attend to what I have so distinctly stated my views to be. . . . Strengthen not the impious against our princes; leave the field open to the anger and judgment of God, which they have so long been calling for with insane eagerness, with laughter and gaiety. At the same time, hold up as an example to our people the conduct of the Maccabees, who followed not those who went forth to defend themselves against Antiochus, but, in the purity of their hearts, allowed themselves to be killed, rather than go against the word of God." (8th Feb. 1539.)

In his treatise *De Seculari Potestate*, dedicated to the duke of Saxony, he says: "In Misnia, in Bavaria, and other places, the tyrants have promulgated an edict, calling upon all persons to deliver up their New Testaments to the magistrates. If the subjects obey this edict, it is not a book which they give up at the peril of their souls, but Christ himself whom they deliver into the hands of Herod. If the authorities, however, seek to take the Testaments by force, they must be submitted to; resistance must not be made to actual violence. *Princes are of this world, and this world is the enemy of God.*

"We must not obey Cæsar, if he makes war upon our party. The

Turk does not attack the Alcoran; the emperor should not attack the gospel." (Cochlæus, 210.)

LXXV. (p. 227.)—The elector had put it to Luther, whether it would be permissible to resist the emperor, sword in hand. He answered in the negative, adding, " If, however, the emperor, not content with being suzerain of the princes' territories, should require of them to persecute, to put to death, or to expel their subjects for the gospel's sake, the princes, necessarily convinced, as they must be, that this would be acting against the will of God, must refuse obedience, as they would be violating their Christian faith, and rendering themselves accomplices in the emperor's crime. Except as to this, they must let the emperor do as he thinks fit, and not defend their subjects against him; he will have to render an account of all he does." Further on, he says, speaking of civil war: " What carnage, what fearful misery, would then cover the whole German land! A prince should prefer to die three times over, to lose his estates three times over, to being the cause of such horrible disorders, even only a consenter thereto. What conscience could support such a reflection! The devil would rejoice in such a state of things. God preserve us from it and him!" (6th March, 1530.)

LXXVI. (p. 229.)—The elector having reprimanded him for an excess of violence in two of his writings, the *Advice to my dear Germans*, and the *Comment on the pretended Imperial Edict*, Luther replied (16th April, 1531), that he had only been answering the still more violent attacks of his enemies, and that it would be unjust to impose silence upon him, and let the others have their swing. " I found it," he says, " quite impossible to be any longer silent upon an affair which concerns me more nearly than it does any one else. Were I to pass over unnoticed so public a condemnation of my doctrines, it would amount to an abandonment, to an abnegation of that doctrine, on my own part. Rather than submit to this, I would brave the anger of all the devils in hell, of the whole world, including the entire imperial council. They say my two writings are sharp and cutting, and they are quite right in that statement: I did not intend them to be otherwise; I am only sorry that their edge was not twice as sharp. Any one who takes into consideration the violence displayed by my enemies, must needs admit that I was not severe enough..... Everybody vociferates against us, the most odious calumnies are circulated to our dishonour, and yet when I, poor man, venture to raise my voice in vindication of my doctrines, I am rebuked for making such a noise, as though nobody had said a word but I.... The short of the matter is, that whatever we do and say is wrong, even though we were to perform miracles, and revive the dead; while all they say and do is right, even though they were to bathe Germany in tears and blood."

LXXVII. (p. 229.)—" Throughout, up to the present period, 1534, and more especially at the diet of Augsburg, we have humbly offered the pope and the bishop to receive consecration and spiritual authority from them, and to assist them in the preservation of this right; but they have always repelled us. If, then, there should, one of these days, befal sacerdotal consecration what has already befallen indulgences, 'twill be no fault of ours. I offered to hold my peace respecting indulgences, if my adversaries were also ordered to hold their peace; they rejected my offer, and now the world cannot sufficiently show its contempt for indulgences; the country is covered, as it were, with torn up indulgences and papal letters, and broken papal seals. Just in the same way will disappear the power of consecrating, and the chrism, and the tonsures, until no one will be able to distinguish which is the bishop and which the priest." (Cochlæus, 245; an extract from Luther's *De Angulari missâ.*)

LXXVIII. (p. 230.)—The anabaptists had long since been in motion in Germany. " We have here a new sort of prophets, come from Antwerp, who pretend that the Holy Ghost is nothing more than the natural reason and intellect." (27th March, 1525.)

" There is nothing new, except that they say the anabaptists are increasing, and extending in every direction." (28th Dec. 1527.)

" The new sect of anabaptists is making astonishing progress; they are people who conduct themselves with very great external propriety, and go through fire and water unflinchingly in support of their doctrines." (31st Dec. 1527.)

" Bavaria is full of disorder. . . . It does not seem to me desirable that you should take any steps for delivering these perturbators into the hands of the magistrate; they will speedily come into his hands of themselves, and then the council will banish them from the town. The words of Munzer are everywhere in circulation, conveying his notion about the future perdition of the wicked, and the reign of the just upon earth. Cellarius is prophesying about this in a book he has just published. He is a spirit of revolt." (27th Jan. 1528.)

LXXIX. (p. 244.)—On the 12th of May, 1528, he writes to Link: " Thou hast seen, I think, my *Antischwermerum*, and my dissertation on the digamy of bishops. The courage of the dying anabaptists resembles that of the donatists, of whom St. Augustine makes mention, or the fury of the Jews at the taking of Jerusalem. The true martyrs, such as our Leonard Keiser, depart hence in fear and humility, and praying for their executioners; the conduct of these men is mere obstinacy, arising in great measure from the malignant hatred of their adversaries."

LXXX. (p. 245.)—*Extract from an old anabaptist hymn book.*— " The words of Algerius are a miracle: 'Here,' said he, at the place of trial, 'here others groan and weep; I am full of joy. In my prison, the army of heaven appeared before me; infinite martyrs have been with me every day. Full of joy, of delight, of the very ecstasy of grace, I saw the Lord on his throne.'

"'But your country,' said those about him, 'your friends, your relations, your profession, can you quit all these without reluctance?' He replied: 'No man can banish me from my country, for it is at the foot of the celestial throne; there my enemies will become my friends, and we shall together sing the same song of praise. As to my profession, physicians, artists, labourers cannot truly succeed here below; he who knows not the power of God has but a blind power.' The judges, furious with him, menaced him with the flames. 'In the strength of the flames,' said Algerius, 'you will discover mine.' (Winderhorn, i.)

LXXXI. (p. 248.)—The following passages from Ruchat's *History of the Reformation in Switzerland*, furnish a good idea of the strange enthusiasm manifested by the anabaptists. "In 1529, nine anabaptists were apprehended at Bâle, and put into prison. They were subsequently brought before the senate, and the ministers were summoned to confer with them. First, Œcolampadius briefly explained to them the Apostles' Creed and that of St. Athanasius, informing them that these comprehended the true and indubitable Christian faith which Jesus Christ and the apostles had preached. Then the burgomaster, Adelbert Meyer, addressing the anabaptists, said, 'You have heard a sound explanation of the Christian faith; it is now for you, who have complained of our ministers, to speak out openly and unequivocally, and fearlessly to say what it is in them or their doctrines that you disapprove of.' But neither of them said a word; all remained silently looking at each other. The chief usher then said to one of them, a turner by trade: 'How is it that thou sayest nothing now, thou who hast never ceased talking everywhere else, in the streets, in the shops, in prison?' As they still remained silent, Mark Hedelin, the chief warden, addressing the principal anabaptist, said: 'What answerest thou, brother, to that which has been put to thee?' The anabaptist replied: 'I do not acknowledge you for a brother.' 'Why so?' returned Hedelin. 'Because you are not a Christian. Amend your life, correct your faith, lay aside your office, and then we may accept you as a brother.' 'Wherein dost thou think I sin so greatly?' asked Hedelin, 'You know very well,' replied the anabaptist.

"The burgomaster here interposed, and ordering the accused to speak more gently and respectfully, pressed him to give an answer to that which had been put to him. The anabaptist replied: 'I deem that no Christian can hold a worldly magistracy, for it is said, *He that takes up the sword, shall perish with the sword.* I hold that the baptism of infants is an invention of the devil and of the pope, and that we ought to baptize only grown persons, according to the order of Jesus Christ.'

"Œcolampadius undertook to refute him, and to show him and his co-religionists, with the utmost possible gentleness, that the passages they cited in defence of their views had a totally different meaning from that which they put upon them, and that all the ancient doctors, as well as Scripture, were against these opinions. 'My dear friends,' he said, 'you evidently do not understand the Holy Scriptures; you handle them most unlearnedly, most uncouthly.' He was about to show them the true meaning of the passages, when one of them, a miller, interrupted him, and calling him a chattering seducer, said, that what he alleged against them was nothing to the purpose; that they had in their hands the pure and real word of God, to which they would cleave in life and death. He said that at that moment the Holy Ghost was speaking through his lips. He excused himself for his inability to speak eloquently, saying that he had never paid any attention to study, that he had been at no university, and that, indeed, from his early youth, he had hated human wisdom, which he regarded as full of deceit and falsehood. That he knew the tricks of the scribes, who were ever seeking to dazzle and blind the eyes of the simple-minded. He then fell to crying and wailing, saying that after having heard the word of God, he had renounced the ill life he before led; and that now, by baptism, he had received the pardon of his sins, he was persecuted of men, whereas, in the time when he was plunged in all sorts of vice, no one chastised him, nor put him in prison, as was done to him now. He had been thrust into a dungeon, like a murderer, he said: what was his crime? &c. The conference having now lasted until dinner-time, the senate adjourned.

"After dinner, the ministers entered into a discussion with the anabaptists, on the subject of the magistracy. One of their number replying in a common-sense way to the questions addressed to him, the rest were quite angry with him, because, as they said, he thereby showed that he was not firm in the faith. They accordingly interrupted him: 'Leave us to speak,' said they, 'we who understand the Scriptures can reply to these questions better than thou who art yet but a novice, and art not capable of defending our faith against these foxes.' The turner then assuming the lead, maintained that St. Paul, (Romans, xiii.,) in speaking of the higher powers, does not mean magistrates, but simply ecclesiastical superiors. Œcolampadius denied this position, and called upon the other to show in what place of the Bible he found any proof of it. The turner replied: 'Rummage the Old and New Testament yourself; you've done so to some purpose, having found a text there which, according to your own interpretation, directs that you are to receive a salary. For my part, I have no time to spare, being obliged to support myself with the labour of my hands, in order to be a burden upon no one else.' This sally giving rise to a laugh in the persons present, Œcolampadius said, gravely: 'Gentlemen, this is no time for laughing, and no matter for jest; if I receive from the church my daily support, I can prove from Scripture that it is reasonable and lawful for me to do so: to controvert this were impious sedition. Rather pray that the Lord, for the sake of His glory, may soften their hard hearts, and enlighten their understandings.'

"After some more discussion of the same kind, the hour of rising came nigh, when, all at once, one of the anabaptists, who had as yet said not a word, began bawling out, in a voice broken by tears and sobs: 'The Last Day is at your gate! Amend your lives! the axe is already put to the tree! Throw no imputations on our doctrine of baptism, for your own sakes! Oh, for the love of Jesus, persecute not the righteous! The Judge is near at hand, and will punish the ill-doer.'

"The Burgomaster interrupted him, saying this noisy lamentation could not be permitted; that he must speak quietly and rationally on the subject of his doctrine, or hold his peace. The man began his vociferations again, but he was silenced. The Burgomaster then stated to the accused, that the senate had caused them to be arrested, not on account of their peculiar opinions, but by reason of their wicked and seditious conduct. One of them, it appeared, had committed a murder, another had preached up the doctrine that it was unlawful to pay debts, a third had sought to excite public commotion, and so on. It was for these crimes they had been arrested, and they would be detained in prison until the law should decide respecting them.

"Thereupon one of them began crying out: 'Brethren, resist not the wicked ones. Even though the enemy stand before your gate, shut it not. Let them go on; they can do nothing against us without the consent of our Father, who has told us that the hairs of our head are numbered. I say even more: I say you should not resist a robber in a wood. Think you that God does not watch over us?' The man would hardly hold his peace, though repeatedly ordered to do so. (Ruchat, ii. 498.)

There was another disputation after this. 'The Zwinglian minister addressed them gently, and in a friendly manner. He remonstrated with them that even were their views true, they did wrong to separate from the church, and preach in woods and fields, and other places apart. He then proceeded to explain to them very plainly and briefly the doctrine of the church, but one of them interrupting him, said: 'We have received the Holy Ghost in our baptism; we need no instruction in the matter.' A member of the senate then said to them:' We are directed to inform you, that out of pity for you as misguided men, we are ready to let you pass without punishment, on condition that you forthwith quit the country, and promise not to return here, at least not until you have amended yourselves.' One of the anabaptists replied: 'What means this order? the magistrate is not a master of the country that he can direct us to quit it, and go elsewhere. God has told us to inhabit the land he has given us. I shall obey his commands, and remain in the country where I was born, and where I have been brought up. This no man has a right to forbid.' However, the senate soon let him know otherwise." (Ruchat, ii. 102.)

"There was at Bâle an anabaptist named Conrad in Gassen, who put forth some strange blasphemies, as for instance—that Jesus Christ was not our Redeemer, that he was not God, that he was not born of the Virgin Mary. He held prayer to be of no account, and when it was urged upon him that Jesus Christ prayed on the Mount of Olives, he replied with brutal insolence: 'Who heard him?' As he was found to be quite incorrigible, he was condemned to have his head cut off. This impious fanatic reminds me of another in our own time, who led astray several persons in my neighbourhood, some years ago, persuading them that neither bread nor wine ought to be used. And when it was objected to him one day at Geneva, that the first miracle performed by our Lord was the turning water into wine, he replied: 'that Jesus Christ was very young at that time, and that it was a juvenile error of his which we must overlook.'" (Ib. iii. 104.)

The Reformation, taking its rise in Saxony, soon gained the banks of the Rhine, and ascending the stream, became associated in Switzerland with the Waldensian rationalism. It even ventured to cross the mountains into catholic Italy. Melancthon, who throughout maintained a correspondence with Bembo and Sadoleti, the two apostolic secretaries, was for some time better known to the Italian literati than Luther, and it was to him they referred the honour of the first attack upon Rome. But the importance of Luther growing with the growth of the Reformation, he soon became recognised in Italy as the leader of the protestant party. It was in this character that he was addressed by Alfieri in 1542, in the name of the protestant churches of the north east of Italy:

"To the most excellent and most upright doctor and master in the Holy Scriptures, Martin Luther, our chief and brother in Christ, the brothers of the church of Venice, Vicenza, and Treiso, wish health.

"We humbly confess our great fault and our ingratitude, in having so long delayed to recognise and acknowledge how vast a debt we owe to thee, who hast opened unto us the way of salvation. We are exposed to all the rage of antichrist, and his cruelty towards God's elected ones becomes, day after day, more terrible. Wandering and dispersed, we await with impatience the coming of the Lord's mighty one. Do thou, whom God has placed in charge of his flock until his coming—do thou watch, we pray thee, do thou drive away the wolves which hover round about to devour us. Solicit the most serene princes of Germany, who follow the gospel, to write on our behalf to the senate of Venice, calling upon it to moderate and suspend the violent measures which it is adopting against the Lord's flock, at the suggestion of the pope's ministers. . . . Thou knowest how our church has increased in these parts, how much wider the gate of the gospel has opened here. Do thou, then, labour on, in the common cause." (Seckendorf, iii. 401.)

" Charles V. himself contributed to spread the name and doctrines of Luther in the Peninsula, by constantly pouring into that country fresh bands of lanzknechts, among whom there were many protestants. It is well known that George Von Freundsberg, the leader of the German troops in the service of the constable de Bourbon, swore to strangle the pope with the gold chain he wore round his neck. The author of a Lutheran history relates that one of these German soldiers openly promised that he would soon eat a piece of the pope. He adds, that after the taking of Rome, some of the Germans turned a chapel into a stable, and, collecting a number of the pope's Bulls, made litter of them for their horses. Then, dressing themselves in sacerdotal habits, they proclaimed as pope one of their comrades, who thereupon holding a consistory with the rest, resigned the popedom to Luther. (Cochlæus, 156.) Luther, indeed, was solemnly proclaimed pope by the Germans on another occasion. A number of these troops assembled one day in the streets of Rome, on horses and mules. One of them, named Grunwald, remarkable for his stature, was apparelled as pope, with a triple crown on his head, and mounted on a mule richly caparisoned. Other troopers were dressed as cardinals, with hats on their heads, the colours of their garments being scarlet or white, according to the persons whom each represented. They then formed, and proceeded through the streets, to the sound of drums and fifes, surrounded by an immense crowd, and, in short, with all the pomp and circumstance usual in pontifical processions. Whenever they came opposite a cardinal's palace, Grunwald blessed the people in the accustomed form. By and by, he got off his mule, and the soldiers, placing him in a chair, carried him the rest of the way on their shoulders. On arriving at the castle of St. Angelo, the mock pope took a large goblet filled with wine, and drank off its contents to the health of Clement, the rest of the party doing the same. He then administered the usual oath to his cardinals, adding, that he called upon them to render homage to the emperor, their legitimate and only sovereign; he made them promise that they would no longer trouble the peace of the empire by their intrigues and machinations, but that, following the precepts of the gospel, and the example of Jesus Christ and his apostles, they would remain submissive to the civil power. After an harangue, in which he recapitulated the wars, the murders, the sacrileges, the crimes of all sorts of which the popes had been guilty, the pretended pontiff solemnly undertook to transfer, by way of will, his authority and power to Martin Luther. 'He alone,' said Grunwald, 'can remedy all these abuses, can put in order the bark of St. Peter, so that it may no longer be the sport of the winds and waves.' Then, raising his voice, he exclaimed: 'Let all those who are of this opinion declare the same by holding up their hand;' whereupon the multitude of soldiers raised their hands, shouting *Long live pope Luther!* All this passed under the eyes of pope Clement VII." (Macrie, Hist. of the Reformation in Italy, 66—7.)

The works of Zwinglius being all written in Latin, circulated more readily in Italy than those of the reformers of Northern Germany, who did not always make use of this learned and universal language. This circumstance, no doubt, was one of the causes of the character which the Reformation assumed in Italy, and, more particularly, in the academy of Vicenza, where Socinianism took its rise. The works of Luther, however, passed the Alps at an early period: "Blaise Salmosius, bookseller of Leipzig, gave me, the other day, some of your treatises. As they received the high approbation of our learned men, to whom I showed them, I have had them reprinted here, and have sent six hundred copies into France and Spain. They are selling greatly in Paris; and my friends write me word, that even in the Sorbonne there are persons who read and like them. Indeed, I know that many of the learned in that country have long desired to see theology placed upon an independent footing. Calvi, the bookseller at Pavia has undertaken to pass a great part of the edition into Italy. He has promised also to transmit to us all the epigrams which shall be composed in your honour by the literati of his country. Such is the favour into which your courage and talents have already brought yourself, and the cause of Christ." (Letter to Luther, dated 14th February, 1519.)

On the 19th September, 1520, Burchard Schenk writes from Venice to Spalatin: "I have read what you sent me of Dr. Martin Luther's. His reputation reached us a long time ago. It is said here, that he need be on his guard against the pope. Two months back, ten of his books were brought to this city, and immediately sold. . . . God guide him in the way of truth and charity." (Seckendorf, 115.)

Some of Luther's productions made their way into Rome—nay, even into the Vatican, under the wing of some orthodox personage, whose name replaced on the title page that of the heretic author. It was in this way that several cardinals had occasion to regret the warm commendations they had unthinkingly passed upon *The Commentary upon the Epistle to the Romans*, and *The Treatise on Justification*, which they deemed to be the works of a certain Cardinal Fregoso, though, in reality, as our readers are aware, they were the production of the arch-heretic, Martin Luther. The case was just the same with the *Common Places* of Melancthon. (Macrie, Hist. of the Ital. Reform. 39.)

"I am engaged," says Bucer, in a letter to Zwinglius, "upon a Commentary on the Psalms. The representations of our brethren in France and Lower Germany have determined me to publish the work under another name, so that the booksellers may be able to sell it; for, as you are aware, it is a capital crime to introduce into either of those countries books bearing any of our names. I shall, accordingly, become a Frenchman for the nonce, and send forth my book in the name of Aretius Felinus." The book was dedicated to the dauphin. (Lugduni, iii. idus Julii, anno MDXXIX.)

LXXXII. (p. 248.) In order to repel the imputations of the catholics, who attributed to the protestant preachers the revolt of the anabaptists, the reformers of all the various sects resolved once more to meet together. The conference took place at Wittemberg, in May, 1536, on which occasion, Bucer, Capito, and several others of the party met the Saxon theologians. The conference lasted from the 22nd to the 25th of the month. On the latter day, the principal personages signed the *articles of agreement* drawn up by Melancthon; and on the 28th, Luther and Bucer preached sermons, in which they proclaimed the union which had been concluded between the two parties. (Ukert, i. 307.)

Before signing the *articles of agreement*, Luther desired that they should receive the explicit sanction of the Swiss reformers: "Least," as he said, "reservations made now, render the *agreement* the source of even greater disagreement than has prevailed." The sanction was accorded. "The Swiss," writes Luther to duke Albert of Prussia—"the Swiss, who hitherto have differed from us on the question of the holy sacrament, are now in a good way. God stand fast by us now! Bâle, Strasburg, Augsburg, Berne, and several other towns, have ranged themselves on our side. We receive them as brothers, and we now have great hopes that God will put an end to the discreditable state of things which has existed, not on our account, for we have done nothing of which we are ashamed, but for the glory of his name, and the still further discomfiture of that abominable pope. The news of all this has terribly alarmed the people at Rome. They are all in a fright, and dare not assemble a council."

At about the same time, negotiations were entered into with Henry, duke of Brunswick, having for their object the attaching him to the Lutheran doctrines; but they remained without effect. On the 23rd October, 1539, Luther wrote to the elector, announcing that similar negotiations with the envoys of the king of England had been equally unsuccessful. The letter containing this information is signed by Luther, Melancthon, and several other Wittemberg divines.

LXXXIII. (p. 249.)—"Dr. John Pomer once told me, that in the Town Hall at Lubeck there had been found, in an old chronicle, a prophecy that in the year 1550, there would arise in Germany a great commotion on account of religion; and that if the emperor interfered in the matter, he would lose all his possessions. But I doubt very much whether the emperor will go to war for the sake of the pope; war is too costly."

The editor of the *Tischreden*, Aurifaber, adds, that Charles V. hung the walls of his retreat of St. Just with twenty pieces of tapestry, representing the principal actions of his reign, which he used to amuse himself every day with walking up and down and looking at. And whenever, says Aurifaber, he stopped opposite that representing the taking of the elector at Muhlberg, he would sigh and murmur, *Ah, if I had let him be as he was, I should have remained what I was.*—(Tischreden, 6.) This observation, which the editor, perhaps designedly, does not seem to understand, simply expresses Charles' regret at the wholly false step he took in giving the electorate to young Maurice.

LXXXIV. (p. 249.)—"I will anticipate your letters, and tell you myself what is passing at Ratisbon. You have been sent for by the emperor, and he has told you to turn over in your mind conditions of peace. You have replied in Latin as well as you could, but have found yourself unequal to so great a matter. Eck, in his usual way, vociferated: 'Most gracious emperor, I will prove against any one, that we are in the right, and that the pope is the head of the church.' And there's all you have to tell me." (25th June, 1541.)

LXXXV. (p. 250.)—The court sought to exercise a sort of control and superintendence over the works even of Luther. In 1531, he had written a book entitled *Against the Hypocrite of Dresden*, and published it, without first submitting the manuscript to the elector. Having been called upon by the chancellor Bruck for an explanation of this omission, he replied: "If all my minor productions were sent to the court prior to their publication, either they would undergo so many critical revisions and alterations that they would not appear at all, or, if they appeared, our enemies would impute the joint-authorship of them to half a dozen people who were not at all to blame in the matter. If I send them straight to the printers, there can be no question but that they are wholly mine, and I stand the brunt of all objections, as I am quite ready to do."

He had on another occasion, of a more serious character, to contend against the interference of the court. Albert, archbishop of Mayence, had put to death one of his officers, named Schauz, in an illegal manner; and, according to the public rumour, to satisfy private animosity. Luther hereupon addressed to the prince two letters, full of indignation. The first of these, dated 31st July, 1535, begins in the following terms: "I do not write to you, cardinal, in the hope of producing any effect upon your utterly depraved heart. That is an idea which I have altogether renounced. I write to you simply to satisfy my own conscience before God and man, and that I may not by my silence appear to sanction the terrible deed you have perpetrated." Further on, he designates the prince, *Cardinal of Hell*, and threatens him with the Eternal Justiciary, who will come and demand from him an account of the innocent blood he has shed. In the second letter, dated March 1536, he says: "The paper I send herewith will let you see that the blood of Schauz is not silent in Germany, whatever it may be in your grace's palace, and amidst your courtiers. Abel lives in God, and his blood cries out against the murderers......I see by your grace's letter to Antony Schauz, that you absolutely seek to throw the guilt of his death upon his family. I have witnessed and I have heard of many a cardinal's villany, but I could not have imagined a viper cruel and insolent enough to outrage in this manner an unhappy family which his own infernal deed had made desolate. I have collected the last words of Schauz, in the moment of his agony. I have down on paper his dying protestations against violence, when your holiness was having his teeth pulled out to extort from him a false confession; I will publish these words, and by God's help, your holiness shall dance to a tune you never heard before......Cain said, indeed, *Am I my brother's keeper?* but the Lord said, too, *Cursed be thou from the earth*......I commend your miserable soul to God, if, indeed, in the insolence of the bloody hat of Rome, you do not think it beneath you to be commended to God."

The elector of Saxony and duke Albert of Prussia, the cardinal's relatives, considering the language of this letter somewhat of the most violent, sent word to Luther, that, in attacking the cardinal thus, he would be attacking the honour of their family, and commanded him to modify what he had to say. Luther, none the less, published the menaced statement some time after.

LXXXVI. (p. 250.)—From the very outset of the conferences, Luther foresaw they would lead to nothing. He was distrustful even of the firmness of Bucer and of the landgrave of Hesse. He says, in a letter to the chancellor Bruck: "I fear the landgrave is allowing himself to be enticed too far by the papists, and that he will endeavour to drag us with him. But he has already led us up and down a great deal more than enough, and I shall no longer follow him. I would much rather take the whole burden on my own shoulders, and walk on alone, at my own risk and peril, as I did in the beginning. We know that it is the cause of God; that it is He who has raised us up, who has brought us thus far; He will give victory to his cause. Those who do not choose to follow us can remain behind. Neither the emperor nor the Turk, nor all the devils together, can effect aught against this cause, whatever they may do to us and our mortal bodies. I am perfectly indignant at their treating this as a mere worldly matter; as a mere affair of the emperor's, of the Turks, of the princes', wherein they may, just as they please, go here, or rest there, or step aside, or come back again. This is a cause in which the devil and his angels are fighting against Satan and his angels. Those who believe not in God may not place themselves in his ranks." (April, 1541.)

LXXXVII. (p. 250.)—" I will go Hagenau, and have a near look at this formidable Syrian, this Behemoth, whom the dweller in heaven laughs at, in Psalm ii.... But they will not comprehend that laugh, until they come to the time *when they shall perish by the way, when the Lord's anger shall have been kindled, for that they would not kiss his Son.* Amen! amen! May that time soon come! They have deserved it—they have insisted upon it." (2nd July, 1540.)

LXXXVIII. (p. 253.)—" The secret marriages of princes and great lords are regular marriages before God, somewhat analogous with the concubinage of the patriarchs." (Tischreden, 320.) This affords an explanation of the consultation in favour of the landgrave.

LXXXIX. (p. 254.)—" The ingratitude of man is the test of good works; if what we do please the world, be assured it will not be agreeable to God." (6th August, 1539.)

" Depression and melancholy proceed from the devil; of that I am quite certain. God neither afflicts, nor intimidates, nor kills; he is the God of the living. He sent us his only Son, that through him we might live, through him overcome death." (Tischreden, 205.)

On Sadness.—" You cannot," says one of the sages—" you cannot prevent the birds from flying over your head; but you may readily prevent them from making their nests in your hair." (19th June, 1530.)

John of Stockhausen applied to Luther for a remedy against spiritual temptations, and against melancholy. The Doctor, in reply, advised him to avoid solitude, and to strengthen his will by an active, laborious life. He recommends him, in addition, to have frequent prayer, and to study the work of Gerson, *De Cogitationibus Blasphemiæ.* (27th Nov. 1532.)

He gave similar advice to the young prince Joachim of Anhalt: " Gaiety," says he, " and courage, innocent gaiety and rational, honourable courage, are the best medicine for young men, and for old men too, for all men, against sad thoughts. I myself, who have passed all my former life in melancholy and depression of spirit, now accept joy and happiness wherever they present themselves—nay, go in search of them. Criminal pleasure proceeds from Satan, and is accursed; but the joy we experience in the intercourse with honest and pious persons is agreeable in the sight of God. Get on horseback and go out hunting with your friends, and partake of all the innocent amusements they suggest to you. Solitude and melancholy are poison to the mind, they are death to man, and more especially to young people." (26th June, 1534.)

Melancthon related the following apologue one day at Luther's table: "A peasant passing through a wood, came to a cavern in which there was a serpent. A great stone which closed the entrance prevented the creature from coming out. He entreated the peasant to roll away the stone, promising him for his compliance a handsome reward. The peasant, induced by this prospect, released the serpent, and then asked for his reward. To which the serpent replied that he would give him the same reward that the world always bestowed upon its benefactors: that he would kill him. The peasant begged and prayed for mercy, but the only concession he could obtain was that they should submit the point to the first animal they met, and abide by his decision. This happened to be an old horse, all skin and bone. His reply was: 'I have spent all the strength I had in the service of man; as my recompence, after starving me almost to death, he is now about to kill me for the sake of my skin.' The serpent consented to refer the matter to one more arbiter. This was an old dog, whose master had just broken half the bones in its body. He gave his decision most emphatically against the peasant. The serpent was then about to kill his benefactor, but the latter induced him to accept one more judge, whose award was to be final. Soon afterwards, they met a fox. The peasant ran up to him, and whispered him that if he would get him off, he would give him all the poultry in his yard. The fox having heard both parties, said that before he pronounced judgment, it was essential for him to see how things had previously stood, and that the serpent must return into the cavern. The animal consented to this, and as soon as he was in, the peasant rolled the stone back to its former position, and there the serpent was fast. The fox came next night to the peasant's to take the poultry that had been promised him, and the peasant killed him for his pains.' When Melancthon had finished his story: 'Ay,' said Luther, 'that is just the image of what we see in the world. He whom we have saved from the gallows puts the rope round our neck. If I had no other example of this, that of Jesus Christ would suffice, who after having redeemed the whole world from sin, death, the devil, and hell, was crucified.'" (Tischreden, 56.)

The pleasantries, the jests, the puns, which we so often come upon in Luther's letters of former years, now entirely disappear; his correspondence becomes sombre, mournful; we scarcely ever see a smile on his lips. The grotesque description of a military expedition of some citizens against a band of robbers, unwrinkles his brow but for an instant: "Here has been a fresh achievement of Kohlhase (a famous brigand whose life forms the subject of a curious historical romance); he has carried off a rich miller of this place. As soon as we heard of the affair, we valorously rushed out into the country, keeping, of course, within safe range of the walls, and, like so many canvas St. Christophers and wooden St. Georges, frightened the crows with sundry musket shots. We have cut down all the trees round about, and carried them into the town, for fear Kohlhase should make a bridge of them, and so get over our little ditch in the night. We are terrible Achilleses and Hectors, I can assure you, fearing no enemy, so long as no enemy presents himself."

XC. (p. 256.)—In 1541, a citizen of Wittemberg, named Cleeman Schobert, followed Luther down several streets, with an arquebuse in his hand, probably with the intention of killing him; he was arrested and punished. (Ukert, i. 313.)

XCI. (p. 258.)—The *Tischreden* (Table Talk,) whence most of the following passages are derived, was first published in 1566, by John Aurifaber, one of Luther's disciples. They form a folio volume of 1254 pages. Luther at his table was always surrounded by his children and friends, Melancthon, Jonas, Aurifaber, and other coadjutors in his labours, and companions of his leisure. A place at this table was an envied distinction: "I would willingly," he writes to Gaspard Muller, "have received Kegel into my family circle, for various reasons; but as young Porse, of Jena, is on the eve of returning here, my table will be full, and I cannot send away my old and faithful companions to make room for new friends. However, it is possible that, after Easter, we may have room, and in that case I will do as you desire—that is, if my lord Catherine will grant us her permission, of which I have no doubt." (19th Jan. 1538.) *Dominus* Ketha is a name by which he used frequently to designate his wife. He begins one of his letters to her thus, (26th July, 1640): *To the rich and noble dame Von Zulsdorf, madame the doctoress Catherine Luther, resident at Wittemberg, but at times taking her pleasure at her estate of Zulsdorf, these from her loving husband.*"

XCII. (p. 258.)—On the 26th August, 1542, we find Luther writing to Mark Cordel: "According to our arrangements, my dear Mark, I send thee my son John, that thou mayst employ him in teaching the children grammar and music, and, at the same time superintend and correct his moral conduct. If thou succeedest in improving him, I will send thee two other sons of mine. For, though I desire my children to be good divines, yet I would have them sound grammarians, and accomplished musicians."

Dr. Jonas observed one day, that the curse of God upon disobedient children was manifest in the family of Luther; the young man just referred to always suffering from illness: "Ay," said Dr. Luther, ''tis the punishment due to his disobedience. He almost killed me once, and ever since I have lost all my strength of body. Thanks to him, I now thoroughly understand that passage where St. Paul speaks of children who kill their parents, not by the sword, but by disobedience. Such children seldom live long, and are never happy. . . . . Oh, God! how wicked is this world! how monstrous the times in which we live! These are the times of which Christ said, *When the Son of Man cometh shall he find faith on the earth?* Happy they who died ere these days came upon the world!" (Tischreden, 48.) It was to this unworthy son, when yet a child, that Luther addressed the following charming letter:—

"Grace and peace to you in Jesus Christ, my dear little child; I perceive with pleasure that you are making good progress in your learning, and that you now give attention to your prayers. Continue to do so, my dear child, and when I return home I will give you beautiful things.

"I know a lovely and smiling garden, full of children dressed in robes of gold, who play under the trees with beautiful apples, pears, cherries, nuts, and prunes. They sing, they leap, they are all joyful; there are also beautiful little ponies, with bridles of gold and saddles of silver. In passing through the garden, I asked a man what it meant, and who were the children. He replied, 'These are the children who love to pray and to learn, who are pious and good children.' I said to him, 'Dear friend, I have also a child, his name is little John Luther: might he not also come here, and eat these beautiful apples and pears, ride on these beautiful ponies, and play with the other children?' The man replied to me, 'If your child, your dear little John Luther, is wise, if he says his prayers, and learns willingly, he may come, and he may bring little Philip and James[1] along with him. He will here find fifes, drums, and other fine instruments to produce music; they will dance and amuse themselves with the cross-bow.' While I was speaking, the man pointed out to me, in the middle of the garden, a beautiful grass park where the children danced, and where the fifes, drums, and cross-bows were all lying. But it was morning; the children had not breakfasted, and I only waited till the dance commenced. I then said to the man, 'Dear sir, I intend to write immediately to my dear little John, and I will tell him to be a good boy, to pray, and learn well, that he may be permitted to come to this garden. He has a dear little sister whom he loves much, her name is Madaline, may he bring her with him?' The man replied, 'Yes, tell him they may both come together.' Be wise, then, my dear little boy; tell Philip and James to be wise also, and you will all be allowed to visit and play in the beautiful garden. I commend my dear child to the protection of God. Salute Madeline, and give her a kiss for me. Your father who loves you, MARTIN LUTHER. 19th June, 1530."

---

[1] The sons of Philip Melancthon. Little is known of them, and it is supposed that they died in early life.

XCIII. (p. 258.)—"Woman is the most precious of creatures. She is full of grace and virtue; she maintains the faith.

"First love is violent, it intoxicates us, and takes away the reason. The intoxication once passed away, well-disciplined and pious souls retain the honourable part of love; the wicked retain nothing.

"Gracious Lord! if it be thy will that I live without a wife, sustain me against temptations; but if it be thy will that I marry, grant me a good and pious spouse, with whom I may pass my days quietly and happily, whom I may love, and who will love me." (Tischreden, 329.)

XCIV. (p. 262.)—"A marriage sanctioned by authority, and not contrary to the word of God, is a good marriage, whatever the degree of relationship of the parties." (Tischreden, 321.)

Luther greatly blamed the lawyers, who, "contrary to their own consciences, contrary to natural law, to divine law, to the imperial law, maintain secret promises of marriage to be valid. In this matter every body should be left to the dictates of his own conscience. No one can be compelled to love another."

"Dower marriage gifts, settlements, and so on, are for the consideration of the civil authority, to which I wholly refer them. We are the shepherds of men's consciences, not of body and goods." (Tischreden, 315.)

On being consulted in a case of adultery, he said: "The parties should be cited to answer for themselves, and then if the case is proved, be separated altogether. These things concern the civil authority, for marriage is a temporal matter, which interests the church in no way except as to the conscience. (Ib. 322.)

On the 1st Feb., 1539, he said: "Though these marriage affairs involve us in a great deal of trouble and anxiety, rendering it necessary for us to study the subject every day, to say nothing of additional reading, praying, writing, preaching, yet I am glad that consistories have been established for the settlement of matrimonial questions. . . . We find constantly parents, particularly fathers-in-law, without any valid reason, forbidding their children to marry. The civil authority and the spiritual minister ought to look to these cases, and favour the contemplated union, if they see fit, even against the will of the parents, supposing that will to be arbitrarily and unreasonably exercised. Children ought to remind their parents of the example of Samson. We are no longer in the times of popery, when people were obliged to follow the law, however it was opposed to equity." (Ib.)

XCV. (p. 266.)—"God knows all trades better than the most accomplished artisans here below. As a tailor, he makes for the stag a coat that lasts him all his lifetime, and hundreds of years after, without tearing. As a shoemaker, he gives him a set of shoes that lasts just as long. And will it be denied that he is a fine cook, seeing how perfectly he cooks, and makes all things ready in the best style, at his great fire the sun? If the Lord were to sell us what he gives us, he would make a large fortune every hour, but as he gives us all things for nothing, we don't even thank him for them." (Tischreden, 27.)

This strange passage, and many others like it, show us in Luther the probable model of Abraham à Sancta Clara. In the seventeenth century, people only imitated Luther's defects.

XCVI. (p. 268.)—"Here have I become a disciple of the Decalogue. I begin to perceive that the Decalogue is the dialectic of the Gospel, and the Gospel the rhetoric of the Decalogue. Christ has all that Moses had, but Moses had not all that Christ has." (20th June, 1530.)

XCVII. (p. 269.)—He thus addresses John Von Sternberg, in dedicating to him his translation of the 97th Psalm: "My reason for placing your name at the head of this little work, was not merely to attract the attention of persons who ordinarily despise all art and all learning; I wished also to afford, in this way, a testimony that there are still pious men to be found among our nobles. Unfortunately, the majority of our nobility at the present time are so insolent and so depraved that they excite the wrath of the poor man. If they desire to be respected by others, they must, in the first place, themselves respect God and his word. If they continue in their present arrogant and wicked course of life, they will soon become lower than peasants; indeed, as it is, they are worse than peasants, though they still bear the name of nobles, and have feathered hats. Let them not forget Munzer.

"I trust that this little book, and others like it, may touch your heart, and that you will, through its pages, make a more useful pilgrimage than that which you heretofore made to Jerusalem. Not that I despise these pilgrimages in themselves; I would readily perform one myself, if I could, and I always hear with pleasure any accounts of them. What I mean is, that they are not made in the proper spirit. I remember, that when I myself went to Rome, I ran about, like a madman, to all the churches, all the convents, all the places of note of every kind; I implicitly believed every tale about all of them that imposture had invented. I said a dozen masses, and I almost regretted that my father and mother were not dead, so that I might have availed myself of the opportunity to draw their souls out of purgatory by a dozen more masses, and other good works of a similar description. 'Tis a proverb at Rome, *Happy the mother whose son says mass for her on the eve of St. John.* How glad I should have been to have saved my mother.

"We did these things then, knowing no better; 'tis the pope's interest to encourage such lies. Now, thank God, we have the gospels, the Psalms, and the other words of God. To them we can make pilgrimages more useful than any others; in them we can visit and contemplate the true promised land, the true Jerusalem, the true paradise. In them we walk, not amid the tombs of saints, or over their mortal relics, but in their hearts, their thoughts, their spirit." (Coburg, 29th August, 1530.)

XCVIII. (p. 270.)—"I sweat blood and water in my efforts to render the Prophets into the vulgar tongue. Good God! what work it is! How difficult 'tis to make these Jew writers speak German. They struggle furiously before they will give up their Hebrew to our barbarous tongue. 'Tis as though Philomela, forgetting her sweet melody, were to imitate the cuckoo's monotonous note." (14th June, 1528.)

He says, elsewhere, that while translating the Bible, he sometimes occupied several weeks in hunting out, and meditating upon the signification of a single word. (Ukert, ii. 337.)

To John Frederic, duke of Saxony, on sending him his translation of the prophet Daniel, he says: "The historians relate, to the honour of Alexander the Great, that he always carried Homer about with him, and at night deposited the precious volume beneath his pillow: how much more just that the same honour, and even greater honours, should be rendered to the prophet Daniel by all the kings and princes of the earth? They ought not merely to place him under their heads; they should treasure him up in their hearts, for he teaches great things indeed." (Feb. or March, 1530.)

XCIX. (p. 270.) "The saints often sinned, often went wrong. What insanity to be always holding up to us their acts and their words as infallible rules of conduct. Let these mad sophists, these ignorant pontiffs, these impious priests, these sacrilegious monks—let the whole vile gang know that we were not baptized in the name of Augustine, in the name of Bernard, of Gregory, of Peter, or Paul, in the name of the benevolent faculty of theology of Sodom (the Sorbonne) of Paris, or of the Gomorrha of Louvain, but in the name of Jesus Christ, our Master, alone." (De Abrogandâ Missâ privatâ. Op. Lat. ii. 245.)

"The true saints are all the authorities, all the servants of the church, all the parents, all the children who believe in Jesus Christ, who commit no sin, and who fulfil, each in his condition, the duties imposed upon them by God."—Tischreden, 134.

Luther had small faith in the legends of the saints, and regarded the anchorites with profound contempt......"If one has committed an excess in eating or drinking, it is soon to be expiated by fasting, and perhaps a touch of fever."

"The legend of St. Christopher is a fine Christian poem. The Greeks, who were a learned, wise, and ingenious people, desired therein to show their idea of a Christian. (*Christoforos*, one who bears Christ.) The legend of St. George is of the same character. The legend of St. Catherine is contrary to the whole Roman history."

C. (p. 271.)—In dedicating to Frederick, abbot of Nuremberg, his translation of the 118th Psalm, Luther says, "This is my own psalm, my favourite psalm. I love them all, I love the whole gospel, for it is my sole consolation, my sole life; but I have more especially attached myself to this psalm, and have, in truth, a sort of right to call it my own. It has deserved well of me; it has saved me from many a difficulty, whence neither the emperor, nor kings, nor wise men, nor saints, could have extricated me. It is, my friend, dearer to me than all the honours, all the power of the earth. I would not exchange it for the whole earth, if I could.

"But, it will be said, this psalm is common to us all, and no one has a right to arrogate it to himself. Ay, and so is Christ common to us all, and yet Christ is mine. I am not at all jealous, however, of this my property; I am willing to share it with the whole world. I only would to God that every man would as eagerly claim this psalm to be his own. It would be a contest most pleasing to God, a competition full of union and perfect charity." (Coburg, 1st July, 1530.)

CI. (p. 273.)—In the commencement of 1519, Luther addressed to Jerome Dungersheim a remarkable letter on the importance and authority of the fathers of the church. "The bishop of Rome, it would appear, is supreme by his dignity. It is to him we must refer all difficult cases, all nice questions. I don't know whether I should be able to maintain this supremacy of his in opposition to the Greeks who controvert it.

"If I acknowledge in the pope the sole right of governing in the church, I must, as a consequence of this admission, treat as so many heretics, Jerome, Augustine, Athanasius, Cyprian, Gregory, and all the bishops of the East; none of these having been instituted by him or under him. The council of Nicea was not assembled by his authority; he presided not over it, either in person or by deputy. What am I to say to the decrees of this council? Which of them are we to acknowledge? Any? All? None?......'Tis a way with you and with Eck to accept as a clear case everything that fell from any of these authorities of yours, and to modify by the fathers' judgment, the words of the gospel, as though the latter were of inferior value to the former. I proceed upon quite a different principle. Like St. Augustine and St. Bernard, while I respect the various authorities, I ascend the stream till I reach the great fountain whence they all take their rise." He then gives several instances of mistakes into which the fathers had fallen, and criticises them philologically, to show that the commentators referred to did not understand the

Hebrew text. "Of how many authorities does not Jerome make abusive application in his controversy with Jovinian; of how many Augustine, in assailing Pelagius! Augustine, for instance, says that this verse in Genesis, *Let us make man in our own image*, is a proof of the Trinity, whereas the Hebrew text is, *I will make man after my own image*. The Master of Sentences affords a sad example of this sort of thing, in his attempt to make the words of all the fathers agree together. The result is that we become the laughing stock of the heretics, when we present ourselves before them with all this obscure or double-meaning phraseology. Eck constitutes himself the champion of the most contradictory opinions. Our dispute will turn upon this subject." (1519.)

"I always wonder on what principle Jerome has had accorded him the title of Doctor of Churches, and Origen, that of Master of Churches. You could not make a Christian out of all their books put together; they were both too much led away by the pomp of works. Augustine himself would not have been much better, had not the Pelagians run him so hard, and compelled him to do his very best in defending the faith." (26th August, 1530.)

"He who likened monachism to baptism was a sheer madman; rather an utter block, than simply a fool. . . . What! Dost thou heed Jerome, when he speaks so impiously of God?—when he lays it down, that next to one's self, one should have the greatest regard for one's parents? Will you listen to Jerome—so repeatedly wrong—so repeatedly sinning? Will you, in a word, rather believe a man than God? If so, go, and believe with Jerome, that we should pass over the bodies of our prostrated parents to flee to the desert." (Letter to Severinus, an Austrian monk, 6th October, 1527.)

CII. (p. 275.)—"Gregory of Rimini has convicted the schoolmen of a doctrine worse than that of the Pelagians; for, though the Pelagians think that one may do a good work without grace, they do not go the length of affirming, that we can, without grace, attain heaven. The schoolmen say, with Pelagius, that without grace we may do a good work, not a meritorious work; but they go infinitely beyond Pelagius, when they affirm that man has the instinct, the inspiration of right natural reason, to which the will may conform itself naturally, for the Pelagians admit that man is aided by the law of God." (1519.)

CIII. (p. 278.)—On the 2nd December, 1536, we find a letter from Luther to the king of Denmark, formally approving of the suppression of episcopacy, and urging that prince to make a good use of the confiscated church property—that is to say, (according to another letter of his, on the same subject, to the margrave, George of Brandenburg, dated 18th July, 1529,) to apply them to the foundation and support of schools and universities.

"The emperor is devouring all the bishoprics in his reach. The nobles must be on their guard. I have done all I could to secure that ecclesiastical property should not be swallowed up in this way, and that a portion of such of it as belonged to noble families should be retained for the poor members of those families; but I cannot achieve this." (Tischreden, 351.)

CIV. (p. 279.)—"In the year 1530, Philip, at Augsburg, was six hours together with that swift-brained cardinal of Saltzburg; and, among other discourses, he had much talk with him about religion. In the end, the cardinal said to him: 'My dear *Domine Philip*, we priests were never yet good; we know that your doctrine is right; but you ought to know, that never yet any man was able to get the better of the priests: you will not be the first to do so.' This cardinal was the son of a horse-jockey in Augsburg, whose father was of an ancient and good family in that place, but, by reason of poverty, came to be a servant. He was the first cardinal we had in Germany. Through his sister's influence, he made himself well known in the emperor Maximilian's court, and was afterwards sent in a legation to the pope to Rome; later, he was made coadjutor of the bishopric of Saltzburg. This cardinal loves his cardinal's hat better than the divine truth; he fears the loss of it, and of his bishopric. He believes not that God is able to put down the mighty from their seat, and to exalt the humble and meek. He is of a cowardly disposition, he cannot hold out long, his conscience pricks him too sorely. The papists differ among themselves, they cannot agree in their own pedlaries. For, *anno* 1530, in the proceeding at Augsburg, they made no mention, no, not so much as one word was spoken, of the article of the pope's supremacy, which was wont to be the chief article of popedom. We ought to set upon such an ungodly and insolent creature, we ought to preach and to write against him. If God spare me life and health but only one half year, I will fetch a dance with that bride over block and stone. I never read such fearful examples of hard hearts, as in these cardinals and bishops; they far surpass the Jews, Pharaoh, and others; in a word, they are next neighbours to the devil. My heart trembles when I think on them. Loving Lord and Saviour Christ, give me life and strength that I may shave the crown of this prelate; for he is a crafty derider of thy name, he is a downright knave, he sticks not to boast that very few of his stratagems have failed him. The good and godly princess electrix of Saxony lately asked me, If any hope were to be had of this cardinal's conversion? I answered: I believe not; however, it would be a great joy unto me, if in time he be won over to the truth, and repent; but there is little hope thereof. I would rather believe and hope the same in Pilate, in Herod, and Dioclesian, who sinned openly.

"I have hitherto prayed for this bishop, *categoricé*, *affirmativé*, *positivè*, with my whole heart, that God might convert him, and I have essayed, by repeated letters, to bring him to repentance. I pray for him now *hypotheticè and desperabunde.* This cardinal wrote often very friendly unto me, thinking to grease my lips, insomuch that I thought he would act upon my advice to take a wife; but he intended with smooth words to deceive me. However, at the diet at Augsburg I learned to know him right; yet, nevertheless, he still pretended great friendship towards me, and in causes of weight would always make choice of me to be an umpire." (Tischreden, 274.)

"At the imperial assembly at Augsburg, in the year 1530, the bishop of Salzburg said unto me, 'Four ways and means there are to make a reconciliation between us and you protestants: One is, that ye yield unto us; to that you say you cannot. The second is, that we yield unto you; but that we will not do. The third is, that the one party, by force, should be compelled to yield to the other; but thereupon a great tumult might be raised: therefore, the fourth way or means were to be applauded and used—namely, that now being here assembled together, the one party should strive to exterminate the other, and that party which shall have the advantage, and be the stronger, the same shall put the other party into a bag.' Whereupon, I answered him, and said: 'This, indeed, were a very substantial course to settle unity and peace, wonderful wisely considered of, found out, and expounded by such a holy and Christian-like bishop as you are;' and thereupon I took letters out of my pocket which, shortly before, I had received from Rome, and gave the same to the bishop to read; which letter related a pretty passage that fell out there, five weeks before, between some cardinals and the pope's fool, as followeth:

"These cardinals had been in serious consultation how, and by what means, the protestants in Germany might be convinced touching their error, or suppressed; but they saw the difficulty of it, in that the protestants, in their books and writings, powerfully cited, against the papists, the sacred Scripture, and especially opposed and withstood them with the doctrines of St. Paul, which were great blocks in the papists' way, insomuch that they found it a business not so easily to be accomplished. Then said the fool unto the cardinals, 'I know how to give you herein an advice, whereby you easily may be rid and quitted of St. Paul, that his doctrines shall not be approved of, as thus: The pope hath power to make saints; therefore let St. Paul be taken out of the number of the apostles, and preferred to be a saint; and then his *dicta*, which are against you, shall be no more held for apostolical.' This and your proposition, I said, are of equal value." (Ib. 19.)

CV. (p. 280.) "The Mendicants alone are divided into several orders, and the Minorites, in like manner, also into seven. All these sects the holy father takes care to feed and nourish, lest they should unite and come together." (Letter to the Diet at Prague, 15th July, 1522.)

CVI. (p. 286.)—In 1530, Luther translated a selection from the fables of Æsop. In the preface, he observes that there probably never was any author of the name of Æsop at all, and that the fables themselves were collected from the mouths of the common people. (Werke, ix. 1455.)

He writes thus to Wenceslaus Link, of Nuremberg, on 20th March, 1536: "If it be not giving you too much trouble, my dear Wenceslaus, I would beg of you to collect for me all the drawings, books, hymns, songs of the minstrels, and rhymes, that have been printed and published in German, in your city, during the past year. Send me all you find of such things: I am most anxious to have all I can get of them. We manage to write Latin books here, but as to German books, we are mere apprentices. However, we are doing our best to improve ourselves in this respect, and I hope we shall soon satisfy you as to our progress."

Luther was incessant in his efforts to raise the character of Wittemberg in every possible way. Writing to the elector John, 20th May, 1530, he says, seeking to raise his courage, and to console him for the various vexations in which the Reformation had involved him: "See how God has manifested his grace and goodness in the states of your highness. In them the gospel has its most pious and faithful ministers, those who teach its word with the greatest purity, zeal, and fruit. You see growing up around you an excellent generation, of good disposition and good conduct, and who will soon be learned in the holy Scripture. It rejoices my heart to see our young people—boys and girls even—understanding God and Christ better, having a purer faith, and praying with more fervent effect than all the episcopal schools and most famous convents put together. This charming youth has been granted you as a sign of divine favour and mercy. God, as it were, has said to you, 'Dear duke John, I confide to thee my most precious treasure: be as a father to these children. I would have thee protect and guide them: be the gardener of this paradise,'" &c.

The duke does not seem to have adopted the charge here suggested to him, for Luther mentions in several of his letters that there were at Wittemberg a great number of students who had scarce anything but bread and water to live upon.

CVII. (p. 287.)—Heine, in the *Revue des Deux Mondes* for 1st March, 1834, observes: "Not less remarkable, not less significant than his prose works, are the poems of Luther, those stirring songs which, as it were, escaped from him in the very midst of his combats and his necessities, like a flower making its way from between rough stones, or a moonbeam glittering amid dark clouds. Luther loved music; he wrote, indeed, a treatise on the art. His versification, accordingly, is in a very high degree harmonious, so that under this head, too, he may be called the Swan of Eisleben. Not that he was by any means gentle or swan-like in the songs which he composed for the purpose of exciting the courage of his people; in these he is fervent, fierce. The hymn which he composed on his way to Worms, and which he and his companions chanted as they entered that city, is a regular war-song. The old cathedral trembled when it heard these novel sounds; the very crows flew from their nests on its towers. That hymn, the Marseillaise of the Reformation, has preserved to the present day its potent spell over German hearts, and we may yet hear it thundered forth again under similar circumstances."

CVIII. (p. 288.)—"The doctor was speaking one day of the genius and skill of the Italian painters. 'They imitate nature so perfectly,' said he, 'independently of the exact colour and form of the object designed, they give such admirable expression to the thoughts and feelings within, as it were, that their pictures seem living things. Flanders follows close upon Italy in this matter. The Flemings are very sharp people, altogether; they learn with similar facility all the foreign languages. 'Tis a proverb, you know: Carry a Fleming in a bag through France or Italy, and he will know the language before he's got a hundred miles.'" (Luther, 424.)

CIX. (p. 292.)—He says in his treatise *De Usuris:* "I call those people usurers who lend money at five and six per cent. The Scripture forbids the lending money at interest; we ought to lend money as we lend anything to a neighbour. Even the civil law forbids usury. 'Tis not an act of charity to exchange a thing with anybody, gaining by the exchange; that's robbery. A usurer deserves to be hanged quite as much as any other thief. Here at Leipzig, 'tis monstrous: a man lends you a hundred florins, and at the end of a single year, you've got to give him forty besides for interest. We should not keep engagements entered into with usurers; usurers should not be admitted to partake of the sacraments, nor be buried in consecrated ground. This is the last advice I shall give usurers: they want money, gold: well, let them address themselves to One who will not give them merely 10 or 20 per cent., but who will give them 100 for 10. He has more than enough to satisfy their utmost avidity; His treasures are inexhaustible; He can give and give without lessening his heap." (Op. Lat. Wittemb. vii. 419.)

Dr. Henning proposed this question to Luther: "If I had amassed money and wished to keep it, and a man came and asked me to lend him some, might I with a good conscience say to him: 'I have no money?' 'Yes,' replied Luther, 'you may do so with a perfectly good conscience; for all it means is: I have no money I wish to part with. Christ, when he orders us to give, does not tell us to give to prodigals and wasters. In this town, the most necessitous people are the students. Their poverty is very great, but their idleness is still greater.... I do not choose to take the bread out of the mouths of my wife and children, to throw it away upon people to whom nothing does any good." (Tischreden, 64.)

CX. (p. 303.)—Still Luther preferred it to the Saxon law. "Dr. Luther, speaking of the great barbarism and severity of the Saxon law, said, that things would go on much better, if the imperial law were observed throughout the empire. But it is a fixed opinion, at least, that such a change could not take place without great confusion and detriment to all classes." (Tischreden, 304.)

CXI. (p. 304.) In the last letter but one he sent to Melancthon, dated 6th February, 1546, Luther says, speaking of the jurists: "O sycophants! O sophists! O pests of the human race! I write to you in anger; but if I were ever so cool, I could say no less to you."

As to the deserving jurists, he desires that their condition should be ameliorated. "The doctors at law do not get enough money, and so are obliged to turn attorneys. In Italy, they give a priest four hundred ducats a-year and more; in Germany, they only have one hundred. They ought to have competent provision, as well as deserving pastors and preachers. For want of this, they are fain to do all sorts of things to support their families, to meddle in farming, and what not." (Tischreden, 414.)

CXII. (p. 304.)—In writing to count Albert of Mansfeldt, in reference to a matrimonial case referred to him, he says: "The peasants, those coarse, rude people, who seek only the liberty of the flesh, and the lawyers, who always decide against the faith, have so worn me out, that I have altogether declined to burden myself additionally with the settlement of these marriage matters, and have already told several people, in the devil's name, to do just what they please about them: *Sinite mortuos sepelire mortuos*. The world insists upon having the pope; so let it. All the lawyers are for him. I hardly know whether at my death they will have the honesty and courage to let my children have my name and what rags I leave behind me. They decide always according to the pope's law. And whose fault is it that they do so? Why the fault of your lords, who puff them up, who support them in whatever they choose to say and decide, who oppress us poor divines, however much reason may be on our side."... (5th October, 1536.)

"There ought to be, in every country, two hundred divines to one lawyer. Meantime, we ought to turn our superfluous lawyers into pastors; and so we shall, as you will see." (Tischreden, 4.)

CXIII. (p. 306.)—"The righteous, which are justified and saved before God only by faith in Christ, do good works willingly of themselves: as St. Paul saith, "Ye are saved by grace through faith, and that not of yourselves, it is the gift of God, not of works, lest any man should boast; for we are his workmanship, created in Christ Jesus unto good works," &c.

"But the reason we do not live without sin, according to the state in which man was first created, is, because we have lost the image of God, and are now become the servants of the devil, through original sin."

CXIV. (p. 308.)—"*Philip Melancthon's Disputation held with Luther, about the article of Justification, Anno* 1536.—"*Philip Melancthon:* The opinion of St. Augustine of justification (as it seems) was more consistent when he disputed not, than it was when he used to dispute; for thus he says: 'We ought to hold that we are justified by faith, that is by our regeneration, or by being made new creatures. Now if it be so, then we are not justified only by faith, but by all the gifts and virtues of God given unto us. That is St. Augustine's opinion. Hence also that *Gratia gratum faciens* of the school divines, grace which makes accepted. They allege also that love is the same grace that makes us acceptable before God. Now what is your opinion, sir; do you hold that a man is justified by this regeneration, as is St. Augustine's opinion?

"*Luther:* I hold this, and am certain that the true meaning of the gospel, and of the apostles is, that we are justified before God *gratis*, only by God's mere mercy, wherewith and by reason whereof, he imputes righteousness unto us in Christ.

"*Melancthon:* I hold not that a human creature is justified only by God's mercy; our righteousness, which is a good conscience, is needful by reason of works: or, will you not allow me to say, man is justified *principaliter*, principally, by faith; *minus principaliter* (in the least measure) by works? yet, in such a way, that faith be in expectation, and the same expectation remaining, the fulfilling of the law is not required, but faith supplies that which is wanting in the law. You will allow that there are two sorts of righteousness needful before God, namely, faith and a good conscience, in which faith supplies what is wanting in the law, which is nothing else than to say: A man is justified not by faith only. For you never understood (as Augustine) that justification is from the beginning of the regeneration; he holds not that a man is saved merely for nothing, but is saved by reason of the virtues which are given unto him. I desire your grave opinion touching this of Augustine; for his opinion of deserts is directly opposite to your meaning, for he takes not deserts away, but only of the ungodly.

"*Luther:* I hold that man is, and remains justified only through God's mercy; for that is the complete righteousness which is placed against God's wrath, sin, and death, and which devours all, which makes a human creature directly holy and innocent, as though he were altogether without sin. For in that God imputes righteousness to mankind *gratis*, the same suffers no sin to remain in the new man: as John, 'Whoso is born of God sinneth not:' for to be born of God, and to be a sinner, the same is contrary the one to the other.

"According to this righteousness of faith, a man is said to be justified, not in the behalf of his works or fruits which God requires, recompences, or rewards; the same I call an external or an outward righteousness, a righteousness of works, which in this flesh and life neither can be pure nor holy.

"*Melancthon:* I ask touching St. Paul after he was regenerated, how he became justified in future—that is, accepted?

"*Luther:* For no other cause, but only by reason of the same regeneration by faith through which he became justified, and remains justified everlastingly.

"*Melancthon:* Was he justified only by reason of God's mercy? or (principally) by reason of the mercy, and (in the least part) by reason of his works and virtues?

"*Luther:* No; but the virtues and works were valued by God to be good and upright for the sake of St. Paul's person, who was justified. Like as a work is pleasing or displeasing, good or evil, for the person's sake that performs it. As also is spoken thereof in Terence. For a good work done by an evil person, has no respect by men, neither is it acceptable.

"*Melancthon:* It seems that Paul was not justified only by mercy. For yourself teach that the righteousness of works is necessary, yea, and that before God. And Paul (who believed and did good works) pleased God; but if he had not done them, then he would not have pleased him. Therefore our righteousness (if no more) is a little piece of the cause that we become justified before God.

"*Luther:* It is necessary, but not out of compulsion of the law, but out of the necessity of a willing mind, which follows without let or hindrance; as the sun of necessity shines, if otherwise it be a sun, not by reason of any law, but by nature, or, as I may say, by reason of the immutability; for thereunto it was created, on purpose to shine; even so one that is justified and regenerated does good works, not by reason of any law, or by compulsion (for no law is given to one that is justified) but out of unchangeable necessity. Moreover, St. Paul says, 'We are God's workmanship; created in Christ Jesus to good works,' &c.

"*Melancthon:* Sadoletus lays the fault in us, in that our doctrine is against ourselves in teaching that we are justified only by faith, and yet that we say that the righteousness of works is necessary.

"*Luther:* Yea; for the hypocrites and false brethren make a show as if they believed; for which cause, works are required, to the end they in their hypocrisy may be confounded. Like as Elias required works of Baal's priests, and said, 'Call upon the name of your God,' &c. Whereby Baal was confounded; for God in such things does nothing by reason of necessity, but of his goodness, and without the law.

" *Melancthon:* When you say: We are justified only by faith, do you understand that only from the beginning of the remission of sins? Or, is it your opinion that Paul was regenerated, and pleased God not by reason of his own obedience or virtues, but only for the sake of God's mercy?

" *Luther:* From the beginning, from the middle, and from the end. The obedience pleased God for Paul's sake who believed; for otherwise, his obedience had not been pleasing. And forasmuch as the person is justified, it is and remains justified so long as faith endure. Therefore this dividing of parts is nothing worth when we bring in three several parts, the beginning, the middle, and the end of the person's justification. The works, therefore, shine through the glass of faith, and for the sake of faith they are acceptable to God, not for the work's sake; otherwise the works following were better and more strong than faith which went before, as those which should make one justified longer, namely, in the midst and end of one's life. Even so, faith would only justify in the beginning, but afterwards would vanish, and so should leave the honour to the works, in that it had left off and ceased.

"*Melancthon:* Sir, you say, Paul was justified—that is, was received to everlasting life, only for mercy's sake. Against which, I say, if the piece-meal or partial cause, namely, our obedience, followeth not, then we are not saved, according to these words, 'Woe is me, if I preach not the gospel,' 1 Cor. ix.

" *Luther:* No piecing or partial cause approaches thereunto; for faith is powerful continually without ceasing; otherwise, it is no faith. Therefore of what value the works are, the same they are through the honour and power of faith, which undeniably is the sun or sun-beam of this shining.

" *Melancthon:* In Augustine these words, *Solâ fide*, directly exclude works.

" *Luther:* Whether it be so or no, these words of Augustine do sufficiently show, that he is of our opinion, where he says: 'I may well be afraid, but I do not therefore despair: for I think upon and remember the wounds of the Lord.' And further, in his Confessions, he says: 'Woe be to the life of that human creature (be it never so good and praiseworthy) that disregards God's mercy.'

" Hereby he shows plainly, that faith is active and powerful in the beginning, middle, and end, that is, continually. As also the Psalm: 'By thee is forgiveness,' &c. Also, 'Enter not into judgment with thy servant,' &c.

" *Melancthon:* Is it proper to say that the righteousness of works is necessary to salvation?

"*Luther:* No; works do not procure nor obtain salvation, but they are present by and with faith, which obtains righteousness; as I of necessity must be present at my salvation. The opinion of Sadoletus may be this: that faith is a work required by God's law, as love, obedience, chastity, &c. Therefore, he that believes has fulfilled the first part of the law, and so has a beginning to righteousness; but when this beginning is present, the other works are required which are commanded in the law, which must be done after and besides faith. Hereby we see that Sadoletus understands nothing in this case: for if faith were a commanded work, then his opinion were right, and faith in that sort would regenerate one in the beginning, as other good works would also renew one afterwards. But we say, that faith is a work of God's promise, or a gift of the Holy Spirit, which indeed is necessary to the fulfilling of the law, but it is not obtained by the law nor by works. But this presented gift, faith, regenerates one continually, so that the regenerated person does new works, but new works do not make a new person. As we see that the works of St. Paul were not pleasing to God because they were good works, but because they were done by Paul, who pleased God, which works had not been pleasing to God, in case Paul's person had not first pleased him.

"Therefore, we can attribute to works in themselves no righteousness before God, although they adorn the person accidentally, and make illustrious by certain and sure recompence, but they justify not the person; for we are all justified one way in and by one Christ; we are altogether acceptable and pleasing, according to the state of the person; one star excels another in brightness, but God loveth no less the star *Saturnus* than he loves the sun and moon.

"A faithful person is a new creature, a new tree. Therefore, all these speeches which in the law are usual, belong not to this case: as to say, 'A faithful person must do good works:' neither were it rightly spoken to say, 'The sun shall shine: a good tree shall bring forth good fruit: or, three and seven shall be ten,' &c. For the sun shall not shine, but it doth shine by nature, unbidden; it is thereunto created. Likewise, a good tree brings forth good fruit without bidding: three and seven are ten already, &c. Insomuch that we speak not of what shall be done, but of what is already done.

"*Melancthon.—Whether those that are justified by faith, do good works of necessity?*

"Luther answered and said, no; first, because 'no law' was or is 'made for the righteous,' 1 Tim. i., whereby it follows not that the righteous must or shall do good works.

"Secondly, they err who speak in this manner: the righteous must do good works, *Fallacia consequentiæ et consequentis;* for they make out the necessity of the cause, or necessity of the law, out of the necessity of the consequence, which already is included; they make a necessity of that which in future shall and must be out of the necessity which is immutable; they made a necessity of compelling and forcing.

"And therefore it is as improperly spoken, as when they say, 'The righteous shall do good works; God shall do good; the sun shall shine,' &c. whereas all these do follow by necessity of the cause, and by consequence of that which is concluded; or, that I may say it more plainly, all these follow by nature and willingly without the commanding of any law, uncompelled and unforced.

"Now in that we do not know how and what we ought to do according to the first creation when Adam and Eve were created in righteousness, therefore God gave the law, thereby to show unto us that both our state and nature are changed, and that we are not now the children of God, but the children of the devil.

"Moreover, God also sent Christ, who hath delivered and sanctified all that believe in him, from the curse, insomuch that now they are justified and saved by faith, &c.

"But those sins and offences which still remain in them, over which they sigh and complain all their life time, the same are not imputed unto them for Christ's sake in whom they believe; according to this article, 'I believe the remission of sins.'"

"I do not think there is any quality which is called *faith* or love, as the dreamers and sophists say, but I refer this altogether to Christ, and I say *mea formalis justitia*, certain, permanent, perfect righteousness, in which there is no defect, nothing wanting, that which is as it ought to be before God; that righteousness is Christ my Lord." (Tischreden, 133.) This passage is one of the many which show us the intimate relationship between the doctrine of Luther and the system of absolute identification.

CXV. (p. 310.)—"The comet gives me a feeling that some calamity threatens the emperor and Ferdinand. It turned its tail first towards the north, and then towards the south, thus pointing to the two brothers." (Oct., 1531.)

CXVI. (p. 311.)—"Michael Stiefel, with his seventh trumpet, is prophesying the Day of Judgment for us on All Hallows Day, this year." (26th August, 1533.)

CXVII. (p. 328.)—"'Tis marvellous," observes Bossuet, "to see how gravely and vividly he describes the devil's coming to him in the middle of the night, and awakening him to have a dispute with him; how closely he describes the fear which seized upon him, the sweat which covered him, his trembling, the horrible feeling of his heart throughout the dispute; the pressing arguments of the devil, leaving no repose to his mind; the sound of the evil one's powerful voice, and his overwhelming method of disputation, whereon question and answer came immediately one upon the other. 'I felt then,' he tells us, 'I felt exactly how it is that people so often die suddenly towards the morning; it is that the devil can come and strangle men, if not with his claws, at all events with his pressing arguments." (*Variations de l'Eglise*, ii. 203.)

Conference between Luther and the Devil, 1521.

"I awoke suddenly at midnight on one occasion, when Satan began to dispute with me in the following terms: "Listen to me," said the fiend; "enlightened doctor, you have, as you know, celebrated mass privately nearly every day during the last fifteen years. What would you say if every one of these masses should prove to be an act of horrible idolatry? What if the body and blood of Christ had never been present, and you had adored, and had induced others to worship mere bread and wine?" I replied to him: "I have been made a priest, I received unction and consecration at the hands of the bishop, all of which I did by the commands of my superiors, and in conformity with the obedience which I owed them. Why, therefore, should I not likewise consecrate, seeing that I have always uttered the words of Jesus Christ in true and perfect seriousness of heart, and that I have celebrated, as you know, the mass in the utmost sincerity of belief?" "That is all perfectly true," said the devil; "but the Turks and pagans perform all the rites of their temples out of obedience, and they conduct their ceremonies in perfect seriousness. The priests of Jeroboam likewise acted in all things with zeal, and with all their heart against the true priests who were at Jerusalem. What if your consecration and ordination proved to be as false and futile as the priests of the Turks, and the Samaritans are false in their lying and impious doctrines? In the first place," continued he, "you know that before your consecration you had no true knowledge of Jesus Christ, nor of the true faith, and that in so far as the faith is concerned, you were no better than a Turk, for the Turk, in common with all the devils, believes in the history of Jesus Christ, that he was born, crucified, died, &c. But the Turk and we condemned spirits have no faith in his mercy, neither do we accept him for our Mediator or our Saviour. On the contrary, we fear him as an inexorable judge. Such was likewise your faith, nor had you any other at the moment when you received unction at the hands of the bishop; and not you alone, but all those who bestowed or who received this consecration entertained the same sentiments with respect to Jesus Christ. They had no other. It is for this reason that, estranging yourself from Jesus as from a cruel yoke, you have resorted to the Virgin Mary and the saints, regarding them as the mediators between you and Jesus Christ. Thus it is that honour and glory have been denied to Christ. No papist can deny this. You have, therefore, received unction; you have received the tonsure; and you have offered the sacrifice of the mass as a pagan, and not as a Christian priest. How is it possible for you to have consecrated the host at the mass, or to have really and truly celebrated mass, since there was wanting for this purpose one who had the power so to consecrate; a radical and essential defect even according to your own doctrine?

"In the second place, you have been consecrated priest, and you have made an abuse of the mass, using it contrariwise to its institution, and to the intention and design of Jesus Christ, who ordained it. For Jesus Christ commanded that the sacrament should be distributed amongst the faithful who communicated, and that the whole church should partake of it, to eat and to drink it. In fact, the true priest was constituted minister of the church, in order that he might preach the word of God, and administer the sacraments as is declared by the words of Jesus Christ at the last supper, and as also is declared by St. Paul, in his 1st Epistle to the Corinthians, wherein he speaks of the Lord's Supper. It is from this that the ancients were in the habit of calling it the Communion, inasmuch as, according to the instititution of Jesus Christ, the priest alone should not reserve the sacraments to himself, but all those Christians, brothers in the faith, present at the time, ought to partake of them with him. And yet you, during fifteen entire years, have kept these sacramental elements to your own self whenever you have said mass, without making those who worshipped with you partake of them! Nay, it was even forbidden you to administer the sacrament completely to them. What sort of a priesthood is that? What is such unction worth? What avail such masses, such consecrations? And what manner of priest are you, who have not been ordained for the church, but for yourself alone? It is most certain that Jesus Christ will neither recognise such sacraments nor this sort of unction.

"In the third place, the thought and design of Jesus Christ, as his words sufficiently indicate, is, that in taking the sacrament we declare and confess his death. 'Do this,' says Christ, 'in remembrance of me;' and, as St. Paul observes, 'Continue to do it until the Saviour comes again.' But you, a mere gabbler of private masses, have never once preached or confessed Jesus Christ in any of your masses. You solely have taken the sacrament, muttering, as if you were whistling between your teeth, the words of the Lord's Supper, keeping them entirely to yourself. Is that the institution of Jesus Christ? Is it by such actions that you prove yourself to be his minister? Is it thus that a Christian priest should act? Was it for this that you were ordained a priest?

"In the fourth place, it is clear that the intentions, the thought, the institution of Jesus Christ were that all Christians should partake of his sacrament. Whereas you have received unction, not in order that you might be duly qualified to administer the sacrament, but for the purpose of offering up a sacrifice. And, contrary to the institution of Jesus Christ, you have availed yourself of the mass as if it were a sacrifice; for what, in reality, do the expressions used by the bishop in giving unction signify, when, according to the ordinary routine of the ceremonial, he places the chalice in the hands of him who is being consecrated, saying to him, 'Receive power to celebrate and to sacrifice for the living and for the dead.' What means this underhand and perverse ordination? Jesus Christ instituted the Lord's Supper as meat and drink for his whole church, to be given by his priests to all who communicate at the same time with him, and you convert it into a propitiatory sacrifice before God. Oh, abomination surpassing all abomination!

"Fifthly, the thought and intention of Jesus Christ is, as I have stated, that the sacrament should be administered in the church to all the communicants, in order to strengthen and revive their faith amidst the divers temptations proceeding from the devil, to secure them from sin, and to renew in their hearts and to preach to them the memory of Christ's goodness. Whereas you have treated this sacrament as if it were something belonging to yourself only, which you could at any time constitute and make without aid from any other person, and that you might either bestow gratuitously, or for money, as to you seemed fit and proper? What can you, let me ask, deny of all this? Have you, then, been made a priest of in this fashion; that is to say, without the participation of Jesus Christ, and in the absence of his faith? For you certainly have received unction and ordination contrary to the design and the institution of Jesus Christ, and not for the purpose of administering the sacrament to others, but merely to offer up a sacrifice for the living and the dead. You have not been ordained to be a minister of the church, &c. Besides, as you have never yet administered the sacrament to others, you have not preached Jesus Christ whilst performing mass, and consequently you have in no respect done that which his institutions require. Have you, then, been ordained, and received unction in opposition to Jesus Christ and contrary to his institution, in order that you might act in contradiction to all that he has ordained? And if it be that the bishops have consecrated you and given you unction against the institution of Jesus Christ, is it not beyond all doubt that your ordination and consecration are alike impious, false, and anti-Christian? I maintain, therefore, that you have never consecrated (the elements) at the mass, for you had no power to do so, and that you have only offered up, and caused to be adored by others, mere bread and wine. You now perceive that there are wanting in your mass—first, a person who has power to consecrate; that is to say, a Christian man; and, secondly, there is wanting a person for whom the elements are consecrated, and to whom the sacrament is to be administered; that is to say, the church, the people, members of the church, who are there present at the same time.

"But you, impious man, wholly ignorant of Jesus Christ, you stand at the altar, all alone, imagining to yourself that Jesus Christ instituted for you only the sacrament, and that you have only to utter a few words in order that the consecration may be complete for the mass, and that you therein offer up the body and blood of Christ, being all the while not only not a member of his church, but his enemy. There is wanting, thirdly, in your mass, the end, the design, the fruit, the uses for which Jesus Christ established this sacrament, for it was instituted by the Saviour on behalf of his whole church, and that it might be eaten and drunk in order to strengthen the faith of his flock, that his goodness might be preached and revealed to all who attend at the mass. Whereas every one who is present is ignorant even of what you yourself say at the mass; they receive nothing from you; they learn nothing of you; you alone, in your corner, mute to the congregation, and scarcely saying anything that you yourself can hear, you eat alone, you drink alone, and ignorant as you are of the words of Jesus Christ, unworthy monk—monk without faith!—you admit no one to communion with you; and, following the custom that prevails amongst your class, you sell for money, as if it were some valuable, the thing that you yourself have created. If thus you are shown to be a person not capable of consecrating the elements, and that you ought not to perform that act; if, likewise at your mass there is no person to take the sacrament; if you reverse the whole ceremony; if you change into an entirely different thing the institution of Jesus Christ,—in short, if you have received unction only that you might thus be empowered to act in every respect contrary to Jesus Christ and his institution, in what does your unction consist? and what do you do by virtue of it, in saying your masses, and in consecrating your elements, but blaspheme and tempt God? So that you are neither a true priest of Jesus Christ, nor are your elements the real body and blood of our Lord. I will give you a comparison: suppose some were to begin to read the ceremony of baptism without having any person on whom to practise that rite; like your bishops, who, following the ridiculous custom that prevails amongst the papists, baptize a church bell, a thing that neither can nor ought to be baptized,—tell me, would this be a real and efficacious baptism? You must perforce admit that this would not be such. For who can baptize that which is not susceptible of baptism? What sort of baptism would it be, if I were to pronounce the words to the empty wind: 'I baptize thee in the name of the Father, the Son, and the Holy Ghost,' and, in so doing, I were to scatter a little water? Who or what would thereby receive a remission of sin, or the Holy Ghost? Would it be the wind? It is obvious that no rite of baptism has been performed, though the words of that ceremony may have been pronounced, and the water sprinkled, inasmuch as a person capable of being baptized was not there. What if the same nonentity really occurs at your celebration of the mass! you therein pronounce certain words, you think you receive the sacrament, whereas all you take is bread and wine; for the church, that is, the congregation, which is that which communicates or receives, does not receive anything, nor does it assist at the ceremony; and you, impious, unbelieving man, are no more capable of receiving the sacrament, under such circumstances, than a bell is of being baptised. This is why your act goes for nothing, in so far as the sacrament is concerned. You will, perhaps, observe to me, that, although you do not offer the sacrament to others who are present in the church, it is not the less a sacrament that you administer to yourself, as there are often found amongst those who receive the sacrament, and undergo baptism, persons utterly incredulous, and unbelievers in Christianity, and yet neither the sacrament and baptism are a whit the less true or efficacious on account of their unbelief. Why, therefore, you will say, cannot there be a real sacrament at the mass. This argument, however, will not stand; for there is no parity between the two cases. In the rite of baptism, even when administered under circumstances of pressing necessity,[1] there are, at the least, always two persons present—namely, the baptizer and he who is baptized; ordinarily, there are several persons who take part in the ceremony. Besides, such is the function of him who baptizes, that he is empowered by that act to confer some thing or gift upon the other persons of his church, whereas he possesses no power to take anything away from them, and to apply his powers exclusively to his own personal use, as you do whilst performing mass. Moreover, the rites, and all parts of the baptismal ceremony, are in strict accordance with the commandments instituted by Jesus Christ, whereas the mass is directly contrary to his institution.

"In the second place, why do you not also teach the doctrine that persons may baptize themselves? Why would you reject or disapprove of such a baptism? Why would you reject the confirmation of a person who had confirmed himself according to the forms of the ceremony practised by yourselves? How is it that the consecration of a priest goes for nothing, if a man consecrated himself? Why would extreme unction be denied to have been given, if a dying person administered it to himself, in the same manner as yourselves perform that rite? Why would there be no marriage if a man married himself, or were to violate a female, and to assert afterwards that the act ought to constitute a marriage in spite of the woman's will? for all these are part and parcel of your seven sacraments. If,

---

[1] *i. e.*, When one person baptizes another in a desert, or at the point of death.

therefore, no person has the power of constituting by himself any one of your sacraments, or of administering them to himself, how is it that you arrogate to yourself alone the sacrament of the Lord's supper? It is certainly most true, that Jesus Christ is himself taken in the sacrament, and also, that the priest, in administering the elements to others, takes them likewise himself. But he does not consecrate them for himself alone; he takes them conjointly with his congregation and with the church, and this is done in conformity to the commandment of Jesus Christ. In speaking here of consecration, I desire to know whether it can be possible for any one to consecrate the elements, and take the sacrament for himself alone; because I am perfectly well aware that every priest can, after the elements are consecrated, take them in common, seeing that the sacrament is a communion, and the Lord's table is for many. As, in like manner, when I asked whether a man could bestow unction, and elect himself thus to the priesthood, I was perfectly well aware that, having been called, and having received unction, he might subsequently enter on his vocation. And, on the other hand, when I asked whether, in the case of a man who had violated a female, it was sufficient for him who had dishonoured her to call this junction a marriage, I knew very well that if the woman consented then to the marriage, the junction which followed after it did in reality constitute a marriage."

In the distress of mind which came upon me during this struggle with the devil, I endeavoured to repulse the fiend with the weapons which I was accustomed to use under the papal authority; I urged, in answer to his arguments, what were the intentions, what the faith of the church, by representing to him that it was acting under the faith of the church, and in the fulfilment of her intentions, that I had celebrated these private masses.

"It may be," said I, "I have not believed as I ought to have believed, and that I am mistaken in my view; the church, nevertheless, has believed, according to the true and right faith; she has not been in error, nor has she been deceived." Thereupon Satan returned upon me with still greater force and vehemence than before: "There it is," said he; "show me where it is written that an impious unbeliever can assist at the altar of Jesus Christ, can consecrate the elements, and administer the sacrament in the faith of the church? Where is it that God has commanded or ordained such an act? How will you prove to me that the church communicates to you her intention that you should say private masses, if you have not the word of God for your act, and if it should happen to be merely men who have enjoined this, without the authority of God's word? The whole of this doctrine is a lie. What audacity are you not capable of? You do these things in darkness. You abuse the name of the church, and then you seek to justify all your abominations, under the pretext that such is the intention of the church. All you have to say is to allege the intention of the church as your excuse. But the church sees nothing, nor does she entertain a thought beyond the words and the institutions of Jesus Christ; much less does she entertain any schemes against his designs and his institutions, respecting which I have already spoken, for Saint Paul says, in the first epistle to the Corinthians, chapter 2, speaking of the church, and of the assembly of the faithful, 'But we have the mind of Christ.' (v. 16.)

"But how are you to know that a thing is according to the design and the intention of Christ and of the church, unless it be by the word of Christ, and by the doctrine and public professions of that church? How do you know the intention of the church to be that manslaughter, adultery, and unbelief are of the number of sins for which a man may be damned? How do you know many other matters similar to these, save by the word of God? If, then, by the word of God, and by his commandments, we learn what the opinion of the church is respecting good or evil works, is it not still more obviously requisite to resort to the same word, in order that we may learn from it what opinion the church holds with respect to his doctrine? Why then, blasphemer, do you dare to contravene, by your private mass, the distinct words and the commands of Jesus Christ, and how it is that you avail yourself of his name, and of the intention of the church, for the purpose of covering your lies and your impiety? You clothe your inventions in these miserable garments, as if the intention of the church could be contrary to the word of Jesus Christ? What prodigious daring is it that enables you thus to profane the name of the church by such mendacious impudence!

"Since, then, the bishop has not constituted you a sayer of mass by the unction which he has bestowed upon you, save only by enabling you, in repeating your private masses, to utter everything that is most opposed to the explicit words and institutions of Jesus Christ, and also most contrary to the design, the faith, and to the public profession of the church, this unction is an utter profanity, and has nothing in it of holy or sacred. It is in itself more idle, more useless, and as ridiculous as the baptism which is bestowed upon a stone or a bell." And Satan, urging to still greater limits this reasoning, exclaimed: "You have, therefore, never yet consecrated the elements; you have only offered bread and wine, as the pagans do. By a traffic, alike infamous and injurious to God, you have sold your own handywork to Christians—serving not God, not Jesus Christ, but your own belly. What unheard of abomination is this! Unheard of under heaven or upon earth."

"I see from hence the holy fathers, who mock at me, exclaiming, 'Hey! what! is this the renowned doctor, who is dumbfounded, and unable to reply to the devil? Do you not perceive, doctor, that the devil is a lying spirit?' Spare me, holy fathers, I should have been in ignorance up to the present moment that the devil is a liar, had you not yourselves, learned theologians, affirmed the fact. Doubtless, if you were compelled to bear his rude assaults, and to dispute matters with him, you would not speak as you do of the examples and of the traditions of the church. The devil tilts somewhat roughly, and he would press you so hardly that you would find it difficult to repel him, unless by the special gift of God. All at once, in the twinkling of an eye, he fills your mind with darkness and misgivings: and if he has to do with a man who is not already forearmed with a text from Scripture, wherewith to reply to him, he can upset him with the turn of his little finger. True it is that the devil is a liar; but he does not lie when he accuses us, for then he attacks us with the double evidence of our own conscience and the word of God. I cannot deny that I am a sinner, neither can I say that my sin is not great, any more than I can deny that I am thereby rendered amenable to death and damnation." [Audin, from whose text I derive this narrative. It is not given by M. Michelet. Refer to the following authorities: *De Missâ Angulari;* Luther, *Op. Lat.;* (Jenæ,) iv. &c.; Cochlæus, in Art. p. 67; Math. Conc. 32; Claude, *Defense de la Reformation*, part ii. ch. 5; Basnage, *Hist. des Eglises Reformées*, &c.—W. H.]

CXIX. (p. 339.) — He wrote to his wife, telling her of this attack. "I was all but dead; I had already recommended thee and our children to God and our Saviour, in the full conviction that I should never see you again; I was greatly affected when I thought of you, thus on the brink of the tomb, as I thought myself. However, the prayers and tears of pious men who love me have found favour before God. This last night has killed my malady; I feel quite as though new born." (27th February, 1537.)

Luther experienced a dangerous relapse at Wittemberg. Compelled to remain at Gotha, he believed himself to be near unto death. He detailed to Bugenhagen, who was with him, his last wishes. He declared that he had combated the papacy in a conscientious spirit alone, and asked pardon of Melancthon, Jonas and Cruciger, for any offence which he might have committed towards either of them." (Ukert, i. p. 325.) Luther was attacked very early in life by the stone, from which painful disorder he suffered severely: he was operated on for it about the 27th Feb. 1537.

"I begin to feel myself convalescent; by the grace of God I resume my drinking and eating, although my legs, my knees, and my frame generally still trembles, supporting myself with difficulty." (21st March, 1537.) "I am," he writes at a later period of the same year, "without particular reference to age or sickness, little more than a benumbed and frozen carcase." (6th Dec. 1537.)

CXX. (p. 348.)—He had before this endeavoured vainly to effect a reconciliation between the counts of Mansfield. "If you desire to bring a tree into the house, you do not force the branches in, for they will spread out and prevent its ingress; you introduce it by the stem, and the branches will bend and yield in following it." (Tischreden, p. 355.)

CXXI. (p. 351.)—*Martin Luther's Confession of Faith.*—"I, Martin Luther, an unworthy preacher of the gospel of our Lord Jesus Christ, thus profess and thus believe; that this article—THAT FAITH ALONE, WITHOUT WORKS, CAN JUSTIFY BEFORE GOD, shall never be overthrown, neither by the emperor, nor by the Turk, nor by Satan, nor by the Persian, nor by the pope, with all his cardinals, bishops, sacrificers, monks, nuns, kings, princes, powers of the world, nor yet by all the devils in hell. This article shall stand fast, whether they will or no. This is the true gospel; Jesus Christ redeemed us from our sins, and he only. This most firm and certain truth is the voice of Scripture, though the world and all the devils rage and roar. If Christ alone take away our sins, we cannot do this with our works; and as it is impossible to embrace Christ but by faith, it is, therefore, equally impossible to apprehend him by works. If, then, faith alone must apprehend Christ, before works can follow, the conclusion is irrefragable, that faith alone apprehends him, before and without the consideration of works; and this is our justification and deliverance from sin. Then, and not till then, good works follow faith, as its necessary and inseparable fruit. This is the doctrine I teach, and this the Holy Spirit and church of the faithful have delivered. In this will I abide. Amen."

CXXII. (p. 352.)—The funeral procession was arranged in the following order:—Four deacons of the church; Dr. Pomer; the officers of the elector, all on horseback; the two counts of Mansfeldt, with their principal attendants; THE CORPSE, in a leaden coffin, covered with black velvet, on a car; Luther's widow in an open chariot, with some female friends; Luther's three sons; his brother James and his wife's two sisters; then, two and two, George and Syriacus the merchant, the chevalier Magnificus and Philip Melancthon, Justus Jonas, Gaspard Cruciger, Jerome Schurf, and other professors and doctors, counsellors, students, men, women, children, of every rank and age, all dissolved in tears. The body being deposited on a bier in front of the altar, Dr. Pomer delivered a funeral discourse, broken by sobs and agonized weeping, preceding one by Melancthon."

The service ended, the body was placed in its final earthly abode, in front of the pulpit. The grave having been filled up and properly secured, a brass plate was affixed upon it with this inscription:—"Martini Lutheri, S. Theologiæ Doctoris Corpus H.L.S.E., qui anno Christi MDLVI., XII. Cal. Martii Eyslebii in patriâ S. M. O. C. V. Ann. LXIII. M.II.D.X."

Some years after this, Wittemberg was besieged and taken. Charles V. on this occasion desired to see the tomb of the Reformer. With folded arms he was reading the inscription, when one of his officers proposed to open the grave, and give the ashes of the heretic to the winds. The monarch's cheek grew red: "I war not with the dead; let this place be respected."—AUDIN.

EPITAPHIUM THEODORÆ BEZÆ IN MARTINUM LUTHERUM.

Roma orbem domuit, Romam sibi Papa subegit
Viribus illa suis, frudibus iste suis
Quanto isto major LUTHERUS, major et illa
Istum, illamque uno qui domuit calamo!
I, nunc! Alciden memorato, Græcia mendax;
Lutheri ad calamum ferrea clava nihil!

EPITAPHIUM PHILLIPPI MELANCTHON, IN MARTINI LUTHERUM.

Occidit omnigena venerandus laude LUTHERUS
Qui Christum docuit non dubitante fide.
Ereptum deflet vero, hunc ecclesia luctu
Cujus erat doctor, verius, imo pater.
Occidit Israel præstans auriga Lutherus,
Quem mecum sanus lugeat omnis homo.
Nunc lactumque suum lacrymoso carmine prodat,
Hoc etenim orbatos flere, dolore decet.

CXXIII. (p. 353.)—We will insert in this place some particulars touching Luther. Erasmus said of him:—"The private life and conduct of this man are universally commended. It is a great testimony in his favour, that even his enemies cannot find subject matter for calumniating him." (Ukert, ii. 5.)

Luther was very fond of simple enjoyments. He often joined his guests, in their musical entertainments, and played at skittles with them.

Melancthon was wont to observe of him: "Whoever was familiarly acquainted with Luther, and knew his habits, must admit that he was an excellent man, agreeable and soft in his social moments, and in no respect dogmatic, or a lover of disputes. To these characteristics, add the gravity becoming one in his position. If he displayed any obduracy or harshness in his struggles with his opponents, that did not arise from the malignity of his nature, but entirely sprung from his ardour and passion for the truth." (Ukert, ii. 12.)

"Although he was neither small in stature, nor of a weakly constitution, he observed the utmost temperance in respect to eating and drinking. I have witnessed him, at a period when his health was excellent, pass four entire days without taking any nourishment; and frequently have I known him to take nothing during the day, save a herring and a morsel of bread." (Life of Luther, by Melancthon.)

Melancthon, in his posthumous writings, observes: "I have on several occasions surprised him by himself in the act of prayer, hot tears streaming down his cheeks, whilst earnestly entreating God for the welfare of the church. He dedicated several hours in each day to the recitation of psalms, and to invocations to the Almighty, uttered in all the fervour of his soul." (Ukert, ii. 7.)

Luther said of himself: "Were I but as rich in eloquence, and endowed with such a treasury of expressions as Erasmus; had I the Grecian lore of Joachim Camerarius; and a knowledge of the Hebrew equal to that of Forscher, what would I not achieve, with a little more youth!" (Tischreden, 447.)

"The licentiate Amsdorf is a theologian by natural endowment. The doctors Cruciger and Jonas are such only by culture and reflection; but it is the doctor Pomer and myself who never threw a chance away in our controversies." (Tischreden, 425.)

To Antony Unruche, a judge at Torgau, he writes thus in the summer of 1538:—"I thank you cordially, dear Antony, for having taken up the cause of Margaret Dorst, and not suffering those insolent clowns to snatch from that poor woman the whole of her means. You are aware that Doctor Martin himself is not merely a theologian and defender of the faith, but that he is likewise the champion of the rights of the poor, who come to him from every quarter, entreating his advice, and soliciting his intercession with the authorities. He willingly gives his assistance to the poor, as you yourself, and those who resemble you, do. All judges ought to be similar to you, who practise piety, fear God, and love his holy word. So, therefore, will not Jesus Christ ever forget you." (12th June, 1538.)

Luther wrote as follows to his wife, respecting an aged domestic who was about to quit his service: "We must dismiss our old John honourably. You know that he has ever faithfully served us, with zeal, and as it behoved a Christian servitor. How much have we not ofttimes bestowed upon good-for-nothing persons, ungrateful students, and others, who have made a bad use of our money? We must not be sordid or parsimonious on this occasion, towards an honest servant; for what we bestow on him, will doubtless prove acceptable in the sight of God. I am well aware we are not rich; I would willingly give him ten florins, if I did but possess them; under all circumstances you must not give him less than five, for he is not properly clad. Whatever you can do in addition, I beg of you to bestow on him. True it is that the city treasury ought to make him a present, for he has been extremely useful in respect to the church services. However, they may do as they please in the matter. See how it will be best to raise this sum. We have a silver goblet, which you can pawn. God will not forsake us, I am sure. Adieu!" (17th Feb. 1532.)

"The prince has given me a gold ring; but, as if to let me see that I was not destined to carry gold, the ring dropped off my finger (for which it was too large), upon which I said to myself, 'Thou art only an earthworm, and not a man; the ring had been better bestowed on Faber or Eck; as for thee, lead and a cord at thy neck would have become thee better.'" (15th Sept. 1530.)

The elector having levied a contribution in aid of the Turkish war, exempted Luther from its payment. The doctor sent him word that he accepted the favour on behalf of both his houses, one of which, (the convent,) said he, cost a good deal to maintain it, and contributed nothing in return; whilst the other was not yet paid for. "But I implore your electoral highness in all submission to permit me to tax some part of my possessions to this contribution. I have a garden, valued at five hundred florins; some land, estimated at ninety, and a little garden, worth twenty florins. I shall prefer doing as others, and fighting the Turk with my farthings, in order not to be altogether excluded from the army which is destined to save us. There are already enough of persons who contribute very unwillingly to this levy: I do not wish to excite envy. Far better will it be to take away all grounds for complaint, and to enable every one to say, 'See how the doctor Martin is obliged to pay his quota, like the rest.'" (26th March, 1542.)

"To the elector John—Grace and peace in Christ Jesus! Serene highness, I have delayed for a long time to offer your highness my thanks for the garments which you were so good as to send me. I now tender them in all sincerity of heart. Nevertheless, I entreat your highness not to credit those who have represented me as entirely destitute. I am, my conscience tells me, only too rich already. It does not become me, a preacher of the gospel, to revel in abundance; I neither require nor wish such a thing. The repeated favours of your highness begin truly to affright me. I do not seek to become one of those to whom Jesus Christ said, *Woe unto you that are rich, for you have received your consolation.*

"I do not desire to be an expense to your highness, whose purse must needs be ceaselessly opened for so many important objects.

There was more than sufficient of the brown stuff which you sent me, but in order not to be ungrateful, I have worn, out of respect to you, the black suit, although far too costly for me. Had it not been a gift from your electoral highness, I would never have consented to appear clad in such garments. I therefore entreat your highness henceforward to permit me to take the liberty of asking when I require anything. Otherwise, this forethought in respect to myself will deprive me of all courage in so far as my intercession with your highness on behalf of others is concerned—others, let me observe, far more worthy of your favour than myself. Jesus Christ will reward your generous spirit. This is my prayer, uttered in all fervency of heart. Amen." (17th August, 1529.)

John the Constant presented to Luther the former convent of the Augustins at Wittemberg; the elector Augustus purchased this site from the doctor's heirs in 1564, in order to bestow it upon the university. (Ukert, i. 347.)

Places in which Luther resided, and objects once in his possession.— The house in which Luther was born no longer exists. It was burnt down in 1689. At the castle of Wartburg there is still shown on the wall of one of the apartments the mark of the inkstand which Luther threw at the devil's head. The cell in the convent of Wittemberg and its furniture are still shown, as Luther left them after his occupation of that dwelling. The walls of the cell are covered with the names of those who have visited the place. Amongst them is that of Peter the Great, written upon the door. At Coburg, tho room which he inhabited during the diet of Augsburg (1530) is still shown.

Luther habitually wore on his finger an enamelled gold ring, on which was represented a skull, with these words inscribed: "Mori sæpe cogita." Around the bevil was written, "Oh mors, ero mors tua." This ring is preserved at Dresden, together with a silver-gilt medal, which his wife used to wear at her neck. The chief device of this medal was the serpent rearing itself over the bodies of the Israelites, with an inscription: "Serpens exaltatus typus Christi crucifixi." The reverse represented our Saviour on the cross, with this legend: "Christus mortuus est pro peccatis nostris." On one side may yet be seen the following record: "D. Mart. Luter, Caterinæ suæ dono. D. H. F.;" and on the other, "Quæ nata est anno 1499, 29 Januarii." He had, in his own possession, a seal, of which he gave a description, in the following letter to Lazarus Spengler: "Grace and peace in Christ Jesus! Dear lord and friend, you tell me I shall give you pleasure by explaining to you the meaning of what is engraved on my seal. I will therefore indicate to you what it is that I have had represented thereon, as symbolical of my theology. First, there is a black cross, with a heart in its centre: this cross recals to my memory that faith in Christ crucified is our salvation. Whoso believes in Him with his whole soul is justified. This cross is black, in order to indicate the mortification and grief which a Christian must necessarily suffer. The heart, however, preserves its natural colour, for the cross does not change our nature; it does not kill, it vivifies. *Justus fide vivit, sed fide crucifixi.* The heart is placed in the centre of a white rose, thereby indicating that faith bestows consolation, joy, and peace. The rose is white, and not red, inasmuch as the peace it indicates is not worldly peace, but the peace of the spirit. Spirits are represented by the colour of white, as also are the angels. The rose is placed on an azure ground, in order to demonstrate that this joy of the soul and in the faith is a beginning of that celestial joy which awaits us. The latter is already comprehended therein; it exists, even now, in hope, but the moment when it is consummated and made perfect is not yet arrived. In this azure field you perceive a golden circle; this indicates that heavenly joys will endure eternally, and that they are superior to all other enjoyments and all other blessings, even as gold is more precious than any other metal. Our Lord Jesus Christ be with you unto eternal life, is my prayer. Amen." (From my desert at Coburg, this 8th July, 1530.)

At Altenburg there was kept, for a long time, a table glass, out of which Luther drank the last time he visited his friend Spalatin. (Ukert, i. 245, *et seq.*)

SELECTIONS FROM THE TISCHREDEN, AS GIVEN BY MICHELET, WITH ADDITIONS.

Of Popes: "Julius was excellent in wars and government; he had altogether a worldly brain and understanding. He waged war against the emperor, the Venetians, and the French; and when he heard his army was defeated before Ravenna, he blasphemed God, and said: 'Art thou, in the name of a thousand devils, now on the side of the French? dost thou in this manner defend and protect thy church?' Then he turned his face towards the ground, and said: Holy Swiss, pray thou for us; and presently sent bishop Langen, the cardinal of Saltzburg, to treat with the emperor Maximilian. He aimed at the empire, and grievously plagued Louis, the French king; insomuch, that he wrote to the universities in France, desiring them by public writings to smother the insufferable pride of the pope. If I had been known then, they would, doubtless, have sent for me to Paris with honour; but I was too young, neither was it God's will at that time I should write against him, to the end people should not think he was thrust from his stool by the strength and power of the French king, but only and alone through God's word. For when God speaks but a word, and says: Jerusalem, fall; Rome, be destroyed, and lie in the ashes; king, yield thyself captive; sir pope, come down from your throne; so is it accomplished immediately. In this sort did God confound that mighty popedom, which was the most powerful of all. Pope Julius would fain have been emperor; pope Alexander would willingly have made his son emperor; likewise pope Leo made his brother king of Naples, but he was destroyed by poison."

Pope Clement was the richest among them all; for he got the great treasure of pope Julius, and was also the craftiest; whatever he took in hand was fraudulent; he was an Italian, and a Florentine, which makes as much as three Italians. Moreover he was a bastard, descended of the house of Medicis, which makes seven Italians. A more offensive knave than pope Clement VII. never was.

"Pope Leo was bribed by the Capuchins with four-score thousand ducats, to the end he might leave them unreformed. When he saw the money they sent lying on the table, he said: 'Who is able to resist so many well-armed potentates?' True it is, money maketh knaves."

"In 1531, the astrologer Gaaric related to the margrave of Brandenburg, Joachim, that some one having reproached Clement VII. with being a bastard, he replied: 'And Jesus Christ?' From that time forth the margrave favoured Luther."

Of Potentates and Princes: "When the people of Bruges held the emperor Maximilian as a prisoner, and thought of cutting off his head, they wrote to the senate of Venice for their advice on the matter. The senate replied: *Dead men don't make war.* The Venetians got up a farce against Maximilian, which used to be played in the streets. First came a person representing the doge; then one representing the French king, with large pockets full of money, which he pretended to throw about him; next came the emperor Maximilian, in a grey coat, and a small hunting-horn round his neck. He had a great pocket too, but when he put his hand in it, his fingers went through the holes. The Florentines had a jest of the same sort against Maximilian. They got a good lesson for it afterwards; the emperor's grandson, Charles V., made them dance to a fine tune. God *put down the mighty from their seat,* in the case of the Florentines, as he has always done for the haughty ones of the earth."

"The emperor Maximilian said that if any one were to put the blood of the princes of Austria and Bavaria into a pot to boil together, it would leap out."

"Maximilian one day suddenly burst out into a great laugh. On being asked the cause: 'Truly,' said he, 'I laughed to think that God should have entrusted the spiritual government of the world, to a drunken priest like pope Julius, and the government of the empire to a chamois-hunter, like me."

"In the castle of Prague, there are the portraits of the kings all in a row along the wall; Ferdinand's is the last, and beyond him there is no room for another. 'Tis the same with the round saloon in the castle of Wittemberg. This bodes no good."

"The emperor Maximilian said: 'The emperor is truly a king of kings, for the princes of the empire do just what they please; the king of France is a king of asses, for his people do just what he tells them; the king of England is a king of men, for his people obey him out of affection.'"

"Maximilian asked one of his secretaries how he ought to treat a servant that robbed him; the secretary replied: 'Hang him.' 'Nay,' returned the emperor, patting him on the shoulder, 'I have need of thy services just now.'"

"After the election of the emperor Charles, the elector of Saxony asked Fabien Von Feilitzsch, his councillor, whether he approved of the king of Spain's having been elected emperor. He answered: ''Tis good that the crows should have a vulture over them.'"

An old prophecy says: "The emperor Charles will subject all Europe, will reform the church under him; the mendicant orders and schismatic sects will be abolished."

"The news came that Antonio de Leyva and Andrea Doria had advised the emperor to march in person against the Turk, and not to take his brother with him, by reason that his brother was unlucky. The truth is, that Ferdinand is too calculating—refines too much upon every point presented for his consideration; he acts only upon long counsel, endless deliberation—never upon divine impulse." The emperor himself is getting unlucky. He does not know how to avail himself of opportunities. He has now lost Milan."

"The king of France is excessively fond of women. Not so the emperor. When the latter was passing through France, in 1544, after a grand banquet that had been held, he found in his bed a beautiful virgin of noble family, whom the king of France had provided for him against his will; but the emperor would not take advantage of her situation, and sent her home in all honour to her parents."

"The emperor invited to his coronation only Italian and Spanish princes, who carried before him the standards and arms of the German electors. I made my observations upon this in a pamphlet; but the emperor bought up all the copies of it."

"The king of France spends quite as much in bribes as he does upon his armies. In consequence of this, in the war against Julius and Venice, he defeated twenty thousand men with four thousand."

"So long as the French king had German men-at-arms in his service, he conquered. They are, in fact, the best soldiers; they content themselves with their pay, and protect the people. It was for this reason Antonio de Leyva, on his death-bed, advised the emperor to attach his German soldiers to his person; for that if he lost them, he would be undone. They stick together as 'twere one man."

"Whatever the king of France may be in the flesh, I like not to see him vanquished and a prisoner; vanquished, perhaps, but captive, that is monstrous. Perhaps the hour of the kingdom of France is come; perhaps 'tis of France as 'twas said of Troy:—

'Venit summa dies et ineluctabile fatum.'

All these are, in my opinion, indications of the coming of the last day. These signs are of graver import than people imagine. There is only one thing pleases me about it, which is the discomfiture of Antichrist, who was beginning to lean upon the king of France."

"The king of France is persuaded that among us Lutherans there is no authority, no marriage, no church, nothing that the world deems sacred. His envoy, Dr. Gervais, assured me positively of this. The reason is, they have not admitted our writings into France, any more than into Italy, while the villain of Mayence pours into both countries as many of his calumnies against us as he chooses."

"There is a Frenchman here, named François Lambert, who two years ago was an apostolic preacher among the Minorites. He has just married a woman of our church, and is going to settle at Strasburg, and make his living by translating my German works into French."

"The kings of France and England are Lutherans in talking but not in giving; they do not seek the interest of God, but merely their own."

"The king of England's divorce has received the sanction of seven universities, but we of Wittemberg, and the people of Louvain, reject it, on the ground of the particular circumstances, the long cohabitation of the parties, there being a daughter," &c.

"Some one who had received letters from England, told Luther that the king had seceded from the gospel. 'I am delighted,' said Luther, 'to be rid of that blasphemer. I am only sorry to see Melancthon wasting his finest prefaces upon the very worst people.'"

"Duke George of Saxony said he would not compel any one to take the communion in one kind, but those who chose to do otherwise must quit his dominions."

"When duke George declared to his brother, duke Henry, that he would allow him to retain his possessions only on condition of his abandoning the gospel, he replied, 'By the Virgin Mary, (his grace's usual affirmation,) before I consent to deny my Christ, I will go, with my wife Catherine, and beg my bread through the land.'"

"I wish the emperor would make duke George pope; the bishops would like his reforms even less than they do mine. He'd soon make the bishop of Mayence keep fewer horses by some score."

"Duke George sucked in Bohemian blood with his mother's milk. She was a daughter of Casimir, king of Bohemia. He would, I dare say, have ultimately joined with the elector Frederic, in smiting the bishops and abbots, and the rest of them, for he is by nature hostile to the clergy; but the letters and flattery of the pope, and the kings of France and England, so puffed him up that he followed where they chose to lead him."

"When duke George saw his son John in his last agony, he consoled him by recalling to him the article of justification by faith in Christ, and exhorted him to look up to the Saviour only, without placing any reliance upon works or upon the invocation of saints; thereupon duke John's wife, sister to the landgrave Philip of Hesse, said to duke George: 'Dear sir and father, why is not this doctrine preached publicly in the country?' 'My dear daughter,' he replied, 'it is a doctrine which we must reserve for the dying; it is not for persons in health.' This duke John had been compelled by his father to swear an eternal hatred and hostility to the Lutheran doctrine. I heard this from Lucas Cranach, to whom duke John mentioned it."

Leipzig being the capital and personal residence of duke George, the protestants, closely watched by the authorities, could not make many proselytes there, a circumstance which made Luther very angry with the town.

"I hate the people of Leipzig more than any other under the sun. They are deformed with arrogance, usury, and wickedness of every description."—"I hate that Sodom, Leipzig; 'tis a sink of usury and evil. I would enter therein upon no consideration, except that of saving its Lot."

"The electorate of Saxony is poor. If the elector had not Thuringia also, he could not maintain forty horse; but this makes up a good income to him, with its tributes from lords and princes, and towns—its rights of convoy, customs, &c. His grace has surrendered for money his royal privileges, among others, the prerogative of mercy."

"The elector Frederic was very economical. He was an excellent hand at filling his cellars and his granaries. He built no fewer than nine castles; and yet he had always money by him. The reason was, he took his fool's advice. One day he was complaining of want of money. The fool said to him: *Be your own collector*, and he adopted the hint. He exacted the strictest nicety of accounts from all his stewards and servants. When he went to one of his castles, he ate, drank, and had his horses tended in the same way as a guest at an inn, on an established scale of charges, and paid the bill when he went away. This deprived his people of the usual excuse: 'Oh, there was so much used when his highness was here!'"

"The elector Frederic-the-Wise said, at Worms, in 1521: 'I find no Roman church in my creed, but I find a common Christian church there.'"

"This prince," says Melancthon, "had near Wittemberg a tame stag, which for many successive years went away, in the month of September, into the neighbouring forest, returning in October. When the elector died, the stag went away and did not return."

"In 1525, the elector John of Saxony asked me whether he should grant the peasants their twelve articles. I told him, Not one."

"Duke John said, in 1525, on learning the revolt of the peasants: "If God will that I remain prince, so be it; but I can very well manage as a private man."

Luther blamed the patience of this prince, who had been told by his confessor to put up with the disobedience of his people, and followed this advice.

He said to Luther: "My son, duke Ernest, has written me a Latin letter, asking me to let him hunt; but I want him to keep to his studies; he can at any time learn how to hang his two legs on a horse."

"This prince had for his body-guard six young nobles, who were always with him, and read the Bible to him six hours a-day, each an hour. His electoral grace sometimes fell asleep, but nevertheless, he would, on awaking, repeat some passage that had particularly struck him. At sermon, he used to have persons near him to take down the preacher's words; nay, he would occasionally do so with his own hand."

"When Ferdinand was elected king of the Romans, at Cologne, the young duke John Frederic was sent by his father to protest against the election. After executing his order, he mounted his horse and galloped off, and only just in time, for he had scarce passed the gates, when people were sent to arrest him."

"It is said the emperor intimated, after hearing our confession and apology, that he wished the same were preached and taught throughout the world. Duke George, too, said he knew very well there were many abuses to reform in the church, but he would not take reform at the hands of an unfrocked monk."

"The last time the elector John went out hunting, he missed all the game. The beasts would no longer recognise him as their master; this was a presage of death to him."

"Duke John Frederic, who was so despoiled by the nobles, learned to appreciate them, though 'twas a costly lesson."

"The elector John Frederic is naturally choleric, but he has a marvellous command over himself. He is greatly given to building, and to drinking too, but, then, he is a large-sized man, and takes more to fill him than other people need. He gives a thousand florins a-year to the university, and two hundred to the minister, with sixty bushels of wheat; besides sixty florins a-year for public lectures." He once sent Luther 500 florins, part of the revenue of a suppressed abbey, as dower for some poor escaped nun.

"Though doctor Jonas earnestly entreated him to do so, Luther refused to apply to the prince for a new visitation of the churches. 'He has got seventy councillors bawling at him, enough to make him deaf: *What good counsel can come from the scribe?* Let us content ourselves with praying God to guide the prince's heart.'"

Of the Landgrave Philip of Hesse.—The landgrave is a pious, wise, and happy man; he maintains peace in his dominions, though it is mostly wood and wild country, so that people travel there in perfect safety. The landgrave is a warrior, an Arminius, though small of person. He listens to sound advice, and when once resolved, is prompt in action. If he would forsake the gospel, then he might obtain of the emperor and pope what he pleased; but God hitherto has steadfastly preserved him. The emperor offered to put him in peaceable possession of the county of Katzeelbogen, and duke George would make him heir of all his countries and people, which the emperor promised to confirm, if he would forsake his religion; but he adheres to the doctrine of the gospel. He hath a Hessian brain, and cannot be idle.

"It was a great boldness in him, that anno 1528, he over-run the bishop's countries; but it was a greater act to put the prince of Wirtemberg in possession of his territories, and hunt king Ferdinand out of them.

"He sent for me and for Philip Melancthon to Weimar, for our counsel and advice touching his intended wars; we endeavoured to dissuade him from his enterprise: we made the best use we could of our rhetoric, and intreated him not with wars to bring a blow or stain upon the gospel; not to infringe and trouble the public peace of the empire; whereupon he grew very red and vexed, although otherwise he was of an upright mind.

"In the colloquy at Marburg, 1539, his highness went dressed in mean apparel, so as no man knew him to be the landgrave; but he had at the same time high cogitations; he asked Philip Melancthon's advice in his affairs, and said, 'Loving Philip! shall I endure this, that the bishop of Mayence by force drive away my preachers of the gospel?' Philip Melancthon said: 'If the jurisdiction of those places belong to the bishop, then your highness may not resist him.' The landgrave replied, 'I hear your advice, but I will not follow it.' I asked Beimelberg, one of his council, why he dissuaded not the landgrave from his plan. He answered, 'Our admonition is nothing: what he intends, from that he is not to be dissuaded.'

"Anno 1530, at the imperial diet, the landgrave openly said to the bishops: 'Make peace, I advise you; we desire it. If ye will not, I will send at least half-a-dozen of you to the devil.' At which the bishop of Saltzburg said to Albert, bishop of Mayence, 'I marvel ye so sorely fear the landgrave of Hesse; he is but a poor prince.' The bishop answered, 'Loving lord bishop! if you dwelt as near him as I, then you would talk otherwise.'

"God has set the landgrave in the midst of the empire; he has four electors inhabiting about him, and also the prince of Brunswick, yet they are all afraid of him; the reason is, he has the love of the common people, and withal, is a valiant soldier. Before he put the prince of Wirtemberg into possession, he went to France, and the French king lent him much money towards his wars."

"The Saxons and the Hessians when once on horseback are perfect heroes. The South German cavaliers are mere dancers in comparison. God preserve the landgrave to us. God preserve us, too, from war; mere war-men are devils incarnate. I refer not merely to the Spaniards, but to the Germans as well.

"After the diet of Frankfort, in 1539, about nine thousand picked soldiers were collected at Bremen and Luneburg, to be employed against the protestant states; but the elector of Saxony and the landgrave of Hesse entered into negotiations with them, through Sir Bernard von Mila, and in consideration of a sum of money in hand, they came over to the elector and the landgrave. Duke George died suddenly soon after this."

"Albert the Unnatural, landgrave of Hesse and Thuringia, was a hard and choleric lord. He was a prisoner to the bishop of Halle, where one night he got out of his window, jumped down a steep descent into the Sals, and swam off. He acted very cruelly towards his subjects. His wife had meat served before him one Friday, and on his refusing to eat any, said—'Dear lord, you fear this sin, and yet every day you commit far greater ones.' She was obliged to fly for it, leaving her children behind her. Previous to her departure at midnight, she stooped to kiss her infant son, who was sleeping in his cradle, blessed him, and, in a transport of maternal love, bit his cheek. Accompanied by a young girl, she let herself down from her tower at Wartburg; a servant was in attendance with horses, and conducted her to Frankfort-on-the-Maine. When the landgrave died, he was wrapped in a monk's frock, at which all his old comrades laughed excessively."

Hospitals.—" In Italy the hospitals are well-built, well-conducted, amply-endowed establishments. The beds and linen are perfectly clean and sweet. There are plenty of attentive servants and able physicians. Many of the apartments are even decorated with fine pictures. As soon as a patient is brought in, his clothes are taken off, and put carefully away, an exact inventory of each article being first made, so that nothing may be lost. A clean bed-gown is then put on him, and he is laid in a comfortable bed; two physicians are in speedy attendance, and servants bring everything that is required, medicine, wine, food in clean bright vessels, which they merely touch with the ends of their fingers. There are also lady visitors to these hospitals—persons of condition, who go through the wards veiled, so that none know who they are, and see that the patients are properly cared for. At Florence, the hospitals are admirably administered. There is a foundling-hospital there, in which poor, deserted children are nourished, taught, and brought up to some business. They are all dressed in a particular costume, and are taken the greatest care of."

" I have got some cloth for breeches, but I have not, as yet, determined upon giving it out to be made up. These I have have been mended four times, and shall be mended once more. The tailors here are very bad, and very dear. Things in this respect are much better in Italy. There one particular class of tailors makes nothing else but breeches."

"In Spain, when the empress was put to bed, four-and-twenty men were flogged till the blood came, to obtain a good time of it for her majesty. Two of the men died from the severe lashing they got, but with no effect to the lying-in woman. What more monstrous superstition than this were the heathen guilty of, I should like to know?"

"In Italy and France, the ministers are, for the most part, mere asses. If you ask them—*Quot sunt sacramenta?* They reply: *Tres.* —*Quæ?* The holy water sprinkler, the censer, and the cross!"

" In France, the people are so sunk in superstition, that all the serfs and peasants wanted to turn monks. The king was absolutely obliged to forbid this monkerizing. France, in fact, is a perfect abyss of superstition. The Italians are either sunk in superstition, or daring freethinkers. 'Tis a common saying there, when they are going to church: 'We must humour the popular prejudice.'"

"A hundred years before Jesus Christ, Rome had a population of four millions; shortly after that epoch, it had nine millions—certes, this was enough to constitute a nation, if, indeed, the statement be true. At Venice, there are three hundred thousand families; at Erfurt, eighteen thousand; at Nuremberg, half that number. Rome now is a mere heap of ashes; its houses now stand on the roofs of old Rome; the ruins on which they are built are two kanzknechts lances deep.* There is nothing commendable in Rome, except the consistorial court, and the court of rota, where cases are decided with great equity."

"Dr Staupitz heard at Rome in 1511, that, according to an old prophecy, a hermit would arise under pope Leo X., and attack papacy. Now, the Augustines were also called hermits.

"There was in Italy a particular order, calling themselves *Brothers of Ignorance.* They all took an oath to know nothing, and to learn nothing. All the monks, in reality, belong to this order."

"One evening, there was at Luther's table an old priest, who related a great many things about Rome. He had been there four times, and had officiated there two years. On being asked why he had gone there so often, he replied: 'The first time, I went in search of a knave; the second time, I found him; the third time, I brought him away with me; the fourth time, I took him back again, and placed him behind the altar of St. Peter.'"

"Christopher Gross, who had resided a long time at Rome as one of the pope's guard, talked a great deal about the countries which lie in the way to the Holy Land, of Aragon, and Biscay. The people in the latter places have as a sign of baptism a little scar on the nose, just below the eyes."

"The Scotch are a very proud people; a great many of them have taken refuge in Germany, and more particularly at Erfurt and Wurtzburg. They admit none but their own countrymen into their convents. The Scotch are looked down upon by other nations, as the Samaritans were by the Jews."

"The English were driven from France, after their defeat at Montlheri, between Paris and Orleans. They do not allow any one to reside at Calais, unless he can learn to speak English in so many hours.

"The plague still rages in England.—England is a piece of Germany. The Danish and English languages are Saxon, that is to say, true German, but the language of Upper Germany is not true German. The Suabians and Bavarians are hospitable people; not so the Saxons. I prefer the dialect of Hesse to all the other German

---

[1] See Montaigne's Journey through Italy, by Hazlitt, p. 572.

dialects, because the Hessians accentuate their words as though they were singing."

"The German language is superior to all others of modern times; its character shows that the Germans are more honest, simple and true than the French, Italians, Spanish, &c. It is honest, clear, and straightforward; while, as to the French, for example, 'tis a proverb: The French write otherwise than they speak, and speak otherwise than they mean. The German is a very complete tongue, and has a great affinity with the Greek. The Latin is dry and thin without double letters. The Saxons and Lower Germans are even more subtle and crafty than the Italians, when they have been a little while with the latter nation. The houses and aspect of countries generally undergo a change every hundred years. Only a short while since, Hesse, Franconia, and Westphalia were mere deserts; on the other hand, round Halle, Halberstadt, and in our own district, you may go three miles and find nothing but heath, where once was cultivated land. God has deprived these districts of their fertility, as a chastisement for the inhabitants.

"We are jolly fellows, we Germans, we eat, and drink, and sing, and break our glasses, and lose at one sitting a hundred, a thousand florins, altogether forgetting the Turk, who yet in thirty days may be with his light horse at the gates of Wittemberg."

"In France, every one has a glass of his own at table. The French are very chary of exposing themselves to the air; if they happen to perspire, they cover themselves all up, creep up to the fire, or go to bed for fear of fever. At their balls, two people dance together, the rest looking on. 'Tis different in Germany. The priests of France and Italy do not even know their own language.

"When I was travelling along the banks of the Rhine, I wanted to perform mass, but a priest said to me, 'You cannot; we follow here the Ambrosian ritual.'"

"George Fægeler, the margrave's chancellor, told me, that in Bavaria there were more than a hundred and twenty-five livings vacant, by reason that no ecclesiastic could be found to fill them. In Bohemia, there are about three hundred livings vacant, and 'tis the same in duke George's territory."

"Thuringia was once very fertile, especially about Erfurt, but now she is labouring under the malediction of God. Corn is dearer there than at Wittemberg. When I was at Schmalkald, a year ago, they had got nothing but very bad black bread. Their vintages are so plentiful, that they sell a pint of wine for a farthing; the quality would be better, if the quantity were less by one half; as it is, they give you the wine for the barrel."

"The electorate of Saxony had twelve Capuchin and Minorite, five Dominican or Pauliner and Carmelite, and four Augustine monasteries. These were Mendicant monasteries, which of themselves are dusted away. Whereupon an Englishman said: 'In England there is scarce a mile square, that has not its seven-and-twenty Mendicant monasteries.' "

"The old elector of Brandenburg, Joachim, once said to the duke of Saxony, Frederick: 'How do you manage to coin so much money, you princes of Saxony?' 'Oh,' replied the other, 'we make money by it!' And so they did, by the quantity of alloy they put into their coin."

"The princess of Anhalt, passing through Wittemberg, visited Luther, and insisted upon discussing various matters with him, though he was ill at the time, and it was at an inconvenient hour. He sought to excuse himself, saying: 'Noble lady, I am rarely well now, suffering almost incessantly in body or mind, or in both.' 'I know it,' she replied; 'but I want to talk to you as to how it is we cannot all live piously.' *Luther:* 'Yet you nobility ought, all of you, to live pious and irreproachable lives; you are few in number, you form a limited circle. We of the commonalty corrupt one another by our multitude; we are the masses, and it is therefore no way wonderful that there should be so few pious persons among us.' And so he went on."

"Luther entertained in his house, for some time, a Hungarian named Mathias von Vai. When the latter returned to his own country, he preached the new doctrine, and was forthwith denounced to the monk George, brother of the Waywode, and who was at this time governing at Buda, as regent. George had two barrels of gunpowder brought into the market-place, and said to the papist who had denounced Mathias, and to Mathias himself: "Each of you say that your particular doctrine is the right one; stand up on these barrels, I will fire the train, and we shall see which of the two remains alive.' The papist refused the test, but Mathias at once took his stand on one of the barrels; whereupon, the papist and his people were condemned to pay four hundred Hungarian florins to the state, and to keep, moreover, two hundred soldiers for a certain time, while Mathias was allowed to preach the gospel."

"A Hungarian noble, named John Huniades, being at Torgau, as ambassador from king Ferdinand to the elector John Frederic, requested the latter to send for Luther, that he might see and speak to him. Luther accordingly came. In the course of conversation, the ambassador said, that in Hungary the priests administered the sacraments sometimes in one kind, sometimes in two, and that they pretended it was quite an indifferent matter. 'Reverend father,' continued the ambassador, 'will you permit me to ask what you think of these priests?' *Luther:* 'I consider them contemptible hypocrites; for if they are convinced that the communion in two kinds is a divine institution, they cannot conscientiously administer it in one kind.' Luther could not long keep to himself the annoyance he felt at the question thus put to him. After a little while, he turned towards the ambassador, and said: 'My lord, I have replied to your lordship's question: will you permit me, in my turn, to put one to you?' *The Ambassador:* 'Yes, assuredly.' *Luther:* 'I am astonished that men like you, the councillors of kings and princes, knowing very well that our doctrine is the true one, should continue to persecute it so determinedly. Can you explain to me how this happens?' The ambassador being very confused at this home question, Andrew Pflug one of the guests, extricated him from the embarrassment by turning the conversation suddenly upon some other topic."

The chapter in the *Tischreden*, where we find collected all that Luther said *On the Turks*, is a curious picture of the terror then pervading every Christian family at the movements of the Mussulmans. Every step taken by the barbarians is marked by a cry of terror throughout Christendom. It is quite the scene in *Goetz Von Berlichengen*, where the knight, reduced to inaction himself, has reports brought him every five minutes of what is passing in the plain below the tower in which he lies; there is just the same excitement about a peril constantly increasing, coming nearer and nearer, but which one is powerless either to avoid or to encounter.

"The Turk will go to Rome, and I don't know that I shall be very sorry if he does. We find it all written in the prophet Daniel...... The Turk once at Rome, the Last Judgment is not far off."

"Christ has saved our souls; he must now save our bodies, for the Turk is about to give Germany a good flanking. I often think of the evils that are coming upon us; they make me sweat. The doctor's wife cried: 'God preserve us from the Turks!' 'Nay,' said he, 'they must needs come and give us the promised shaking.'"

"Who would ever have said that I should see the two emperors, the kings of the south and of the north, facing each other!

......"O pray, friends, for our war-men are too presumptuous; they rely too much upon their strength and upon their numbers. This cannot have a good ending." And he added: "The German horses are more powerful than those of the Turks, which are active, but very light. Ours will overthrow them easily enough."

"I don't rely on our walls, nor on our arquebuses, but on the *Lord's Prayer*. That's what will vanquish the Turks; the *Decalogue* would not be sufficient."

Luther tells us, that after a long search for the Alcoran, he at last came across a bad Latin version of it, dated 1300, which he translated into German, the more effectually to unmask before all men the Mahometan imposture. In his *Opinions derived from the Alcoran*, he "proves that Mahomet was not Antichrist, (for his imposture was too flagrant and palpable,) but the hypocritical pope. Three years ago, a Mauritanian monk passed this way. We disputed with him by an interpreter, and he was quite confounded on all points by the Word of God. 'Truly,' he said to us, at last, 'your doctrine is a good one.' "

The Jews, as Jews and as usurers, were in very bad odour with Luther.

"We ought not to permit the Jews to remain amongst us. We ought not to eat or drink with them.' 'But,' said some one, 'it is written that the Jews shall be converted before the Last Judgment.' 'It is written, too, observed Luther's wife, 'that there shall be but one sheep-fold and one shepherd.' 'Ay,' dear Catherine,' replied the doctor, 'but that prophecy was accomplished when the pagans embraced the Scripture.' "

"If I were in the duke's place, I would collect all the Jews together, and I would ask them why they call Christ a bastard, and St. Mary a prostitute. If they made out their case, I'd give them a hundred florins; if they did not, I'd tear their tongues out.' "

"A servant woman had been for a number of years regularly visited by an invisible spirit, which sat down by her at the fire, and talked with her night after night. One evening, the woman asked Heinzchen, as she called him, to appear before her in his real form. He would not, at first, but as she persisted, he told her to come down with him into the cellar, and there he would appear to her. The servant took a candle, and went down into the cellar, where, in an open cask, she saw a dead infant, floating in its blood. Now, many years before, this servant had had a child, killed it, and concealed it in a cask."

Of Forms and Ceremonies.—Luther thus writes to George Duchholzer, an ecclesiastic of Berlin, who had asked his opinion respecting the changes recently introduced into Brandenburg. "As to the chasuble, the processions, and other external matters that your prince will not abolish, my opinion is this: If he allows you to preach the gospel of Jesus Christ in its purity, without any human additions, to administer baptism and the communion in the way appointed by Christ; if he allows you to suppress the adoration of saints and masses for the dead, to relinquish the blessing of water, salt, and herbs; no longer to carry the host in processions, and to sing only the divine canticles, pure from all human doctrine, then I say, Go through whatever ceremonies he requires, whether they relate to carrying a gold or silver cross, to chasuble of velvet, of silk, or linen, to cope, or what not. If he is not satisfied with one cope or chasuble, put on three, after the fashion of the high priest Aaron, who wore three robes, one upon the other, all beautiful and gorgeous garments. If his grace does not think one noisy procession enough, make your progress seven times over, after the fashion of Joshua and the children of Israel, who marched seven times round the walls of Jericho, singing and sounding trumpets. And if his grace has any particular fancy that way, by all means let him himself head the procession, dancing before the rest to the sound of harps and timbrels, as David did before the ark of the Lord; I have no sort of objection to his doing so. These things, when kept free from mischievous abuse, neither take from nor add to the gospel. All we need do, is to guard ourselves from deeming them essentials, from making them chains and fetters for the conscience. If I could only achieve this last point with the pope and his adherents, how thankful should I be to God! His holiness, in that case, might ask me to carry whatever he pleased.

The following are Mr. Roscoe's observations upon Luther's letter to the pope, referred to in page 64:

"In assigning to the important letter from Luther to Leo X. the date of the *sixth of April*, 1520, I have been accused of having displayed a manifest prejudice against the character of Luther, and even of not having paid a due attention to the authors whom I have cited. From this circumstance some persons have also affected to draw conclusions unfavourable to the general authenticity of my history. How far these charitable inferences would justly follow from the discovery of a single mistake in a narrative of such extent, I am happily not under the necessity of inquiring, as I have it in my power to give the most satisfactory evidence of the correctness of my former statement. If in this vindication I should trespass on the indulgence of the reader, I must beg him to observe that the question is of considerable importance, as it respects the character and conduct of Luther on one of the most trying occasions of his life.

This question commenced with Seckendorf, who, in his Commentary on the History of Maimbourg, has attempted to show that the letter from Luther, which I have considered as bearing the date of the 6th of April, 1520, and as having been the cause of such great offence to the pontiff, was not written until October following, about four months after the issuing of the papal bull, which bears date the fifteenth of June, in the same year. This letter Seckendorf also considers as conciliatory, and as intended to soften the animosity of the pontiff, and to throw the blame on Eccius, and the cardinal of Gaeta. If these conjectures were well founded, it would follow of course, that after the issuing of the bull, Luther still wished and endeavoured to bring about a reconciliation with the Roman see; and that the character and conduct of the great reformer must, in this instance, be viewed in a different light from that in which they have been placed in the following work.

For the establishment of his proposition, Seckendorf has chiefly relied on the letters of Charles Miltitz, the papal envoy to Luther, of which he had obtained a sight after the publication of the first edition of his work. From these he presumes, that Miltitz had a conference with Luther on the eleventh of October, 1520, in which Luther promised, within twelve days, to write to the pontiff *modestly* and *humbly*, and to prefix his letter to a book which he was then writing, and intended to send to the pope; dating his letter on the sixth day of September preceding; with which date it is said the letter now under consideration is published in the German edition of the works of Luther. Seckendorf has also stated, that on the twenty-eighth day of August, 1520, a general chapter of the Augustine order was hald at Isleben, when a deputation was sent to Luther to prevail upon him to write to the pope in moderate and conciliatory terms, which he promised to do. On the third of October, it seems however that Luther had again changed his mind, and determined not to write to the pontiff; until he was again prevailed upon to undertake that task by the persuasions of Miltitz, as before related.

In the narrative which I have had occasion to give of the early part of the reformation, I have considered the letter which has given rise to this discussion as actually written on or about the sixth of April, 1520, the date which it bears in the Latin edition of the works of Luther. This decision is strongly supported by the internal evidence of the letter itself, which for various reasons, could not have been written by Luther after the issuing of the papal bull.

This letter, it must be observed, contains a sort of history of the opposition of Luther to the Roman see, and of the violent and oppressive measures adopted by his adversaries against him; terminating with an account of the disputations at Leipsic in the month of June, 1519. Could Luther then, in a narrative of this nature, have omitted to notice the proceedings of the papal see from June, 1519, to September or October, 1520, and particularly the bull, which had then been published throughout Europe, and by which his doctrines were condemned and himself declared a heretic, unless he made his submission within a limited time? To advance such an assertion, is to attribute to Luther an absurdity of which he was surely never guilty, and a dereliction of his principles, which would have degraded him in the estimation both of his friends and his foes.

There is indeed great reason to believe, from the manner in which Luther refers in this letter to the disputation at Leipsic, that the application made to him by the Augustine fathers, occurred in the year 1519, and not in 1520, as stated by Seckendorf and his followers. "These disputes," says Luther, (which the reader will please to observe took place on the twenty-seventh of June, 1519,) "having had no other result than the greater confusion of the Roman see; in the third place, Charles Miltitz applies to the fathers of the Augustines, assembled in their chapter, and asks their advice about conciliating matters, which were then in a most deranged and dangerous state. Some of the most distinguished of them, when violence was found to be of no avail, were sent to me, and desired that I would at least honour the person of your holiness, and by humble letters demonstrate both your innocence and my own. That matters were not yet desperate, if Leo X. in accordance with his mild disposition, would endeavour to remedy them." From which it should appear that Miltitz, finding that the disputation at Leipsic had produced no good effect to the cause of Rome, applied soon afterwards to the Augustine fathers, as the next or succeeding measure, probably at their general chapter in the month of August, 1519; and that as matters were not yet desperate, (which could not surely be said after the issuing of the papal bull) Luther might still entertain hopes of a reconciliation. The result of the disputes at Leipsic, and the application of Miltitz to the Augustine fathers, are stated by Luther in the same sentence, a cause and effect; the latter being the immediate consequence of the failure of the former. On any other supposition it would appear that Miltitz had remained in Germany upwards of a year after the disputes at Leipsic, without any effort to forward the business on which he came, and on which he was only employed about two years in the whole. The letters of Luther which appear without a date, but which Seckendorf, *of his own authority*, refers to the year 1520, apply with much greater propriety to the year 1519, when Luther had frequent meetings with Miltitz, and promised to write in humiliating terms to the pope; and are in perfect unison of sentiment and language with his other letters written at that period; but by no means agree with his temper and circumstances after the issuing of the bull in 1520.

Again, it can scarcely escape notice, that Luther, in his letter to the pope, enters into a vindication of the part which he had taken in the disputes at Leipsic; asserting that he was reluctantly dragged into the debate respecting the supremacy of the holy see, by Eccius, who had taken advantage of an unguarded expression of his on this subject. Admitting this letter to have been written about the time it bears date in the Latin edition, this explanation is sufficiently consistent with the character of Luther, and with his temper at this period; but to suppose that after his doctrines had been condemned by the papal bull, he would have apologized to the pontiff, for an expression which he had used at Leipsic fifteen months before, tending to impeach the supremacy of the Roman see, is not less remote from all probability of truth, than it is derogatory from the character of Luther.

It is indeed remarkable that Seckendorf himself has not pretended to do more than to suggest some doubts as to the real time when the letter in question was written;[1] and it is still more remarkable, that in the second edition of his history, he has not ventured to adopt his own previous suggestions, by giving, or even mentioning this letter in the place where, according to chronological order, it ought to occupy so conspicuous a station, and where it would place the conduct of Luther, after the issuing of the bull, in so very different a light. On the contrary, he has assented to the narrative of Maimbourg, with whom he so seldom agrees in other respects, as to the uniform perseverance, and even violence of Luther after the issuing of the bull, without attempting in any manner to show that Luther endeavoured to effect a reconciliation with the papal see. He refers only to the new appeal of Luther—to a general council, in which Luther personally attacks the pope as *a tyrant, a heretic, an apostate, and as Antichrist himself*,[2] and to the two tracts published by Luther against the bull, which are dated the first of December, 1520, and are replete with the most violent invectives against the Roman see.[3]

But independent of either the internal evidence of the letter, or any other conjectural proof, a due consideration of the following circumstances will

---

[1] "De tempore tamen quo tradita Epistola est *dubitationem quandam* infra aperiam. (Seck. i. 27, 98.)

[2] "Sed nunc commotior Lutherus Pontificem ipsum, *ob editam Bullam*, pro *tyranno, hæretico, apostata, antichristo*, et superbo concilii contemtore habet." (Seck. i. 31, 117.)

[3] One of these is entitled, "*Adversus execrabilem Antichristi Bullam;*" the other, *Assertio articulorum Martini Lutheri, per Bullam Leonis X. novissime damnatorum.* These tracts are of considerable extent, and must have engaged the attention of Luther for several months before their publication.

fully decide the question. The letter of Luther was not a separate or occasional production, but was the dedication to Leo X. of the treatise of Luther *De Libertate Christiana*, actually prefixed to, and published with that work in the early part of the year 1520.[1] In this form it is also given in the Jena edition of the writings of Luther, where it immediately precedes the treatise, and is inscribed, *The Epistle of Luther to the Roman Pontiff Leo X.* PREFIXED TO HIS BOOK ON CHRISTIAN LIBERTY.[2] The dedicatory words to the pontiff at the close of the letter admit of no doubt. *That I may not*, says he, *approach your holiness with empty hands, I bring with me this tract*, PUBLISHED UNDER THE SANCTION OF YOUR NAME, *as an auspice of returning peace and favourable expectations.* That this work preceded, in the order of publication, the treatise of Luther, *De Captivitate Babylonica*, is not only apparent from the very different tenour of those writings, but is expressly stated by all the authors on this subject, and even by Seckendorf himself;[3] and the latter tract had made its appearance in the month of August, 1520.[4] The precise time of the publication of the treatise *De Libertate Christiana*, is therefore, most probably, marked by the dedicatory letter itself—viz., the sixth of April, 1520, about two months before the issuing of the papal bull, when such language was not unsuitable to the dignity and character of Luther; but at whatever time it was published, it is evident that as it preceded the treatise *De Captivitate Babylonica*, which was published in or before the month of August, 1520, it could not on its first appearance have been accompanied by a letter which Luther is said not to have written till the ensuing month of October; and further, that the book which Luther is said by Miltitz to have been writing in the month of October, 1520, with the intention of sending it to the pope, could not have been the treatise on Christian Liberty.

Whether Luther did or did not promise to write to Leo X. after the issuing of the papal bull; whether he did or did not actually write to him, are not the present subjects of inquiry. The question is, whether Luther

---

[1] An edition was published at Wittemberg, in 1520, and entitled, EPISTOLA LUTHERIANA *ad Leonem Decimum summum Pontificem* TRACTATUS DE LIBERTATE CHRISTIANA. The Letter and Tract were also printed at Antwerp in the same year; *per Michael. Hillenium.* And again at Wittemberg, in 1521, under the following title. DE LIBERTATE CHRISTIANA, *Dissertatio Martini Lutheri, per autorem recognita.* EPISTOLA *ejusdem ad Leonem Decimum summum Pontificem.*

[2] Epistola Lutheri ad Leonem X. Rom. pontificem, LIBELLO DE LIBERTATE CHRISTIANA præfixa. Luth. op. tom. i. 385.

[3] Sleidan ii. in prin. Maim. ap. Seck. 28, Seck. ibid. et in Indice, Script. Lutheri, an. 1520.

[4] "Ad hæc Elector. d. 24 *August*, respondet. *Lutheri librum jam editum esse; si id præscivisset, impediturum publicationem libenter fuisse.* Non dubito libellem hunc esse eum, quem *de Captivitate Babylonica* conscripsit." Seck. i. 27. 98. But in the interval between the publication of these two tracts, Luther also published a treatise in German, addressed to the emperor and the German nobility, in terms of such violence against the Roman see "ut etiam amici ejus libellum istum pro classico belli haberent." After noticing the contents of this work, Seckendorf adds, "Alter libellus *mense Augusto* prodiit, titulum habens *De captivitate Babylonica*," &c. Seck. i. 38. 112.

in the month of October wrote to him the letter printed in his Latin works, with the date of the 6th of April, and this it is apparent he could not have done; the work to which the letter was annexed as a dedication having been published at least before the month of August, and most probably in April, 1520. But as some attempts have been made to impeach the accuracy of the Latin edition of the works of Luther, I shall offer a few remarks which may tend to prove its correctness, and more clearly to demonstrate that the date of the sixth of April is the genuine date of the letter in question.

This edition, which was begun in the year 1554,[1] was superintended by particular friends of Luther soon after his death, and is preceded by a preface, written by his faithful adherent Nicholas Amsdorf. From this it appears that the writings of Luther had been previously collected without any proper attention to their order and arrangement; although it is of great importance, as Amsdorf observes, "to know *at what time* each of them was published by their author." "For many persons," adds he, "not having duly considered *the time*, have erred most scandalously, whilst under the pretext of the writings of Luther, they have undertaken *to reconcile Christ and Belial.* Nor can it be denied that Luther, in the commencement of the controversy, whilst he was still fascinated by the received opinions, imprudently conceded many things to his adversaries."

"These and similar errors," says he, "which deformed the writings of Luther, excited the pious mind of the son of our late illustrious elector to devise some method by which the works of this holy man might be given to the public in a pure, uncorrupt, entire, and regular order, for the general use of the church; and might be transmitted to posterity faithfully, and free from blemish. For this purpose he called from Denmark the venerable and learned Georgius Rorarius, to whom Luther himself had deputed this task, and established a printing-office at Jena, that all his works might be published with exact attention to the order of time, entire and unadultrated, and without any interference from the comments of other persons.

In the subsequent part of the preface, Amsdorf again insists upon the accuracy of this chronological order in the publication of the writings of Luther, as the great excellency of the work. "The reader must be informed," says he, "that by this first volume of the tracts of Luther, published in the years 1517, 18, 19, 20, and 21, a history is formed, which shows the beginning and progress of the disputes about religion, the causes that impelled Luther to the contest, and that the light of the Holy Spirit became gradually stronger and clearer in his mind. After such declarations is it possible to suppose that the letter in question, prefixed to the treatise on Christian Liberty, printed with that treatise, with the date of the 6th of April, and followed in the works of Luther, at a considerable distance, and after several intervening publications by the papal bull, was not written until after such bull had been issued? and even not until after the tract *De Captivitate Babylonica*, which was published in August, 1520, and appears in its proper place in the Jena edition of the works of Luther?

It is, indeed, surprising that any person who has paid the least attention to the subject, should not have perceived how inconsistent it would have

---

[1] It was carefully reprinted from the first edition, at Jena, in 1612, in four volumes; to which latter edition the references in this work are made.

been with the character of Luther, and how contradictory to his known declarations and conduct, to have addressed himself to the pope, after the issuing of the bull, in terms which could, on any construction, be supposed to have been pacific and conciliatory. From his own letters, it appears that he knew of the bull early in the month of July, and that he then formed a resolution never more to be reconciled, or hold communion with the church of Rome. "The die is now cast," says he; "the Roman fury and the Roman favour are alike despised; I never more will be reconciled with them, nor communicate with them in future. Let them condemn and burn my writings. I, in return, unless fire shall be wanting, will condemn and publicly burn the whole pontifical law; that is, that Hydra-heresy; and there shall be an end of my hitherto fruitless obedience." Whether Luther deviated from this his first resolution, sufficiently appears by his subsequent conduct.

Another striking indication of the disposition of Luther, appears in his treatise, *De Captivitate Babylonica*. At the close of this work he also admits that he had heard of the bull and of the sentence of excommunication issued against him, unless he should renounce his errors; to which he ironically adds, "If this be true, let this book be taken as a part of my retractation; and lest they should think that their tyranny has produced no effect, I shall soon, Christ willing, publish the remainder, which shall abundantly testify my obedience, in such a manner as the Roman see never saw or heard of before."

Thus far the declarations of Luther during the months of July and August next after the issuing of the papal bull. But it is yet more remarkable that in the month of October, and at the precise time when he is supposed to have written the letter in question, he still adhered to his former resolution, never more to be reconciled to the Roman see. In a letter of the thirteenth of that month, he declares that "as to the bull, respecting which others wrote so much to the Roman court, he despised it, and would attack it as false and impious, and in every respect *Eccian*." If the supposition of my opponents were well founded, Luther assured Miltitz that he would write to the pope within twelve days from the *eleventh* of October, *modestly* and *humbly*, and would date such letter on the sixth day of September preceding, and prefix it to a book which he was then writing, and intended to send to the pontiff. What the sentiments of Luther were on the *thirteenth* of October we have just now seen, and that no alteration took place between the thirteenth and the thirtieth of the same month may be inferred from another letter, said to be nearly in the same words as the former;[1] and yet we are required to believe that during this precise interval Luther wrote to conciliate Leo X.

It must also be observed that from several passages in the letters of Luther at this period, it is evident that he was then preparing his two tracts before mentioned as an answer to the bull, which he published, and which appear in his works, with the date of the first day of December, 1520.[2] In the preface to the first of these, *Adversus execrabilem Antichristi Bullam*, he

[1] Seck. i. 29, 115.

[2] It does not appear that Luther wrote any book after the publication of the bull, and before December, 1520, except these two tracts, neither of which could surely be the work which, as Miltitz informs us, he was then writing, *and intended to send as a peace-offering to the pope.*

treats the bull as a surreptitious production: pretending that he is uncertain whether the papists are mocking him, or whether they are really so insane at Rome as to have issued such a bull. He declares, in the presence of God and of Jesus Christ, the holy angels and the whole world, that he wholly dissents from the damnable doctrines of the bull, which he anathematizes and execrates, as the sacrilegious and blasphemous adversary of our Lord Jesus Christ. He asserts his own articles condemned by the bull, and proposes them to be believed by all Christians, under pain of eternal damnation; declaring that he shall consider all those who assent to the bull as antichrists and as heathens. Nor is he less severe, or less violent, in the work itself than in the preface. He there calls upon the pope and his cardinals to repent of their errors, and put an end to their diabolical blasphemies, "otherwise," he adds, "be it known to you, that I and all other Christians shall consider your see as the seat of Antichrist, possessed by Satan himself; which not only will we not obey, nor own ourselves subject to, or incorporated with, but shall detest and execrate, as the chief enemy of Christ: being prepared in this our decision not only to bear with joy your stupid censures, but even to request that you will never absolve us, or number us among your followers, as we would rather fulfil your cruel tyranny by offering up to you our lives. If, then, the spirit of Christ and the vigour of our faith be of any avail, we in return condemn you, if you persevere in your fury, and deliver over you and your bull, with all your decretals, to Satan, that by the destruction of the flesh, your souls may be liberated in the coming of the Lord. In the name of him whom ye persecute, Jesus Christ our Lord—Amen."

In the foregoing passage, Luther again refers to his invariable resolution of committing the bull, with the Roman decretals, to the flames; a resolution which he carried into effect at Wittemberg on the tenth day of Decem ber, 1520; and thus accomplished, in their full extent, the threats which, as we have seen, he had thrown out as early as the month of July preceding.

The real feelings and conduct of Luther on this occasion are to be judged of, not from the letters of the papal agent, who might misrepresent him to the pope, but from his own undoubted declarations and writings, which form an almost uninterrupted series, and in which he uniformly attacks the Roman court with a degree of violence wholly inconsistent with the idea that he had ever, from the issuing of the bull, entertained the slightest hope or wish for reconciliation. By this bull it must be remembered that forty-one points of doctrine, asserted by Luther, were condemned as heretical and scandalous. Can it then be supposed that he would have deserted the defence of his opinions, to write, as is pretended, a humble letter to the pope, for the purpose of bringing about a reconciliation? If he could have been guilty of such a dereliction of his principles, it would have subjected him, in reality, to the hypothetical animadversions of Mosheim, which, although applied to Luther after the confirmatory bull of excommunication, in 1521, would have been equally proper on this occasion. "To submit to the orders of a cruel and insolent enemy, would have been the greatest degree of imprudence imaginable; and to embrace anew errors that he had rejected with a just indignation, and exposed with the clearest evidence, would have discovered a want of integrity and principle worthy only of the most abandoned profligate."[1]

---

[1] Mosheim's Eccl. Hist. by Macleane, vol. ii. p. 29.

After this explicit statement, I might in my turn accuse my opponents of having engaged in this discussion without having previously paid sufficient attention to the subject, and of having rashly contended for such a construction of the conduct of Luther as would have led to consequences of which they were not aware; but I am so far from retorting their censures, that I feel gratified by the opportunity which their remarks have afforded me, of obviating the only charge of an error in point of fact, which has been brought against my work; and at the same time of examining, still more particularly, the conduct of Luther, at one of the most critical and active periods of his life, and removing from the records of ecclesiastical history an important error, highly injurious to the great reformer, and to which several protestant writers, subsequent to Seckendorf, have incautiously given their support.

I cannot, however, finally quit this subject without some notice of the charges which have so generally been connected with those before mentioned, and by which it has been insinuated, or asserted, that I have endeavoured to discredit the characters of the early reformers, and to depreciate the beneficial effects of the Reformation, as well by a reference to the well-known persecution of Servetus, as on other occasions. In answer to this I must be allowed to observe, that the idea that the following work is hostile to the Reformation, is a misrepresentation, industriously circulated by those who, under the pretext of a warm attachment to the cause of protestantism, are as adverse to all religious liberty as the most bigoted Roman catholic; and that whoever peruses the following pages with an impartial eye, cannot fail to discover, that so far from depreciating the beneficial effects of the Reformation, I have only had to regret that it was not carried to the full extent for which its promoters originally contended. To this I can add, with great sincerity, that in adverting to the persecutions of which protestants have been guilty, my only object has been to excite that abhorrence of persecution, under every form and pretext, which is the surest safeguard against its return. If it should appear, as has been imputed to me, that I have animadverted with more severity on the protestants than on the papists, it is because better things were to have been expected from them; because they who asserted the right of private judgment in themselves, ought not to have denied it to others; because they who have represented the cruelties and persecutions of the church of Rome as the greatest of her abominations, ought to have been peculiarly cautious how they gave rise to similar charges against themselves; and lastly, because it is more painful to perceive a disgraceful blot among those with whom we are nearly associated, than among those who are further removed from us in principles and opinions. Hence the persecution of Servetus, conducted by Calvin, and approved by Bullinger and Melancthon, has been exhibited in those colours which it so justly merits; and should, if it were in my power, be still further raised up, as a perpetual beacon, to guard mankind against the possible recurrence of an event which outrages at once the feelings of humanity, the dictates of common sense, and the religion of Christ. It is not on the doctrinal tenets of any established church, whatever its adherents may believe, that we are to rely for the rejection of those intolerant and persecuting principles which have for so many ages disgraced the Roman see. 'Luther, Calvin, Cranmer, Knox, the founders of the reformed church in their respective countries, inflicted, as far as they had power and opportunity, the same punishments which were denounced against their own disciples by the church of Rome, on such as called in question any article in their creeds.'[1] To have freed the human race from the dread of violence and persecution, in the exercise of religion and in the pursuit of truth, would have conferred greater honour on Luther than the enforcement of any dogmatical opinions whatever. To his good intentions and incorruptible integrity, the following work bears uniform and ample testimony; but with the restraints of his superiors, Luther could not shake off the trammels of his education; and his highest aim was only to establish another despotism in the place of that from which he had himself escaped. In thus sanctioning, by his opinion and example, the continuance of an exterior and positive control over the consciences of mankind, he confirmed the pretensions of the Roman see; and may more justly be said to have shared its authority, than to have invalidated its unjust assumptions. But the principles of toleration are derived from higher views; from an enlarged idea of the wisdom, the goodness, and the impartiality of the Supreme Being, from the cultivation of generous and social affections; and, in short, from the exercise of the Christian religion as taught by its great founder, and not as perverted by the ambition, the obstinacy, or the ignorance of his erring followers."

[1] Robertson's Charles V., book ii.

INDEX.

THE END.

T. C. Savill, Printer, 4, Chandos Street, Covent Garden.